Arshile Gorky

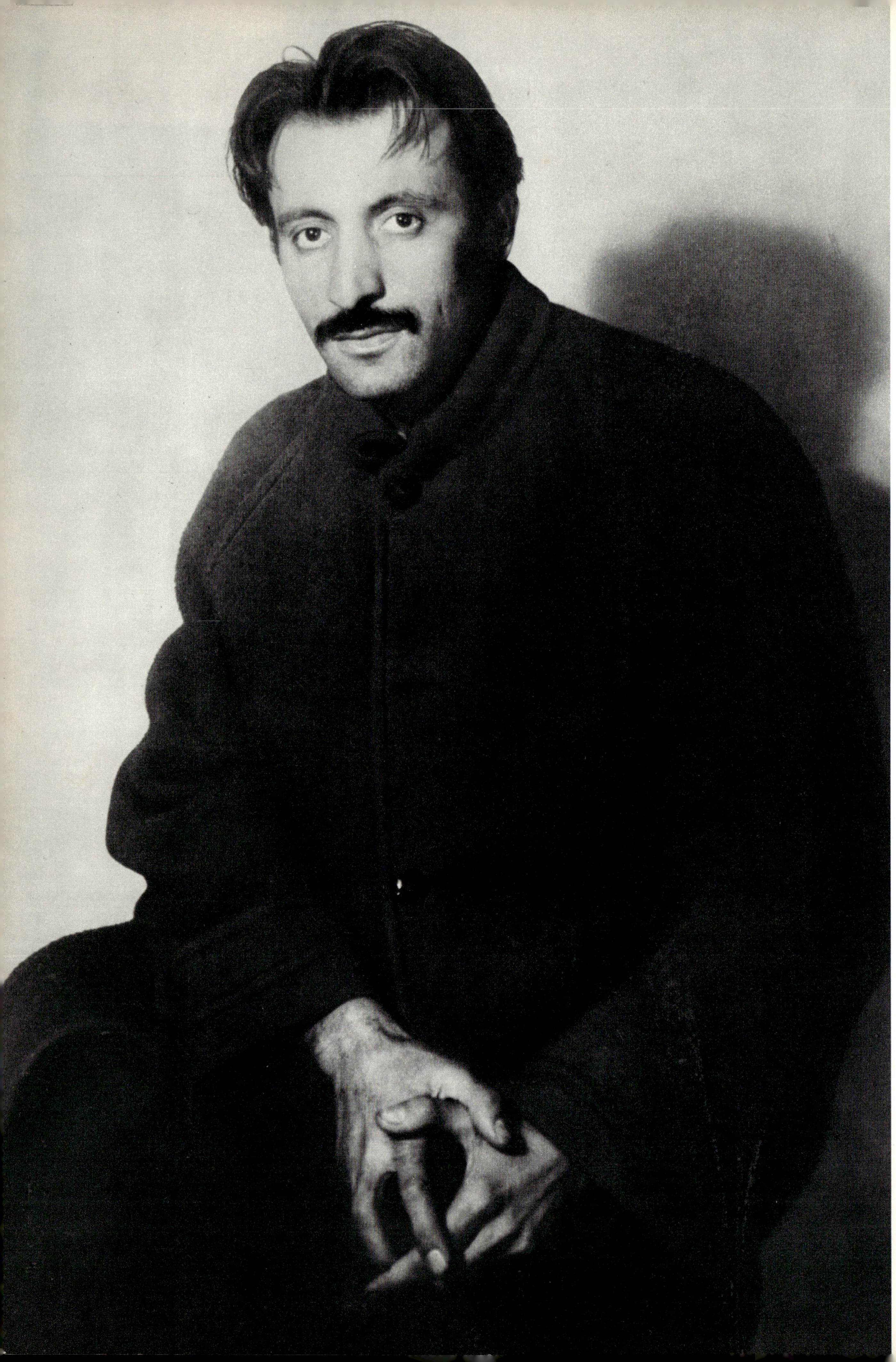

Diane Waldman

Arshile Gorky

1904–1948

A Retrospective

This project is supported by the National
Endowment for the Arts in Washington, D.C.
and Knoll International
Published by Harry N. Abrams, Inc., New York,
in collaboration with
The Solomon R. Guggenheim Museum, New York

front cover:
The Liver Is the Cock's Comb. 1944
Collection Albright-Knox Art Gallery, Buffalo, New York
Gift of Seymour H. Knox, 1956

back cover:
One Year the Milkweed. 1944
Collection National Gallery of Art, Washington, D.C.
Ailsa Mellon Bruce Fund

frontispiece: Arshile Gorky, ca. 1933

Book Design: Nai Y. Chang

Editor: Carol Fuerstein

ISBN 0-89207-025-0

Library of Congress Catalog Card Number: 80-52992

Published by Harry N. Abrams, Incorporated, New York, in collaboration with The Solomon R. Guggenheim Foundation, New York, 1981

Printed and bound in Japan

Lenders to the Exhibition

Mrs. Charles Abrams, New York
American Broadcasting Companies, Inc., New York
Mr. and Mrs. Harry W. Anderson
Satenig Avedisian, Connecticut
Mr. and Mrs. Walter Bareiss
Mr. and Mrs. Michael J. Berberian, Connecticut
Mr. and Mrs. E.A. Bergman
Marilyn and Bernard Brodsky
Ann Dunnigan
Stefan Edlis
Gerald S. Elliott, Chicago
Richard Estes, New York
Dr. and Mrs. Martin L. Gecht
Mr. and Mrs. Philip Gersh, Beverly Hills
Milton A. Gordon, New York
Mr. and Mrs. Chaim Gross
Graham Gund
Mr. and Mrs. Michael de Havenon, New York
Edwin Janss, Jr.
Barbara and Donald Jonas
Mr. and Mrs. Jacob Kainen
Mary Judith Kanner
Dr. and Mrs. L. Keoshian, California
Mr. and Mrs. Sidney Kohl
Steingrim Laursen, Copenhagen
Mrs. M. Victor Leventritt, New York
Julien Levy
Mr. and Mrs. H. Gates Lloyd
Duncan MacGuigan, New York
Menil Foundation, Houston
Dorothy C. Miller
C.A. Muschenheim, Evanston, Illinois
Mr. and Mrs. S.I. Newhouse, Jr.
Mr. and Mrs. Gifford Phillips, New York
Mrs. Walter L. Portnoff, New York
Dr. and Mrs. William Rattner, Huntington Woods, Michigan
Michael M. Rea
Mr. and Mrs. Edmond Ruben, Minneapolis
Christopher C. Schwabacher, New York
Ethel K. Schwabacher, New York
Mr. and Mrs. Joseph Randall Shapiro, Oak Park, Illinois
Rebecca and Raphael Soyer Collection
Thyssen-Bornemisza Collection, Lugano
Mrs. Joseph Douglas Weiss, Chappaqua, New York
Frederick Weisman Family Collection
Nicholas Wilder, Los Angeles
Sue and David Workman
Albright-Knox Art Gallery, Buffalo
Allen Memorial Art Museum, Oberlin College, Oberlin, Ohio

The Art Gallery of Ontario, Toronto
The Art Institute of Chicago
Australian National Gallery, Canberra
The Baltimore Museum of Art
Sarah Campbell Blaffer Foundation, Houston
The Brooklyn Museum
The Cleveland Museum of Art
Grey Art Gallery and Study Center, New York University
The Peggy Guggenheim Collection, Venice, The Solomon R. Guggenheim Foundation
The Solomon R. Guggenheim Museum, New York
The High Museum of Art, Atlanta
Hirshhorn Museum and Sculpture Garden, Smithsonian Institution, Washington, D.C.
Indiana University Art Museum, Bloomington
Los Angeles County Museum of Art
Lowell Art Association, Lowell, Massachusetts
The Metropolitan Museum of Art, New York
Musée National d'Art Moderne, Centre National d'Art et de Culture Georges Pompidou, Paris
The Museum of Modern Art, New York
National Collection of Fine Arts, Washington, D.C.
National Gallery of Art, Washington, D.C.
National Gallery of Canada, Ottawa
Nelson Gallery—Atkins Museum, Kansas City
Newark International Airport Art Collection, The Port Authority of New York and New Jersey
Philadelphia Museum of Art
San Francisco Museum of Modern Art
Seattle Art Museum
The Tate Gallery, London
The University Art Museum, The University of Texas at Austin
Washington Art Consortium, Eastern Washington State Historical Society
Whitney Museum of American Art, New York
Yale University Art Gallery, New Haven

Xavier Fourcade Inc., New York
Susanne Hilberry Gallery, Birmingham, Michigan
Sidney Janis Gallery, New York
David Nisinson, Inc.
Allan Stone Gallery, New York

Table of Contents

Lenders to the Exhibition, p. 7

Thomas M. Messer Preface, p. 10

Diane Waldman Acknowledgements, p. 11

Diane Waldman Arshile Gorky: Poet in Paint, p. 13

Plates, p. 62

Lisa Dennison Tabak Chronology, p. 255

Selected Exhibitions and Reviews, p. 268

Selected Bibliography, p. 279

Photographic Credits, p. 284

Preface

ARSHILE GORKY, seen as the end product of a historical evolution, becomes the last link in a chain of modern painters who have compelled our vision since the late nineteenth century. But at the same time and not inconsistent with such a view, we endow Gorky today with the attributes of a pioneer. For it was his painterly insights and attributes that helped shape the generation of Americans who, having waged their first decisive battles at about the time of his death, were carried to prominence and victory in the 1950s as the martyrs or heroes of the New York School.

Equipped with a native poetic talent which searched for visual equivalents, Gorky subjected himself in the twenties and thirties to a schooling that consisted of conscientious imitation of the modern masters and of a deliberate avoidance of self-assertion and original expression. The forties witnessed Gorky's emergence as a major and innovative figure in American painting, even as his tragic life moved relentlessly toward catastrophe. Only in that last phase of his creative life does Gorky emerge powerfully in his own terms and speak to us through forms that are uniquely his.

Gorky's contribution lies in that special realm that seeks to enlarge and materialize human awareness. Like others who have followed this road before and after him, Gorky, attempting to explore the unknown, first perfected the methods that served in the domain of the known. As he moved into *terra incognita*, he modified the graphic tools in accordance with newly emerging modes of thought. The thought, of course, remains invisible, but the adaptation of tools constitutes the painter's style and becomes a visible projection on a widened human horizon. As viewers we stand before this manifestation confounded and moved.

It would have been impossible to realize a retrospective of such encompassing scope without substantial financial assistance. We are therefore deeply grateful to the National Endowment for the Arts which has demonstrated its continuing commitment by giving us essential support for this project and to Knoll International for its generous grant.

Thomas M. Messer, Director
The Solomon R. Guggenheim Foundation

Acknowledgements

AN EXHIBITION OF THIS MAGNITUDE AND COMPLEXITY would not have been possible without the generous support and cooperation of numerous individuals. Above all I am most grateful to the family of the artist—Mrs. Alexander Fielding, Maro and Matthew Spender and Natasha Gorky Young—for their encouragement and their enthusiastic help with every aspect of the project. I am indebted as well to the artist's nephew Karlen Mooradian for his extensive research on Gorky's life and his many insights into his Armenian heritage. Gorky's sister Satenig Avedisian and his niece Florence Berberian shared their reminiscences with me. Special thanks are also due to Ethel Schwabacher whose monograph remains the single most insightful and comprehensive volume on the artist.

My gratitude must be expressed to Xavier Fourcade, dealer for the Gorky Estate, and to the following individuals who have been most generous in contributing their time and providing me with invaluable information: Harold Diamond, Richard Feigen, Carroll Janis, Allan Stone and Joan Washburn.

In the course of my researches on the artist's life and work I have obtained much new and valuable information, both in conversation and in the form of previously unpublished documentary material from critics and scholars and friends and colleagues of Arshile Gorky: Will Barnet, Peter Busa, Dorothy Dehner, Clement Greenberg, Jim Jordan, Lillian Kiesler, Eila Kokkinen, Elaine de Kooning, Lee Krasner, Julien Levy, Rook McCulloch, George McNeil, Dorothy Miller, Isamu Noguchi, Gordon Onslow-Ford, Harry Rand, V. V. Rankine, Mrs. Alexander Sandow, Meyer Schapiro, Vaclav Vytlacil and Anna Walinska.

Thanks are also due to Ari Manijikian and Maedo Soghomian of the Armenian Prelacy in New York and Susan Kelekian of *Ararat* for providing me with useful information on the history of the Armenian people. Others who have aided me in documentation on the artist and are owed thanks are: Lee Andrukiewicz, Superintendent of Schools, Rhode Island; David Boyce of the Sidney Janis Gallery; Mae Fitzgerald, Librarian, Whitney Museum of American Art; Janet Hynes, Art Reference Section Librarian, Boston Public Library; Annette Fields of Sotheby Parke-Bernet; Nancy Little and Katherine Moore of Knoedler & Co; Vlasta Odell and Brian Wallis of the Registrars Department of The Museum of Modern Art; Margaret Ann Parker and Jill Weinberg of Xavier Fourcade Inc.; and Lee Smith of the Art Students League.

An undertaking as far-reaching as the current exhibition and catalogue involves all levels of the Museum's organization. Therefore, the Guggenheim's staff as a whole should be thanked for their diligence and devotion. The following staff members were most directly concerned with the preparation of the exhibition and catalogue: Lisa Dennison Tabak, Exhibition Coordinator, who contributed to all aspects of the exhibition and publication; Carol Fuerstein, Editor, who edited the catalogue and saw it through the presses; and volunteers Maud Lavin, Merope Lolis, Nina Nathan, Estelle Goodman and Leila Taghinia-Milani.

My last and perhaps most important acknowledgement is addressed to the lenders who have made this retrospective possible. Unless they wish to remain anonymous, their names are cited elsewhere in this catalogue. I am most grateful to them for their truly generous support and commitment to this exhibition.

D.W.

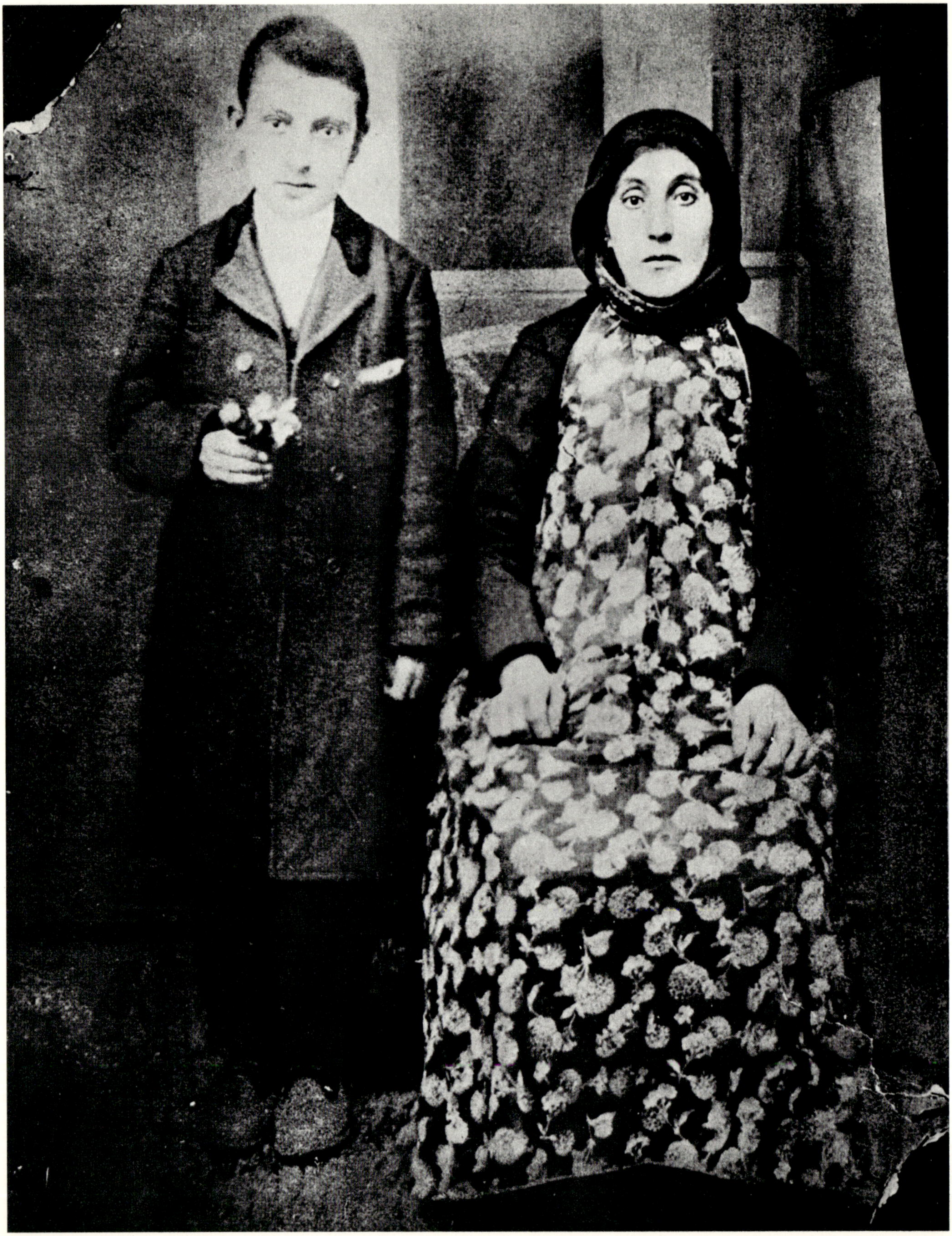

1. Vosdanik and Lady Shushanik, Van City, 1912

Arshile Gorky: Poet in Paint

ARSHILE GORKY died at the age of forty-four on July 21, 1948. An aspiring poet as well as a painter, Gorky was a man of many moods and facets, at once shy, warm and exuberant, a gentle, adoring father, a compassionate teacher, a student of the great painting of the past, a seminal figure in the forging of the new American painting that emerged in the late 1940s, the author of some of the great paintings of our time. A proud and melancholy man who had experienced extreme poverty and suffering, he was both sensitive and high-spirited. A man of many contradictions, he was passionate about his Armenian heritage and loved the art of the past yet was engaged in a monumental struggle to create a new direction in painting. To his friends and admirers his relationship to the art of the 1950s was comparable to Cézanne's relationship to the revolutionary painting of the early twentieth century. As Cézanne foretold and inspired the Cubism of Picasso and Braque, so Gorky heralded the coming of age of an independent and progressive American art.

Arshile Gorky was born Vosdanik Adoian on April 15, 1904, in Khorkom, a small village on the southeast shore of Lake Van in the Van Province of Armenia. He was born into a family of peasants and priests, the first son of Sedrak Adoian, a trader and occasional carpenter, and Shushanik der Marderosian, a woman of noble birth descended from a long line of clergy. Vosdanik was named after his mother's birthplace, Vosdan, the ancient Armenian city situated on the southernmost shore of Lake Van. He later was given the middle name Manuk (or Manook), after his paternal grandfather, for, according to Armenian tradition, the eldest son receives the name of the clan's patriarch upon his death. Gorky was generally known by this name among Armenians, although he reportedly disliked it.[1]

He was exposed to Armenian art at a very early age when his mother took him to her family's fifth-century ancestral Vank (an Apostolic church-monastery-academy complex), to shrines and tombs in the area and to the Church of the Holy Cross on the Island of Akhthamar. The latter was a renowned tenth-century structure adorned with friezes portraying Biblical themes and saints. Alternating with these religious subjects is a bestiary of real and fantastic creatures, surmounted by vines and wild beasts. Although Gorky was too young to have formed more than a vague impression of these treasures, the memory of them stayed with him throughout his life.[2]

In 1908 Sedrak Adoian emigrated to the United States to avoid conscription into the Turkish Army—many Armenians fled at this time to escape the violent discrimination of the Turks, who forced them to fight against their own countrymen. He left behind a wife and four children: Akabi (Akho), born 1896, Shushanik's daughter by a former marriage; Satenik, born 1901; Vartoosh, born 1906; and Vosdanik. On leaving, the elder Adoian presented his son with red Armenian slippers; these same slippers appear throughout Gorky's oeuvre. From 1909 to 1910 the young boy attended St. Vardan's Armenian Apostolic School in Khorkom. There he studied drawing, writing and vernacular Armenian; from his mother he learned classical Armenian. In the spring of 1910, with his uncle Grikor Adoian, Vosdanik visited the city of Van for the first time. A land of ravishing beauty, Van is evoked by an Armenian proverb: "Van in this world, paradise in the next." The summer of that year he attended the funeral of his maternal grandmother, Lady Hamaspiur, purportedly the source of his 1947 canvas *The Orators* (cat. no. 238). Lady Shushanik and her three children moved to the city of Van in September of 1910, where Vosdanik studied at the Husisian Armenian Apostolic School. Van, one of the oldest seats of culture in the world, with its vast repository of ancient manuscript and wall paintings, sculpture and architecture, provided young Gorky with a rich artistic legacy on which to draw throughout his life. Later that year the family moved to Aikesdan, a suburb of Van. The famous Vank of Varak, widely known for its priceless collection of medieval Armenian illuminated manuscripts, was close-by, and the young Gorky visited it frequently. (Varak and its manuscripts were destroyed by the Turks in 1915.) At this time he met and became friendly with Manuk (Moorad) Mooradian who later married Vartoosh. From 1910 to 1915 the boy attended The American Mission School in Aikesdan. In 1912 in Van city Gorky and his mother posed for the local photographer (fig. 1). The photograph he took was sent to the father in America and ultimately became the inspiration for two masterful paintings entitled *The Artist and His Mother* (cat. nos. 75,76).

The Turkish siege of Van, which began in November of 1914, forced the Adoians to flee Aikesdan on June 15, 1915. Burying their belongings in the ground at home in the mistaken belief that they would be able to return, they took with them only a small amount of money and a few days supply of bread. One month later they reached Erevan (now Yerevan), some hundred miles from Van. Years later Vartoosh recalled their journey:

Naturally, the day they told us we must escape, all of the city panicked and the streets filled with people . . . . There was nothing but parched earth when we left Van. The Armenian commandos placed those who could not walk on caravans. But all of us walked . . . . We marched along the east end of Lake Van, a very mountainous area, passed Bergri Dasht where later the Turks massacred 50,000 Armenians. We walked day and night with little rest. We had no food to speak of. If mother found anything she would give it to Gorky because you take more care of a boy than girls and he was the only boy and he was very thin. My mother always worried about him. He was her favorite. Even when we kept fasts in Van, Mother would give him food. Some Vanetzis journeyed to Persia and then on to Baghdad. But we journeyed to Yerevan, to Caucasian Armenia.[3]

Amid massacres, war and starvation caused by the Turkish blockade of Armenia, Gorky, his sisters and his mother managed to eke out a meager existence. Gorky found various odd jobs, including carpentry, at which he was apparently very skilled, and printing. He attended the Temagan boys' school of St. Sarkis Church and learned to speak Caucasian Armenian. In the fall of 1916 Akabi and Satenik left for America, while Vosdanik remained behind with his mother and Vartoosh. Conditions for the impoverished Adoians gradually worsened, and on March 20, 1919, the mother died of starvation at the age of thirty-nine. Gorky, fifteen, and Vartoosh, thirteen, became virtual orphans. In May of 1919 with the help of an old family friend, Kertza Dikran, the children journeyed by train to Tiflis. In August they left Tiflis for Batum on the Black Sea, but stayed there only three weeks. In September brother and sister sailed to Constantinople, where they were befriended by Sedrak and Verghinay Kelekian. In February of 1920 Gorky and Vartoosh boarded a merchant ship bound for Athens, went on to Patras for fifteen days and finally took the liner S.S. *Presidente Wilson* sailing for America via a one-day layover in Naples.

Gorky and Vartoosh arrived at Ellis Island on February 26, 1920. Three days later they traveled to Watertown, Massachusetts, which had a large Armenian community, to stay with Akabi. In April of that year Gorky moved to Providence to stay with his father, whom he had not seen for twelve years. Records indicate that he attended the Old Beacon Street School and Bridgham Junior High School, but he decided to move back to Watertown in the summer of 1921. Although Gorky soon found work at the Hood Rubber Company there, he was fired after several months for drawing on the frames in which the shoe soles were transported. He also angered his employers by drawing on the factory roof. By the winter of 1922–23 Gorky was studying at Boston's New School of Design. Katherine O'D. Murphy, a fellow student, remembered Gorky as:

. . . a tall, serious young man in his twenties of great ambition who spent most of his free time in museums and who washed dishes in a restaurant for his meals. Afternoons he worked in a small portrait class where he could relax, walking back and forth with intricate dance steps, telling his long fanciful delightful tales of his boyhood in Russia.

Among his stories was one, that he was the nephew of Maxim Gorky. That caused considerable embarrassment to the school director who had introduced him as such to a friend of the author.

During the noon recesses, Gorky used to sketch outdoors and one dull day, Gorky painted a small panel of the Park Street Church. A parishoner passing by offered Gorky five dollars for the painting if he would make his figures more distinct and less like peasants. Naturally Gorky was furious

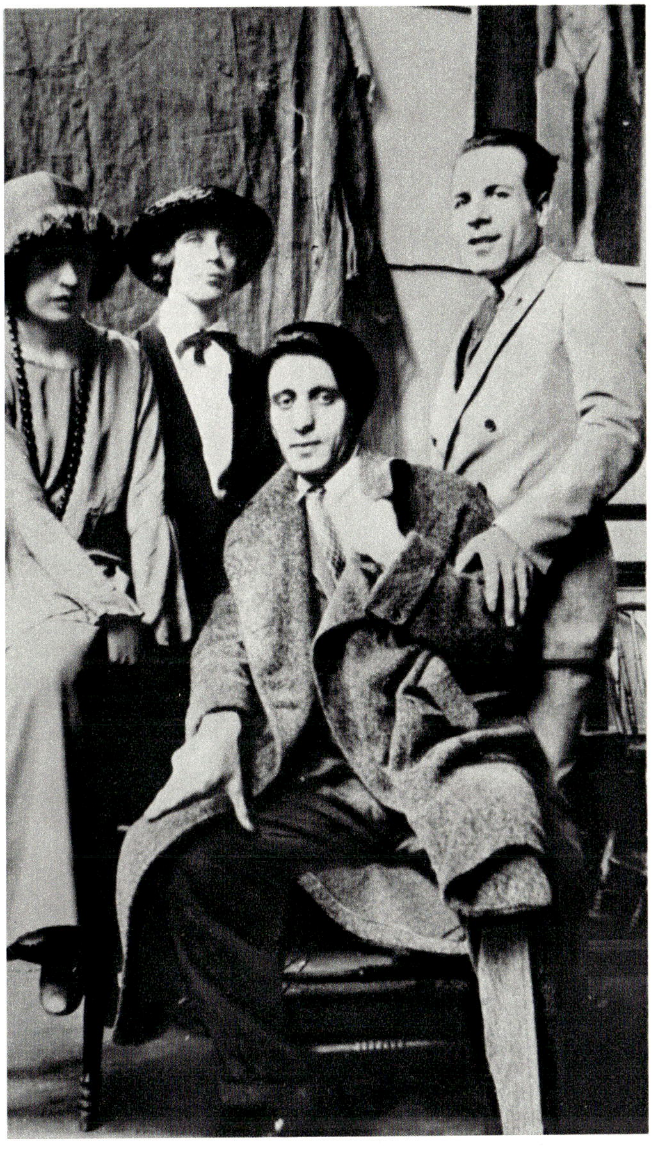

Gorky (seated) with Miss Lisle, Ethel M. Cooke, friends from New School of Design, and Felix Chooligian, friend from Van, 1924

> *and returned to the school enraged but sorry that he had not sold the little oil for $5.00 and offering it at that price. So I gave him $10.00 for the little oil and $10.00 was quite a sum to me then.*[4]

This modest and charming little canvas of 1924 (cat. no. 1), painted in a Post-Impressionist style, is one of the few remaining works of this time. The rosy brick and lavender hues of the church, the pale lilac sky, the odd greens and deep yellow of the foreground foretell Gorky's future color preferences. Clearly the work of a young artist, it is nevertheless adroit in its painterliness.

Gorky drew constantly from childhood. Vartoosh remembered her brother always drew pictures on the sand and did a great deal of wood carving. She recalled, "When Mother was alive in Yerevan she would encourage him and give him some money to purchase paper and pencils."[5] The late Yenovk der Hagopian, a sculptor and close friend of the artist from their boyhood days in Van, recalled their early shared love of art: "In Khorkom, we would go together to the shrine of Vart Badrik and become thrilled by the *khatchkars* all around it. You know, the ancient Armenian tombstones with miniature Armenian drawings carved on them. We were always so amazed. Neither I nor he had any advanced ideas about art at such an early age naturally. At that time all we knew was that they were beautiful and we would go there and touch them with our hands."[6] Der Hagopian remembered telling his father about the beautiful tombstones; in turn his father showed him the paintings in the family Bible. After relating this to Manuk, "Manuk asked his mother to show him the paintings in their family's Armenian Bible. And his family had a great deal of art because Manuk's grandfather was the head of the Vank of Charahan Surp Nishan in Vosdan. And I remember that Manuk had a knife with which he carved flutes in the early spring from the willow trees which we call *uri*."[7]

Gorky and der Hagopian caught up with one another after World War I in Watertown. At Gorky's initiation, the two would often take their painting boxes to the Charles River and other sites to work. Der Hagopian wrote that Gorky often found unusual places to set up an easel, once choosing a busy intersection, disrupting traffic and nearly getting himself arrested. Gorky continued to carve and made miniature versions of the plows of Van—a subject that still occupied him in the 1940s. Der Hagopian, who worked with Gorky on one plow, recalled the artist's obsession with craftsmanship at this time.

Gorky's Armenian heritage always remained meaningful to him. To his Armenian friends and family he often spoke of his desire to return to the old country, a wish that was never fulfilled. The lengthy correspondence he carried on with Vartoosh and her family from 1937 to 1948 reveals his longing for Armenia. His memories of childhood came to people his canvases, and the expression of his love for his country grew even more profound when he returned to nature in 1943. To der Hagopian Gorky said, "That which we used to have in our country, in Van, we weren't mature enough to fully appreciate. We couldn't understand everything. Now I know my way. Now I know where I'm standing."[8] As late as 1946, when this conversation took place, Gorky was directed toward Armenia—in der Hagopian's words, "toward an even greater appreciation of the natural beauty of the old country . . . he realized fully what we had and what we had lost."[9]

But in 1924 thoughts of Armenia were not uppermost in Gorky's mind. He decided to leave the Boston area, to move to New York to become a great artist. He had already taken a new name: the surname he adopted was inspired by that of the Russian writer Maxim Gorky. As a given name he first took Arshele, then Archele or Archel, finally settling on Arshile.[10] He liked to explain that in Russian Gorky means "bitterness" or "the bitter one" and Arshile, "Achilles."[11] Gorky was no stranger to romantic legend, forever telling exotic and conflicting stories about his origins, passing variously as Russian, Georgian, Armenian; speaking of himself as a relative of Maxim Gorky and as a pupil of Kandinsky, a student of the Polytechnical Institute in Tiflis, a student at the Académie Julian in Paris or at Brown University, when, in fact, he was far too young to have undertaken such advanced studies. There exist a few clues about the reasons the young painter chose the name Gorky. The most obvious are that the Russian writer was known to an American audience, that Gorky felt both alienated and estranged as a refugee from a country so little known and with so little meaning here and, wishing to be famous, adopted the name of a famous author, although he had determined to make a name for himself as an artist and ultimately reveal himself as an Armenian (a fact he confided to Vartoosh). He probably felt justified in taking a pseudonym because Maxim Gorky was itself a pseudonym, and, moreover, it was common for many of his colleagues to change their names (John Graham for one, Mark Rothko for another). Gorky differed from these painters in that he assumed the name of an artist who already existed, while they abbreviated or anglicized their own names. (Marcel Duchamp went even further than Gorky, choosing to assume an entirely new identity, a disguise, in the persona of Rrose Sélavy.)

Gorky's quest for identity not only led him to assume a new name but to seek out a new art in New York. Vartoosh recalled that: "He went to New York because it was the center of art in America, even though he was not very impressed with America's art, and he felt there they might understand him better. Everyone was against his going except me. They all thought that he should work in a factory, that he couldn't live from art. What will you do in New York? No, he replied. I want to draw. And he left."[12] Although it is commonly believed that he settled in New York in a studio at 47a Washington Square South at the corner of Sullivan Street, he probably moved about at first, possibly staying with friends. Vartoosh, who had married in 1923, visited as often as she could. She said they spoke:

> *About Armenia, about Van, and about art. Always about art . . . . At that time he was painting and showing me his works. "This is how I am going to do things, Vartoosh, and try to arrange an exhibition." His art then was more realistic. But he began to change. We would go to Washington Square and sit together. There many children played, and he named one of them Uccello. "Vartoosh," he said, "this one draws just like Uccello." And he would put a chalk in the child's hand, he was hardly two years old, and the child would just draw on the sidewalk. "These are the authentic artists," he told me, "who draw lines in their day of purity and thereby release naivety. When we try to do that we have a very difficult time, but for them it is very easy."*[13]

Shortly after Gorky first moved to New York, he enrolled as a student in the Grand Central School of Art. By 1926 he had been recognized for his exceptional talent and asked by the head of the school, Edmund Greacen, to join the faculty. An article published in the *New York Evening Post* on September 15, 1926, notes that ". . . today he became an active member of the faculty of the Grand Central School of Art." Amusingly titled "Fetish of Antique Stifles Art Here, Says Gorky Kin," it is both fanciful about Gorky's origins and informative about his art. "The young Russian hears occasionally from his famous cousin, Maxim," is said to believe that America is obsessed with the antique, often at the expense of modern art and is quoted as follows: "in Paris and in Germany, a painting done this year is exhibited this year." The reporter describes his visit to Gorky's West 50th Street studio (that this studio existed is a little-known fact), where he saw still lifes, portraits and paintings and observed the artist working on a study of a few glass objects and fruit. Most important, we are informed that Gorky considers Cézanne, Matisse and Picasso the major painters of our time and, in fact, thinks that Cézanne is the greatest artist of all time.

An inspired teacher, Gorky taught at the Grand Central School of Art until 1931. To supplement his earnings, into the early 1940s he also gave lessons in his studio to many private students, among them Ethel Schwabacher, Betty Parsons, Walter Murch and Hans Burkhardt. His teaching paralleled his own growth and development as an artist, reflecting a thirst for experiment and change which was all the more remarkable given the conservative climate of the period. Many of his students have spoken or written of his teaching. One of the most interesting accounts is that of Murch, as related by Daniel Robbins:

> *Gorky prescribed a certain size of paper—large—about 14 × 18, and made everyone begin with lead pencil, then charcoal. Murch's first drawing for Gorky, of a nude, was done in his best O.C.A. manner. Gorky looked at it sympathetically and said, "Never more draw like that." It was an attempt to duplicate the observed thing: Murch believed that the artist was supposed to be able to do . . . every detail, especially in pencil. But Gorky said, "You don't use a pencil like that!" Gorky explained that the medium or the artist must be allowed to take over . . . that the medium was interesting in itself, not merely a vehicle for something else . . . . When, at the end of the semester, Gorky left the Grand Central, Murch studied painting with him privately for about two years, at his studio on Washington Square South. They went out a lot, on ferries, up to the Bronx, in Central Park, around the docks. Gorky would look down side streets and at groups of rocks and trees often waving his hand and saying, "all wrong." He meant that the given, the observed could be wrong; he criticized views that were dull, or insipid. He dared to criticize nature! Murch thus began to learn what art was, and how it could be superimposed on the given; he began to sense the infinite possibilities and endless relationships between the observed, himself, and something that Gorky was certain about: Art.*[14]

The 1920s was not an auspicious time for the young and aspiring painter. During the postwar era the mood of the nation engendered a feeling among

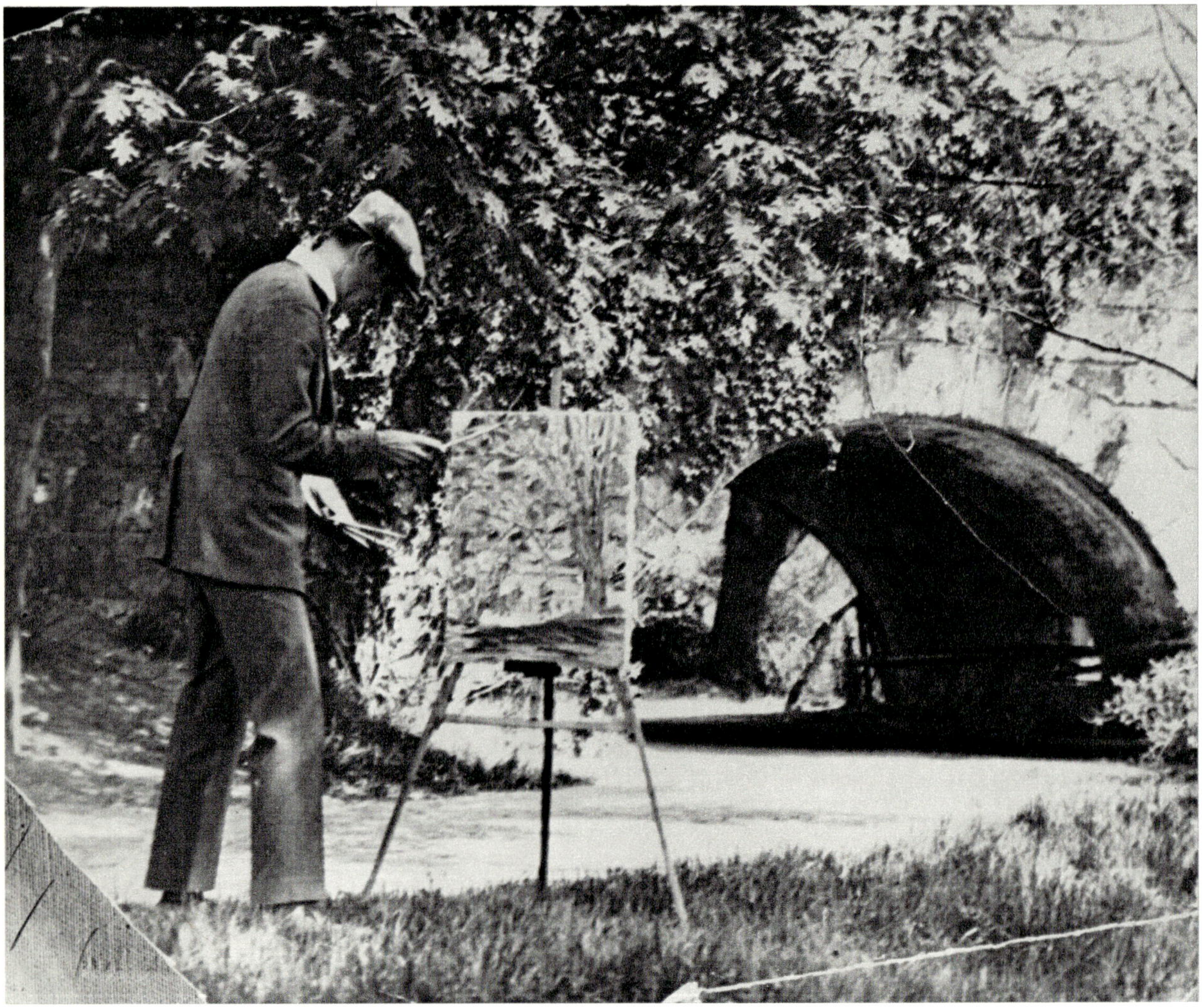

Central Park, ca. late 1920s

many artists that their occupation was utterly frivolous: to be an artist was to avoid facing the abysmal social and political realities of the day. Further, to be an *abstract* artist was anomalous in terms of the prevailing aesthetic temper in America. In may ways this temper coincided with the contemporaneous conservative retreat from abstraction and experimentation in Europe, where artists like Picasso, Braque, Gris, the Futurists and Matisse returned to more traditional modes of painting. This retrogression, which began in the middle of World War I, was to last until the middle 1920s there; in the United States it continued well into the 1930s. The collapse of the American avant-garde was not only of longer duration but was more complete—Americans simply did not have a formidable enough tradition of advanced painting to sustain them.

Provincialism as embodied in Regionalism, American Scene Painting and Social Realism prevailed in the States during the 1920s and 1930s. Thomas Hart Benton and a number of other popular representational painters had once embraced avant-garde art but renounced abstraction entirely after World War I. Their intense reaction was symptomatic of America's political, social and aesthetic conservatism, its isolationism and chauvinism, its disillusionment born of the war and deepened by the Depression. Even Georgia O'Keeffe, Marsden Hartley and Stanton MacDonald-Wright, who had been among the most advanced abstract artists in America, returned, at least for a time, to representation. Few artists continued to work in vanguard modes—Arthur Dove and Morgan Russell from the first generation, Stuart Davis, the only major American to emerge during the twenties, and Josef Albers and Hans Hofmann, Europeans who came to this country in the early 1930s. The great majority of painters, however, depicted the poverty and despair of the urban masses or celebrated a fictional rural utopia. Everyday reality (or a fantasy thereof) was the accepted artistic subject, as painting often became topical, journalistic, illustrational.

Why Gorky rejected these conservative, insular models and almost from the beginning of his artistic development found his inspiration in sophisticated European painting is uncertain. When he was already looking toward Europe, contemporaries such as Rothko and Adolph Gottlieb continued to paint in a representational manner rooted in Social Realism and Expressionism, although they admired the great European art of the past and present as intensely as Gorky. It may be that Rothko and Gottlieb felt compelled to express their deep commitment to social and political issues through representational painting, despite their love of abstraction. Gorky, on the other hand, participated only marginally in social and political causes. These speculations aside, it is certain that by absorbing the lessons of the most advanced art of the time Gorky was able to forge his personal style well before most of his colleagues in New York had begun to formulate their own aesthetics.

While Social Realism and Expressionism were the most visible and predominant influences upon the majority of young artists of Gorky's generation, alternatives were to some extent accessible in New York. If Stieglitz's gallery "291" and his magazine *Camera Work* had foundered by 1920, the forces of change were encouraged elsewhere. Katherine Dreier's Société Anonyme, whose motto was "Traditions are beautiful—but to create them—not to follow," had opened on April 20, 1920, at 19 East 47th Street. Dreier gave one-man shows (in most cases, the artist's first in the United States) to Kandinsky, Klee, Léger, Miró, Ernst, Mondrian, Malevich and others. In addition, Dreier and her friends sponsored lectures on the psychology of modern art as well as a symposium on Dada, and published the English translation of Apollinaire's volume on Cubism. By mid-decade activity began to intensify: the first issue of *Cahiers d'Art,* with articles on Léger, Miró, Picasso and de Chirico, appeared in Paris in 1926, the Gallatin Collection opened in New York, the Quinn Collection was shown, the Montross, Daniel and Valentine galleries and Neumann's New Art Circle exhibited advanced art and, finally, The Museum of Modern Art opened to the public in 1929.

Gorky's paintings of the mid to late twenties are dominated by Cézanne. He had the opportunity to see a small number of Cézannes in Boston at the Museum of Fine Arts and surely could have encountered others in New York. At the Metropolitan Museum he would almost certainly have seen the French master's *View of the Domaine Saint-Joseph*, which had been purchased from the Armory Show and was on view during the twenties. Durand-Ruel, the Reinhardt Galleries and Wildenstein all showed the artist's work throughout the late 1920s. The opening show of The Museum of Modern Art featured Cézanne together with Gauguin, van Gogh, Seurat. The Havemeyer bequest to the Metropolitan in 1929 contained several Cézannes.

Gorky would have seen other Cézannes in reproduction and might well have read about his work in essays such as William Huntington Wright's "What is Modern Painting," in which the artist is discussed at considerable length; this particular text was published in conjunction with *The Forum Exhibition*

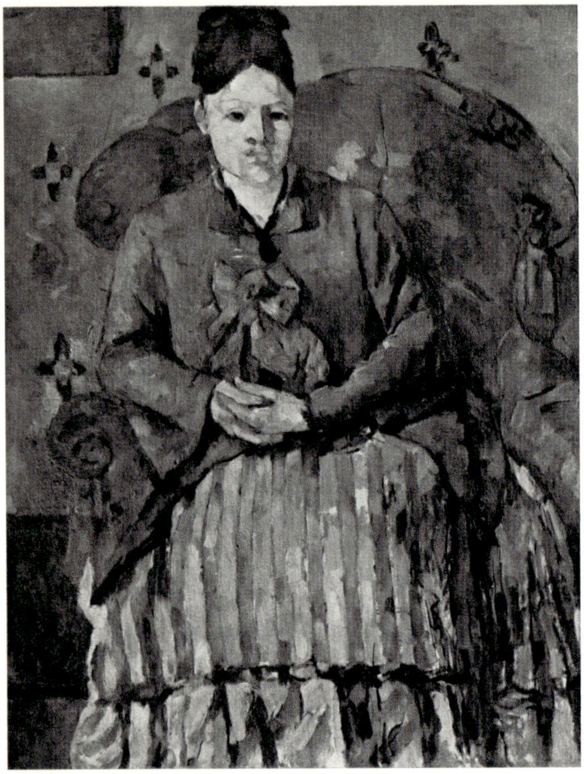

2. Paul Cézanne
Madame Cézanne in a Red Armchair. ca. 1877
Oil on canvas, 28 1/2 × 22″
Collection Museum of Fine Arts, Boston

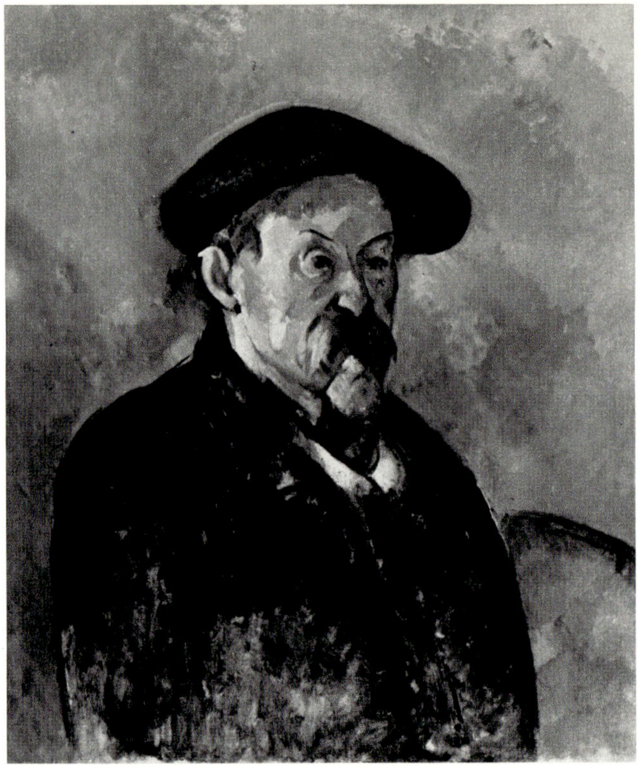

3. Paul Cézanne
Self-Portrait with Beret. ca. 1900
Oil on canvas, 25 1/4 × 21″
Collection Museum of Fine Arts, Boston

of Modern American Painters held in March of 1916 at the Anderson Galleries. Although there is no record of Gorky's attending the Art Students League, he frequented it. Gorky must also have known Max Weber and his Cézannesque paintings, since he later asked the older artist to recommend him for a Guggenheim grant.

Gorky owed Cézanne a profound debt: from him he learned concepts of space and tactility and to analyze nature in terms of form, structure, light. To fully experience Cézanne, Gorky painted still lifes, landscapes and portraits in the master's style, usually adopting a specific model or composites of several works he knew either in the original or in reproduction. Gorky's *Self-Portrait at the Age of Nine*, ca. 1927 (cat. no. 8), is very similar to portraits by Cézanne such as *Madame Cézanne in a Red Armchair,* ca. 1877 (fig. 2). In each, the shape of the face is defined by a few bold outlines, the forms are built up of deftly articulated patches of color, the features accentuated or de-emphasized according to their importance as shape and volume within the total composition. Gorky's self-portrait differs from *Madame Cézanne in a Red Armchair* and indeed much of Cézanne's oeuvre in an important respect: its aura of sadness and melancholy contrasts markedly with the stoic calm and emotional objectivity that often characterize Cézanne's work.

A later, equally fascinating example of Gorky's Cézannesque portraiture is *Self-Portrait* of ca. 1928–31 (cat. no. 9). It reflects Cézanne's later, loosely-brushed style as epitomized in his *Self-Portrait with Beret*, ca. 1900 (fig. 3). The Gorky has quiet authority; the gaze is commanding; the artist portrays himself as a somewhat romantic nineteenth-century figure, costumed in the manner of that time. In another Cézannesque *Self-Portrait* of ca. 1931 (cat. no. 13), Gorky depicts a more defiant personality, bohemian, collar loosened, vest unbuttoned, face saddened by the forces of destiny. During this period he turned also to Gauguin and Matisse. His *Self-Portrait* of ca. 1928–31 (cat. no. 12) seems a composite of Matisse's *Self-Portrait* of 1906 (fig. 4) and elements drawn from Gauguin's self-portraits. From Matisse he took pose, costume and heavy outlines, from Gauguin, treatment of hair and beard, a sense of directness and stylized background forms. Of all the early self-portraits, this is the most primitive in its impetuous brushwork, its heightened color and bold, staring eyes. Significantly, none of these rather

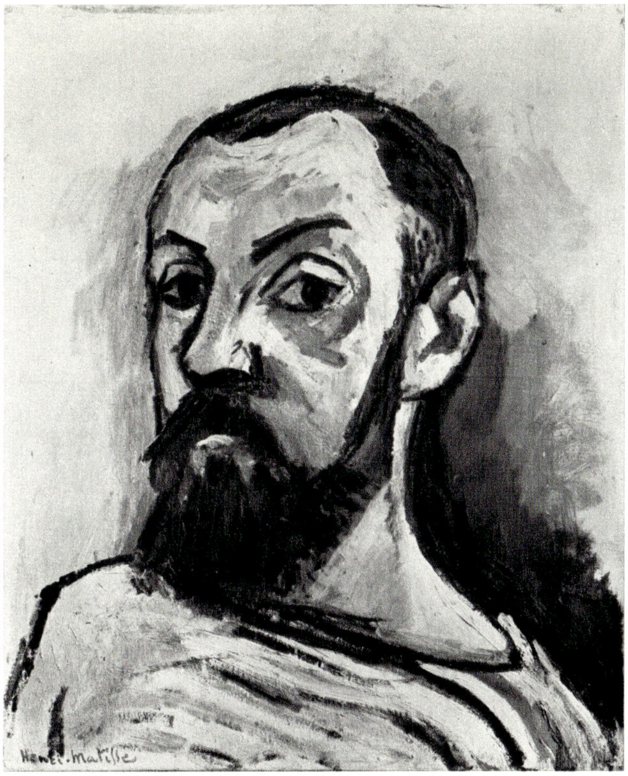

4. Henri Matisse
Self-Portrait. 1906
Oil on wood, 21 5/8 × 18 1/8″
Statens Museum for Kunst, Copenhagen, J. Rump Collection

idealized portraits resembles Gorky very closely. For not until he began to rely upon his personal memories as his primary inspiration could he reveal himself in his self-portraits. Thus, in the *Self-Portrait* of 1931–33 (cat. no. 67) he discloses his true identity by delineating his distinctive physiognomy and by referring to conventions of Armenian wall paintings and manuscripts, such as ornamental stylization of facial features and emphatic patterning of curves.

Gorky's landscapes are among his most literal adaptations of Cézanne. He made no attempt to disguise his reliance upon the master, titling one of his paintings *Landscape in the Manner of Cézanne.* Other works of the mid to late 1920s, such as *Untitled* (*Landscape*), late 1920s (cat. no. 4), clearly derive from Cézanne forest paintings. The Gorkys lack Cézanne's pronounced vertical elements and his extraordinary integration of line and color. Nevertheless, these early works display a directness, intensity and, above all, a formal awareness unusual for so young an artist. Gorky could not duplicate Cézanne's exquisite touch, his feathered brushstroke, his tenuous balance of bare and painted areas of canvas, his sense of captured light; but he understood their structural function and the essential principles of Cézanne's style. Gorky was at his best when he painted directly from nature, even as he referred to the model of Cézanne. Vaclav Vytlacil remembered that Gorky sometimes studied reproductions of Cézanne landscapes, then painted at the pond in the park opposite the Plaza Hotel and finally compared the finished product with the reproductions.[15] *Landscape, Staten Island,* 1927–28 (cat. no. 7), is one of the most successful examples of this genre, revealing Gorky's skills in the massing of shapes, use of warm earth tones, cool dark greens, equally cool, lighter-valued blues, some understanding of Cézanne's adroit manipulation of foreground, middle and background space, and an excellent grasp of the master's brushwork.

It is indisputable that Gorky's evolution was uneven. Many of his Cézannesque still lifes of the 1920s and 1930s are energetic but clumsy. By far the most unusual of the still lifes of this category is the macabre, uncharacteristically expressionist and rather unresolved *Still Life with Skull* of the late 1920s (cat. no. 3), based on a number of Cézannes of the same subject in the Barnes Foundation and the National Gallery (figs. 5,6). The bulky cloth and skull and the dense impasto in Gorky's painting are very much in the manner of the French artist, but the relationships are confusing and the composition is a curious amalgam of still life and interior. The forms, although awkward, prefigure the curvilinear shapes of the later work. Moreover, certain distinctive colors, such as red-brown, chrome green and lavender, as well as the powerful sense of gravity evident here become important elements in subsequent paintings.

Pears, Peaches and Pitcher, late 1920s (cat. no. 15), is as convincing a statement as an artist working in the style of another can produce. Far more interesting than the Cézannesque manner, however, is the original organization of space and form: the horizontal compartmentalization of the canvas which evokes the divisions of landscape, the interruption of these horizontal areas by the vertical of the pitcher, the punctuation of the surface with the forms of the fruit. The velvety surfaces, luminous color and rich facture reveal that at this imitative phase of his development Gorky could handle paint with extraordinary skill. When he achieved his breakthrough in 1941–42, he recaptured in his new and personal language the evanescent beauty of much of the early work.

Although Gorky painted his way through Cézanne, the lessons of the French master remained with him throughout his life to emerge once again, transformed, in the last great stage of his career. Gorky's early Cézannesque attempt to paint the

5. Paul Cézanne
Young Man with a Skull. 1896–98
Oil on canvas, 51 1/8 × 38 1/8″
© The Barnes Foundation, Merion, Pennsylvania

6. Paul Cézanne
Still Life with Apples and Peaches. ca. 1905
Oil on canvas, 32 × 39 5/8″
National Gallery of Art, Washington, D.C.
Gift of Eugene and Agnes Meyer

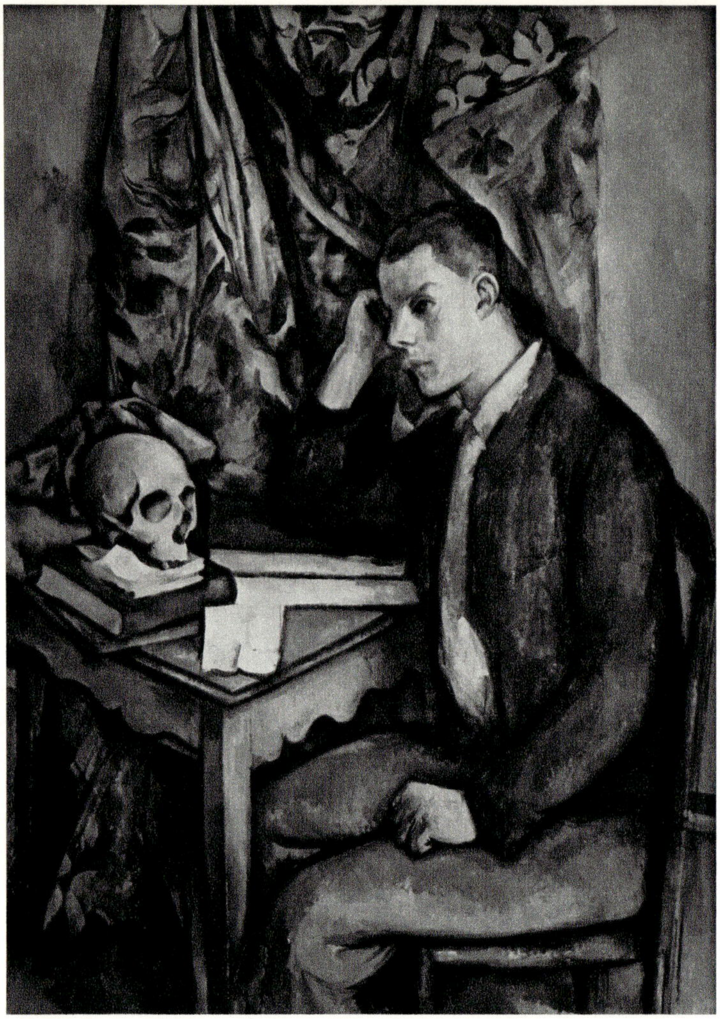

space in and around objects, to paint the atmosphere, became crucial to his mature style. For the fundamentals of Cézanne's teaching are visible in Gorky's late work: in his return to nature and his re-creation of that nature into abstractions which embody a vivid sense of reality.

Most critics see in Gorky's work of the 1920s and 1930s an almost total abnegation of self, a denial not only of individuality but of originality. They see his career in two unconnected phases: a highly imitative period followed by a brief great original style. But the flowering of Gorky's genius did not occur as an abrupt transformation of the imitative into the innovative. His evolution was, rather, a series of sometimes faltering but ultimately progressive steps leading to an art which is a synthesis of the traditional and the revolutionary. Gorky did not believe in "originality," at least not insofar as the term signifies newness for its own sake. In these early years Gorky haunted the museums, seeking nourishment for his own art, proselytizing the great art of the past. He was an equally avid devotee of the most modern and the most ancient art. For him great art was truly timeless. Because its forms are constant, Gorky could draw from all periods, basing his painting on sources as diverse as Greek sculpture and Matisse in a work such as *The Antique Cast,* 1926 (cat. no. 2). (Curiously, the Matisse which served as model here is itself based on an antique sculpture.) He put himself at the service of the great art of the past in order to learn the language of art. Only after mastering this old language did he feel he could invent a new one. His was not the ambition of an imitator but of an artist who felt he had the makings of a great painter. He would, by means of imitating the great painters of the past, ultimately rival those masters.

If most critics did not understand why Gorky chose to draw from the artists of the past, his fellow painters were more sensitive. Stuart Davis, who, after his return from Europe, met the artist sometime in 1929, said: "I have never raised any question

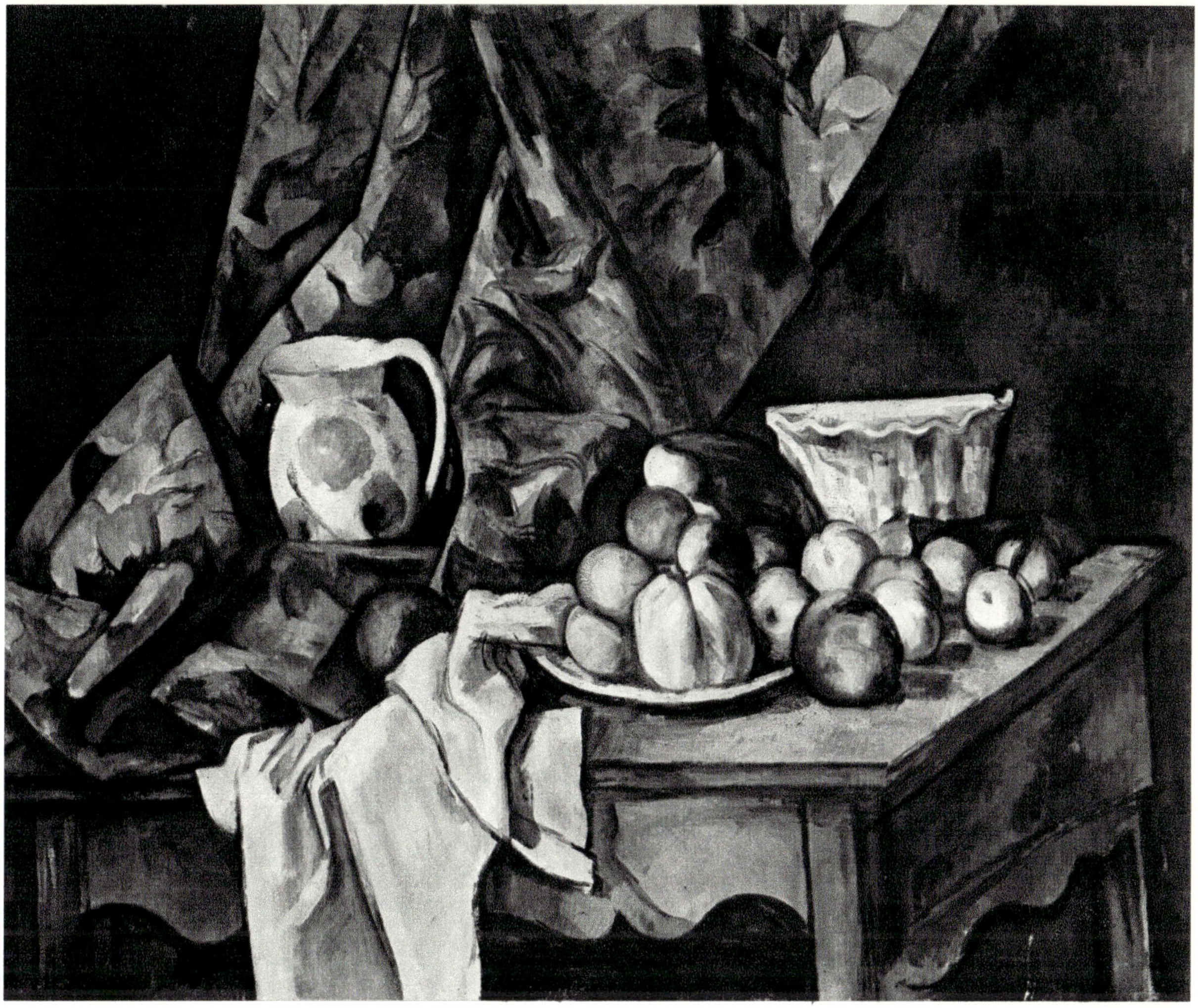

about Gorky's unusual gifts as an artist, nor do I do so now. In the beginning he chose the strongest painters in modern art as the models for his development. I always supported him, against the charges of 'imitation' that accompanied this valid process."[16]

Davis' recollections offer us an illuminating glimpse of Gorky's personality and daily life. He recalled visiting Gorky in his studio on Sullivan Street:

He had many unique qualities but poverty was not one of them. In spite of this situation he was the only artist I can recall who always had a real studio. Most, including myself, painted in their bedrooms or temporary makeshift quarters. In addition, he managed to keep these studios stocked with a supply of art materials worthy of a small retail store, and used them up with abandon and unconcern for cost in accord with his temperament. The periods without paint and canvas when he could only draw . . . were mainly the product of orgies of consumption rather than a permanent state of attrition. In brief, he galloped around the Village like a mountain goat with his pauper peers and got off better than most.[17]

Davis and Gorky remained close friends for several years. Together with John D. Graham (whom Gorky had met shortly after he moved to New York—the date is variously given as 1928 or 1929), they were often referred to as the "Three Musketeers." Although Davis was ten years Gorky's senior and Graham was much older, their unswerving devotion to modern art cemented the friendship and gave them strength and stability during an uncertain time.

Davis encouraged younger artists and commanded their respect as a painter dedicated to the most advanced concepts when these ideas were generally in disrepute. Davis' longstanding commitment to abstraction, which dated back to the time of the Armory Show, was extremely meaningful to less experienced artists in the late 1920s and early 1930s. Both Graham and Davis were important sources of intellectual support for Gorky.

The aristocratic Graham, born Ivan Dombrovski in Kiev, Russia, in 1887, was the most sophisticated and erudite of the three. Forced to flee Russia when the counterrevolution failed, he came to New York via Warsaw in 1920, the same year Gorky arrived in America. By the late 1920s he had made several trips to Paris and had begun collecting art. He frequented avant-garde circles, meeting Picasso, André Breton, André Gide, Paul Eluard and the critic Waldemar George. Although a gifted painter in his own right, Graham was important to younger artists here for his firsthand knowledge of contemporary European art. Graham's willingness to convey this knowledge to his American colleagues, his ability to formulate current ideas into systematic theory (he published the provocative and influential *System and Dialectics of Art* in 1937), his extraordinary generosity and his encouragement of younger men like Gorky, Willem de Kooning, David Smith and Jackson Pollock made him a figure of great consequence in the 1920s and 1930s. During the 1930s Graham championed Marxism, psychoanalysis, primitive and abstract art. He believed in the unconscious as a source of creativity, in the use of accident and automatism in art. For Graham, Uccello was the next step in the evolution of the two-dimensional expression of Graeco-Egyptian and Byzantine art that culminated in Picasso. He called this two-dimensional expression "pure painting." Graham maintained that artists must evolve through three phases: apprenticeship to the old masters, the confusing search for one's own path and, finally, mature resolution. These ideas, more than Graham's painting, were absolutely fundamental to Gorky's growth throughout the thirties.

At this time both Graham and Davis were dedicated to Picasso's Cubism. Years later when Davis commended Gorky for having "the intelligence and energy to orient himself in the direction of the most dynamic ideas of the time,"[18] he was referring to Cubism. And Gorky himself exclaimed, "Has there been in six centuries better art than Cubism?"[19] For as Gorky had emulated Cézanne, he turned to Picasso as a revered teacher and example during the succeeding stage in his evolution towards maturity. Gorky's need to grow, to change and experiment was manifested in a systematic absorption of modern painting as it unfolded chronologically from Cézanne to the art of his own time. Picasso was the inevitable next step in this progression; Gorky acknowledged as much when he said, "I was *with* Cézanne for a long time and now naturally I am *with* Picasso."[20] He modeled his art closely upon Picasso's, painting in the Spaniard's many styles, emulating the Blue and Rose Periods and Synthetic Cubism, even imitating his numerous signatures and their varied placement on the canvas.

Gorky did not work through Picasso's styles in their actual chronological order; rather he selected what intrigued him or what he needed at a given time. For example, he painted in a Synthetic Cubist style before exploring collage, thus reversing the evolutionary order of Picasso's and Braque's own work. Except in a few sketches, Gorky chose not to emulate Analytical Cubism, the style which represents Picasso's most original and revolutionary contribution. In his study of Cézanne, Gorky had explored what might be called proto-Cubism, and certainly understood the impact of Cézanne's revolutionary paintings upon Picasso's own development. Yet neither the Analytical Cubists' experimentation with volume, their assembling and reassembling of forms in space, their architectonic compositions nor their monochromatic color interested him. He was, however, attracted to the organization of flat shapes on the picture plane, the vivid color and tactile pigment that characterized the succeeding phase of the style, Synthetic Cubism.

In his still lifes of the late 1920s Gorky interpreted and explored the Synthetic Cubism of both Braque and Picasso, and to a lesser extent that of Gris. The original Cézannesque still-life motif now becomes increasingly schematic, and the guitar from the standard Cubist repertory joins the fruit, pitcher and bottle as subjects. Gorky largely ignores the subject matter of the café and daily life: the pipes, dice, calling and playing cards, newspapers and lettering which had so enriched the paintings and collages of Braque and Picasso. He avoids the topicality of subjects drawn from everyday reality in favor of more classical, timeless motifs. He simplifies and abstracts from the profusion of images offered by the Cubist iconography. In contrast to works like *Pears, Peaches and Pitcher,* late 1920s, discussed above, *Composition with Vegetables,* 1928, and *Still Life,* ca. 1928 (cat. nos. 21, 22), are emphatically flat. Although Gorky retains the tilted plane of the table from his Cézannesque composition, he now treats it differently. As it had previously, the extremely tilted tabletop thrusts the objects toward the viewer. However, the table no longer bridges the gap between rounded objects and flat background, nor does it act as a foil for these shapes, but serves as a framing device and is one flat shape among many. The composition has become an organization of interlocking shapes and abstract color patterns. As space becomes flatter and more compressed, Gorky's interest in tactility and surface effect increases as paintings such as *Still Life with Pears,* 1928, and *Still Life,* ca. 1928 (cat. nos. 19, 20), reveal. He builds forward from the canvas with heavier impasto; he emulates Picasso's characteristic incised crosshatching and attempts to simulate materials such as chair caning and marbelized paper in the manner of both Picasso and Braque.

Gorky found inspiration for the use of curved shape and intense color in a number of Picasso's boldly geometric and relatively simplified compositions such as the Synthetic Cubist *Harlequin,* late 1915, and *Guitar,* autumn 1919 (figs. 7,8). In each of these paintings Picasso heightens the vividness of his colors by effectively contrasting them with dramatic areas of black and white. Gorky either could not achieve or did not wish to achieve the clarity of Picasso's color and black and white, or the precision with which he manipulates curve and straight edge. His rounded shapes and his space remain indeterminate, never attaining the crispness or flatness of Picasso's; his color, rich as it is, is soft, subtle, nuanced in comparison to Picasso's intense, sometimes harsh palette. Gorky's innately lyrical sensibility did not allow him to attain the dramatic impact of Picasso, despite his attempts at emulation.

Still Life, 1928 (fig. 9), is a fine example of the Braque-like Gorkys of 1927–31. The format of the painting, an extended horizontal, the deep blues and greens of the objects and the touching of them with white, the layering of paint, the decorative stippling are all characteristic of the French painter. While Gorky was able to capture much of the spirit of Braque's work and certainly understood the formal aspects of his composition, he never achieved the Frenchman's decorative touch, exquisite scumbled surfaces or sense of perfect scale.

While it is sometimes difficult to identify the source of Gorky's inspiration as Picasso or Braque, *Still Life,* 1929–32 (cat. no. 23), clearly derives from the Spaniard's *Mandolin and Music Stand* of 1923 (fig. 10). This is perhaps Gorky's most successful and interesting early adaptation of Picasso, as well as a key to his future development. Here Gorky has used many shapes identical to Picasso's own, most notably the trefoil motif at the left. But he has transformed the guitar into a composite that is part face, part boot, introducing the slipper or boot motif which appears throughout the later work. Emotional tenor is transformed as well: the mundane reality suggested by Picasso's guitar is replaced by a powerful sense of enigma which issues from the ambiguous hybrid boot-face. Cubist structure underlies proto-Surrealist content.

During the late 1920s and early 1930s Gorky and Graham worked in similar directions. Gorky's *Still Life with Palette* and Graham's *Still Life,* both 1930 (figs. 11, 12) share the Cubist vocabulary of motifs—the jug, the palette, the tabletop, as well as such Picassoesque forms as eye-like shapes, circles which represent holes—and techniques of execution. However, Gorky is invariably more painterly than Graham, his shapes are more curvilinear, his lines more fluid.

Gorky intermittently explored collage beginning in the early thirties. Will Barnet recalled an incident of this time:

> *. . . I made a visit to Arshile Gorky's Washington Square studio. I knocked timidly on his door, and it soon opened and before me was a scene of great commotion. Gorky was evidently upset and I soon learned why; the previous evening he had designed a collage painting of which a part was composed of a piece of cheese. Gorky had gone to bed and in the morning awakened to find that a village mouse, enamored by the choice of materials used in this work had proceeded to re-design the canvas by eliminating the cheese. Of course Gorky was livid.*[21]

Among the few experiments in this medium that survive is a fascinating work of 1934–35 (cat. no. 18). Gorky's collage is a fairly literal adaptation of Picasso's *Still Life: Bottle, Playing Cards, Glass* of 1914 (fig. 13), which he could have seen in the Gallatin Collection. (Or he may have known it in reproduction from the March 1929 issue of *Creative Art* or in the Gallatin Collection's catalogue, published in 1933.) To Picasso's composition Gorky has added the bird's head at the left, a bizarre image probably derived from Ernst. This and the few other collages extant reveal jarring and discordant juxtapositions of subjects which are more closely related to Dada than to Cubism and are unusual in Gorky's work at this time. Collage was a convenient and appropriate medium in which to combine images of different orders. Although he did not pursue his experiments in this medium, he continued to explore strange and unusual juxtapositions of images in his drawings of the thirties and in his paintings of the forties.

Gorky reveals his subjects in a rich variety of guises, transforming his shapes from still-life objects to human figures to abstract images to evocative organic hybrids. The shapes of *Abstraction*

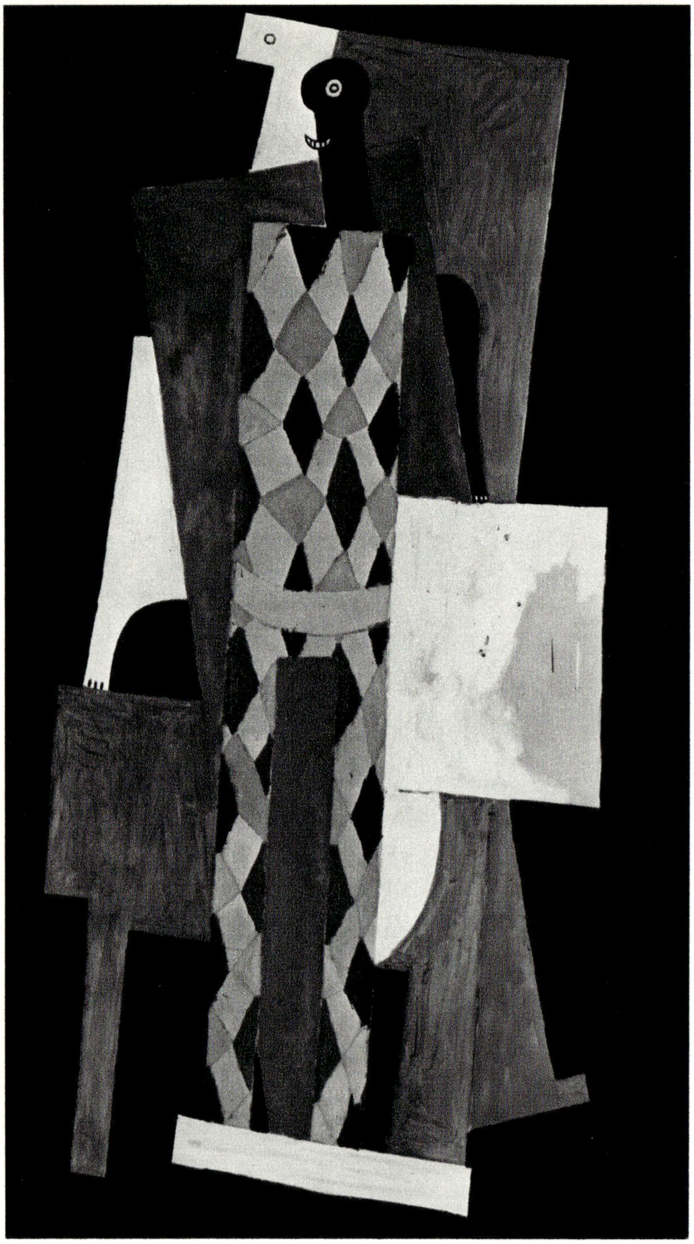

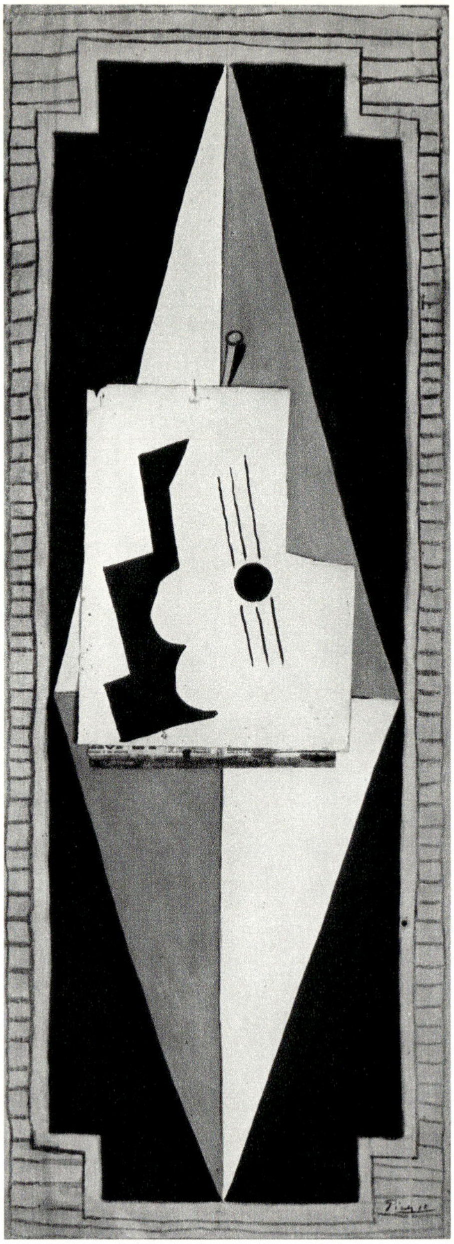

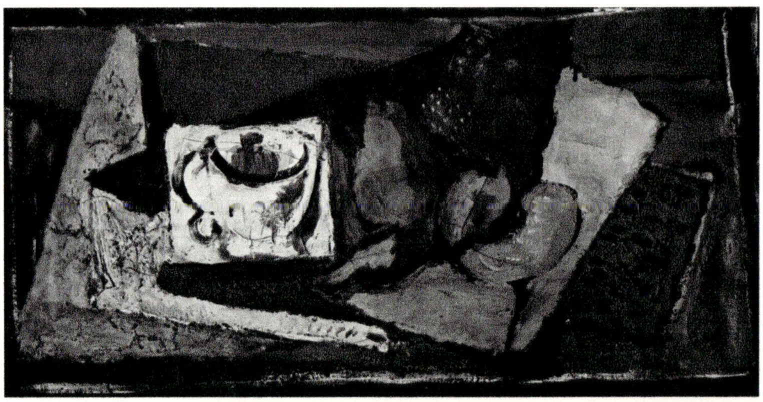

7. Pablo Picasso
Harlequin. Late 1915
Oil on canvas, 72 1/4 × 41 3/8″
Collection The Museum of Modern Art, New York, Acquired through the Lillie P. Bliss Bequest

8. Pablo Picasso
Guitar. Autumn 1919
Oil, charcoal and pinned paper on canvas, 85 × 31″
Collection The Museum of Modern Art, New York, Gift of A. Conger Goodyear

9. Arshile Gorky
Still Life. 1928
Oil on canvas, 14 1/2 × 29″
Collection Mr. and Mrs. Chaim Gross

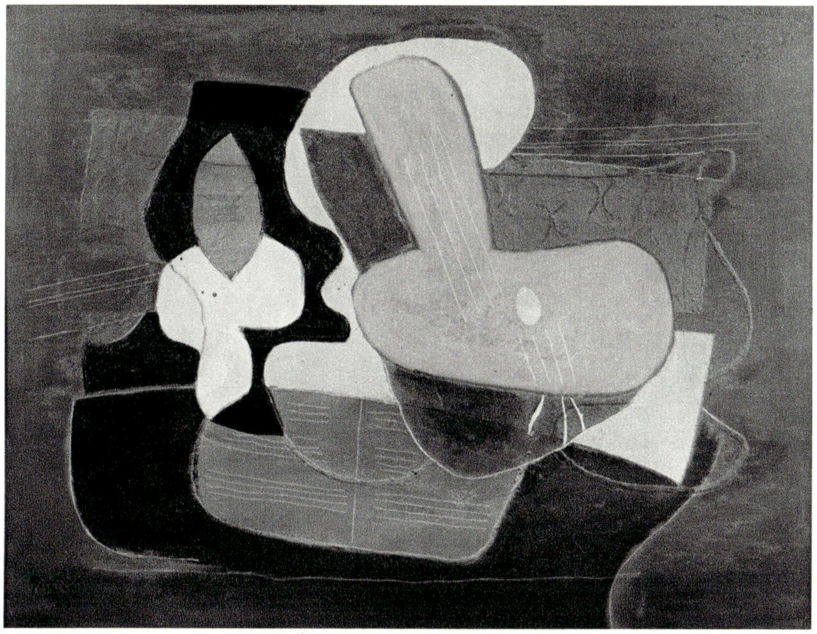

10. Pablo Picasso
Mandolin and Music Stand. 1923
Oil on canvas, 38 1/4 × 51 1/4″
Private Collection

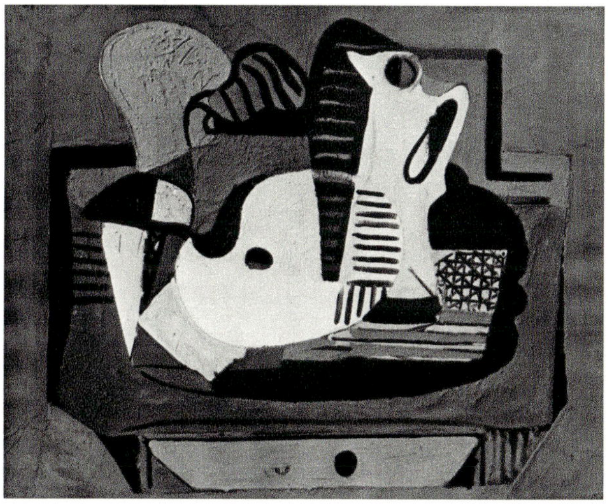

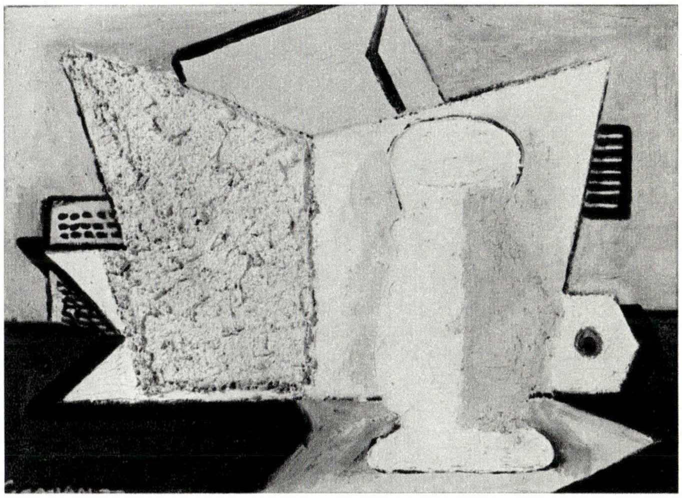

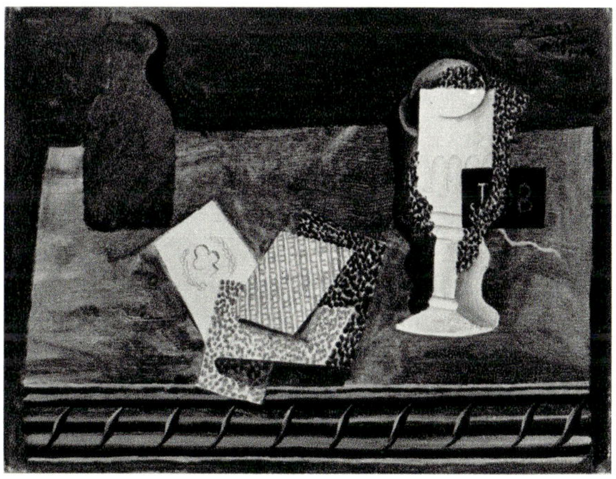

11. Arshile Gorky
Still Life with Palette. ca. 1930
Oil on canvas, 28 × 36″
Whereabouts unknown

12. John D. Graham
Still Life. 1930
Oil on canvas, 19 3/8 × 26″
Yale University Art Gallery, New Haven,
Gift from the Estate of Katherine S. Dreier

13. Pablo Picasso
Still Life: Bottle, Playing Cards, Glass. 1914
Oil on wood, 12 3/8 × 16 7/8″
Philadelphia Museum of Art:
A.E. Gallatin Collection

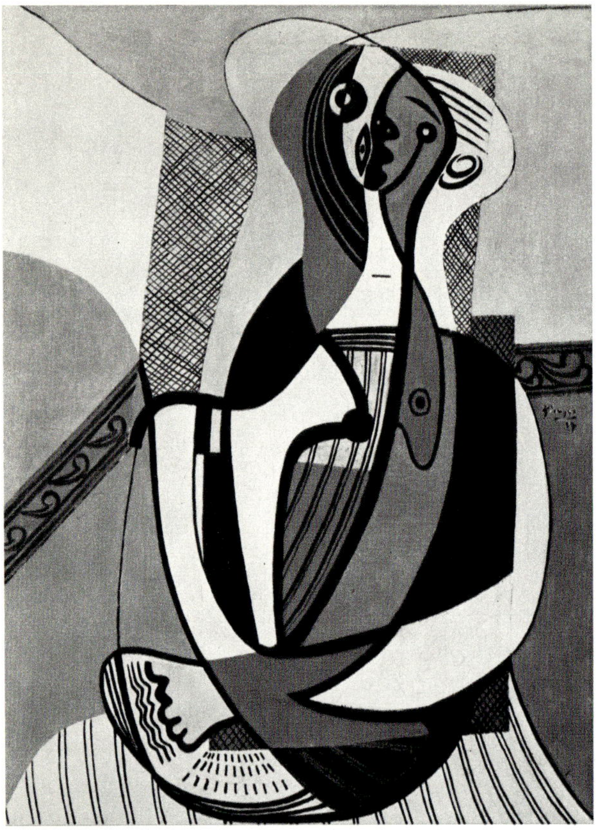

14. Pablo Picasso
Seated Woman. 1926–27
Oil on canvas, 51 1/2 × 38 1/2″
Collection Art Gallery of Ontario, Toronto

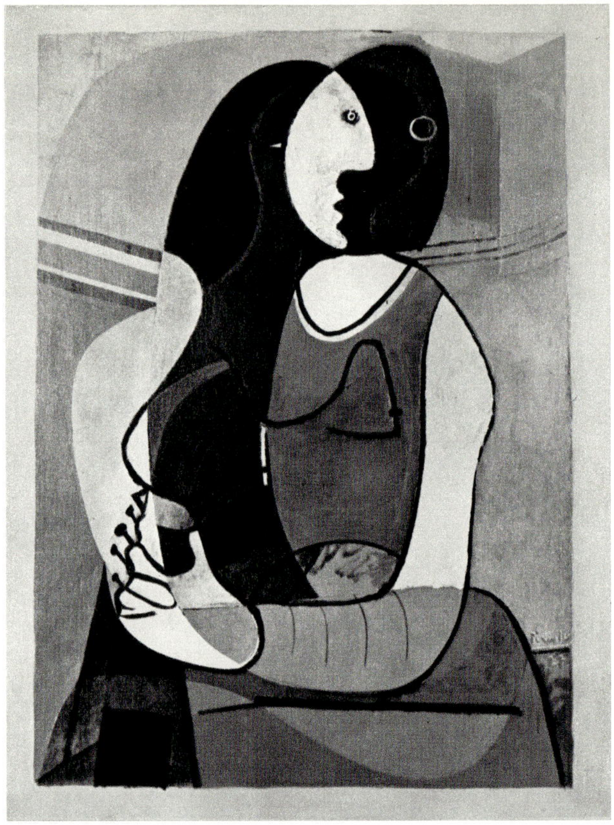

15. Pablo Picasso
Seated Woman. 1927
Oil on wood, 51 1/8 × 38 1/4″
Collection The Museum of Modern Art, New York; James Thrall Soby Bequest, 1979

with Palette, 1930 (cat. no. 24), reappear with slight modifications in a lithograph of 1931 (cat. no. 25), in numerous drawings of the period (see cat. nos. 36–46) and again in the painting *Blue Figure in Chair,* ca. 1931 (cat. no. 26). The recurring forms relate the various works, yet the two paintings, which reflect Gorky's interest in Synthetic Cubism, are linked to his past evolution, while the lithograph and drawings prefigure a new direction. The prototype for the blue figure is Picasso's *Seated Woman* of 1926–27 (fig. 14), a painting Gorky could have seen reproduced in *Cahiers d'Art* (no. 6, 1927). Both canvases bear some resemblance to Picasso's aforementioned *Harlequin* of 1915 and his *Three Musicians* of 1921; both are constituted of flat, overlapping shapes with contrasting curved and straight edges and decorative touches that suggest, among other objects, a harlequin's costume or balustrade. In the lithograph and drawings Gorky has replaced integrated but autonomous shapes with an overall pattern in which certain previously significant features—breast, eyes, hand, front and profile head, light and shadow—have become secondary, if not inconsequential. The looping curves that unify these features are much more important and emphatic in the small drawings than in the larger paintings, where they serve primarily as counterpoints to the predominant rectiliniarity. Mirroring Picasso's own redirection toward Surrealism in the 1920s, Gorky came to use the curve increasingly and with growing authority in his works on paper, most notably in the magnificent drawings now loosely grouped together as the Nighttime, Enigma and Nostalgia series of 1931–32 (cat. nos. 36–42). In fact, Gorky's fluid and generous arabesques are often more graceful than those of Picasso.

Another Picasso *Seated Woman,* this one of 1927 (fig. 15), reproduced in the same issue of *Cahiers d'Art* as *Seated Woman,* 1926–27, moved Gorky deeply. The painting was shown in 1930 at The Museum of Modern Art in the important *Painting in Paris* exhibition, where he undoubtedly saw it. Peter Busa has recently said it was his friend Gorky's favorite painting and that when they saw it together in 1939 at the Modern's exhibition *Forty Years of Picasso,* Gorky "would stand in front of it for an hour at a time."[22] Picasso simplified the complex curves of his earlier *Seated Woman* in the second version, and Gorky followed suit, adopting a portion of the reduced image for his similarly simplified work *Painting*, ca. 1932, and related gouaches of the early 1930s (cat. nos. 27, 28). Significantly, Gorky used Picasso's forms, often quite literally, yet he rejected Picasso's characteristic brutality. Picasso's *Seated Woman* is part human, part predatory animal, part Inquisitor, part Crucifixion; her hooded, mask-like visage, the configuration of her nails generate a sense of danger typically terrifying, typically Picasso. In Gorky's *Painting*, however, there is no violence, no brutality: the deformation of the woman is modified, the implicit volume of the figure and thus its physical presence are suppressed, the forms are flatter, simpler, clearer and, above all, more abstract. The immense power, the severity and intense drama of Picasso's art are absent from Gorky's oeuvre. For Gorky's sensibility is exquisite and lyrical. Despite his debt to Picasso, this painting is imbued with the grace, idealism and poetry which mark his lifelong oeuvre.

During the early 1930s Gorky restricted himself almost entirely to drawing, only occasionally painting the subjects he first explored in his works on paper. Why he limited himself to this medium is unknown; Ethel Schwabacher believes he could not at this time afford the extravagant amounts of paint and canvas of the quality he required. It is possible, however, that Gorky freely chose to restrict himself, as he did again for periods in 1943, 1944 and 1945, because drawing allowed him to change rapidly: it was his means and perhaps his impetus for change. Certainly, Gorky's most significant stylistic redirections have issued from his drawing rather than from his painting. In December of 1935 Gorky showed eighteen abstract drawings at the Guild Art Gallery. Among them were *Enigmatic Tryptich, Night Time Nostalgia, Composition, Detail for Mural* and fourteen works without title. These were members of a rich and varied sequence of drawings, begun around 1931, which are now loosely grouped together as the Nighttime, Enigma and Nostalgia series. The drawings shown at the Guild elicited generally favorable reviews. Carlyle Burrows in the *Herald Tribune* cited the "intensity and clarity of effect he usually gains in his designs" and lauded him as "a skillful and ingenious pen craftsman," but noted his sources in Picasso, Braque and others and observed that it was difficult to "tell where originality begins and where inspiration leaves off."[23] Burrows' unfortunate comments typify the insensitive reviews that plagued Gorky throughout his life. To be sure, there are references in these drawings to other artists (although Braque is not among them), but there are unique and personal characteristics Burrows failed to perceive. And these drawings mark a significant turning point in Gorky's development, a breakthrough into improvisation, a loosening of the rigid structure of Synthetic Cubism, a Surrealist-inspired turn towards darkness and dream, towards enigma and the nether side of reality. This new direction was interrupted, possibly because Gorky was forced by harsh economic realities to work for the WPA. The WPA required its artists to paint the American Scene, resulting in a retreat from experiment and abstract form on the part of Gorky and many other participants in the program. Ultimately, however, the resources of Surrealism were to free him and inspire his great personal vision.

The Nighttime, Enigma and Nostalgia drawings are the first instance of a series in Gorky's oeuvre. De Chirico's Metaphysical Interiors may have provided the impetus for working in series, a practice Gorky continued in his Khorkom and Sochi works. Indeed, the use of series then became essential to him, providing the connective threads for most of his mature oeuvre. However, the Nighttime, Enigma and Nostalgia drawings should be considered a series only in the broadest sense, for they are exceptionally varied, although loosely linked by theme and format.

For the Nighttime variations Gorky drew from a number of artists, including, as before, Picasso, and new sources of inspiration such as Max Ernst, de Chirico, Dali and Uccello. Study for *Nighttime, Enigma and Nostalgia*, ca. 1931–32 (cat. no. 36), the prototype for the sequence, relates in both its form and content to Max Ernst's paintings *One Night of Love*, 1927, and *The Kiss*, 1927 (fig. 16). Gorky reproduces Ernst's sweeping fluid curves and suggests his subject, the coupling of male and female, love and procreation. The figures derive as well from Picasso's Surrealizing works of the period, such as his Crucifixion drawings (fig. 17) and illustration of the painter with a model knitting from Balzac's *Unknown Masterpiece* (fig. 18). There is about these drawings a dark, rich eroticism which springs from lushly tactile surfaces and almost obsessional imagery suggesting breast, phallus, seed and seductively reclining curvilinear forms.

From de Chirico, Gorky learned to order real objects in an unreal world. De Chirico had taken the ruler, the glove, the biscuit, the statue and organized them in a strange new space, in a mysterious and dreamlike environment beyond ordinary time and place. The world of strictly compartmentalized

16. Max Ernst
The Kiss. 1927
Oil on canvas, 50 3/8 × 63″
The Peggy Guggenheim Collection, Venice, The Solomon R. Guggenheim Foundation

17. Pablo Picasso
Study for Crucifixion. 1927
Whereabouts unknown

18. Pablo Picasso
Painter with a Model Knitting. 1927
Etching, 7 5/8 × 11 3/8″,
illustration for Balzac:
"Le Chef-d'Oeuvre Inconnu," 1931
Collection The Museum of Modern Art, New York
Gift of Henry Church

19. Pablo Picasso
Seated Bather. Early 1930
Oil on canvas, 64 1/4 × 51″
Collection The Museum of Modern Art, New York
Mrs. Simon Guggenheim Fund

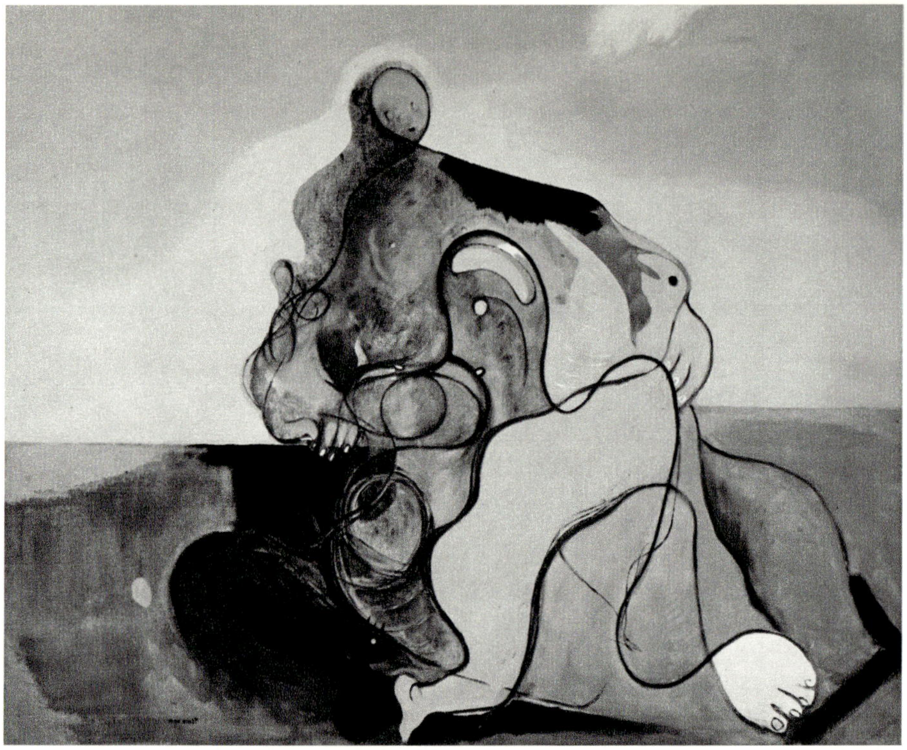

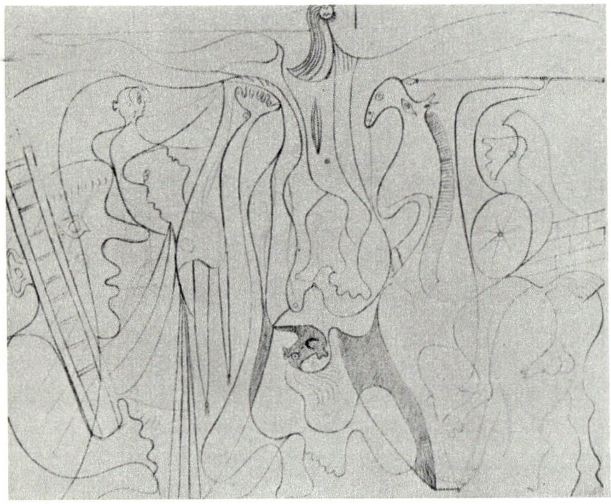

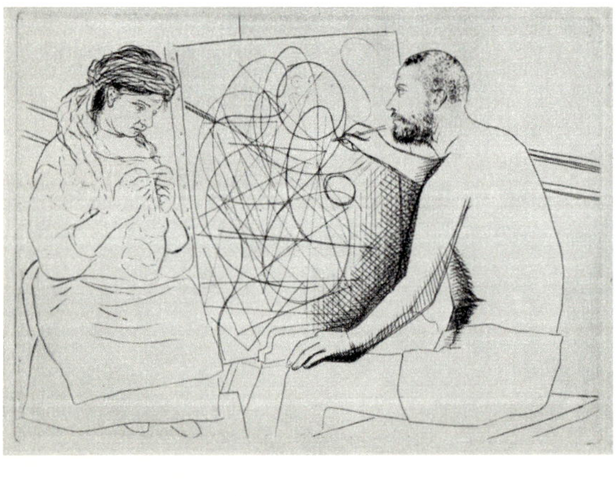

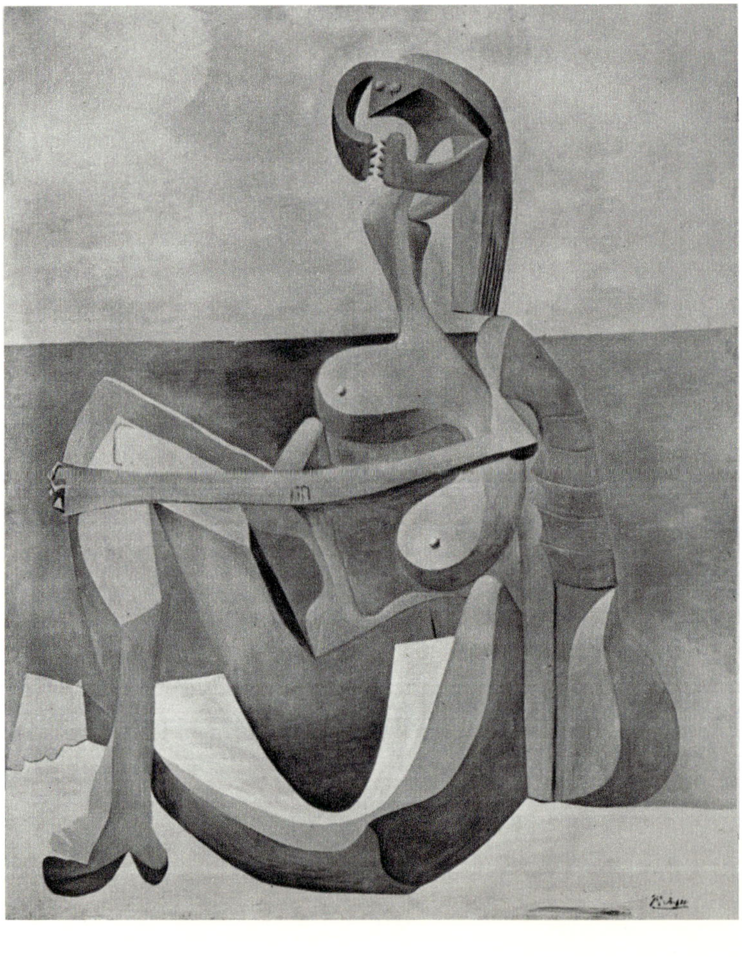

space, the silence, the dream, the lengthening shadows, the enigma and the timelessness of de Chirico's universe pervade Gorky's own metaphysical drawings. The source for a number of the Nighttime drawings as well as certain specific images therein is a de Chirico in the Gallatin Collection (fig. 20), with which Gorky was undoubtedly familiar. From this painting Gorky took the fish-like form and the half-lit, half-shadowed profile that frequent many of his compositions (fig. 21, cat. nos. 44, 46). (The double head was, of course, also an image favored by Picasso and Léger.) Gorky could have appropriated the antique cast that inhabits a number of his drawings and his untitled painting of 1936 (cat. nos. 54–57) from any one of a number of de Chiricos or from Picasso's *Studio with Plaster Head* of 1925 (fig. 22). Two paintings Sidney Janis acquired from Julien Levy in 1930, de Chirico's *Evangelical Still Life* of 1916 and Dali's *Illumined Pleasures* of 1929 (figs. 23, 24), were surely known to Gorky and may also have inspired him. De Chirico's compartmentalized space is evident in *Nighttime, Enigma and Nostalgia* of ca. 1931–32 (cat. no. 45). Here, however, forms are set in a number of deeply recessed niches, while in drawings such as *Untitled,* ca. 1931 (fig. 21), and *Objects,* 1932 (cat. no. 39), they are disposed across a flat, horizontal plane superimposed on a deep background space. In drawings of this type, Gorky takes images such as the palette-pelvis and breast-like shapes and recombines them into a newly structured space. The bold shadows, the play of starkly contrasting light and shade as well as positive and negative areas and the use of rapidly diminishing perspective which produces an effect of vast space are clearly derived from de Chirico and from Dali by way of de Chirico.

Certain of the Nighttime drawings have a sculptural reality and are concerned with the play of flat against volumetric shapes. Their images, specifically the pelvic shapes, relate to Picasso's bone figures such as his *Seated Bather* (fig. 19) and to Arp's reliefs of concave and convex forms. They often feature reclining figures juxtaposed with a round form which suggest Picasso's reclining bathers with beach balls. Clearly, Gorky was now extremely adept at unifying two and three-dimensional forms into a powerful totality.

When Gorky bothered to use titles in his early work, he usually paraphrased Picasso's very general titles *(Composition, Painting)*. Exceptional are the evocative names he gave his Nighttime variations, after de Chiricos such as *Nostalgia of the Infinite* and *The Enigma of a Day*. Only later in the forties,

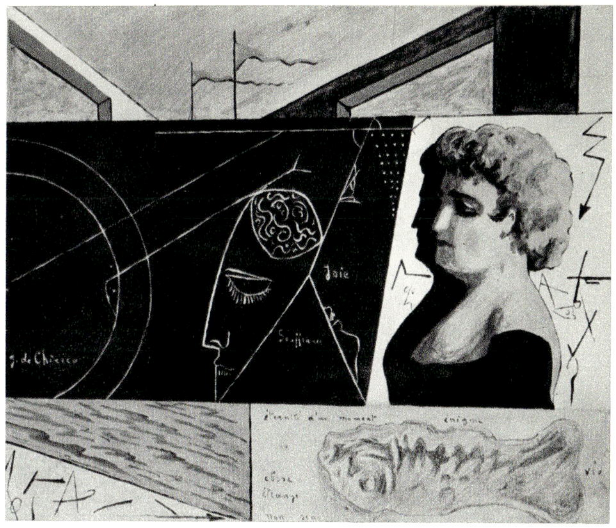

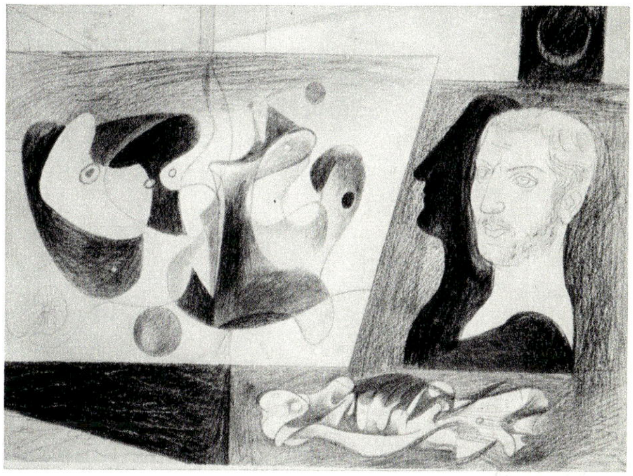

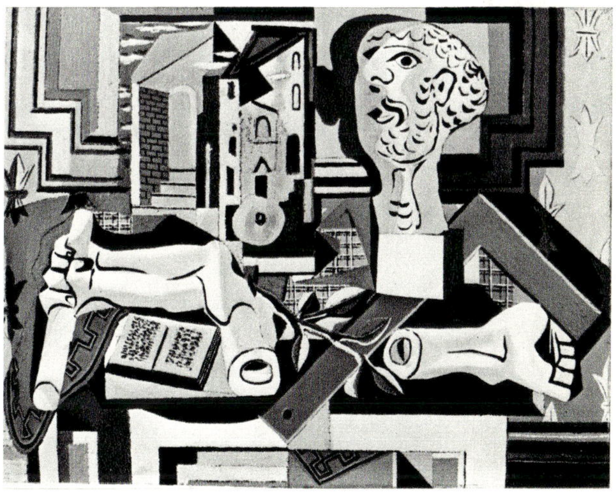

20. Giorgio de Chirico. *The Fatal Temple.* 1913
Oil on canvas, 12 3/4 × 15 1/2″
Philadelphia Museum of Art: A.E. Gallatin Collection

21. Arshile Gorky. *Untitled.* ca. 1931
Pencil on paper, 21 1/2 × 29 7/8″
Private Collection

22. Pablo Picasso. *Studio with Plaster Head.* Summer 1925
Oil on canvas, 38 5/8 × 51 1/8″
Collection The Museum of Modern Art, New York, Purchase

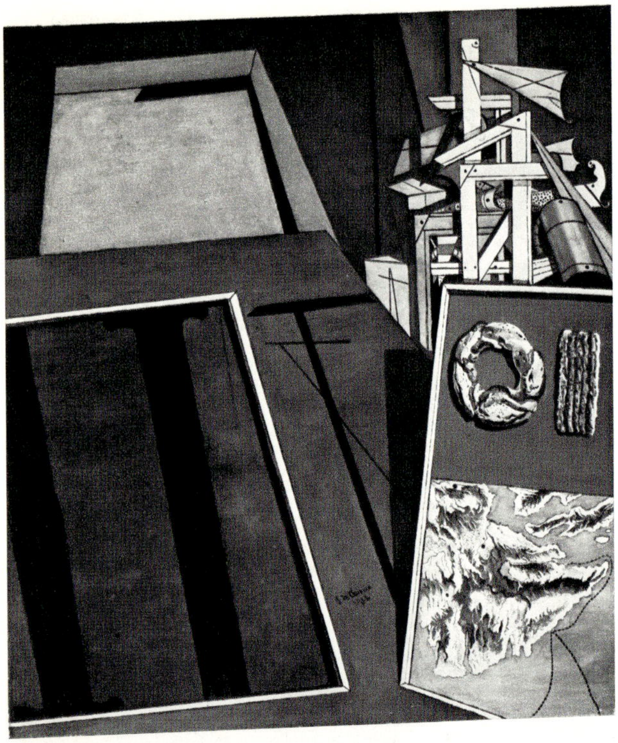

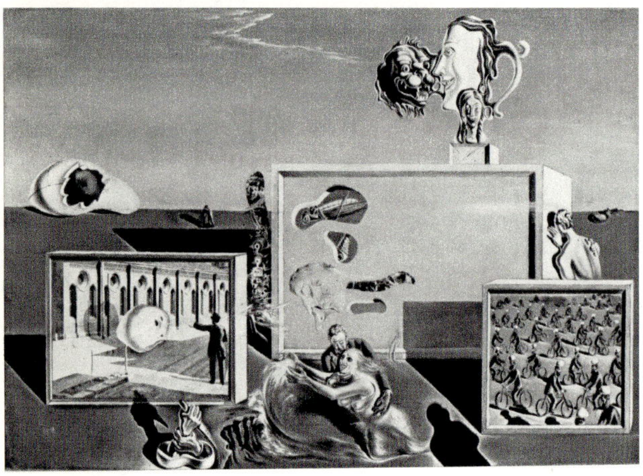

23. Giorgio de Chirico
Evangelical Still Life. 1916
Oil on canvas, 31 3/4 × 28 1/8″ (irregular)
The Sidney and Harriet Janis Collection (fractional gift), Gift to The Museum of Modern Art, New York

24. Salvador Dali
Illumined Pleasures. 1929
Oil and collage on composition board, 9 3/8 × 13 3/4″
The Sidney and Harriet Janis Collection
Gift to The Museum of Modern Art, New York

however, did Gorky become intrigued with the metaphorical possibilities of titles and begin to invent for each canvas a unique and poetic name.

Gorky executed the majority of his Nighttime drawings in pen and ink, restricting them to black and white, but occasionally enhancing them with brown ink (for example, cat. no. 41). Several others are executed in pencil or crayon. Some are almost rude, some smooth and highly finished. *Forms* of ca. 1931–32 (cat. no. 40), is one of the most spectacular examples of the period. Purchased by Katherine Dreier for the Société Anonyme from the Guild exhibition of 1935, it is one of the few works Gorky sold in his lifetime. The drawing reveals Gorky at his most inventive. He works the surface of his paper in many ways, washing, scraping, rubbing off both ink and the nap of the support, producing brilliant tonalities from ink alone. Elsewhere he creates overlapping washes of ink. His use of crosshatching, derived from Picasso, is extraordinarily varied and features evenly-spaced grids, free patterns, dense and open areas. He cultivates a dense, velvety black that unifies the composition and creates a sense of different spatial levels almost comparable to the effect of collage. His skill recalls that of two masters of the medium, Max Ernst and Paul Klee, whose innovatory techniques supported the inventive qualities of their forms. Gorky's manipulation of positive and negative space, skillfull variation of texture, virtuoso handling of materials, exquisite adjustment of line in proportion to the scale of images, the sureness of his freehand line (he never used a ruler) are exceptional here.

Two versions of *Study for a Mural,* ca. 1931–32 (cat. nos. 50, 51), are conceived as a sequence of separate frames which unfold horizontally. The compartmentalized scheme and certain forms and details, such as a column in the center of the sequence and the diamond-patterned marble floor are directly inspired by *The Miracle of the Host* (fig. 25) by Uccello, an artist idolized by the Surrealists, Graham and Gorky. Gorky's attraction to Uccello is significant evidence of his brief turn towards Surrealism in this period. He imbues his dark and dreamlike Nighttime drawings with the spirit of Uccello, whom he called the painter of moonlight: in his abstract studies he evokes Uccello's airless, sealed-off spaces, his haunting silences, his frieze-like disposition of figures which seem suspended in time, his air of heraldry and pageant, his sense of drama and hallucination.

Gorky's truly eclectic drawings reveal his ability to adapt elements from artists as disparate as Uccello, de Chirico, Ernst and Picasso and to syn-

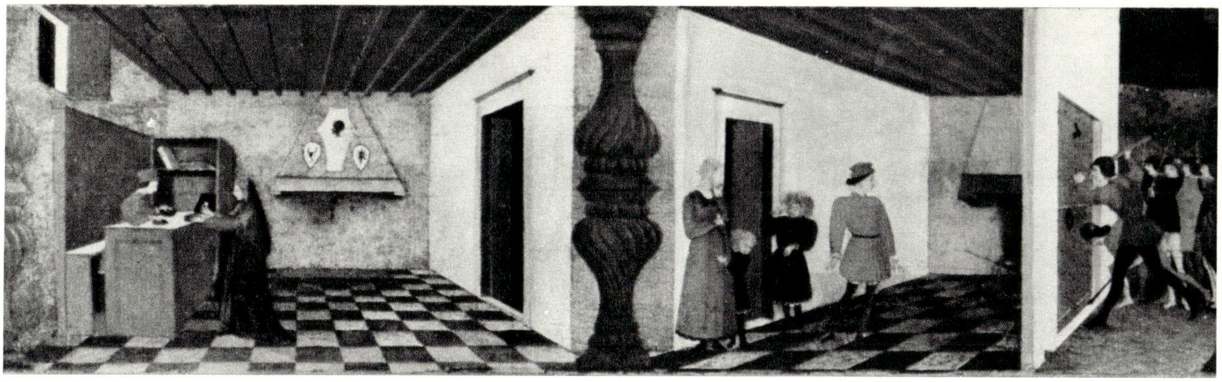

25. Paolo Uccello *The Miracle of the Host*. ca. 1467–68
Tempera, 17 × 138 1/2″
Galleria Nazaionale della Marche, Palazzo Ducale, Urbino

thesize them into works that bear the stamp of his individual genius. A lesser artist might have become the mere imitator Gorky is reputed to be. But these drawings of the early thirties offer evidence not only of an enormous appetite for the art of others, but also of the talent to transform borrowed forms and concepts, as Picasso had done before him, into a unique personal vision.

It would be convenient to read Gorky's development as a simple progression from figuration to abstraction. This is not possible, however, for Gorky remained concerned with portraiture and naturalistic drawings of figures and landscapes into the 1940s. The dating of all his early work is problematic and the portraits are particularly difficult to place, because Gorky appears to have started some in the 1920s and continued to work on them into the 1930s. At least one of the two versions of *The Artist and His Mother,* probably the painting now at the National Gallery, is known to have been in his studio in the early 1940s; Gorky was still working on it at the time of his marriage to Agnes Magruder in 1941. Others have been dated to the early 1920s, when in all probability they were executed years later. For example, *Portrait of Vartoosh* (cat. no. 66) is dated 1922, which seems highly unlikely as Gorky was only seventeen and recently arrived in America at the time. Moreover, in a letter of 1938 to his sister, he referred to a series of portraits of Vartoosh which he was then painting.[24] Aware of the precocity of Cézanne and Picasso, Gorky may have felt compelled to backdate some of his work.

Gorky's portraits are distinguished from his other early work in an extremely significant respect: they are based primarily upon deeply personal sources—a photograph of his mother and himself, drawings of Vartoosh, his memories—rather than the images of other artists. To be sure, Gorky continued to seek certain formal solutions for his portraits in Picasso, Ingres and Corot, but their essential, fundamental inspiration is personal. The artist himself referred to these paintings as his "Armenian Portraits" and spoke of them as the beginning of his true self-expression. Gorky drew upon himself—his past and feelings—to create statements of eloquence and passion.

The two variants of *The Artist and His Mother* (cat. nos. 75, 76) are the first signals of Gorky's break with his artistic past. Although the imagery of Picasso's Blue and Rose Periods inspired a certain physical milieu as well as formal elements and mood, these are basically intensely personal visions closely modeled on Gorky's own photograph. For the first time he has overcome his need to identify with the great artists of the past and has engaged, instead, in a quest for contact with his own past and personal identity. The extraordinary emotional intensity and formal economy of these two canvases are unsurpassed in Gorky's oeuvre, save for the great work of the 1940s.

Although they are the same size, the two versions differ in several ways. The National Gallery portrait adheres most closely to the photograph in details such as the position of the feet and the relationship between the boy's left arm and his mother's right arm; in the Whitney canvas the child draws further away from the mother. Of the two, the Whitney painting is the more finished, the figures are more stylized, the facial features more fully modeled, the spatial definition more exact. Moreover, the palettes of the two canvases are very different: the Washington painting is a study in warmish roses, lavender, lime green, putty grey, beige, tans, reds; the Whitney portrait, a harmony of ochers and brown, greys, muted greens, peach and yellow. Yellow is one of

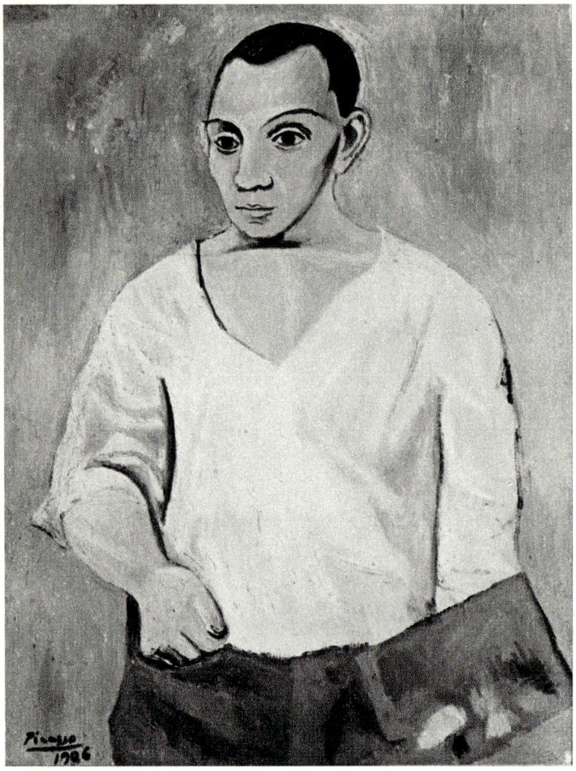

26. Pablo Picasso
Self-Portrait. 1906
Oil on canvas, 36 × 28″
Philadelphia Museum of Art: A.E. Gallatin Collection

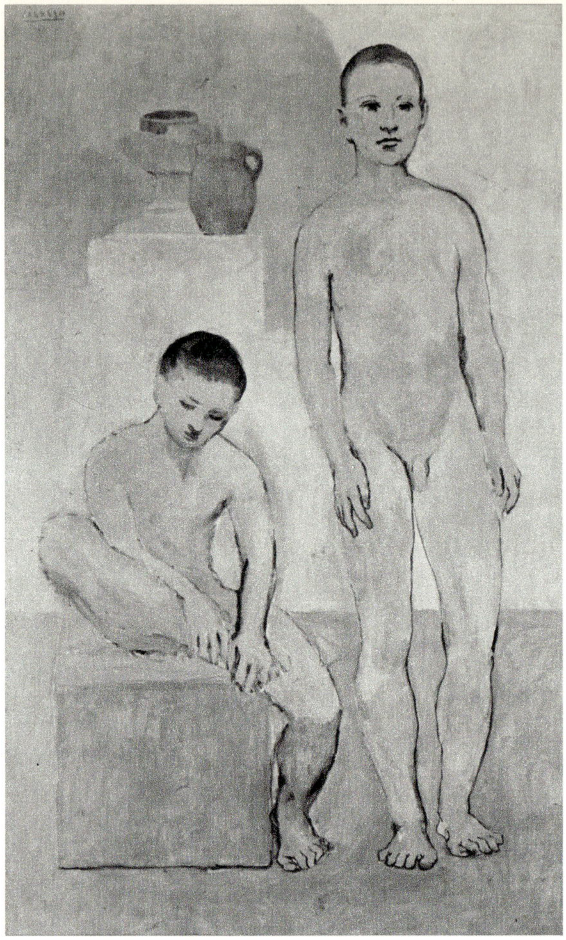

27. Pablo Picasso
Two Youths. 1905
Oil on canvas, 59 5/8 × 36 7/8″
National Gallery of Art, Washington, D.C.
Chester Dale Collection

many colors that reminded Gorky of Armenia—according to Vartoosh, he wanted to paint the "yellow that is produced when we cooked the roots of the Van dandelion."[25] Both paintings are somber and haunting, the subjects melancholy and introspective.

Picasso's *Self-Portrait* of 1906 in the Gallatin Collection (fig. 26) is a prototype for *The Artist and His Mother* as well as for Gorky's *Self-Portrait* of ca. 1937 (cat. no. 77). With similar economy of means Gorky has re-created the wide-eyed gaze and solemn austerity, the dreamlike melancholy, the sense of figures frozen in time and space characteristic of Picassos of around 1906. Gorky has also borrowed Picasso's cursory rendering of hands. However, Picasso's undefined hands are deliberately schematic and therefore remain consistent with the other stylized forms in his compositions, while Gorky does not always successfully integrate them into his paintings. He has, for example, only with great difficulty adapted the hand and palette motif from Picasso's *Self-Portrait* in his own *Self-Portrait* and the otherwise extraordinary *Portrait of Master Bill* of 1929–30 (cat. no. 78). Moreover, Gorky's portraits are often marked by other inconsistencies, undoubtedly the result of their intermittent execution over long periods of time. Thus, in the Whitney version of *The Artist and His Mother,* the faces are quite finished and other areas, such as the mother's apron, are roughly brushed. Despite this inconsistency, the paintings are unified through compelling imagery and unsurpassed use of evocative color.

Fascinating parallels can be drawn between the National Gallery's *The Artist and His Mother* and Picasso's Rose Period *Two Youths* of 1905 (fig. 27). The paintings are similar in color, with the Picasso a more consistent tonality throughout, rather more earthen and a bit lighter in its range of roses and pinks. Gorky's palette is at once more pastel and more intense, as his lavender heightens the painting's sensuous impact. The canvases are close formally as well: the linearity of the figures, their manner of juxtaposition, the use of the floor line to locate the figures in shallow space, the description of detail

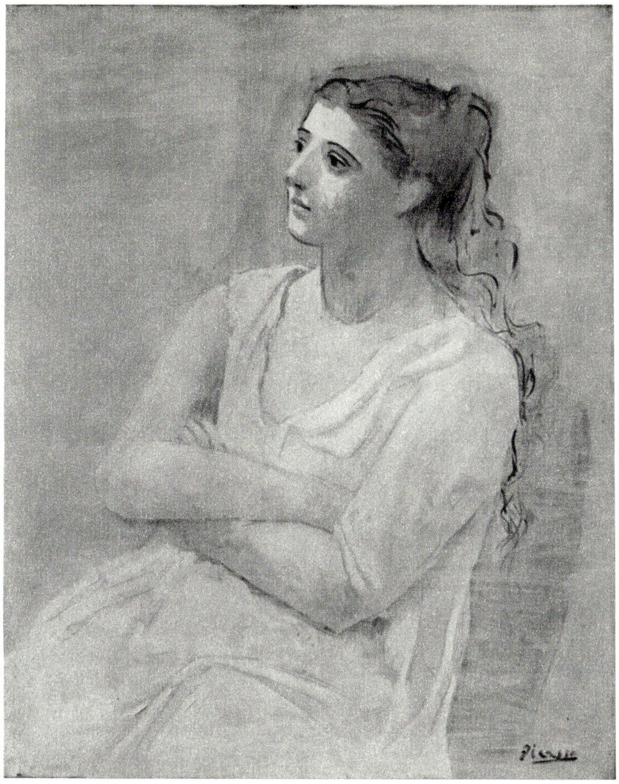

28. Pablo Picasso
Woman in White. 1923
Oil on canvas, 39 × 31 1/2″
The Metropolitan Museum of Art, New York
Purchase, Rogers Fund

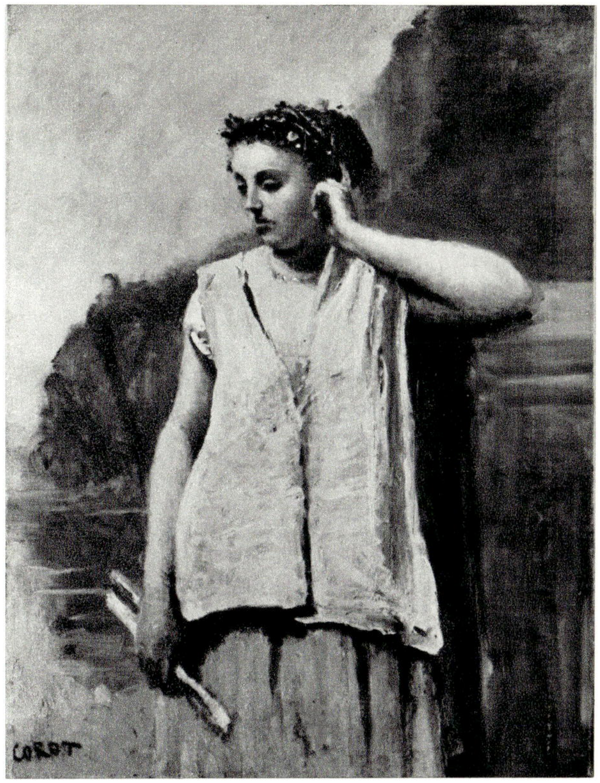

29. Jean Baptiste Camille Corot
The Muse—Comedy. ca. 1865
Oil on canvas, 18 1/8 × 13 7/8″
The Metropolitan Museum of Art, New York
Bequest of Mrs. H.O. Havemeyer, 1929
The H.O. Havemeyer Collection

with a few effective linear accents are comparable. *The Artist and His Mother* is, however, the more disquieting work: its pervasive sense of alienation and sadness is closer to the mood of Picasso's Blue Period than to the dreamy reverie of his Rose Period figures.

Certain portraits, among them *Portrait of Vartoosh,* with their bluish-green cast and almost ghostly presence are reminiscent of the wan and sickly subjects of Picasso's Blue Period. Still others, for example, the charming small *Seated Woman with Vase,* mid-1930s (cat. no. 62), relate to neoclassic paintings such as Picasso's *Woman in White* of 1923 (fig. 28) and Corot's *Sibylle* and *The Muse—Comedy* (fig. 29); indeed, they belong to a succession of neoclassic figures which begin with Ingres and evolve through Corot and Picasso to de Kooning and Graham.

Gorky's "Armenian Portraits" are related to prototypes in Armenian manuscript illumination as well as to models of Western European portraiture. Specific parallels may be drawn between the distinctive almond-shaped eyes, the solemnity, dignity and frontality of many of Gorky's subjects and the figures of Near Eastern manuscripts. Hieratic stance and intensity of gaze lend religious overtones to certain portraits. These overtones are enhanced in *The Artist and His Mother* by the architectural background which recalls the settings of Renaissance Annunciations. The versions of *The Artist and His Mother* are at once contemporary portraits, imaginative interpretations of a photograph and original conceptions which refer to Ingres and Picasso and resonate with the sense of religious icons.

Gorky's friends have described his technique of scraping painted surfaces with a razor blade or sandpaper and repainting them to produce a smooth, porcelain-like surface. This opalescent, reflective finish clearly derives from Ingres, whom Gorky revered. In combination with the soft, evanescent colors of the portraits, it creates a spectacular effect of unreal light. But Gorky looked to Ingres for much more than finish. Ingres' consummate draftsmanship, his exquisite contours, his delicate and precise line moved and inspired him. In Ingres, as in Cézanne

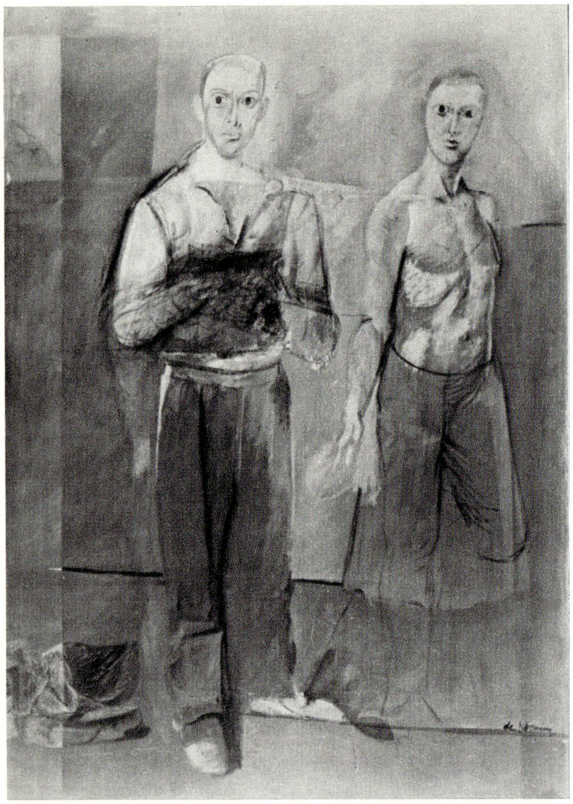

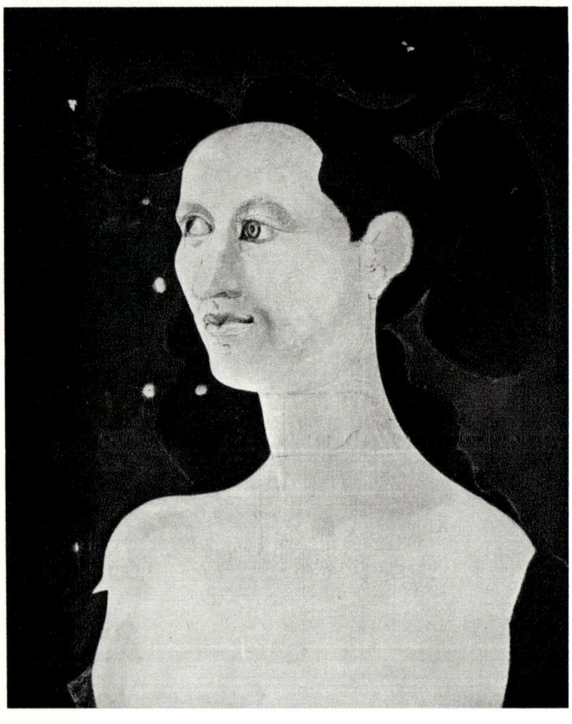

30. Willem de Kooning. *Two Men Standing*. ca. 1938
Oil on canvas, 61 1/8 × 45 1/8". Private Collection

31. John D. Graham. *Kali Yuga*. ca. 1952
Oil, casein, chalk and ballpoint pen on cardboard
25 × 20 3/4" Collection Whitney Museum of American Art, New York; Promised gift of Richard S. Zeisler

and Picasso, he sought the purely formal relationships underlying representational imagery. The transition from the fully-modeled head to two-dimensional picture plane by means of the curved line and flattened surface of the arm is less explicit in Ingres than in Cézanne and Picasso, but no less compelling for Gorky.

Like Gorky, Graham and de Kooning admired the women of Ingres. Both interpreted Ingres' vision through Gorky's eyes in portraits of the thirties and forties. *Portrait of Master Bill* and *The Artist and His Mother* prefigure a number of de Koonings, including *Two Men Standing*, ca. 1938 (fig. 30), and Grahams such as *Kali Yuga*, ca. 1952 (fig. 31). They, as Gorky had done before them, emulated Ingres' contours and surface finish and adapted his synthesis of volumetric and flat form. Both employ the compelling gaze and sense of remoteness first encountered in Gorky's portraits. De Kooning, like Gorky, worked from real subjects to produce portraits which seem part real, part imaginary. As Gorky painted a *Portrait of Myself and My Imaginary Wife*, mid to late 1930s (cat. no. 65), so de Kooning executed a drawing entitled *Portrait of Myself and My Imaginary Brother*, ca. 1938 (which is remarkably similar in composition to *The Artist and His Mother*). De Kooning's works are more direct and brutal, however; their agitation and roughness contrast with the monumental calm and stability of Gorky's portraits. Graham's obsessive, cryptic symbols place his subjects in the realm of mysticism and the occult. His figures, unlike Gorky's, are not portraits but embodiments of a strange and mysterious order.

A number of Gorky's portraits and line drawings of the mid-thirties (for example, cat. no. 60) are extraordinarily close to Matisse's drawings around the same period. Gorky appears to have looked at Matisse intermittently throughout his life, occasionally emulating specific paintings by the master, such as *Self-Portrait*, 1906, *Still Life with a Greek Torso*, 1908, and *Girl with Green Eyes*, 1909. In addition, traces of the French artist's felicitous line and heightened color sometimes appear in his work. He is unable to capture the fluidity of Matisse's line, however, and does not seem particularly interested in his flat shapes, broad flat areas of color, decorative patterns and sculptural form. Above all, the order and harmony which inform Matisse's art are conspicuously absent from Gorky's work. Yet he was attracted to Matisse's meandering line, exotic color and orientalism, which he was able to exploit fully only in his mature painting, once he was free of the restraints of architectonic form.

During the early 1930s Gorky moved from Greenwich Village to 36 Union Square. Ethel Schwabacher described Gorky and his studio at this time:

[He scrubbed] the floor weekly so that it finally had the bleached tone of driftwood; the large palette on the table, under the frosted slanting window, was left in just the state of lowlustered sheen he liked best. There was nothing haphazard about the piles of left-over or unused paint; there was no bit of material that he was indifferent to; the brushes, of which he had great quantities, bristle, camel's hair, of various sizes, round, flat, worn or new, were washed with soap and water after work; there were bottles of ink, pens, quill pens, crayons in profusion; a Greek head and hand, a porcelain fruit dish, a vase or so, stood or lay about; also a few art books, an old small phonograph and a half-dozen records of Russian songs. And on the wall, where he would certainly have liked to hang the paintings of his choice, were the nearest substitute he could afford—life-size photographs of the works of Uccello and Ingres.

The great excitement of 36 Union Square lay in the feeling it evoked of work done there; work in progress day and night, through long years of passionate, disciplined and educated effort. Gorky took pride in the massive pile of his work. Some two hundred of his paintings were carefully stacked, stretcher against stretcher, in a separate room off the foyer used only for storage. He knew where each painting was and could find any given one when he wanted to revise it, as he so often did; or to use some detail in a new effort to solve some problem, whether of this year or fifteen years earlier, that in the actual moment was absorbing his attention.[26]

On December 20, 1933, in the depths of the Depression, Gorky joined the Public Works of Art Project (PWAP), a government program funded by Harry Hopkins' Civil Works Administration. This was a short-term project designed to help indigent artists through the winter 1933–34. In New York the PWAP employed some eight hundred artists who produced close to four hundred designs for murals. Few of the designs were executed under the aegis of this program, however: the majority were transferred to a project supported by the College Art Association in New York with funds supplied by the Temporary Emergency Relief Administration between June 1934 and August 1935. Many of these designs were developed into the earliest murals painted for the Works Progress Administration's Federal Art Projects (WPA/FAP). Gorky submitted to the PWAP a proposal for a mural, the sketch for which was to measure thirty by one hundred and twenty-three inches and to be executed in pen and ink. In his letters to Vartoosh, Gorky criticized America's industrial society, its worship of material objects and emphasis on technology. Because the WPA required that all subjects be related to the American Scene, however, he was now forced to treat urban and industrial themes in his work. Gorky described his proposal as follows:

My subject matter is directional. American plains are horizontal. New York City which I live in is vertical. In the middle of my picture stands a column which symbolizes the determination of the American nation. Various abstract scenes take place in the back of this column.

My intention is to create objectivity of the articles which I have detached from their habitual surroundings to be able to give them the highest realism.[27]

Gorky was dropped from the project on April 29, 1934, and was not transferred to the payroll of the Temporary Emergency Relief Administration. He then subsisted on the meager earnings from his teaching and the sale of a few works until he received home relief from the Emergency Relief Bureau in July 1935.

In August 1935 Gorky was hired by the Works Progress Administration/Federal Art Project. Between that August and July 1937 he executed a monumental series of murals. Titled *Aviation: Evolution of Forms Under Aerodynamic Limitations,* the enormous project, consisting of ten huge panels (all but two of them [cat. nos. 87, 88] destroyed by the military during World War II), covered 1,500 square feet. Initially intended for Floyd Bennett Field, the series was to include photomurals by Wyatt Davis (the brother of Stuart Davis) and murals which incorporated photographs by Davis and paintings by Gorky. At some point, the idea of using photographs was abandoned, and the destination of the murals was changed to the Newark Airport Administration Building.

Gorky wrote about his conception of mural art in a commentary intended for publication in *Art for the Millions:*

I am definitely opposed to the interior decorator's taste in mural painting which seems to be that everything must "match." Mural painting should not become part of the wall, because the moment this occurs the painting loses its identity.

In these times, it is of sociological importance that everything should stand on its own merit, always keeping its individuality. I much prefer that the mural fall out of the wall than harmonize with it.

Mural painting should not become architecture. Naturally, it has its own architecture and limits of space, but should never be confused with walls, windows, doors, or any other anatomical blueprints.[28]

In order to prevent his murals from losing their identity and merging with the wall, Gorky rejected the fresco technique and, like over sixty percent of his WPA colleagues, executed his panels in oil on canvas. Gorky's close friend Frederick Kiesler has noted also that the artist probably chose to work in this medium because of "lack of material, the lack of proper wall preparation, the shortness of time, or the necessity for a 'mobile,' mural painting due to short-lived building structures as a whole. . . ."[29] He remarked that "Gorky tried to invent a new oil paint technique for this departure from common mural treatment. He uses oil paint in an outflattened, equalizing cover, paralleling in this manner the super individual objective expression of the room-enclosing surface."[30]

Gorky's first gouaches for the murals (cat. nos. 83, 86) reveal that he relied heavily upon Wyatt Davis' pictures as well as those of Leo Seltzer, another photographer who worked under the WPA. Nevertheless, the panels are linked stylistically with the paintings and drawings that directly preceded them (see, for example, *Abstraction with Palette*, 1930 [cat. no. 24]). Whereas Gorky had not pursued his early experiments with Cubist collage, in these murals he approximates a form of collage inspired by the principles of photomontage. (He and Wyatt Davis actually executed a collage study for the murals.) Doubtless, the juxtaposition of disparate images in the panels derives from these explorations. The urban, technological theme of the murals moved Gorky to search for appropriate new models. He turned to Stuart Davis' *Egg Beater* paintings and gouaches and his related works of the late twenties as well as Amédée Ozenfant's Purist still lifes. (Ozenfant was living in New York at this time and Gorky is known to have visited his studio.) In Davis' work Gorky found sharp edges, smooth surfaces and bright color; in Ozenfant's paintings he saw matte finish, soft, chalky hues and precise form. But, above all, it is the Cubism of Léger, specifically the images of *The City*, 1919, which engaged Gorky. For Gorky found that Léger's urban imagery, his machine forms, his bright and vivid colors—red, blue, yellow, black, grey, brown—were particularly appropriate to express the spirit of aviation. Although Gorky uses flat shapes together with modeled forms in the manner of Léger and combines illusions of deep recession and shallow space, the overwhelming effect of the panels is of intense compression and flatness: two-dimensional shape and vivid color are paramount.

It is perhaps unfair to assess the two extant murals away from the site for which they were intended and out of the context of their destroyed companions, for their cumulative effect cannot now be measured. On their own, however, the remaining panels seem ungainly, lacking Gorky's characteristic grace as well as the power and energy of Léger's masterful evocations of the machine age. The preparatory gouaches are another matter altogether; their jewel-like perfection indicates that Gorky was far more comfortable working in the very small scale of studies or in easel scale, rather than on monumental murals.

The murals were far too abstract for their audience and met with only reluctant official acceptance. In fact, the committee charged with approving the panels tried unsuccessfully to find an excuse to reject them. Stuart Davis described this effort:

There was nothing to it after the first broadside fired by our oratorical professors, Doctors and Experts. One of the locals quickly joined our side, and the rout was complete. But their unhorsed chairman made a final convulsive effort by whistling for an air ace pilot who charged into the room. "Tell these Yankees what you think of these so-called modernistic murals," the chairman gasped. The ace surveyed the huge pieces of canvas. . . . But the chairman's ace-in-the-hole, blasted his last hope by saying he didn't know nothin' about art but thought they were right pretty. He said he was reminded of wonderful things he had seen, and began to recite recollections of beautiful cloud formations observed on his numerous flights. . . . An official surrender was signed, and our cavalcade sped back victorious to the taverns of New York to celebrate.[31]

The WPA engendered a sense of community among artists who had formerly been isolated. Abysmal conditions impelled these artists to band together into protective associations. Davis and many other painters of Gorky's generation were deeply involved with radical politics and artists' groups. Although

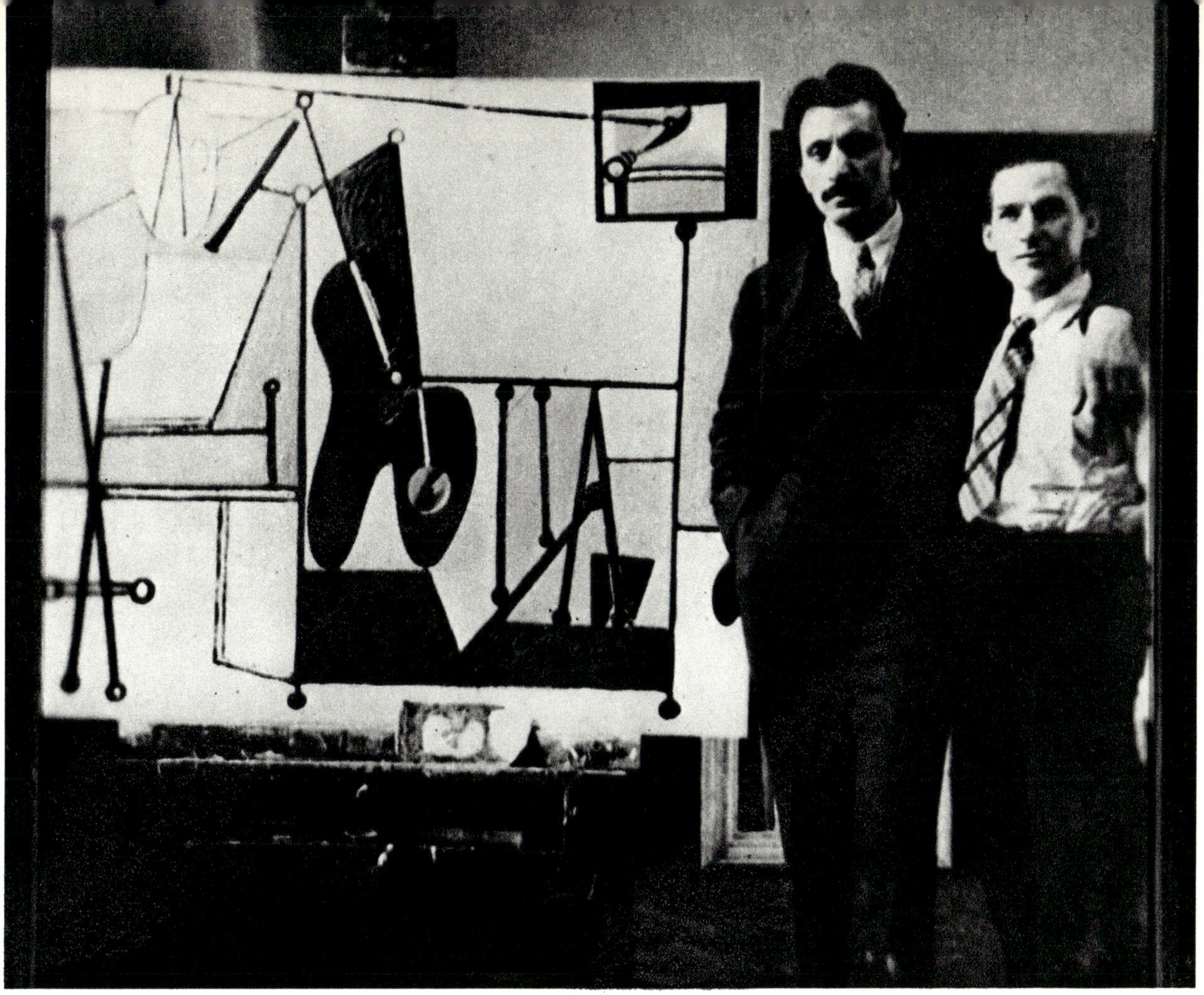

Gorky and de Kooning with Organization, *ca. 1934*

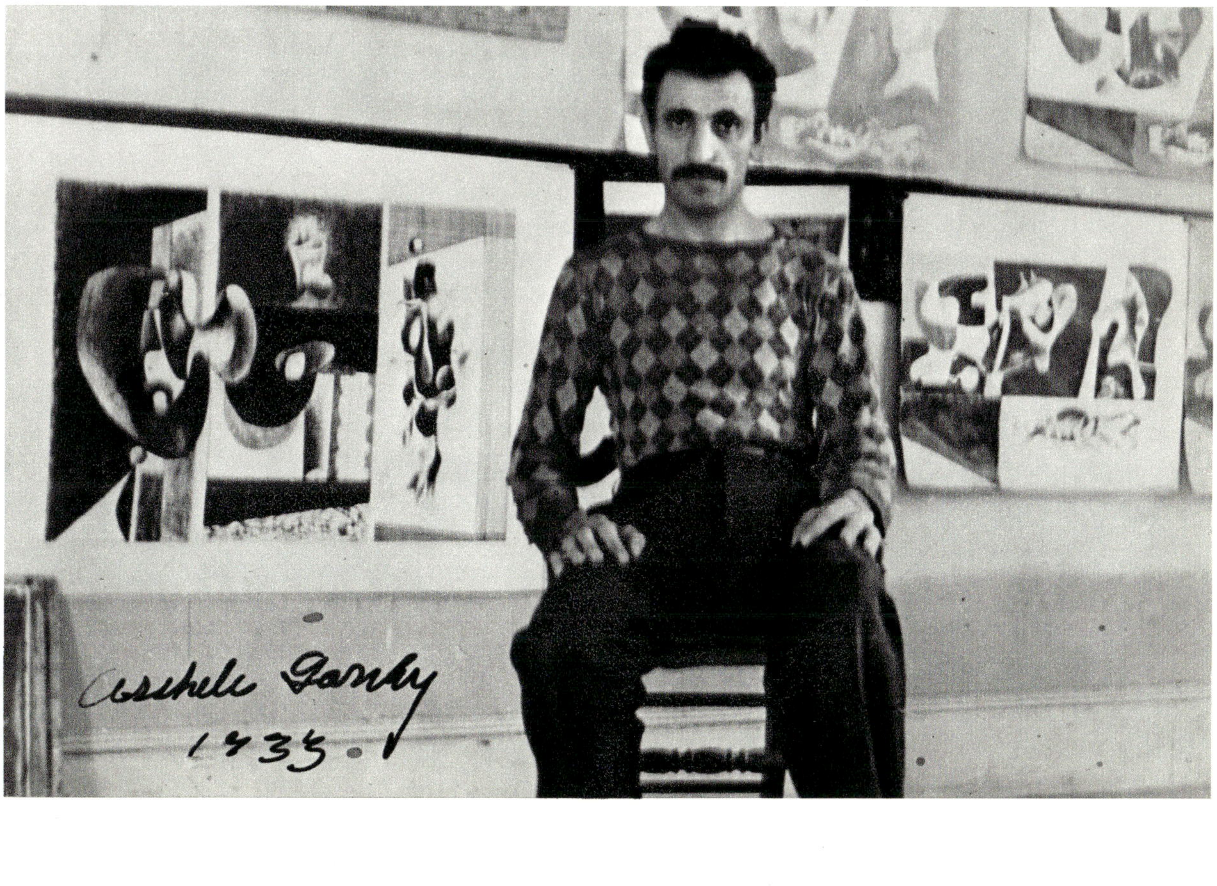

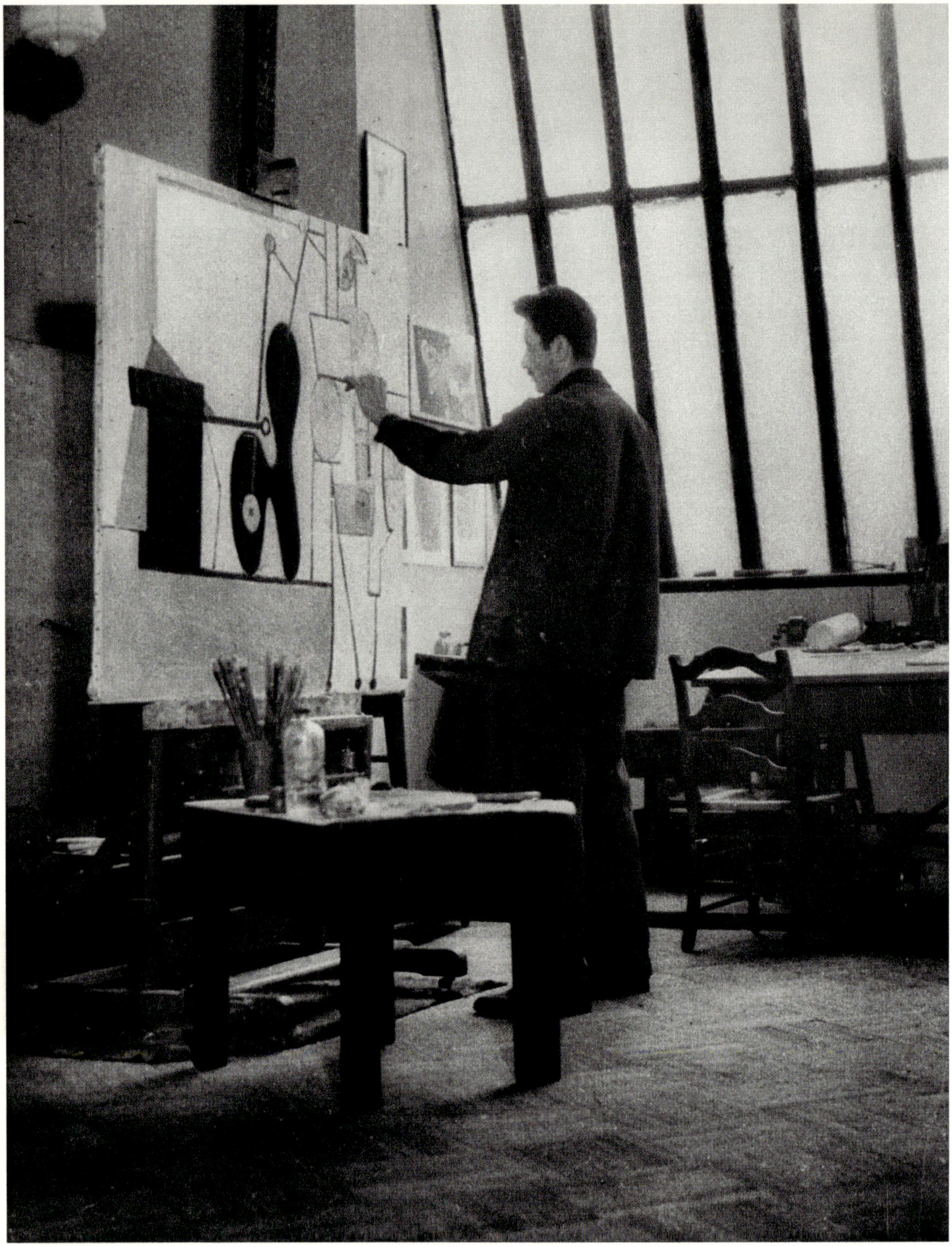

At work on Organization *in 36 Union Square Studio, 1934–35*

Gorky participated initially in the Artists' Union, he was unwilling to allow political activity to encroach upon his life as an artist. Davis, angered by what he considered Gorky's frivolous attitude, terminated their friendship in 1934. Gorky disdained to make what he termed "poor art for poor people" and was, above all, committed to the act of painting and producing art of the highest quality. As Balcomb Greene has pointed out, he refused to capitalize upon the power to be derived from a group activity.[32] He attended the first meeting of the American Abstract Artists, but would not join because the group refused to confine its discussions to aesthetic issues and sought instead to become a weapon for reform of the art world. Despite his sociability and his occasional forays into group activities, Gorky remained an outsider and alone.

Gorky was on the WPA/FAP payroll through 1941. Although the sums allotted to participants in the Easel and Mural Divisions were meager, these funds, which were supplied with dependable regularity, together with proceeds from occasional sales, allowed artists like Gorky to subsist. It is difficult to imagine how the painters who became known as the New York School could have survived the 1930s without government assistance. Gorky himself was able to continue with his own painting while working on the Newark murals—sympathetic officials apparently did not insist that artists work exclusively on government projects. Yet Gorky spoke of the period with despair. According to his widow Agnes:

> *Gorky described it as the bleakest, most spirit-crushing period of his life and spoke with bitterness of the futility of such paralyzing poverty for the artist. Towards the end of the 30's, he felt a terrible isolation which no amount of subsequent friendliness on the part of the surrealists or anyone else could eradicate. He often said that, if a human being managed to emerge from such a period, it could not be as a whole man and that there was no recovery from the blows and wounds of such a struggle to survive.*[33]

During this prolonged struggle, Gorky still managed to put painting ahead of all else, often going without food to buy materials. At this time he made his paintings as physical as possible, building out from the canvas with a heavy, textured impasto. He followed Graham's theories about the "absolutely spontaneous and final" nature of edges and the visibility of the artist's touch. Several of Gorky's friends have commented upon his technique. Stuart Davis remarked:

> *He would squeeze out a half-dozen tubes of each color he used in great piles on several palettes. These were left standing around for a certain number of days to acquire a viscous consistency. When ready to paint, he transferred this small fortune in pigment to one or more canvases with palette knives in a heat of creative excitement. But as his percentage of hits and misses was no better than average, he would often scrape it all off the next day and start again with a new batch of colors. Where the initial painting escaped this fate and was continued day by day to completion, the weight of the canvas increased proportionately. The finished product had an astounding weight. Persons uninformed about this would innocently approach a canvas to heft it at his invitation. Members of the weaker sex and anemic men would retreat from the dangerous experience with minor but none the less painful sprains and bruises. A standing joke around the Gorky studio, this never failed to get a laugh.*[34]

And Balcomb Greene, Gorky's neighbor at Union Square, spoke of the artist's adamant attitude about technique and materials:

> *When friends protested to him that his half-inch masses of pigment would some day crack, he denied this. He insisted, against all authorities, that pure zinc white was more permanent than any titanium or lithapone product. When the evidence seemed against him, he undertook to grind and prepare his own paints, with the aid of a machine built for him by Giorgio Cavallon. It was necessary that his paintings be laboriously made. The issue about physical permanence, which he kept undecided, surely was related to the pain which he nursed and of which he spoke so often to those who knew him. His acceptance of technical hazard, I believe, was an attitude which could extend immortality to him proportionately as he deserved it. The pain may at some time have seemed to him partial evidence of his ability. Sure of this, he could let himself go into a kind of automatism, and I believe it is from these works, his very worst, that the lyricist will emerge.*[35]

Concurrent with the production of the Newark murals, he executed a number of paintings based on Picasso's studio interiors of 1927–28. *Composition with Head* of ca. 1934–36 (cat. no. 79), is clearly modeled after Picasso's *The Studio* of 1927–28 (fig.

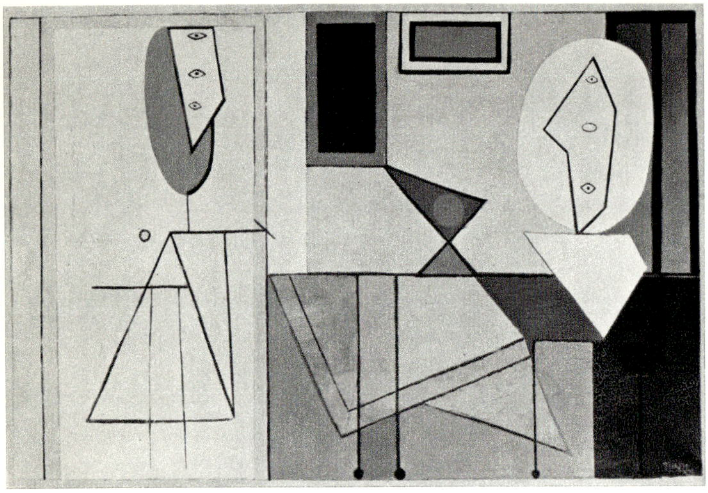

32. Pablo Picasso
The Studio. 1927–28
Oil on canvas, 59 × 91″
Collection The Museum of Modern Art, New York
Gift of Walter P. Chrysler, Jr.

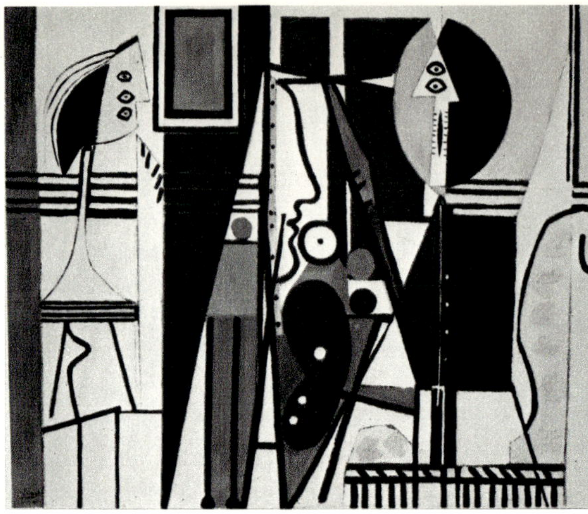

33. Pablo Picasso
Painter and Model. 1928
Oil on canvas, 51 1/8 × 64 1/4″
The Sidney and Harriet Janis Collection (fractional gift), Gift to The Museum of Modern Art, New York

32), which he could have seen at the Valentine Gallery, and *Painter and Model* of 1928 (fig. 33), in the collection of Sidney Janis. Gorky has paraphrased Picasso's spare geometry, using similar triangular shapes, rectangles for window frames and circles for breasts. He repeats the Spanish artist's combination of female and male sexual attributes in a single figure and adopts his color scheme of grey and yellow with accents of red, blue and green. However, Gorky rejects Picasso's effects of transparency in favor of his habitual preference for heavily layered paint. He also ignores Picasso's use of trapezoidal shapes and intersecting diagonals to suggest spatial recession: as in the past, Gorky's painting remains resolutely flat.

Organization of ca. 1936 (cat. no. 81) follows even more closely Picasso's example—yet, unlike *Composition with Head,* which retains the overlapping and interlocking forms of Synthetic Cubism, it hints at a new openness. This openness is evoked by the areas of white which suggest expansion and the separation rather than the overlapping of forms. The punctuation of the surface with widely dispersed forms of varied shape, size and color are the first instance of what Gorky would later call "spotting." And, despite the presence of biomorphic forms, there is a far greater emphasis upon geometric structure than previously encountered in Gorky's work. The dynamism of the composition is carried by its asymmetrical arrangement, a type of equilibrium Gorky undoubtedly saw in Mondrian. However, the enclosing outlines and heavily impastoed surfaces tend to contradict the flow of movement. Gorky's interest in rigorous geometry was short-lived, for he soon turned towards freer expression and more fluid organic form.

Crucial to the evolution of this new direction was the influence of Surrealism, which ultimately liberated him from his past and allowed him to crystallize his great, original vision. Surrealism, which had been lauched officially in 1924 with the publication of André Breton's first *Surrealist Manifesto,* exploited the bizarre, the irrational, the accidental in an assault on the formal and rational order of Cubism. This order the Surrealists felt to be a major barrier to the expression of the unconscious, which they were convinced was the essential source of art and life. Thus, the Surrealists set out to explore the hidden recesses of the unconscious mind: its dreams, its spontaneous workings. Breton stated his belief in the ultimate unification of two seemingly contradictory states, the dream and reality, into one reality called "surreality." To rid the mind of preconceived ideas, to free words from their accustomed contexts, to renovate poetic imagery, the Surrealist poets and painters employed illogical, always surprising and often shocking associations of words and images.

Automatism and the estrangement of the object from its normal context became basic techniques of Surrealism. Objects that formerly belonged to separate spatial and conceptual planes were placed in unexpected juxtaposition. In the researches of Freud and his explorations of the subconscious, the Surrealists discovered ideal tools for their own experiments; out of his theories they developed the technique of automatism, which they applied to both painting and poetry, creating automatic texts and drawings. The purpose of automatism was to free art of conscious control and to liberate the imagination. In 1924 Breton had defined Surrealism as:

> *SURREALISM noun, masculine. Pure psychic automatism by which one intends to express verbally, in writing or by other method, the real functioning of the mind. Dictation by thought, in the absence of any control exercised by reason, and beyond any esthetic or oral preoccupation.*
>
> *ENCYL Philos. Surrealism is based on the belief in the superior reality of certain forms of association heretofore neglected, in the omnipotence of dreams, in the undirected play of thought. . . .*

The growing influence of Surrealism upon Gorky is dramatically revealed in the Khorkom drawings and paintings. This series, based upon Gorky's memories of Armenia, is rooted in the art of the Surrealist André Masson. Masson's work was readily accessible to Gorky: examples of it were reproduced in *Cahiers d'Art* in 1929 and 1931, in *Transition* in 1930; his *Cock Fight*, 1930 (fig. 34), was on view in the Gallatin Collection, and the artist was included in important group shows such as *Newer Super-Realism* at the Wadsworth Atheneum in 1931 and presented in a major one-man exhibition at the Pierre Matisse Gallery in 1933. Gorky bases his biomorphic forms in both the drawings and paintings upon Masson's characteristic heart and kidney shapes, and appropriates as well the French artist's cursory and spontaneous calligraphy, whipping line divorced from form and his sense of weightlessness. Gorky's seemingly spontaneous calligraphy is particularly significant here, for improvisation, as we have seen, is a fundamental premise of Surrealism. Masson's part-animal, part-abstract creatures which seem to do battle in nature foreshadow Gorky's own hybrids. Thus, the wedding of discrete form and meandering line, prefigured in the Nighttime, Enigma and Nostalgia drawings, reemerges emphatically in the Khorkom variations. Close as the Khorkom works are to their prototypes, Gorky's individual sense of form, his fluidity of line set them apart: his feeling for overall composition, for the grouping of forms, for rhythm and harmony, nowhere more evident than in the superb drawings of this sequence, is far superior to that of Masson.

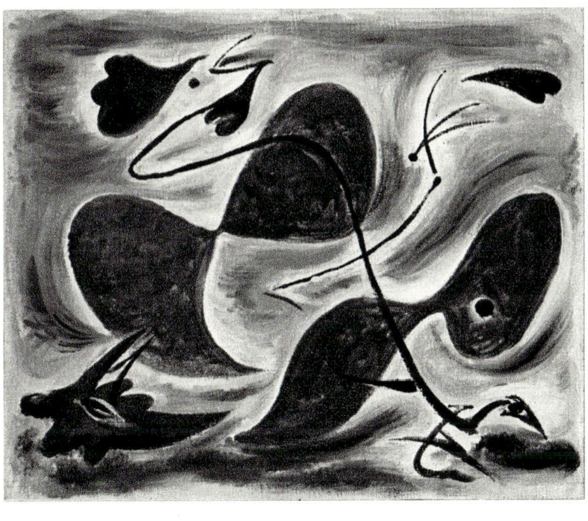

34. André Masson
Cock Fight. 1930
Oil on canvas, 8 1/2 × 10 1/4″
Philadelphia Museum of Art: A.E. Gallatin Collection

The Khorkom paintings are not nearly as improvisational as the studies—Gorky continues to be preoccupied with heavily built-up paint surfaces, and tactility and texture still dominate shape and space. Nonetheless, in these canvases there is a new freedom of structure and color, an uncharacteristic element of playfulness and whimsy which are strikingly apparent in comparison to the paintings based on Picasso's studio interiors which immediately preceded them.

The reduced palette of primaries and complimentaries, the clear and separate identities of form, line, plane and color, the grid structure of the studio interiors have disappeared from the Khorkom canvases. Instead the discrete but intertwined forms and the play of positive and negative space announced in the Nighttime and Khorkom drawings are embodied in vivid reds, oranges, yellows, greens, lavenders, browns, greys and strong value contrasts, bright and dark shapes set off by light or white images or fields. In *Image in Xhorkom,* 1934–36 (cat. no. 99), forms flow within the shallow space of the picture field; in place of a grid, Gorky suppresses the activity of these forms with an allover pattern of convex and concave shapes and a heavy blanket of gestural strokes and surface texture. Here there is an even greater conflict between fluid form and heavy facture and outline than in *Organization.* Despite their mobility, these shapes are ultimately as stable as the static geometric figures of *Organization.*

Image in Xhorkom is a study in equivocal imagery: like Masson, Gorky has created a series of hybrid images which are basically abstract but allude to human or animal forms. What seem to be birds, breasts, eyes, hearts (symbols which become central to the mature work) imbue the composition with erotic overtones and are rendered more ambiguous in the context of entirely non-representational shapes. Meaning is even further diffused in *Image in Xhorkom Summer,* 1936, and in *Xhorkom,* 1936 (cat.

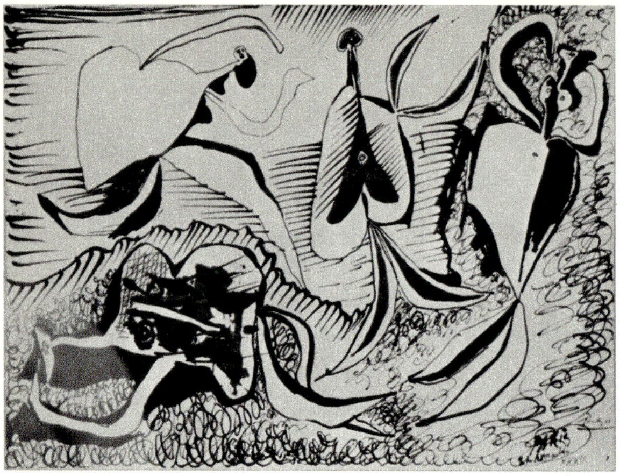

35. Pablo Picasso
Women Playing at the Edge of the Sea. Paris, November 25, 1932. India ink, 9 7/8 × 13 3/4″
Collection Mr. and Mrs. Victor W. Ganz, New York

no. 100), where the images are more nearly abstract. The sense in these and subsequent paintings is of a new family of forms—animate, organic, enigmatic.

Of the three Khorkom canvases, *Image in Xhorkom* is the least disciplined and resolved. Figure and ground, foreground and background planes are far more successfully integrated in *Image in Xhorkom Summer.* Because forms are more widely dispersed here, lateral spread rather than recession into depth is stressed. In the later *Xhorkom,* Gorky brings the background plane even further forward and enhances its physical presence and autonomy—by reducing the size of the images in relation to the field, by lightening the color of the field and emphasizing its tactility. The distinction between figure and field is therefore blurred. He was in the next years to cultivate this ambiguity to achieve a great breakthrough: the unification of foreground and background leading to the ultimate submerging of the image into the field.

Gorky's experimentation with accident in *Image in Xhorkom*—he enlivens its surface with a small number of drips—is significant in terms of the later work. The Dada artists had introduced the element of chance into art, the Surrealists, among them Miró, had expanded its role and Picasso had dripped paint in his own Surrealist-inspired canvases of the 1930s. Gorky, of course, knew these works and was clearly aware of the potential uses of accident. However, in this period he experimented with chance effects only rarely, no doubt because they are out of keeping with the heavily-built up and relatively static surfaces he still favored. Not until the 1940s, when he loosened and lightened his surface treatment, would random effects play a vital role in his art.

Significantly, these are the first abstractions in which Gorky makes specific reference to his Armenian origins. For from this time forward, the twin threads of memory and Surrealism begin to run through his art. Gorky was to intertwine these threads in a letter of 1942 to Vartoosh evoking the images of the Khorkom sequence as well as those which emerge in the Sochi paintings:

> *Sweet Vartoosh, loving memories of our garden in Armenia's Khorkom haunt me frequently. Recall Father's garden down the path from our house and the Tree of the Cross upon which the authentic Armenian villagers attached the colorful pennants of their clothing. Within our garden could be found the glorious and living panoply of Armenian nature, so unknown to all yet so in need of being known. Beloved sister, in my art I often draw our garden and recreate its precious greenery and life. Can a son forget the soil which sires him?*
>
> *Beloveds, the stuff of thought is the seed of the artist. Dreams form the bristles of the artist's brush. And as the eye functions as the brain's sentry, I communicate my most private perceptions through art, my view of the world. In trying to probe beyond the ordinary and the known, I create an inner infinity. I probe within the confines of the finite to create an infinity. Liver. Bones. Living rocks and living plants and animals. Living dreams. Vartoosh dearest, to this I owe my debt to our Armenian art. Its hybrids, its many opposites. The inventions of our folk imagination. These I attempt to capture directly, I mean the folklore and physical beauty of our homeland, in my works.*[36]

In a letter of 1943 Gorky describes the beautiful Armenian slippers that he and his father used to wear and his mother's butterchurn, "that pearl in the crown of our hard-working village women."[37] Such imagery might have been the basis for literal paintings; but through the medium of Surrealism, Gorky was able to transform his private memories of homeland into visions of poetic fantasy.

Shortly after the inception of the Khorkom series, Gorky began a group of paintings based upon Picasso's Surrealist-inspired works. They evolved from drawings related to the Nighttime, Enigma and Nostalgia variations. Like several other Gorky drawings of the period, they seem to have been directly inspired by Picasso's *Women Playing at the Edge of the Sea* (fig. 35). This drawing, whose playful figures have evolved into hybrid plants and animals, is unique in Picasso's oeuvre, where women are usually altered but not transformed. Gorky borrows these fanciful creatures, reshaping them somewhat, for his studies (cat. nos. 96, 98) for *Painting* of 1936–37 (cat. no. 102), the best-known canvas of the series. He also adapts Picasso's random scrawl, his incisive crosshatching and his wonderfully ebullient spirit. This spirit, rare in Picasso's own work, Gorky was not yet able to capture in his painting. Just as the Khorkom drawings are freer than the paintings they precede, so these studies are far less inhibited than the canvases which issue from them. In fact, the difference in degree of spontaneity is even more marked in this instance, for Gorky reverts in the present paintings to certain ideas he had assimilated from Picasso's studio interiors. In *Painting,* for example, he relies on a semblance of rectilinear structure similar to that in *Organization*, incorporating a few crucial intersecting verticals and horizontals to anchor his free-floating biomorphic forms. In comparison to the Khorkom variants, *Painting* is relatively static and represents a synthesis of earlier experiments rather than a break with the past.

In *Enigmatic Combat* of ca. 1936–37 (cat. no.104) Gorky expresses his appreciation of Picasso with new intensity. He models the painting after *Girl Before a Mirror* of 1932 (fig. 36), referring to the double head, disconnected anatomical parts, sweeping arabesques, whiplash curves and heavy impasto which characterize Picasso's work of the early thirties in general and this canvas in particular. Gorky appropriates as well the master's "cloisonné Cubism" of heavy black outlines and stained-glass color and he even emulates his retracing of black outline with white. Although he has adopted these formal devices, he rejects the painting's explicit Vanity theme. Moreover, he does not bisect the canvas into two vertical compartments or portray forms as if they were in front of a background. Instead, inspired by Masson, he atomizes his figure and begins to synthesize its parts into a more fully unified entity. The ground is as important and palpable as the figures; these figures become extremely difficult to read, so intertwined are they with the ground. Although Gorky still provides some suggestions of three-dimensional space, he has created a far more abstract composition than Picasso's, one which foreshadows his canvases of the 1940s.

Gorky's paintings of the thirties are airless spaces in which increasingly mobile, ever more fanciful organic forms begin to undermine Cubist-derived structure. The sense of forms inhabiting real space diminishes as Gorky works with a new freedom and impulsiveness. Line, which had formerly defined form and structure, becomes wayward, labyrinthean. More impetuous brushwork and vivid color animate highly tactile, heavily impastoed surfaces. Form is no longer contained by line, and brushstroke alone creates shape. Paint takes on an independent life. Gorky is about to liberate himself from his past; he is on the threshold of his personal vision.

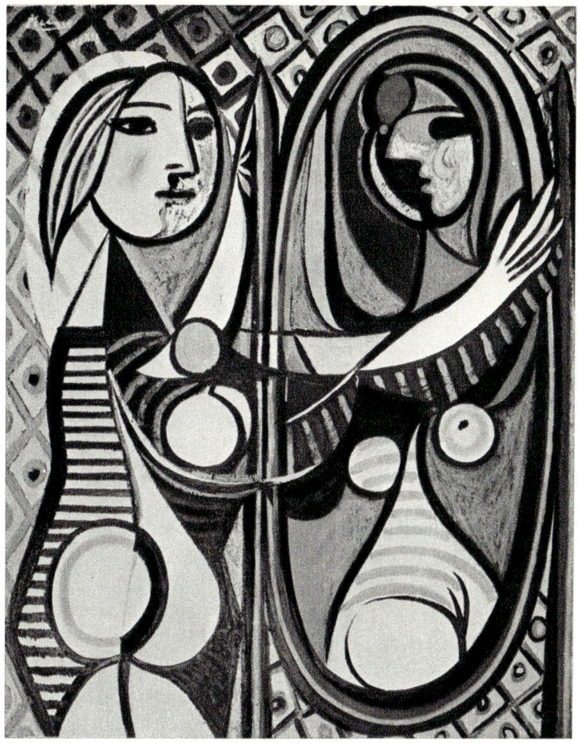

36. Pablo Picasso
Girl Before a Mirror. 1932
Oil on canvas, 64 × 51 1/4″
Collection The Museum of Modern Art, New York
Gift of Mrs. Simon Guggenheim

Gorky continued to seek inspiration from Picasso in this period, as reflected in such outstanding paintings as *Abstraction* of ca. 1936, *Portrait* of 1936–38 and *Grey Painting* of 1937 (cat. nos. 90, 89, 103). Yet a new and decisive influence, that of Miró, now began to inform his work. More than any other single artist, Miró at last freed him from the restraints of Cubism. Undoubtedly, Gorky felt a kinship with Miró on various levels: Miró's art owed much to his Catalan heritage—the Romanesque frescoes and Catalan manuscripts of his native province—as Gorky was committed to the medieval manuscripts and ancient tomb sculpture of his own Armenia; and both artists were united by an extraordinary sense of fantasy. Gorky could have seen Miró's work as early as 1927 in an exhibition organized by the Société Anonyme at The Brooklyn Museum; in 1930 at the Valentine Gallery, in a presentation of the Gallatin Collection at The Gallery of Living Art and in *Painting in Paris* at The Museum of Modern Art; and in 1932, 1933–34, 1935 and 1936 at the Pierre Matisse Gallery. Moreover,

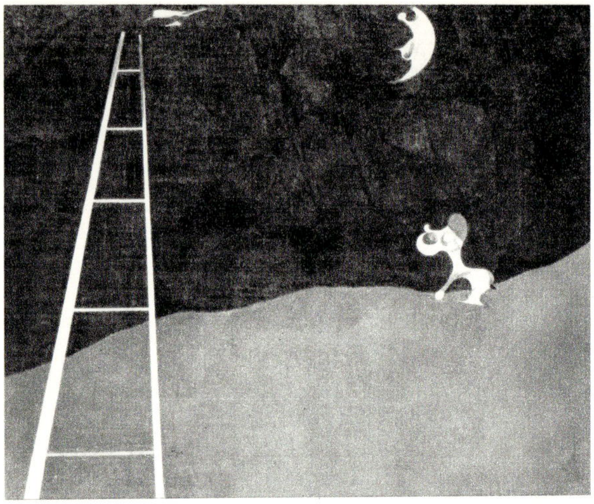

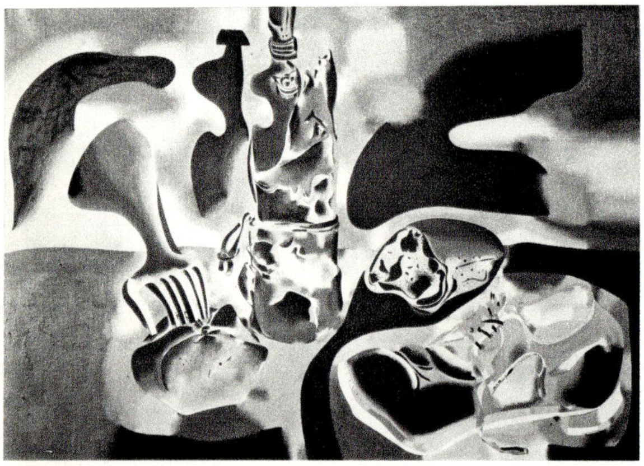

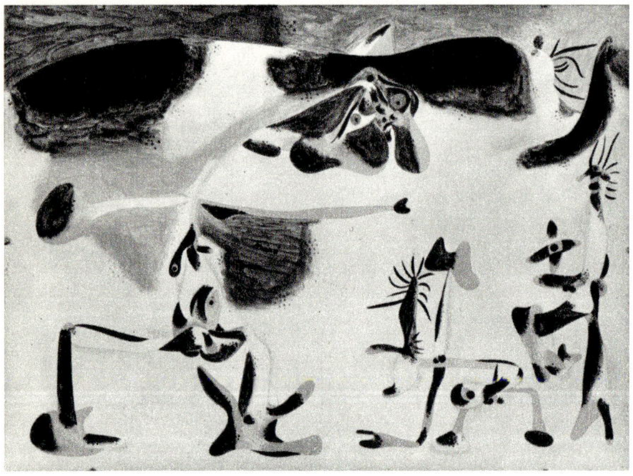

37. Joan Miró. *Dog Barking at the Moon.* 1926
Oil on canvas, 28 3/4 × 36 1/4″
Philadelphia Museum of Art: A.E. Gallatin Collection

38. Joan Miró
Still Life with Old Shoe. Paris, January 24–May 29, 1937
Oil on canvas, 32 × 46″
Collection The Museum of Modern Art, New York; James Thrall Soby Bequest, 1979

39. Joan Miró. *Two Personages in Love with a Woman.* 1936
Oil on copper, 10 × 14″
Courtesy Pierre Matisse Gallery, New York

Mirós were reproduced in *Cahiers d'Art* in 1926, 1929, 1934 and 1936. That Gorky knew and admired Miró paintings such as *Dog Barking at the Moon*, 1926 (fig.37), is evident, for he incorporated a number of the Spaniard's images in his own canvases at an early date: the fanciful face that enlivens an otherwise orthodox Cubist *Composition with Head,* ca. 1934–36 (cat. no. 79); the recurring eye, pinwheel or star motifs in the Nighttime, Enigma and Nostalgia drawings; the bootlike form which already occurs in *Still Life* of 1929–32 (cat. no. 23); the ladder forms in *Painting,* 1938 (cat. no. 119). These isolated motifs appeared in Gorky's canvases before Miró's formal influence became pervasive in the Garden of Sochi series.

Gorky's most personal and formally resolved paintings, other than *The Artist and His Mother, Portrait of Master Bill* and the *Self-Portrait* of ca. 1937, are three canvases and related works on the Garden in Sochi theme (cat. nos. 121–125), begun in 1940. Gorky has identified the theme as a memory vision of the garden of his youth. His poem, written in 1942 at the request of Dorothy Miller when The Museum of Modern Art acquired *Garden in Sochi* (cat. no. 124), illuminates the meaning and evokes the mood of the series:

> *I like the heat, the tenderness, the edible, the lusciousness, the song of a single person, the bathtub full of water to bathe myself beneath the water. I like Uccello, Grünewald, Ingres, the drawings and sketches for paintings of Seurat, and that man Pablo Picasso.*
>
> *I measure all things by weight.*
>
> *I love my Mougouch. What about papa Cézanne! I hate things that are not like me and all the things I haven't got are God to me.*
>
> *Permit me—*
>
> *I like the wheatfields, the plough, the apricots, the shape of apricots, those flirts of the sun. And bread above all. . . .*
>
> *About 194 feet away from our house on the road to the spring, my father had a little garden with a few apple trees which had retired from giving fruit. There was a ground constantly giving shade where grew incalculable amounts of wild carrots, and porcupines had made their nests. There was a blue rock half buried in the black earth with a few patches here and there like fallen clouds. But where came all the shadows in constant battle like the lancers of Paolo Uccello's paintings? This garden was identified as the Garden of Wish Fulfillment and often I had seen my mother and other village*

women opening their bosoms and taking their soft and dependent breasts in their hands to rub them on the rock. Above all this stood an enormous tree all bleached under the sun, the rain, the cold, and deprived of leaves. This was the Holy tree. I myself don't know why this tree was holy but I had witnessed many people, whoever did pass by, that would tear voluntarily a strip of their clothes and attach this to the tree. Thus through many years of the same act, like a veritable parade of banners under the pressure of wind all these personal inscriptions of signatures, very softly to my innocent ear used to give echo to the sh-h-h-sh-h of silver leaves of the poplars.[38]

The painting believed to be the earliest in the Garden in Sochi series as well as its related studies (cat. no. 121) are based primarily on Miró's *Still Life with Old Shoe*, 1937 (fig. 38). Considered Miró's response to Picasso's allegorical masterpiece *Guernica,* this is a simple composition of four symbolic objects—an apple pierced by a fork, an old shoe, a gin bottle wrapped in paper and part of a loaf of bread. It is an impassioned protest against the horrors of war, against the Spanish Civil War and the anguish and poverty it engendered. While most advocates of Miró's abstraction were disappointed with the picture's realism, the Surrealists embraced its representational and symbolic content. Gorky perceived its innate abstract form and translated the singularly realistic objects into an arrangement of organic shapes, suppressing Miró's modeling of form and spatial illusionism in favor of flatness. Even where Gorky does imply modeling, he shades only portions of forms and he merely alludes to depth by overlapping figures. Shapes remain basically flat, held in a single plane with horizontally and vertically disposed forms. He closely follows Miró's composition, subdividing the canvas into four zones, without, however, alluding to either landscape or horizon line. Like Miró, Gorky ties his forms to the edges of the canvas, integrating figure and ground into one surface plane, allowing the field to encroach upon the autonomy of his forms. Gorky transforms the emotional as well as the descriptive content of Miró's canvas. While he uses Miró's basic palette, he changes its emphasis. Miró's ominous black field is now light-filled yellow ground. Night becomes day and a dark and angry vision becomes a hot summer garden. The nervous staccato of Miró's contours, the tortured forms and flickering light, suggestive of gunfire, war and flames, are transformed into lyrical, smoothly flowing forms, evoking a pastoral mood of rich and sensuous beauty.

Gorky referred to a number of other Mirós in the Sochi series, among them *Two Personages in Love with a Woman,* 1936 (fig. 39). In the *Garden in Sochi* of 1941 (cat. no. 123) he paraphrases the Spaniard's creatures: compare, for example, the strange figures in the lower right of the Miró with the similar configurations in Gorky's canvas; moreover, the face of Miró's woman may inspire Gorky's slipper and eye motif. Gorky also emulates Miró's alternating play of light and dark shapes spotted over the canvas. He eliminates the key component of Miró's abstract or naturalistic line from his Garden in Sochi paintings, but nevertheless retains the sense of gravitational pull which accompanies this element. Critics have commented that Miró's figures appear to float in a single plane in front of a backdrop, while Gorky's seem firmly anchored in place. However, in this and other Personage paintings of 1936, Miró uncharacteristically layers his figures in an irrationally ordered landscape space or aligns them with the canvas edge to produce an effect of relatively stable shapes. The basic compositional arrangement of *Garden in Sochi,* 1943 (cat. no. 125), is very close to that of the first version. It is, however, far more painterly and abstract. Color is brushier and, like line, begins to assume independence. Edges of shapes are more active; forms, with their boundaries blurred, begin to dissolve into the medium of the field. Images retain the sense of animal life but become more schematic, as details such as eyes and tails are eliminated.

Despite the many parallels that may be drawn between the Sochi variants and Miró's oeuvre, important differences exist. Miró's line is more even, his color more strident and intense. There is little evidence, as yet, in Gorky's work, except for the Nighttime series, of the erotic subjects which inhabit Miró's painting. Gorky does not organize his shapes into groups of teeming figures as Miró often does, nor does he employ the Spaniard's abrupt changes of scale. And Gorky's compositional phrasing is unique: the spaces between the forms themselves do not serve as mere background. Miró's backgrounds are impenetrable and definite; Gorky's are as ambiguous as his figures. Miró's Boschian figures are schematized but still representational, imbued with magical, religious and narrative overtones entirely absent from Gorky's more generalized, mysterious forms. For, despite his symbolic allusions to personal memories, Gorky is far more abstract and far more painterly than Miró.

By the early 1940s Gorky had clearly started to evolve a language of signs, symbols and form that corresponded to the intricate complexities of his inner vision. Whereas his primary inspiration came from the poetic abstractions of Miró and Masson, he nevertheless admired the literal dreamscape illusionism of Dali and Tanguy and was intrigued and nourished by the Surrealist love of the dream, the landscape of the mind and the imagination. In 1945 Gorky stated that ". . . art is a language that must be mastered before it can be conveyed."[39] Cubism represented the language he mastered, Surrealism, the freedom to reinvent it.

During the war years Gorky faced both spiritual and economic hardship. No longer receiving funds from the WPA/FAP, his poverty was extreme. He tried without success in the fall of 1940 to get a class together at the Grand Central School of Art. Deeply disturbed by the war, he volunteered to serve in the camouflage section of the army, but was rejected as overage. He organized a camouflage class at the Grand Central School of Art in the fall of 1941 and, in an announcement for the course, articulated his hopes that art might serve the war effort as well as an aesthetic function:

> *An epidemic of destruction sweeps the world today. The mind of civilized man is set to stop it. What the enemy would destroy, however, he must first see. To confuse and paralyze this vision is the role of camouflage. Here the artist and more particularly the modern artist can fulfill a vital function for, opposed to this vision of destruction, is the vision of creation.*
>
> *Historically, it has been the artist's role to make manifest the beautiful inherent in all objects of nature and man. In the study of the object, as a thing seen, he has required a profound understanding and sensibility concerning its visual aspects. The philosophy as well as the physical and psychological laws governing their relationships constitute the primary source material for the study of camouflage. The mastery of this visual intelligence has been the particular domain of the modern artist. Intent on the greatest exploration of the visible world it was the cubist painters who created the new magic of space and color that everywhere confronts our eyes in new architecture and design. Since then the various branches of modern art through exhaustive experiment and research have created a vast laboratory whose discoveries unveiled for all the secrets of form, line and color. For it is these elements that make an object visible and which are for the artist the vocabulary of his language.*
>
> *This course is dedicated to that artist, contemporary in his understanding of forces in the modern world, who would use this knowledge that will deepen and enrich his understanding of art as well as make him an important contributor to civilian and military defense.*[40]

Despite Gorky's enthusiasm, the course was soon abandoned because of insufficient enrollment. Gorky sold very little during his lifetime: in letter after letter to Vartoosh he complains he cannot sell his paintings. Not until 1945, three years before his death, was he able to write his sister that he was working for the first time without financial worries. However, in 1941 several of his friends, independent of one another, donated some of his works to museums. Bernard Davis, an early supporter, gave *Argula*, 1938 (cat. no. 120), to The Museum of Modern Art; Mr. and Mrs. Wolfgang S. Schwabacher gave *Garden in Sochi*, 1941, to the same museum; the mosaicist Jeanne Reynal gave *Enigmatic Combat* to the San Francisco Museum of Art.

In 1941 Gorky met Agnes Magruder and immediately fell in love with her. (He had been married, very briefly in 1935 to Marny George, a young mid-Westerner living in New York.) Agnes, an admiral's daughter, strikingly beautiful and considerably younger than he, was very different from him in background, temperament and physical appearance. In the summer of 1941 Gorky and Agnes, together with the sculptor Isamu Noguchi and three other friends, traveled across country to San Francisco. The trip was prompted by Jeanne Reynal's suggestion to Gorky that a change in environment might benefit his painting. She offered him the use of a studio and promised to try to arrange an exhibition for him on the West Coast.

The journey was in may ways a revelation for Gorky: for the first time he saw the vast expanses of the American landscape and he was introduced to the culture of the American Indian, so completely unlike the European aesthetic traditions in which he was immersed. Reynal's efforts were successful and a one-man exhibition of Gorky's work of 1921 to 1941 was held at the San Francisco Museum of Art in August. The show met with favorable notice from critics who noted his sources in Picasso, Braque and Miró and praised his lushly tactile surfaces, his fluidity of design and spontaneity of movement. Most interesting were Alexander Fried's comments in the *San Francisco Examiner* of August 17, 1941, for at this early date, he saw Gorky as a Surrealist.

Gorky and Agnes were married in Virginia City, Nevada, on September 15. They returned to New York and to 36 Union Square. For the first time in

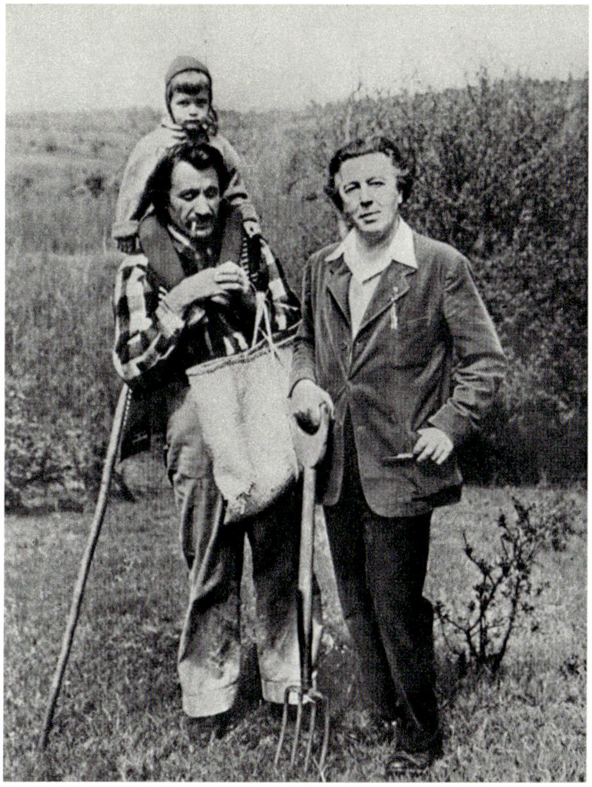

Gorky with daughter Maro and André Breton, ca. 1946

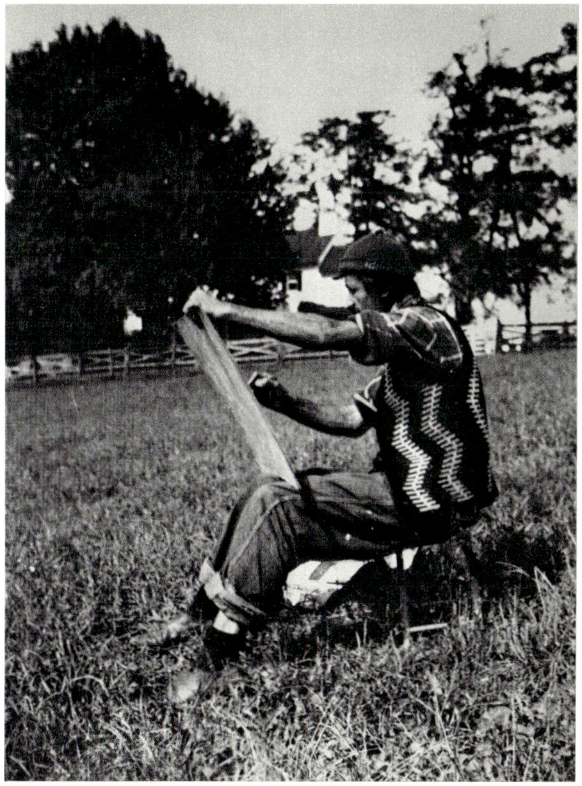

Crooked Run Farm, 1943 or 1944

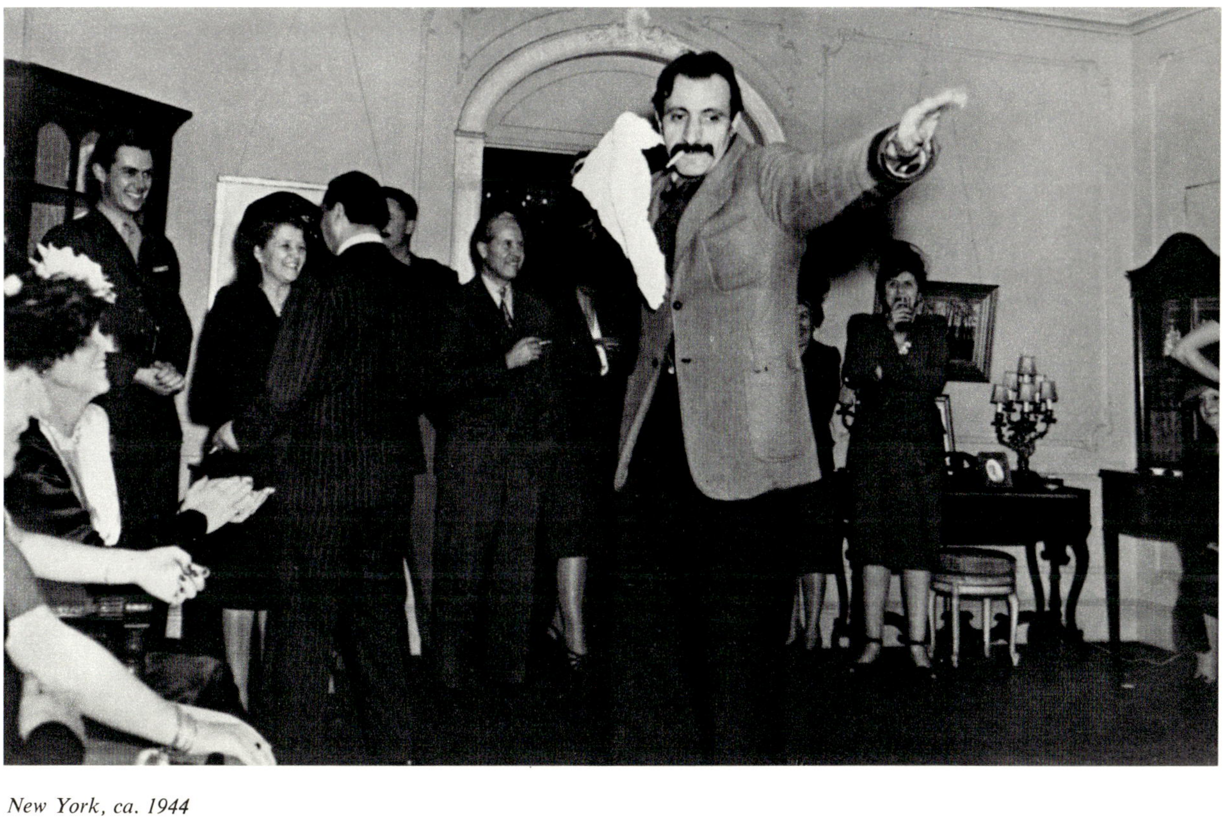

New York, ca. 1944

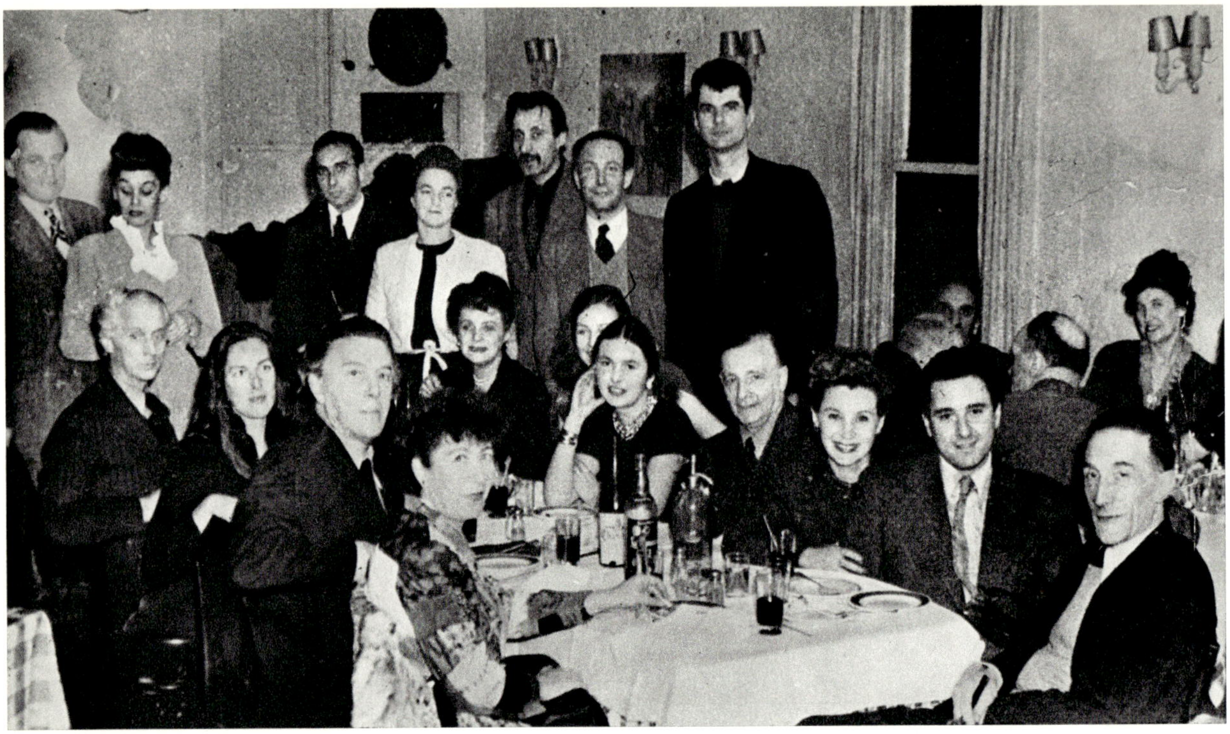

Standing, l. to. r.: Bernard Reis, Irene Francis, Esteban Francis, Elena Calas, Gorky, Enrico Donati, Nicolas Calas. Seated, clockwise: Steffi Kiesler, André Breton, Agnes Gorky, Max Ernst, Becky Reis, Elisa Breton, Patricia Matta, Frederick Kiesler, Nina Lebel, Matta Echaurren, Marcel Duchamp, New York, 1945

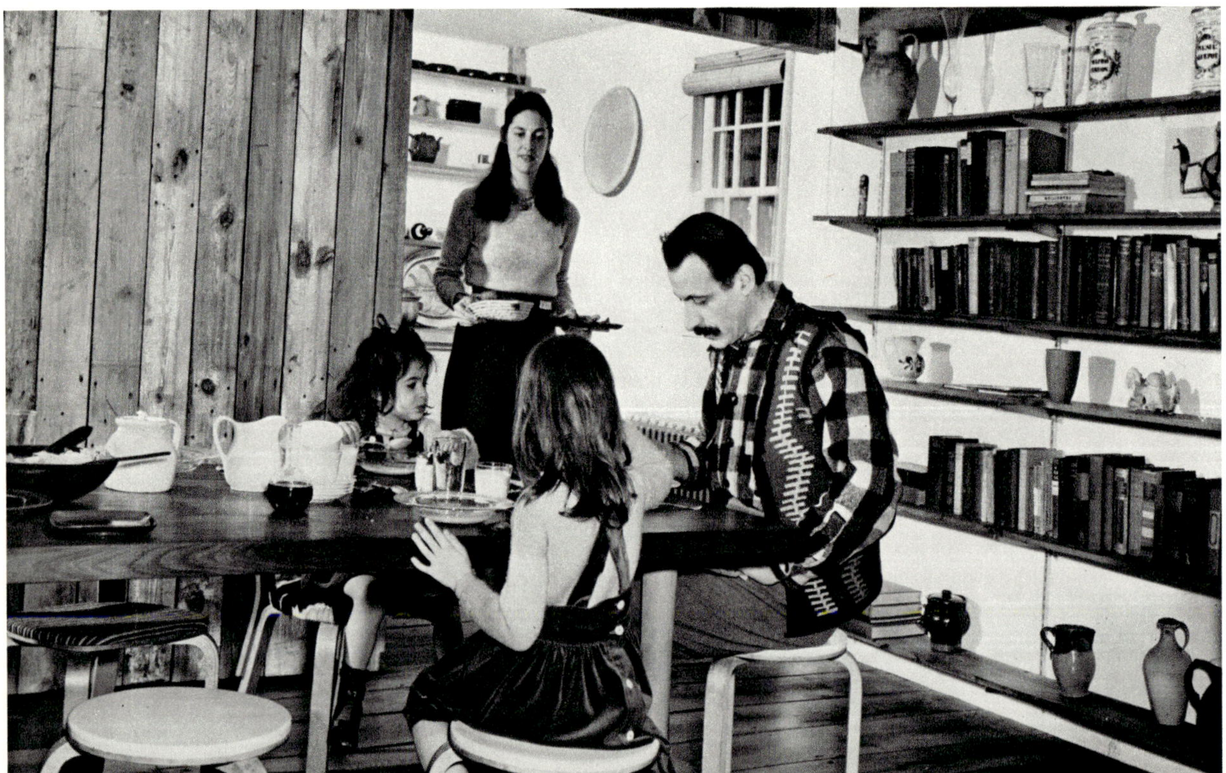

Gorky and family in Sherman, Connecticut, February 1948

his letters to Vartoosh Gorky expressed optimism, even happiness. He continued to work on his Sochi paintings and this year met and became friendly with the Chilean artist Matta Echaurren. He was increasingly drawn into Surrealist circles.

The influence of Surrealism had emerged in the United States in the early 1930s and grew throughout the decade. As early as 1931 the first important Surrealist exhibition in America, *Newer Super Realism,* was mounted by Arthur Everett Austin at the Wadsworth Atheneum in Hartford. The show traveled to Julien Levy's gallery in New York in 1932. Levy vigorously supported the movement, showing its important painters throughout the 1930s and publishing a major anthology, *Surrealism,* in 1936. That same year Alfred H. Barr, Jr. presented the crucial *Fantastic Art, Dada, Surrealism* at The Museum of Modern Art.

Nothing Gorky and his colleagues had seen previously prepared them for the revolutionary aesthetic of Surrealism which now caused them to rethink their own positions during the 1930s. The real catalyst for the younger artists' revolt was, however, the arrival in New York at the time of World War II of many of the major Surrealists—Max Ernst, Yves Tanguy, Matta Echaurren, André Masson and the poet laureate of the movement, André Breton. These artists, exiles like himself, brought with them a vitality, a commitment to the new, the experimental, the unorthodox. Their spirit, their imagery, their automatic techniques inspired Americans like Pollock, Rothko, Gottlieb, Newman, Still and de Kooning to throw off the past. They purged their art of political and social content and with it figuration, they abandoned the Neo-Plastic dogma of the American Abstract Artists and they abandoned Cubism, a movement that was already moribund in Europe. (A similar phenomenon was to occur in the early 1960s when Pop Art destroyed the last vestiges of a derivative Abstract Expressionism.) For all of the fledgling Americans it was an exhilarating moment in history that gave them the freedom and the challenge they needed to cut their bonds to a provincial American past and an outmoded European tradition. From this alliance with European Surrealist art and thought they forged, in a monumental effort, a brilliant new American art. For Joseph Cornell, who had practiced a form of Surrealism since 1932, and for Gorky, who had already experimented with the idiom in the thirties, the actual presence of these emigrés in New York was particularly significant: their personal encouragement helped them persevere in their search for new means of expression. when Gorky was on the verge of a breakthrough and desperately needed critical approval, the Surrealists were there to support him. Gorky's new alliance was disdained by Stuart Davis who, as an unyielding Cubist, felt that his drift toward Surrealism was a betrayal of his innate gifts as an artist, a capitulation to a frivolous and decadent movement. But Breton's position as the founder and leader of Surrealism had earned him the respect of many younger American artists. Thus, when he voiced his admiration for Gorky's work in his preface for the catalogue of the artist's exhibition at the Julien Levy Gallery in 1945, his words reached a receptive audience. In Breton, Gorky found a mentor he revered; from him he received a kind of acclaim he had never before known and was not to experience again. For a few years Breton, poet and critic, was Gorky's Apollinaire.

The year following their marriage, Gorky and Agnes spent three weeks at the home of Saul Schary in Connecticut. Working in the landscape reawakened Gorky's deep feeling for nature. *The Pirate I* of 1942 (cat. no. 126) was an early response to the intense pleasure of this long-postponed moment. It is a delicate painting, a study in pale washes of color: soft greens, pale lavenders, delicate blues. The surface treatment is vastly different from anything the artist had ever before attempted. According to Julien Levy, this radical change in technique may be ascribed to the influence of Matta. Matta described his "relationship with Gorky as one of unreserved exchange but basic misunderstanding."[41] Nevertheless, the exchange was mutually rewarding. As Levy explains:

> *Matta urged Gorky to mix turpentine freely in his paints and thus achieve the liberty of fresh, airy improvisation. He encouraged him to profit from the inevitable dripping of such a fluid medium, and to use the accidental splotches as suggestive forms for further elaboration, as Leonardo da Vinci used the stains on the wall plaster of his room. And, admiring Gorky's leaping and inventive line, a line like the flight of a fly, Matta borrowed for long study one of Gorky's most profuse drawings . . . so that for one or two years the drawings of Matta and those of Gorky had quite a family resemblance. But, as Matta explains, their "meanings were different." Matta was working toward a vocabulary of his personal outer space and Gorky toward his inner space. Matta, the nihilist, was increasingly cynical at this time; Gorky, warm and vulnerable.*[42]

While critics have noted that there is little substance

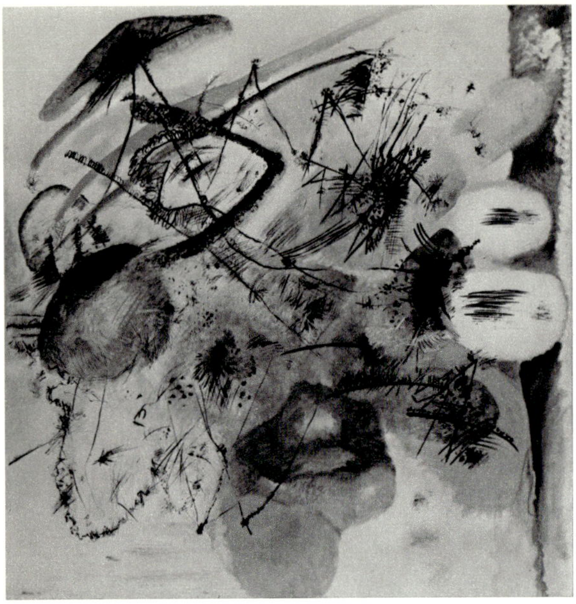

40. Vasily Kandinsky
Black Lines. December 1913
Oil on canvas, 51 × 51 1/4″
Collection The Solomon R. Guggenheim Museum, New York

in Matta's work, he was a spectacular draftsman and superb technician. Gorky was attracted to his charismatic presence and dazzling if inherently superficial style; he gave meaning and substance to many of Matta's ideas.

The "Old Pirate," Gorky explained to Julien Levy, was a mongrel which visited his yard. And Levy has, in fact, discovered the image of a dog sitting placidly in the center foreground of the canvas, as well as the rump of a horse at the upper left. As Levy points out, Gorky at this time began his paintings from nature but proceeded to disguise or camouflage his images as they developed. A comparison of *Pirate I* with another version of the theme, *Pirate II* of 1943 (cat. no. 127), reveals the intensification of the camouflage process. In *Pirate II* the amorphous imagery of the earlier painting has become even more ambiguous, although the dog in the center foreground is still barely discernable. Moreover, the ground is brushier and more active in *Pirate II* and hence appears to encroach further upon the figures. This ground speaks less of natural atmosphere than of painterly expression. However, the clustering of forms in a centralized image within this field is regressive in terms of the evolution of Gorky's more allover compositions. Both paintings are like sketches, graced with spontaneous, flickering line which animates and unifies evanescent form.

Waterfall of ca. 1943 (cat. no. 129) is one of Gorky's most intense evocations of nature. It retains certain recognizable landscape elements but affords the viewer an immediate and satisfying apprehension of nature through basically abstract means—cool, dense greens and blues, the smooth watery flow of paint and liquid forms. We can sense the path of the water as it cascades down the fall, flows in and around the rocks and comes to rest in the eddies and pools at its base. Here Gorky responds to his surroundings directly, as he captures the essence of nature.

Waterfall and other paintings of the period, such as *Housatonic Falls,* 1943–44 (cat. no. 138), reveal the powerful influence of Kandinsky. While it is unlikely that Gorky saw Kandinsky's one-man show at the Société Anonyme in 1923, he had ample opportunity to become familiar with the Russian's work in later years: at the *Blue Four* exhibition at the Daniel Gallery in New York in 1925; at the Société Anonyme in 1926 and 1927; at J.B. Neumann's New Art Circle in 1936; at Nierendorf in 1937; at the Museum of Non-Objective Painting; and at another *Blue Four* exhibition at the Buchholz Gallery in 1944. Kandinsky's art served as an antidote to the literary and literally realistic painting of many Surrealists and reinforced Gorky's own inclinations toward abstraction. And most important was Kandinsky's painterliness, upon which Gorky drew throughout the remainder of his brief life. In both *Waterfall* and *Housatonic Falls,* Gorky adapts Kandinsky's peaked forms and, to a certain extent, his highly-charged line. However, he is now more interested in touch and strong color harmonies than in the independent line exemplified in Kandinskys such as *Black Lines,* December 1913 (fig. 40); thus, his line does not exist for its own sake but has structural and spatial relevance, giving shape to a rock, a slope, a ledge, establishing shallow planes which position forms in space. *Waterfall* and *Housatonic Falls* also suggest Kandinsky in their random juxtaposition and fanning out of forms. Yet passages in which form is built up of massed strokes recall Cézanne. And the spirit of Cézanne is evoked as well in the palpable and living atmosphere of these canvases.

Waterfall is far more painterly than any of the artist's preceding work. Here, with utmost virtuosity, Gorky manipulates large and small forms, dark and pastel colors, spontaneous line. He contrasts random surface treatment with precise form, delicately etched line with washes of color and drips of paint. He applies paint in overlapping layers or allows it to soak into the canvas; he bleeds one color into another and lightens a dark mass with diaphanous plumes of white. He defines amorphous forms by juxtaposing them against secondary shapes and weaves his changeable line in and out of color areas. His extraordinary loose painterly style prefigures such brilliantly realized abstract canvases as *Water of the Flowery Mill,* 1944 (cat. no. 160), and *How My Mother's Embroidered Apron Unfolds in My Life,* 1944 (cat. no. 164).

In the summer of 1942 Gorky visited his in-laws at their newly acquired home in Virginia, Crooked Run Farm. The Gorkys took with them their daughter Maro, born in April of that year. Here he started a series of drawings inspired by nature; he began, in in his own words, to "look into the grass."[43] These works, which James Johnson Sweeney describes as "a series of monumentally drawn details of what one might see in the heavy August grass,"[44] together with numerous others Gorky executed on subsequent visits to Virginia became the source for many of his most magnificent paintings. Now Gorky studied nature with a passion he had heretofore reserved for the study of art, examining closely the forms of flowers, leaves, insects, observing the wind as it ruffled the tall grasses that grew in that region. He captured the appearance of living organisms and the sense of the sun, shadow and heat around him; and, above all, he captured the poetry and beauty of nature. From these observations of the flora and fauna of external reality, his studies of past art, the inspiration of other artists and from his inner life of memories and emotions, Gorky created a vocabulary of new forms. In his well-known essay, "The Eye-Spring," written for the catalogue of Gorky's show at Julien Levy's, Breton defined these forms as "hybrid" and described their genesis in the context of Surrealism:

> *By "hybrids" I mean the resultants provoked in an observer contemplating a natural spectacle with extreme concentration, the resultants being a combination of the spectacle and a flux of childhood and other memories, and the observer being gifted to a rare degree with the grace of emotion. In short it is my concern to emphasize that Gorky is, of all the surrealist artists, the only one who maintains direct contact with nature—sits down to paint* before *her. Furthermore, it is out of the question that he would take the expression of this nature as an end in itself—rightly he demands of her that she provide sensations that can serve as springboards for both knowledge and pleasure in fathoming certain profound states of mind. Whatever may be the subtle ways by which these states of mind choose to express themselves they stem from the wild and tender personality which Gorky hides, and share the sublime struggle of flowers growing toward the light of day. Here for the first time nature is treated as cryptogram. The artist has a code by reason of his own sensitive anterior impressions, and can decode nature to reveal the very rhythm of life.*[45]

Breton saw no difficulty in classifying Gorky as a Surrealist although his initial inspiration was in nature, while the Surrealists' was, by definition, in pure automatism. This was indeed a significant difference however, one that set Gorky apart from the Surrealists, just as it later was to separate him from the Abstract Expressionists. In fact, Gorky and the Surrealists proceeded in opposite directions. The Surrealists began without specific images in mind but discovered and cultivated those that emerged in the process of applying their random marks. In Breton's term they were "moving in favor of the subject." Gorky, however, was moving from nature toward abstraction.

The eroticism of Gorky's drawings and paintings relates to the Surrealist obsession with sexuality and their use of Freudian symbolism to express sexual content. Sexual content in Surrealist art took various forms. For Miró, sex means procreation, birth and renewal; his approach is positive and humorous, except at the time of the Spanish Civil War when his imagery becomes grotesque and bestial. Matta's sexual imagery, on the other hand, is aggressive, equated with violence and death, and Dali's speaks of voyeurism and impotence. The sexual imagery in Gorky's erotic paintings—depictions of male and female genetalia—may in some instances be compared to the forms in Matta's paintings. Most often it is similar in its form and playfulness to Miró's imagery. Frequently, however, these paintings convey a mood of profound frustration and despair. Occasionally, the images, heightened color and exquisite line express erotic ecstacy, as in the sublime *The Liver Is the Cock's Comb,* 1944 (cat. no. 161).

Many drawings of these years are dense and impacted, rich in color and nuance, complex in imagery. Gorky produced the most intricate drawings of 1943–44 with the simplest means: pencil, pen and ink, wax crayon, pastel. Rarely using all media in a single drawing, usually working in a horizontal format, with limited means he cultivates a variety of effects. He at once reveals the inherent characteristics of individual materials and combines them into an integrated totality, creating the appearance of interpenetrating levels of space. In examples such as *The Housatonic* and *Composition I* of 1943 (cat. nos. 134, 136) he continues to explore the biomorphic forms and the play of positive against negative space which engaged him in the Khorkom and Nighttime, Enigma and Nostalgia series. He also combines the crosshatching of the Nighttime drawings with a more random circular pattern of lines. Entirely new, however, is the importance accorded to contouring line—line which indicates a horizon, defines a plane or shapes an amorphous figure. New also is the freedom with which shapes float, drifting towards the top of the paper, stabilized only by the residual horizon line.

Pastel and crayon or crayon and pencil drawings of 1943, among them *Drawing, Untitled, Carnival* (cat. nos. 154, 157, 159), display a coloristic brilliance not attained in the paintings until the following year. Drawings of this type are the models upon which Gorky based such major canvases as *The Liver Is the Cock's Comb*. Their lush, velvety surfaces and intense hothouse color recall the pastels of Redon, although Gorky's mixture of mediums gives them more varied texture and subtler modulation. In the most successful works of this genre, Gorky achieves an effect of color washes that is more characteristic of painting than drawing. Indeed, these drawings rival the oils in their beauty and perfection.

Other drawings (see cat. no. 178, for example) of the period are as lean, spare and resistant as *Composition I, Carnival* and its companions are rich, complex and ingratiating. Here, Gorky used only a minimum of means—pencil and occasionally a trace of crayon, working the nap of the paper to create an effect comparable to embossing. These extraordinarily subdued drawings require close scrutiny to reveal the subtle complexities of patterns and nuances. Yet another category of works on paper, among them *Composition II, Untitled, Anatomical Blackboard,* all of 1943 (cat. nos. 145, 146, 148), display greater clarity than the extremely complex or colored drawings and are more sensuous than the austere pencil drawings. Here Gorky employs a variety of forms, techniques and concepts. In drawings such as *Untitled,* forms are veiled by a series of misty areas in the foreground which confound our reading of spatial relationships. In *Anatomical Blackboard* there is a play between effects of recession into space and horizontal movement across the flat surface plane of the paper, between flat and volumetric form, between precise and sketchy line, between line which encloses shape and freely meandering line. And *Drawing* is comprised of plant and animal forms, vaguely phallic shapes, pinwheels, dashes, plumes of color, all disposed frontally on the flat surface plane in the manner of Miró. On the other hand, Matta's forms, his spatial illusionism and adaptations of his automatist painting techniques are apparent in a number of the drawings (see cat. no. 140). However, no matter how closely the Chilean's example is followed, Gorky's drawings are far softer, more sensitive and poetic, free of Matta's illustrational overtones and brittle effects.

The study for *They Will Take My Island,* 1944 (cat. no. 180), is a superb example of an additional group of Gorky's works on paper, the preliminary drawings for paintings. Characteristically direct and spontaneous, it lacks the attention to finish, the exquisite perfection of the other drawings, for Gorky is concerned with ideas and planning, not subtleties of execution. The more generous forms and open areas convey a sense of scale not apparent in the denser, impacted drawings of the period. This drawing, like others before it, attests to Gorky's concern with flatness: despite some layering of space, the forms remain basically two-dimensional. To enhance this sense of flatness Gorky aligns most of his shapes in rectilinear fashion, referring to an implicit or explicit grid. Often he crops forms at the edges of the paper, thereby tying them, no matter how active they are, to the surface of the support. These are his most nearly abstract drawings, for he seldom refers to landscape in them. Yet the sense of landscape continues to inform them, for Gorky created new and magical metaphors for nature with the line, shape and color of the exquisite drawings of this year.

Like the drawings of 1944, *The Liver Is the Cock's Comb* contains numerous elliptical forms gathered together into small groups which are scattered across the flat field of the support. Tiny pointed forms cap several of these configurations: they function almost abrasively, interrupting the smooth flow of movement, contrasting with the scale and rounded contours of the major shapes. A number of verticals act as sentinels or stanchions, unifying the composition and locking its mobile figures securely in place. Line plays a vital if supporting role, defining portions of shapes, enhancing the vertical thrust of bands of color, linking forms. In addition, Gorky duplicates or approximates the shapes of certain color-forms with line. He positions these linear echoes so that the forms seem off-register. *The Liver Is the Cock's Comb* is at once a grand summing up of ideas generated in the drawings and paintings of the preceding years and a forerunner of concepts Gorky would explore in future work. For example, the pointed ocher and green shape at the upper right is developed more emphatically in the late masterpiece *Agony,* 1947 (cat. no. 220), and the feathering of paint becomes an essential component of the great series of 1947, The Plow and the Song and *The*

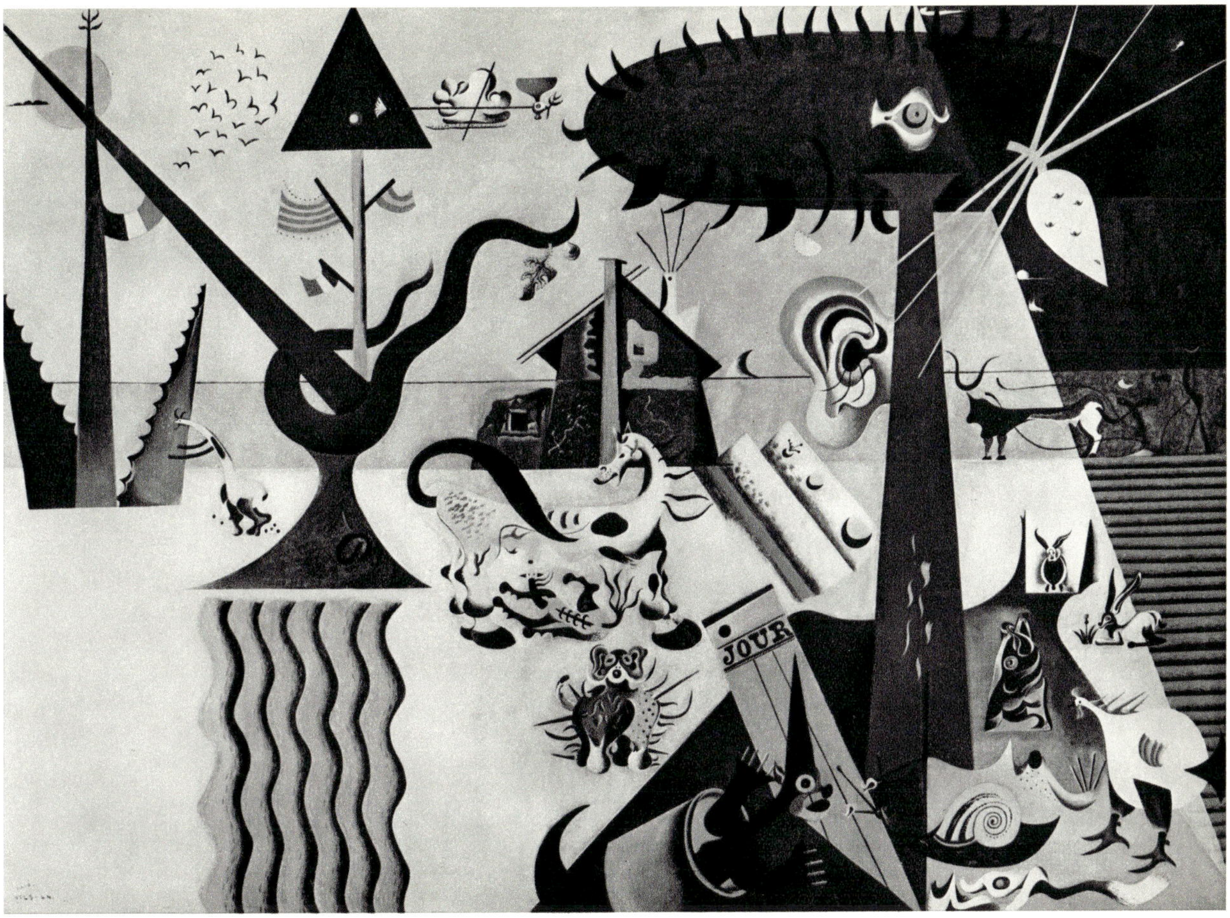

41. Joan Miró. *The Tilled Field.* 1923–24
Oil on canvas, 26 × 36 1/2″
Collection The Solomon R. Guggenheim Museum, New York

Orators (cat. nos. 203–205, 238). Tactility is enhanced, spotting of light and dark areas intensified, as the rich and varied hues of earlier canvases proliferate into a luxuriant garden of color. As in the earlier *Waterfall,* a profusion of organic shapes is organized in a series of shallow overlapping planes. The planes are tied to the canvas surface with a narrow column of pale lemon yellow which, like Mondrian's black bands, stops just short of the bottom edge of the support. Grouped to the right of these planes is a cluster of smaller forms, some oval, one resembling a bird in profile. The disposition of those small forms, tightly jammed together and overlapped, reading in shallow depth, contrasts with that of the larger figures which are set somewhat further apart and read up and down the surface plane.

Gorky looks beyond his own earlier work for formal precedents for *The Liver Is the Cock's Comb.* The influence of Kandinsky is pervasive in the flowing forms, pointed shapes, the charged field of oriental colors scattered against greys, the feathery brush stroke. While the model of Kandinsky is central, Gorky sought inspiration as well in a myriad of sources in the art of the past. The telescoping of near and far distances recalls Grünewald's *Isenheim Altarpiece;* the jumps in scale suggest parallels with Renaissance donor portraits where the importance of the subject, rather than its position in space, determines its size. As if to support this reference, Gorky's painting even contains, in the best Renaissance tradition, a "window" (just off-center at the top of the canvas). In addition, Miró's *The Tilled Field*, 1923–24 (fig. 41), may have inspired Gorky in its utilization of objects of inconsistent scale to suggest flatness and depth and create a sense of a landscape space. Whereas Miró's fanciful and abstract landscapes retain a feeling of natural reality, Gorky gives us a world of another order. His is at once a visceral interior and a landscape that, as Julien Levy has so aptly said, "unfolds in full daylight." An extraordinary coupling of visceral forms and animal imagery, interior and exterior spaces, it speaks eloquently of his intense involvement with both

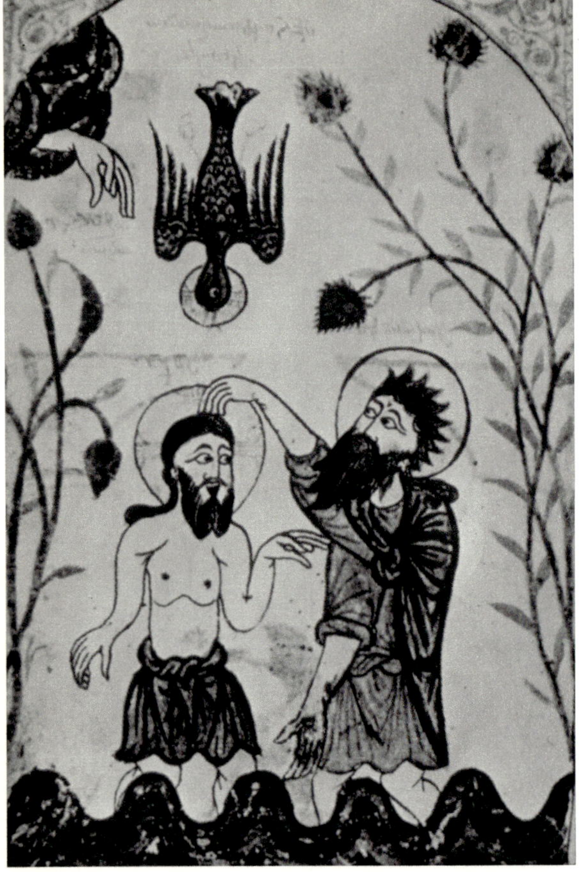

42. Armenian Manuscript: Hovhannes of Hizan. *Baptismal Scene*, 1402. Whereabouts unknown

Surrealism and nature. In true Surrealist fashion, he places objects from separate spatial and conceptual planes in unexpected juxtaposition, for his joining of the animal and the visceral is, as Max Ernst expressed it, "the fortuitous encounter upon a non-suitable plane of two mutually distant realities."[46]

Not only Western European art but Armenian stone carving, mural and manuscript painting significantly influenced Gorky's mature painting. For Eastern European art nourished his abstract art as profoundly as it had his portraits. He often referred to the medieval manuscript painters Sarkis Pidzak and Toros Roslin, to the splendors of the sculptures of Akhtamar and to the art of the family's Vart Badrik shrine in Khorkum. He said this shrine "is as vivid before my eyes as in my youth" and "I trace with my hand the lacework of the Katchkar, the abstract work of centuries of innocent Armenian artists, trained and untrained, each carving speaking its own language."[47] He spoke also of his memories of "Medieval Armenian manuscript paintings with their beautiful Armenian faces, subtle colors, their tender lines and the calligraphy. . . . And to this day I can still feel the chill of excitement at being introduced to a whole new world of plasticity. I love the School of Lake Van. I love the School of Cilicia of our Toros Roslin and Sarkis Pidzak."[48] And he maintained that "Toros Roslin is the first. But Uccello is the next step. The beginnings of what are considered modern paintings, the coming to grips with color and dimensionality and space. . . ."[49] Gorky loved to recite tales of Armenia's past and trace its culture from the beginnings of civilization, to point to its art and the land as the true sources of his own art. He repeatedly referred to the Armenian plows, the butterchurns and clay baking tools, the rugs, the gardens, wheatfields and orchards of the Adoian family, noting, for example, how the "dimensionality of our three houses coalesces with red orchards and blue gardens," describing "purple mountains and Lake Van's white salt shores and the sweet valleys and animals,"[50] reminding Vartoosh of his earliest paintings "when I used Armenia's authentic colors. Painting on *Gunick* eggs was my introduction to the use of color. Nature in Armenia was an inexhaustible paint tube. And brushes once dipped in it can dance to their own songs."[51] More importantly, he recognized in Armenian art a universal language of form. He wrote:

> *Beloved ones, I am forever fascinated by the universality of art. I mean that sometimes I will paint a thought or concept and then see the very same one for the first time in an ancient work. . . . Such inexplicable occurences lead me to conclude that certain similarities in art can arise independently in various regions on earth. . . . It is why I feel that tradition in art is so important for progress. The sensitivity of the Armenian world seems to flow out of my hands and mind. When I see ancient Armenian art I feel that I am a part of it . . . . It is as if that ancient artist felt and thought as I do. Yet both of us thought and felt in an identical manner quite independent of each other. . . . Strange, that thousands of years of separation produce the sinew of identity.*
>
> *Dearest ones, it is my feeling that form is the language of a given time, and it is that which must be constantly sought. Many emotions and experiences are ageless. Some are more readily conveyed than others. . . . I seek a form or language which will express my ideas for our time.*[52]

Gorky's heightened color, rhythmic forms, his combination of a rectilinear structure and meandering line, his attention to silhouette and to detail, his fluid calligraphy, his disregard of Renaissance perspective in favor of a hieratic ordering of forms, indicate much more than a profound regard for specifically Armenian tradition, art and architecture, more than a revival of an art of the past and the incorporation of the aesthetic of an ancient tradition into his paintings and drawings. In the medieval manuscripts, mural painting and stone carving of his homeland, Gorky discovered a timeless language of form (see fig. 42). In Armenian art, as in Surrealism, Gorky found an art that combined the worlds of the inner imagination and exterior reality, the sacred and the profane, the fantastic and the sublime. Gorky achieved his extraordinary ambition: he created a new language within the context of ancient Near Eastern tradition, Western European art and the avant-garde.

If *The Liver Is the Cock's Comb* epitomizes Gorky's emotional expressivity, *They Will Take My Island,* 1944 (cat. no. 181), is the ultimate embodiment of of his rational artistic intelligence. As *The Liver Is the Cock's Comb* resonates with seductive heat, so *They Will Take My Island* is tough, astringent and comparatively inaccessible. For the latter work and *Painting,* also 1944 (cat. no 182), show the artist adapting his leanest drawing style to canvas and restraining the spontaneous flow of his feelings in favor of conscious control. Of these canvases, Gorky said, "Any time I was ready to make a line somewhere, I put it somewhere else. And it was always better."[53] And shortly after his death his widow wrote, "When he painted from his drawings it was different from drawing from nature because he was editing his own emotion and adding and using all his conscious knowledge of his art. This produced some wonderful paintings but he sometimes said he wished he could eliminate that art and make the paintings as direct on the canvas as the emotion was within him in front of nature. . . . he would like to eliminate the artistic and conscious selection."[54]

Both paintings feature a sort of rude drawing and reveal little attention to detail or exquisite effects—an approach typical of a number of studies but rare in his canvases to date. Where *The Liver* and *Water of the Flowery Mill,* 1944 (cat. no. 160), display a rich and varied range of color, *They Will Take My Island* and *Painting* are almost colorless. What little color they contain is laid on cursorily and is as unyielding as their line. Here line is urgent and abrupt where elsewhere it is full of liquid grace; here there is anger and defiance where elsewhere there is harmony. Significantly, the model for *They Will Take My Island* is not the work of Kandinsky or Miró (although certain of its forms are Miróesque), but Picasso's *Guernica,* which Gorky very much admired. The clenched fists, contorted face, flame-like forms, like the motifs of *Guernica,* all speak of death and destruction. Like *Guernica,* it is a statement about homeland; as in *Guernica,* the style is graphic rather than painterly. *They Will Take My Island* and *Painting* are pivotal in their linearity. They are tough and demanding works in which Gorky begins to explore line in a manner that anticipates Pollock's allover painting by several years. And they are equally noteworthy in anticipating Gorky's own paintings such as *Nude, Charred Beloved I* and *Charred Beloved II,* all of 1946 (cat. nos. 194, 195, 196), which are emptied of all but a few form-defining lines and spare touches of color.

By now Gorky began to explore the uses of poetic titles for his paintings. A number of these titles were suggested by friends, among them Breton, Max Ernst and Julien Levy. Ernst, for example, proposed *Diary of a Seducer,* which was a chapter heading in Kierkegaard's *Either/Or.* And the painting *Days,etc.* was inspired by Paul Eluard's "Days like fingers, twist their battalions." Gorky has elaborated upon a number of his titles, illuminating layers of their meaning:

> *The song of a cardinal, liver, mirrors that have not caught reflection, the aggressively heraldic branches, the saliva of the hungry man whose face is painted with white chalk.*
>
> *The Liver Is the Cock's Comb*
>
> *. . . down the road, by the stream, that Old Mill, it used to grind corn, now it is covered with vines, birds, flowers. Flour Mill—Flowery Mill. That's funny! I like that idea . . .*
>
> *Water of the Flowery Mill*
>
> *. . . one image leads to another, one wisdom leads to another when you look into it, like peeling an artichoke. . . the leaves lying in the plate like feathers. . . and of course the silhouette of an artichoke leaf is quite simply that of an owl. . . .*
>
> *The Leaf of the Artichoke Is an Owl*
>
> *I tell stories to myself, often, while I paint, often nothing to do with the painting. Have you ever listened to a child telling that this is a house and this is a man and this is a cow in the sunlight. . . while his crayon wanders in an apparently meaningless scrawl all over the paper? My stories are often from my childhood. My mother told me many stories while I pressed my face into her long apron with my eyes closed. She had a long white apron like the one in her portrait, and another embroidered one. Her stories and the embroidery on her apron got confused in my mind with my*

eyes closed. All my life her stories and her embroidery keep unraveling pictures in my memory. If I sit before a blank white canvas. . . .

How My Mother's Embroidered Apron Unfolds in My Life

. . . I have been so lonely, so exasperated, and how to paint such empty space, so empty it's the limit!. . . .

The Limit[55]

While Gorky's titles are evocations of memories, of present objects, of poems, of insights and feelings—they are not descriptions of the forms and events in his paintings. It is, of course, possible to see in many of the paintings and drawings specific subject matter such as plant and animal forms, domestic interiors, funeral orations, particularly when they are suggested by the titles. Because the figures are so ambiguous and the compositions so complex, however, they elicit a variety of reactions; each viewer is stimulated to provide an individual interpretation. Gorky did not wish his paintings stripped of their complexity but welcomed unique and imaginative responses. He was, after all, not a painter of the ideogram or the pictograph like many of his contemporaries. Nor was he a painter of emblems like the Pop artists who followed in the next generation. He was, as William Rubin has noted, a painter of poetic allusion.[56] He was a painter of nature filtered through memory and fantasy who moved from representation toward abstraction, from the realm of the exterior world to the inner imagination. It is best to read his work with caution, as Levy has noted,[57] citing Breton's remarks in this context:

Truly the eye was not meant to take inventory like an auctioneer not to flirt with delusions and false recognitions like a maniac. . . . Easy-going amateurs will come here for their meager rewards; in spite of all warning to the contrary they will insist on seeing in these compositions a still life, a landscape, or a figure instead of daring to face the hybrid forms in which all human emotion is expressed.[58]

As the forties progressed, Gorky continued to seek change and, painting as one possessed, experimented with a variety of techniques and formal possibilties. He recalls Klee in the delicate tracery of line, the tonal nuances, the floating, disembodied forms and sense of fantasy of some works. He develops the lean, graphic style announced in *They Will Take My Island* in paintings such as *Impatience, Hugging, Landscape Table,* all 1945 (cat. nos. 184, 185, 189). Here Gorky turns once again to the example of Miró, highlighting shape with a line of contrasting color, blending one color area into another, dissolving solid surfaces into transparent veils with overlays of line. The power and poetry of Gorky's drawing, however, far surpasses the expressiveness of Miró's line. And Gorky does not emulate Miró's primitive shapes nor their disposition in space. Miró's forms are solid and complete, self-contained and bounded on all sides, and are usually confined to a single plane in a fairly legible space or floated in front of an atmospheric field. Only rarely does Miró introduce the background into the fabric of his images. Gorky, on the other hand, has evolved a very different concept of form, movement and space. His forms are not bounded but, rather, are amorphous entities, linked to one another and always flowing in and out of a yielding, complex, ambiguous spatial continuum.

In January 1946, a fire in Gorky's studio destroyed much of his work: drawings, sketches, books were reduced to ashes. In February of the same year he underwent an operation for cancer. Perhaps sensing that he had little time left to live, he began working even more compulsively. That summer the Gorkys, now a family of four (their second daughter Natasha was born in 1945), returned once more to the Magruder's farm in Virginia. Gorky produced 292 drawings, again working in the fields. New skeletal forms inhabit the landscape drawings, joining the familiar floral and palette, bird and animal motifs. Also among the drawings of this summer was a group of small interiors, some of which became the basis for important late paintings such as *The Calendars,* 1947 (now destroyed).

The drawings are superb, yet the paintings that followed in 1946 and 1947 are even more extraordinary. Ranging from the spare linearity of *Nude,* 1946 (cat. no. 194), to the pure painterly expression of The Plow and the Song series, they are in general more open and direct than the canvases of the past. It is as if the fire and his operation had released him from his obsessional concern with perfection of detail and finish. Shapes grow more attenuated, line more nervous, color more evanescent. He employs many techniques, thinning paint so it soaks into the canvas in *Charred Beloved I* and *Charred Beloved II,* feathering it in *The Betrothal II* and *The Betrothal*, 1947 (cat. nos. 198, 200), rubbing it with his brush into the canvas in *Year After Year,* 1947 (cat. no. 212). Mooradian has pointed out that Gorky often wet his canvas down before painting so it would become taut and then, after working on it, wet it down again, removing much of the paint. Gorky said, "I prefer not to see the strength of my arm in the paint-

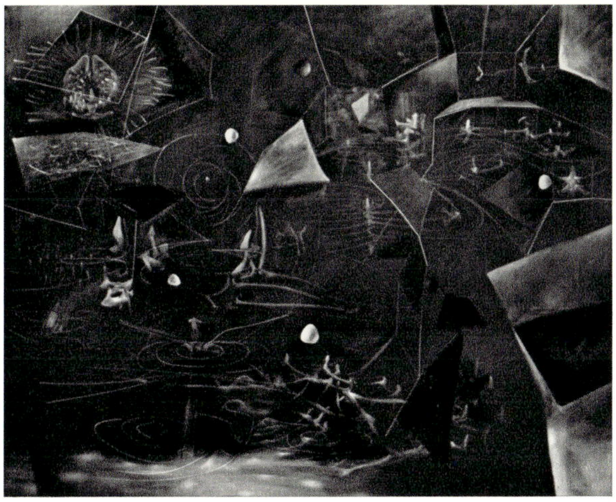

43. Matta Echaurren
Le Vertige D'Eros. 1944
Oil on canvas, 77 × 99″
Collection The Museum of Modern Art, New York
Given anonymously

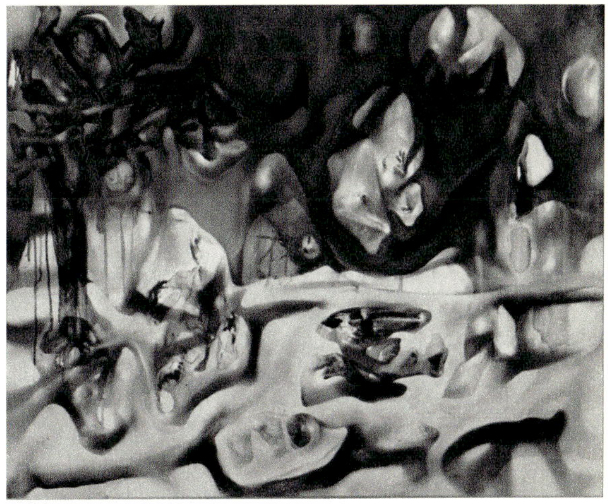

44. Matta Echaurren
Fabulous Race Track of Death (Instrument Very Dangerous to the Eye). n.d.
Oil on canvas, 27 1/2 × 35 1/2″
Yale University Art Gallery, New Haven,
Gift of the Société Anonyme

ing but only the poetry of my heart. The trouble is everyone uses their arms too much, that is too many brushstrokes. And I prefer, after the scrubbing, to be able to move into the painting and reform it. I want to leave only the ghost of the painting to spur imagination."[59] He explores numerous formal possibilities as well, in a single year, 1947, submerging figure into ground in *Agony* (cat. no. 220), returning once again to intricate linear expression and spatial agitation in *Summation* (cat. no. 247), enveloping figures and field in a liquid atmosphere and evoking infinite spaces extending beyond the canvas boundaries in *The Limit* (cat. no. 248); floating his forms in an ambiguous, indefinable space in *The Orators* (cat. no. 238).

The sense of movement and flux in these canvases calls to mind Matta's work of the late 1930s and early 1940s (see, for example, figs. 43, 44). Gorky borrows Matta's roughly ovoid and trapezoidal shapes. Like Matta, he makes them radiate from a central point, but he flattens the Chilean's deep space. Moreover, Matta's space is labyrinthean and chaotic, while Gorky's compositions, random and varied as their scattered images may appear, are in actuality highly organized and far simpler. For, like many great artists, Gorky understands that simplicity and clarity must underly a complex vision. Matta's fondness for theatrical effects and his preference for mechanical form rather than natural phenomena set him very much apart from Gorky. Both Matta and Gorky were intrigued by Duchamp's machines: Matta used them as the point of departure for a series of paintings with robot subjects. But when Gorky referred to *The Bride Stripped Bare by Her Bachelors, Even* in *The Betrothal* and *The Betrothal II,* he converted Duchamp's soft machine into a new anatomy of organic forms. He transformed *The Bride* into a despairing and moving commentary on courtship, love and death. Like many artists attracted to modern science, Matta succeeded only in producing rather literal approximations of mechanical forms and futuristic visions of space. Gorky's vision of nature and space was enacted as a drama in the language of abstract form.

Nude, Charred Beloved I and *Charred Beloved II* are masterpieces of understatement, composed of a small number of intensely evocative forms. Gorky's command of line and color allows him to shape forms and articulate the space between them with a minimum of means—a few bold strokes, a few touches of pigment. Like Miró, Gorky is able to place his figures slightly off-center or align them with the edges of the canvas without disrupting the tenuous equilibrium of his compositions. Although he rarely explored field painting as we now conceive of it, throughout his late work he fuses field and image into a continuum. Just as he joins image and ground into a single entity in his last paintings, so he synthesizes forms and motifs from various stages of his evolution: antique casts, bird, animal and floral forms, Armenian slippers, butterchurns exist together in the unified vision of his final statements. Toward the end of his life, Gorky became disillusioned with Surrealism. In a letter to Vartoosh he said:

. . . Surrealism is academic art under disguise and anti-aesthetic and suspicious of excellence and largely in opposition to modern art. Its claim of liberation is really restrictive because of its narrow rigidity. To its adherents the tradition of art and its quality mean little. They are drunk with psychiatric spontaneity and inexplicable dreams. . . . Their ideas are quite strange and somewhat flippant, almost playful. Really they are not as earnest about painting as I should like artists to be. Art must always remain earnest. . . . Art can remain marvelous when it is not conquered by frivolity.[60]

As he had freed himself from Cézanne, from Cubism, from Picasso, Gorky had now moved beyond Surrealism into a new realm.

Julien Levy related that Masson once told Gorky "I do not paint in front of, but from within nature."[61] Gorky might have said this about himself. As both Schwabacher and Levy have pointed out, Gorky and, hence, the viewer seem to be within the field of many of his paintings. This feeling of immersion in nature is intensified in the last works. The figures are now more rudimentary, fragmented and disconnected, the brushstrokes larger and more impetuous, the drawing rougher: like Monet at the end of his life, Gorky seems impatient in his search for meaning. Although his forms dissolve and the rhythm and flow of his line and images are interrupted, the paintings are about death only in the sense that death is part of life: they are a celebration of life, of the forces of nature and art. Gorky said "Even death expands. Death and life are two moving planes in eternal existence."[62] Human life, nature and art are one. Gorky is within nature and within art.

Gorky's terrible childhood experiences may have strengthened his will to survive his grave illness and the destruction by fire of his studio and his work, or it may ultimately have contributed to his collapse. His marriage, which had been troubled, now began to disintegrate. He had endured years of poverty and lack of recognition, but he could not withstand the final event in the succession of tragedies that befell him. On June 26, 1948, the car in which he was riding with Julien Levy and his wife Muriel crashed. Gorky's neck was broken. When he returned home from the hospital ten days later, his painting arm was paralyzed. Agnes left with the children for her parents' farm. Driven by despair, anger, jealousy, frustration in his love of family and art, Gorky killed himself on July 21, 1948.

In his too brief life Gorky produced some of the most sublime paintings of our time. He reached his artistic maturity several years before his friends and colleagues of the future New York School and introduced a complex of ideas and problems he did not live to resolve. This and the standard of greatness he set was his legacy to succeeding generations of painters. In concerning himself with the formal problems of pure painting—color, flatness, frontality—he anticipated both Abstract Expressionism and stain painting, although he used color in relation to line and form, according to the traditions of easel painting. In *One Year the Milkweed* of 1944 he drips paint with an abandon worthy of the action painters; in *The Liver Is the Cock's Comb* he treats broad area in a manner that prefigures Newman; he experiments with allover patterning before Pollock; he gives disembodied color an independent life before Rothko; he exploits the physicality of paint as de Kooning, who describes him as his mentor, came to present it. While he explores the relative values and tonalities of colors, he predicts the stain painting of Morris Louis by using thin, almost transparent washes of color.

Gorky has been called the last Surrealist and the first Abstract Expressionist. There is some truth in each judgement, but neither is accurate: he was both and he was neither. He did not participate in either the Surrealist movement proper or the formation of the Abstract Expressionist group yet represented Surrealism's last great plastic expression, and in his formal concerns and painterliness he anticipated Abstract Expressionism. He differed from the Abstract Expressionists in his lifelong commitment to the Old Masters; in his careful preplanning of his paintings with complete and fully rendered sketches; in his combination of the rational order of Cubism with the irrational dream of Surrealism. Moreover, his choice of easel scale and his presentation of small images in a large landscape contrasts with the Abstract Expressionists' use of large marks or areas on monumental canvases. His is the Boschian or Miróesque cosmos of vast expanses inhabited by fantastic organisms. Gorky's dialogue with the masters of the past such as Uccello, Ingres, Cézanne set the tone of his own art. His paintings are not topical statements, records of the present, but a vision of timeless, enduring tradition. Within this tradition, faithful to its values, Gorky created a new and original art.

He loved art and willed painting in America in our time into existence as a statement of greatness.

Diane Waldman

FOOTNOTES

1. Karlen Mooradian, *Arshile Gorky Adoian*, Chicago, 1978, p. 112
2. Ethel K. Schwabacher, *Arshile Gorky*, New York, 1957, p. 26
3. Karlen Mooradian, "A Sister Recalls: An Interview with Vartoosh Mooradian," *Ararat: A Special Issue on Arshile Gorky*, vol. 12, Fall 1971, p. 10
4. Letter to Ethel Schwabacher, July 21, 1951
5. Mooradian, "A Sister Recalls," *Ararat*, 1971, p. 14
6. Karlen Mooradian, "Remembrances of Gorky," *Ararat: A Special Issue on Arshile Gorky*, vol. 12, Fall 1971, p. 54
7. *Ibid.*
8. *Ibid.*, p. 55
9. *Ibid.*
10. Mooradian, *Arshile Gorky Adoian*, 1978, p. 13
11. Elaine de Kooning, "Gorky: painter of his own legend," *Art News*, vol. XLIX, January 1951, p. 41
12. Mooradian, "A Sister Recalls," *Ararat*, 1971, p. 15
13. *Ibid.*
14. Daniel Robbins, *Walter Murch: A Retrospective Exhibition*, exh. cat., Museum of Art, Rhode Island School of Design, Providence, 1966, pp. 21–23
15. Interview with Vaclav Vytlacil, June 1980
16. Stuart Davis, "Handmaiden of Misery," *Saturday Review*, vol. 40, December 28, 1957, p. 17
17. *Ibid.*
18. Stuart Davis, "Arshile Gorky in the 1930s: A Personal Recollection," *Magazine of Art*, vol. 44, February 1951, p. 58
19. Arshile Gorky, "Stuart Davis," *Creative Art*, vol. 9, September 1931, p. 213
20. Julien Levy, *Arshile Gorky*, New York, 1966, p. 56
21. Letter from Will Barnet, May 1, 1980
22. Letter from Peter Busa, May 2, 1980
23. Quoted in "Arshile Gorky Exhibits," *The Art Digest*, vol. 10, January 1, 1936, p. 21
24. Letter to Vartoosh, October 18, 1937. On deposit in Gorky file, Whitney Museum of American Art, New York
25. Mooradian, "A Sister Recalls," *Ararat*, 1971, p. 18
26. Schwabacher, *Arshile Gorky*, 1957, p. 48
27. Francis V. O'Connor, "Arshile Gorky's Newark Airport Murals: The History of Their Making," *Murals Without Walls*, exh. cat., The Newark Museum, 1978, p. 22
28. *Ibid.*, p. 13
29. Frederick T. Kiesler, "Murals Without Walls: Relating to Gorky's Newark Project," *Murals Without Walls*, exh. cat., The Newark Museum, 1978, p. 31
30. *Ibid.*
31. Stuart Davis, *Magazine of Art*, February 1951, p. 58
32. Balcomb Greene, "Memories of Arshile Gorky," *Arts Magazine*, vol. 50, March 1976, p. 110
33. Letter from Agnes Gorky Phillips to Patricia Passloff in *The 30's: Painting in New York*, exh. cat., Poindexter Gallery, New York, June 1957, n.p.
34. Stuart Davis, *Magazine of Art*, February 1951, p. 57
35. Greene, "Memories," *Arts Magazine*, March 1976, p. 110
36. Karlen Mooradian, "The Letters of Arshile Gorky to Vartoosh, Moorad and Karlen Mooradian," *Ararat: A Special Issue on Arshile Gorky*," vol. 9, Fall 1971, p. 28
37. *Ibid.*, p. 29
38. Schwabacher, *Arshile Gorky*, 1957, p. 66
39. Mooradian, "The Letters of Arshile Gorky," *Ararat*, 1978, p. 34
40. *Grand Central School of Art Catalogue*, New York, 1942. Reprinted in Schwabacher, *Arshile Gorky*, 1957, p. 82
41. Levy, *Arshile Gorky*, 1966, p. 24
42. *Ibid.*
43. James Johnson Sweeney, "Five American Painters," *Harper's Bazaar*, vol. 78, April 1944, p. 122
44. *Ibid.*
45. André Breton, "The Eye Spring: Arshile Gorky," *Arshile Gorky*, exh. cat., Julien Levy Gallery, New York, March 1945, n.p.
46. Max Ernst, "Inspiration to Order," *This Quarter*, vol. V, September 1932, p. 8
47. Mooradian, "The Letters of Arshile Gorky," *Ararat*, 1971, p. 27
48. *Ibid.*, p. 34
49. *Ibid.*
50. *Ibid.*, p. 32
51. *Ibid.*
52. *Ibid.*, p. 20
53. Jerry Tallmer, "Watch that paint," *New York Post*, June 7, 1980, p. 13
54. Letter to Ethel Schwabacher. On deposit in Gorky file, Whitney Museum of American Art, New York
55. Levy, *Arshile Gorky*, 1966, pp. 34–35
56. William Rubin, "The New York School—Then and Now, Part II," *Art International*, vol. 2, May-June 1958, p. 20
57. Levy, *Arshile Gorky*, 1966, p. 34
58. *Ibid.*
59. Mooradian, *Arshile Gorky Adoian*, 1978, p. 208
60. Mooradian, "The Letters of Arshile Gorky," *Ararat*, 1971, p. 39
61. Levy, *Arshile Gorky*, 1966, p. 30
62. Mooradian, "The Letters of Arshile Gorky," *Ararat*, 1971, p. 30

1. *Park Street Church, Boston.* 1924
Oil on canvasboard, 16 × 12″
Collection Lowell Art Association,
Massachusetts, Gift of
Katherine O'Donnell Murphy

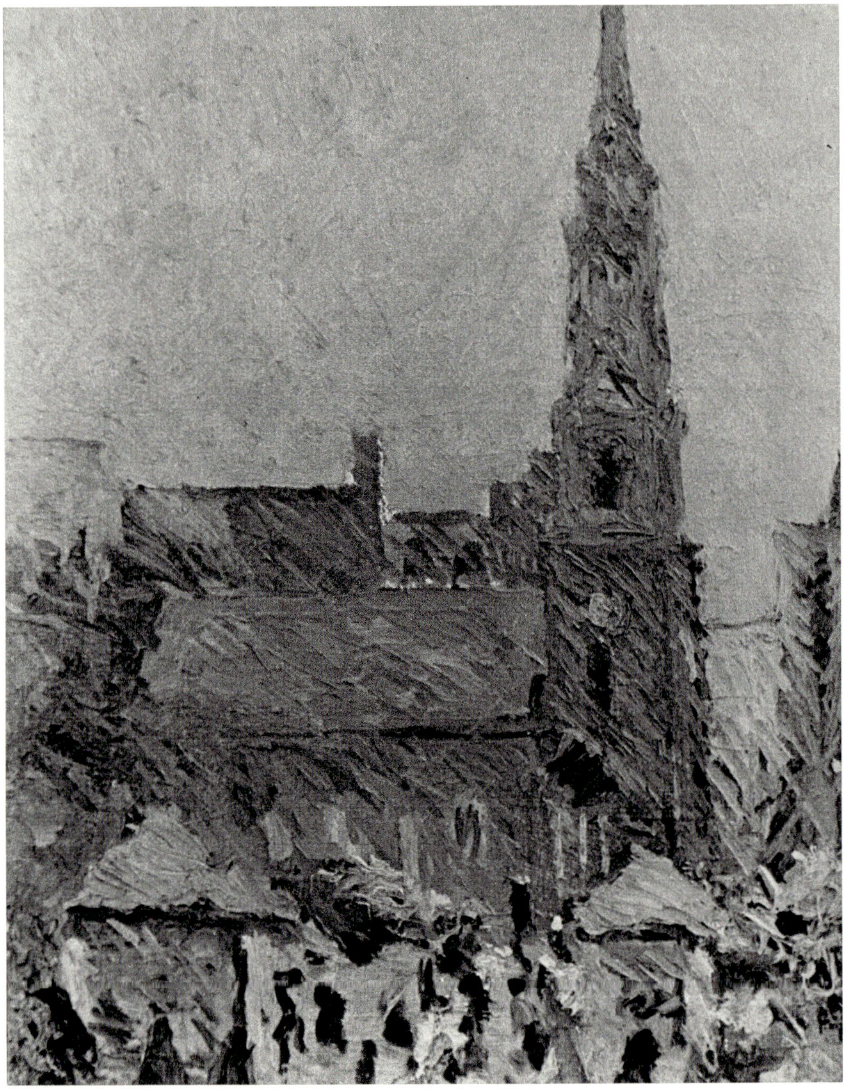

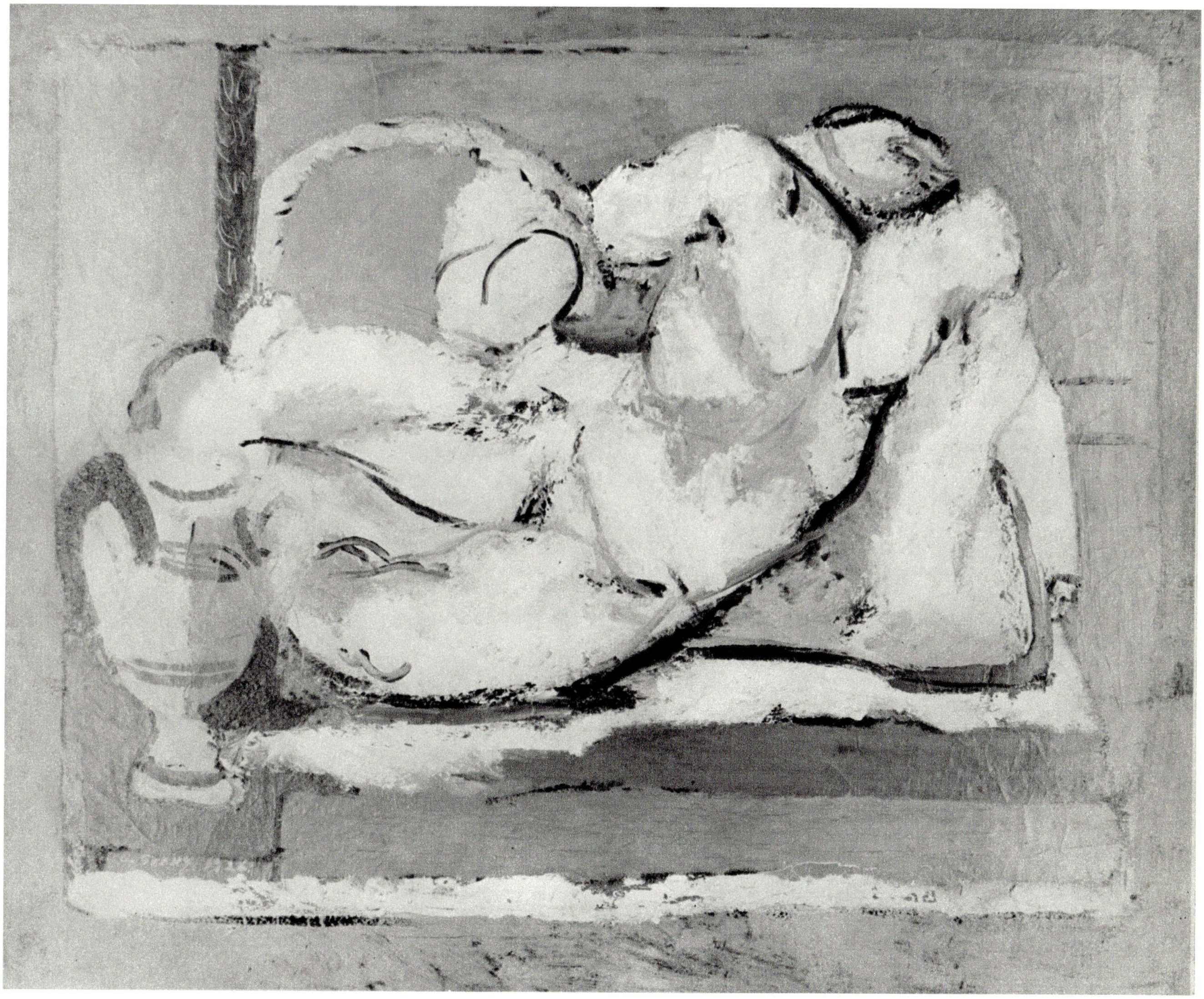

2. *The Antique Cast*. 1926
Oil on canvas, 36 1/8 × 46″
Private Collection

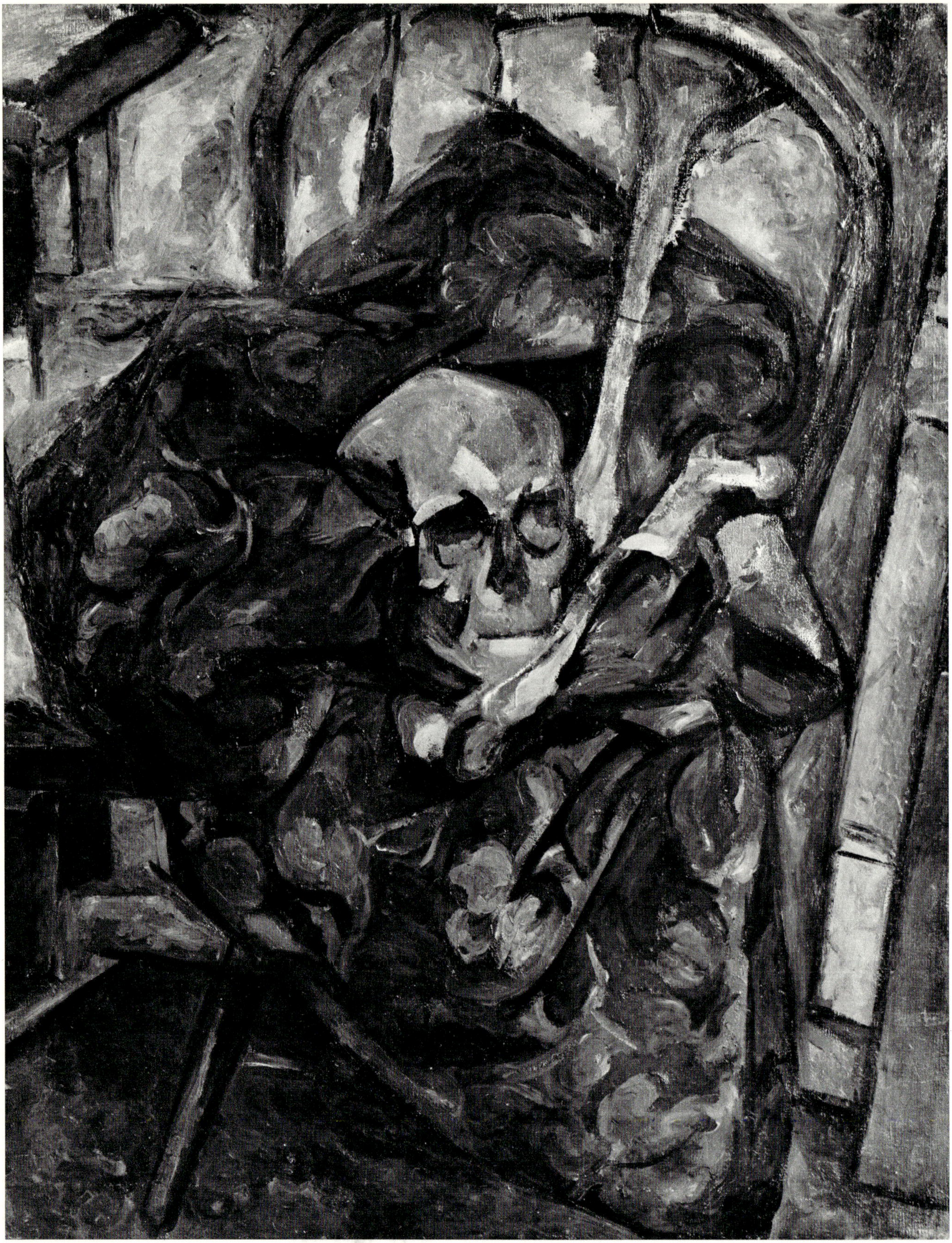

3. *Still Life with Skull.* late 1920s
Oil on canvas, 33 × 26″
Private Collection

4. *Untitled* (*Landscape*). late 1920s
Oil on canvas, 21 1/2 × 17 1/4″
Private Collection

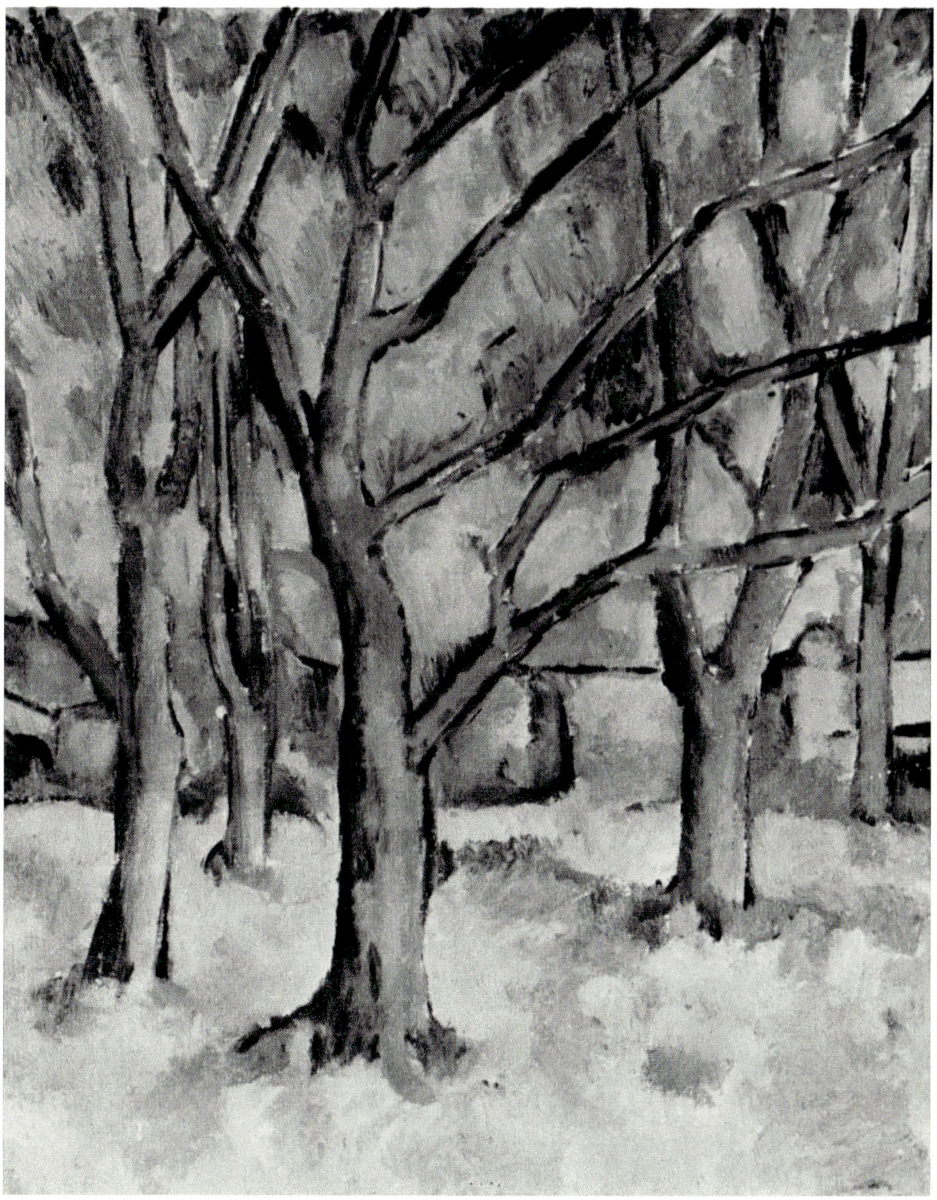

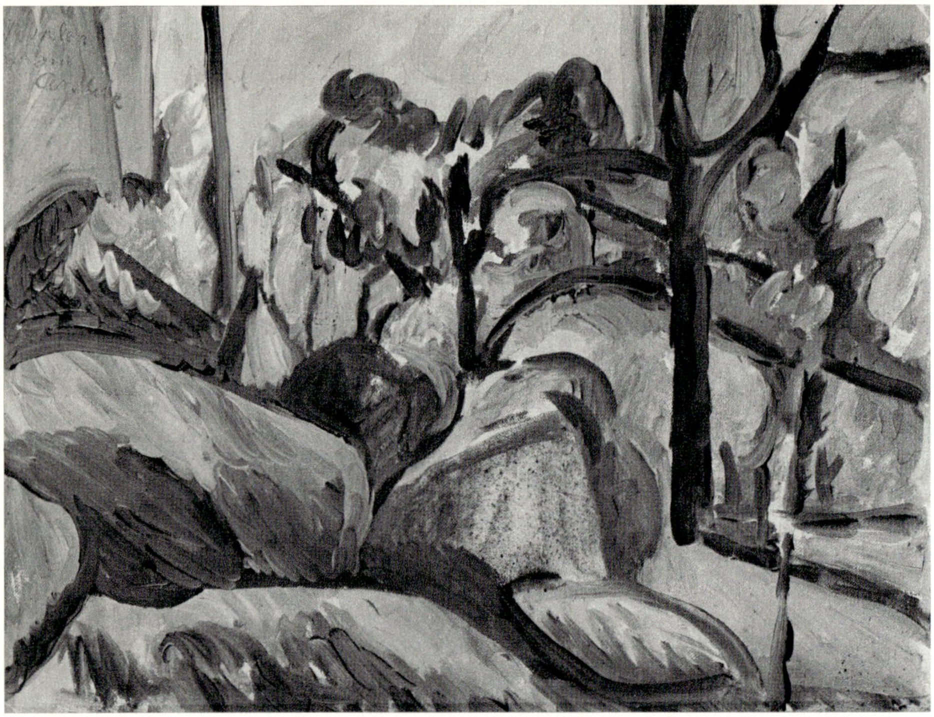

5. *Untitled* (*Central Park*). 1933–34
Oil on canvas, 11 1/2 × 16″
Private Collection, New York

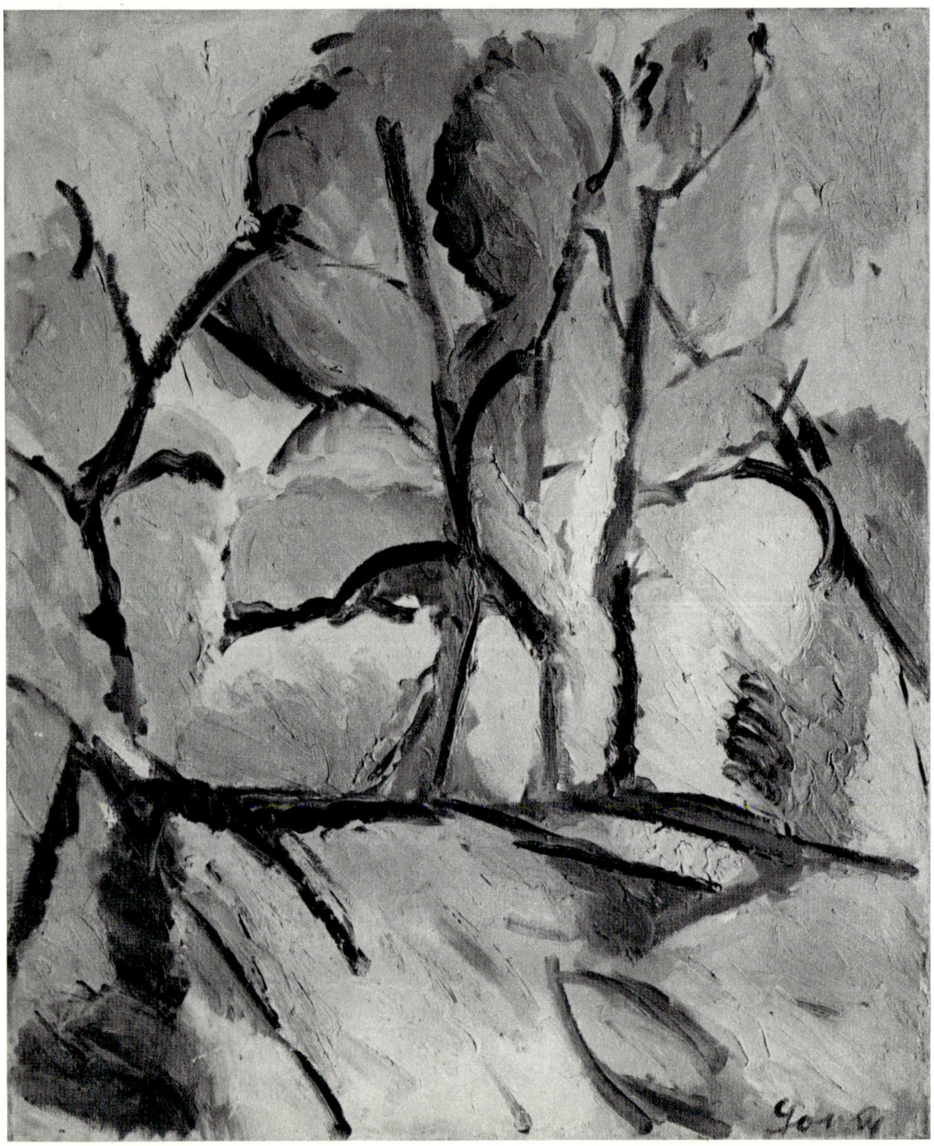

6. *Landscape*. 1933
Oil on canvas, 24 3/4 × 21″
Collection The Metropolitan Museum of Art, New York, Gift of Dr. Meyer A. Pearlman, 1964

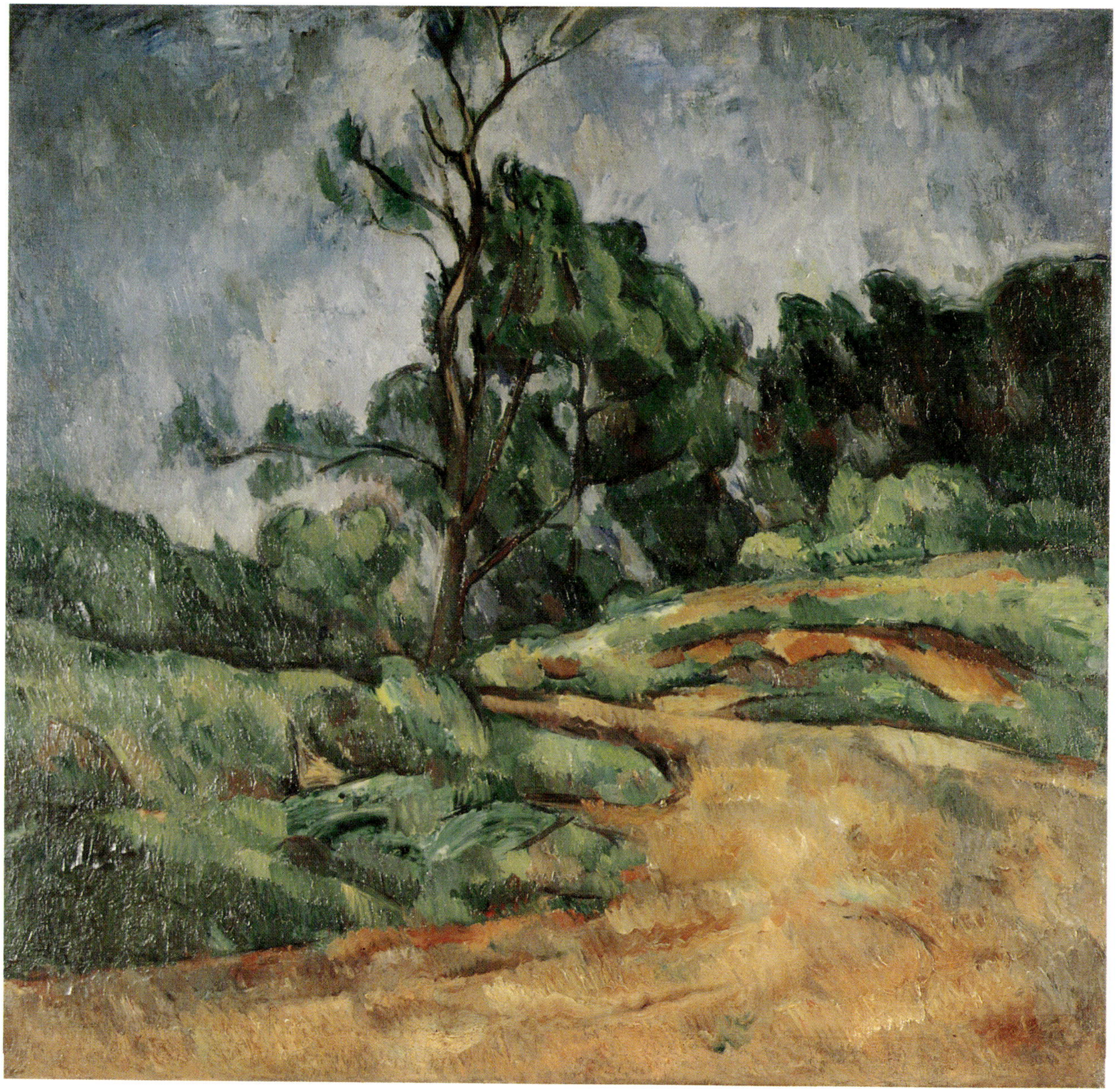

7. *Landscape, Staten Island.* 1927–28
Oil on canvas, 32 1/8 × 34″
Collection Richard Estes, New York

8. *Self-Portrait at the Age of Nine.* ca. 1927
Oil on canvas, 11 3/4 × 9 5/8″
Collection Nicholas Wilder, Los Angeles

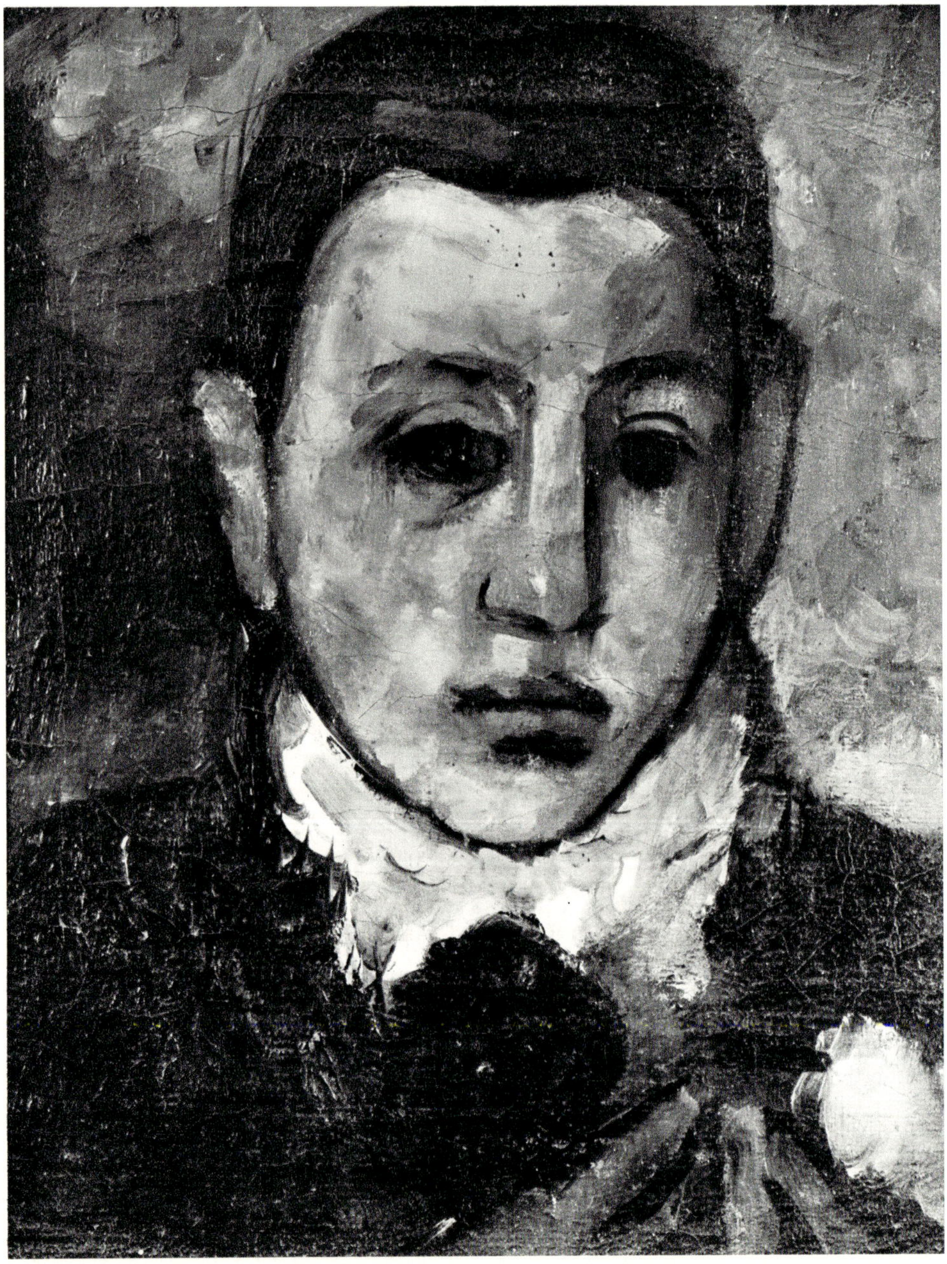

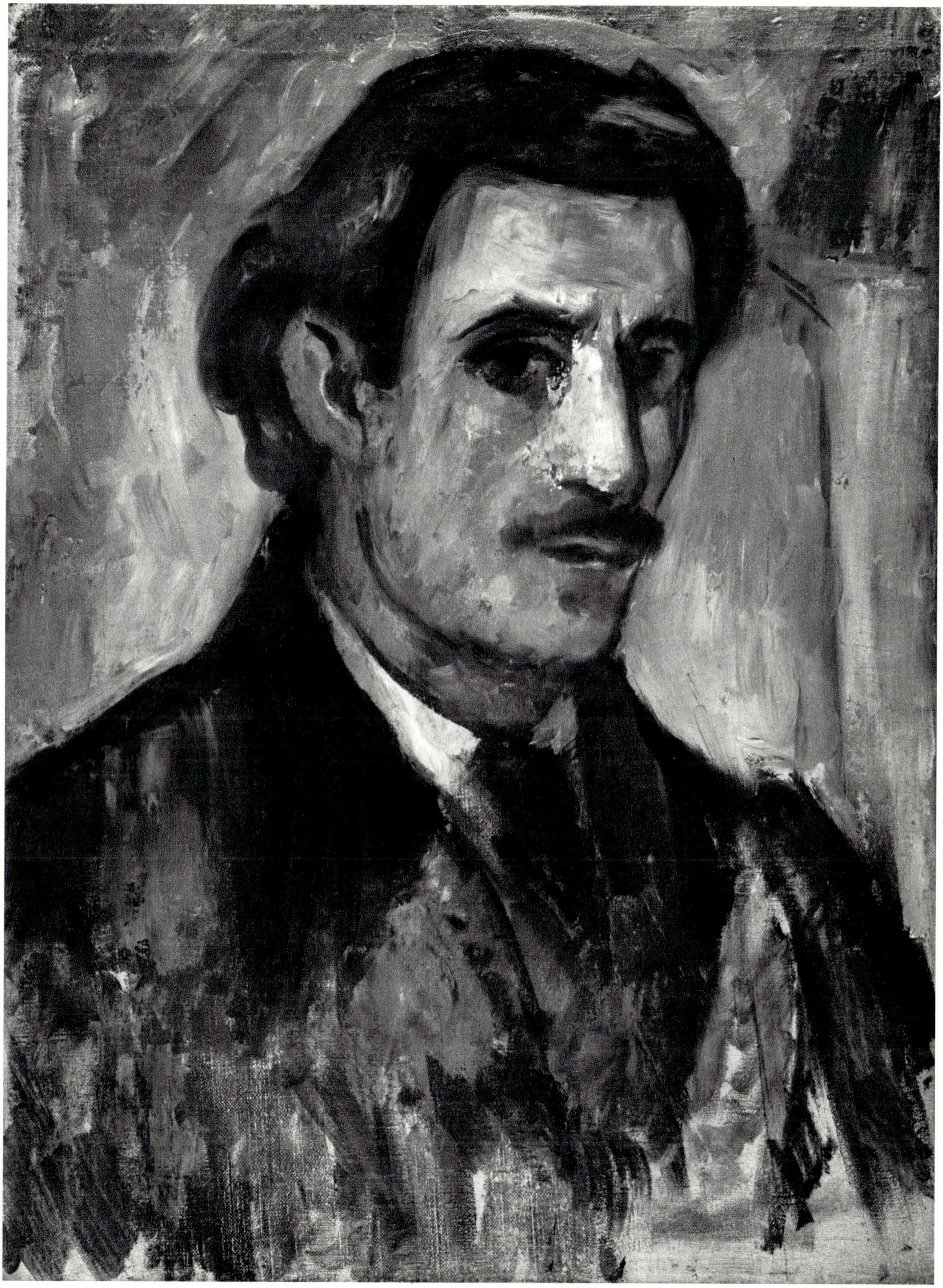

9. *Self-Portrait*. ca. 1928–31
Oil on canvas, 19 3/4 × 15 1/8″
Collection Mr. and Mrs. E. A. Bergman

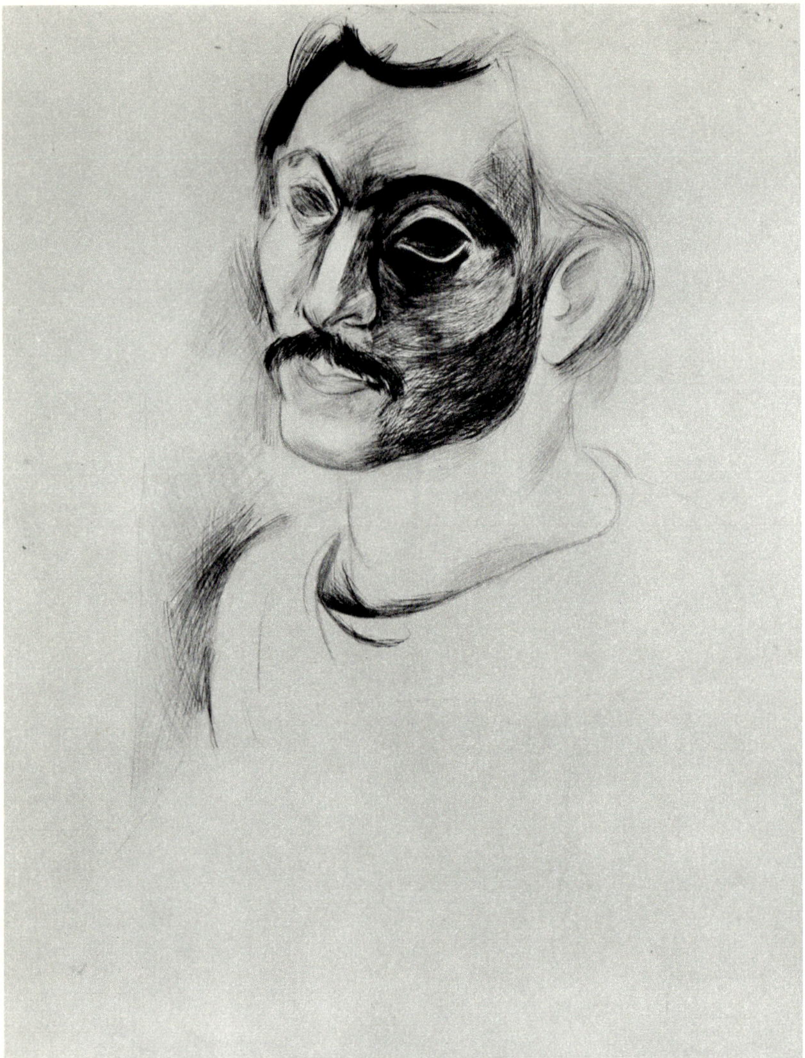

10. *Self-Portrait*. 1933
Pencil on paper, 29 1/2 × 22″
Private Collection

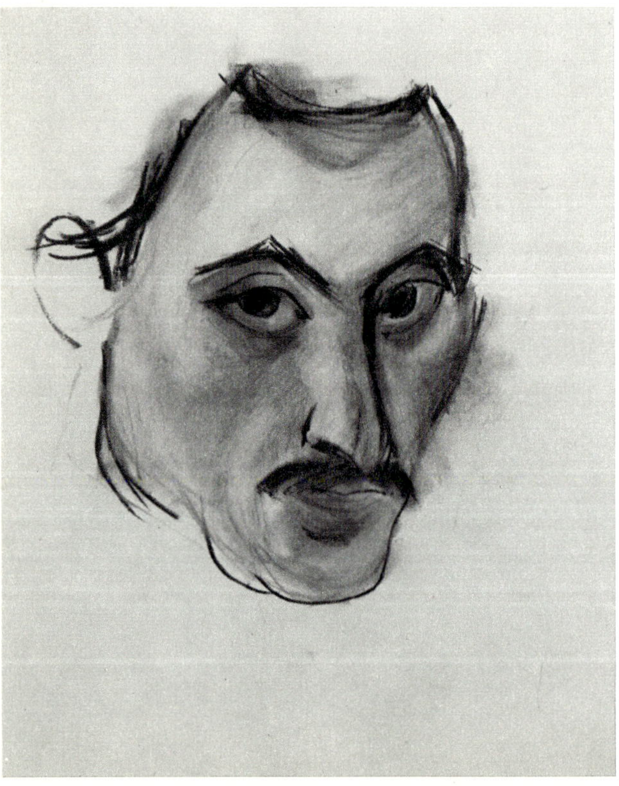

11. *Self-Portrait*. mid-1930s
Pastel on paper, 13 × 11″
Collection Mr. and Mrs. Harry W. Anderson

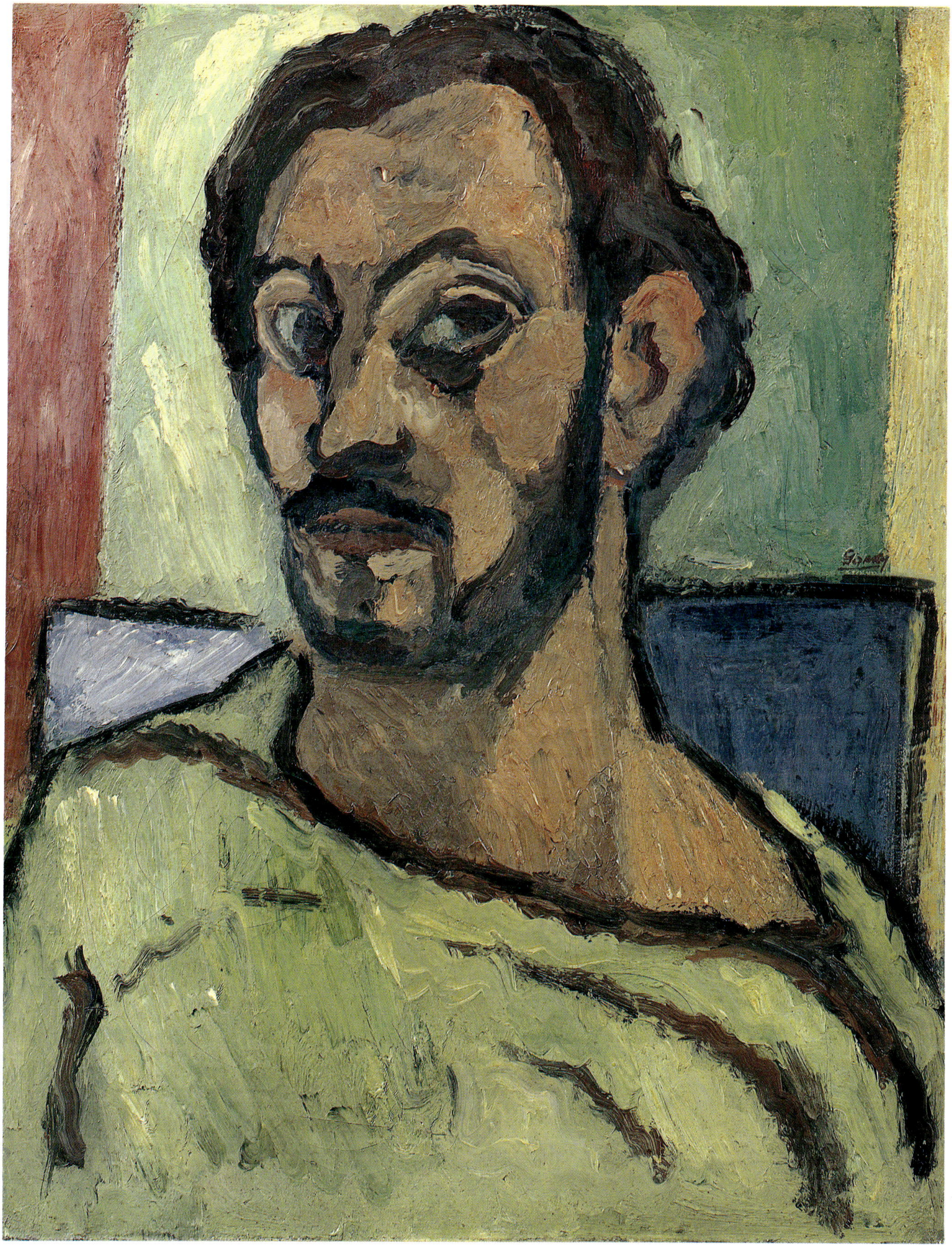

12. *Self-Portrait*. ca. 1928–31
Oil on canvas, 20 × 16″
Private Collection

13. *Self-Portrait.* ca. 1931
Oil on canvas, 24 × 16″
Los Angeles County Museum of Art:
Gift of Mr. and Mrs. Hans Burkhardt

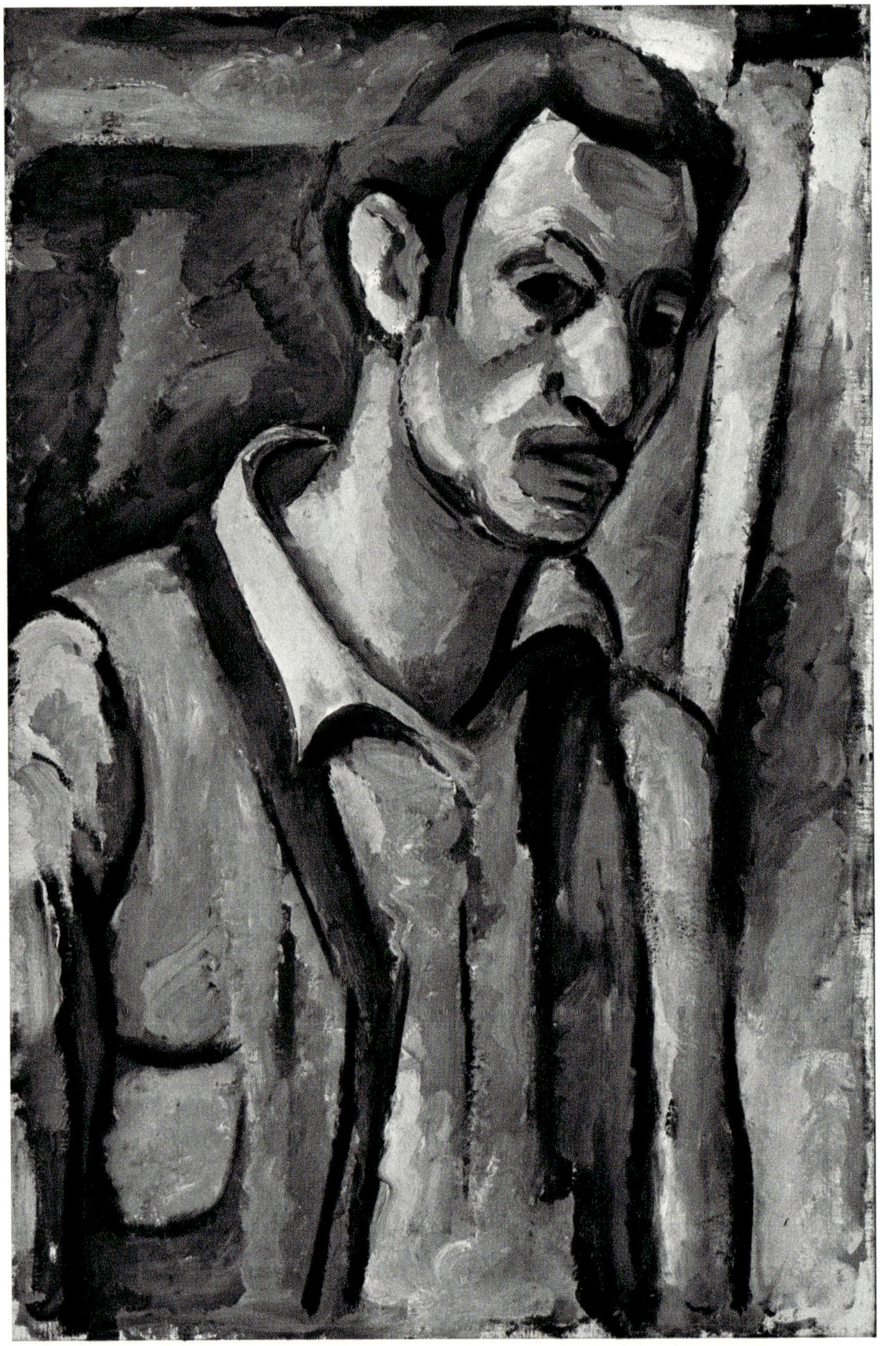

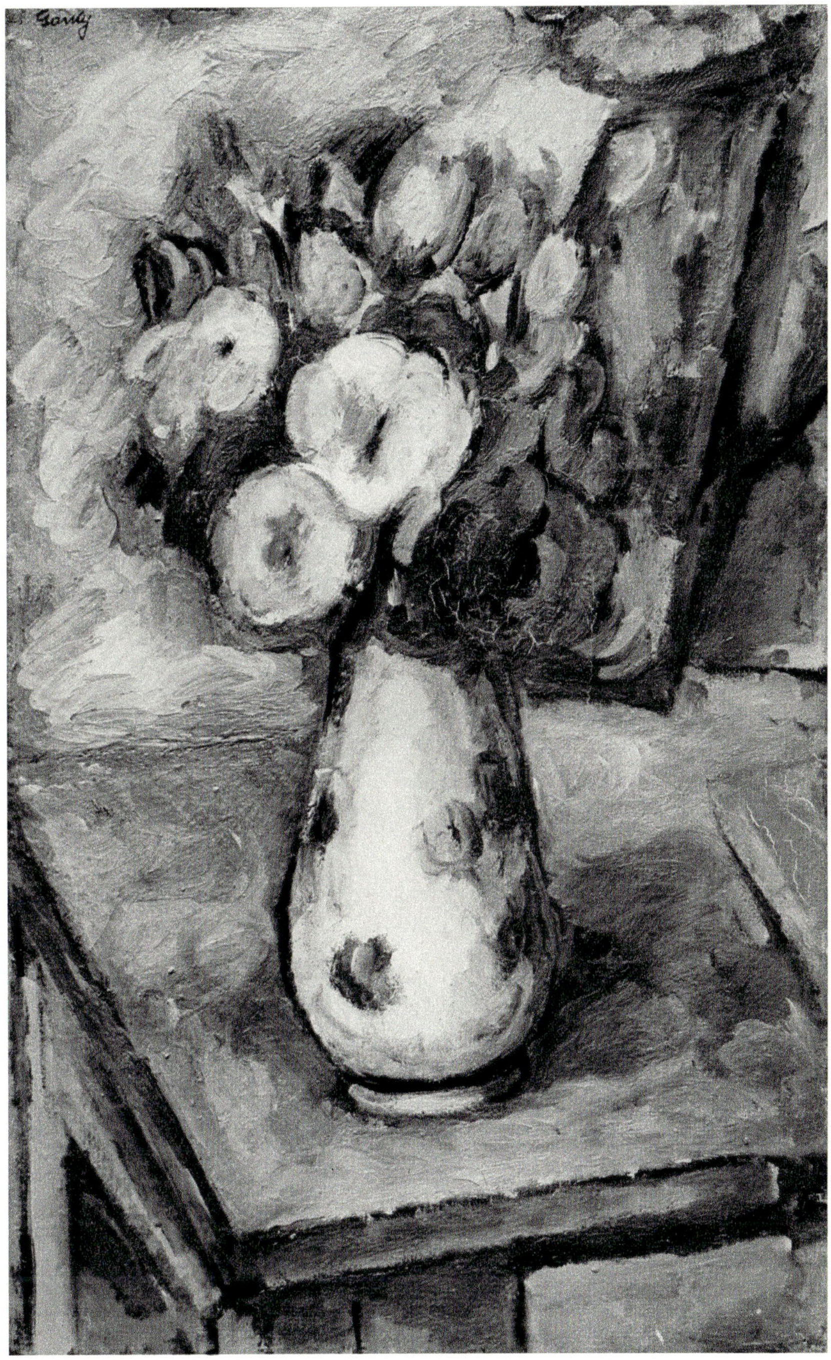

14. *Still Life of Flowers.* 1928
Oil on canvas, 20 × 13 1/8″
National Collection of Fine Arts, Smithsonian Institution, Washington, D.C., Gift of Mr. and Mrs. Nathan I. Bijur

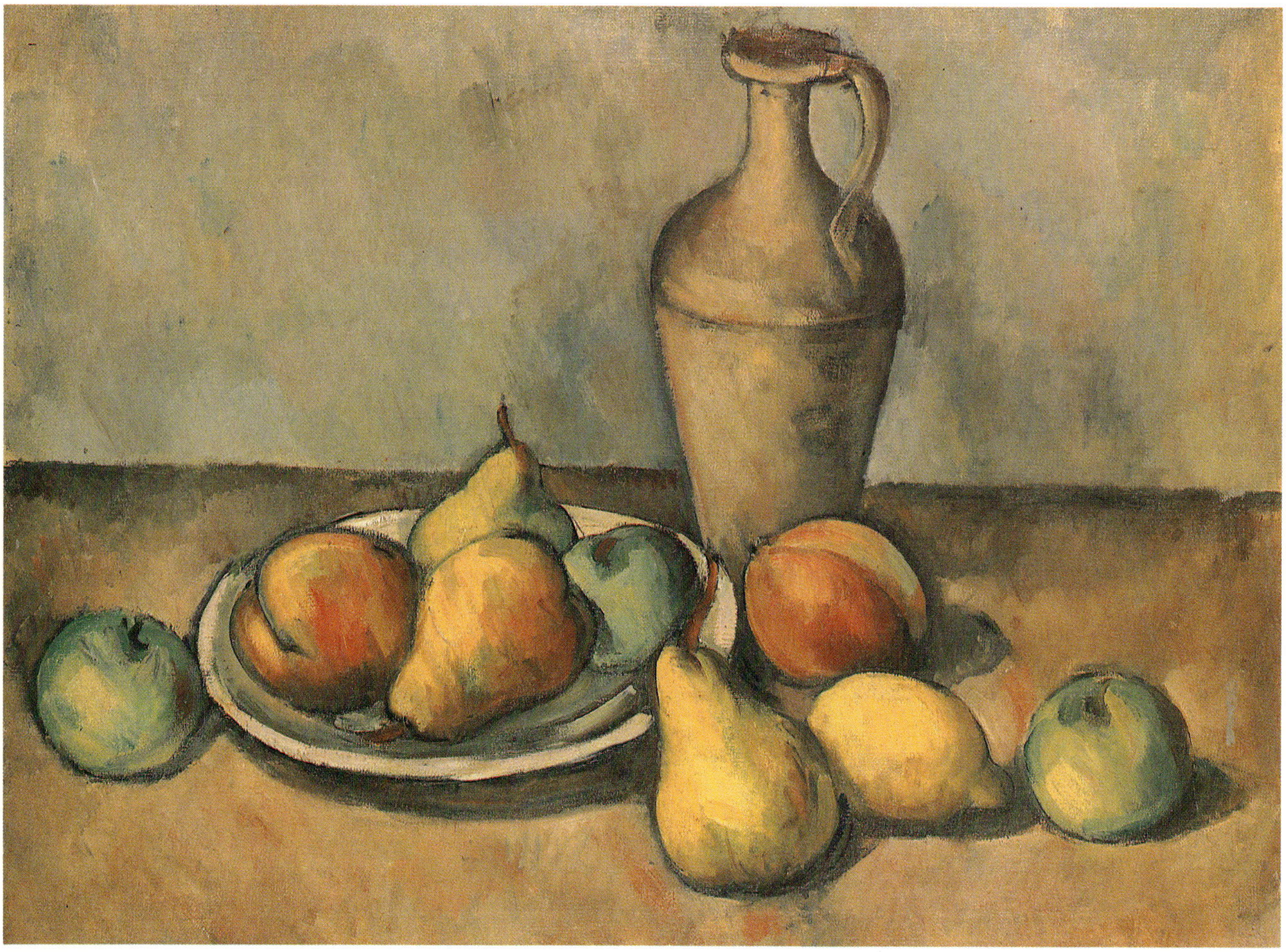

15. *Pears, Peaches and Pitcher*. late 1920s
Oil on canvas, 17 1/4 × 23 5/8″
Private Collection

16. *Still Life*. 1927
Oil on canvas, 20 1/8 × 24 1/4″
Private Collection

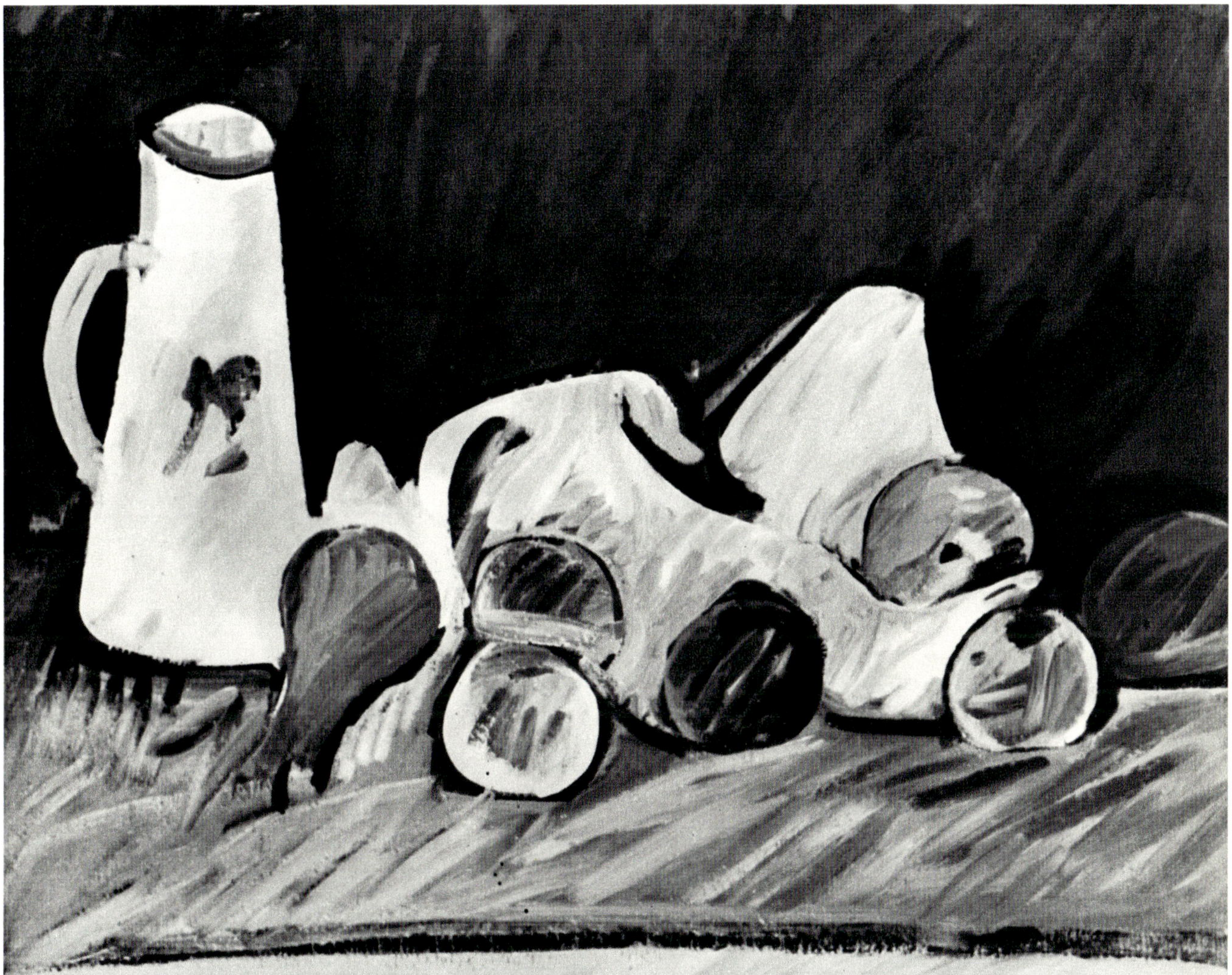

17. *Still Life*. 1928
Oil on canvas, 21 × 16″
Collection Dr. and Mrs. Donald R. Nielsen

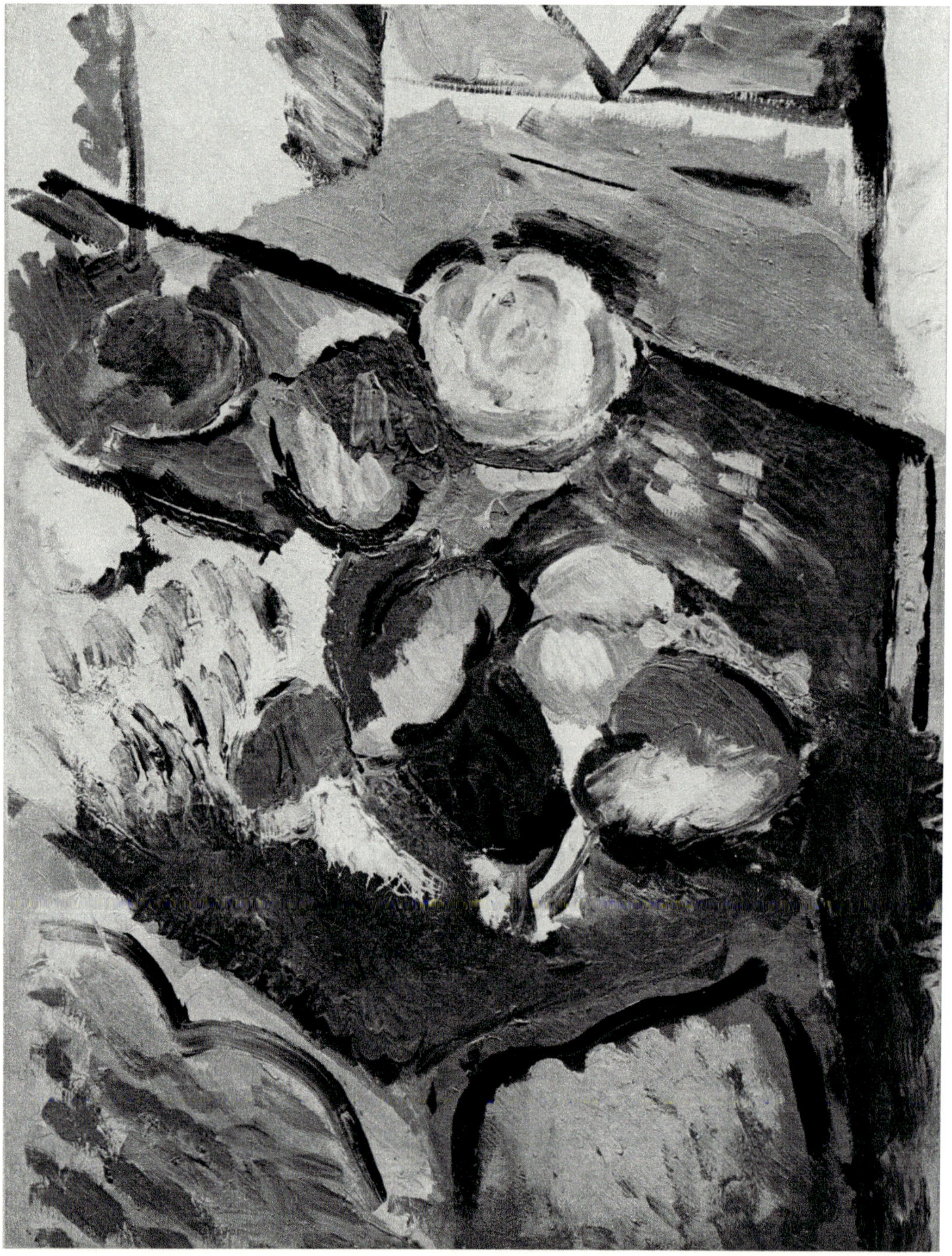

18. *Still Life*. 1934–35
Oil and collage on canvas, 11 × 10″
Private Collection

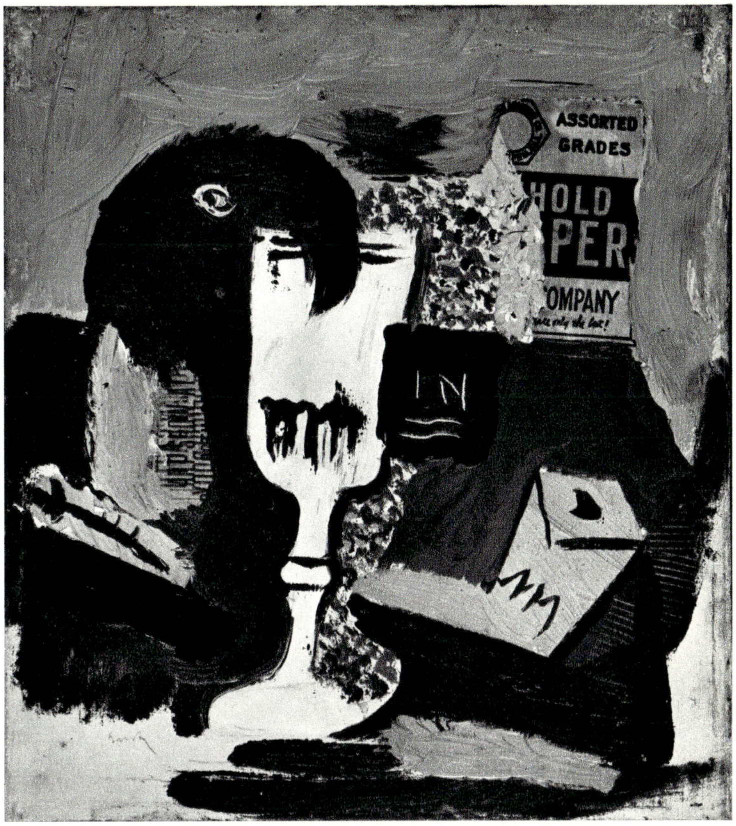

19. *Still Life with Pears*. 1928
Oil on canvas, 16 × 24″
Courtesy Allan Stone Gallery, New York

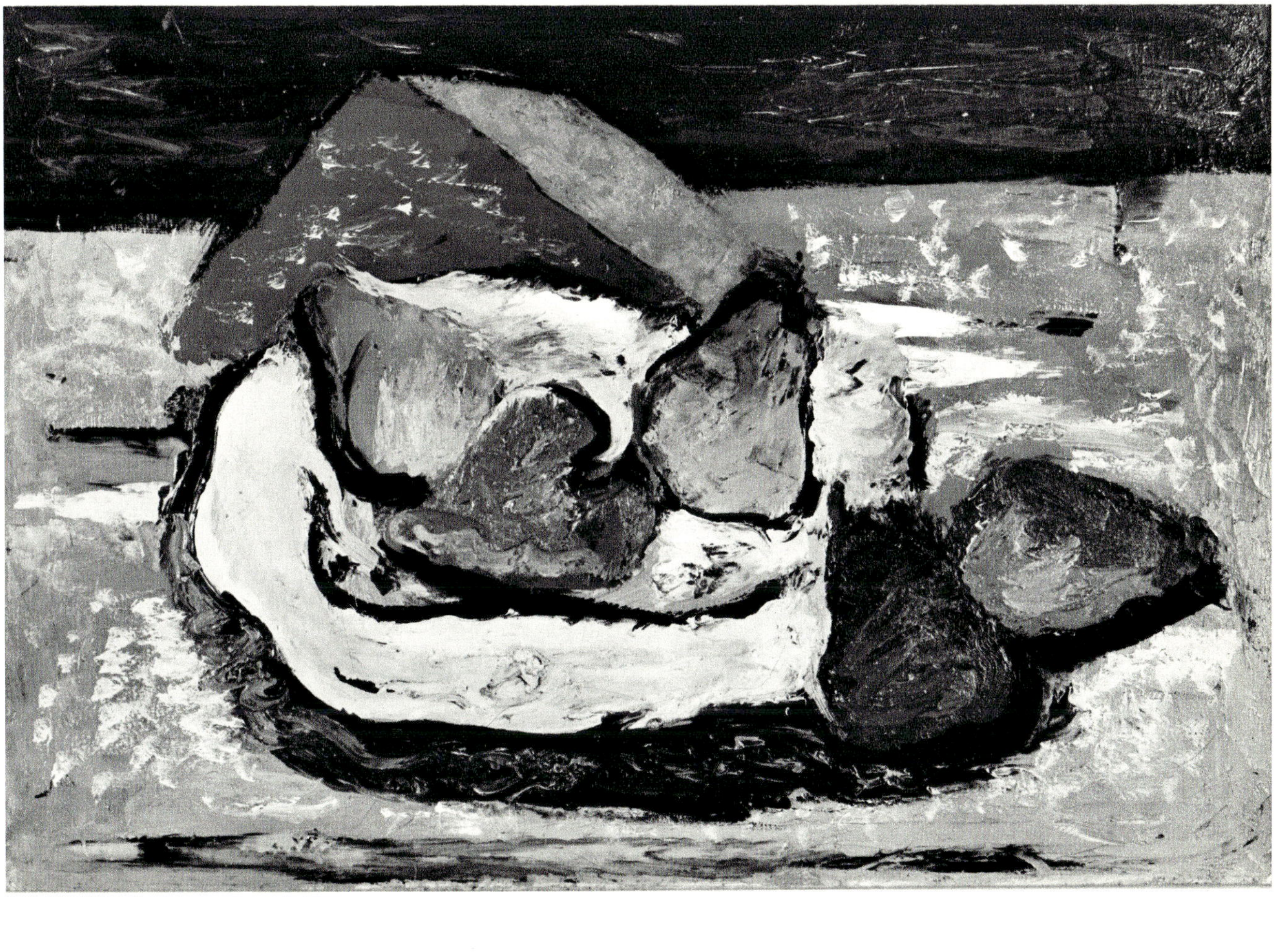

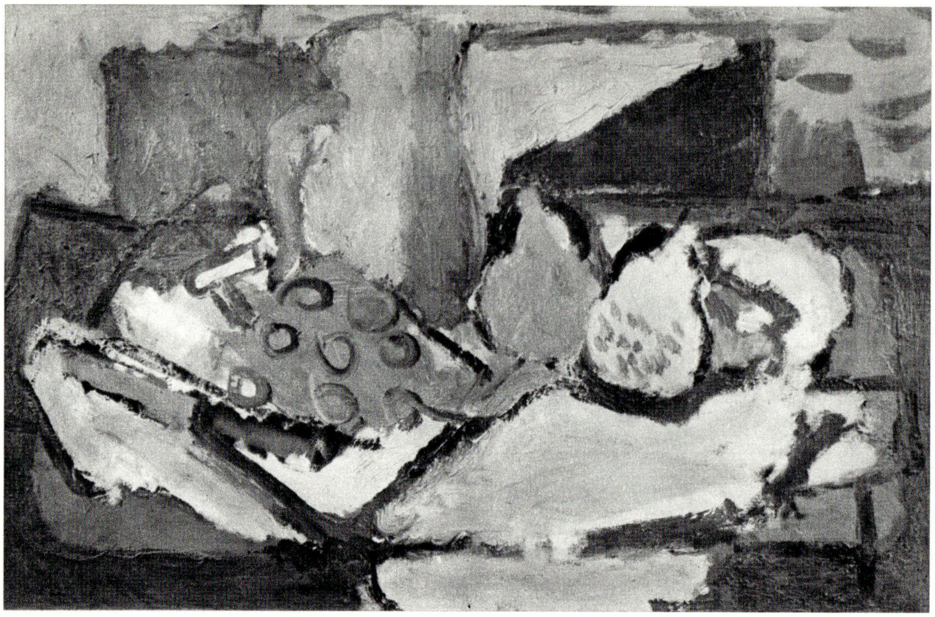

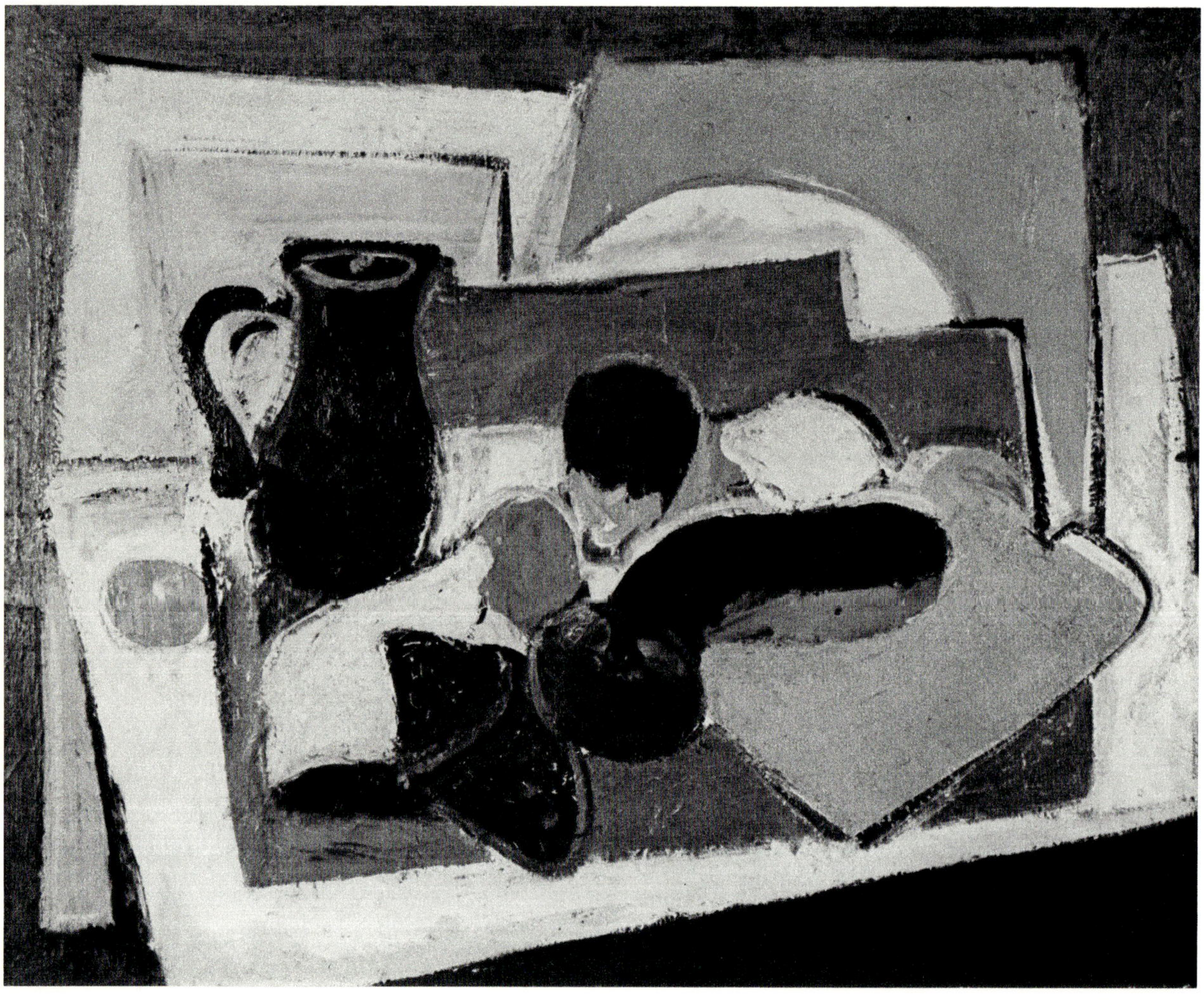

20. *Still Life.* ca. 1928
Oil on canvas, 18 × 28″
Collection Mrs. Joseph Douglas Weiss,
Chappaqua, New York

21. *Composition with Vegetables.* 1928
Oil on canvas, 28 × 36″
Gift of Mr. Erskine to The James
and Mari Michener Collection;
The University Art Museum,
The University of Texas at Austin

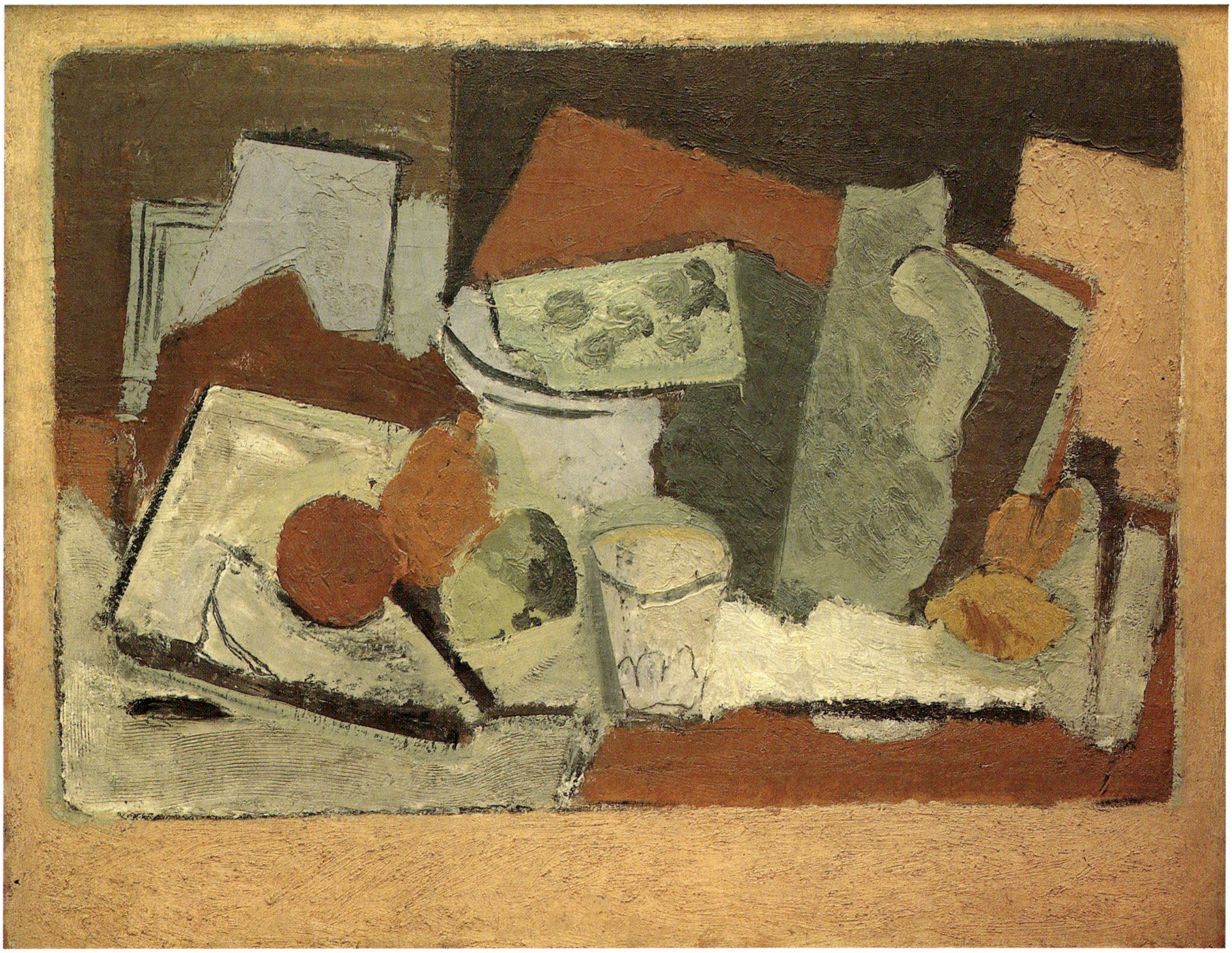

22. *Still Life.* ca. 1928
Oil on canvas, 25 1/2 × 33 1/2″
Collection Mrs. M. Victor Leventritt,
New York

23. *Still Life*. 1929–32
Oil on canvas, 42 7/8 × 60 1/2″
Private Collection

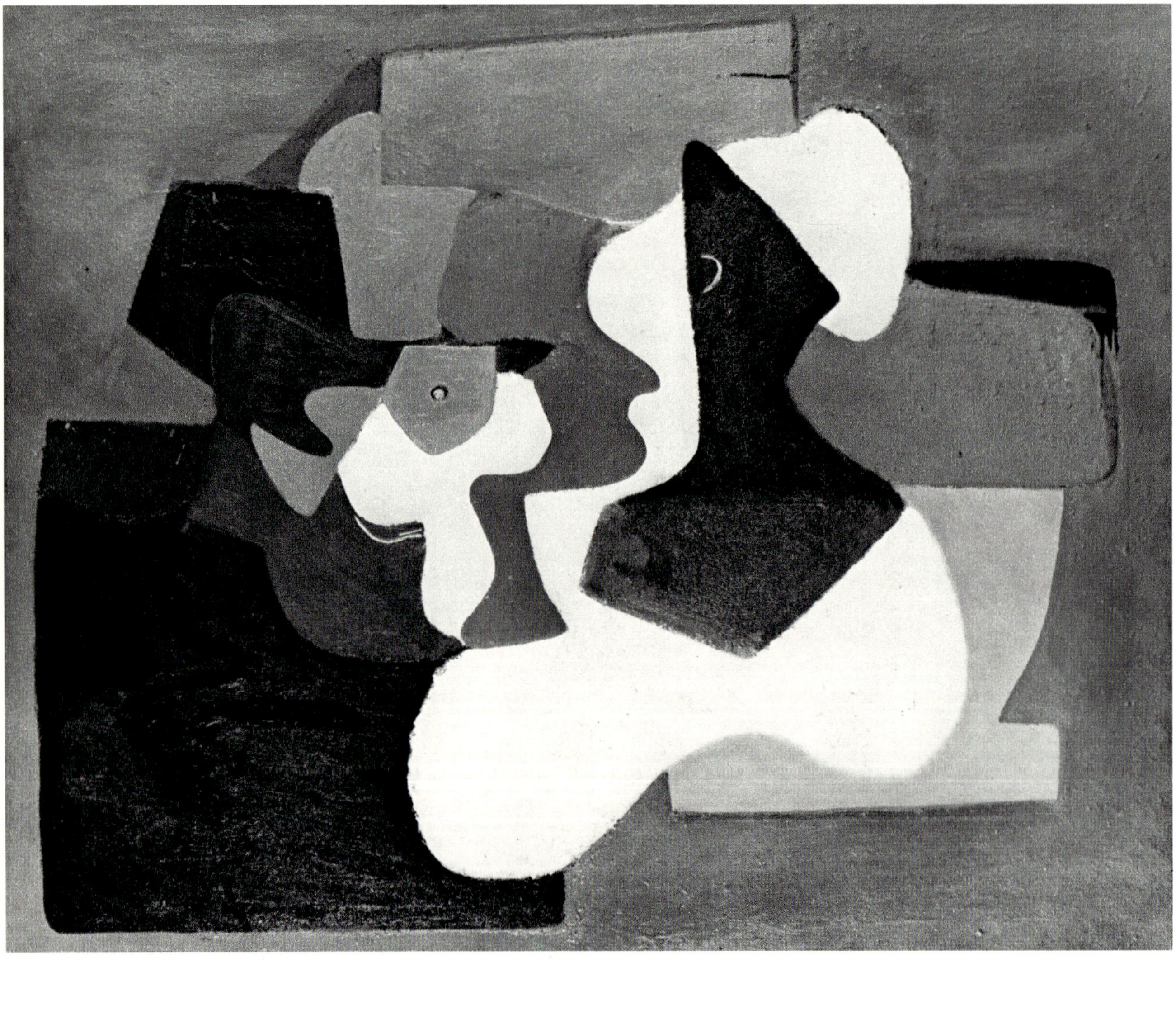

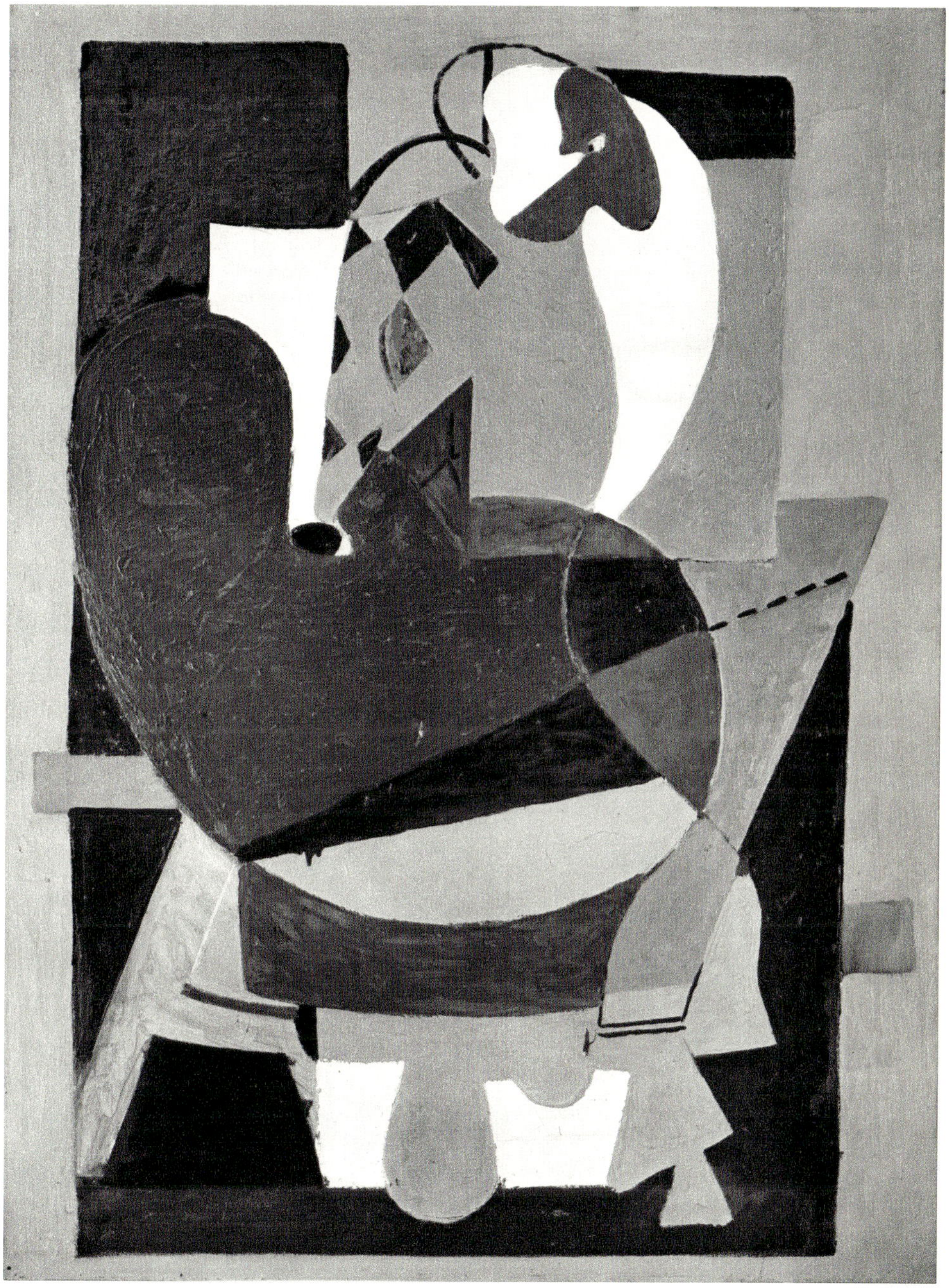

24. *Abstraction with Palette.* 1930
Oil on canvas, 47 1/2 × 35 1/2″
Philadelphia Museum of Art: Given by Bernard Davis

25. *Untitled.* 1931
Lithograph, 13 × 11″, edition 17/25
Private Collection, New York

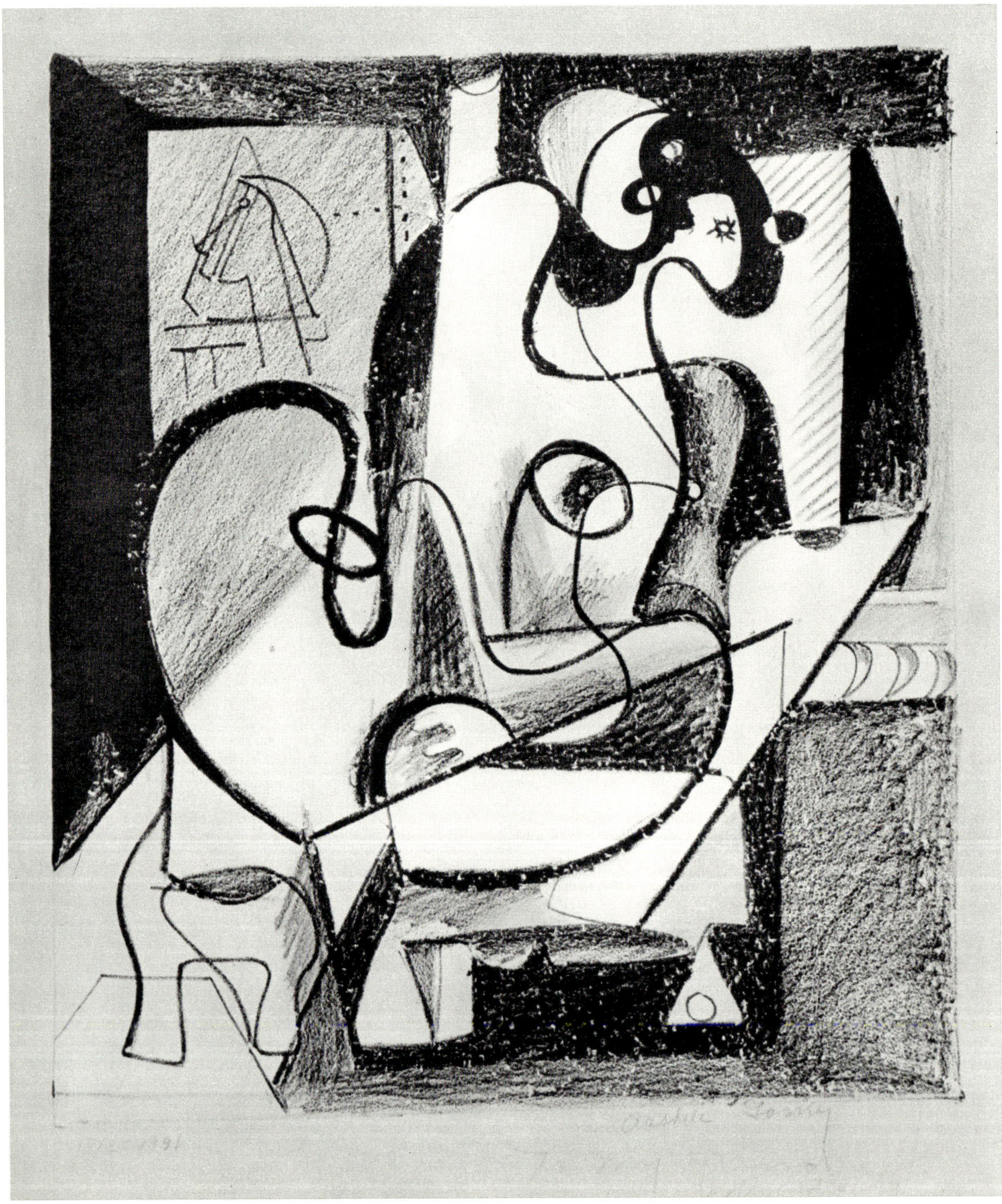

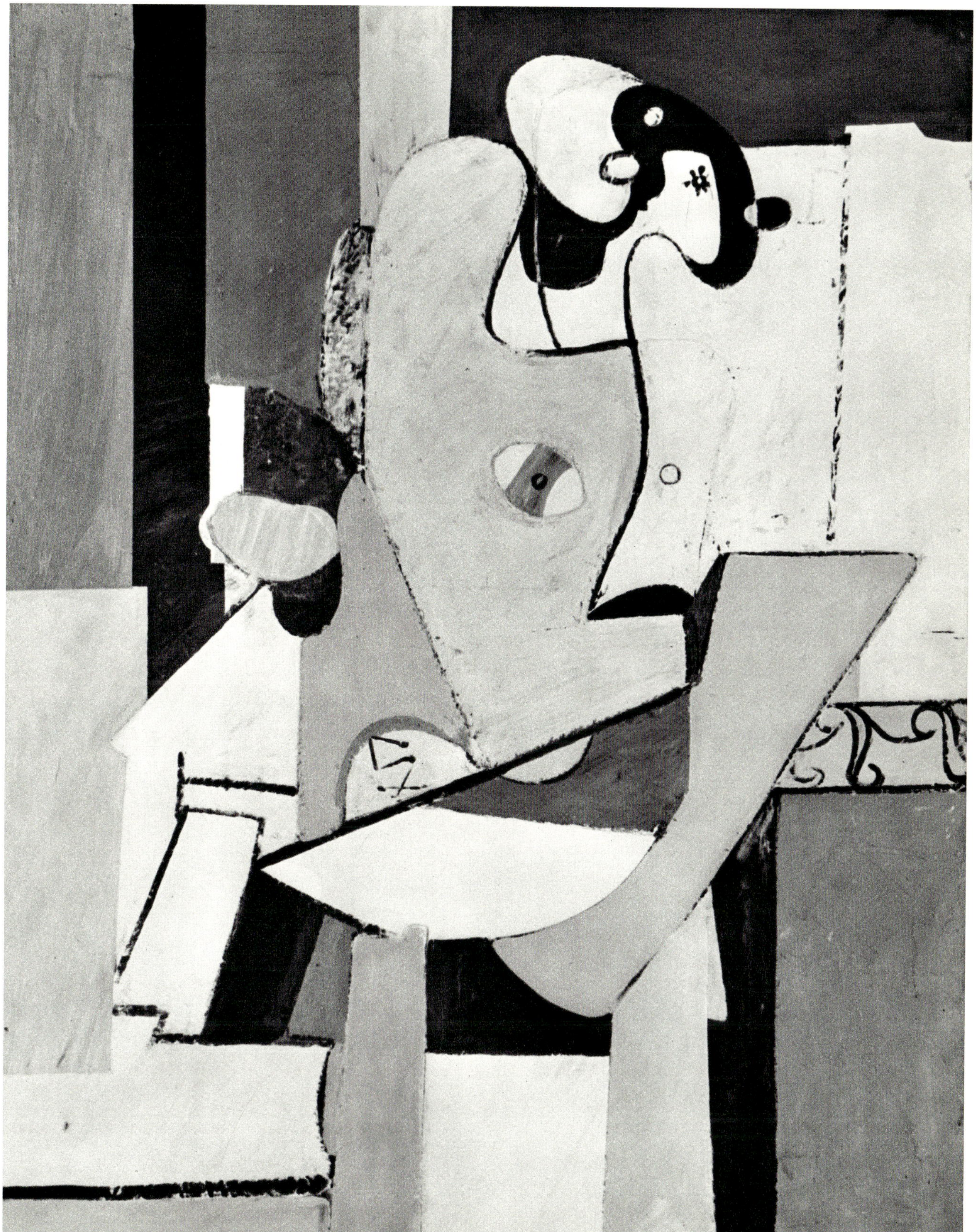

26. *Blue Figure in Chair*. ca. 1931
Oil on canvas, 48 × 38″
Private Collection

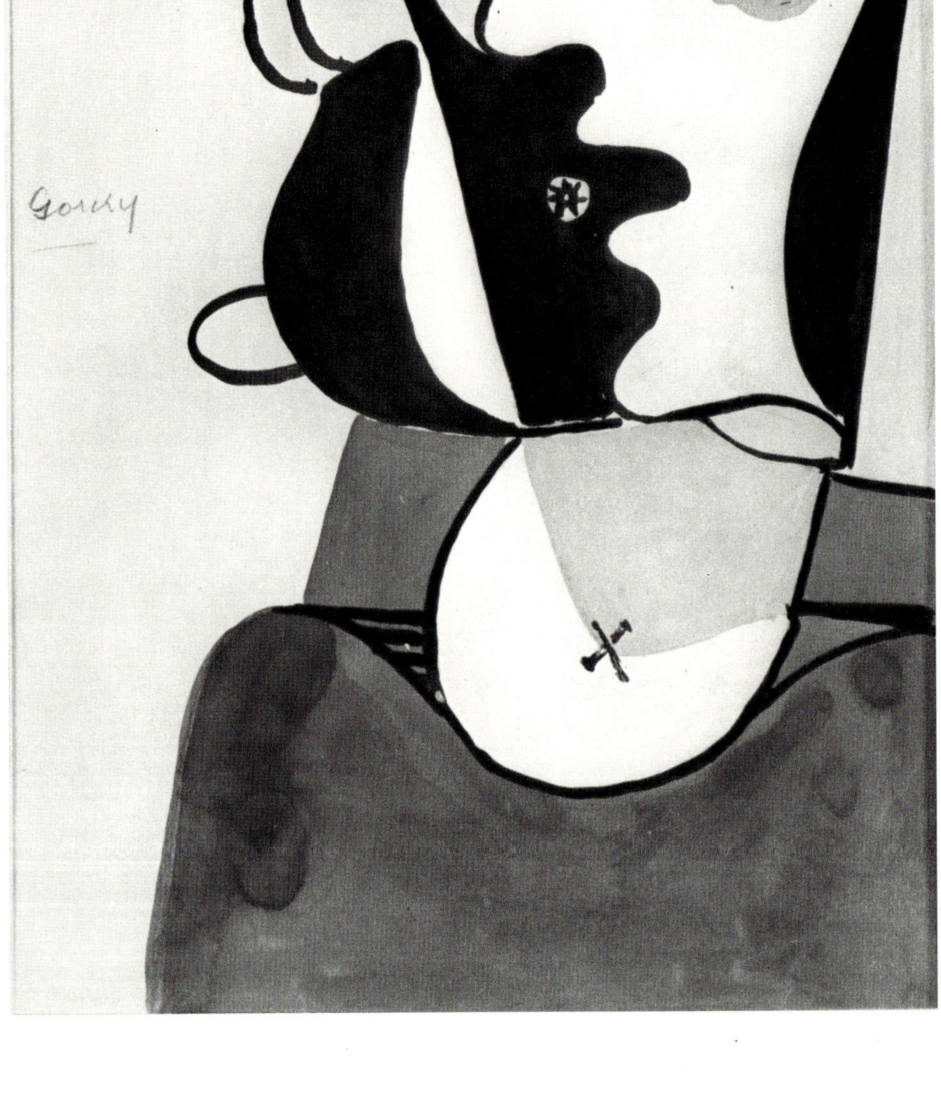

27. *Head.* early 1930s
Gouache on cardboard, 12 1/2 × 8 3/4″
Private Collection

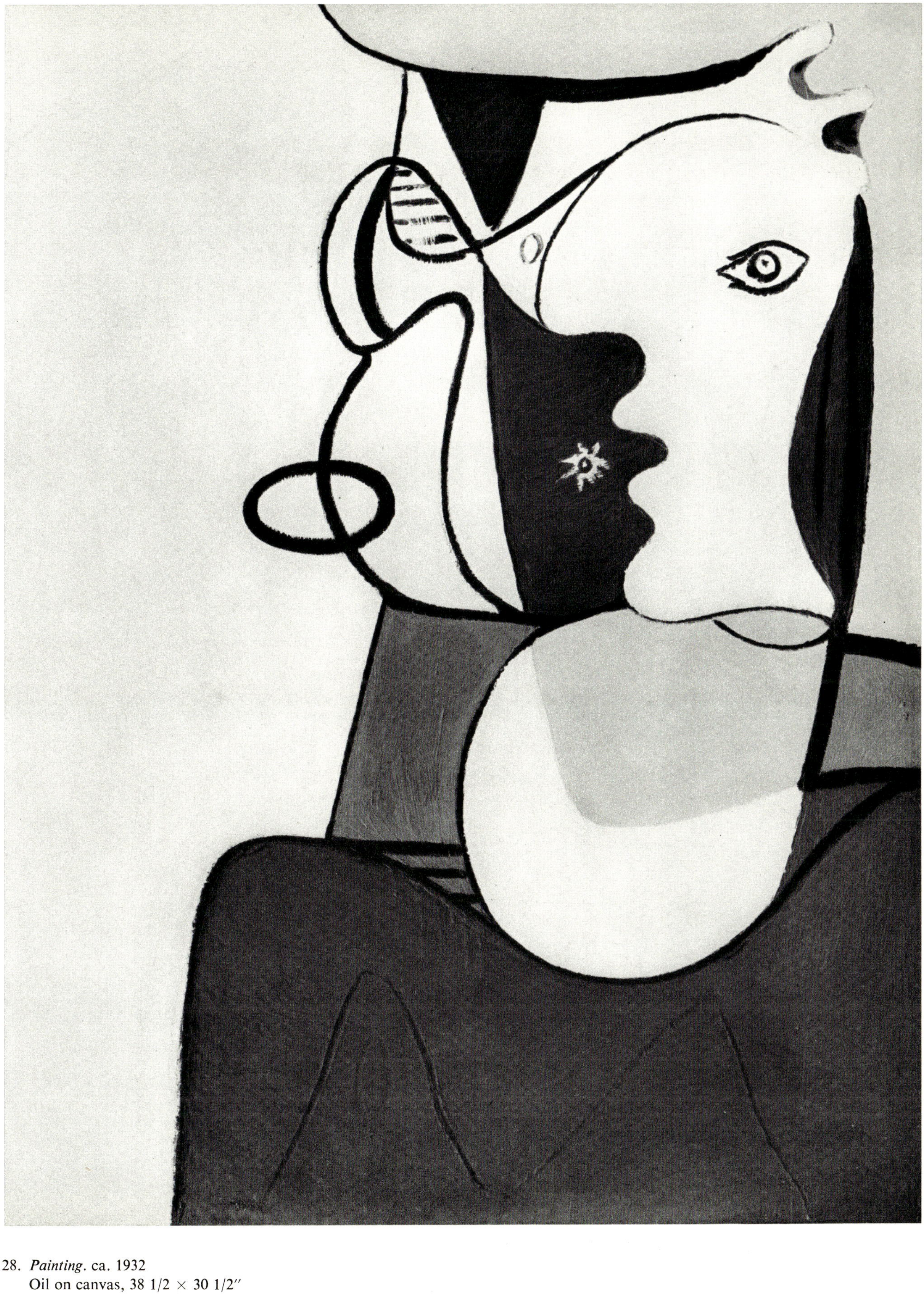

28. *Painting*. ca. 1932
Oil on canvas, 38 1/2 × 30 1/2″
Courtesy Sidney Janis Gallery, New York

29. *Untitled* (*Drawing from a 1931 Sketchbook*). ca. 1931
Pen and ink on paper, 12 3/4 × 9 1/2″
Collection Julien Levy; Courtesy Richard L. Feigen & Co.

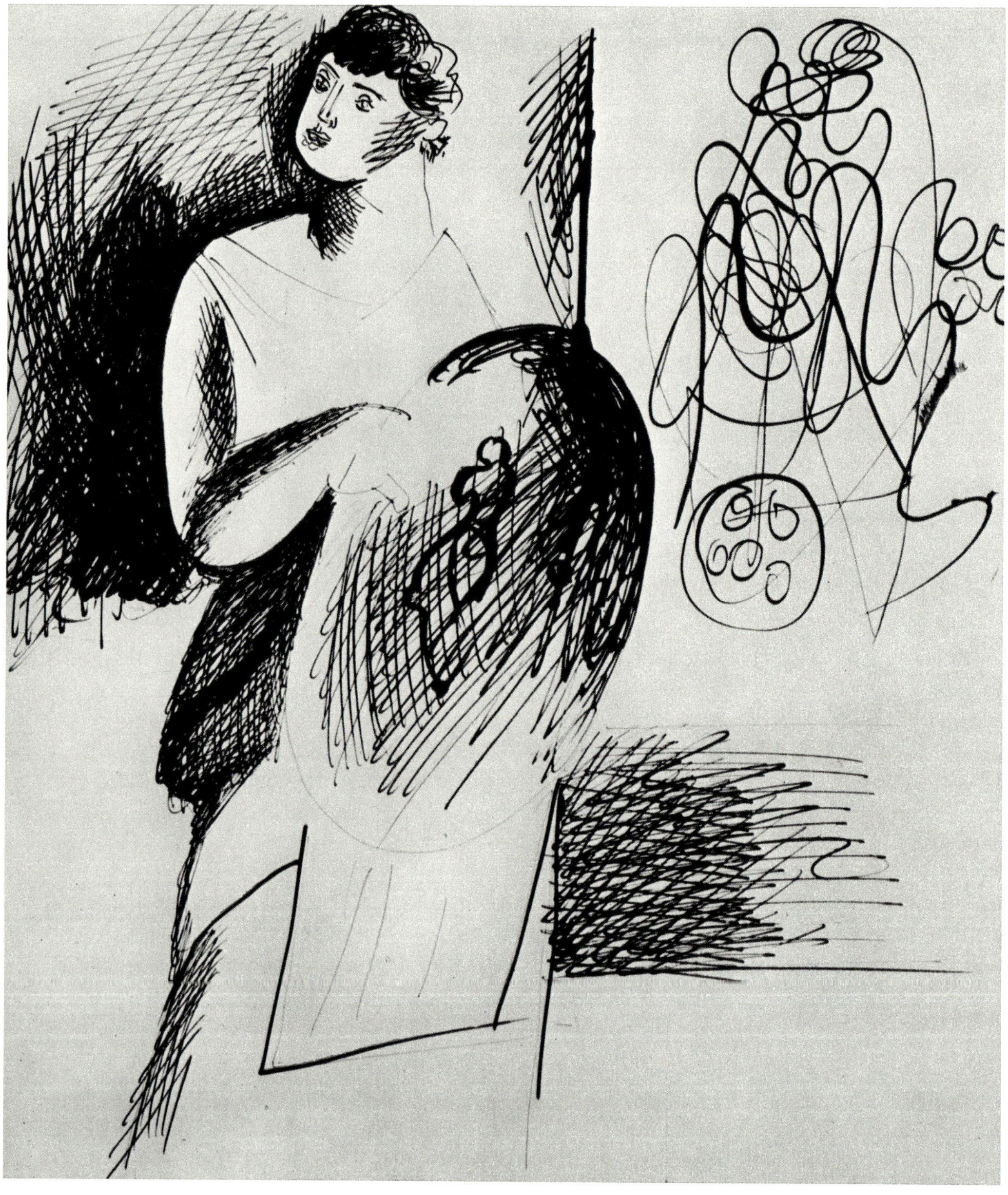

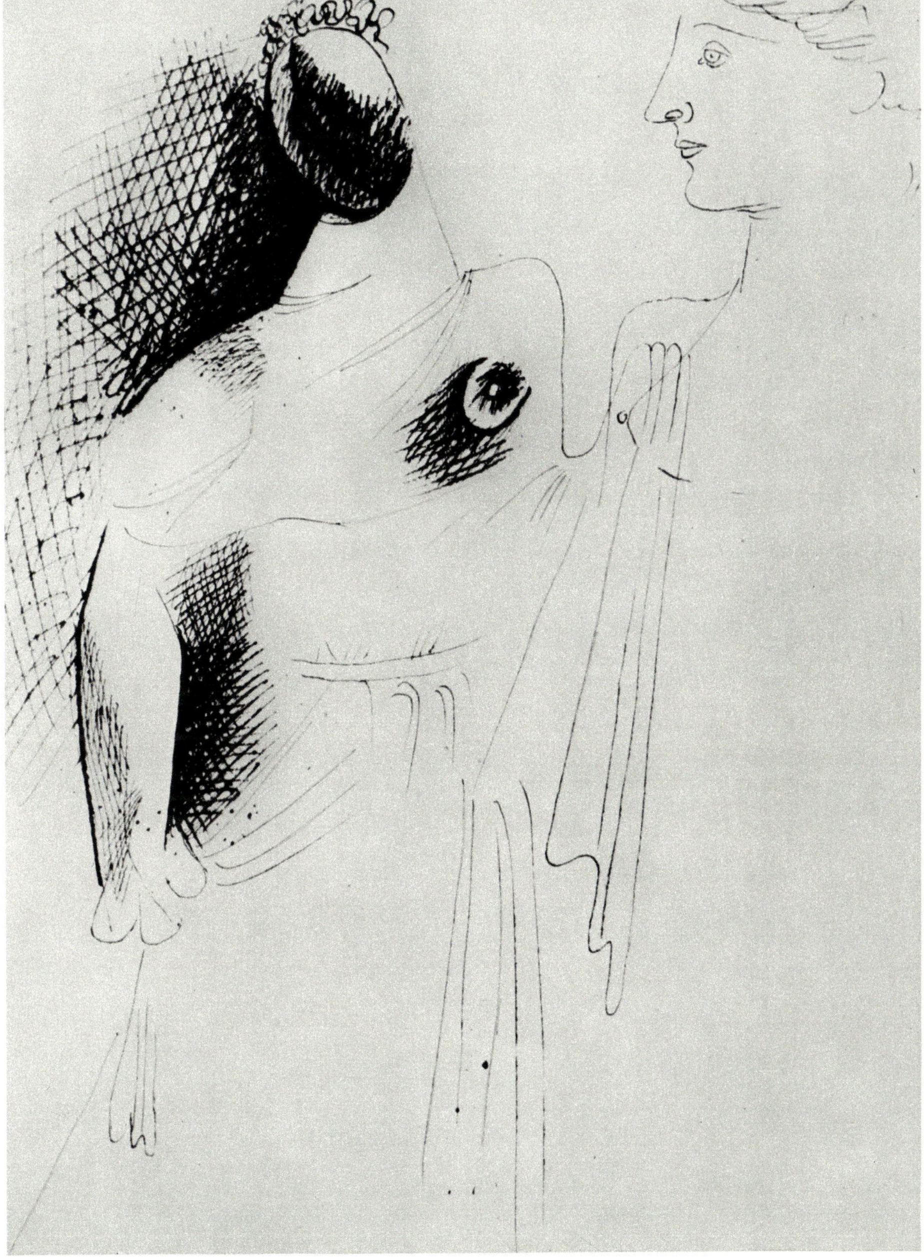

30. *Untitled* (*Drawing from a 1931 Sketchbook*). ca. 1931
Pen and ink on paper, 12 3/4 × 9 1/2″
Collection Julien Levy; Courtesy Richard L. Feigen & Co.

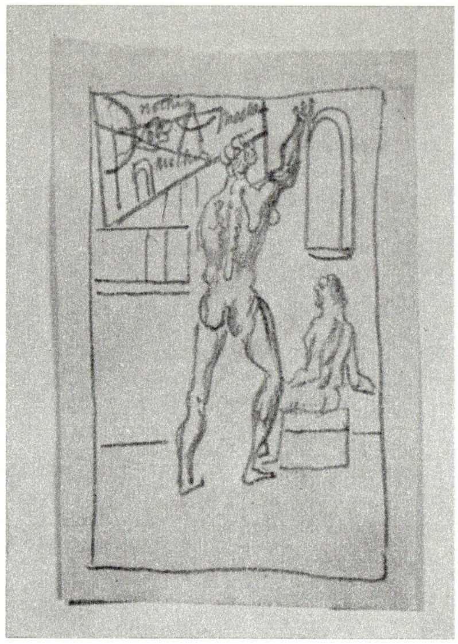

31. *Untitled.* ca. 1930–35
Pencil on paper, 2 5/8 × 1 5/8″
Collection The Museum of Modern Art, New York; Gift of Mr. and Mrs. Abraham L. Chanin

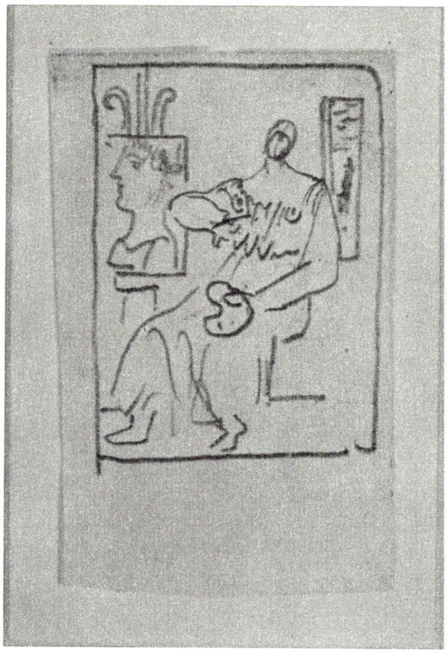

32. *Untitled.* ca. 1930–35
Pencil on paper, 2 3/8 × 1 3/8″
Collection The Museum of Modern Art, New York; Gift of Mr. and Mrs. Abraham L. Chanin

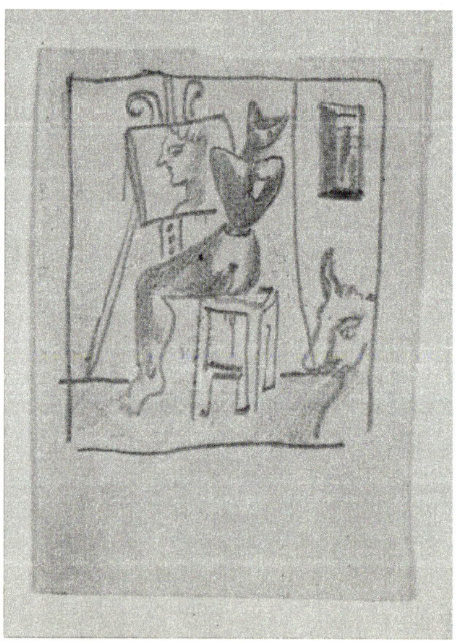

33. *Untitled.* ca. 1930–35
Pencil on paper, 2 1/2 × 1 3/4″
Collection The Museum of Modern Art, New York; Gift of Mr. and Mrs. Abraham L. Chanin

34. *Untitled.* ca. 1930–35
Pencil on paper (menu), 6 × 4″
Collection Mr. and Mrs. Chaim Gross

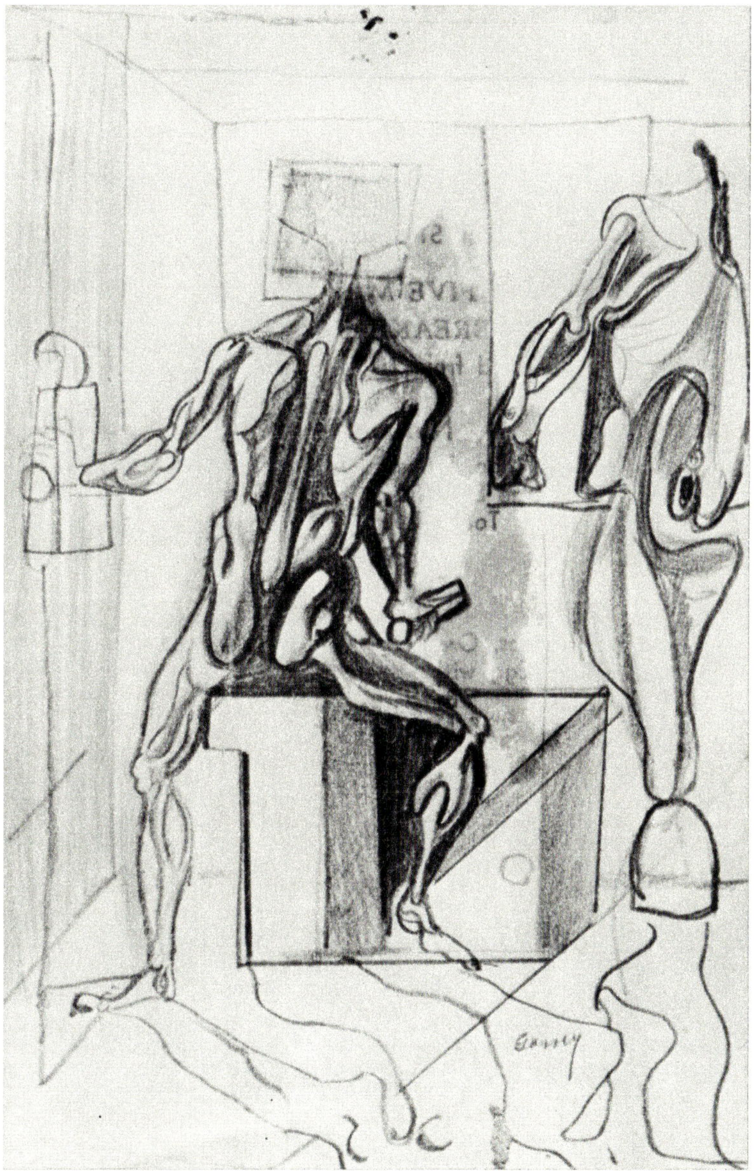

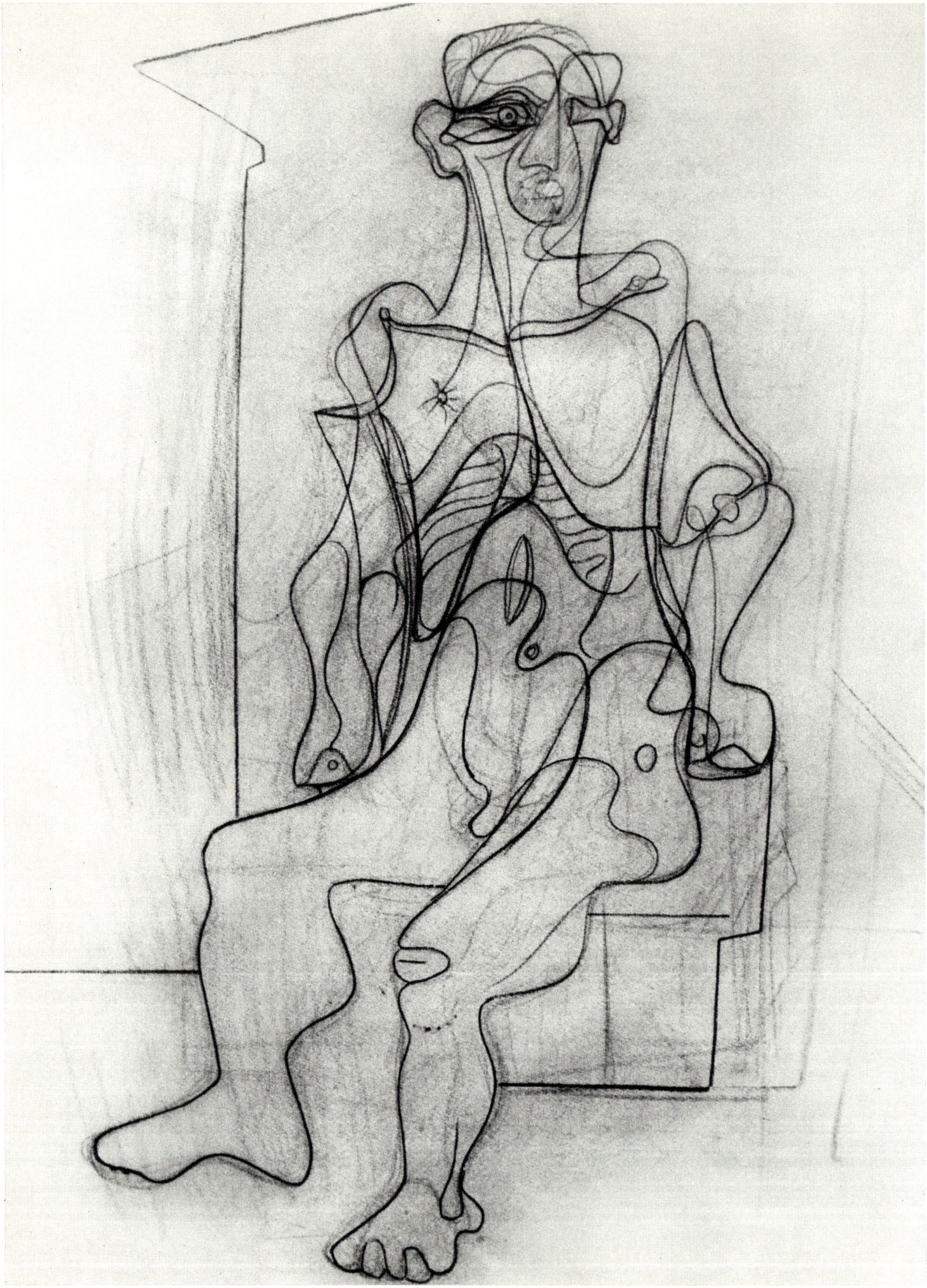

35. *Figure Drawing*. ca. 1930–35
Pencil on paper, 24 1/2 × 18 1/4″
Private Collection

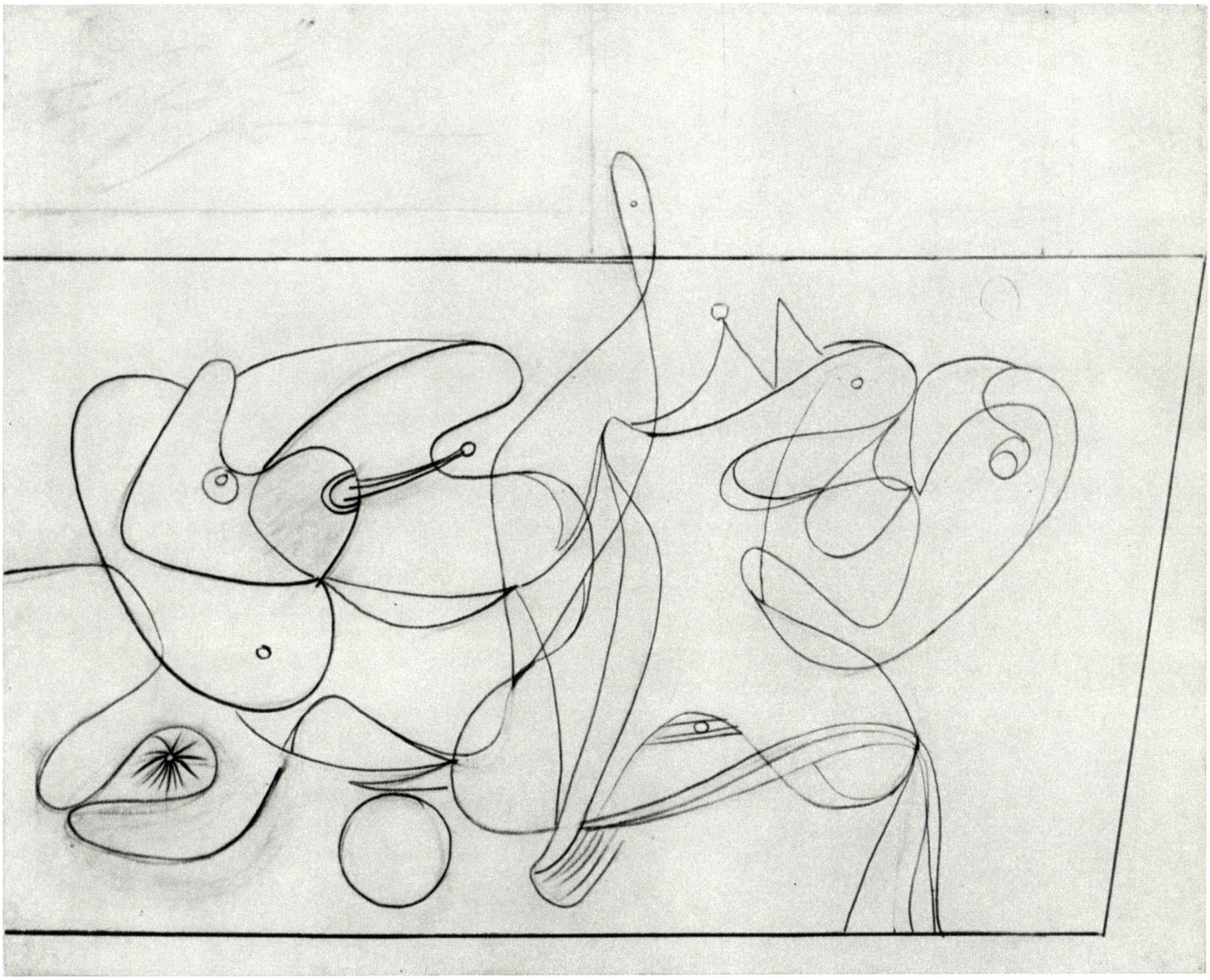

36. Study for *Nighttime, Enigma and Nostalgia*. ca. 1931–32
Pencil on paper, 22 1/4 × 28 3/4″
Collection The Museum of Modern Art, New York;
Gift of Richard S. Zeisler

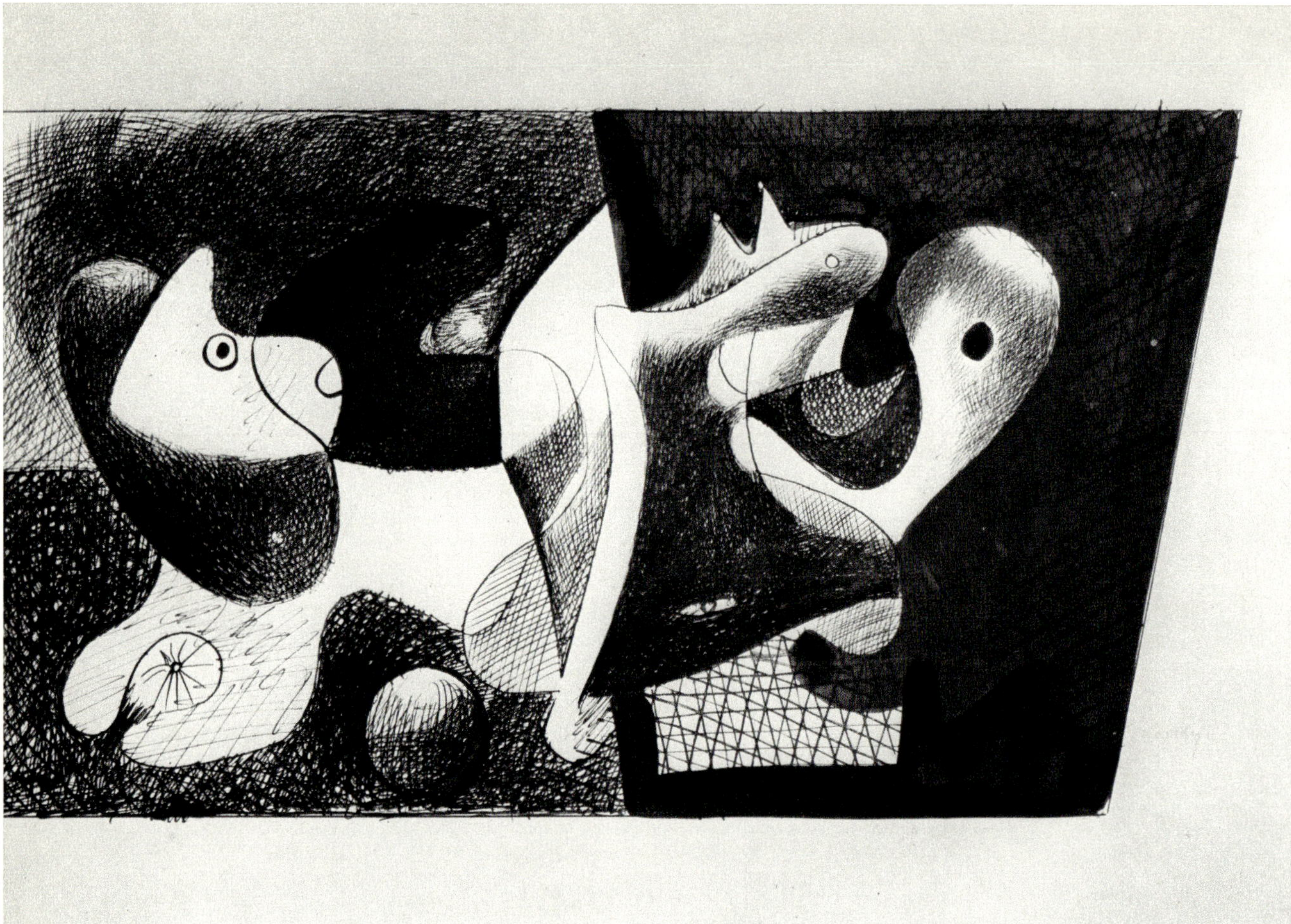

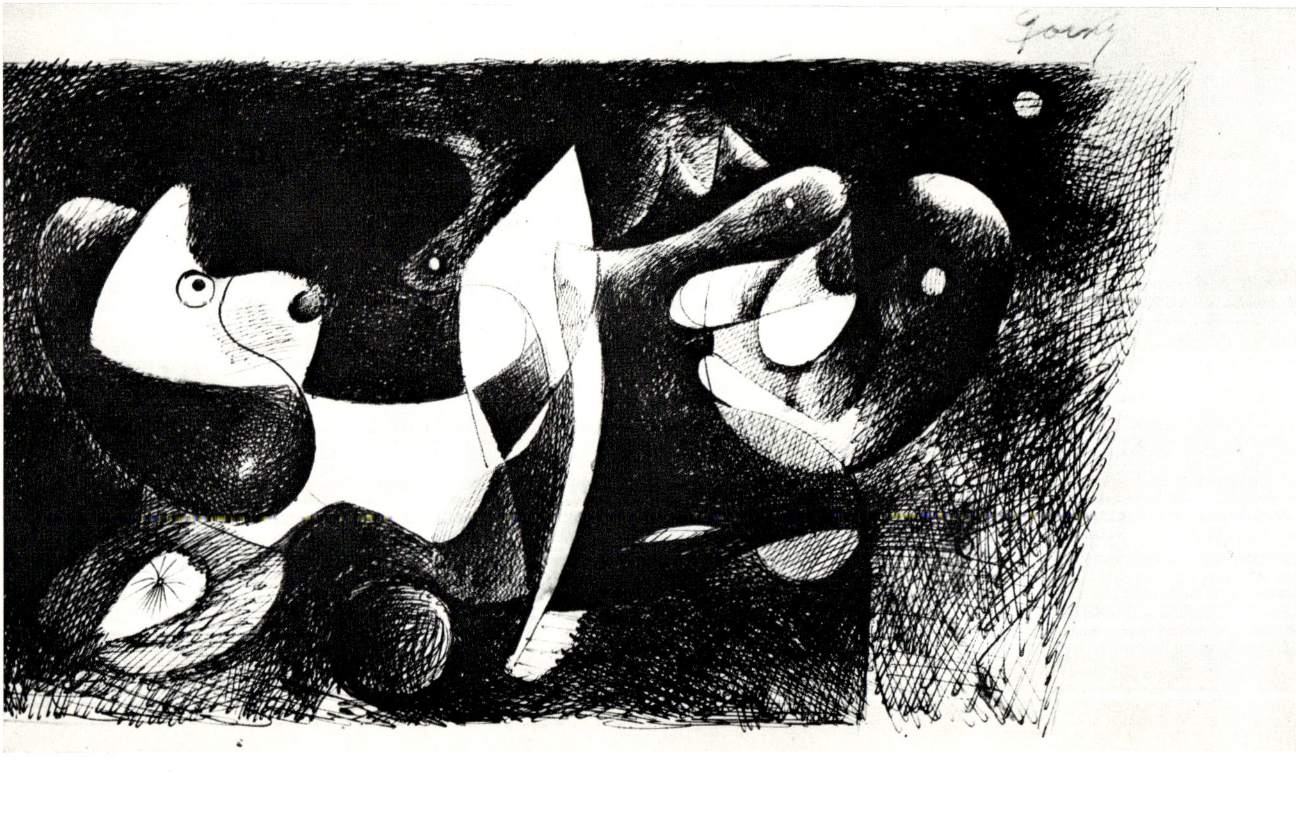

Gorky

37. *Untitled.* 1932
Pen and ink on paper, 14 7/8 × 21 1/4″
Private Collection

38. Study for *Nighttime, Enigma and Nostalgia.* ca. 1931–32
India ink on paper, 12 3/4 × 21 3/4″
Collection Mr. and Mrs. Philip Gersh, Beverly Hills

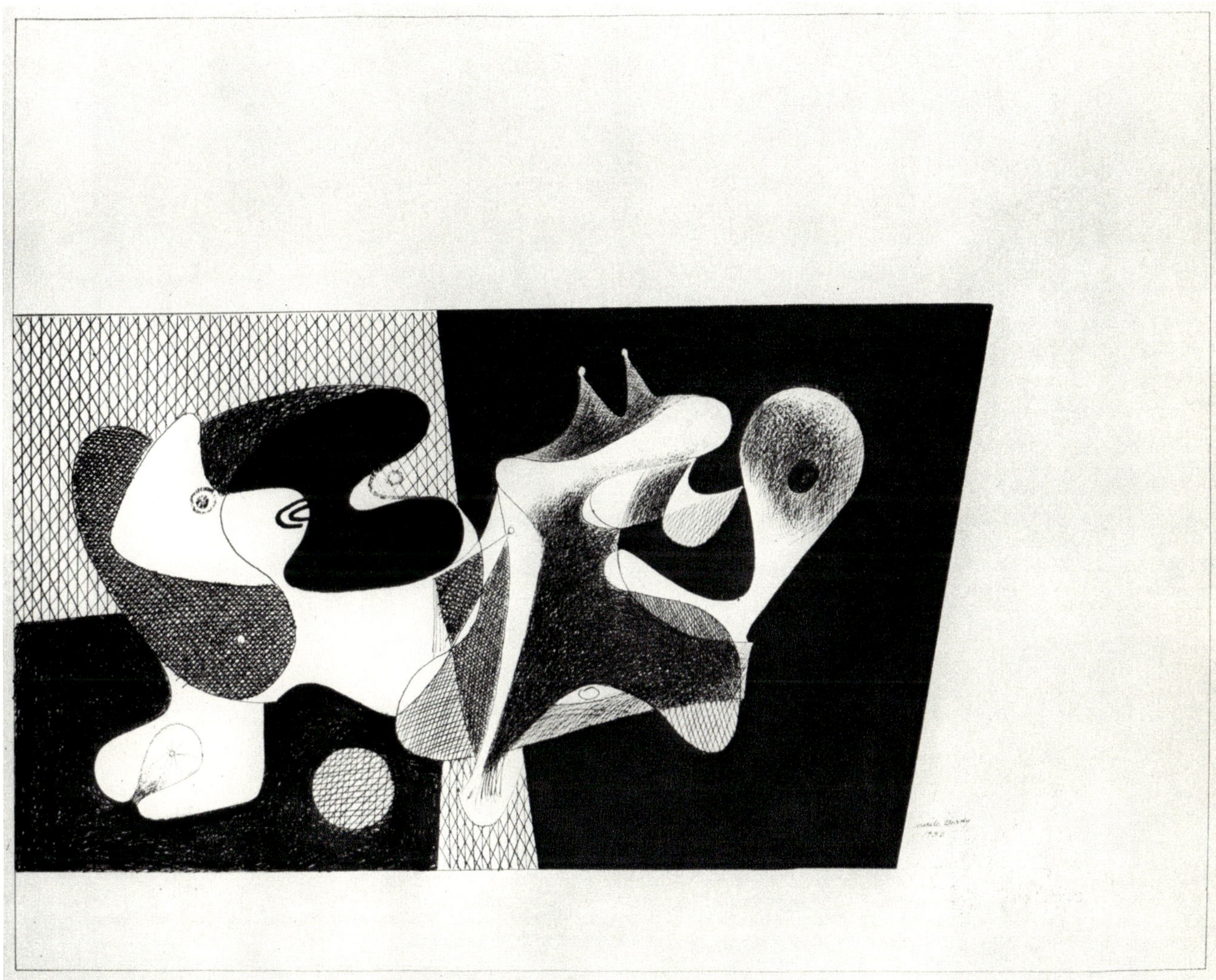

39. *Objects.* 1932
Pen, brush and ink on paper, 22 1/4 × 30″
Collection The Museum of Modern Art, New York,
Vincent van Gogh Purchase Fund

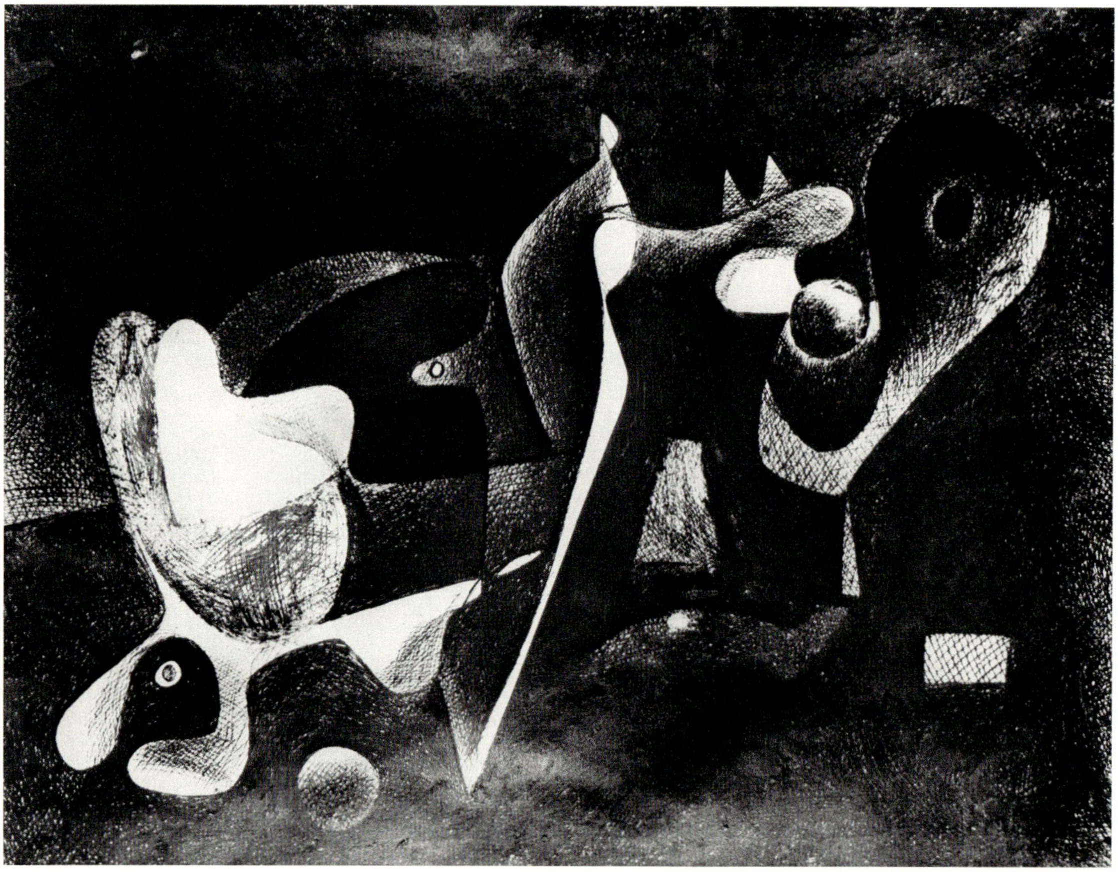

40. *Forms*. ca. 1931–32
Pen and ink on paper, 18 3/16 × 24 5/16″
Yale University Art Gallery, New Haven,
Gift of the Société Anonyme

41. *Nighttime, Enigma and Nostalgia.* ca. 1931–32
India ink and sepia on paper, 21 5/8 × 28″
Collection National Gallery of Art, Washington, D.C.,
Ailsa Mellon Bruce Fund

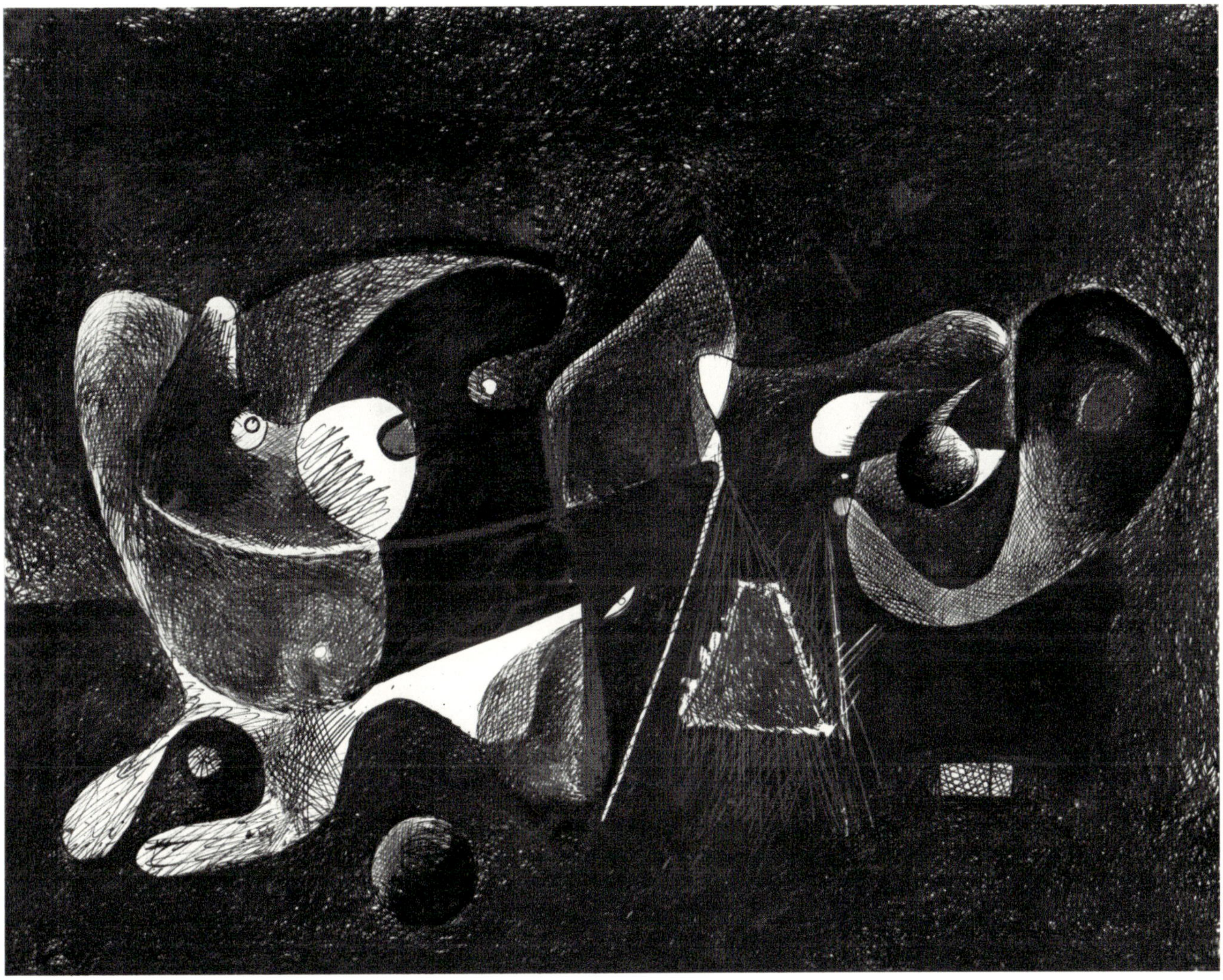

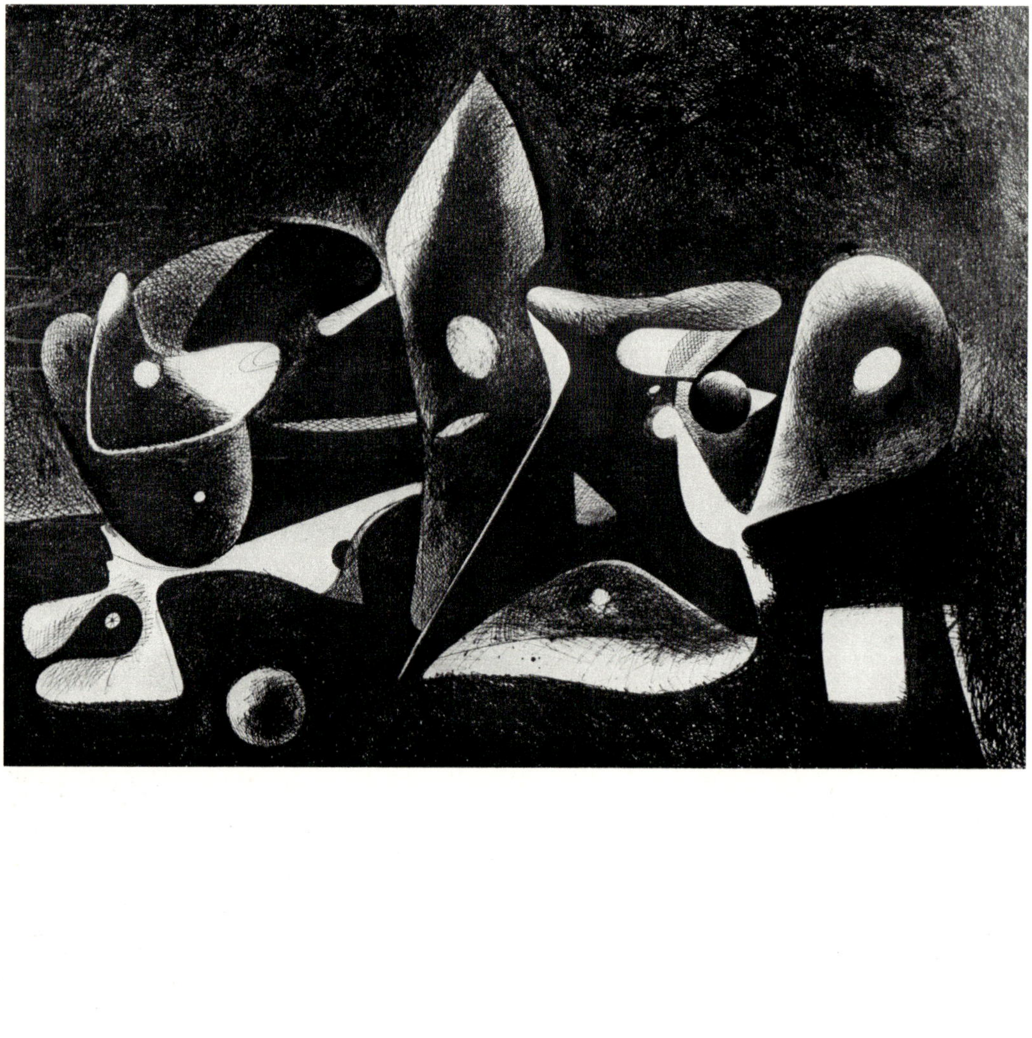

42. Study for *Nighttime, Enigma and Nostalgia.* ca. 1932
Pen and ink on paper, 28 1/2 × 38″
Courtesy Sidney Janis Gallery, New York

43. *Nighttime, Enigma and Nostalgia.* 1933–34
Oil on canvas, 36 × 48″
Private Collection

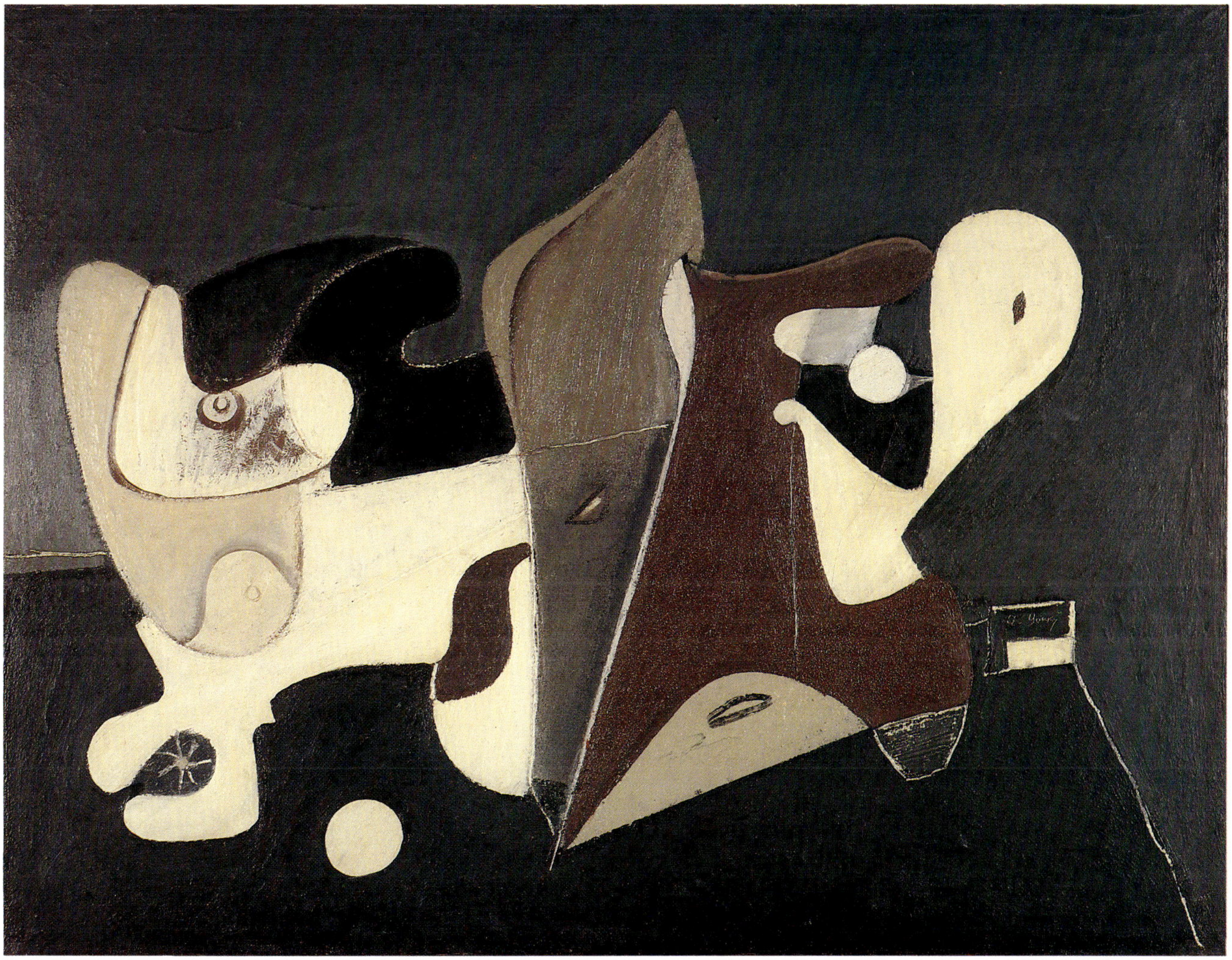

44. *Abstract Composition.* 1931–32
India ink on paper, 22 × 28 3/4″
Collection The Art Institute of Chicago: 1968. 35
The Grant J. Pick Memorial Fund

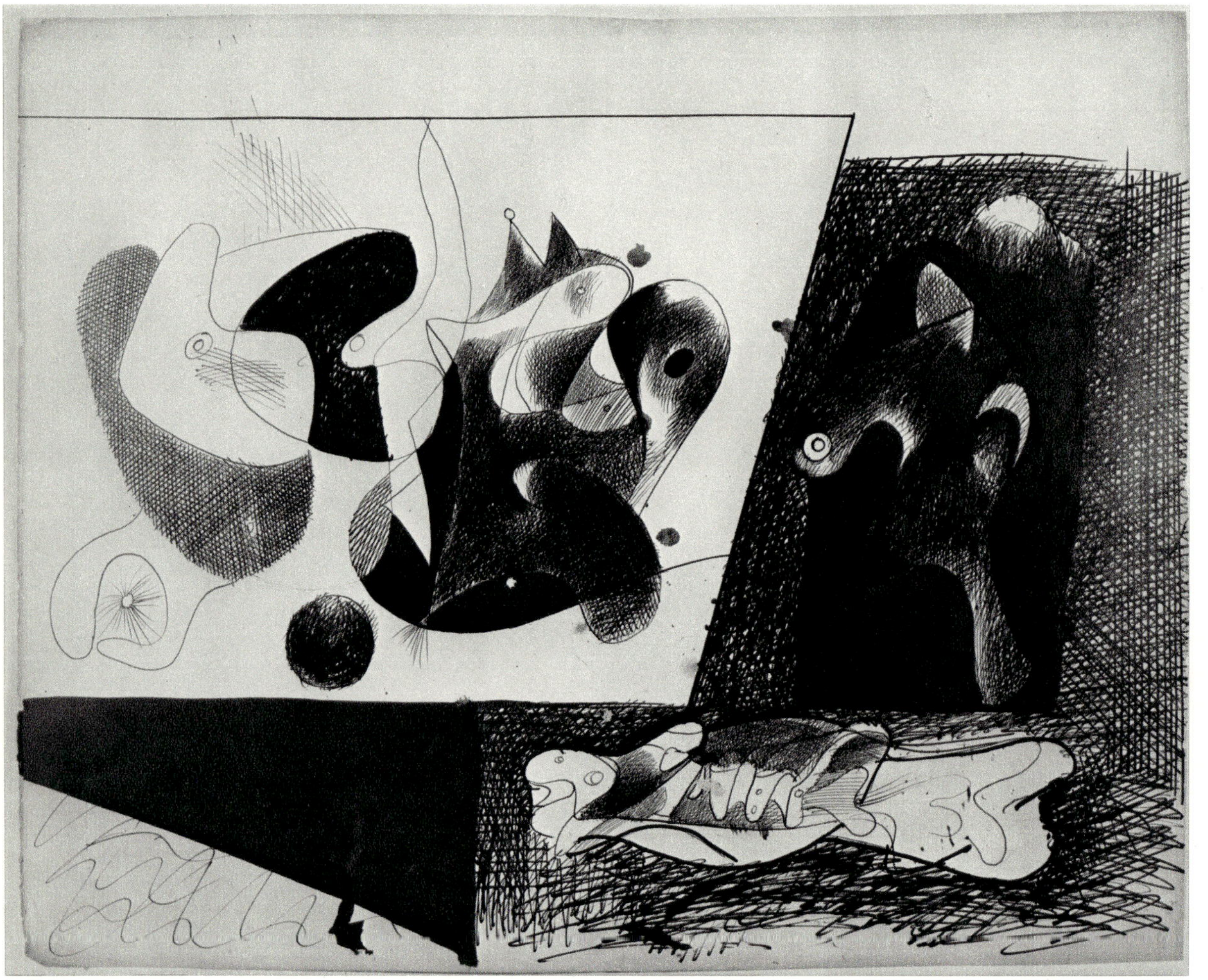

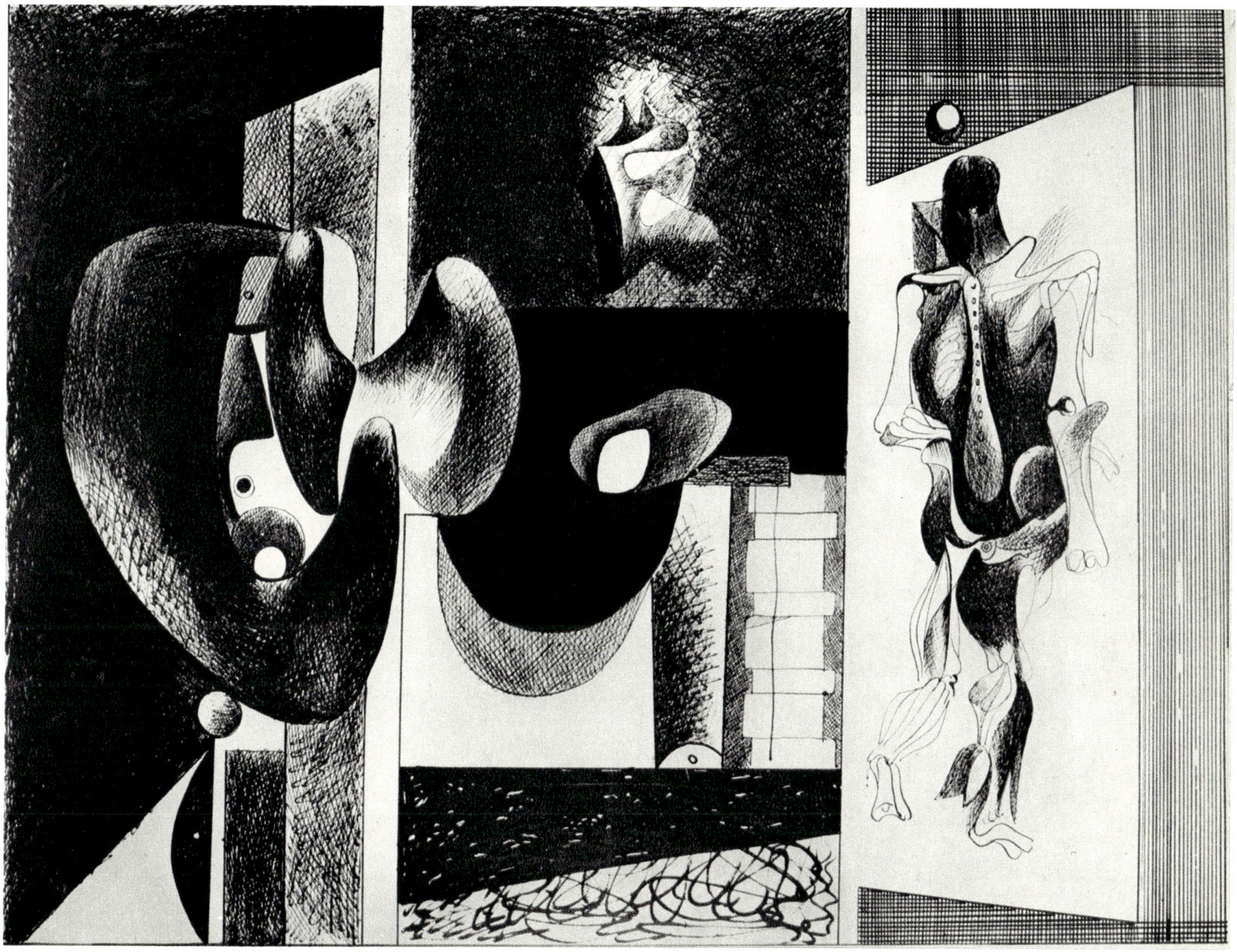

45. *Nighttime, Enigma and Nostalgia.* ca. 1931–32
Pen and ink on paper, 23 1/8 × 31 1/4″
Collection Mr. and Mrs. E. A. Bergman

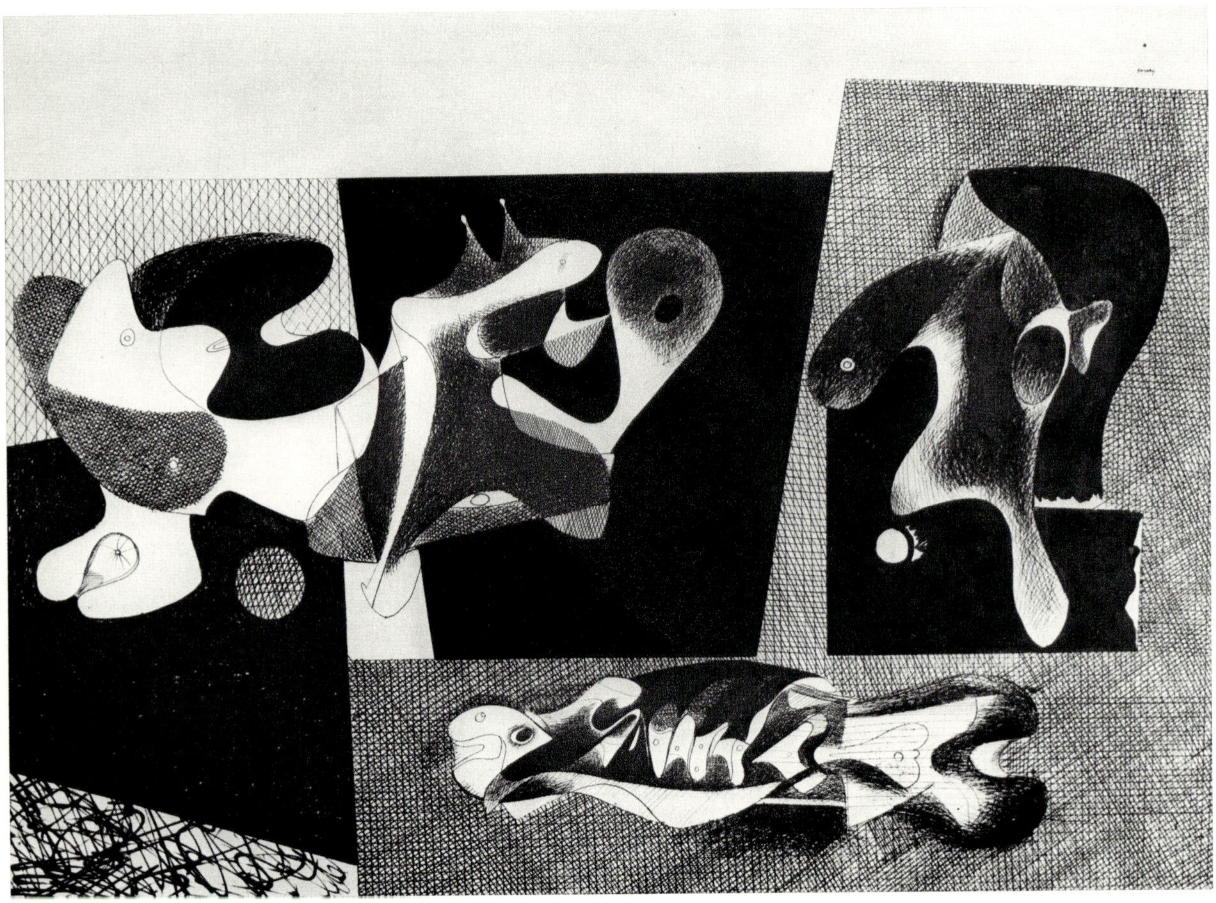

46. Study for *Nighttime, Enigma and Nostalgia*. ca. 1932
Pen and ink on paper, 19 3/4 × 28 1/4″
Courtesy Sidney Janis Gallery, New York

47. *Composition.* 1931–32
Pen and ink on paper, 22 × 30 1/8″
Private Collection

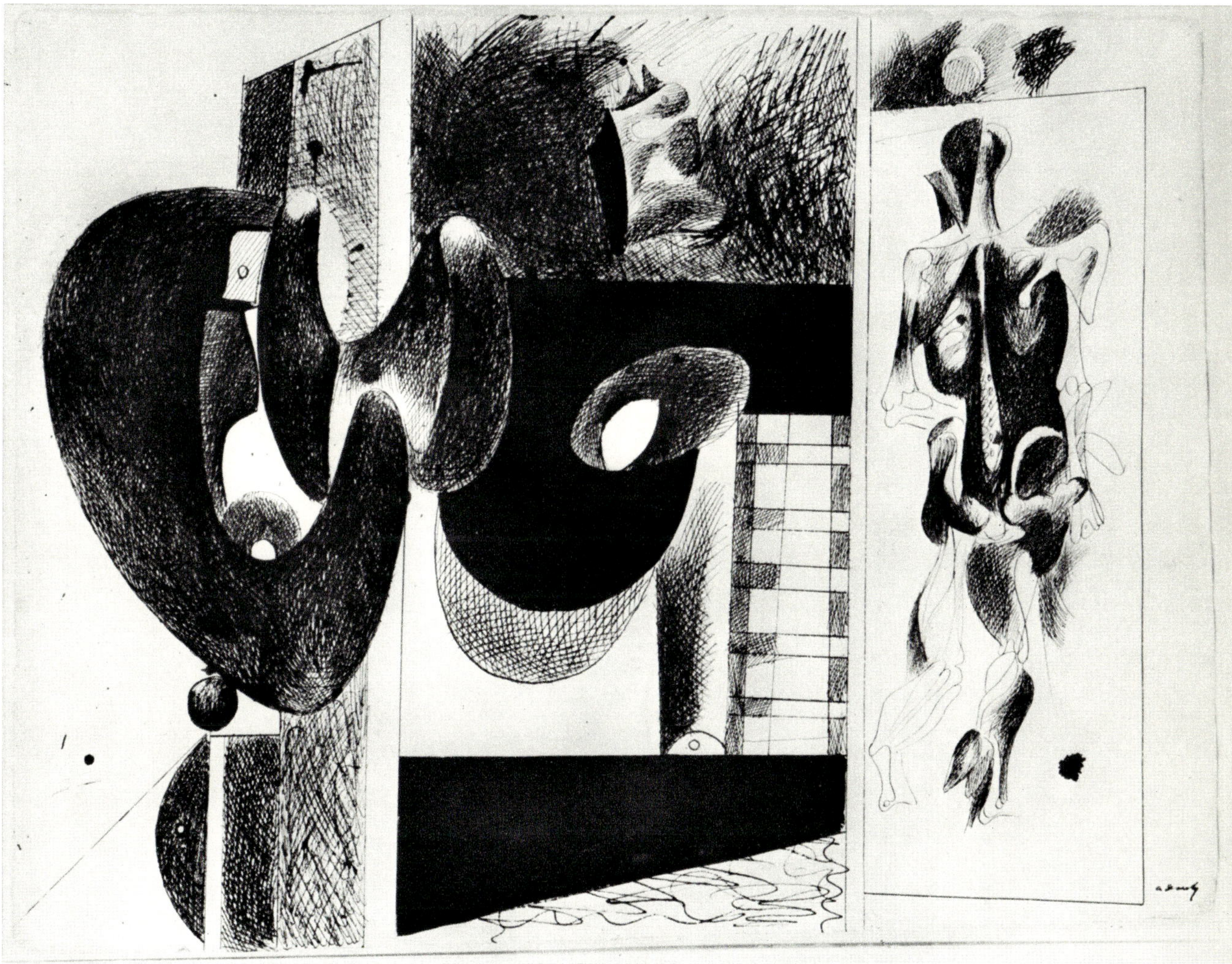

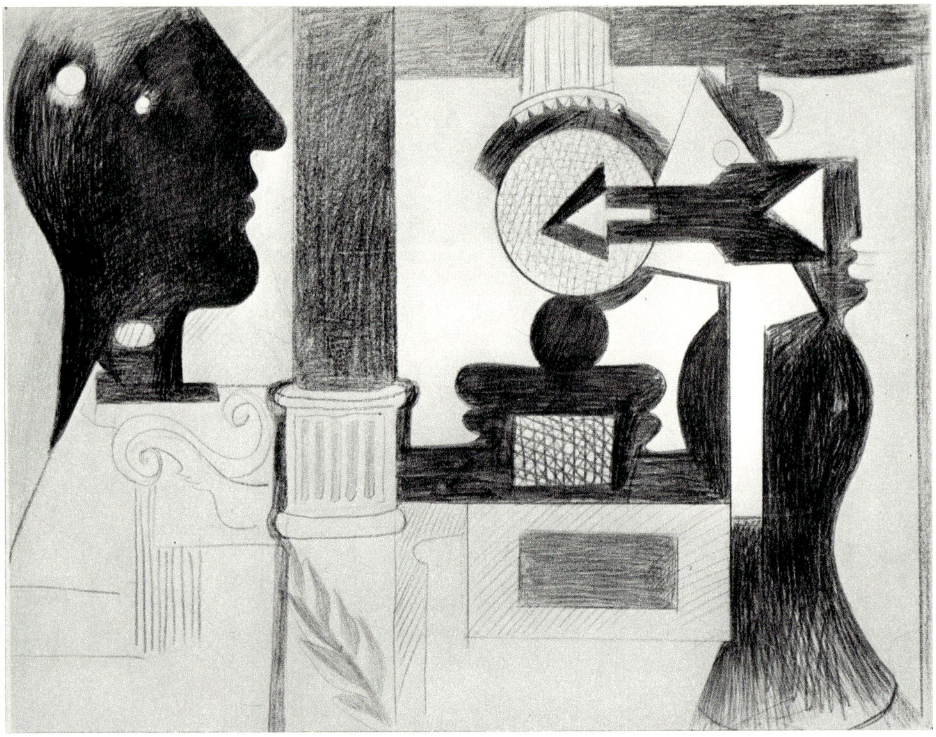

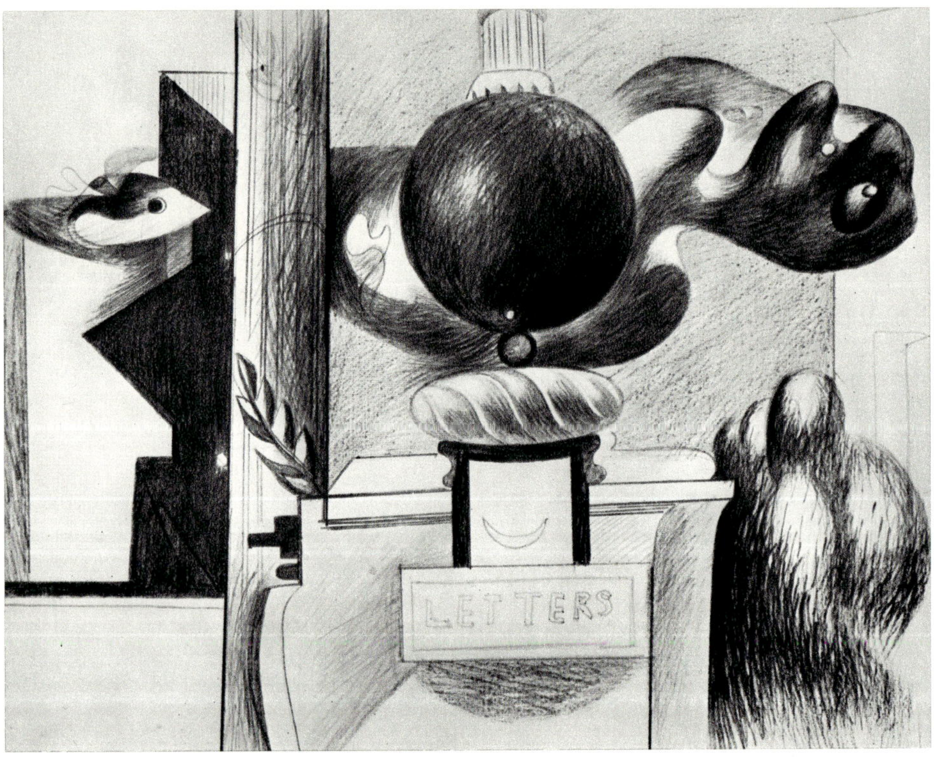

48. *Untitled*. ca. 1932–34
Pencil on paper, 18 1/2 × 24″
Private Collection

49. *Untitled*. ca. 1932–34
Ink and pencil on paper, 18 1/2 × 24 1/4″
Private Collection

50. *Untitled* (*Study for a Mural*). ca. 1931–32
Pen and ink on paper, 9 1/2 × 29″
Private Collection

51. *Untitled* (*Study for a Mural*). ca. 1931–32
Pen and ink on paper, 7 1/4 × 26″
Courtesy Allan Stone Gallery, New York

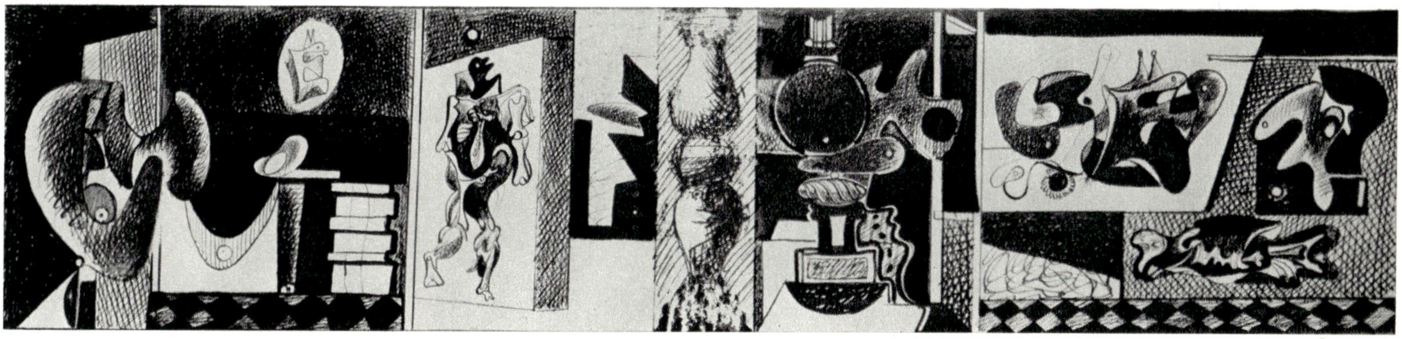

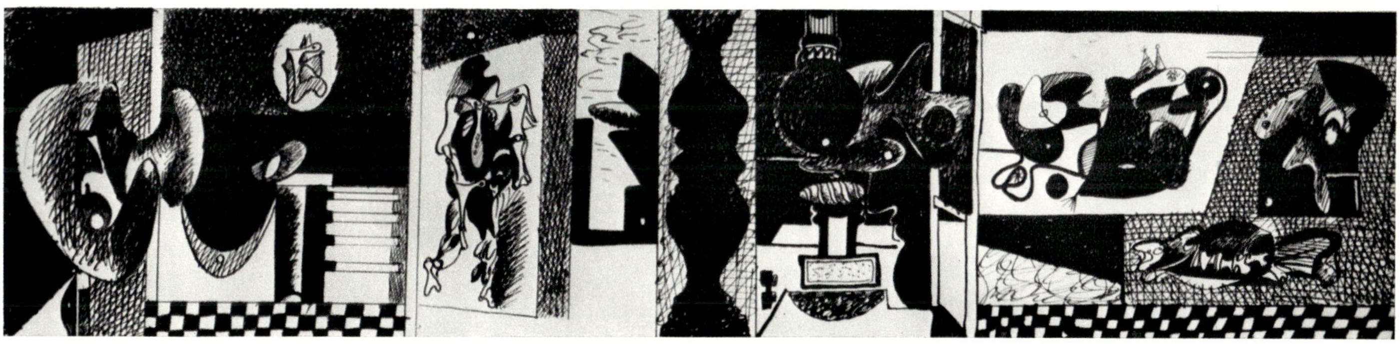

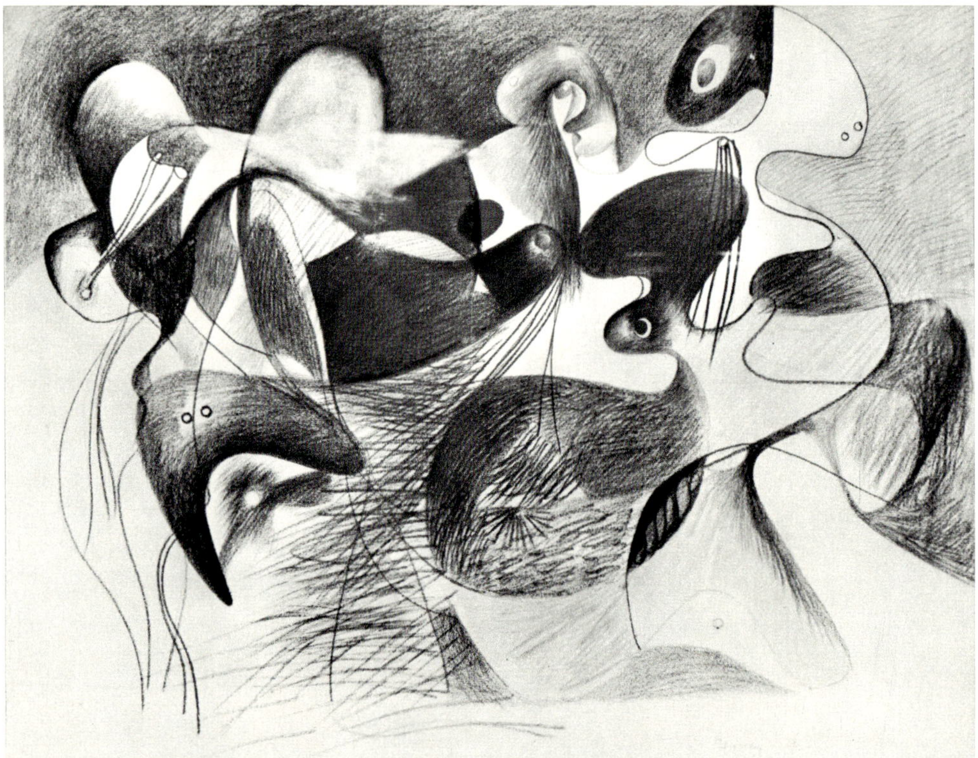

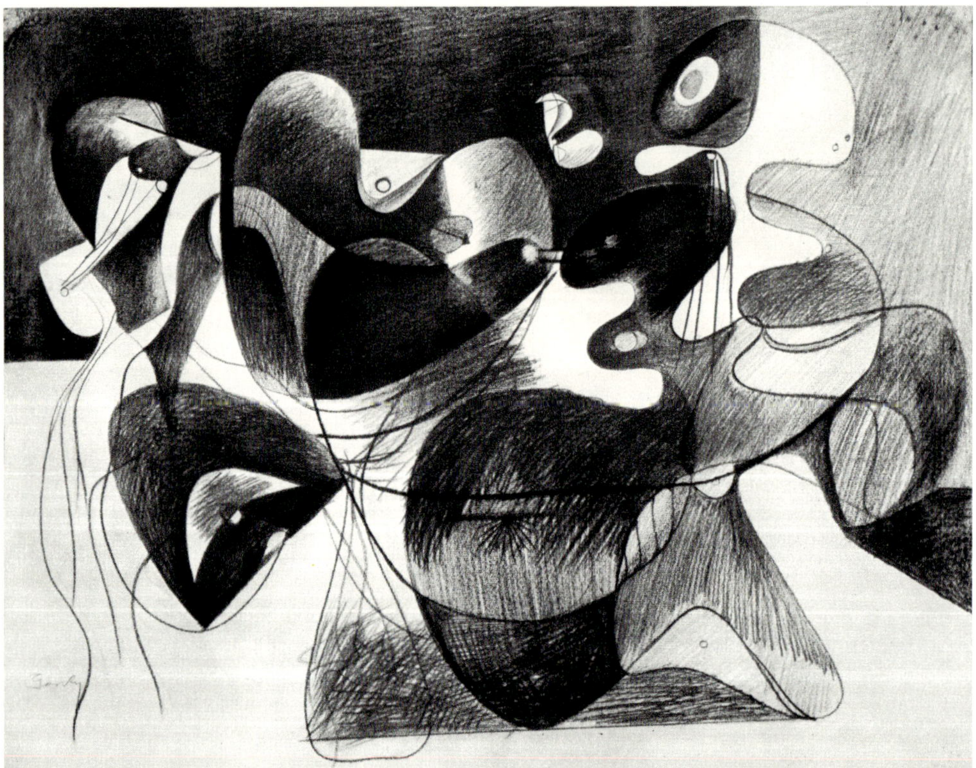

52. Study for *Image in Xhorkom.* mid–1930s
Pencil on paper, 18 1/2 × 24 3/8″
Private Collection

53. Study for *Image in Xhorkom.* mid–1930s
Pencil on paper, 19 × 24″
Courtesy Allan Stone Gallery, New York

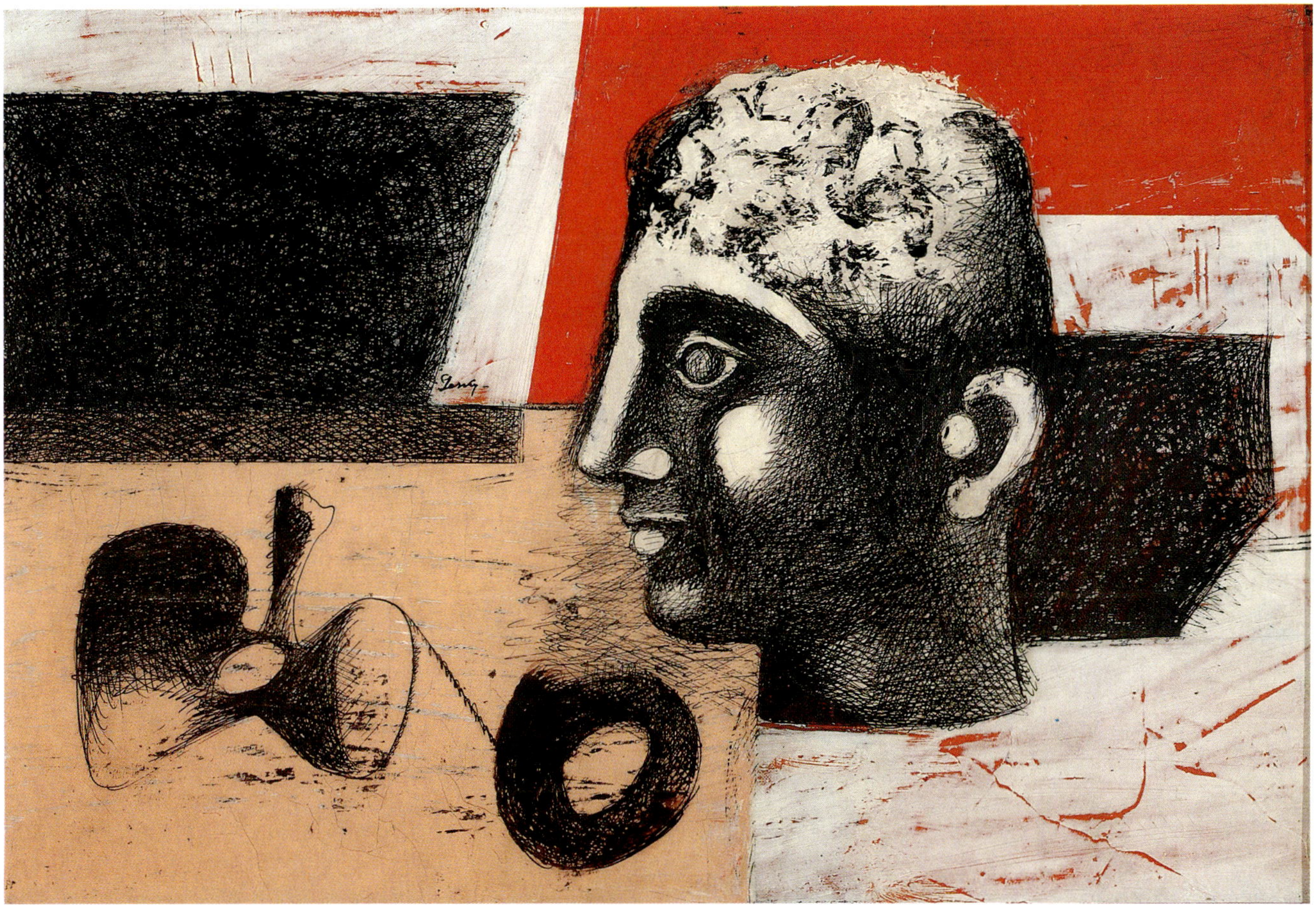

54. *Untitled*. ca. 1936
Oil on canvas with superimposed ink drawing, 15 1/2 × 23 1/2″
Collection Christopher C. Schwabacher, New York

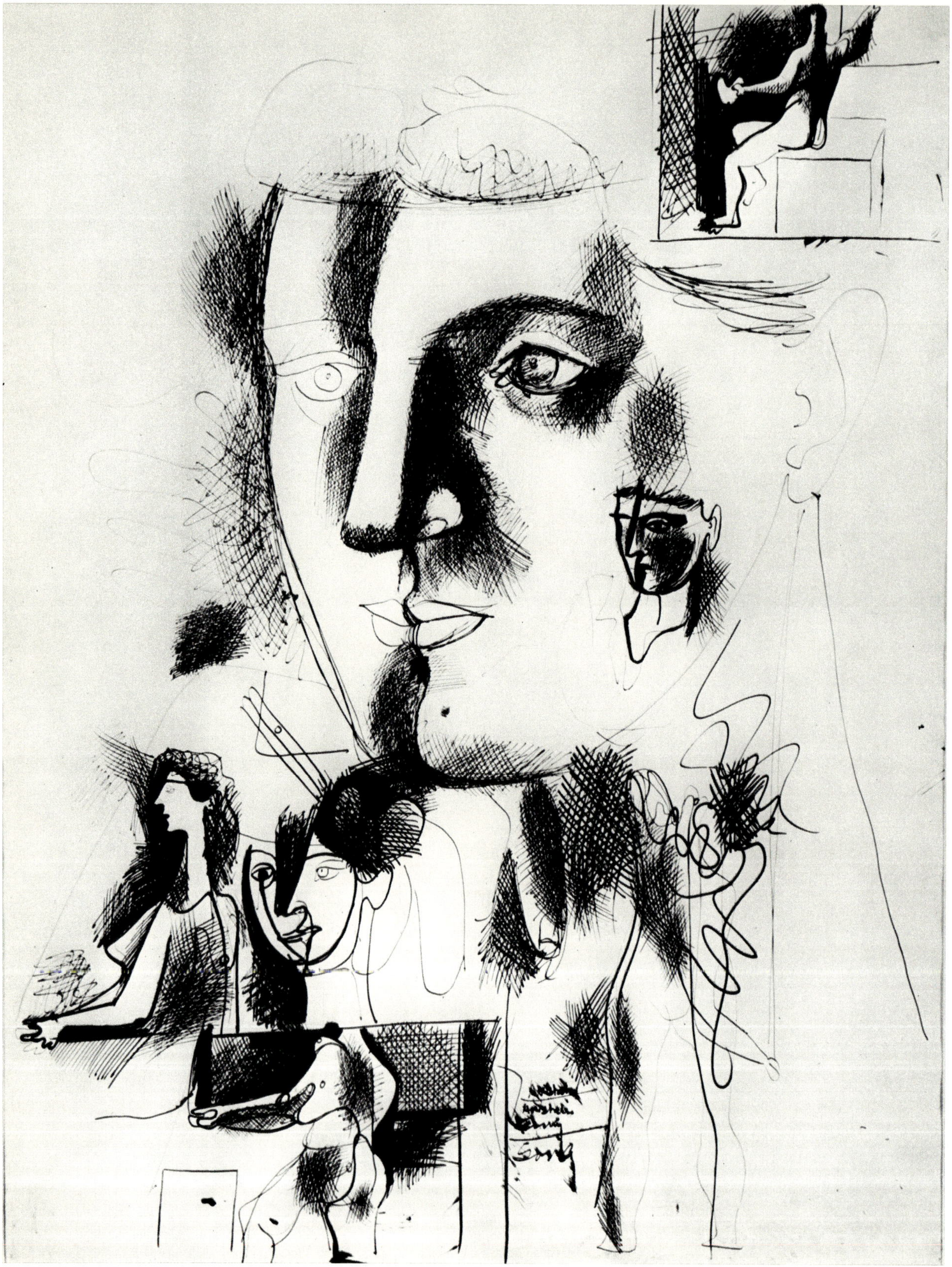

55. *Untitled.* ca. 1938
Pen and ink on paper, 25 1/2 × 19 1/2″
Collection Dr. and Mrs. William Rattner,
Huntington Woods, Michigan

56. *Untitled.* 1932–34
Pen and ink on paper, 14 × 17″
Private Collection

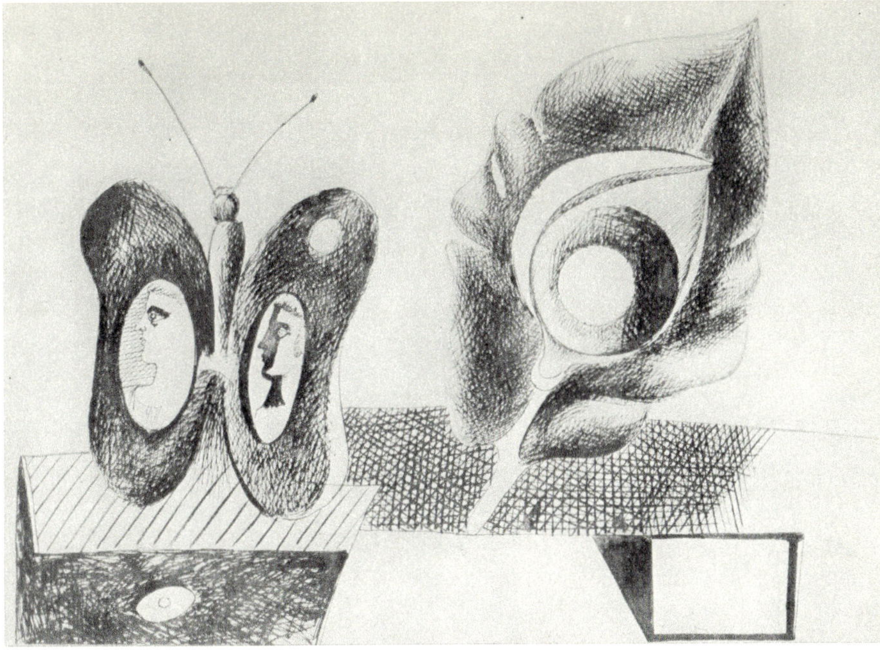

57. *Untitled.* ca. 1936
Ink on paper, 14 1/2 × 10 1/2″
Courtesy Allan Stone Gallery, New York

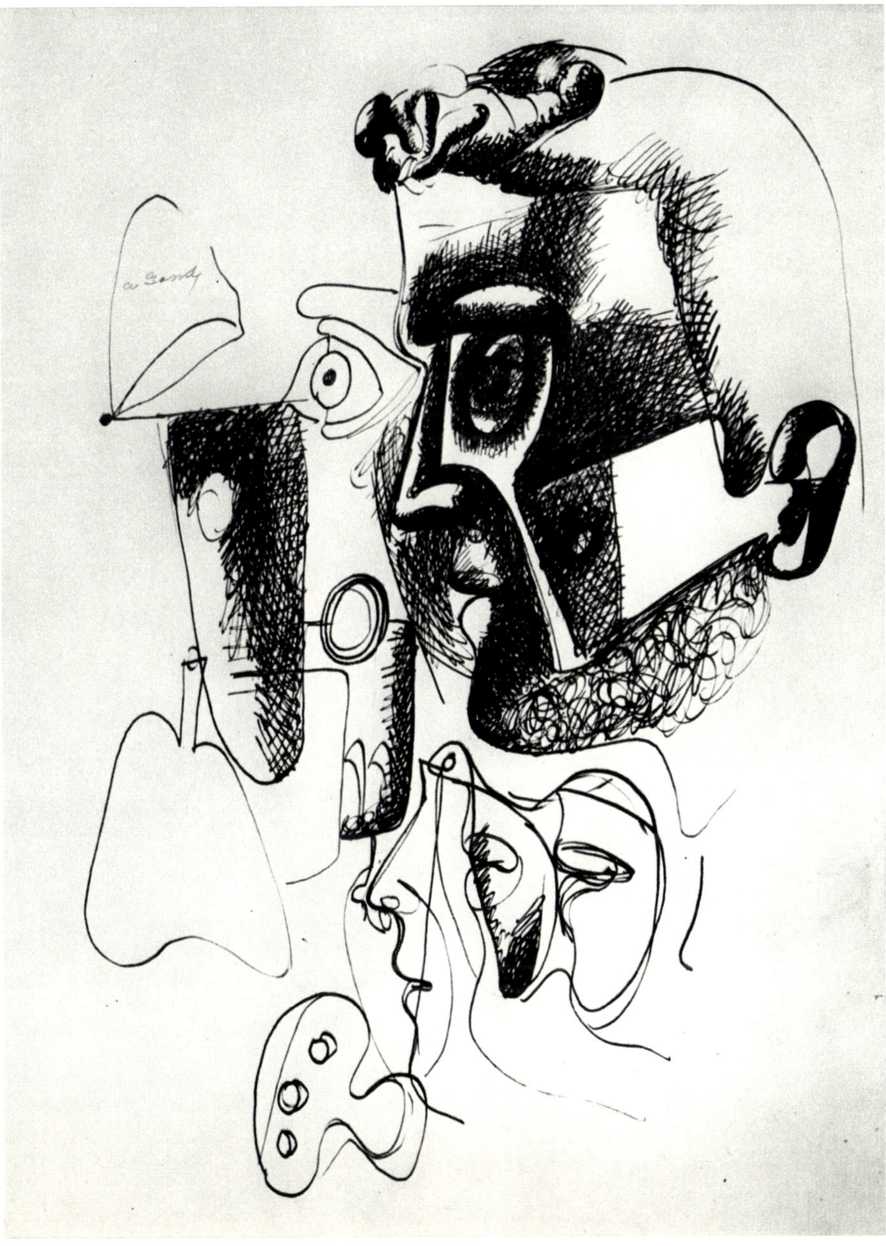

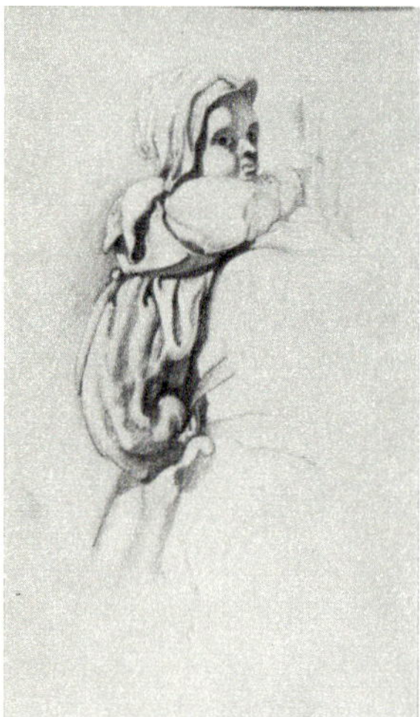 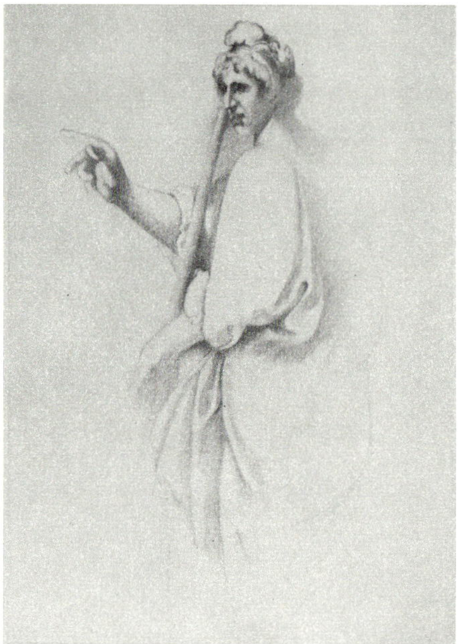 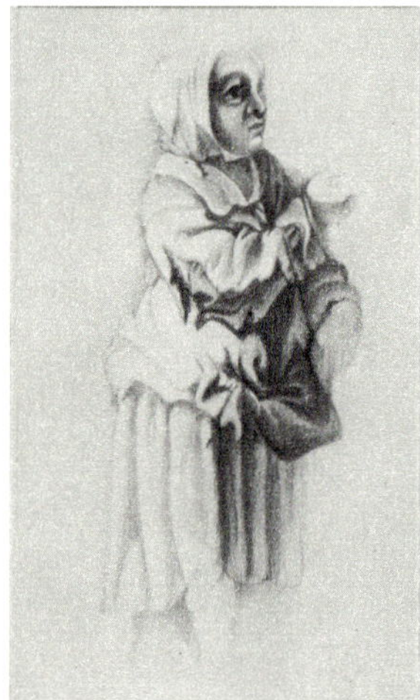

58a,b,c. *Three Drawings* (*After Le Nain*) (*After Millet*)
(*After Le Nain*). mid-1930s
Pencil on paper, 7 1/2 × 4 1/4″,
9 × 6 1/2″, 7 1/2 × 4 1/4″
Collection Ethel K. Schwabacher, New York

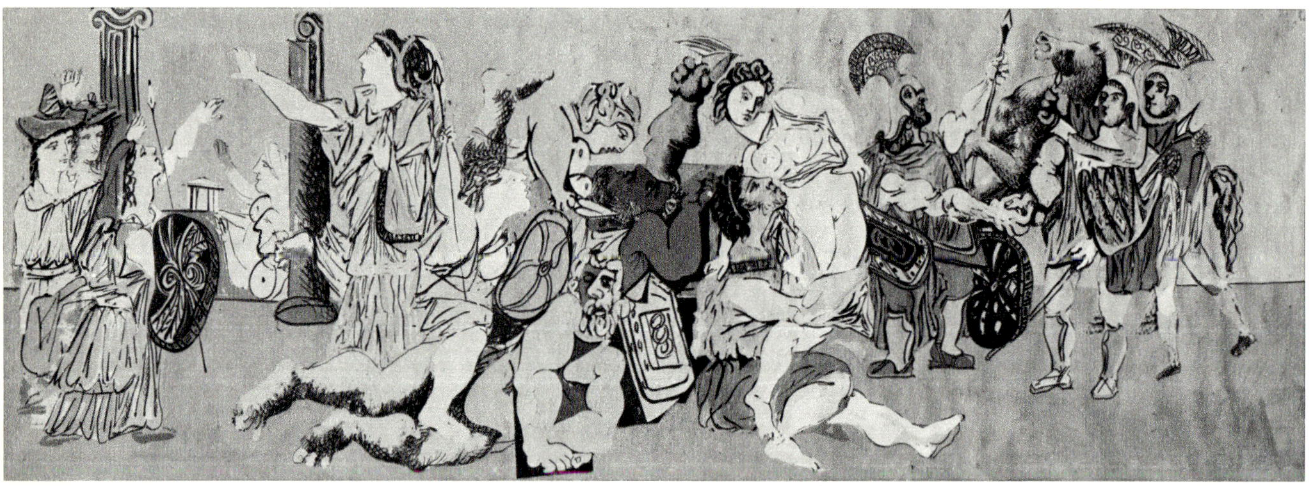

59. *Untitled.* mid-1930s
Gouache on paper, 8 1/4 × 23 1/4″
Collection Ethel K. Schwabacher, New York

60. *Untitled*. ca. 1933–34
Pencil on paper, 11 1/2 × 9″
Private Collection, New York

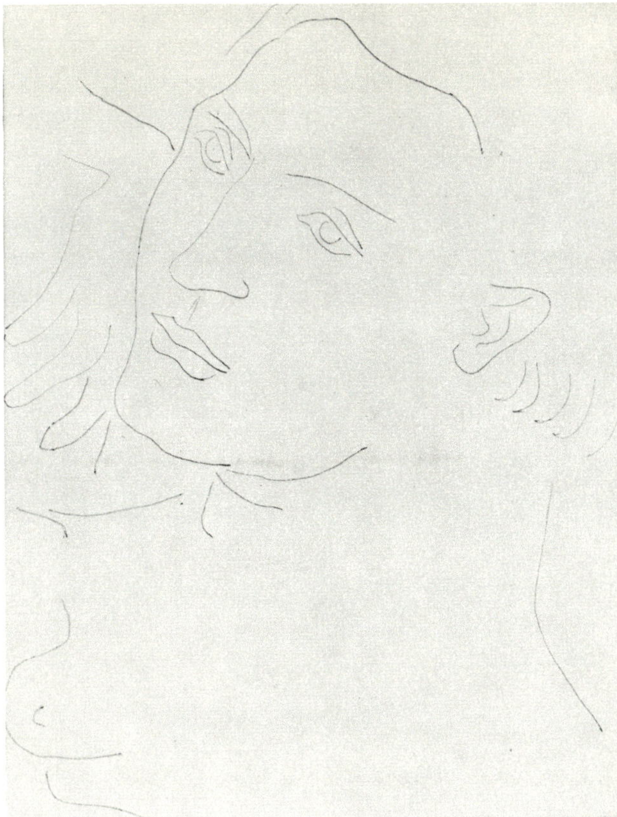

61. *Untitled* (*Head of a Woman*). 1932–34
verso of *Nighttime, Enigma and Nostalgia*
Pen and ink on paper, 25 × 19″
Courtesy Susanne Hilberry Gallery,
Birmingham, Michigan

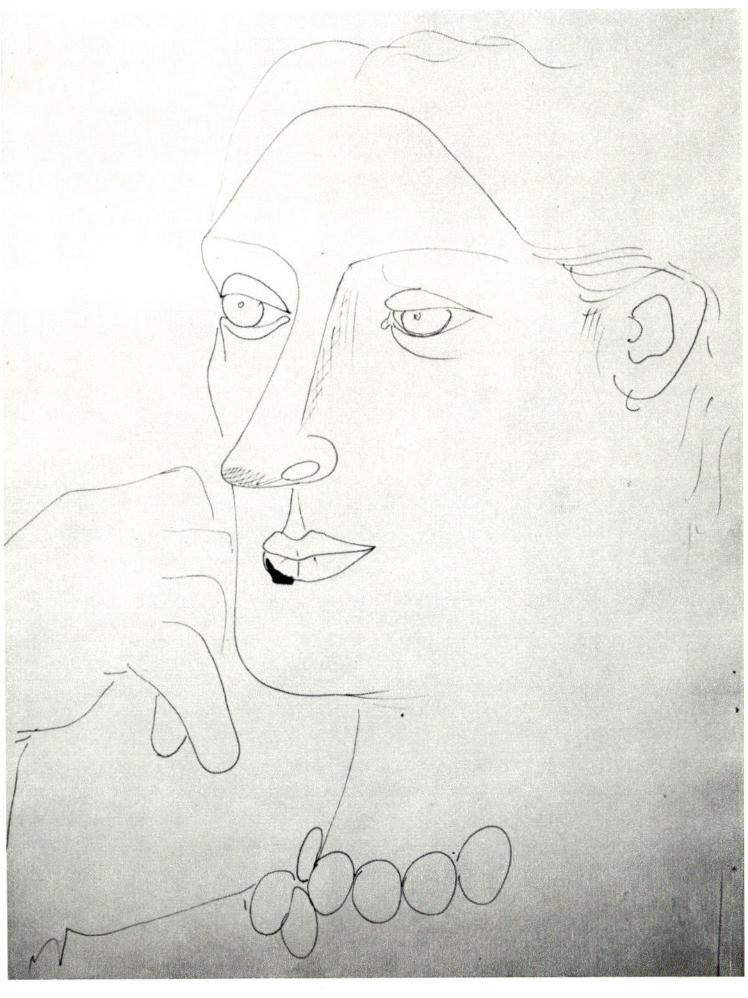

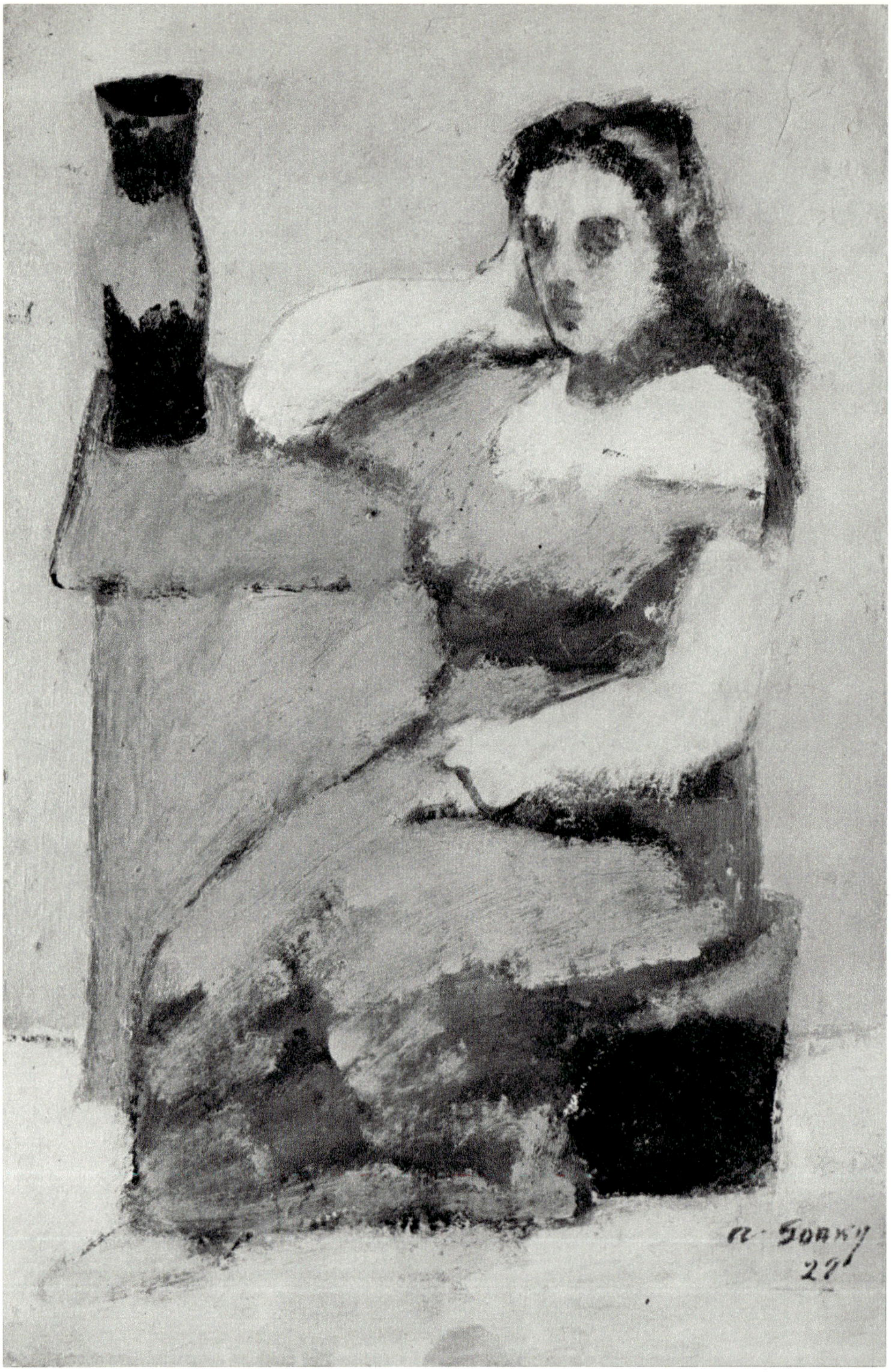

62. *Seated Woman with Vase.* mid-1930s
Oil on paperboard, 11 1/2 × 7 7/8″
Collection Hirshhorn Museum and Sculpture Garden,
Smithsonian Institution, Washington, D.C.

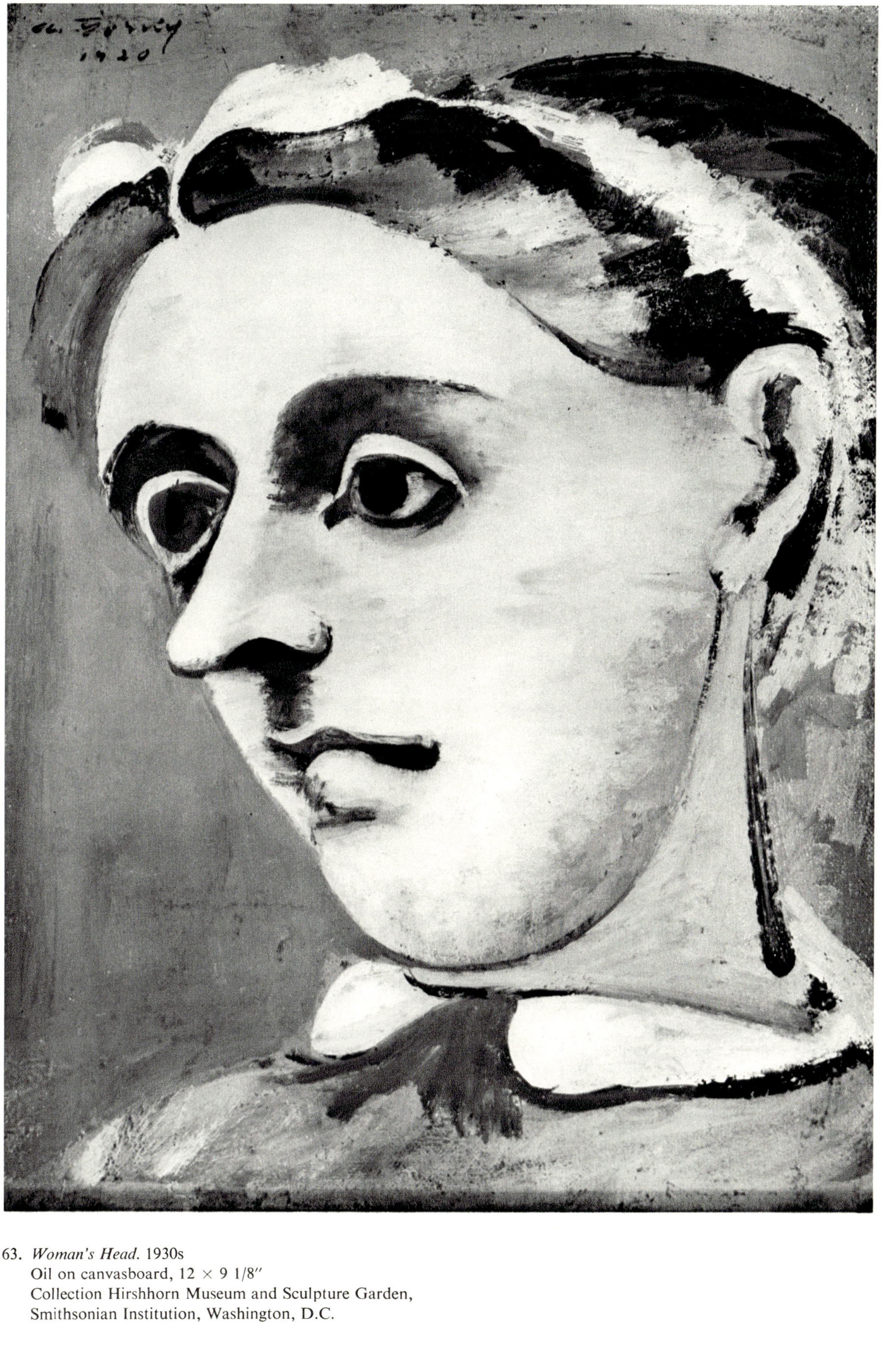

63. *Woman's Head.* 1930s
Oil on canvasboard, 12 × 9 1/8″
Collection Hirshhorn Museum and Sculpture Garden,
Smithsonian Institution, Washington, D.C.

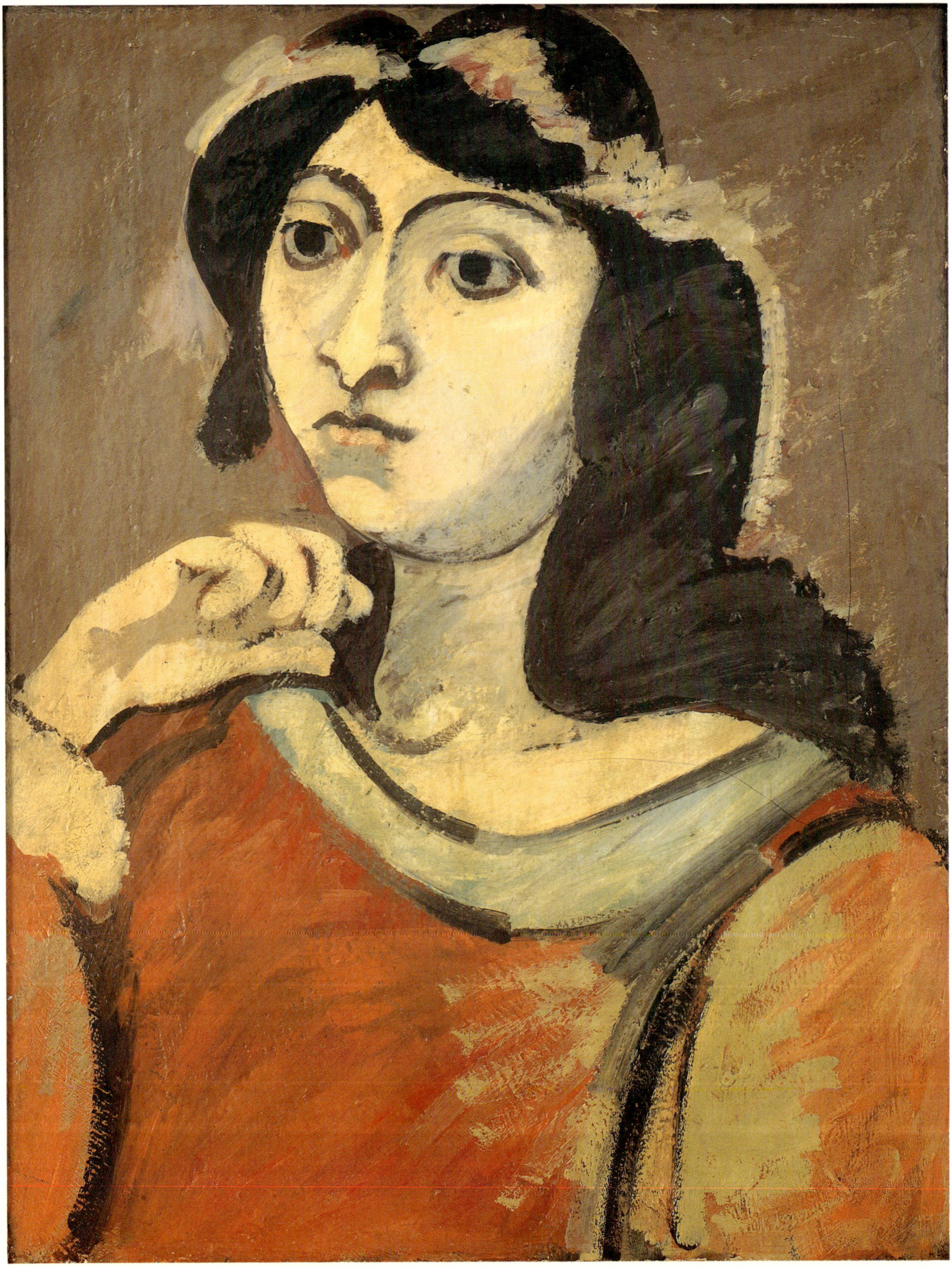

64. *Portrait of Akko.* ca. 1937
Oil on canvas, 19 1/4 × 15″
Private Collection

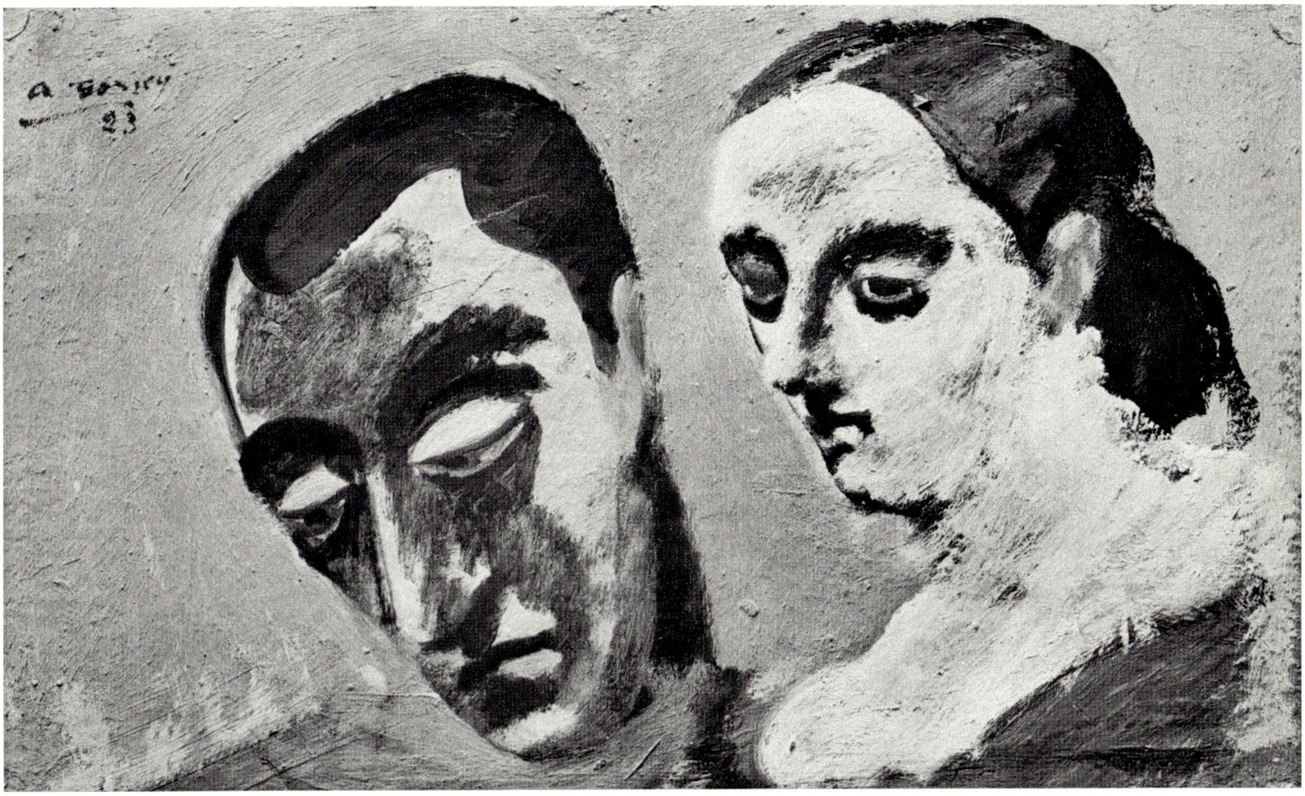

65. *Portrait of Myself and My Imaginary Wife.* mid to late 1930s
Oil on paperboard, 8 5/8 × 14 1/4″
Collection Hirshhorn Museum and Sculpture Garden,
Smithsonian Institution, Washington, D.C.

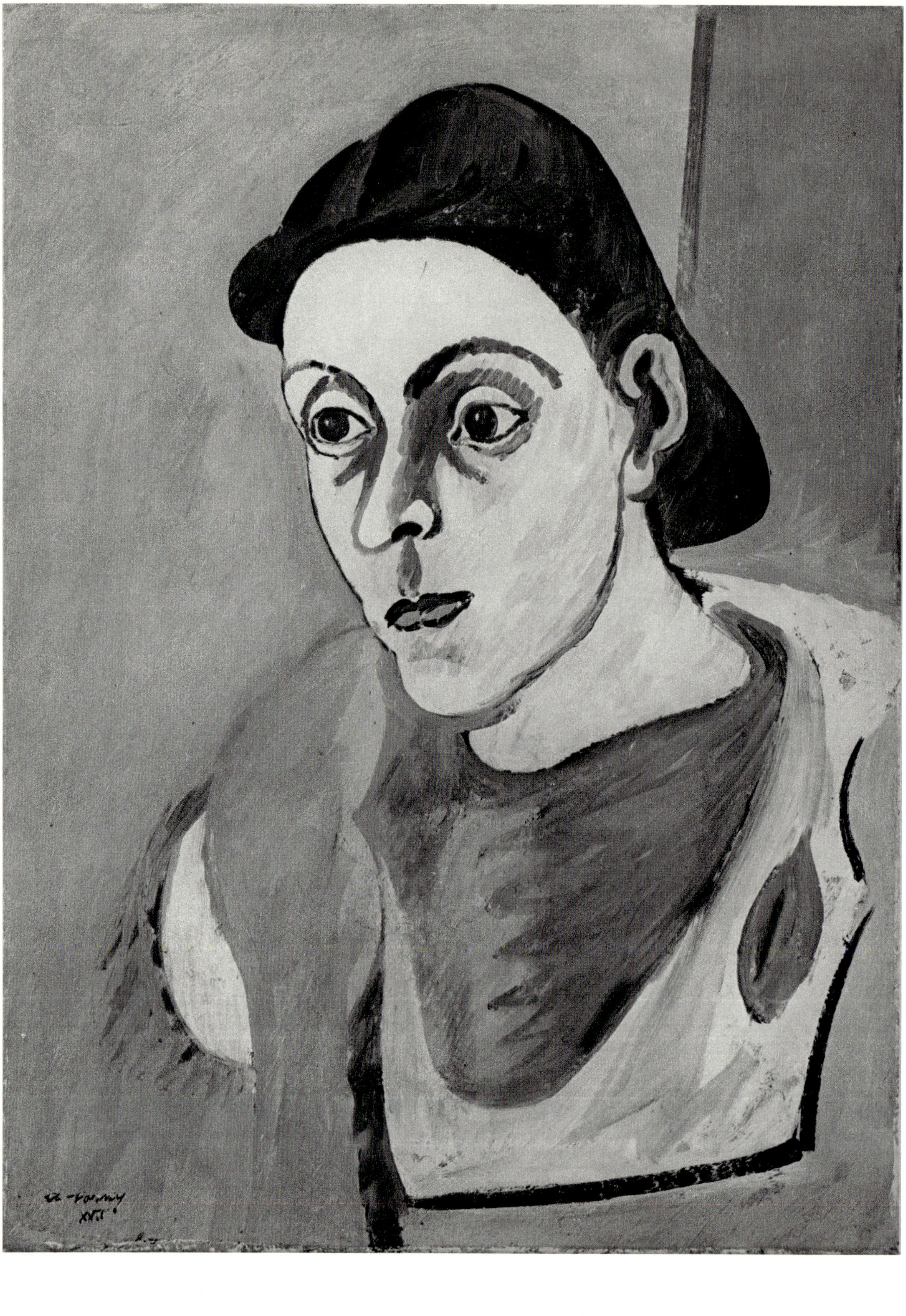

66. *Portrait of Vartoosh.* mid to late 1930s
Oil on canvas, 20 1/4 × 15 1/8″
Collection Hirshhorn Museum and Sculpture Garden, Smithsonian Institution, Washington, D.C.

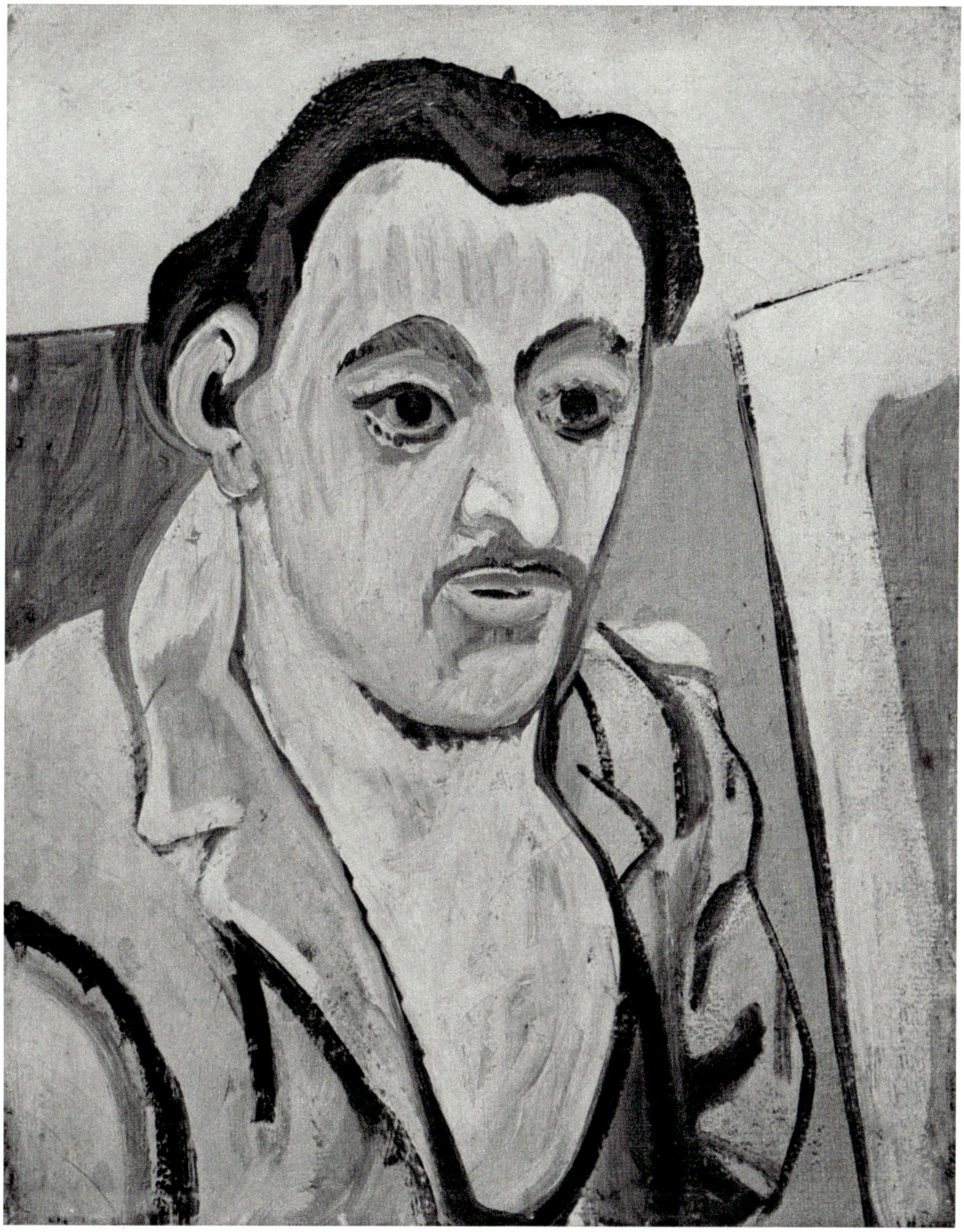

67. *Self-Portrait.* 1931–33
Oil on canvas, 10 × 8″
Rebecca and Raphael Soyer Collection

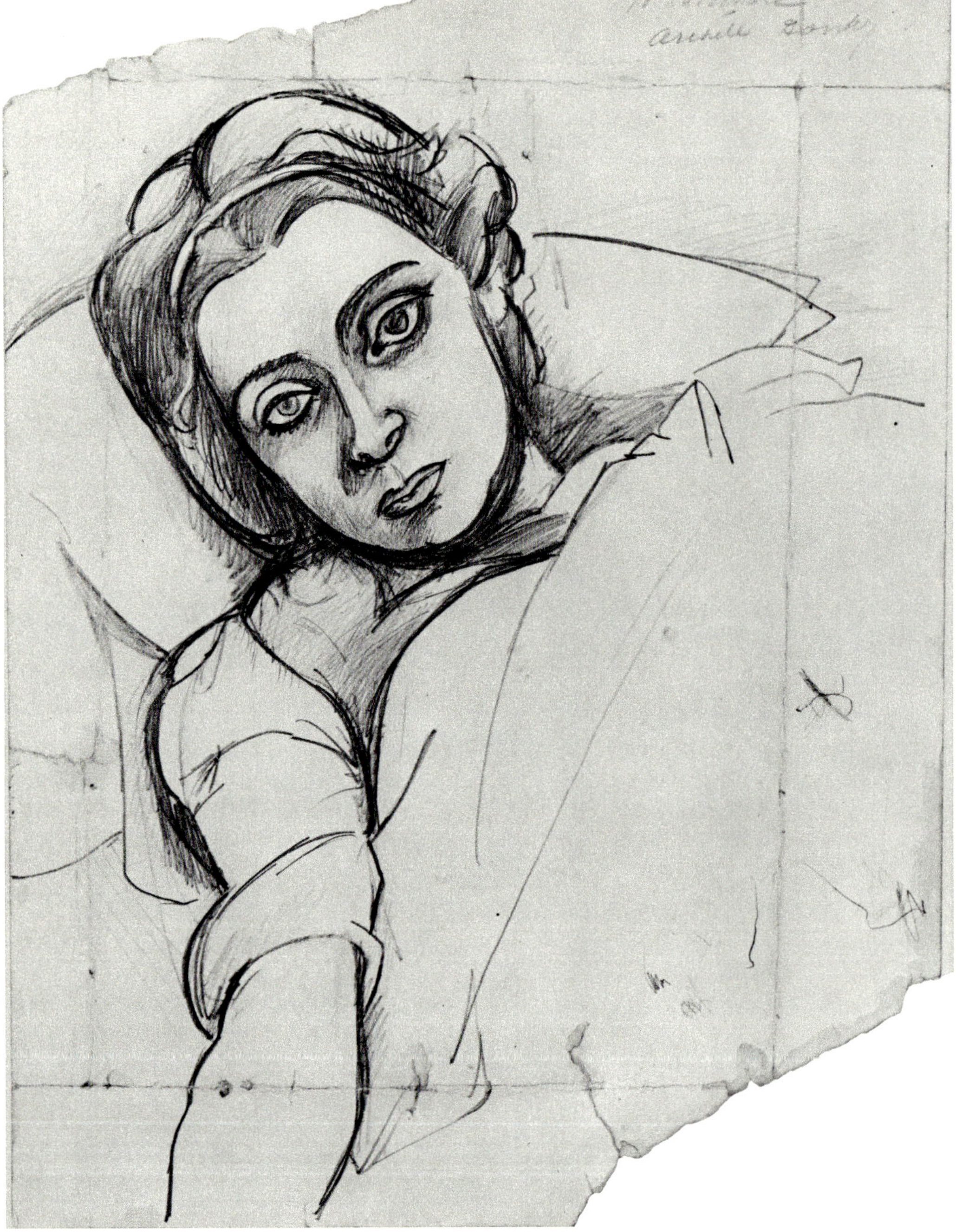

68. *Vartoosh Mooradian.* ca. 1935–36
Pencil on paper, 12 1/4 × 9 1/2″
Collection The Museum of Modern Art, New York,
The Kay Sage Tanguy Bequest

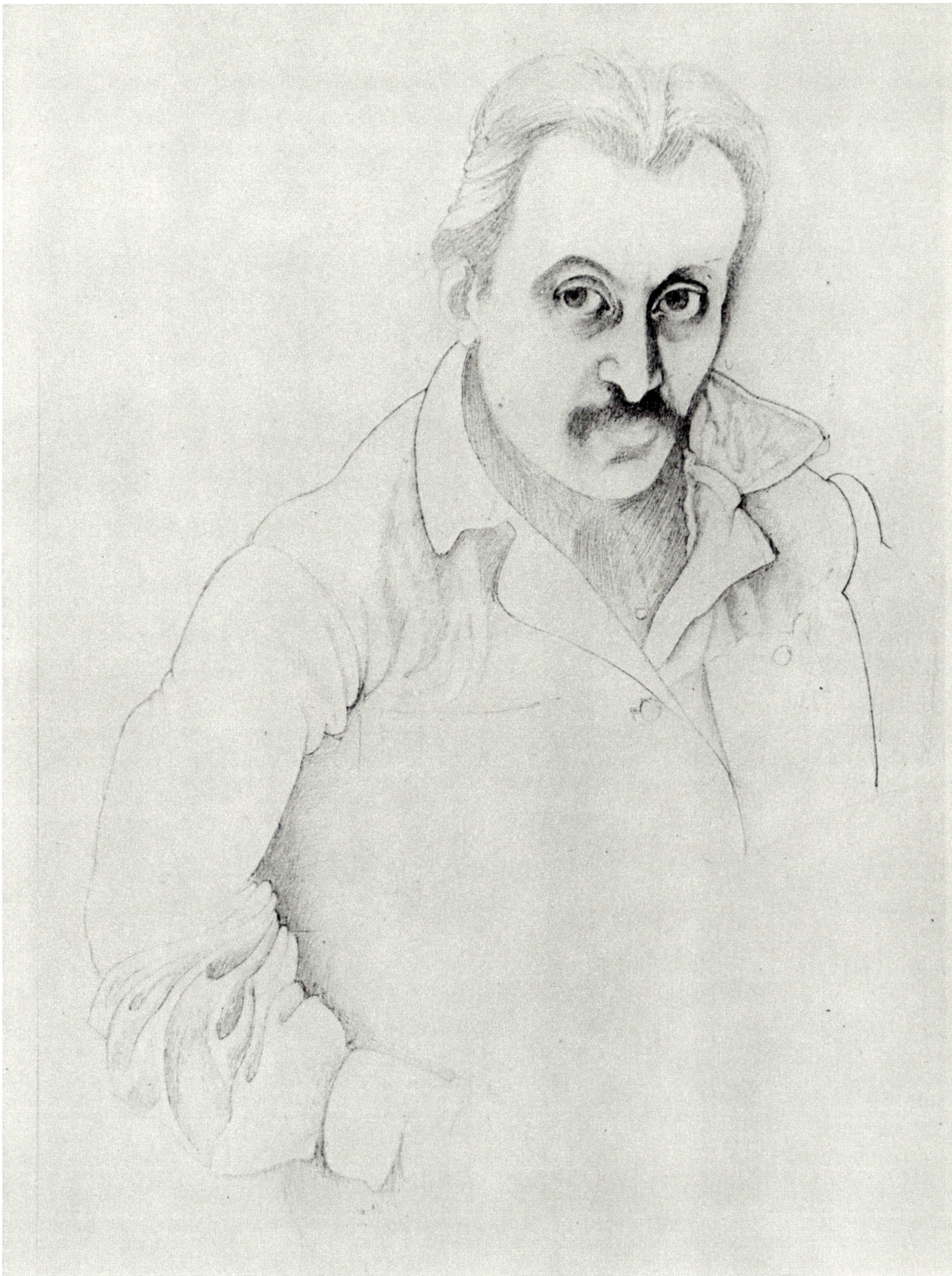

69. *Self-Portrait*. ca. 1936
Pencil on paper, 9 × 6 1/2″
Collection Ethel K. Schwabacher, New York

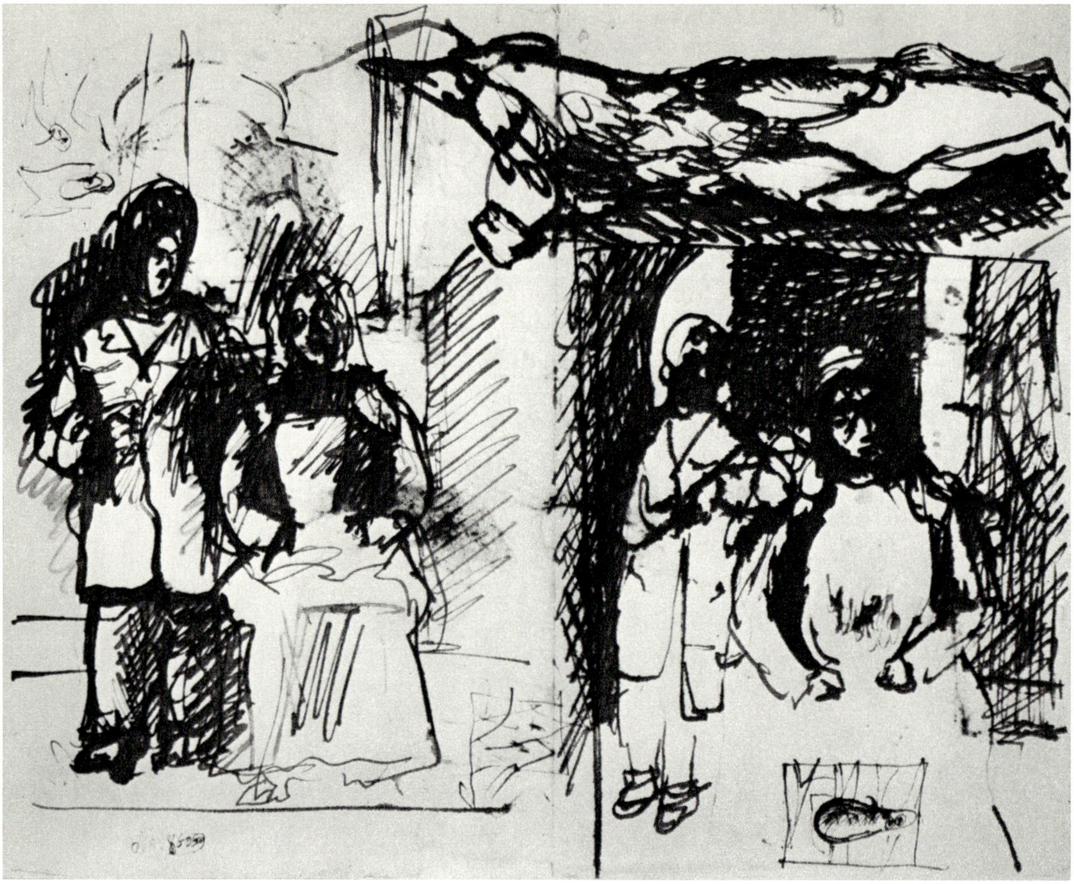

70. *The Artist and His Mother*. ca. 1936
Pen and ink on paper, 8 5/8 × 11″
Private Collection

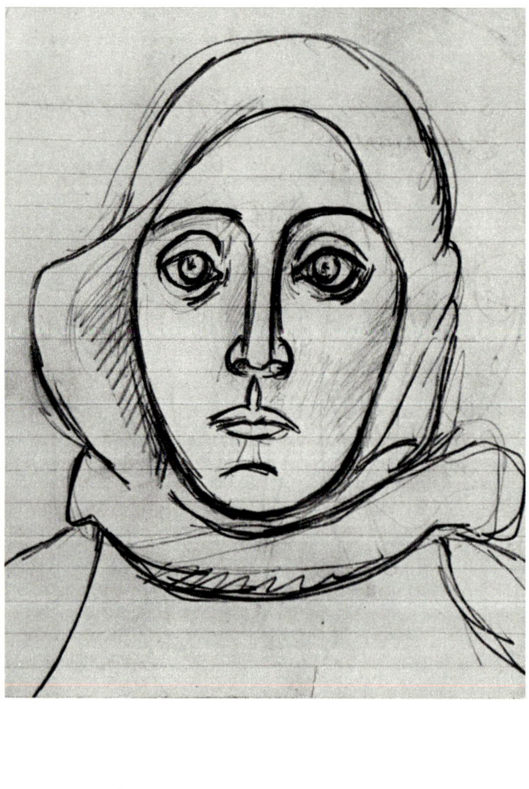

71. *Study for Mother and Son*. ca. 1936
Pencil on paper, 8 × 7″
Collection Mary Judith Kanner

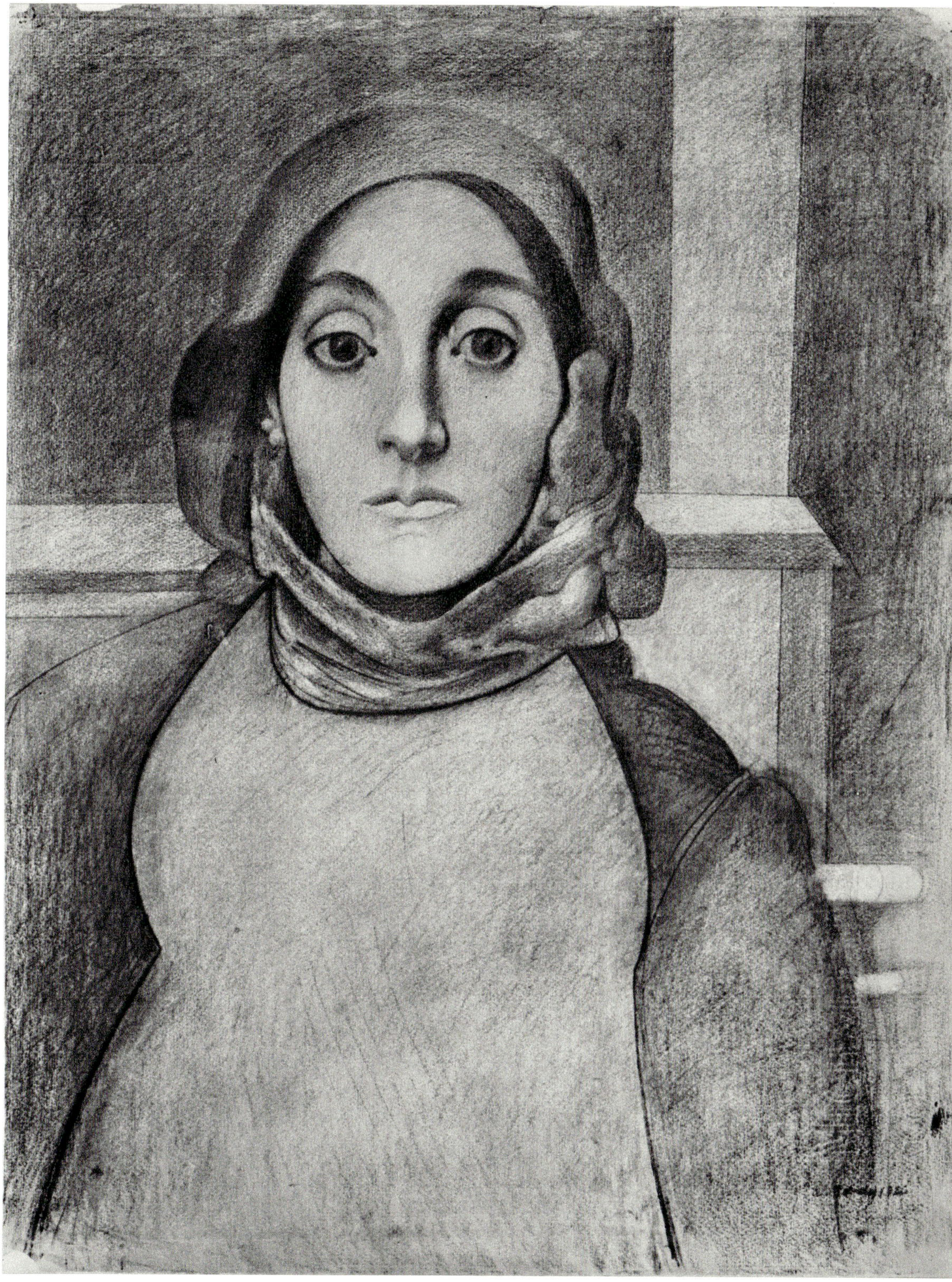

72. *The Artist's Mother*. 1938
Charcoal on paper, 24 × 18 1/2″
Courtesy of The Art Institute of Chicago: 1965. 510. The Worcester Sketch Collection

73. *Standing Figure*. ca. 1936
Pen and ink wash on paper, 11 × 8 1/2″
Private Collection

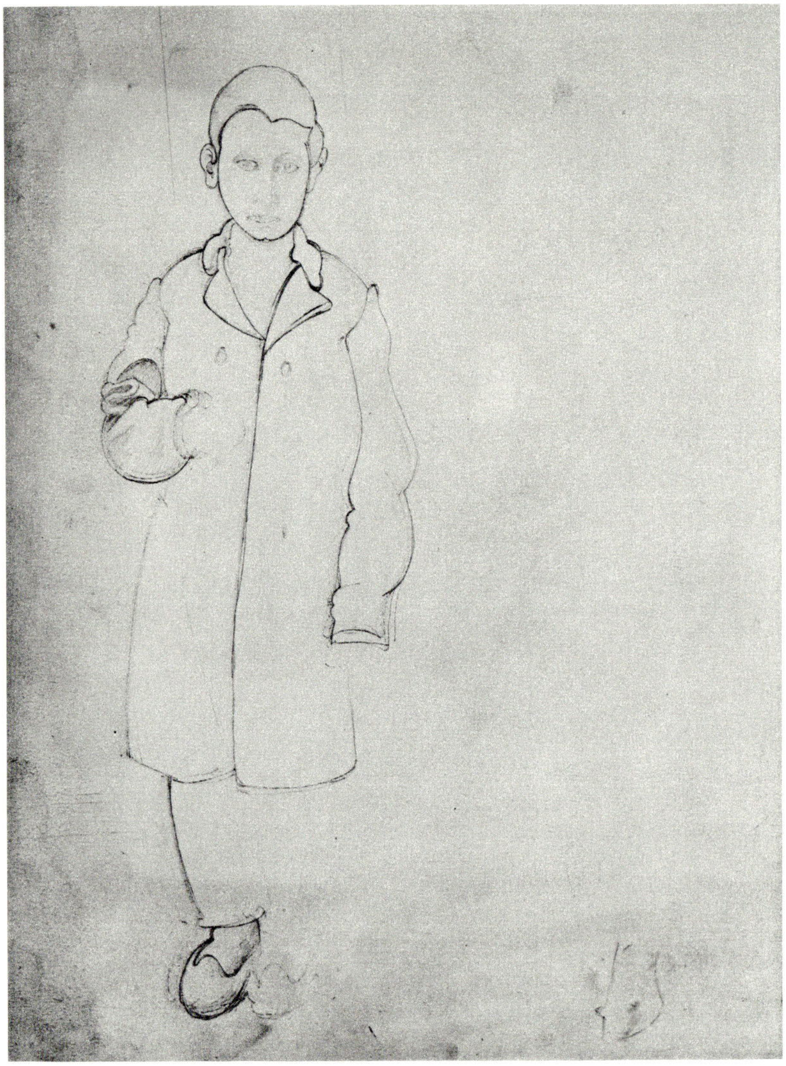

74. *Portrait of The Artist and His Mother*. ca. 1936
Pencil on paper, 29 × 19″
Collection National Gallery of Art, Washington, D.C., Ailsa Mellon Bruce Fund, 1979

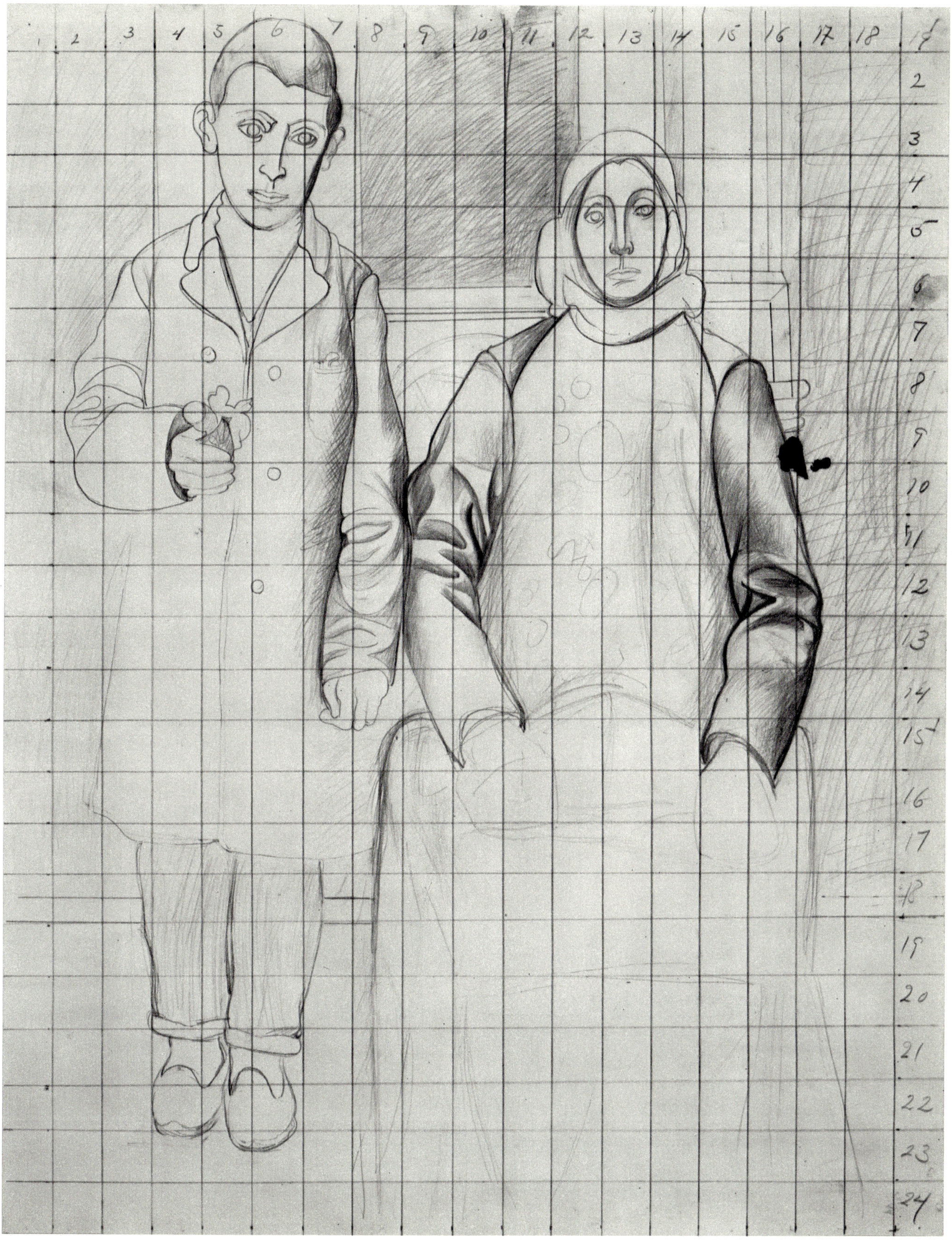

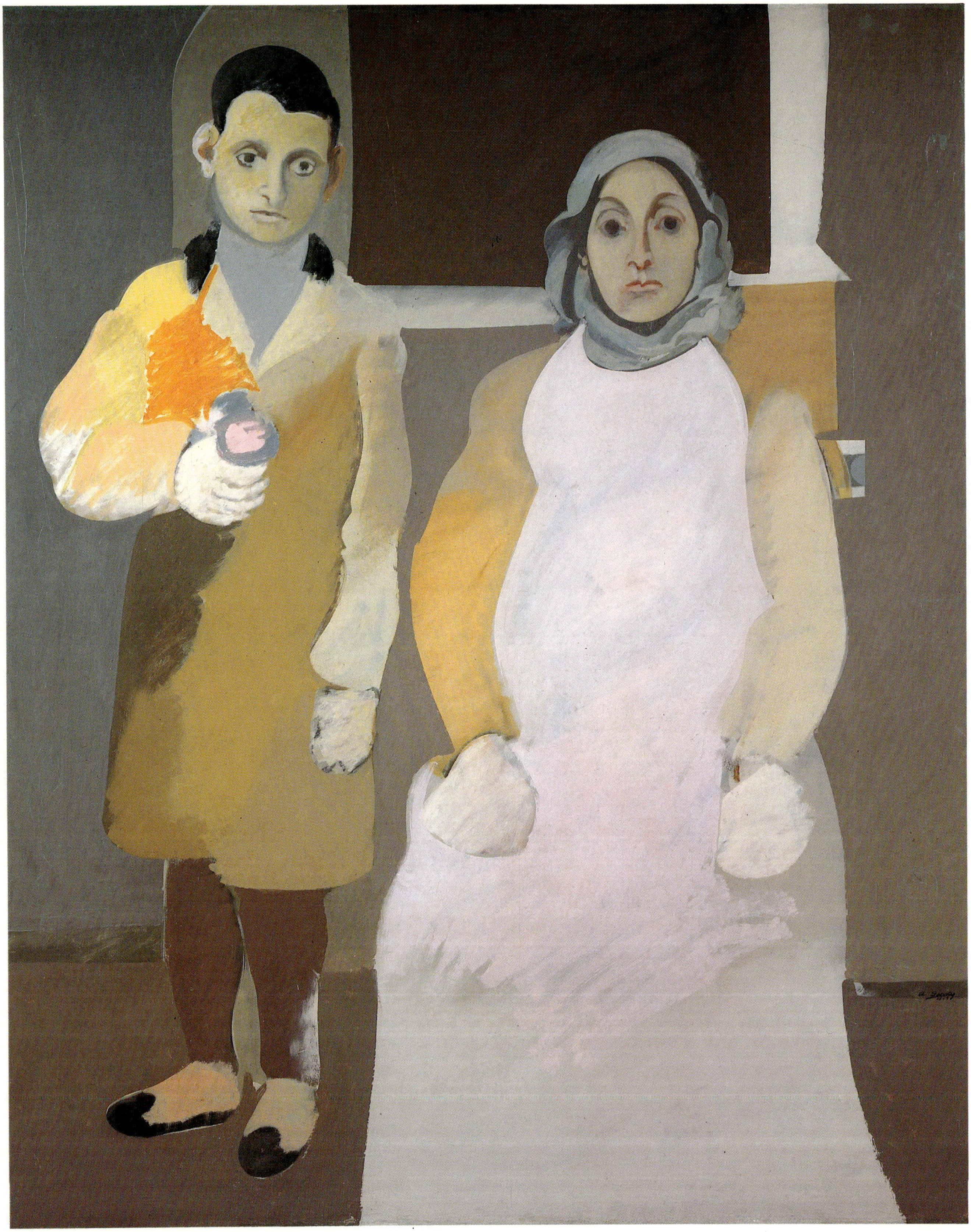

75. *The Artist and His Mother*. 1926–36
Oil on canvas, 60 × 50″
Collection of the Whitney Museum of American Art, New York.
Gift of Julien Levy for Maro and Natasha Gorky in memory of their father

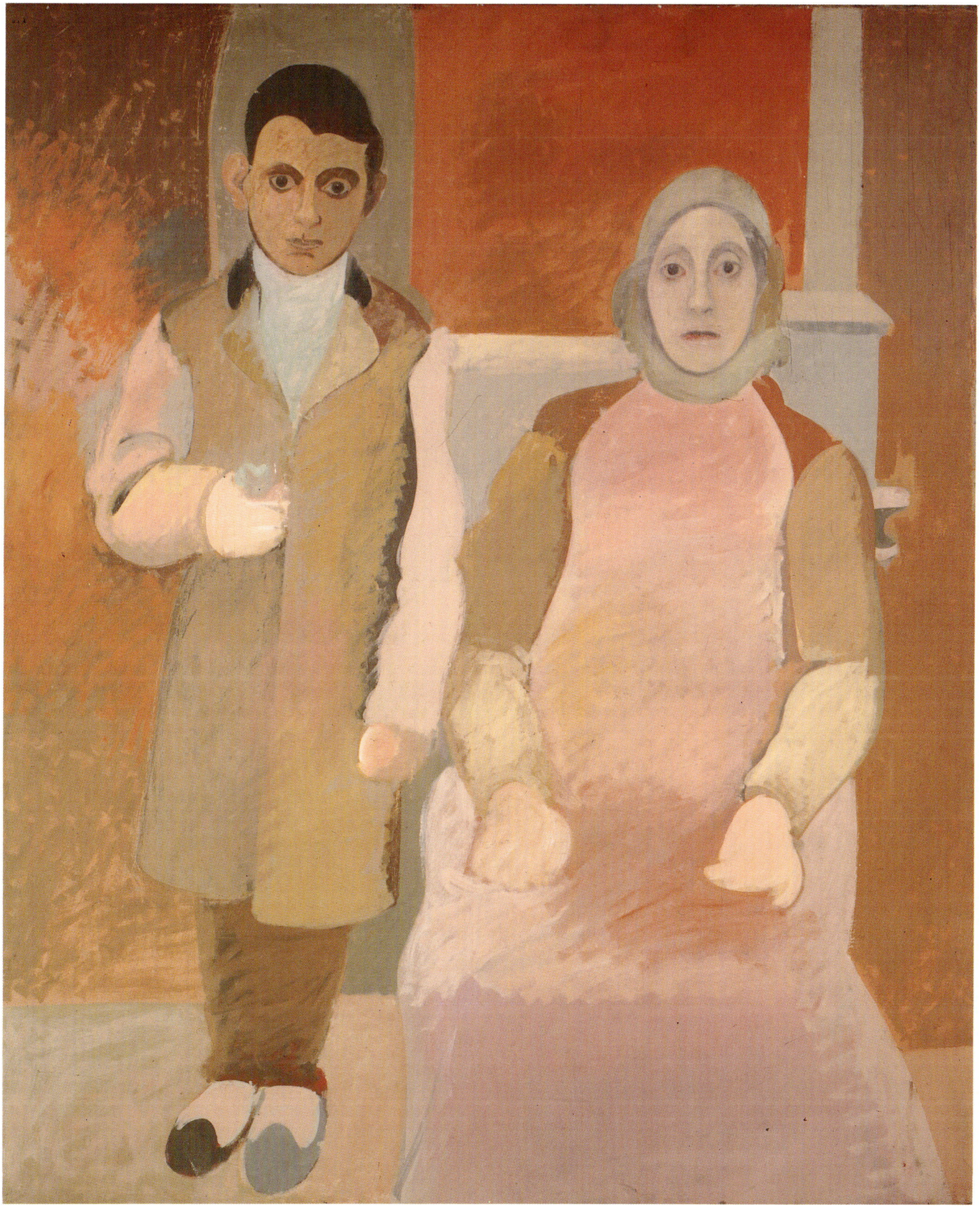

76. *The Artist and His Mother*. ca. 1929–42
Oil on canvas, 60 × 50″
Collection National Gallery of Art, Washington, D.C., Ailsa Mellon Bruce Fund

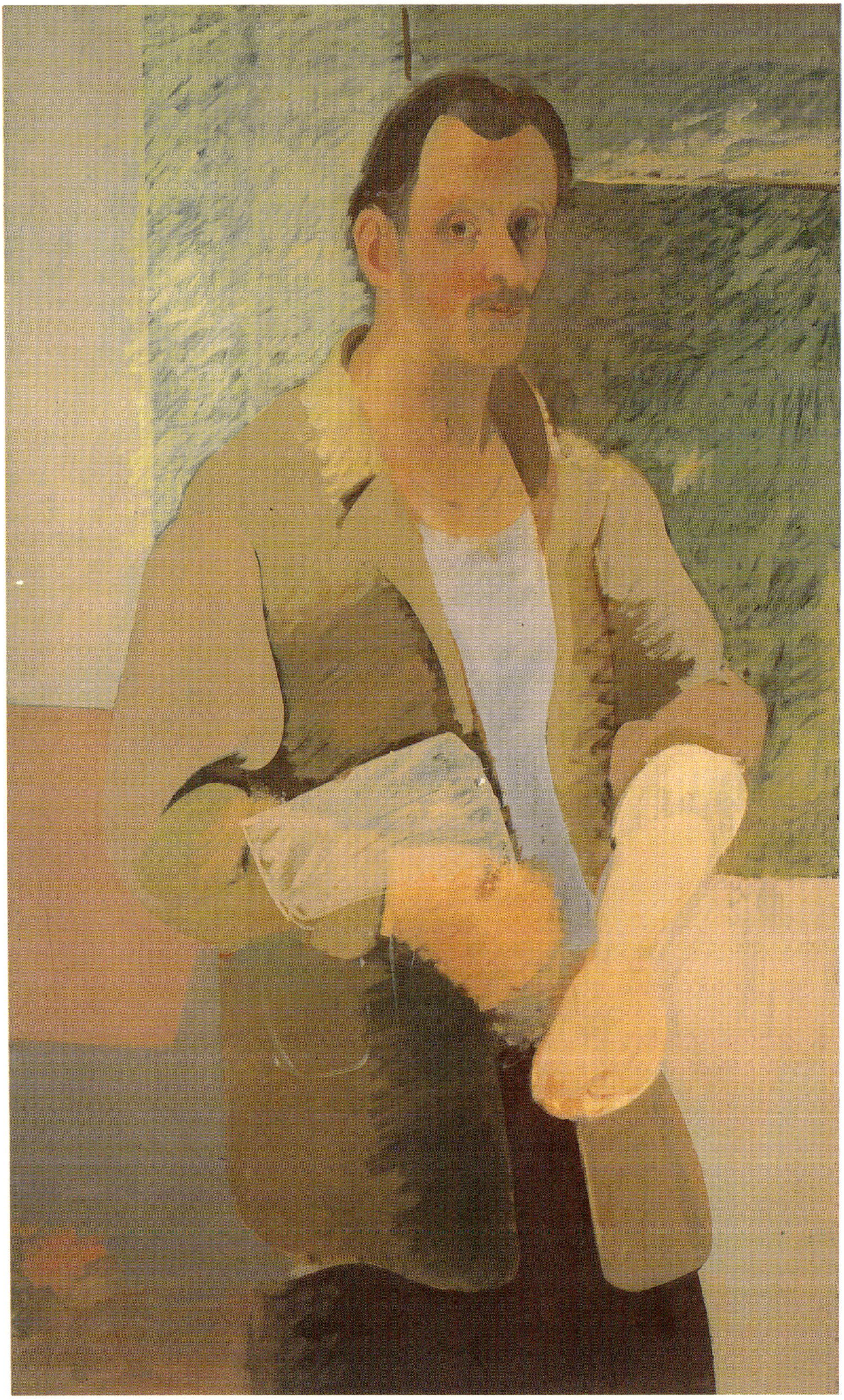

77. *Self-Portrait*. ca. 1937
Oil on canvas, 55 1/2 × 23 7/8″
Private Collection

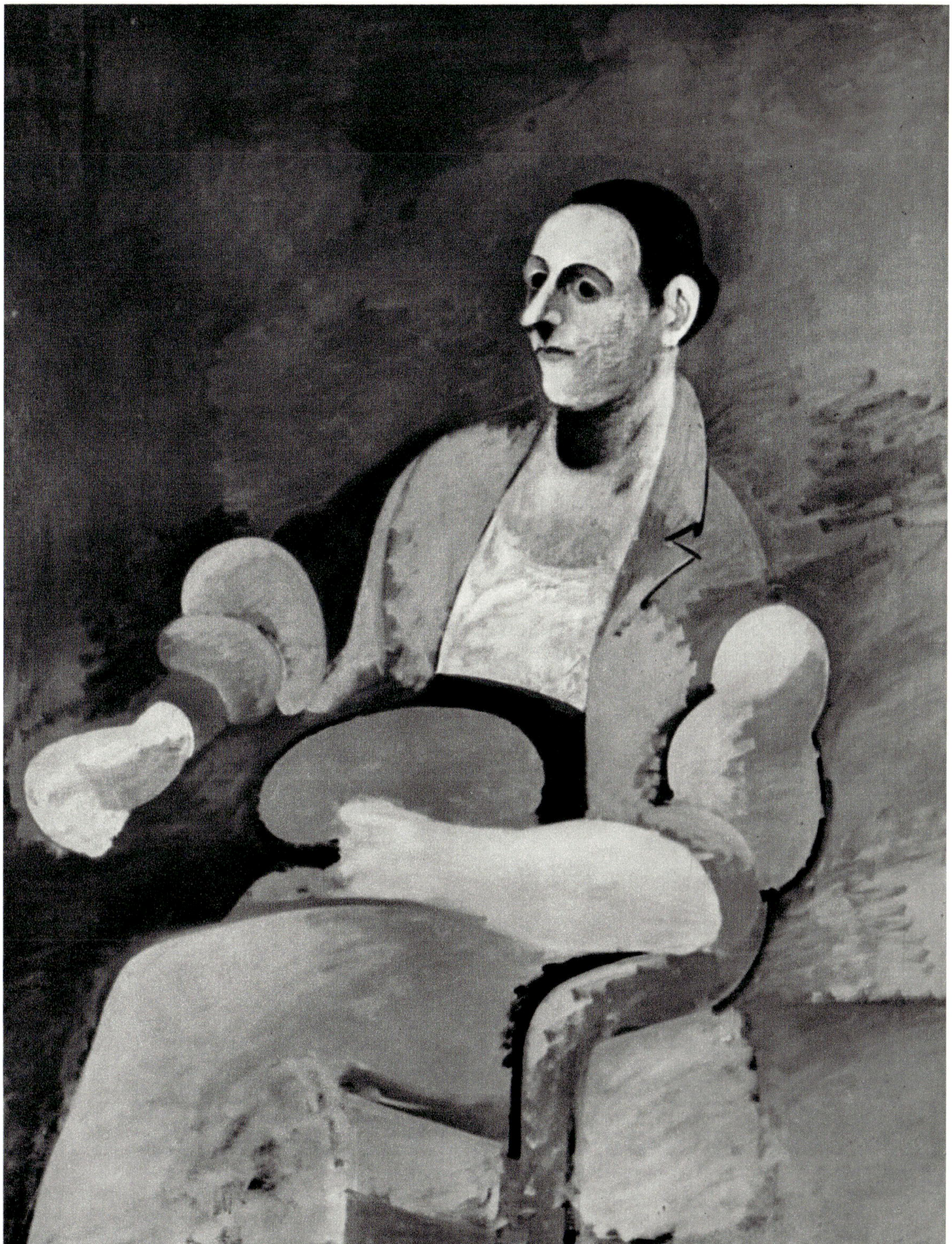

78. *Portrait of Master Bill*. 1929–39
Oil on canvas, 52 × 39 1/2″
Private Collection

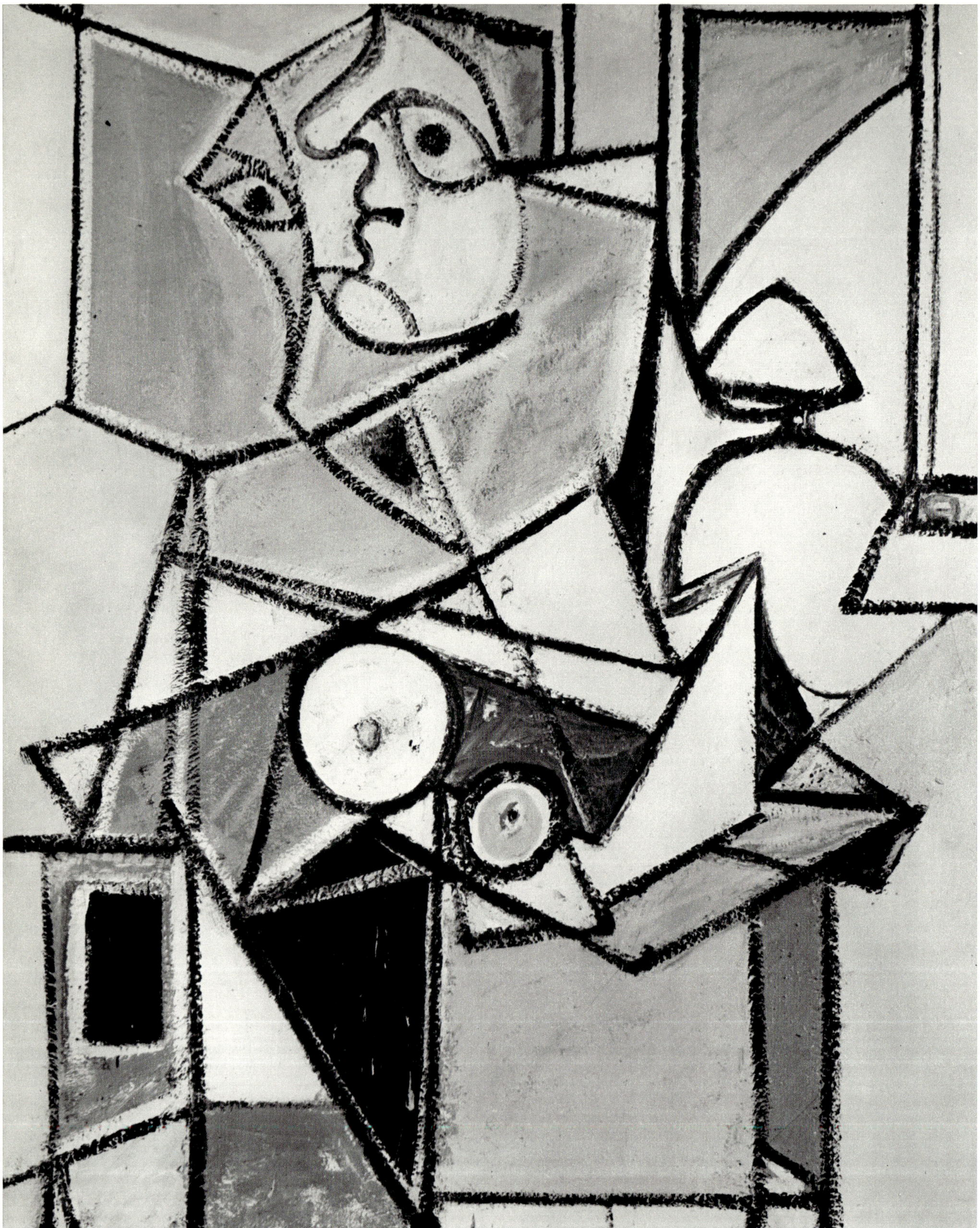

79. *Composition with Head.* ca. 1934–36
Oil on canvas, 78 × 62 1/4″
Private Collection

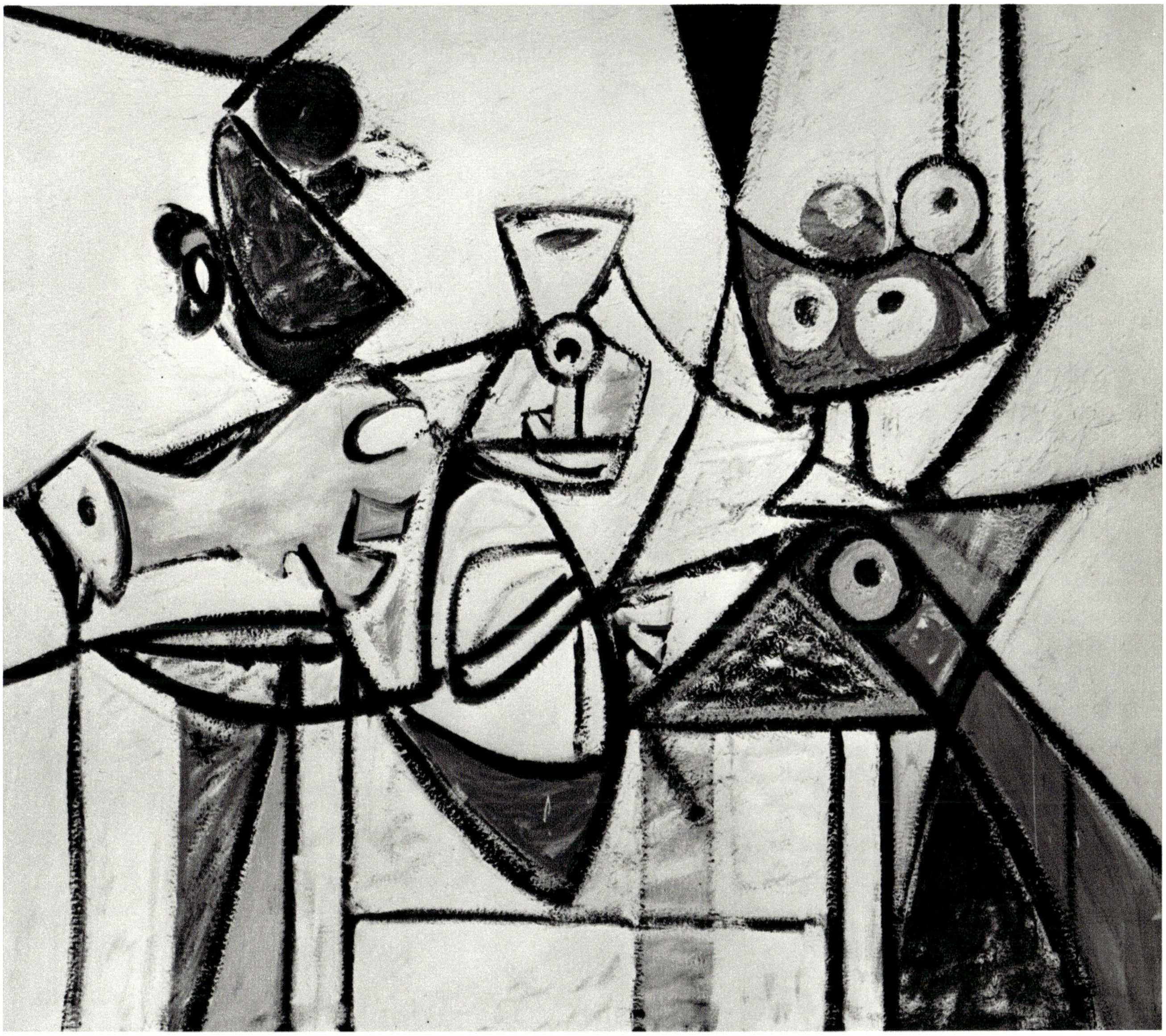

80. *Still Life on the Table.* ca. 1935
Oil on canvas, 54 × 64″
Private Collection

81. *Organization*. ca. 1936
Oil on canvas, 49 3/4 × 60″
Collection National Gallery of Art, Washington, D.C.,
Ailsa Mellon Bruce Fund

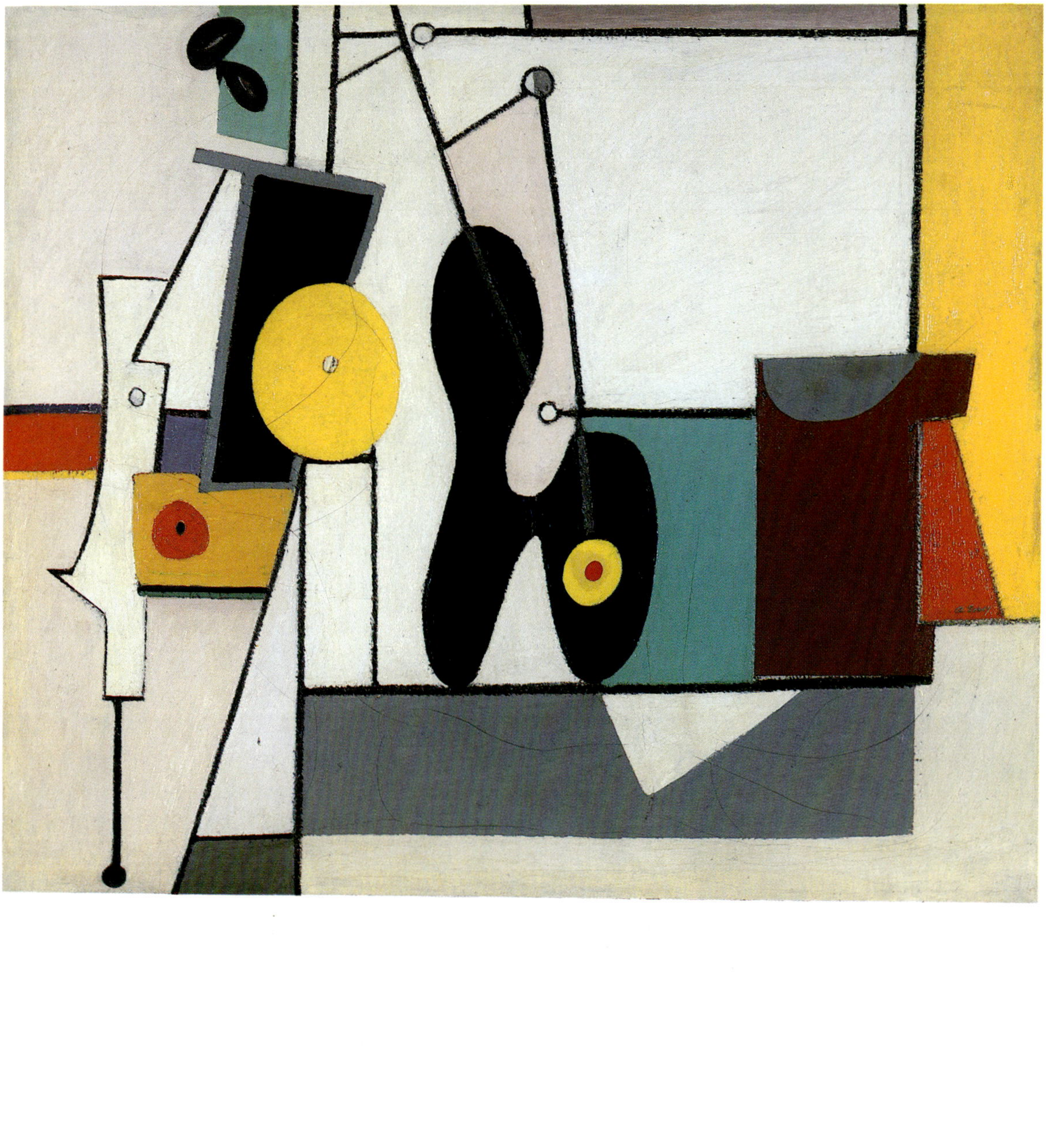

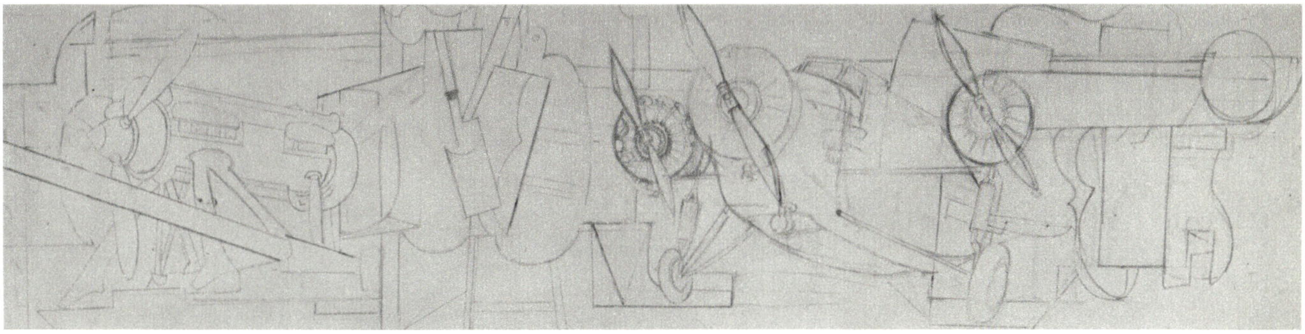

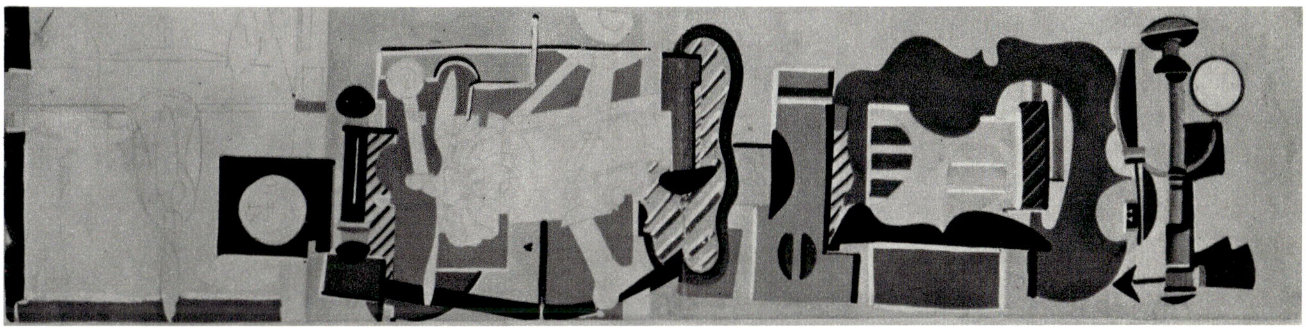

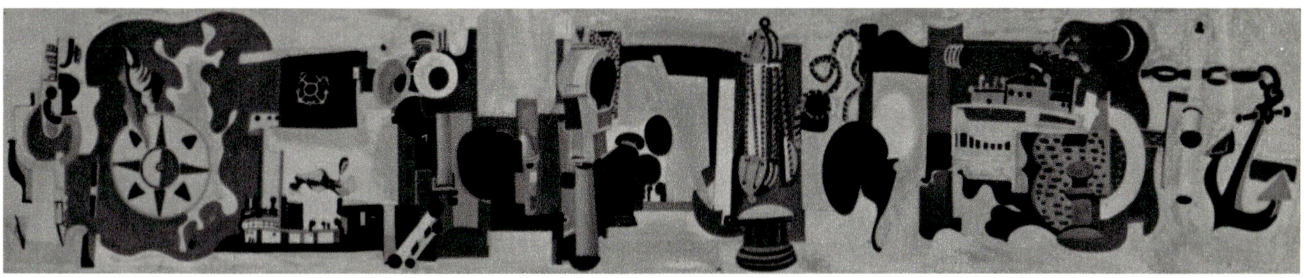

82. Study for Newark Airport Mural. 1935–36
Pencil and pen and ink on paper, 5 7/8 × 23″
Private Collection

83. Study Related to Newark Airport and
World's Fair Aviation Building Murals. 1935–36
Gouache and crayon on paper, 5 7/8 × 23 7/8″
Private Collection

84. Sketch for Mural for Marine Transportation Building
at New York World's Fair. 1938
Tempera on cardboard, 9 × 44 1/2″
Collection C. A. Muschenheim, Evanston, Illinois

85. *Untitled* (*Mural Study for Newark Airport*). ca. 1935–36
Oil on canvas, 30 × 35″
Collection Grey Art Gallery and Study Center,
New York University, Gift of Miss May E. Walter

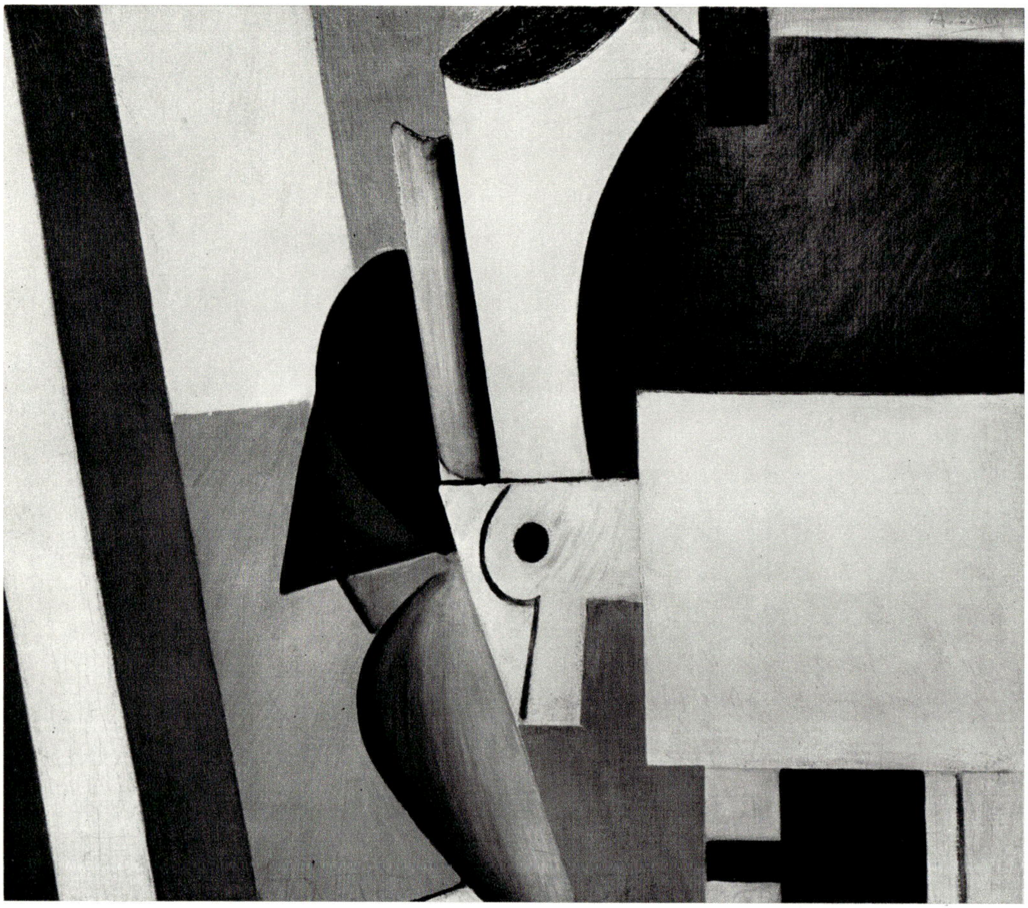

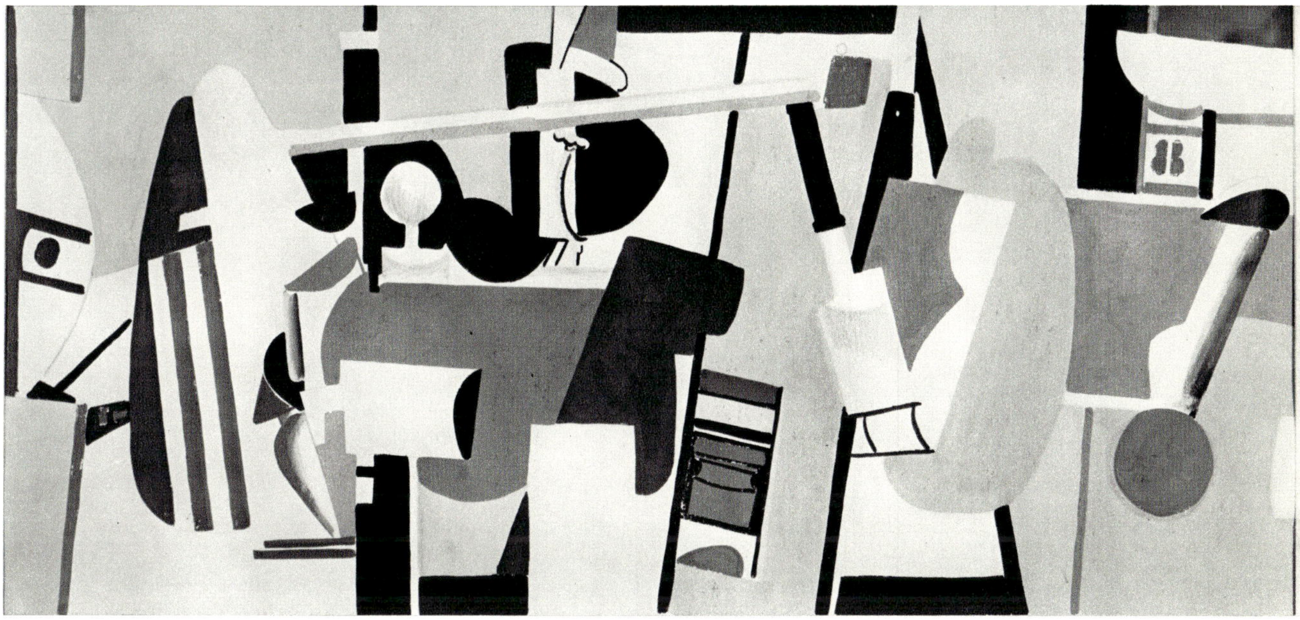

86. Study for a Mural for Administration Building,
Newark Airport, New Jersey. 1935–36
Gouache on paper, 13 5/8 × 29 7/8″
The Museum of Modern Art, New York; Extended loan
from the United States WPA Art Program

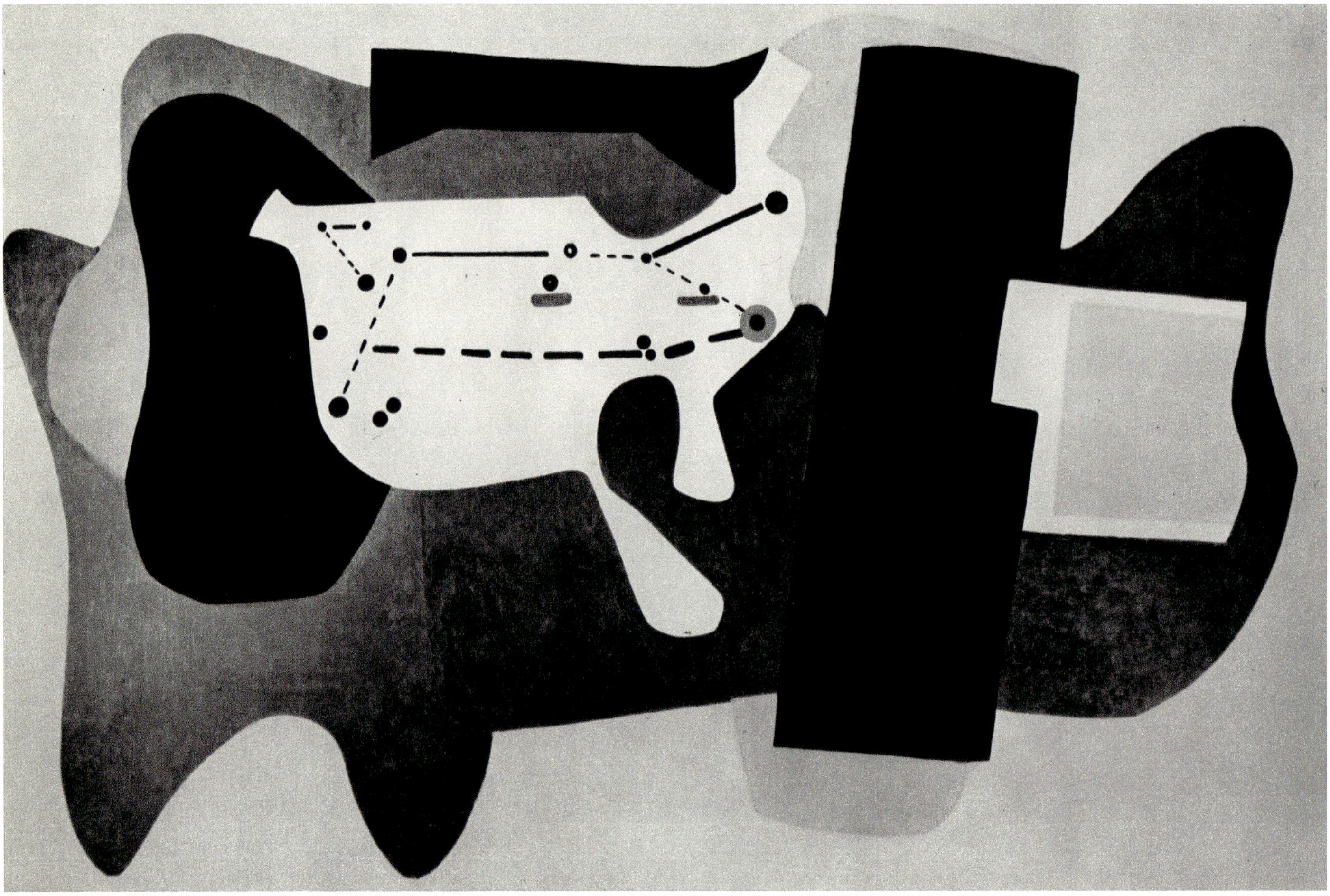

87. *Aerial Map*. 1936–37
Oil on canvas, 77 × 121″
Newark International Airport Art Collection, The Port
Authority of New York and New Jersey

88. *Mechanics of Flying*. 1936–37
Oil on canvas, 108 × 133″
Newark International Airport Art Collection, The Port Authority of New York and New Jersey

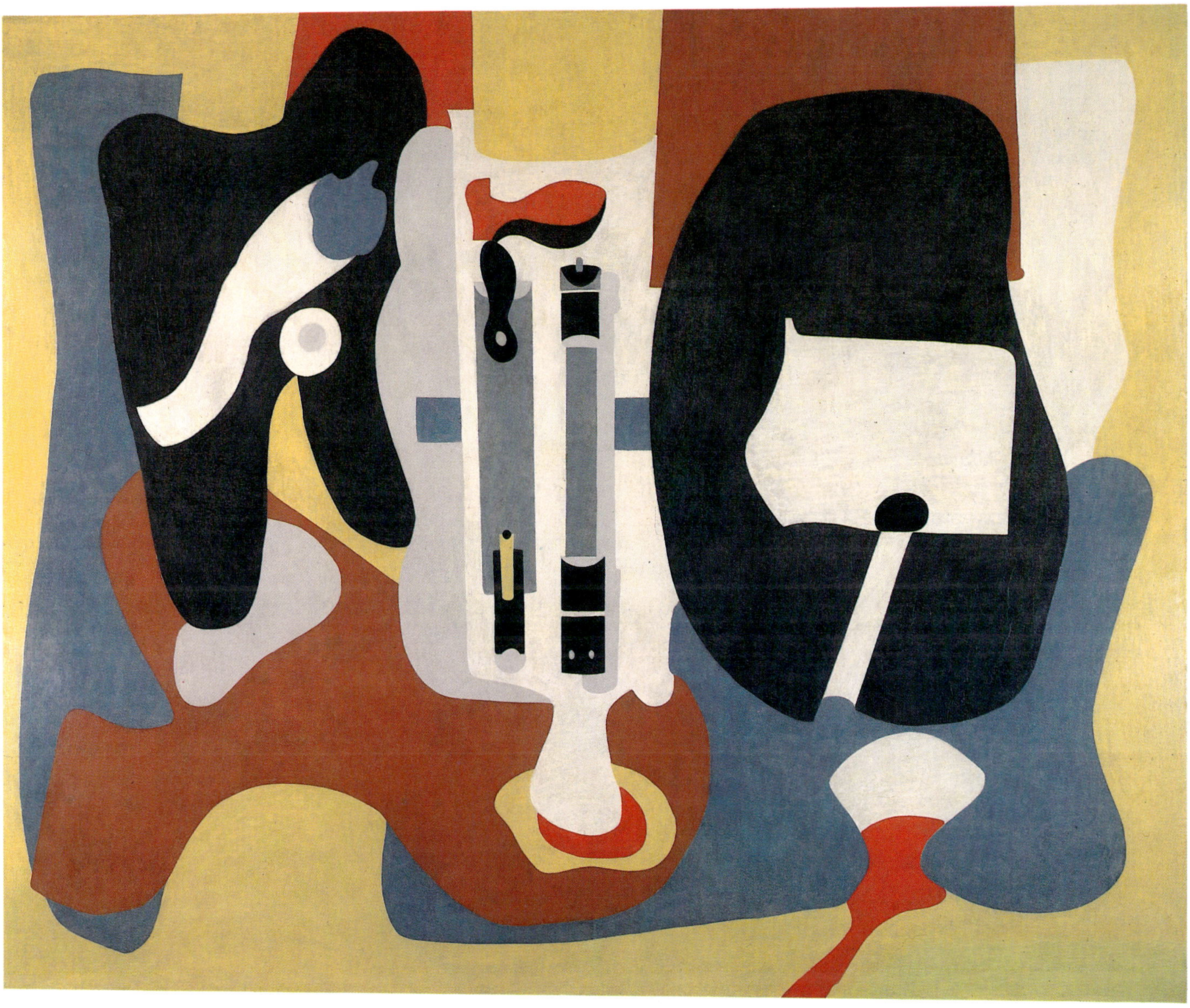

89. *Portrait*. 1936–38
Oil on canvas, 29 1/2 × 23 5/8″
Private Collection

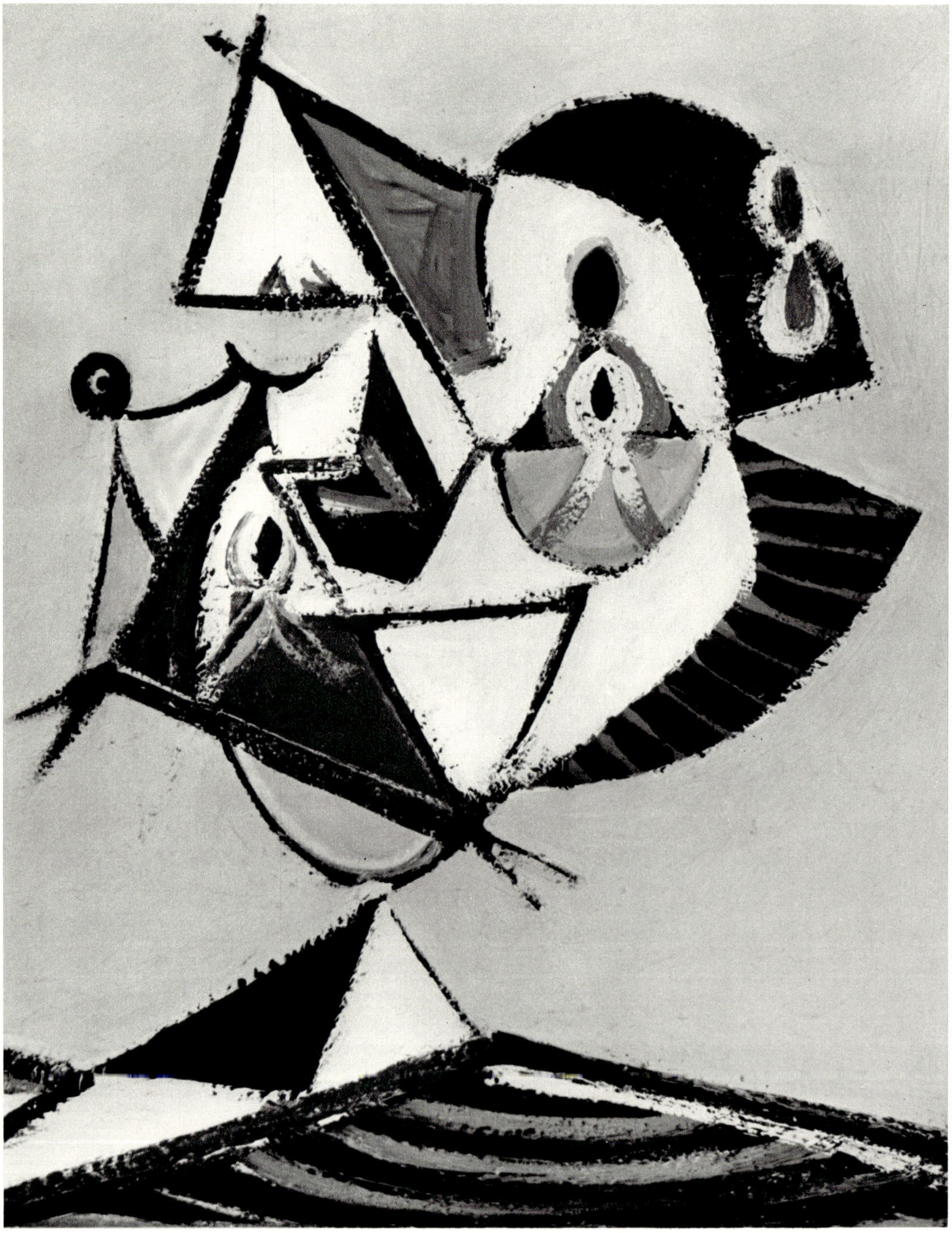

90. *Abstraction*. ca. 1936
Oil on canvas, 34 1/4 × 26 1/4″
Collection Ethel K. Schwabacher, New York

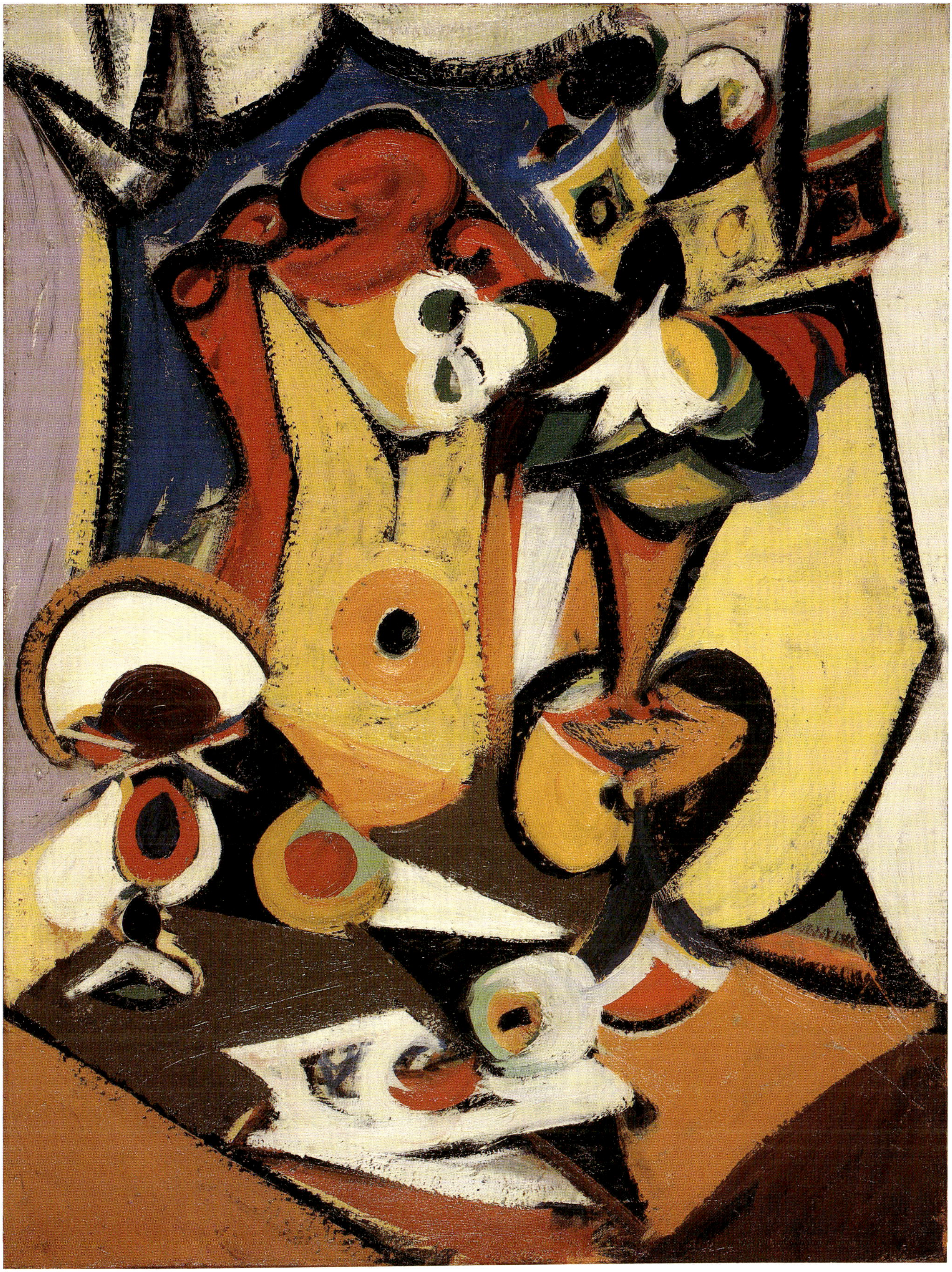

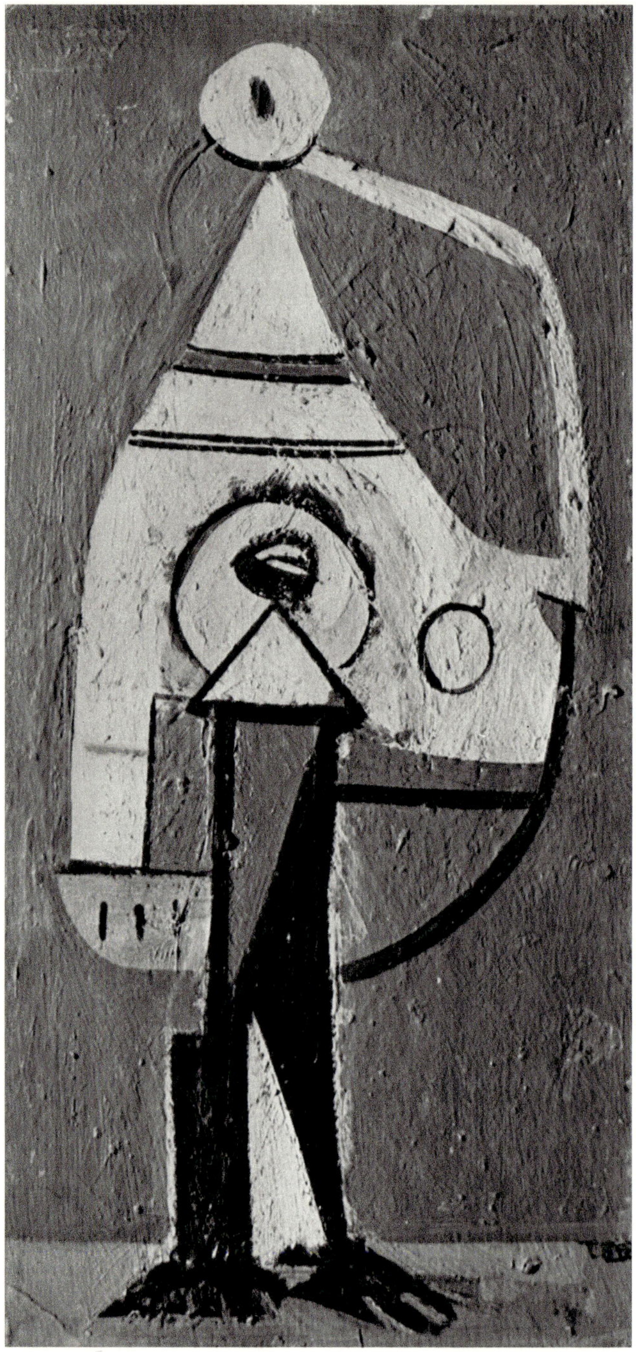

91. *Composition No. 5.* 1933
Oil on paperboard mounted on paperboard, 17 1/2 × 8 1/2″
Collection Hirshhorn Museum and Sculpture Garden,
Smithsonian Institution, Washington, D.C.

92. *Untitled.* 1936
Oil on canvas, 29 1/2 × 23 5/8″
Private Collection

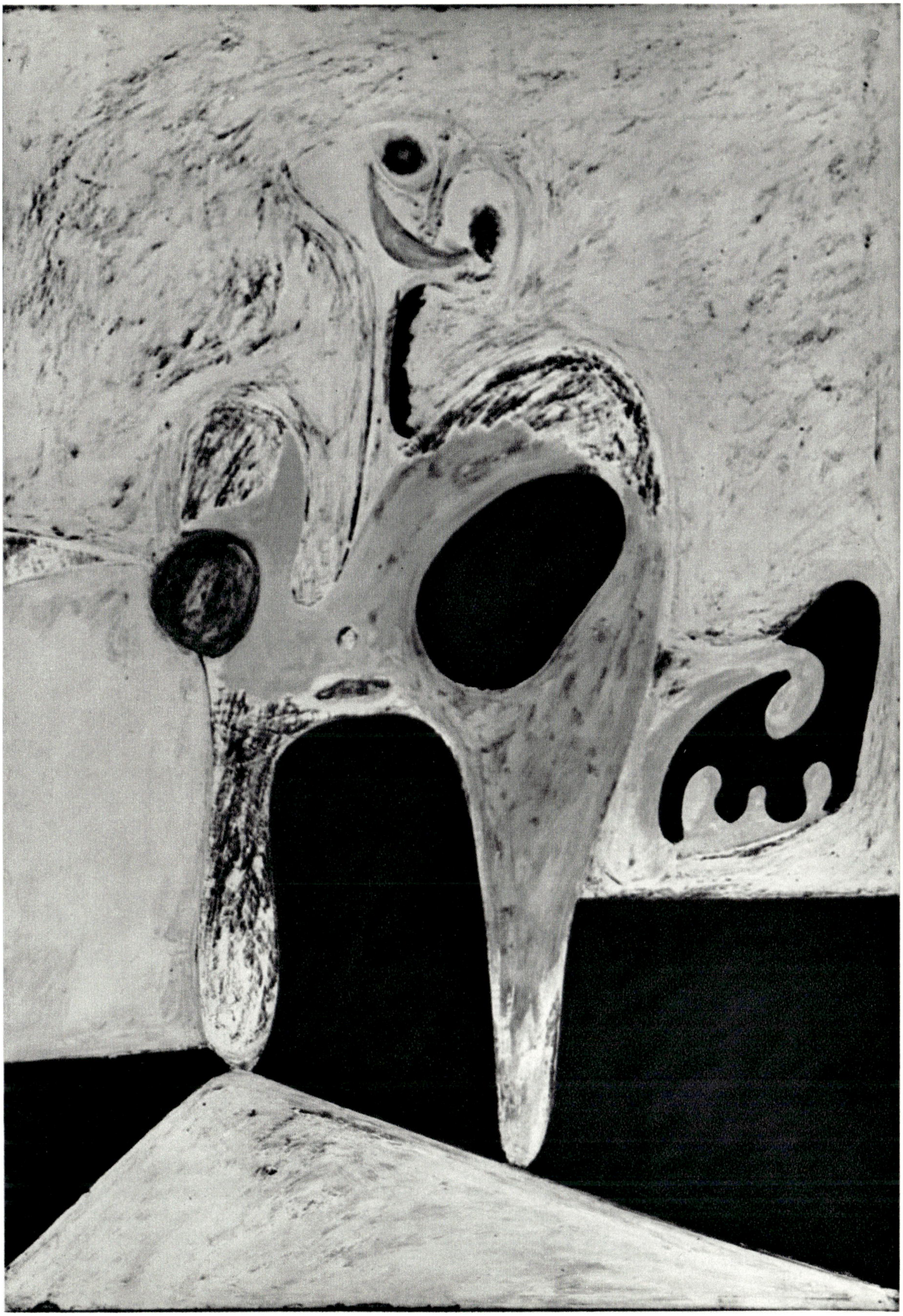

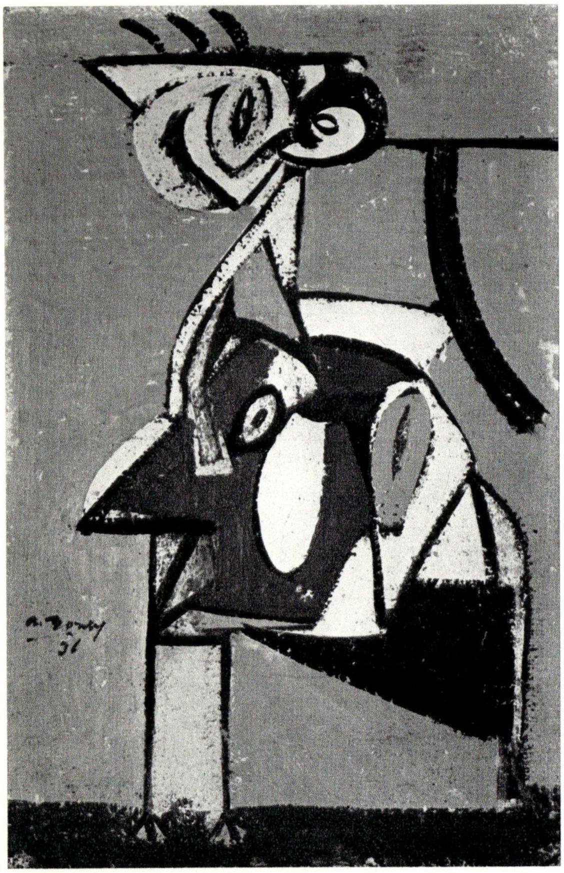

93. *Child of an Idumean Night.* 1936
Oil on burlap mounted on
paperboard, 12 × 8 1/8″
Collection Hirshhorn Museum and Sculpture Garden,
Smithsonian Institution, Washington, D.C.

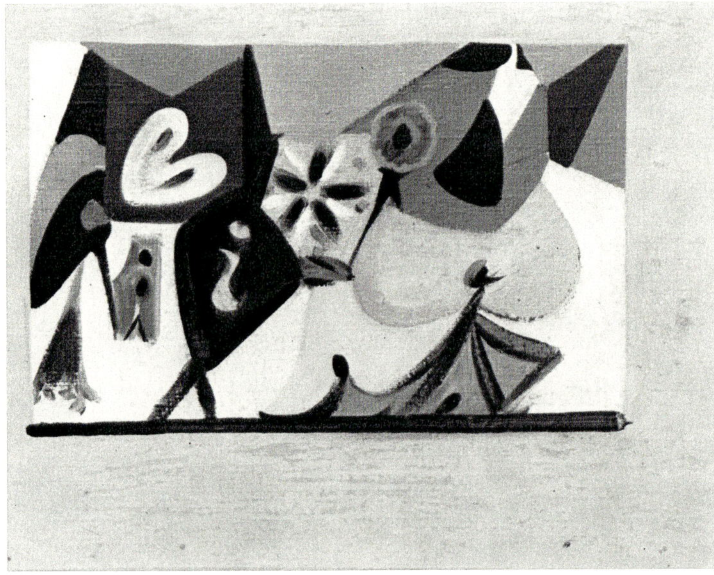

94. *Battle at Sunset with God of the Maize.* mid-1930s
Oil on canvas, 7 1/2 × 9 1/2″
Collection Ethel K. Schwabacher, New York

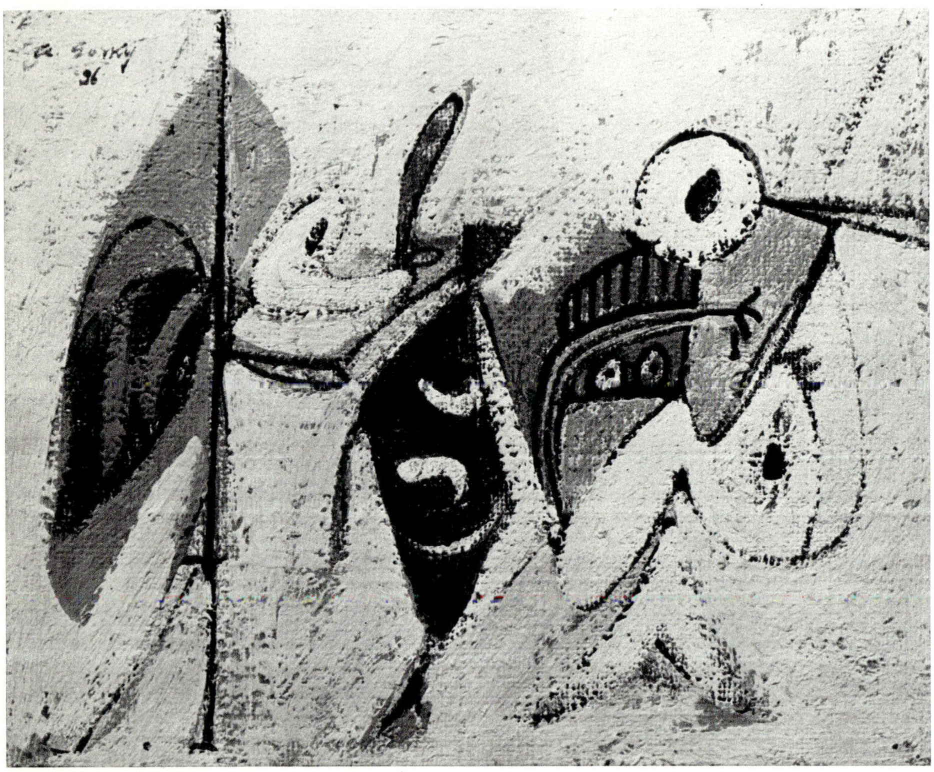

95. *Battle at Sunset with God of the Maize.* 1936
Oil on canvas mounted on
wood, 8 × 10 1/4″
Collection Hirshhorn Museum
and Sculpture Garden, Smithsonian
Institution, Washington, D.C.

96. *Untitled.* mid–1930s
Pen and ink on paper, 5 × 6″
Courtesy Allan Stone Gallery, New York

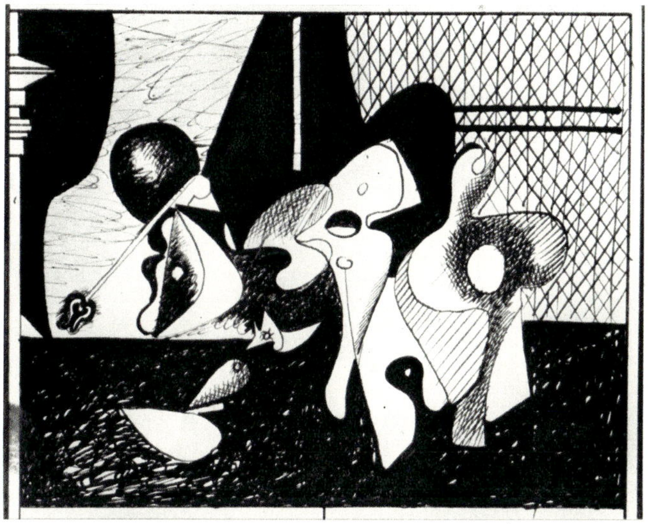

97. *Abstract Composition.* ca. 1931
Pen and ink on paper, 8 3/8 × 11 3/4″
Collection Mr. and Mrs. Jacob Kainen, Washington, D.C.

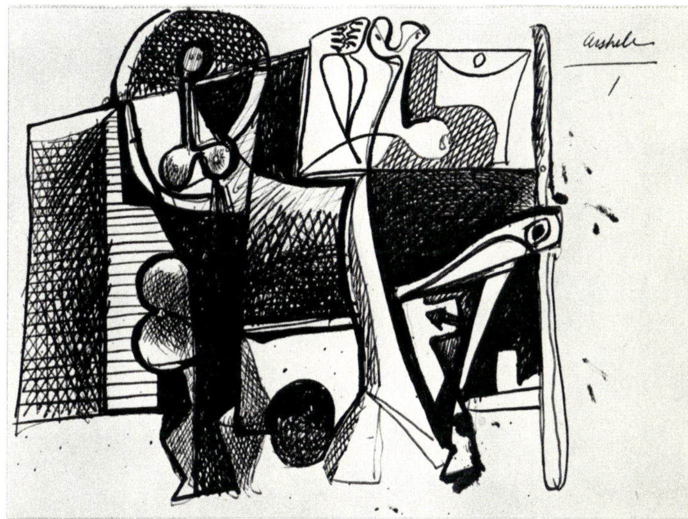

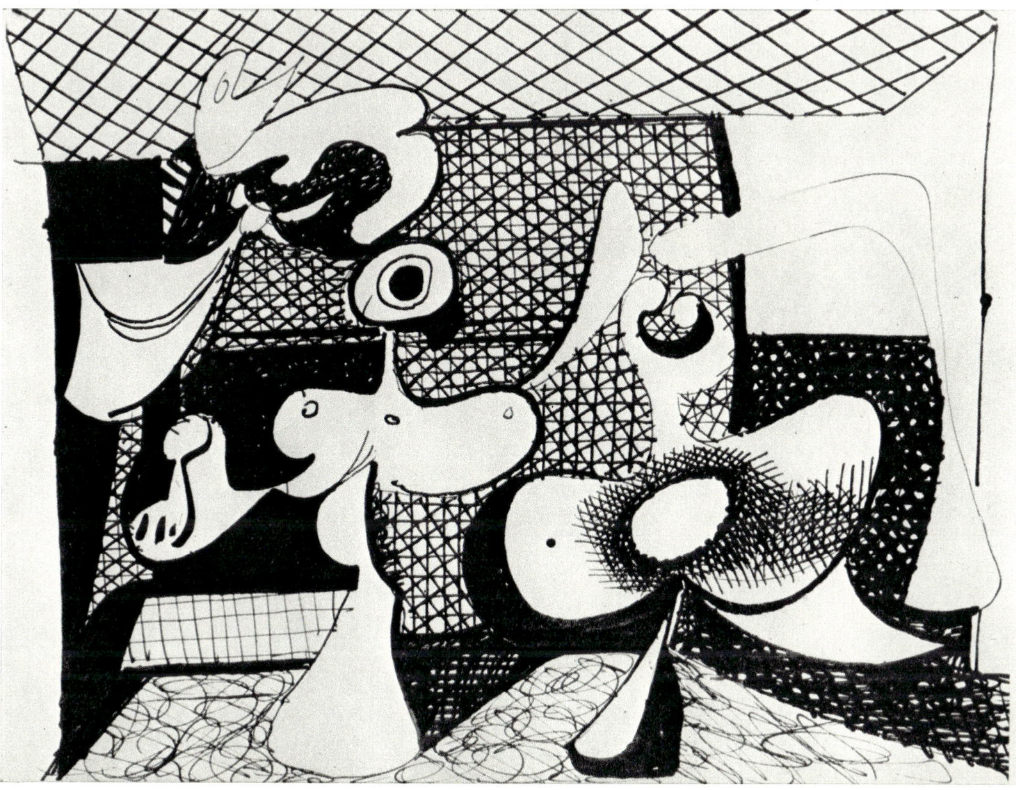

98. *Untitled.* mid-1930s
Pen and ink on paper, 9 × 12″
Courtesy Allan Stone Gallery, New York

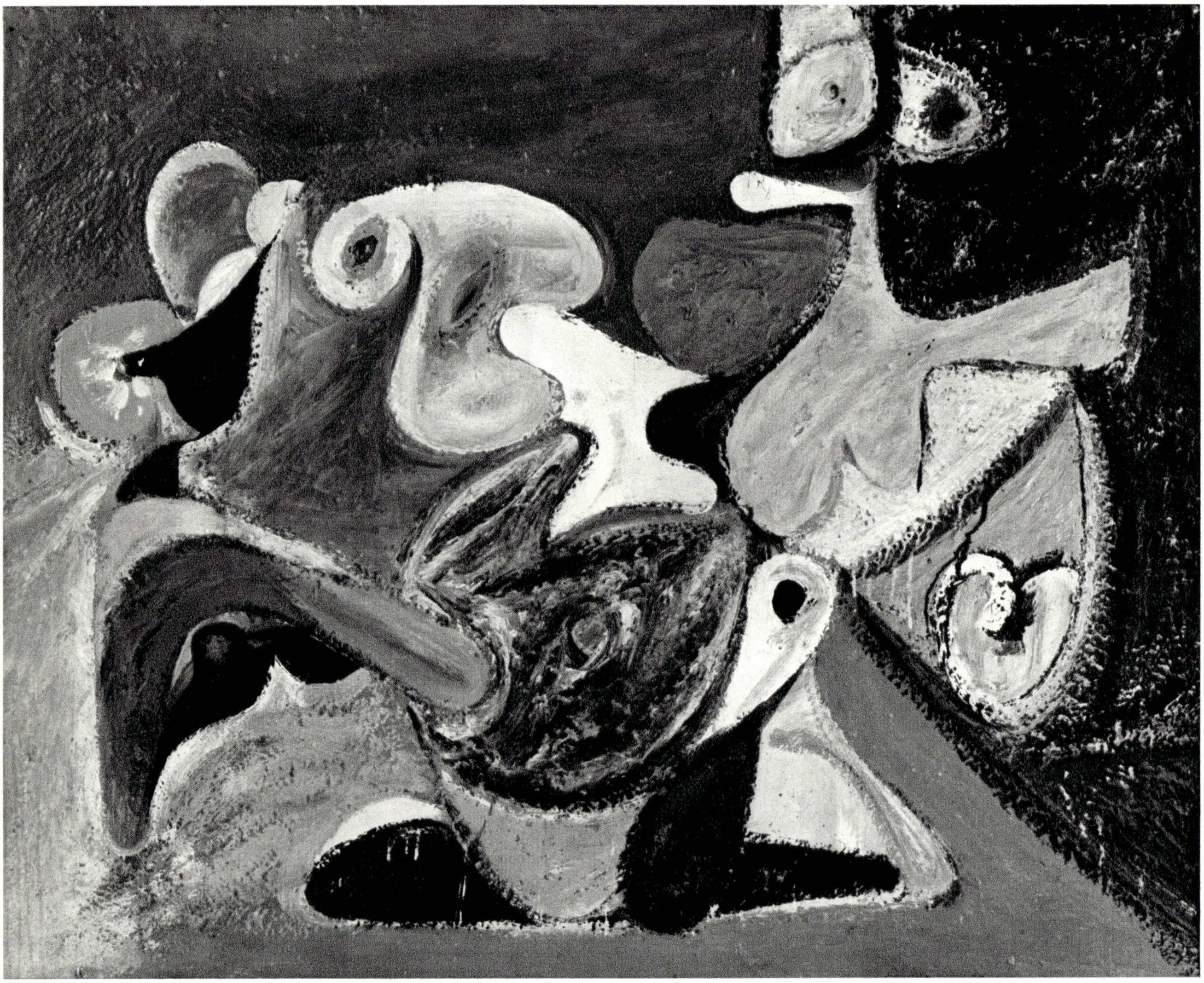

99. *Image in Xhorkom.* 1934–36
Oil on canvas, 33 × 43 1/8″
Private Collection

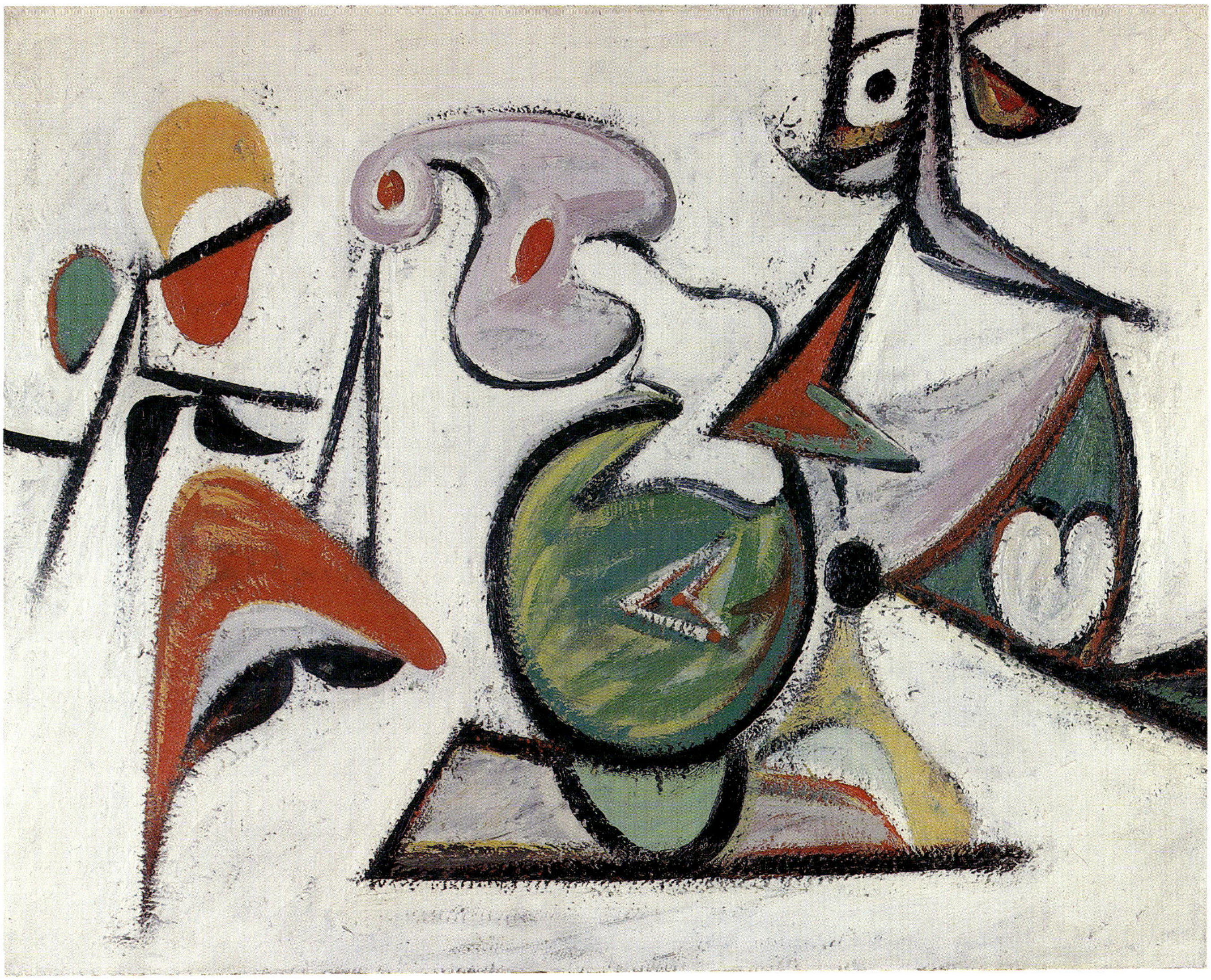

100. *Xhorkom*. 1936
Oil on canvas, 40 × 52″
Private Collection

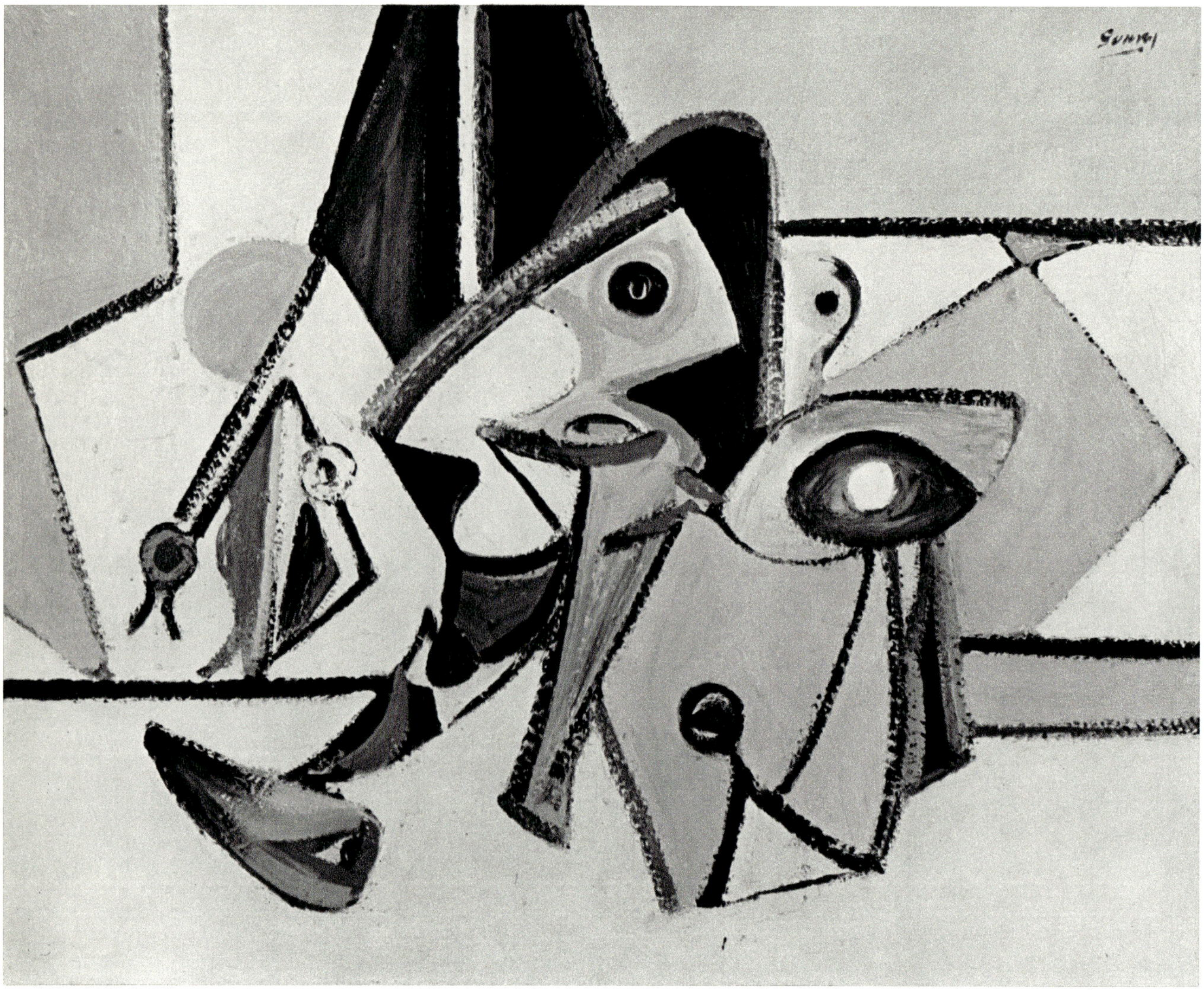

101. *Organization II.* 1936–37
Oil on canvas, 28 × 38″
Private Collection

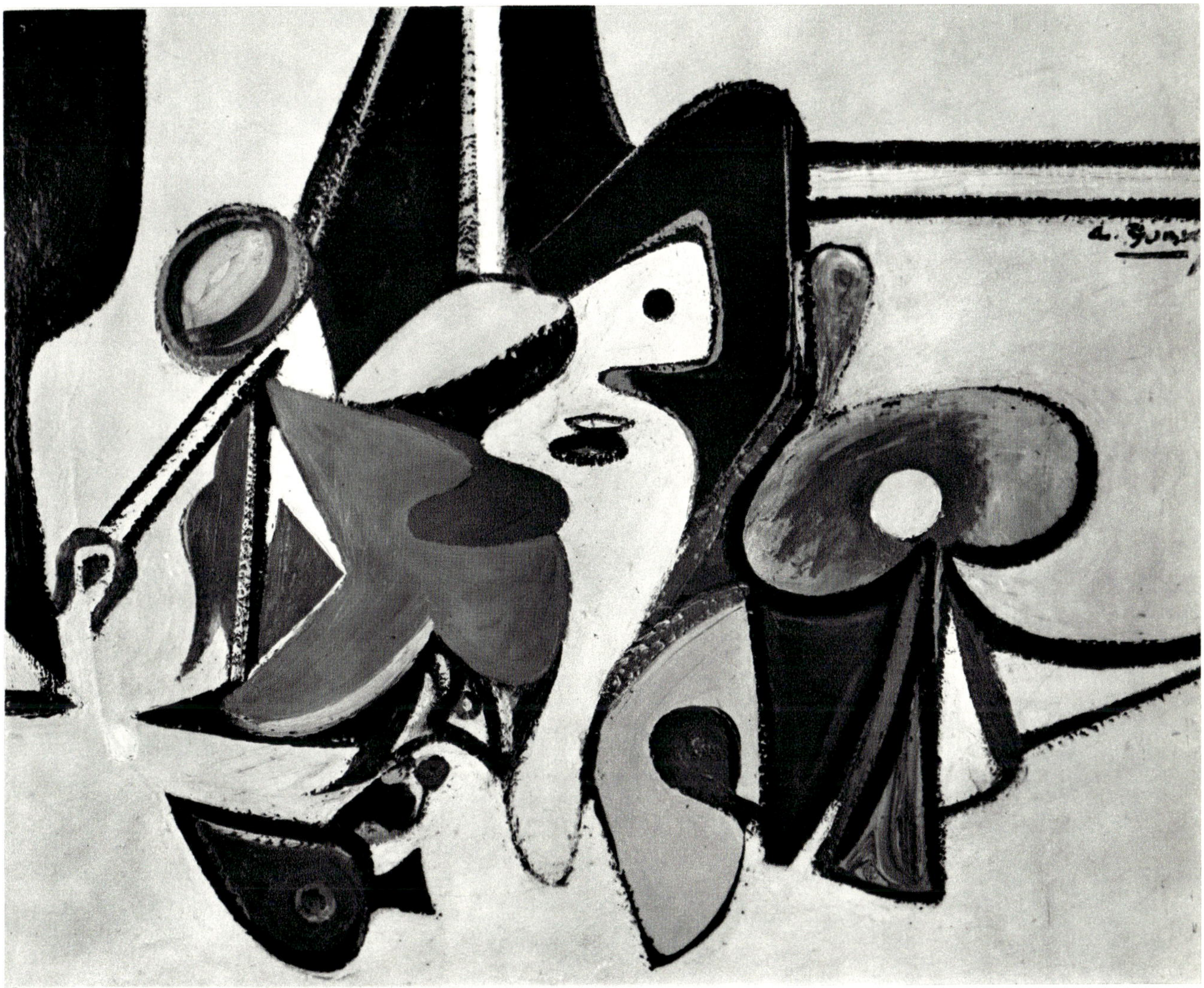

102. *Painting*. 1936–37
Oil on canvas, 38 × 48″
Collection of the Whitney Museum of American Art, New York

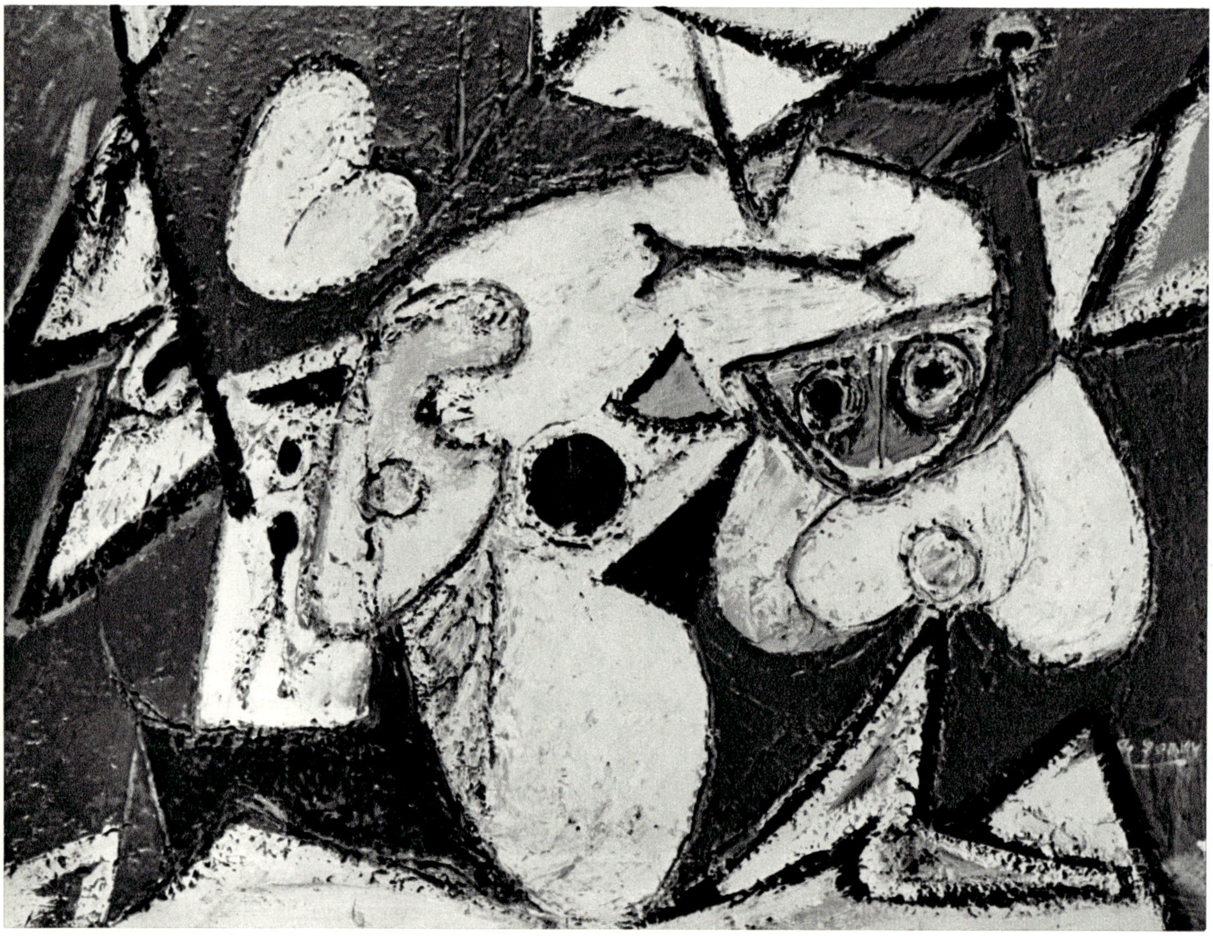

103. *Grey Painting*. 1937
Oil on canvas, 29 1/8 × 40 1/8″
Private Collection

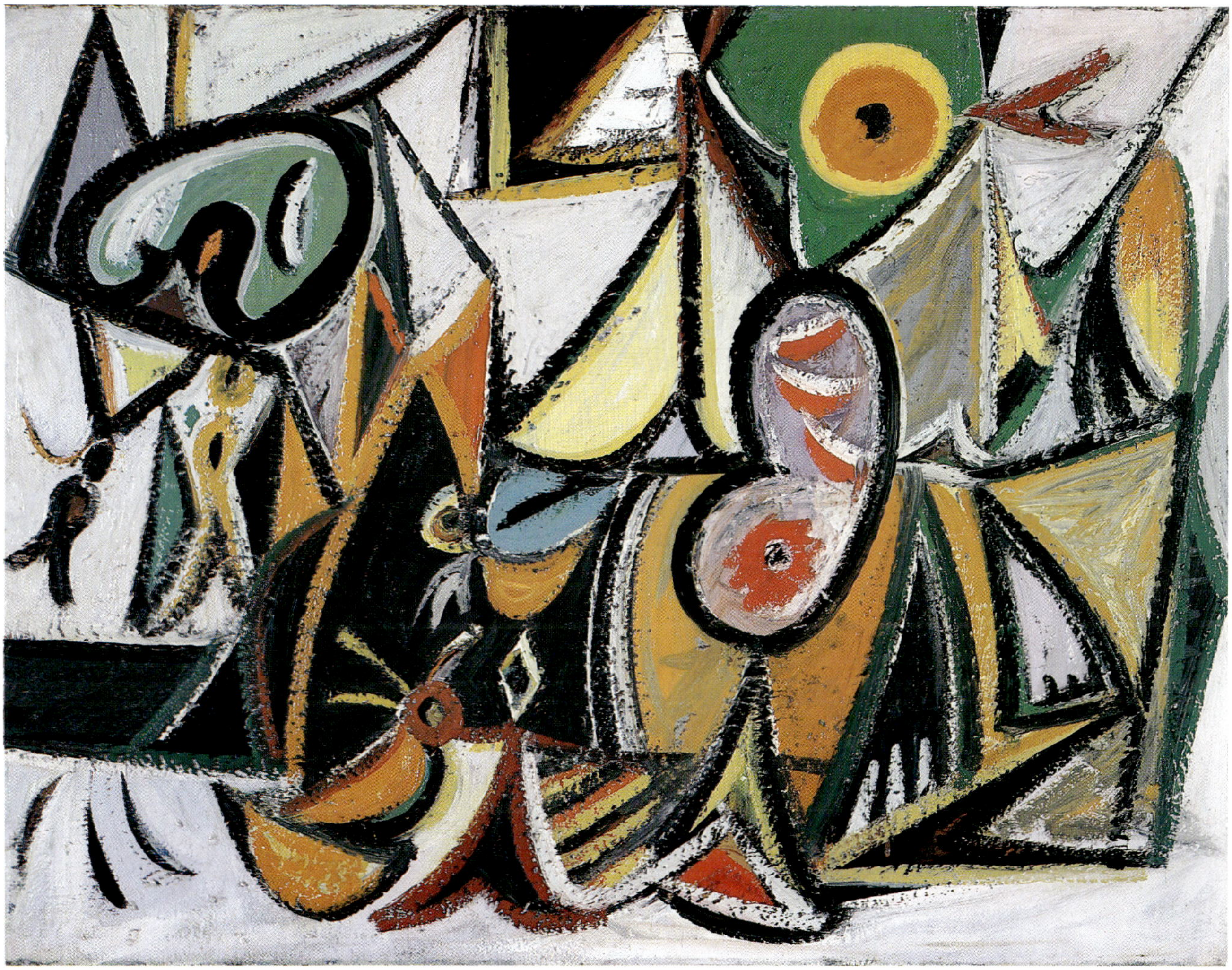

104. *Enigmatic Combat*. ca. 1936–37
Oil on canvas, 35 3/4 × 48″
San Francisco Museum of Modern Art, Gift of Jeanne Reynal

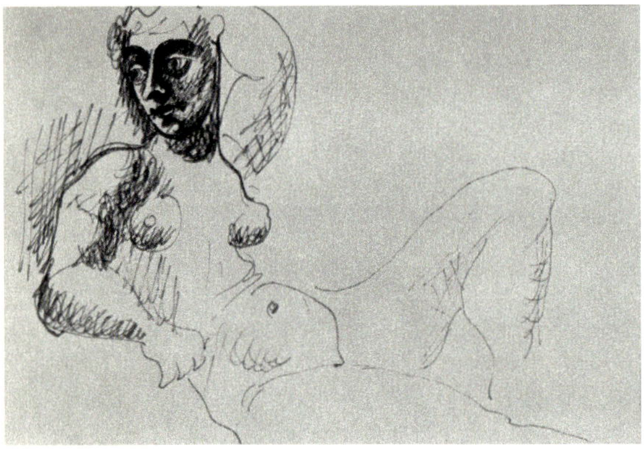

105. *Reclining Nude*. late 1930s
Pen and ink on paper, 4 3/4 × 6 3/4″
Collection Mrs. Walter L. Portnoff, New York;
Courtesy M. Knoedler & Co., Inc.

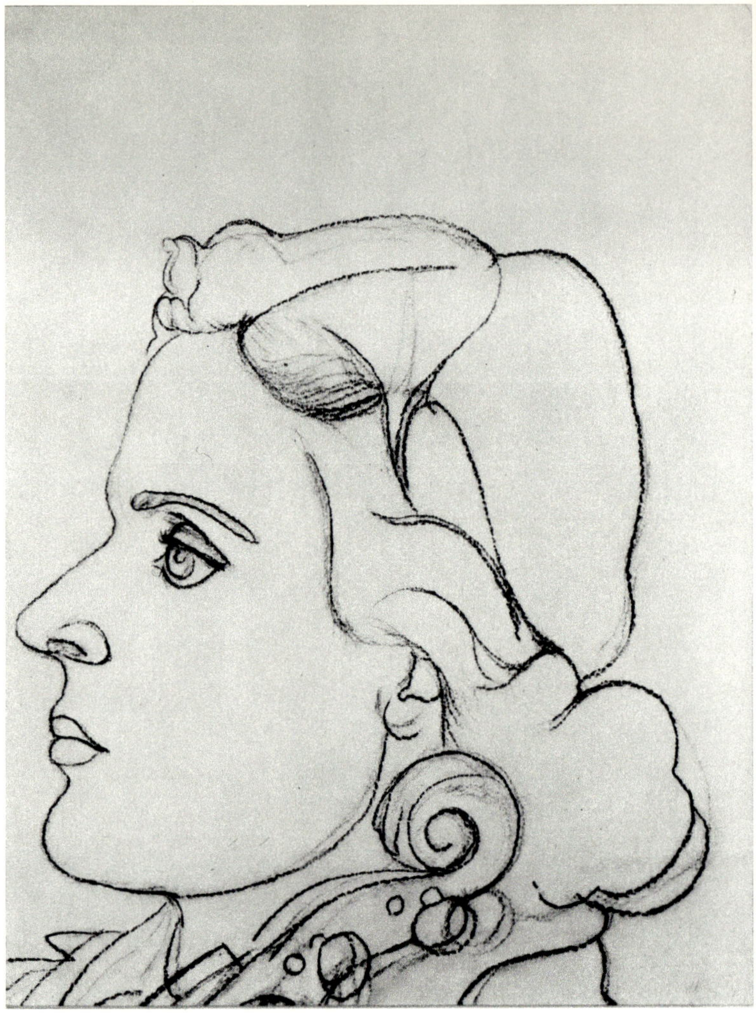

106. *Portrait of Leonora Portnoff*. 1938–40
Crayon on paper, 13 1/2 × 10 1/4″
Private Collection

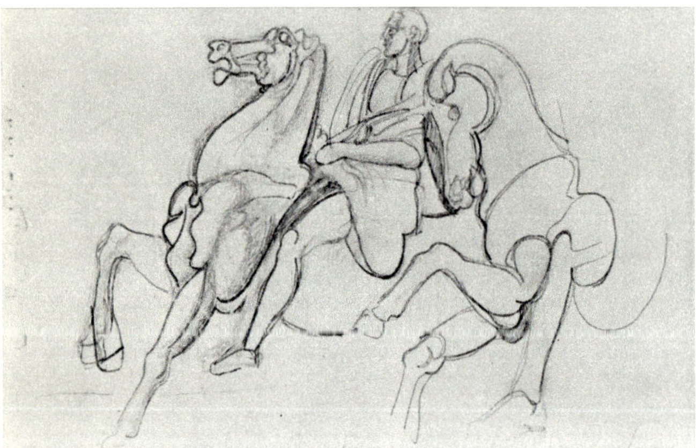

107. *Parthenon Horses*. ca. 1939
Pencil on paper, 6 7/16 × 9″
Collection Fogg Art Museum, Harvard
University, Cambridge, Massachusetts,
Purchase—Anonymous Fund for Acquisitions

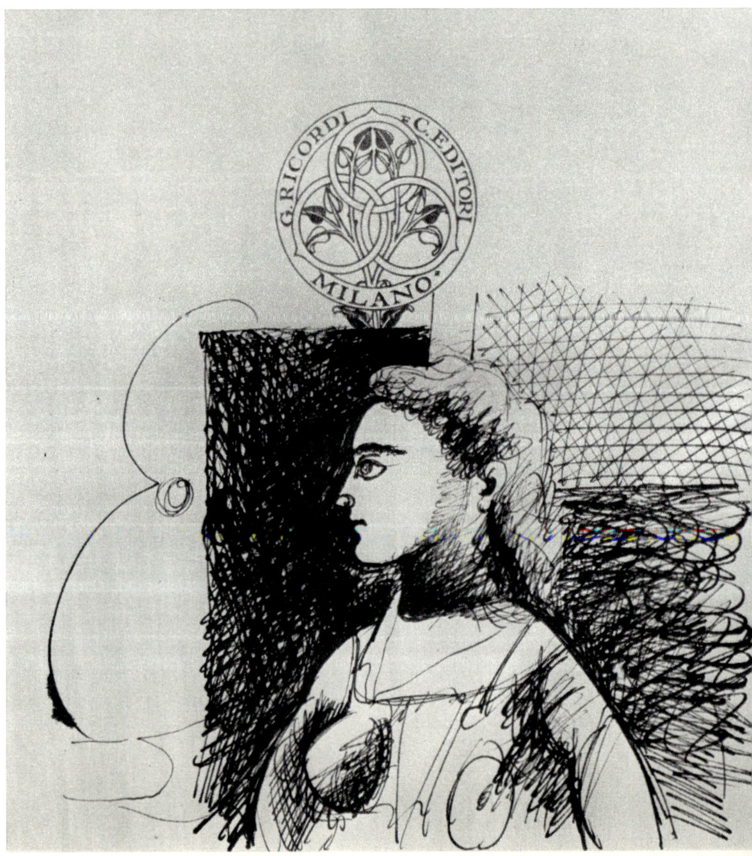

108. *Portrait*. late 1930s
Pencil on paper, 10 3/4 × 9 3/4″
Collection Mrs. Walter L. Portnoff, New York;
Courtesy M. Knoedler & Co., Inc.

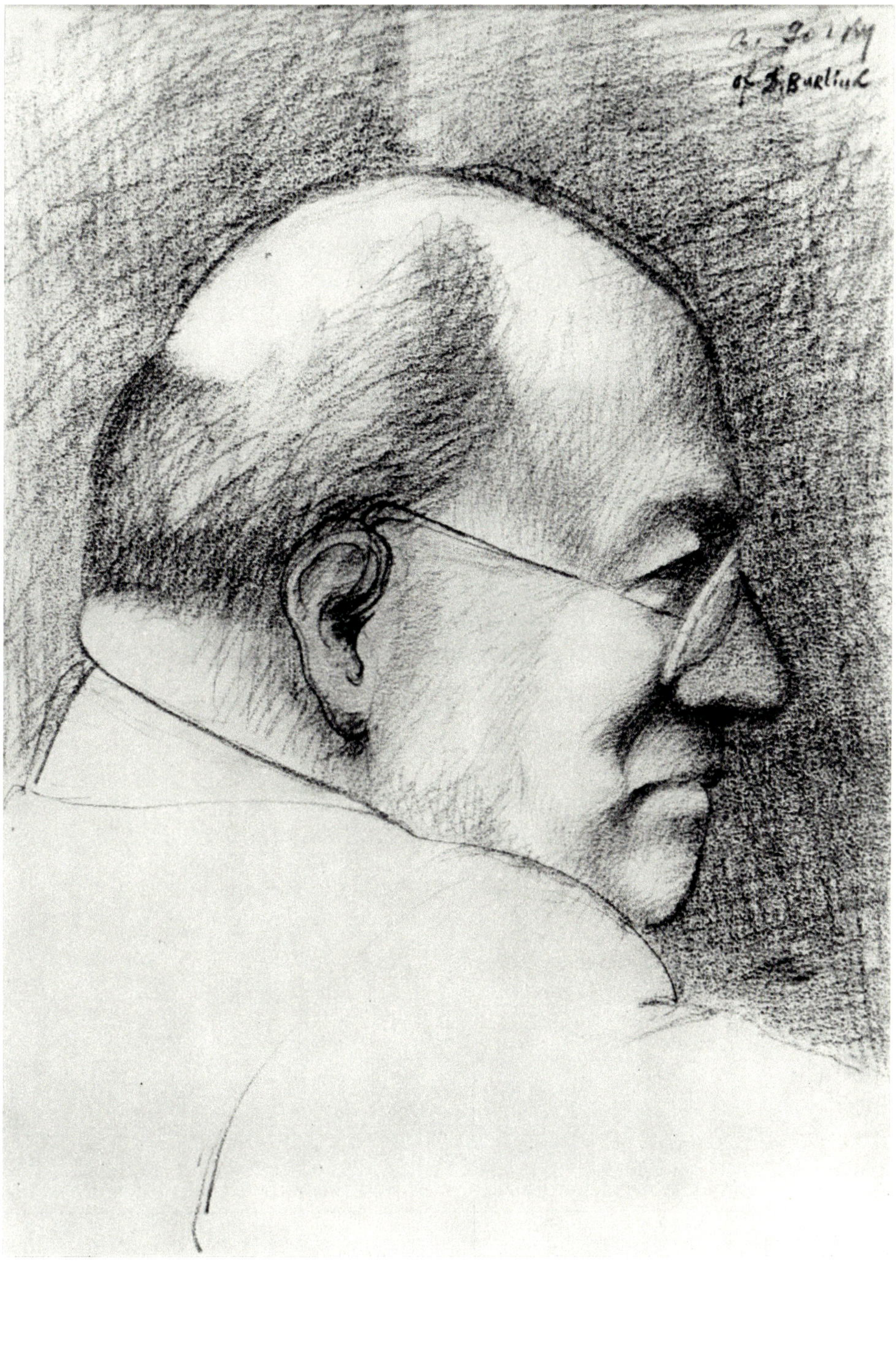

109. *Portrait of David Burliuk*. ca. 1940–41
Pencil on paper, 12 × 8 1/2″
Rebecca and Raphael Soyer Collection

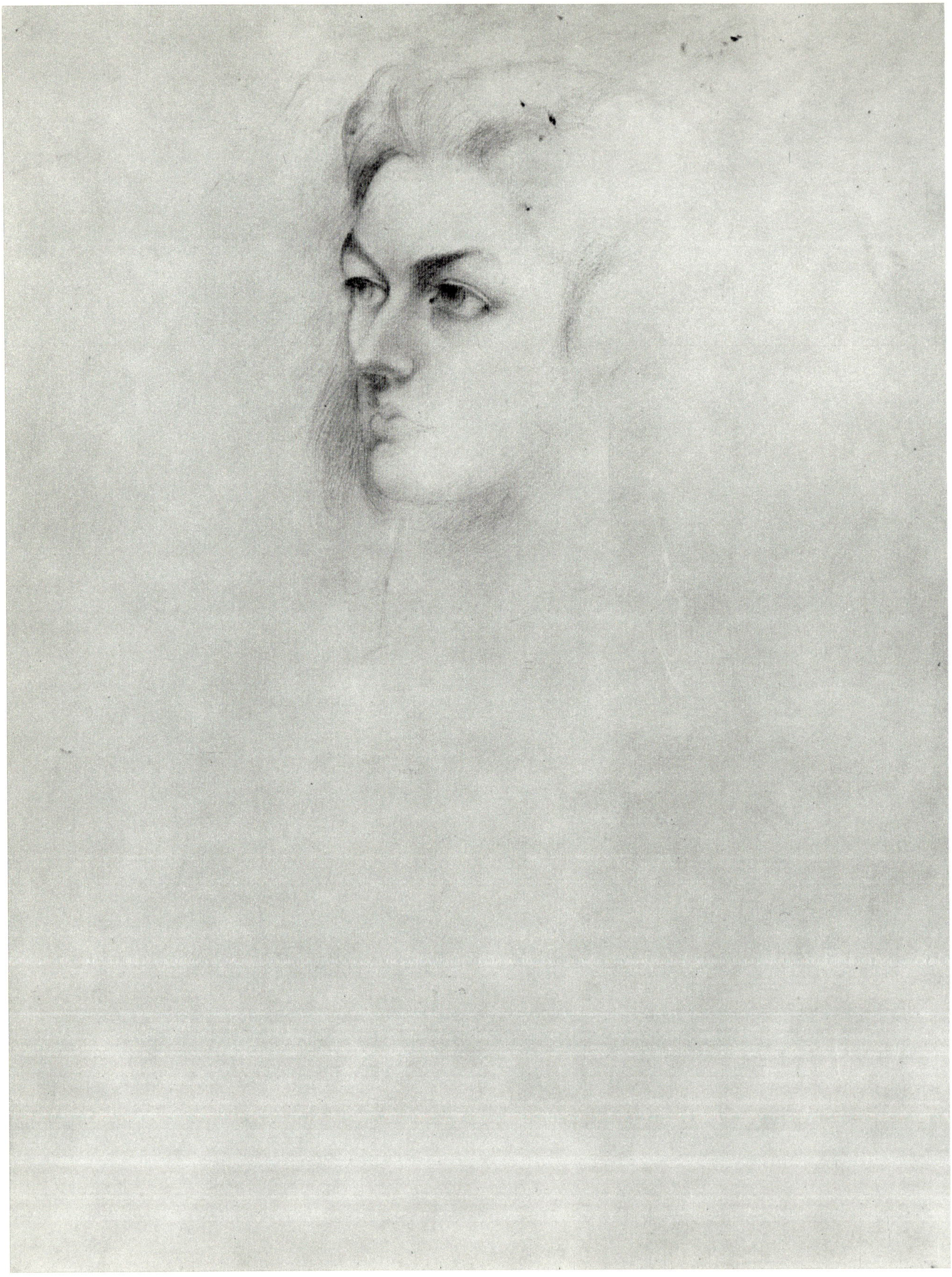

110. *Portrait of a Woman.* ca. 1941
Pencil on paper, 24 3/4 × 19″
Private Collection

111. *Portrait of a Man with Pipe.* ca. 1943
Pencil on paper, 12 1/2 × 9 1/2″
Private Collection

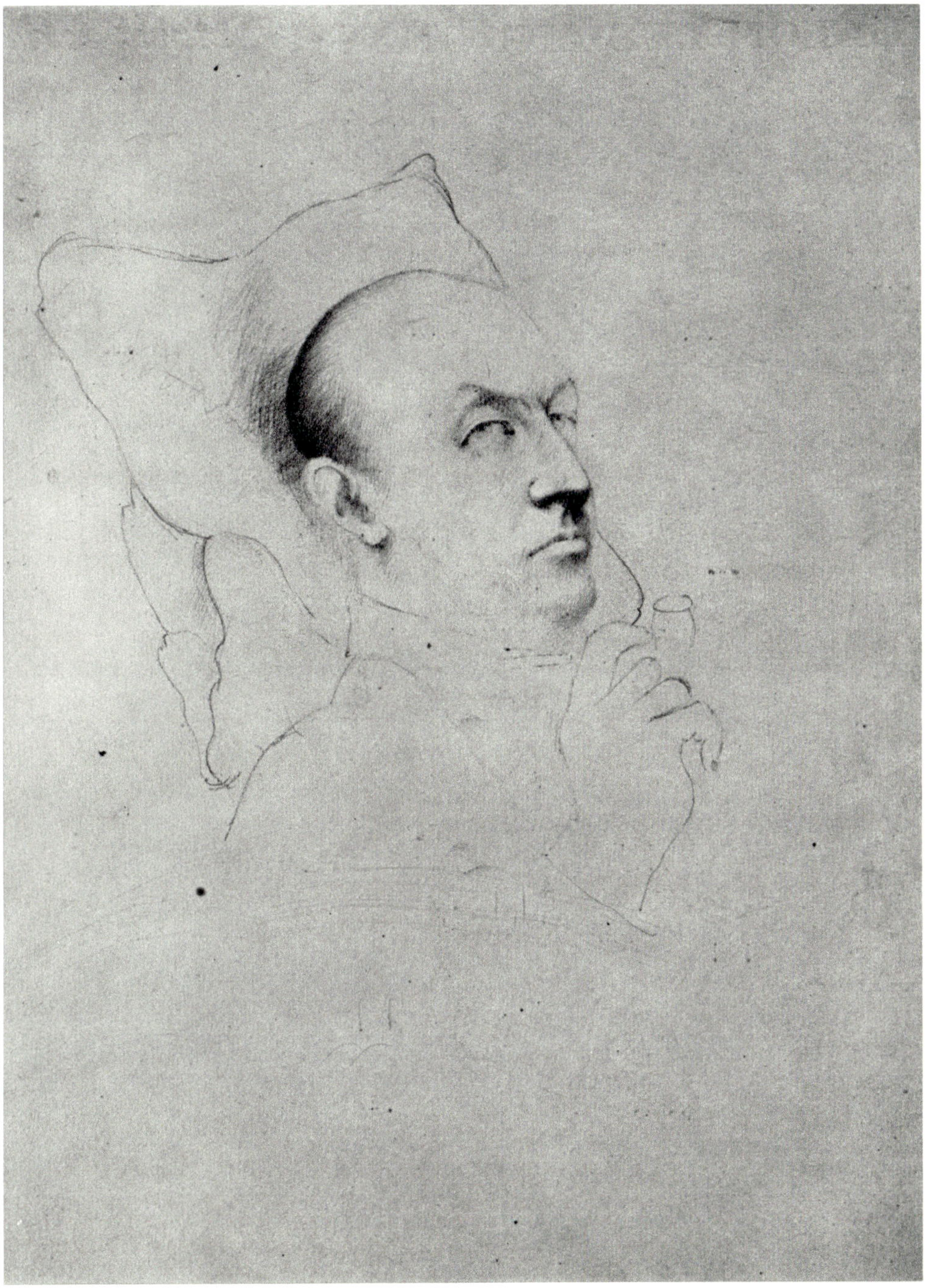

112. *Untitled*. ca. 1941
Pen and ink on paper, 18 1/4 × 12″
Private Collection

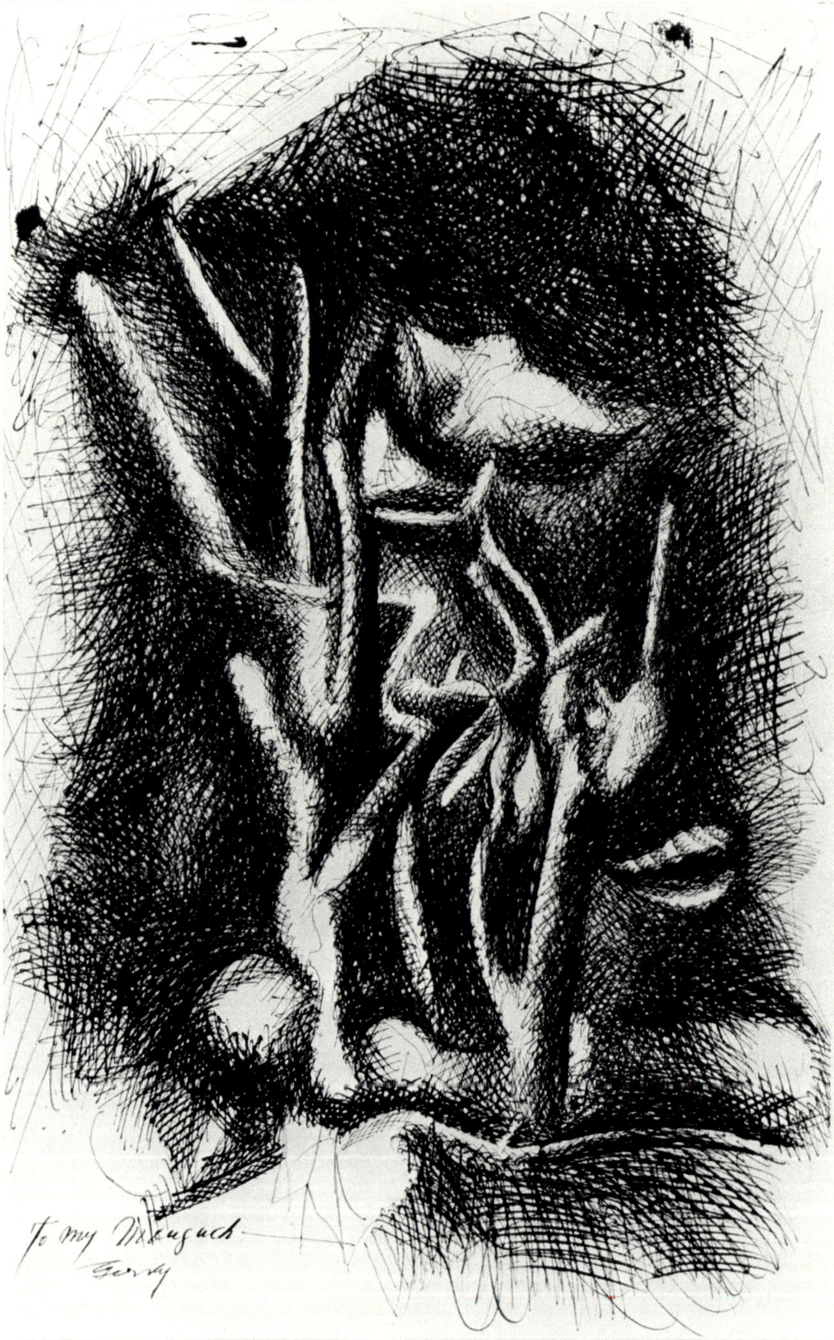

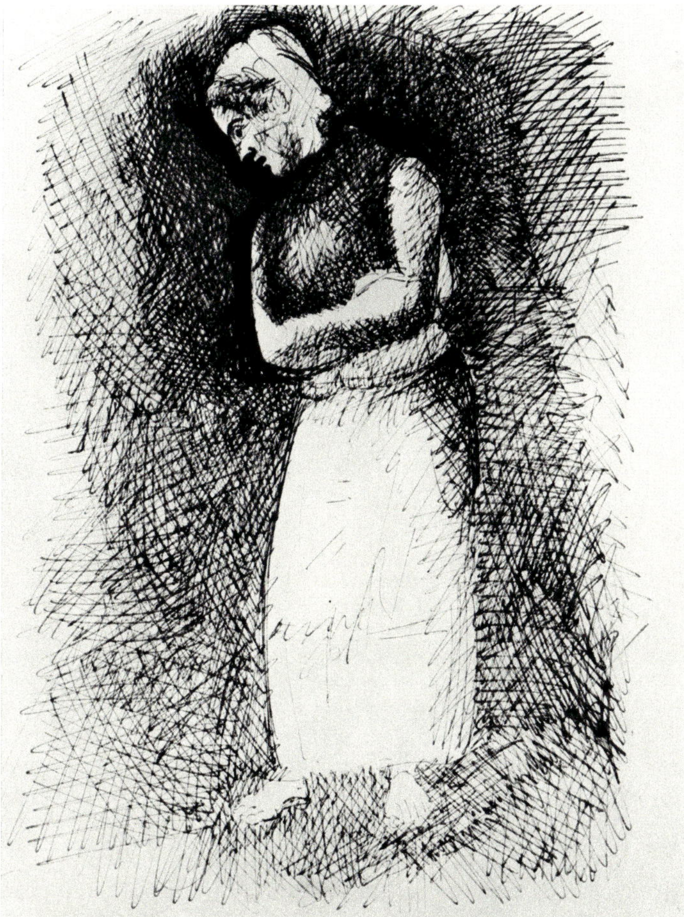

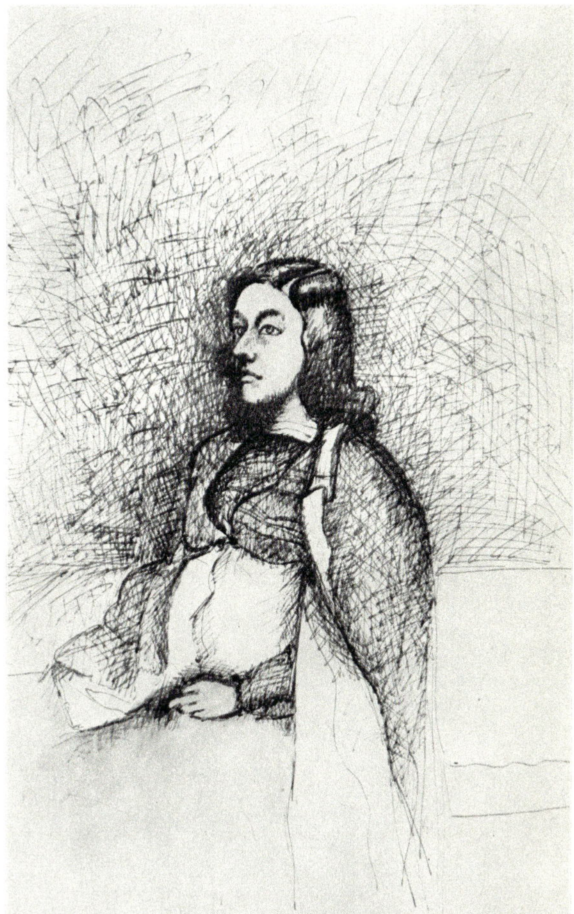

113. *Standing Woman with Folded Arms.* 1941–42
Pen and ink on paper, 11 1/2 × 9 1/4″
Private Collection

114. *Portrait of the Artist's Wife.* 1943
Pen and India ink with sepia and wash on paper, 13 3/4 × 9 1/4″
The Baltimore Museum of Art, Thomas E. Benesch Memorial Collection 63.110

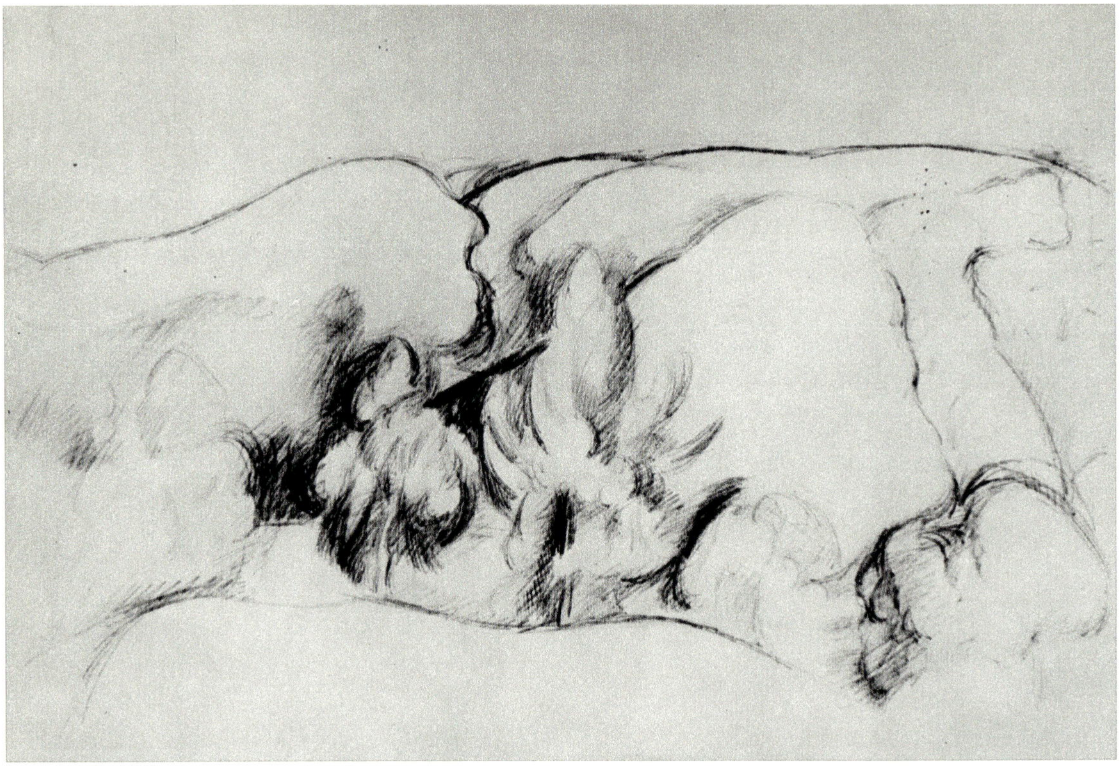

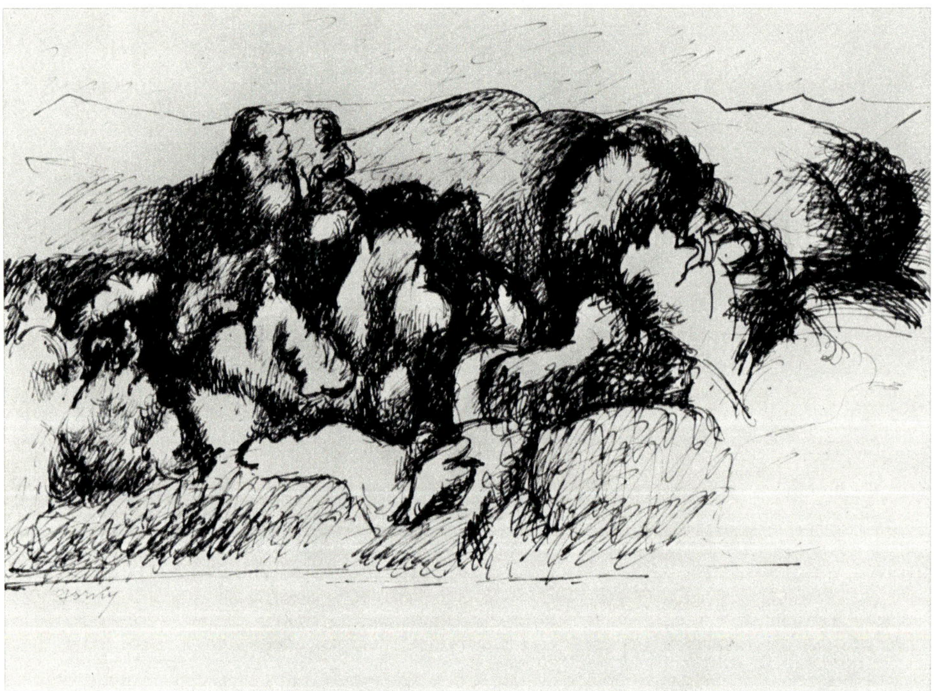

115. *Landscape.* late 1920s
Pencil on paper, 12 5/8 × 17 7/8″
Private Collection

116. *Mountain Landscape.* ca. 1942
Sepia on paper, 10 1/8 × 14″
On loan to The Solomon R. Guggenheim Museum, New York, from the Arthur Ross Foundation

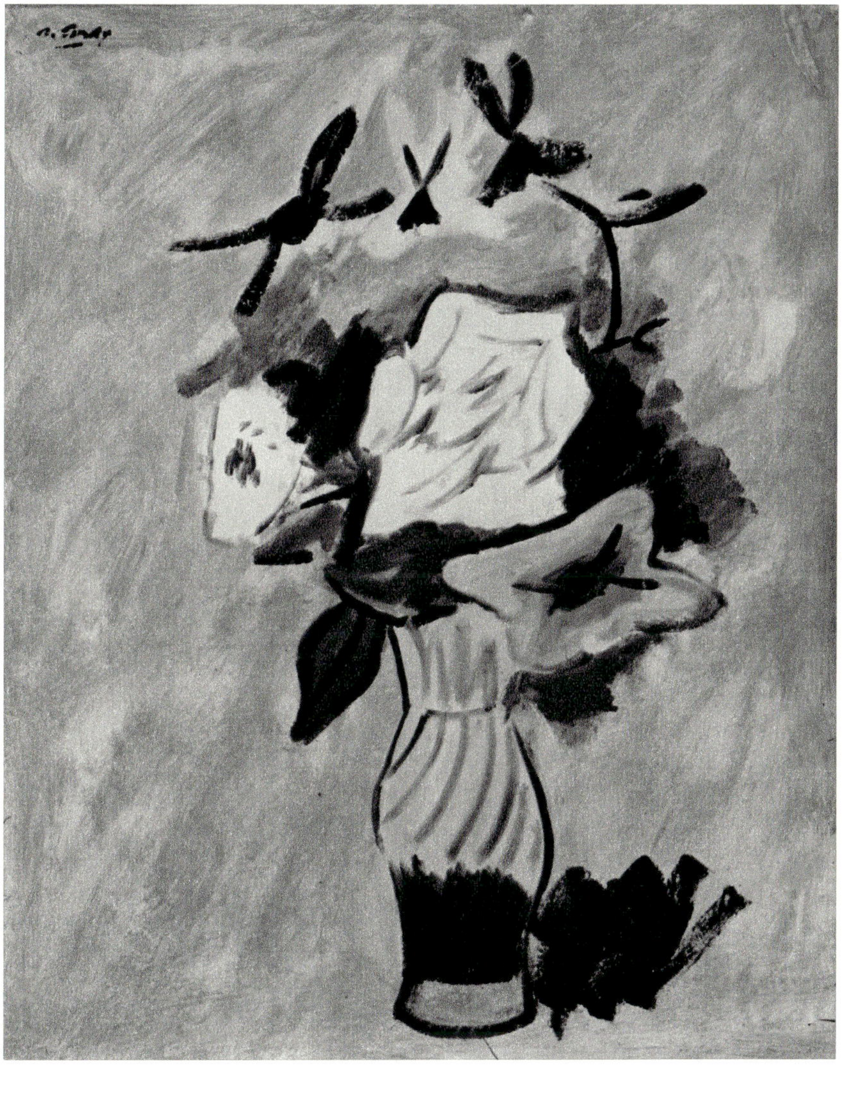

117. *Still Life.* 1939
Oil on canvas, 20 × 16″
Private Collection

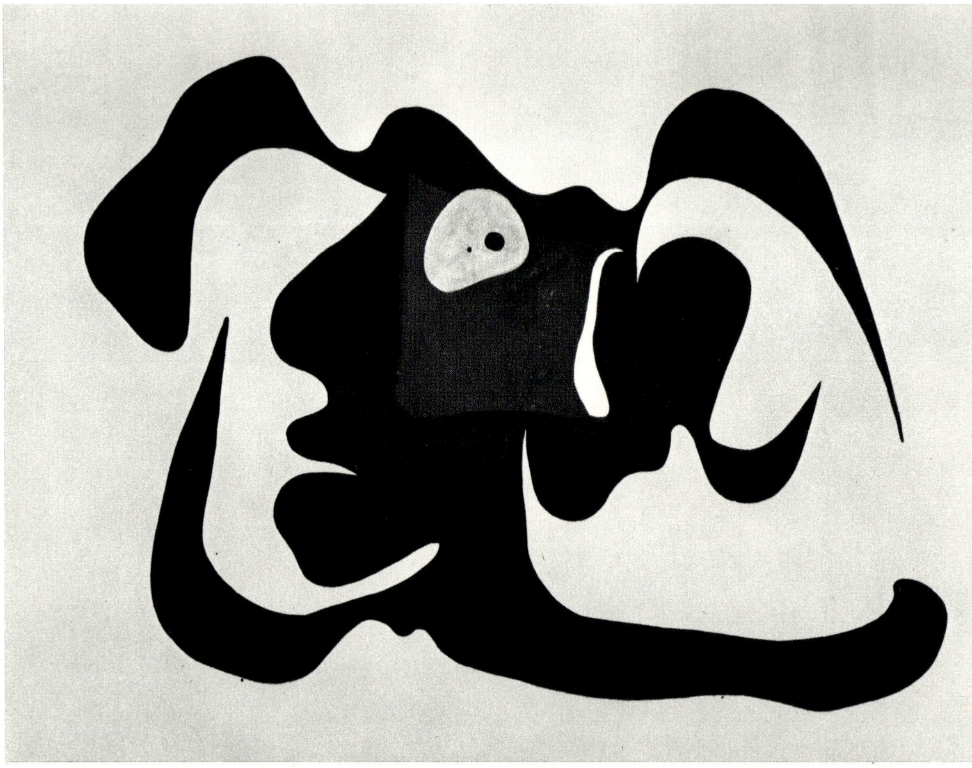

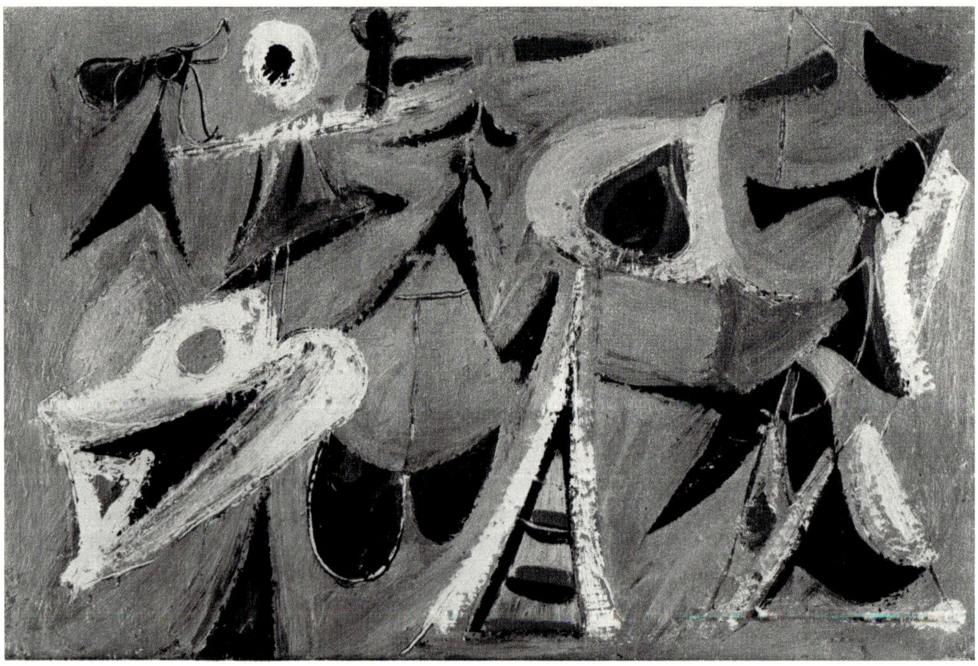

118. *Bull in the Sun*. 1942
Gouache on paper, 18 1/2 × 24 3/4″
Collection The Museum of Modern Art, New York;
Gift of George B. Locke

119. *Painting*. 1938
Oil on canvas, 18 1/8 × 28″
Collection Dorothy C. Miller

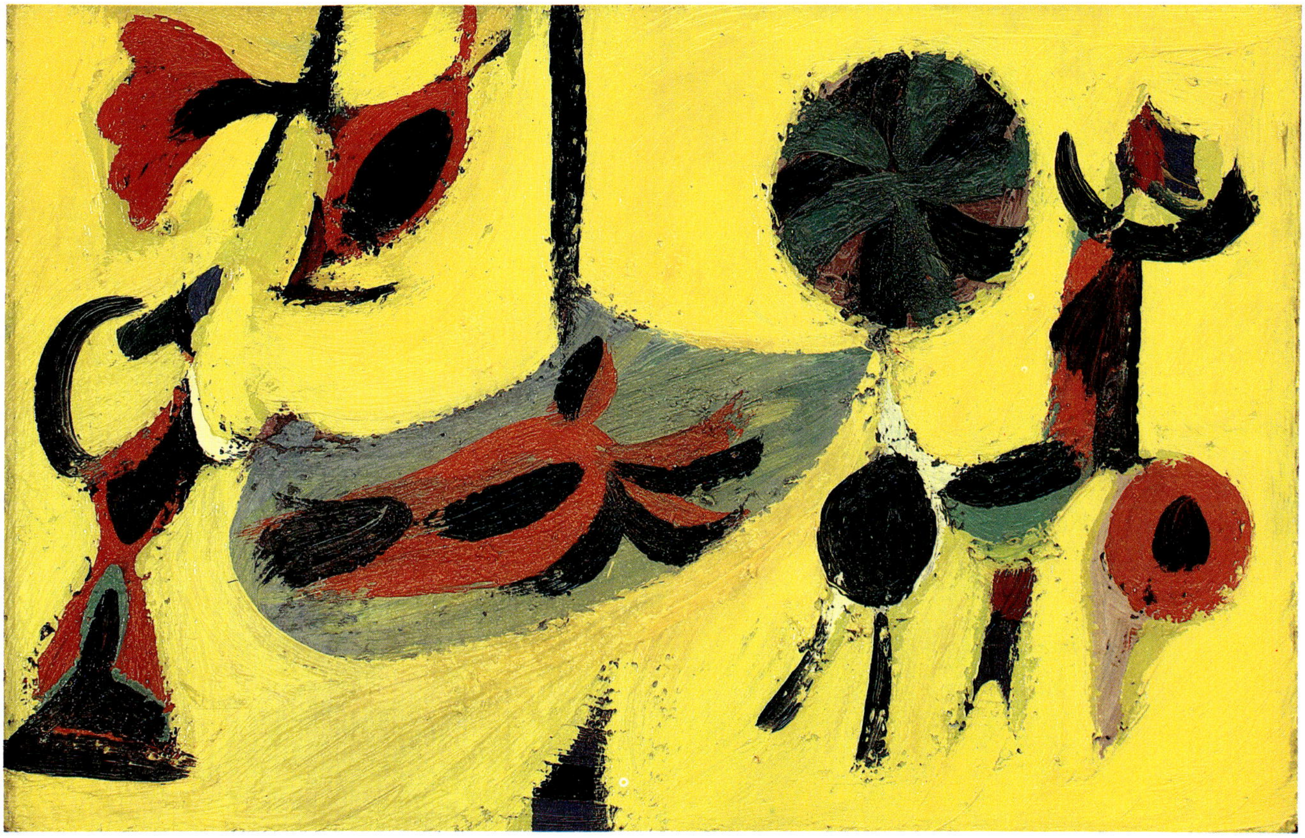

120. *Argula*. 1938
Oil on canvas, 15 × 24″
Collection The Museum of Modern Art, New York;
Gift of Bernard Davis

121. *Garden in Sochi*. 1940–41
Gouache on board, 22 × 28″
Museum Purchase with bequest of C. Donald Belcher, 1977
Permanent Collection of The High Museum of Art, Atlanta

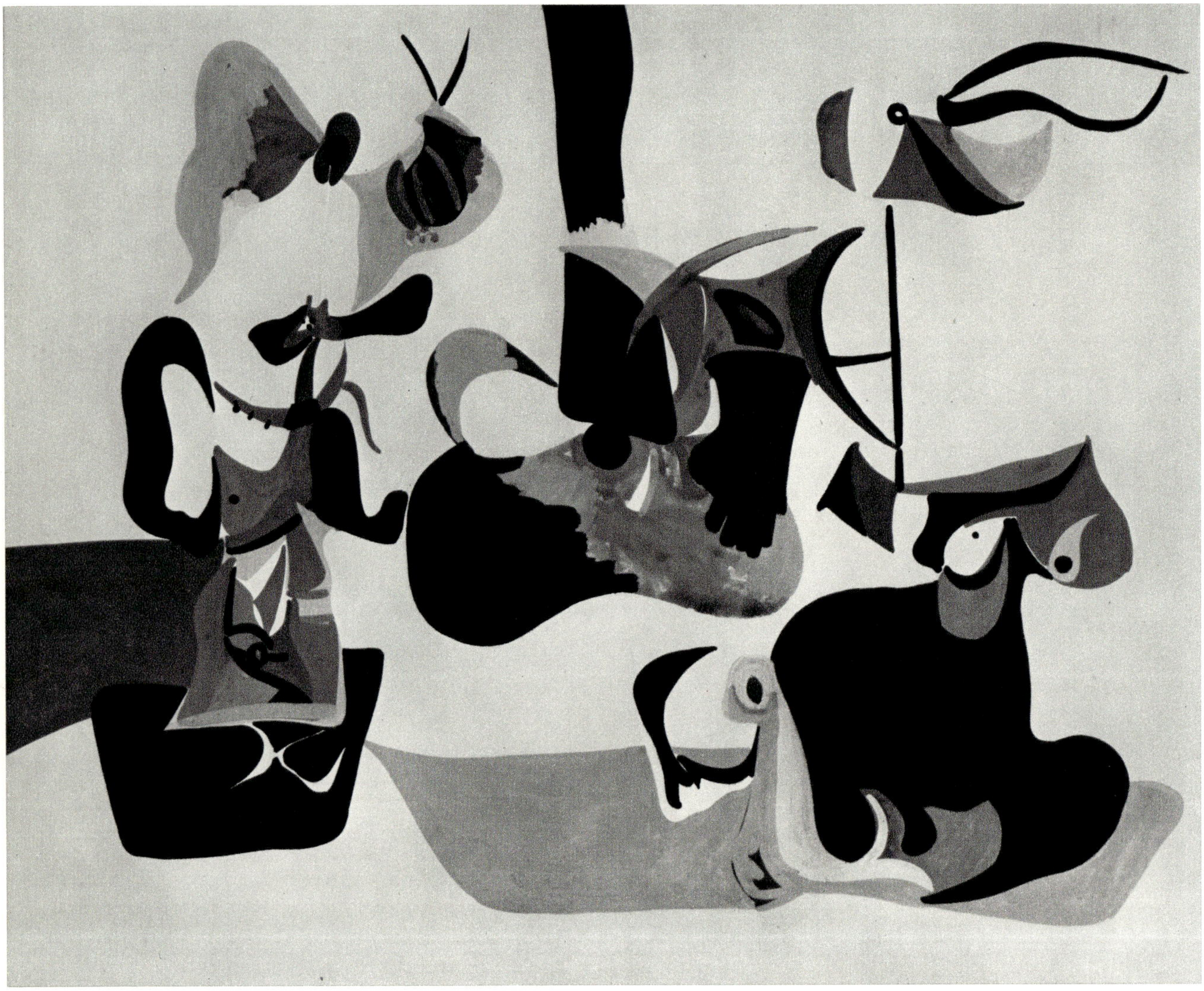

122. *Untitled*. 1940
Watercolor and gouache on gessoed wood panel, 4 × 7 1/8″
Collection Mr. and Mrs. Michael J. Berberian
on loan to Museum of Fine Arts, Boston

123. *Garden in Sochi*. 1941
Gouache on paper, 13 3/4 × 17 3/4″
Private Collection

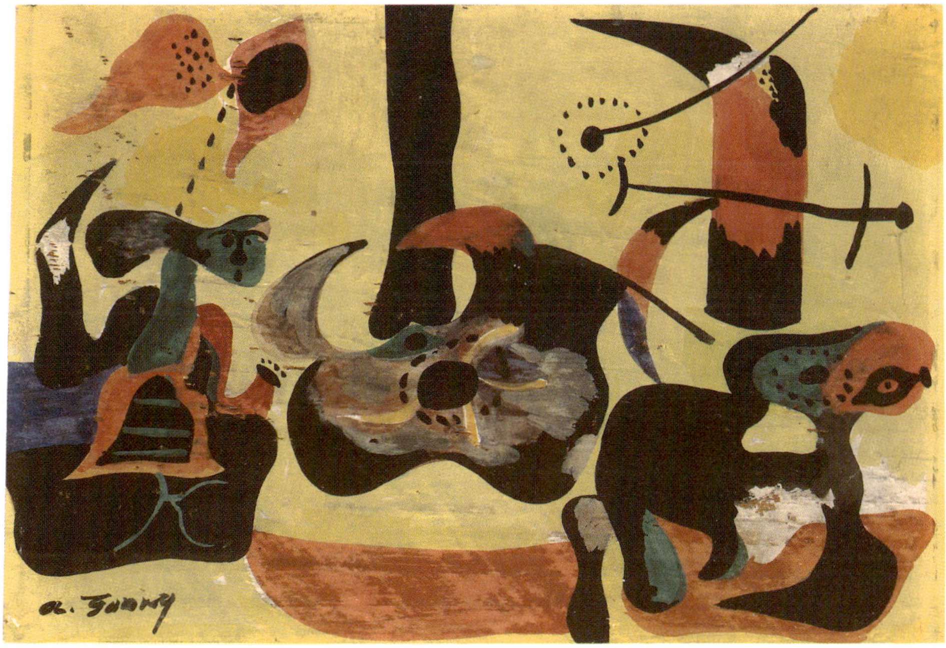

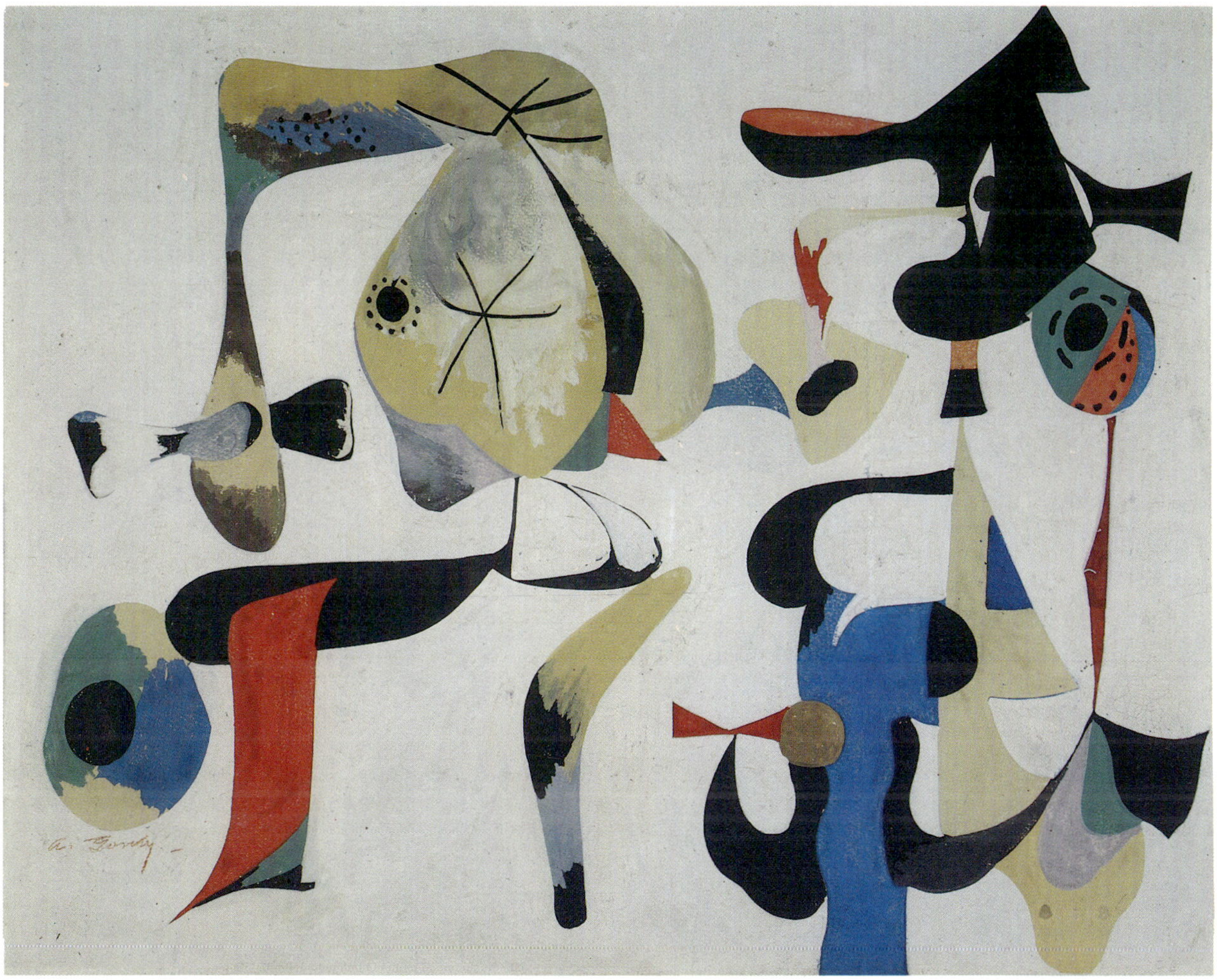

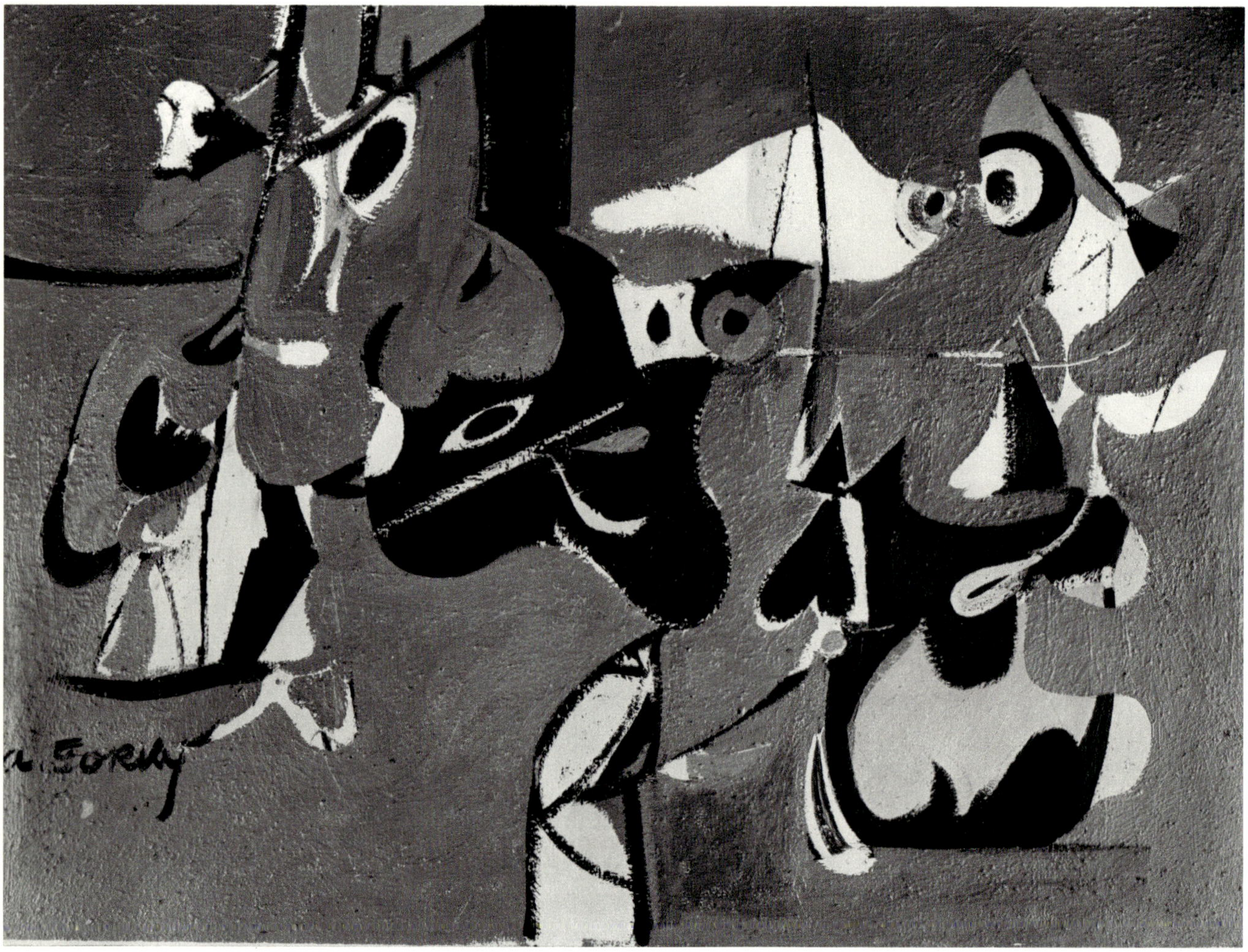

124. *Garden in Sochi*. 1941
Oil on canvas, 44 1/4 × 62 1/4″
Collection The Museum of Modern Art, New York; Purchase
Fund and gift of Mr. and Mrs. Wolfgang S. Schwabacher

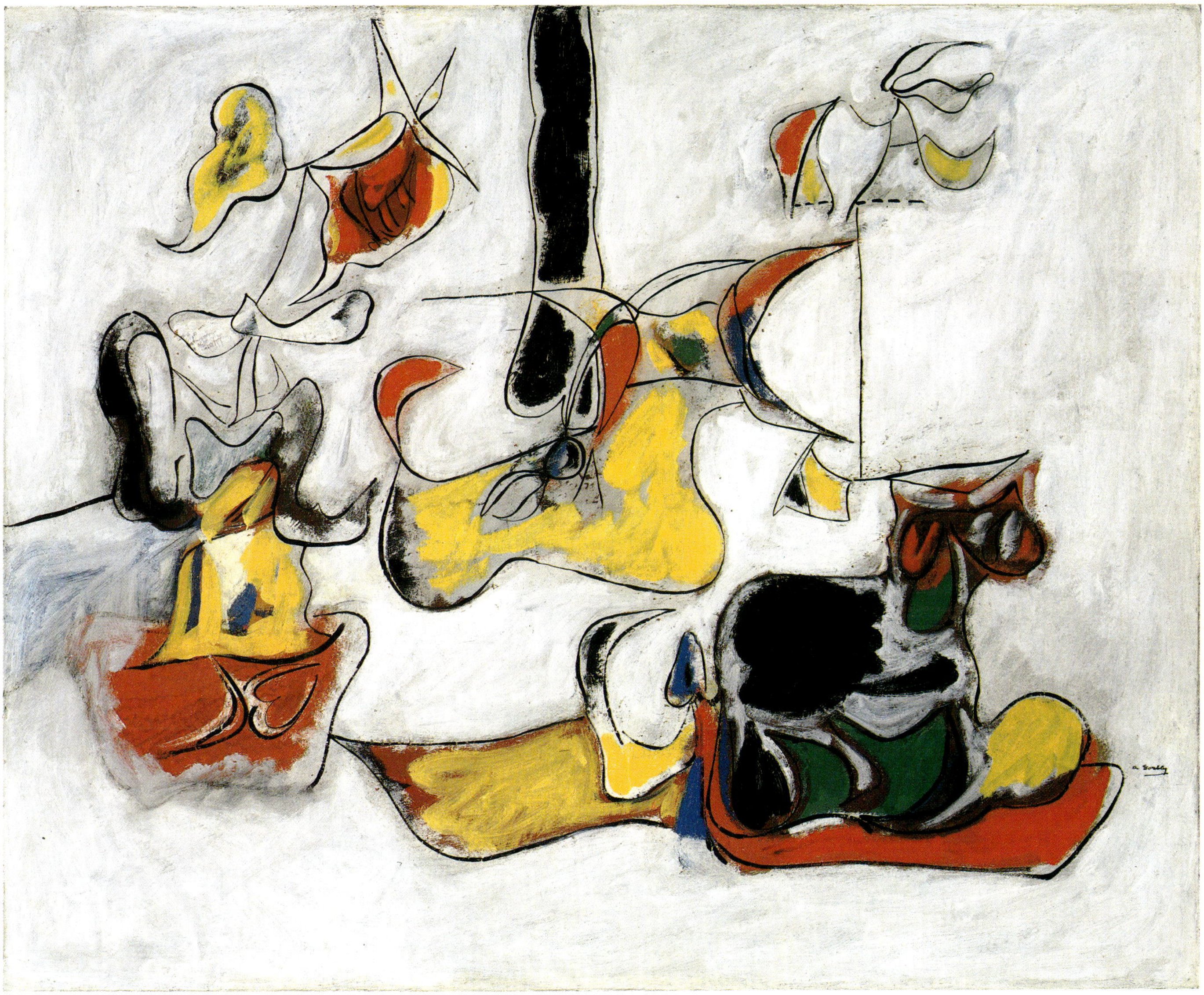

125. *Garden in Sochi*. 1943
Oil on canvas, 31 × 39″
Collection The Museum of Modern Art, New York,
Acquired through the Lillie P. Bliss Foundation

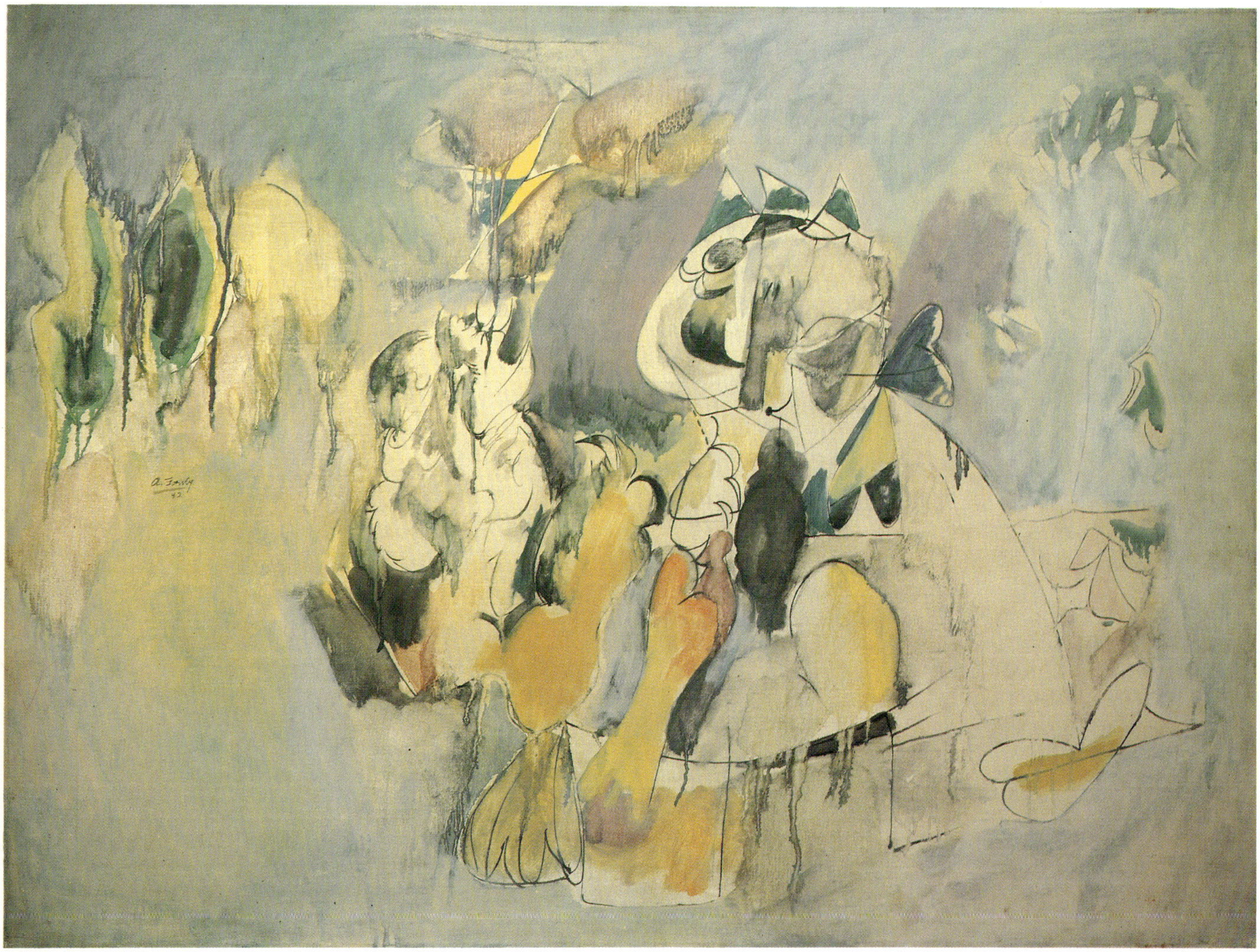

126. *The Pirate I.* 1942
Oil on canvas, 29 1/4 × 40 1/8″
Collection Julien Levy; Courtesy Richard L. Feigen & Co.

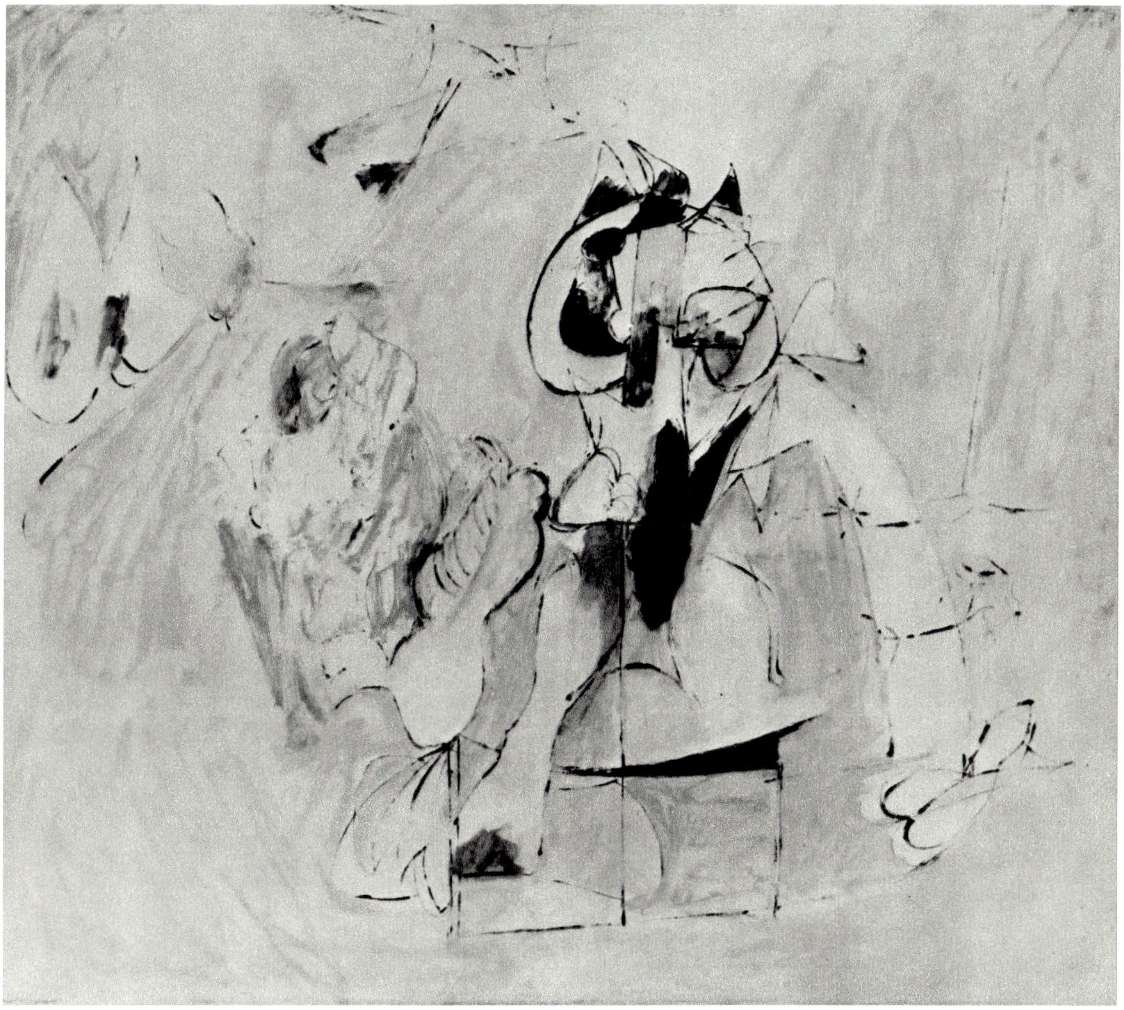

127. *The Pirate II.* 1943
Oil on canvas, 30 × 36″
Collection Julien Levy; Courtesy Richard L. Feigen & Co.

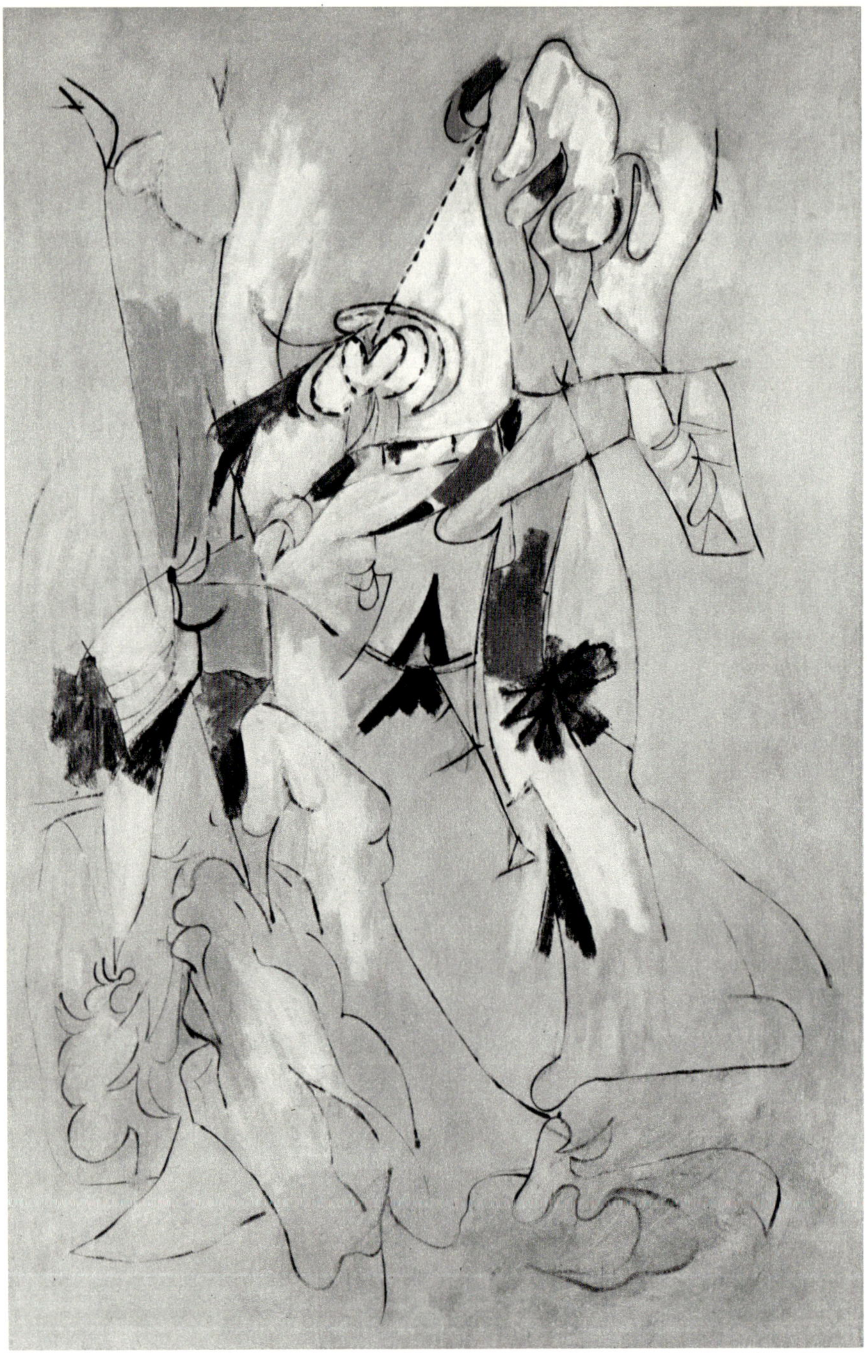

128. *Waterfall*. ca. 1943
Oil on canvas, 38 1/8 × 25 1/8″
Collection Hirshhorn Museum and Sculpture Garden,
Smithsonian Institution, Washington, D.C.

129. *Waterfall*. ca. 1943
Oil on canvas, 60 1/2 × 44 1/2″
Collection The Trustees of the Tate Gallery, London

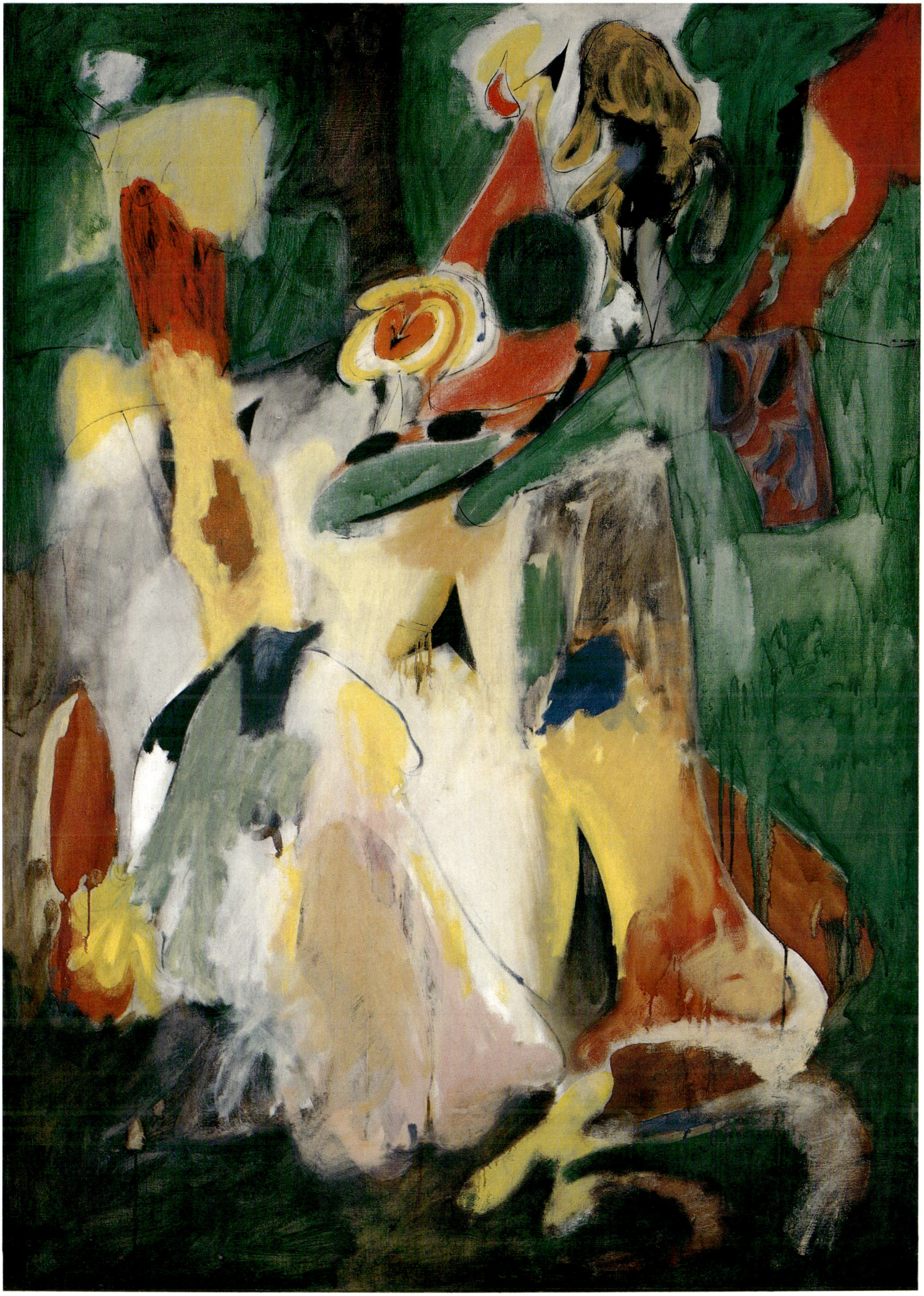

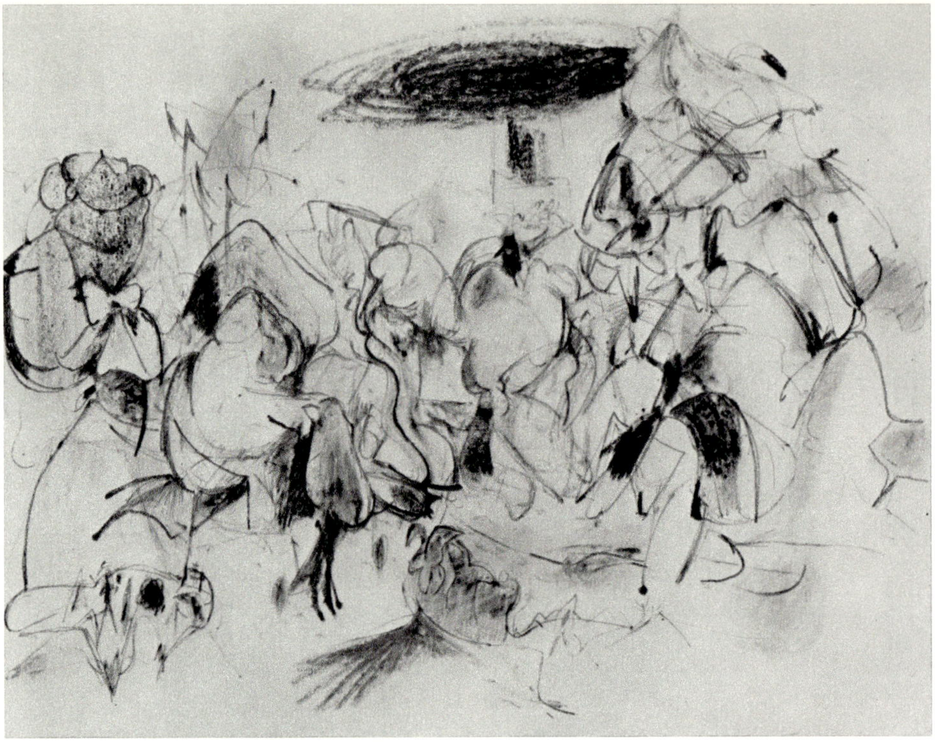

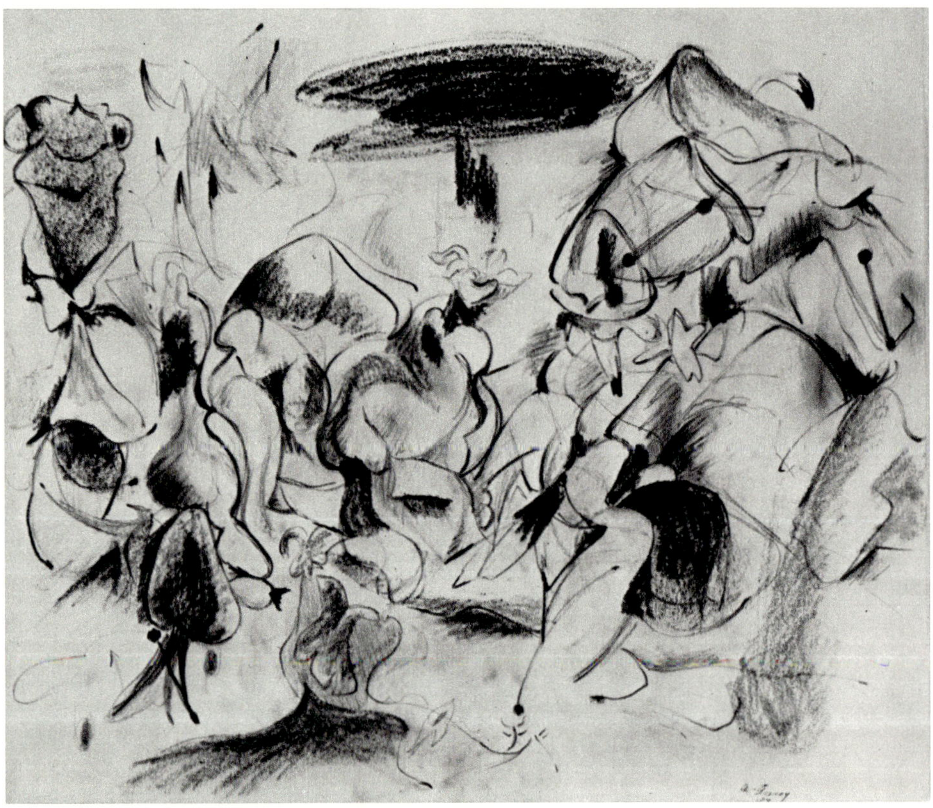

130. *Connecticut Sketch*. 1943
Pencil and crayon on paper, 13 × 17″
Collection Mrs. Charles Abrams, New York

131. *Sochi*. 1943
Pencil and crayon on paper, 14 1/4 × 16 3/4″
Collection Mr. and Mrs. Edmond Ruben, Minneapolis

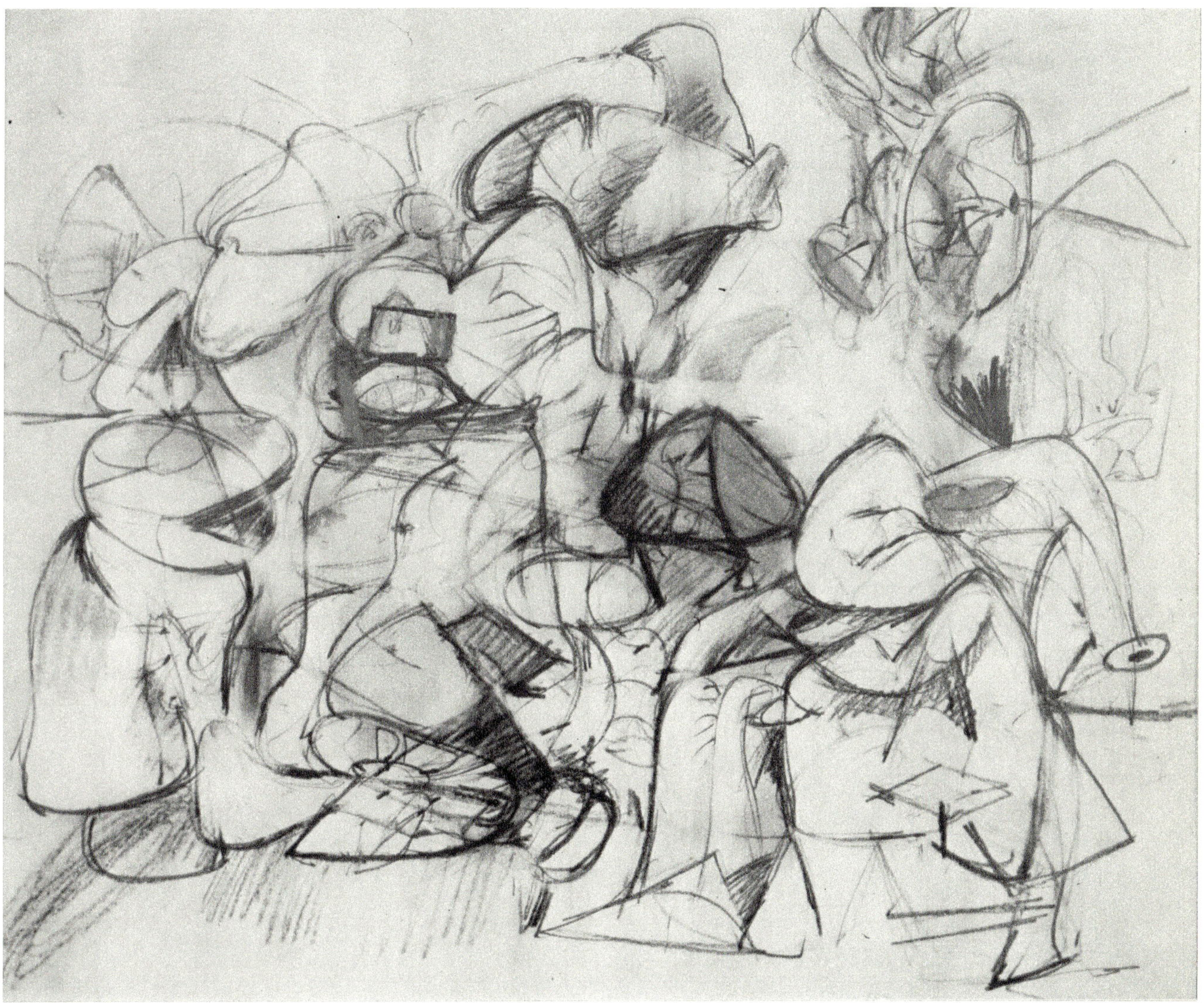

132. *Landscape—Virginia*. 1945
Pencil and crayon on paper, 19 × 24″
Collection Marilyn and Bernard Brodsky

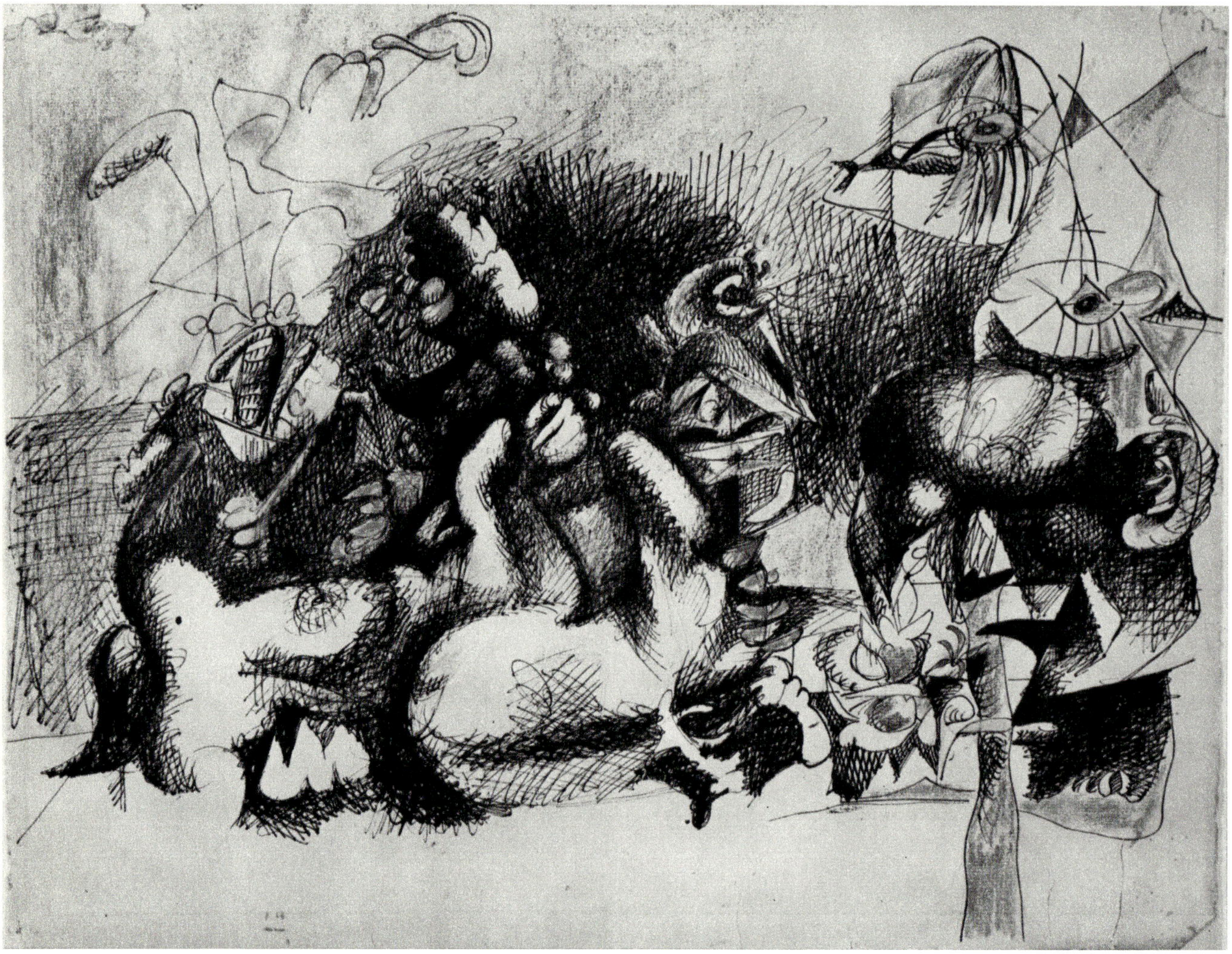

133. *Untitled.* 1943
Pen and ink and pastel on paper, 17 1/4 × 23″
Collection Mr. and Mrs. E. A. Bergman

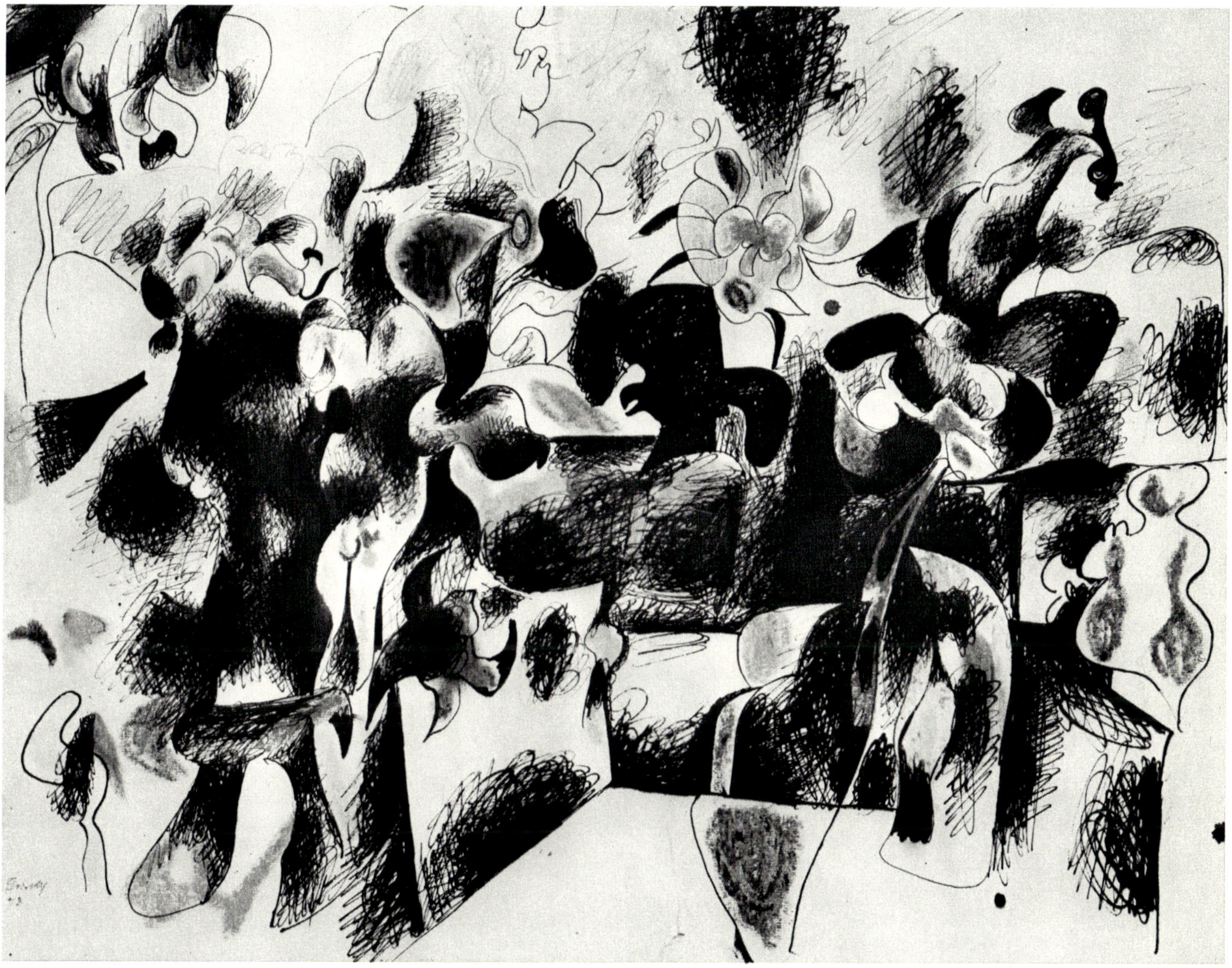

134. *The Housatonic*. 1943
Ink and crayon on paper, 18 × 23 1/2″
Private Collection

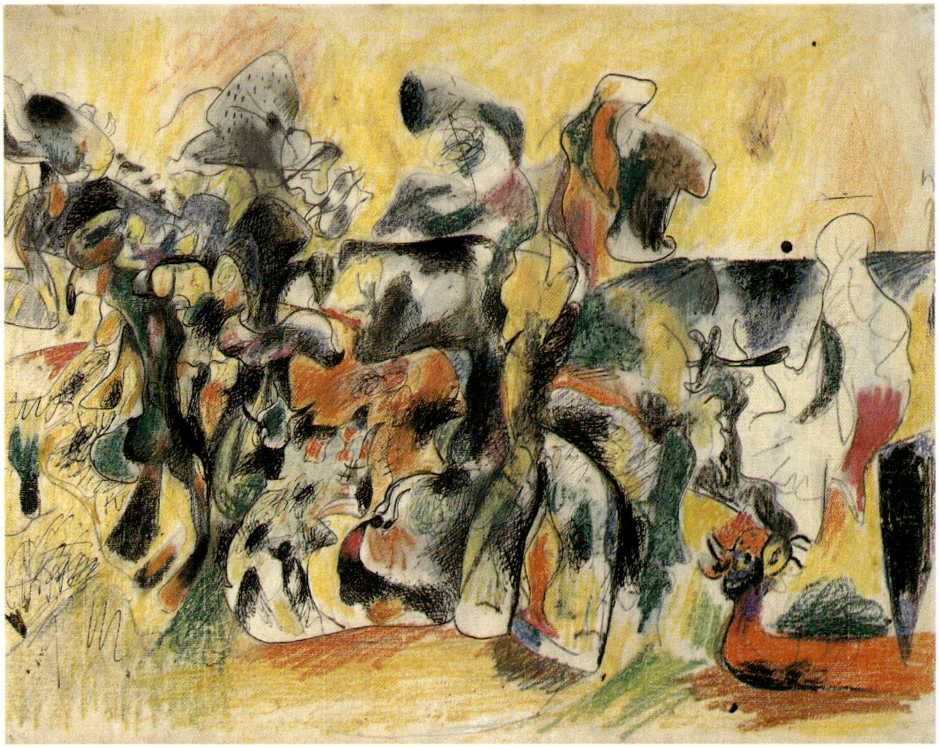

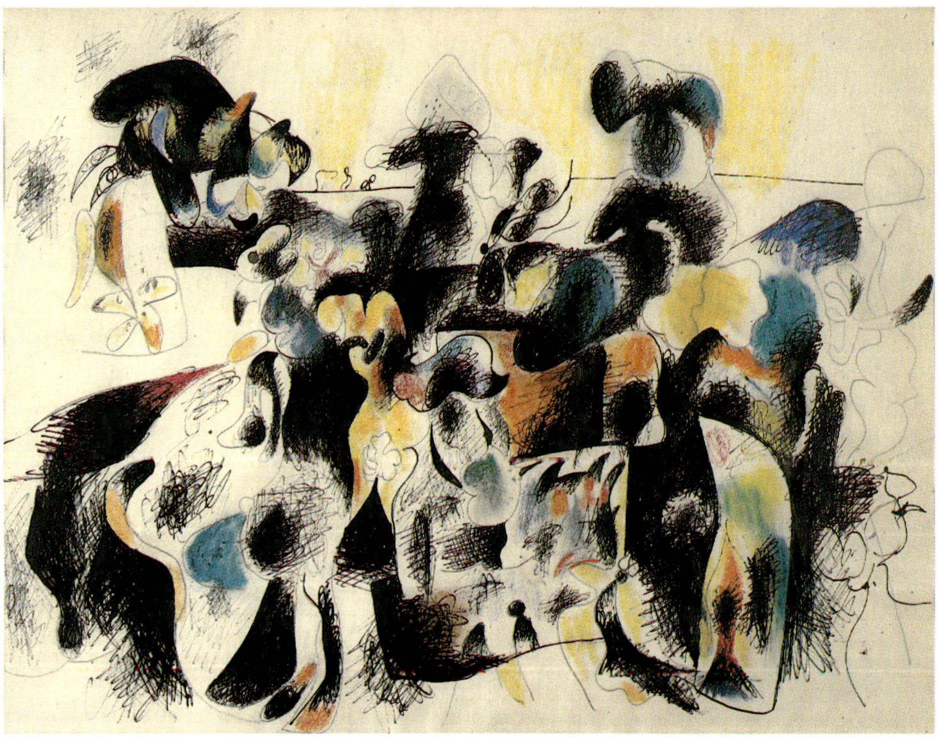

135. *Untitled*. 1943
Crayon, pen and ink and pencil on paper, 17 1/8 × 22 1/16″
Private Collection

136. *Composition I*. 1943
Pencil, ink and wax crayon on paper, 18 1/2 × 24 1/2″
Collection Ann Dunnigan

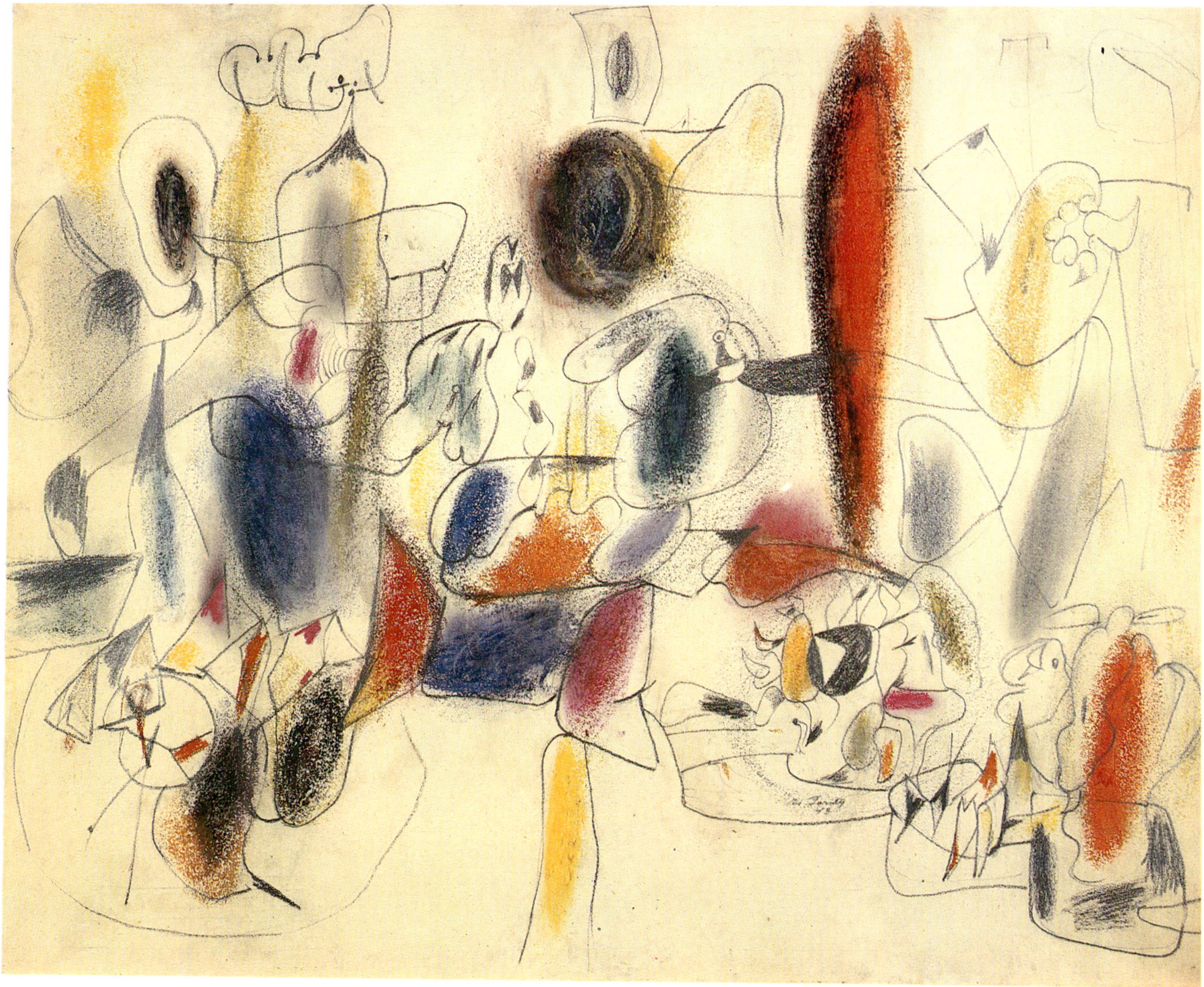

137. *Untitled*. 1943
Pencil and crayon on paper, 19 1/2 × 25″
Courtesy David Nisinson, Inc.

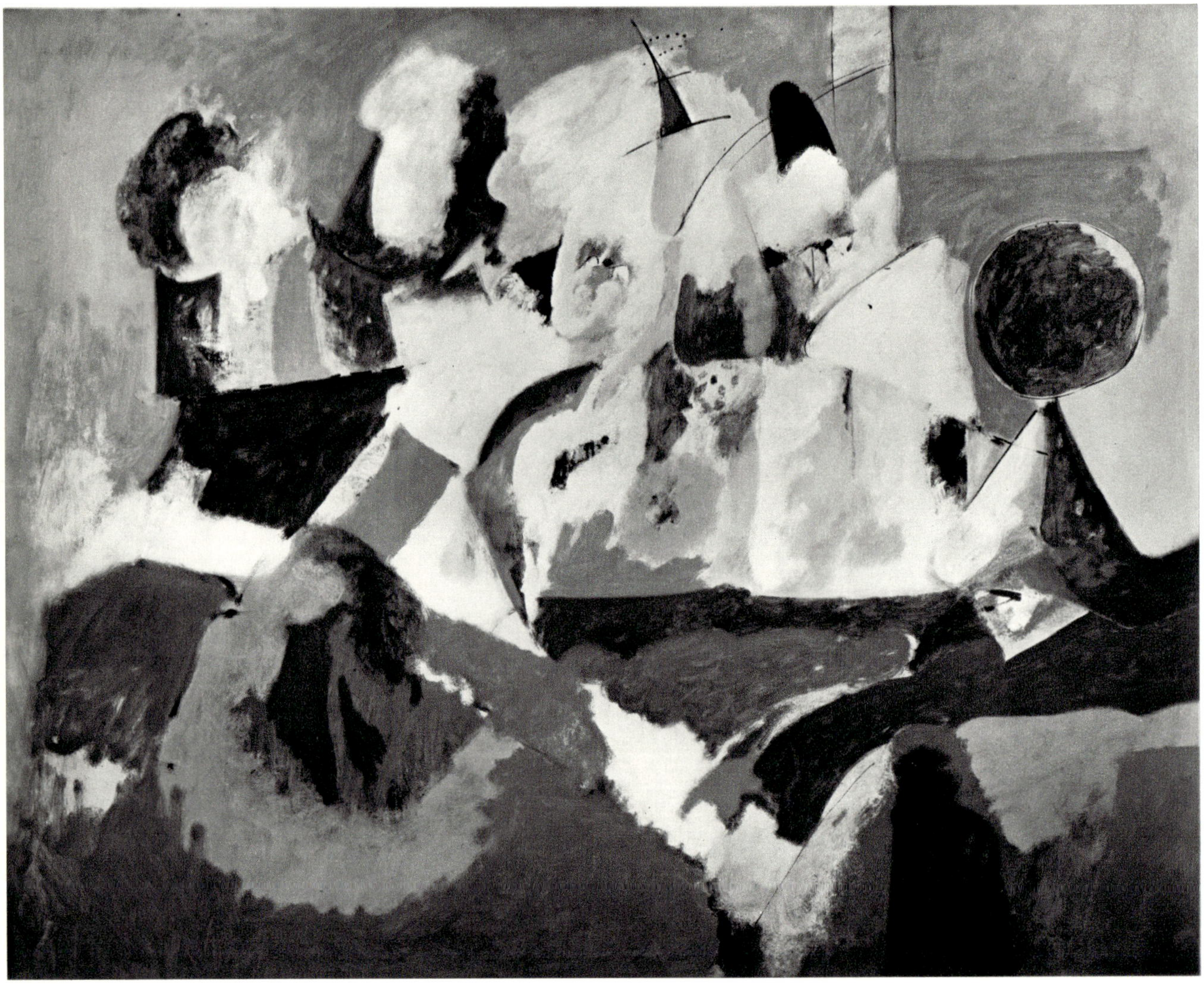

138. *Housatonic Falls*. 1943–44
Oil on canvas, 34 × 44″
Private Collection

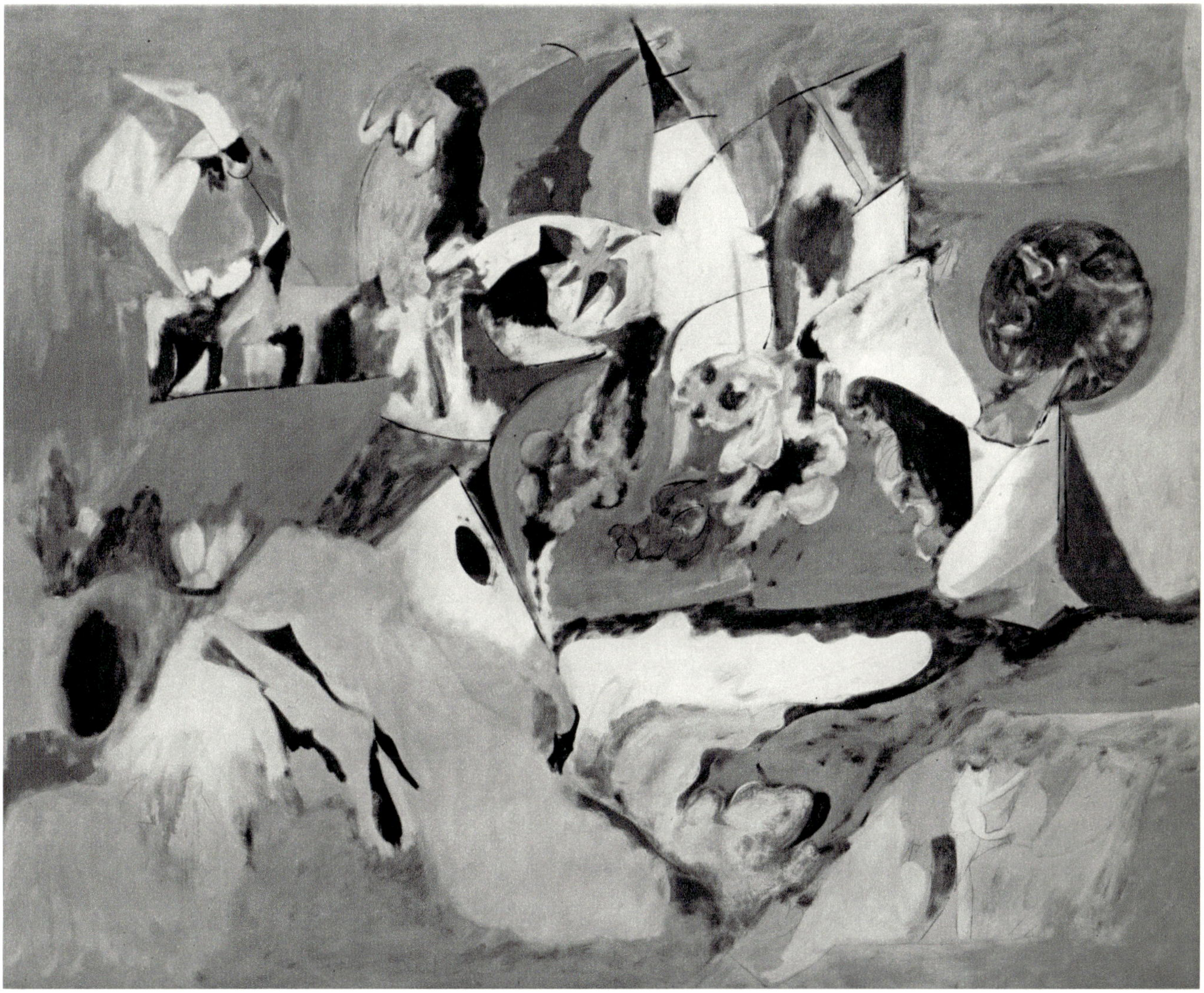

139. *Golden Brown.* mid-1940s
Oil on canvas, 43 1/2 × 56″
Collection Washington University, St. Louis

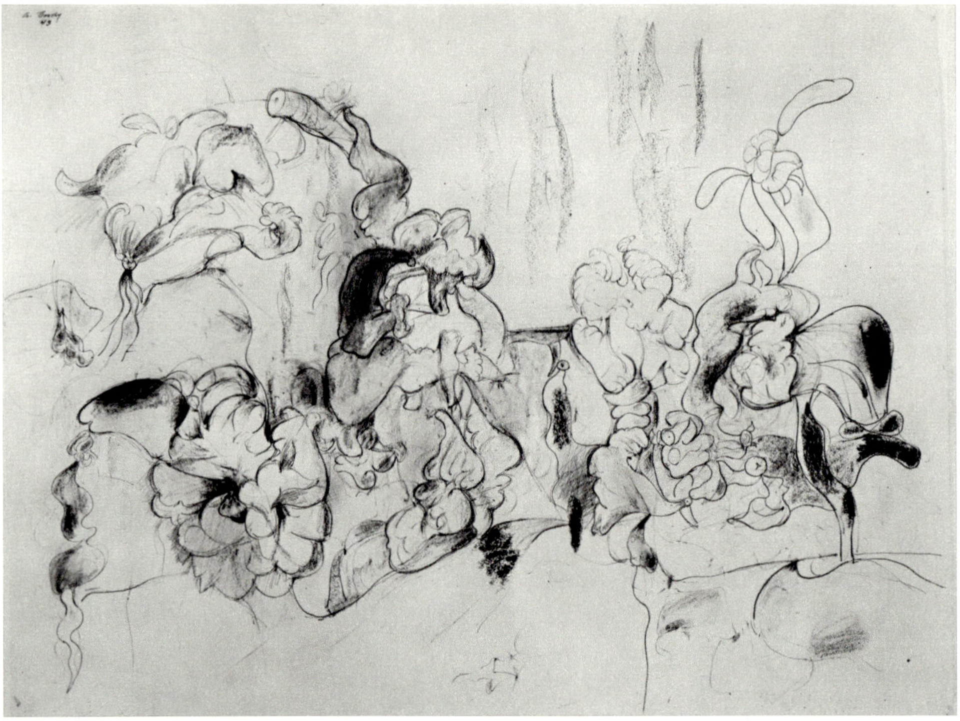

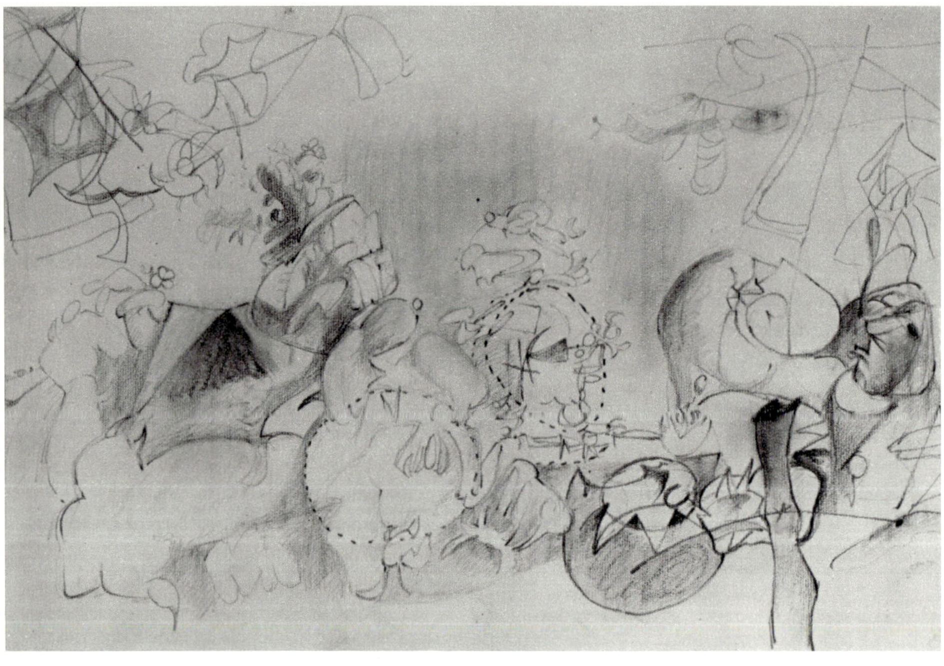

140. *Landscape.* 1943
Pencil and crayon on paper, 20 1/4 × 27 3/8″
Private Collection

141. *Untitled.* 1943–44
Pencil on paper, 12 × 17 7/8″
Private Collection

142. *Virginia Landscape*. 1943
Pencil and wax crayon on paper, 18 1/2 × 23 1/2″
Private Collection

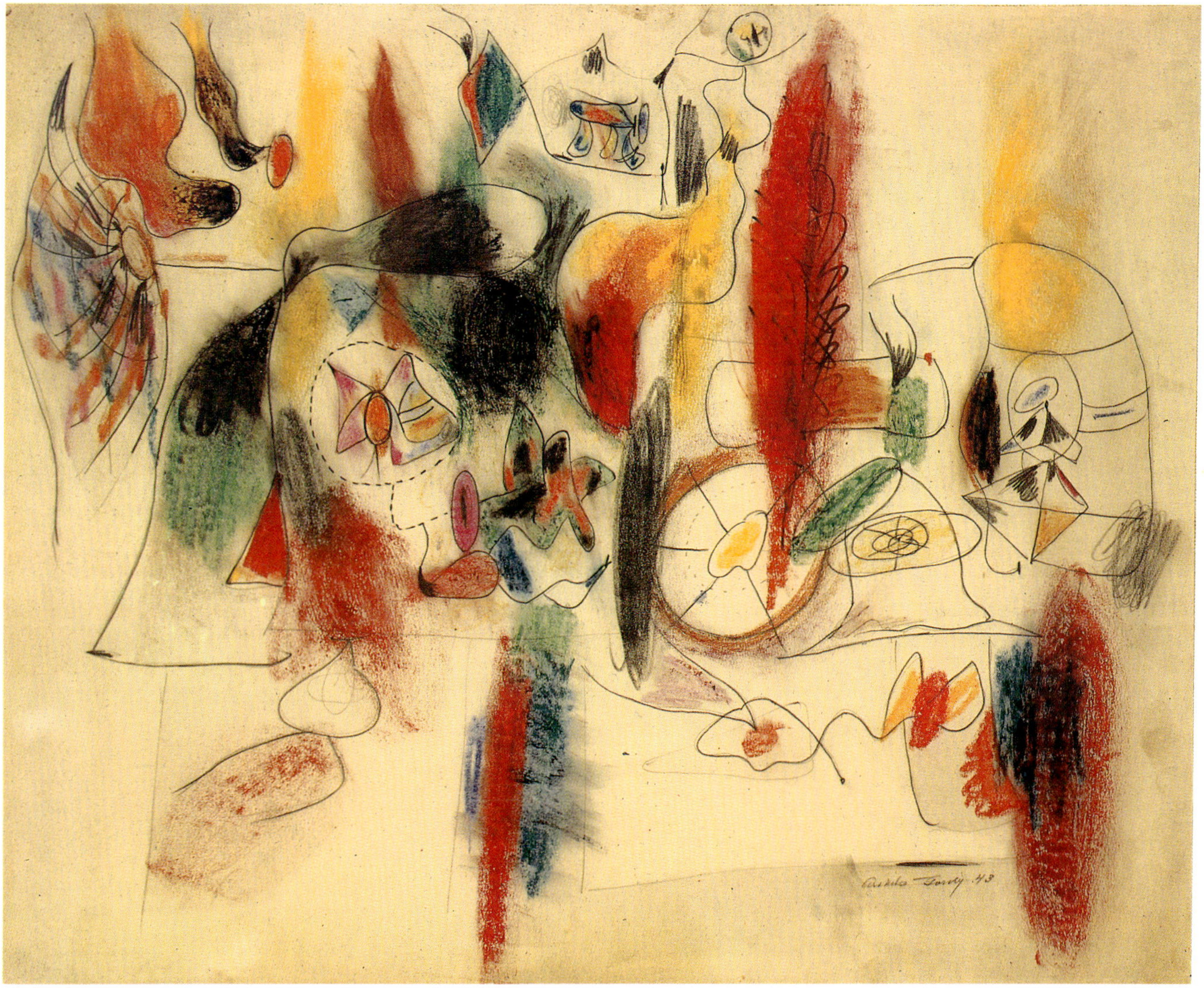

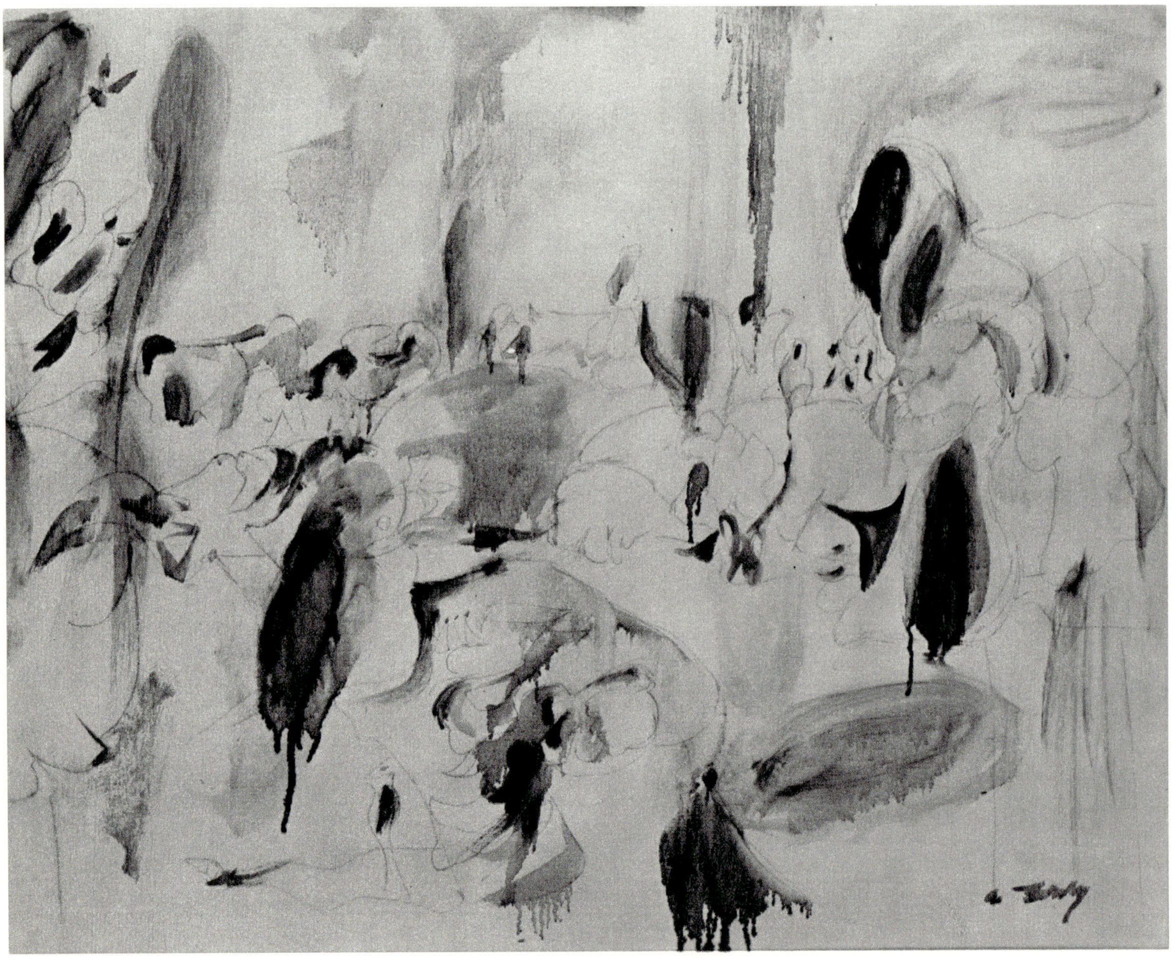

143. *Untitled (Landscape?).* 1943
Oil and pencil on canvas, 19 1/2 × 25″
Contemporary Collection of The Cleveland Museum of Art

144. *Love of the New Gun*. 1944
Oil on canvas, 29 1/2 × 37 5/8″
Menil Foundation Collection, Houston

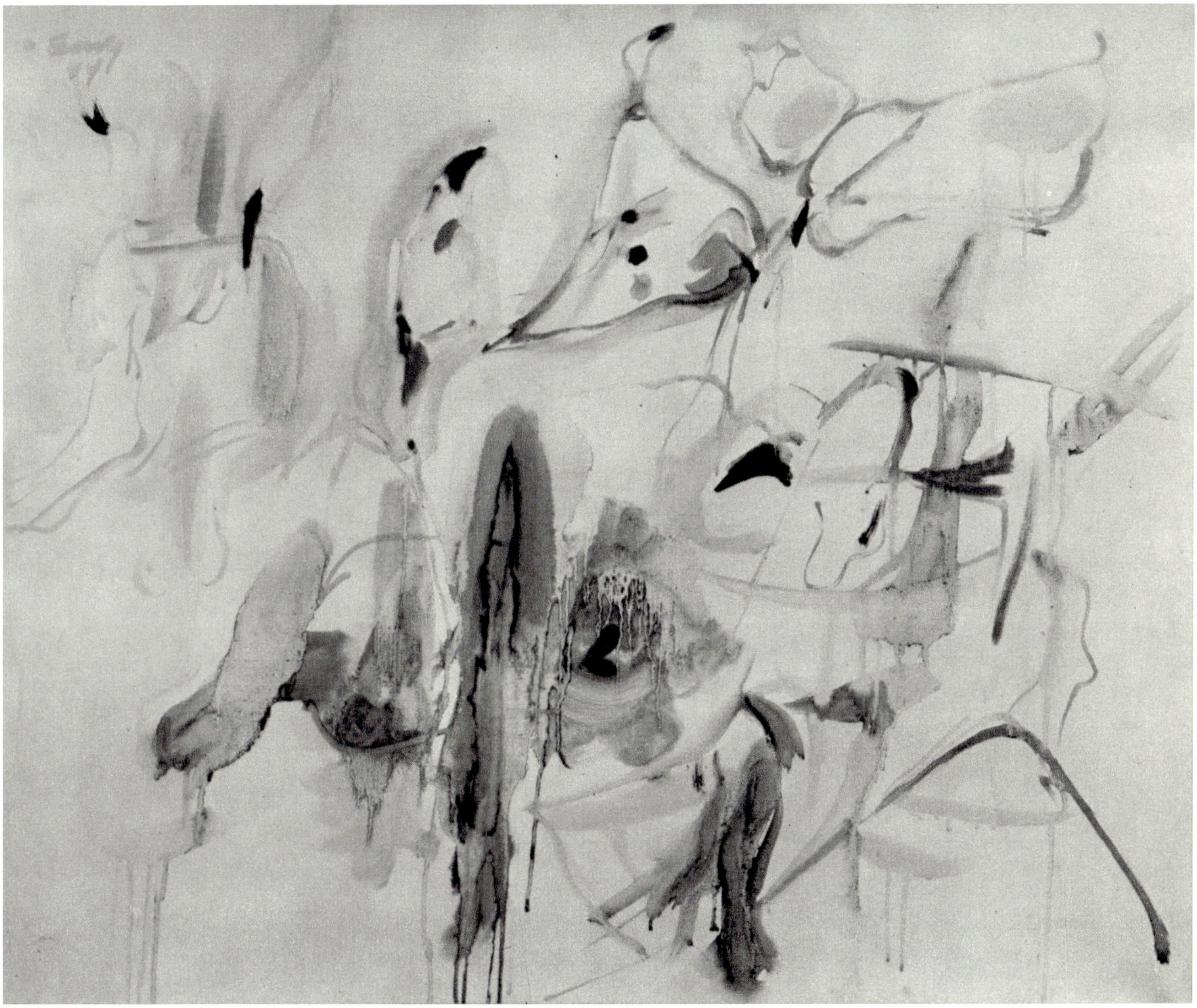

145. *Composition II.* 1943
Pencil and wax crayon on paper, 22 3/4 × 29″
Collection Barbara and Donald Jonas

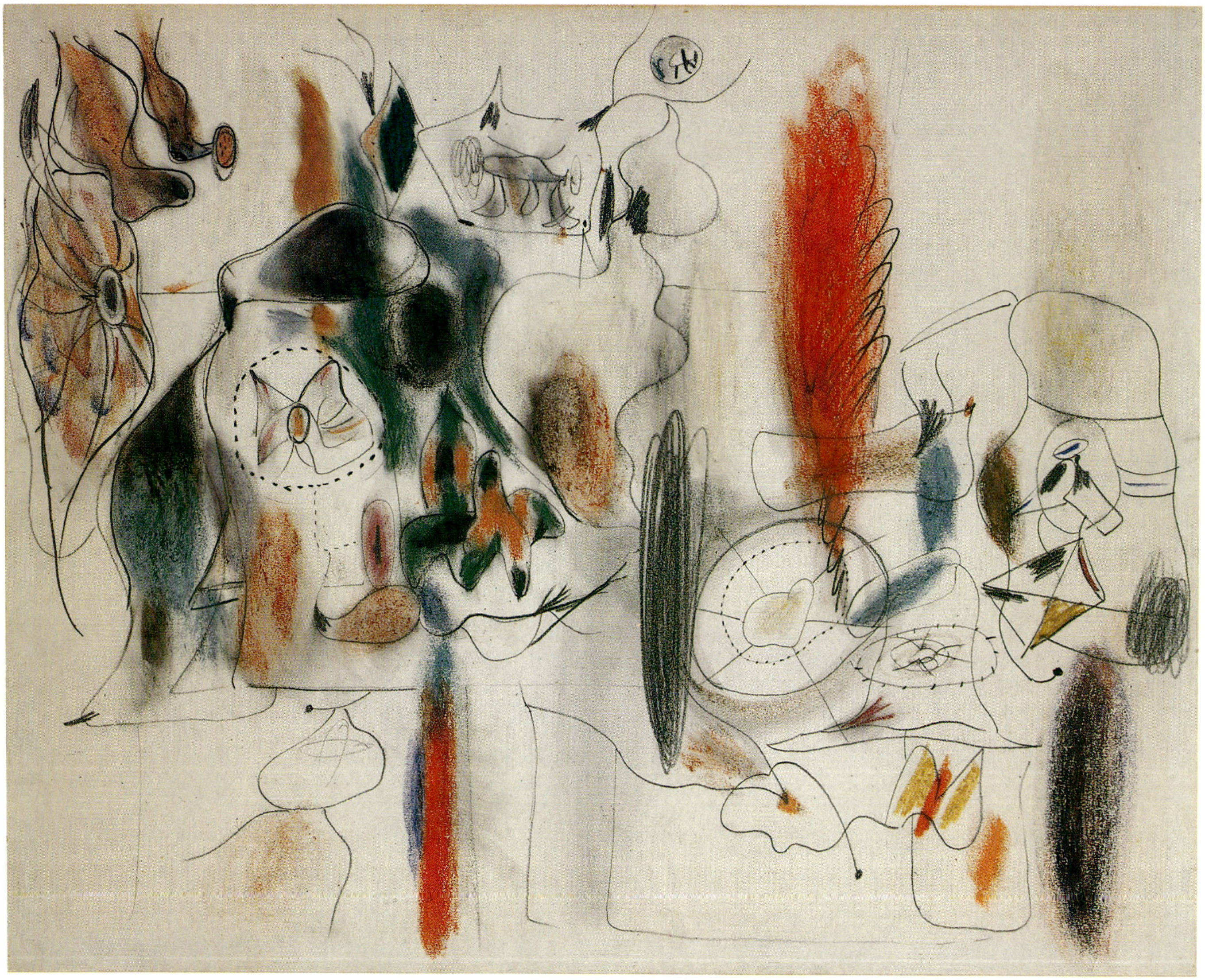

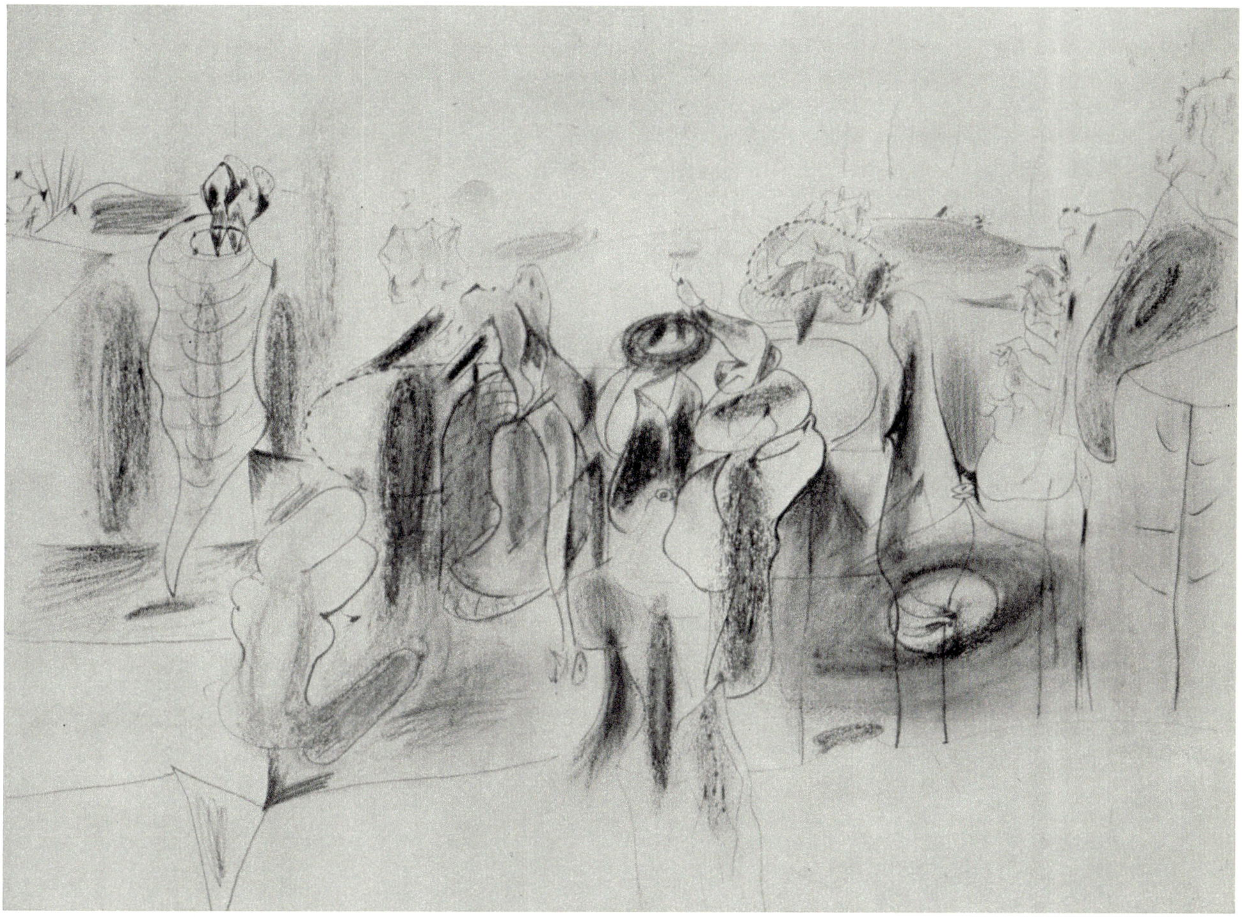

146. *Untitled*. 1943
Pencil and pastel on paper, 19 9/16 × 26 3/4″
Collection Mrs. Satenig Avedisian
on loan to Museum of Fine Arts, Boston

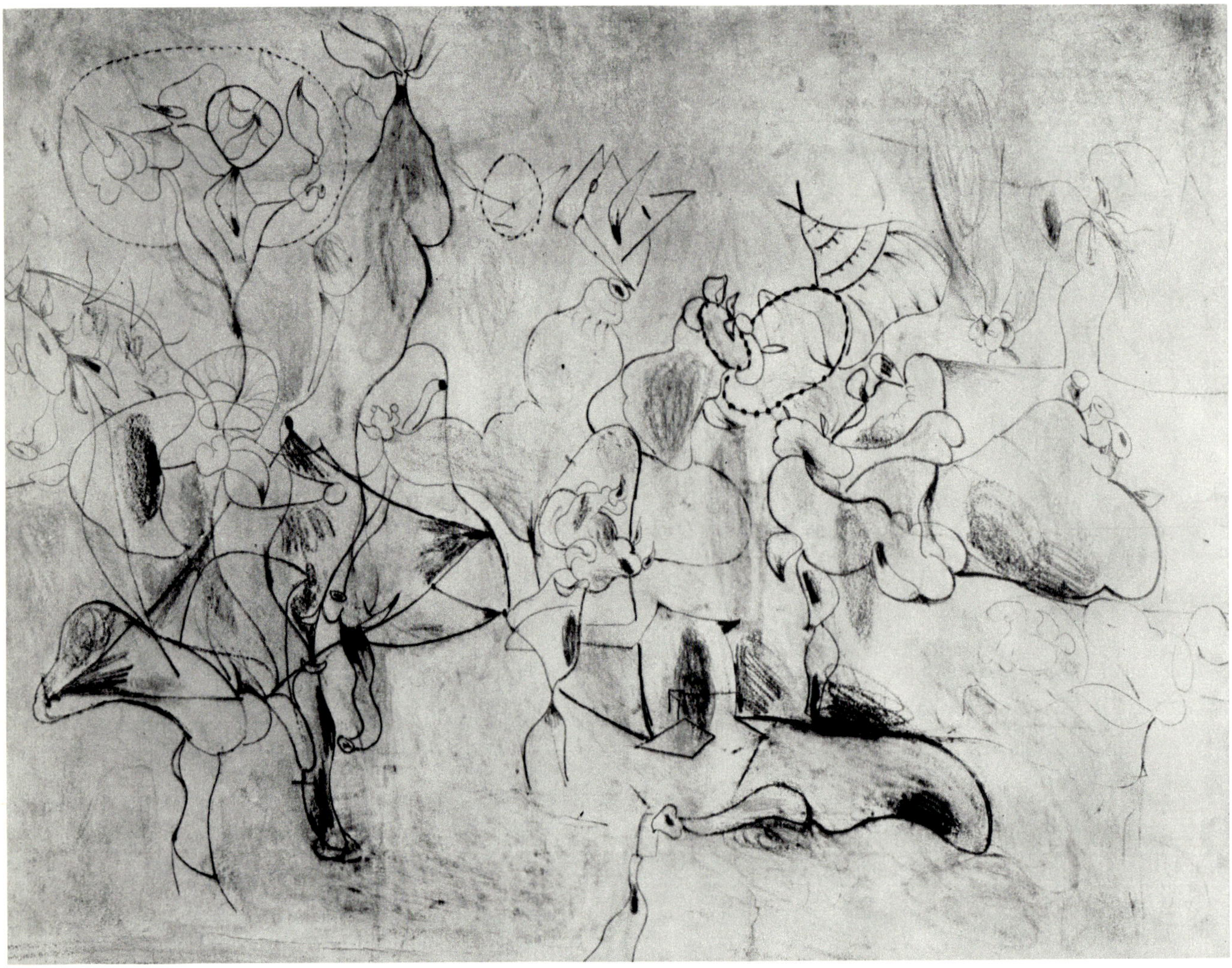

147. *Untitled*. 1944
Watercolor and pencil on paper, 19 3/4 × 26 1/2″
Collection Mr. and Mrs. Michael de Havenon

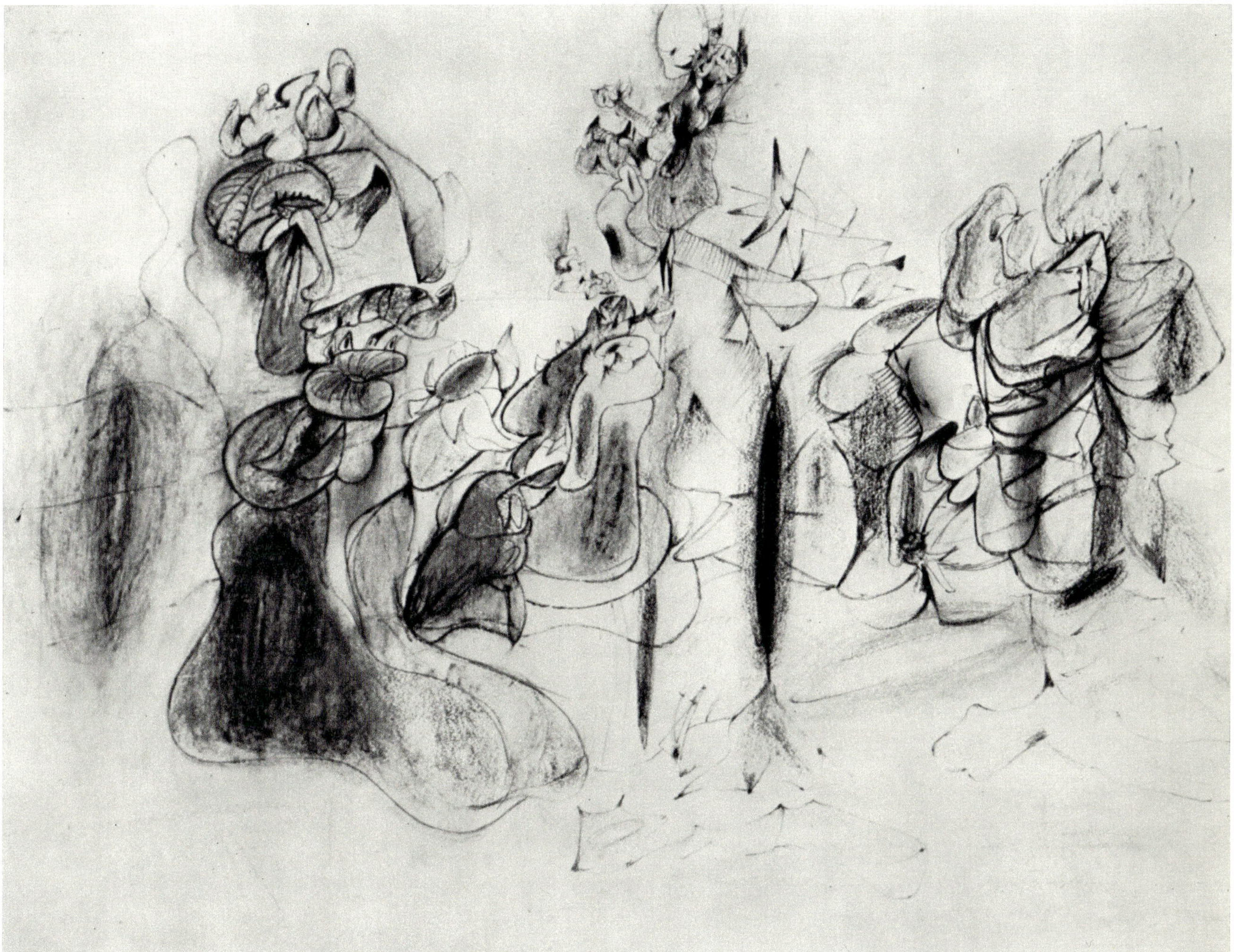

148. *Anatomical Blackboard.* 1943
Pencil and wax crayon on paper, 20 1/4 × 27 3/8″
Collection Mr. and Mrs. Walter Bareiss

149. *Good Afternoon, Mrs. Lincoln.* 1944
Oil on canvas, 30 × 38″
Courtesy Allan Stone Gallery, New York

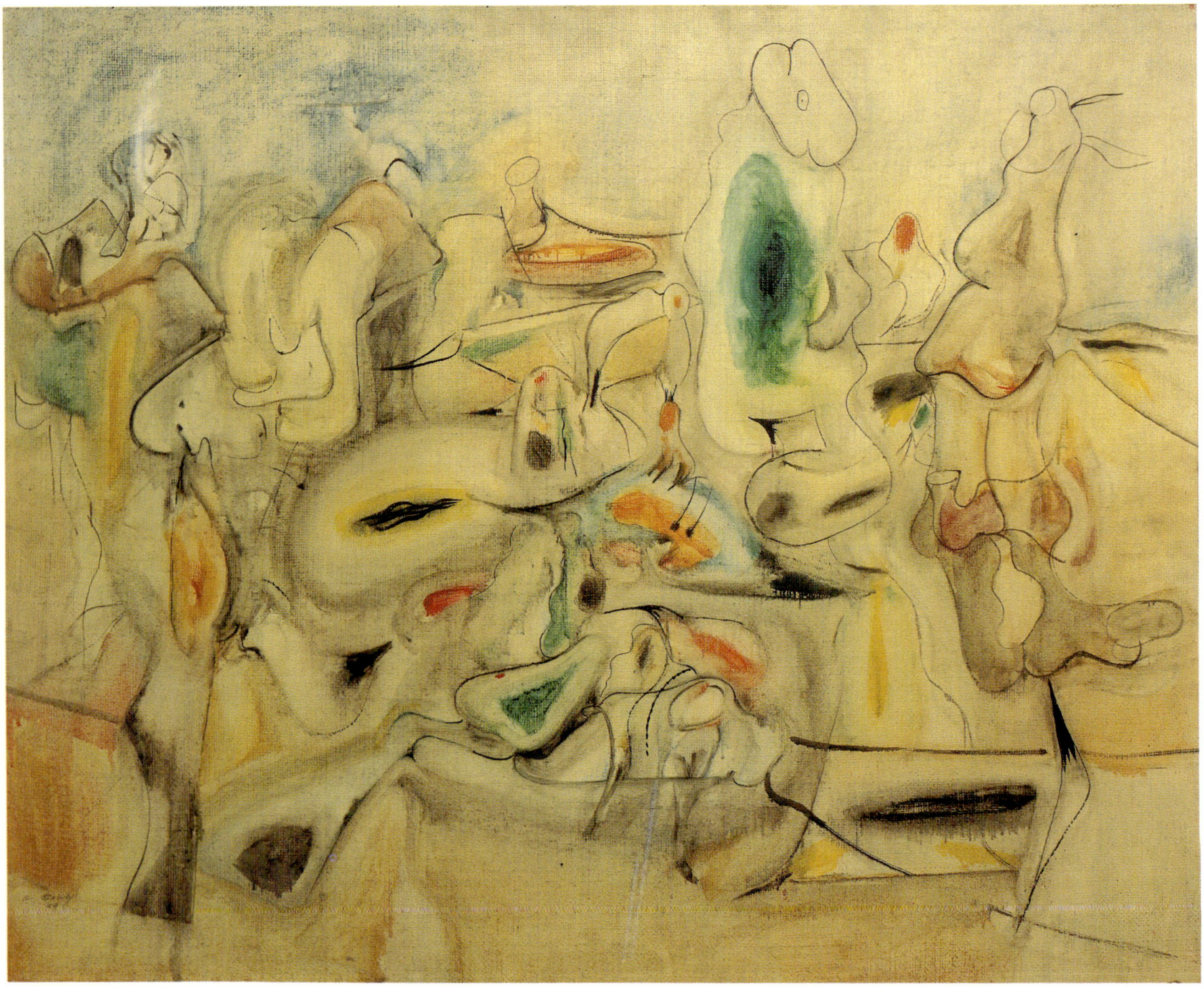

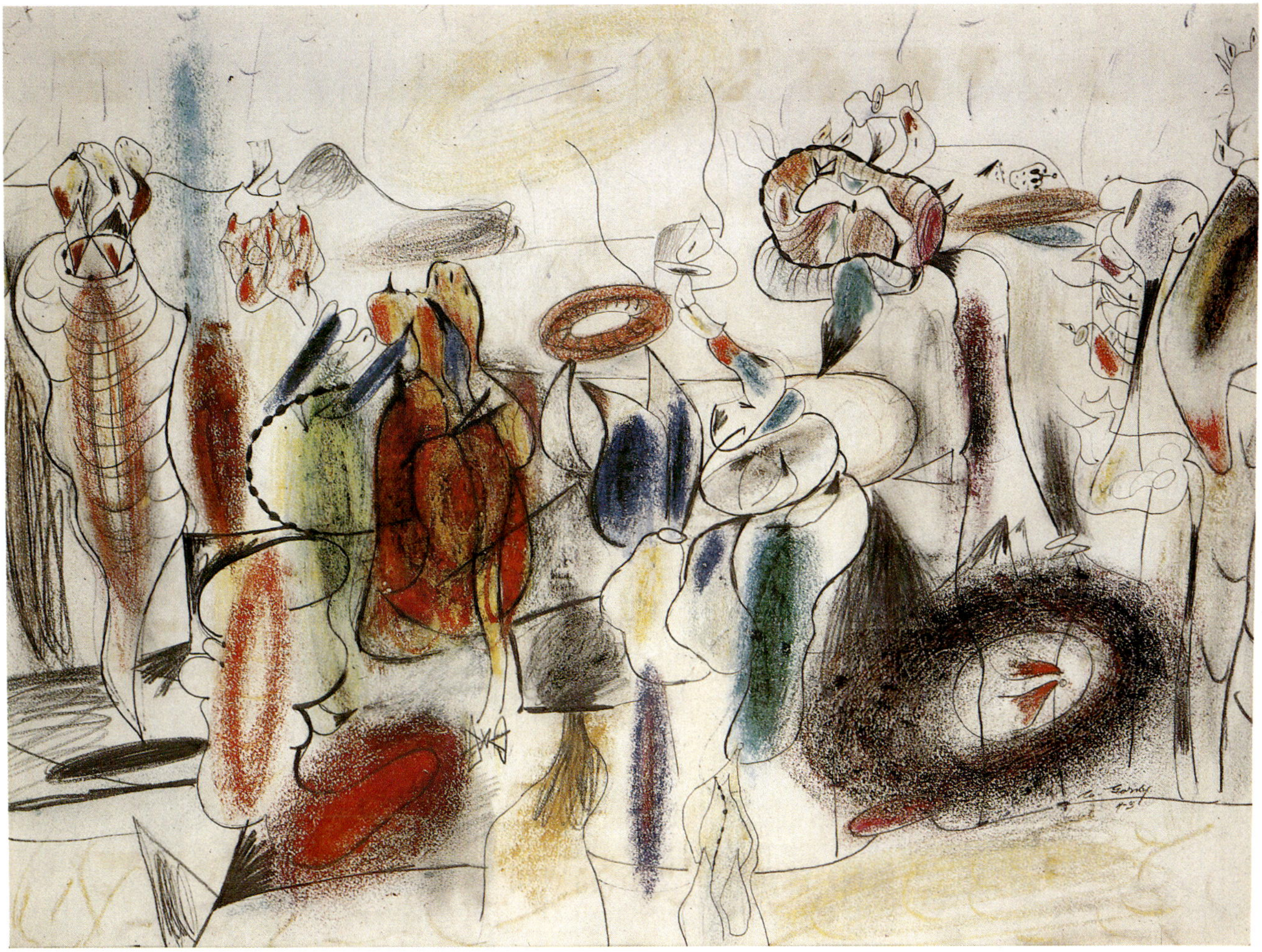

150. *Virginia Landscape*. 1943
Pastel and pencil on paper, 19 3/4 × 26 1/2″
Private Collection

151. *Virginia Landscape.* 1943
Pencil and wax crayon on paper, 20 × 27″
Private Collection

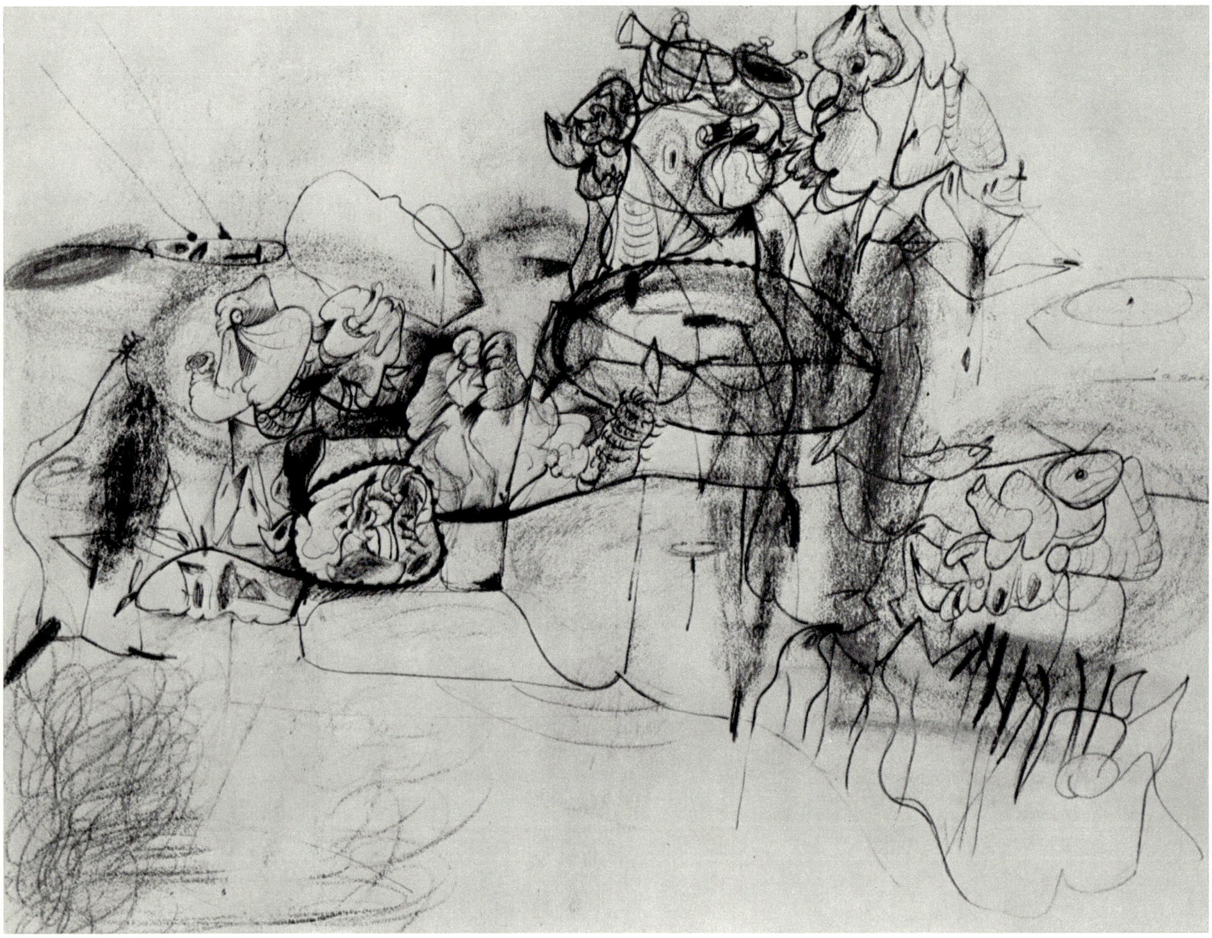

152. *Virginia Landscape.* 1944
Pencil and sargent crayon on paper, 19 × 25″
Collection Stefan Edlis

153. *Virginia Pastel.* 1943–44
Pastel and crayon on paper, 20 1/4 × 27 1/2″
Private Collection

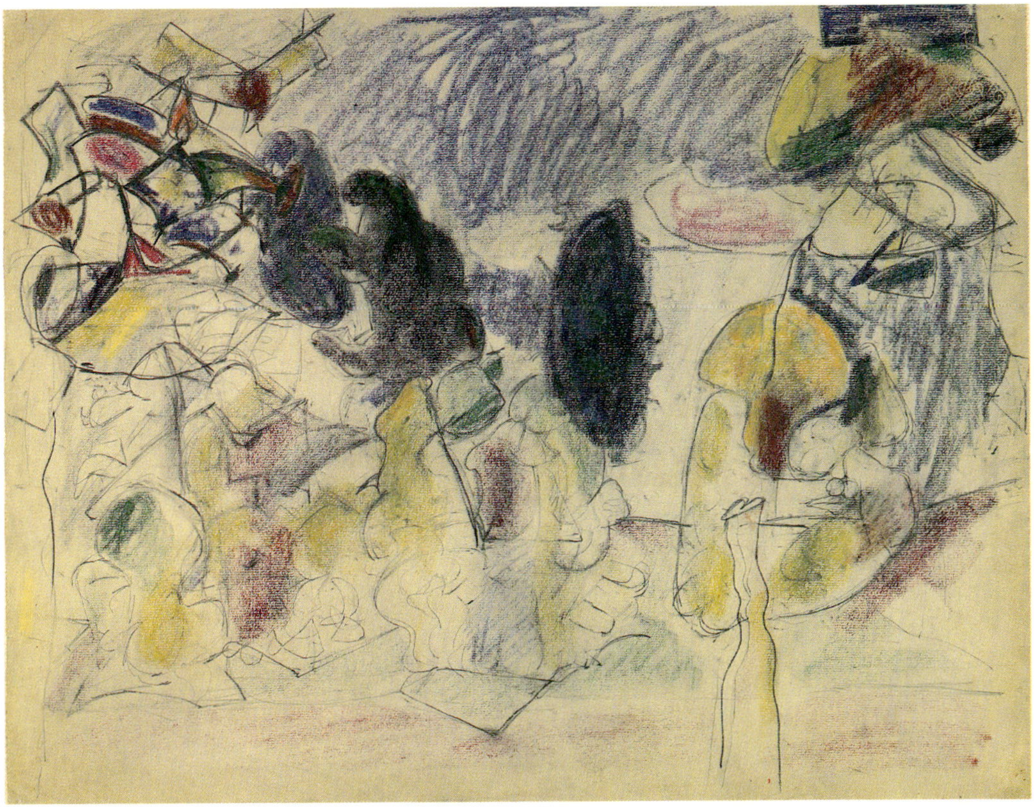

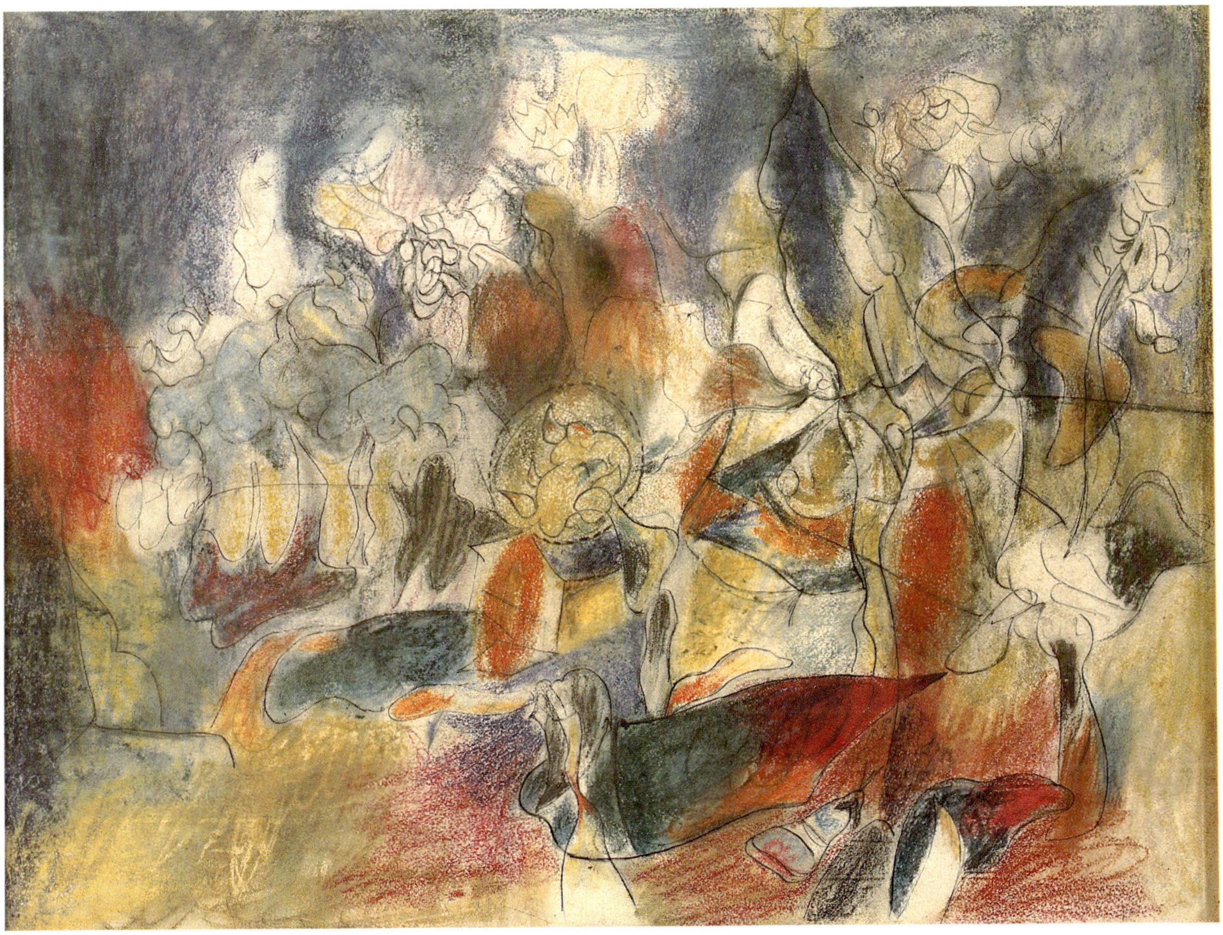

154. *Drawing*. 1943
Pencil and wax crayon on paper, 22 × 27 1/4″
Courtesy Allan Stone Gallery, New York

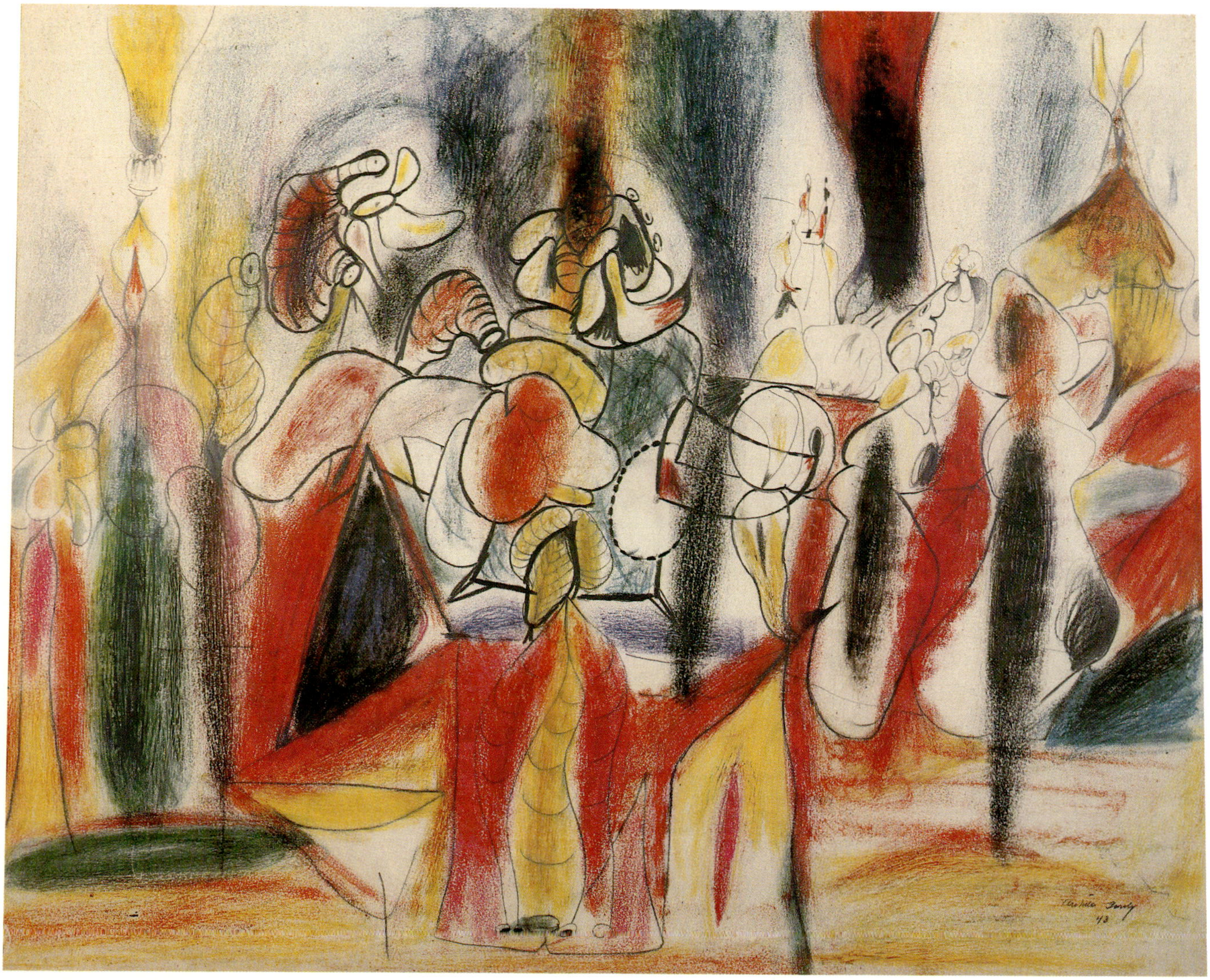

155. *Untitled*. 1943
Pencil and crayon on paper, 22 3/4 × 29″
Courtesy of The Art Institute of Chicago: 1963. 571
Gift of Ada Turnbull Hertle; Joseph R. Shapiro;
Peter Bensinger; Helen Regenstein

156. *Untitled* (Study for *The Liver is the Cock's Comb* [?]). 1943
Pencil and crayon on paper, 20 3/4 × 27 11/16″
Collection Hirshhorn Museum and Sculpture Garden,
Smithsonian Institution, Washington, D.C.

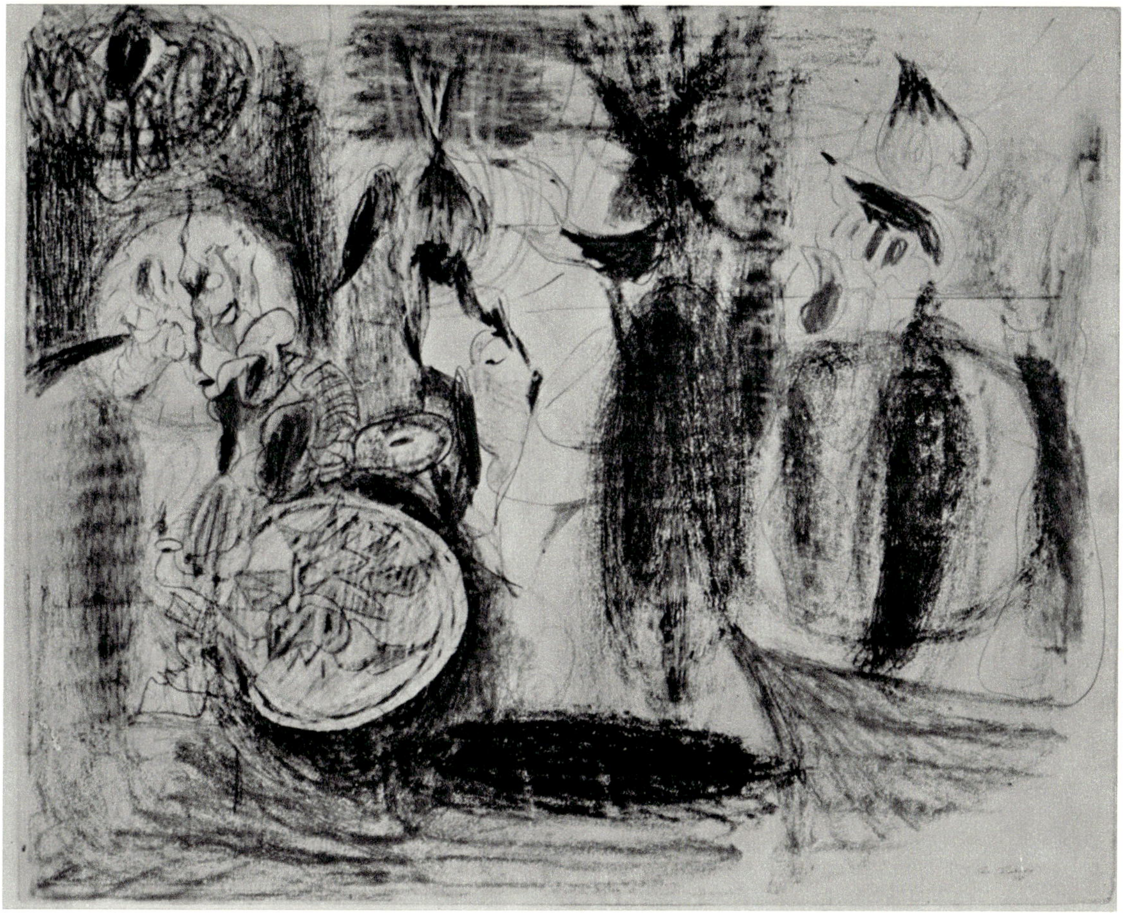

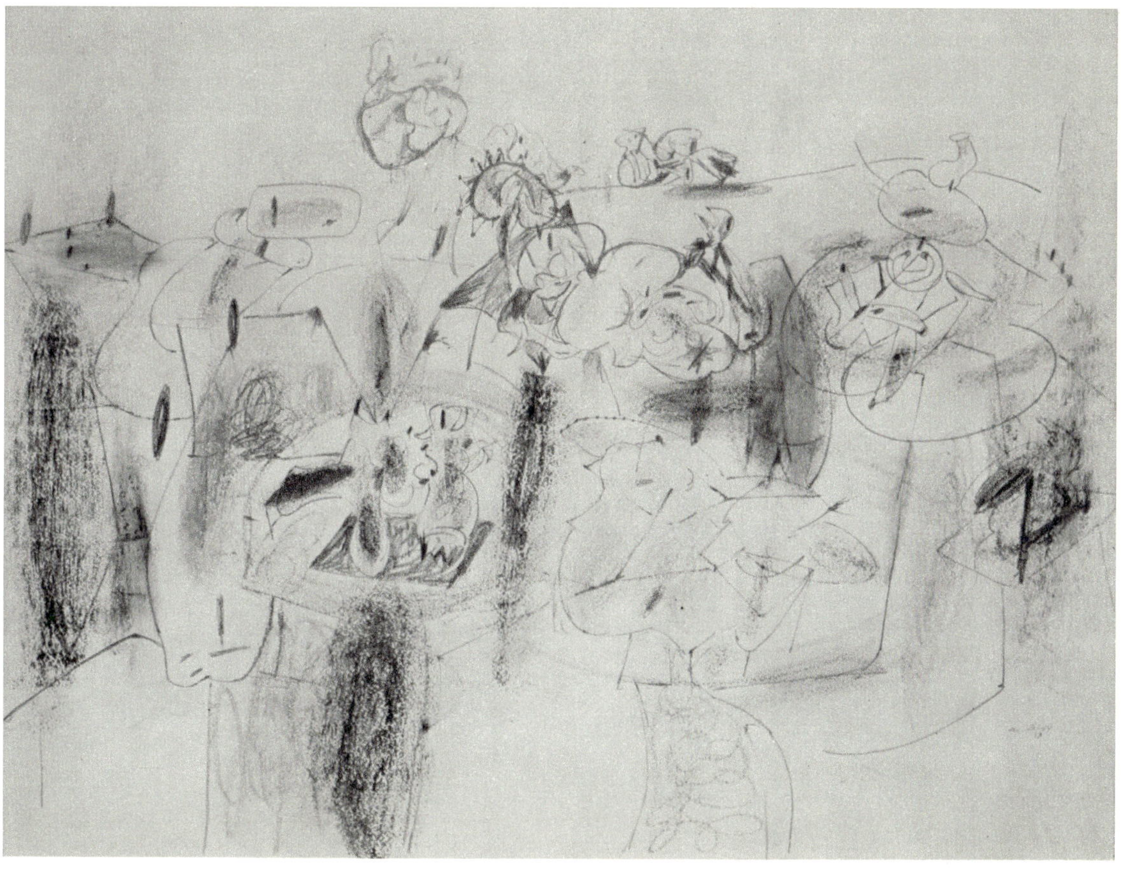

157. *Untitled.* 1943
Wax crayon and pencil on paper, 20 × 26 3/4″
Collection The Solomon R. Guggenheim Museum, New York,
Gift, Rook McCulloch 77.2332

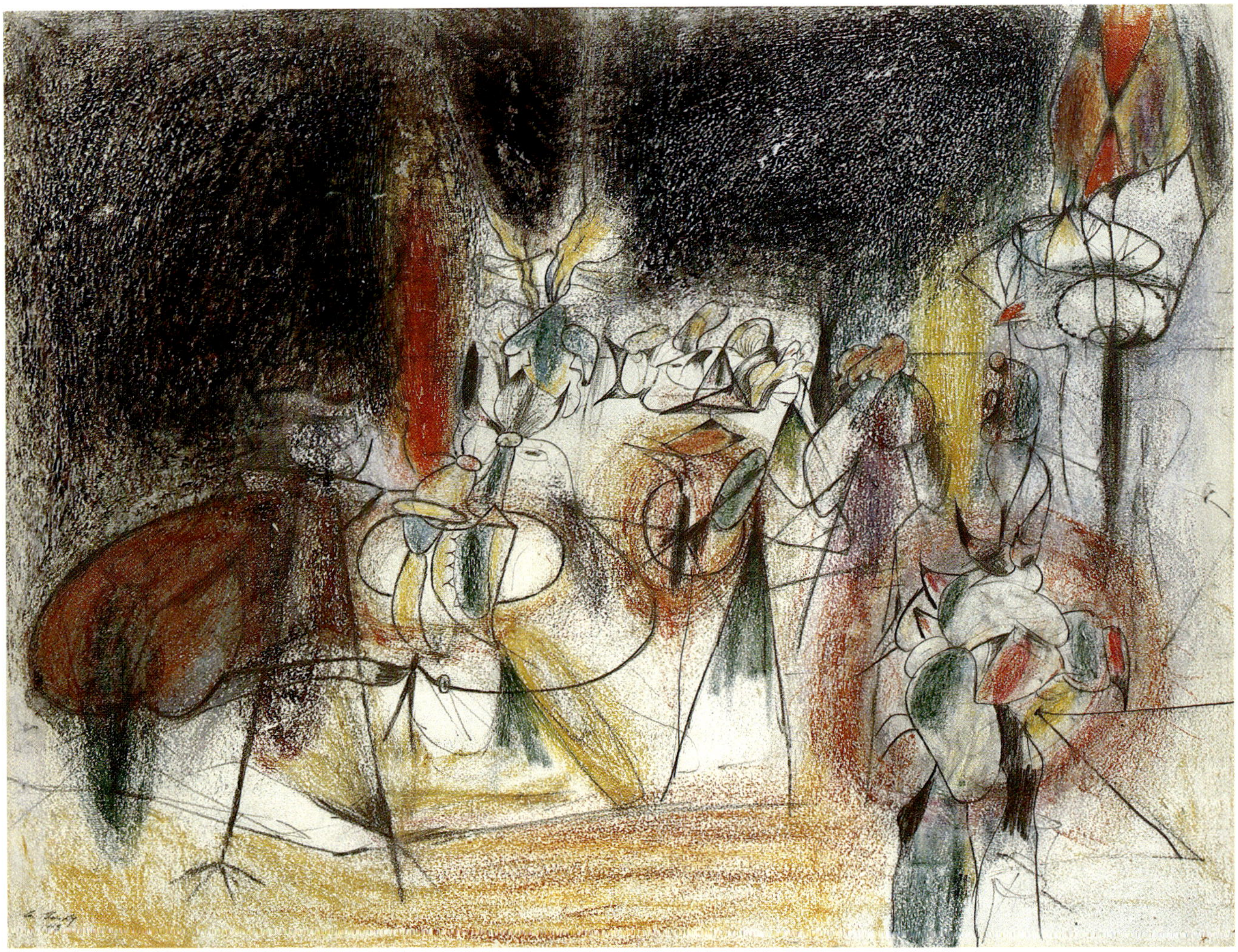

158. *Study for the Liver is the Cock's Comb.* 1943
Ink, pencil and crayon on paper, 19 × 25 1/2″
Frederick Weisman Family Collection

159. *Carnival.* 1943
Crayon on paper, 22 × 28 3/4″
Collection Mr. and Mrs. E. A. Bergman

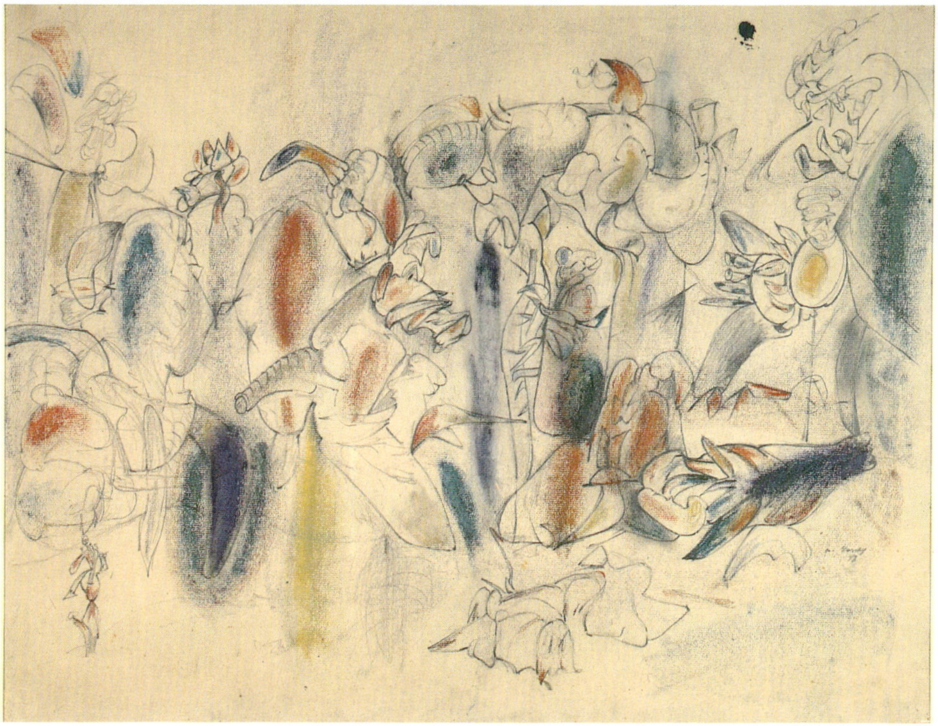

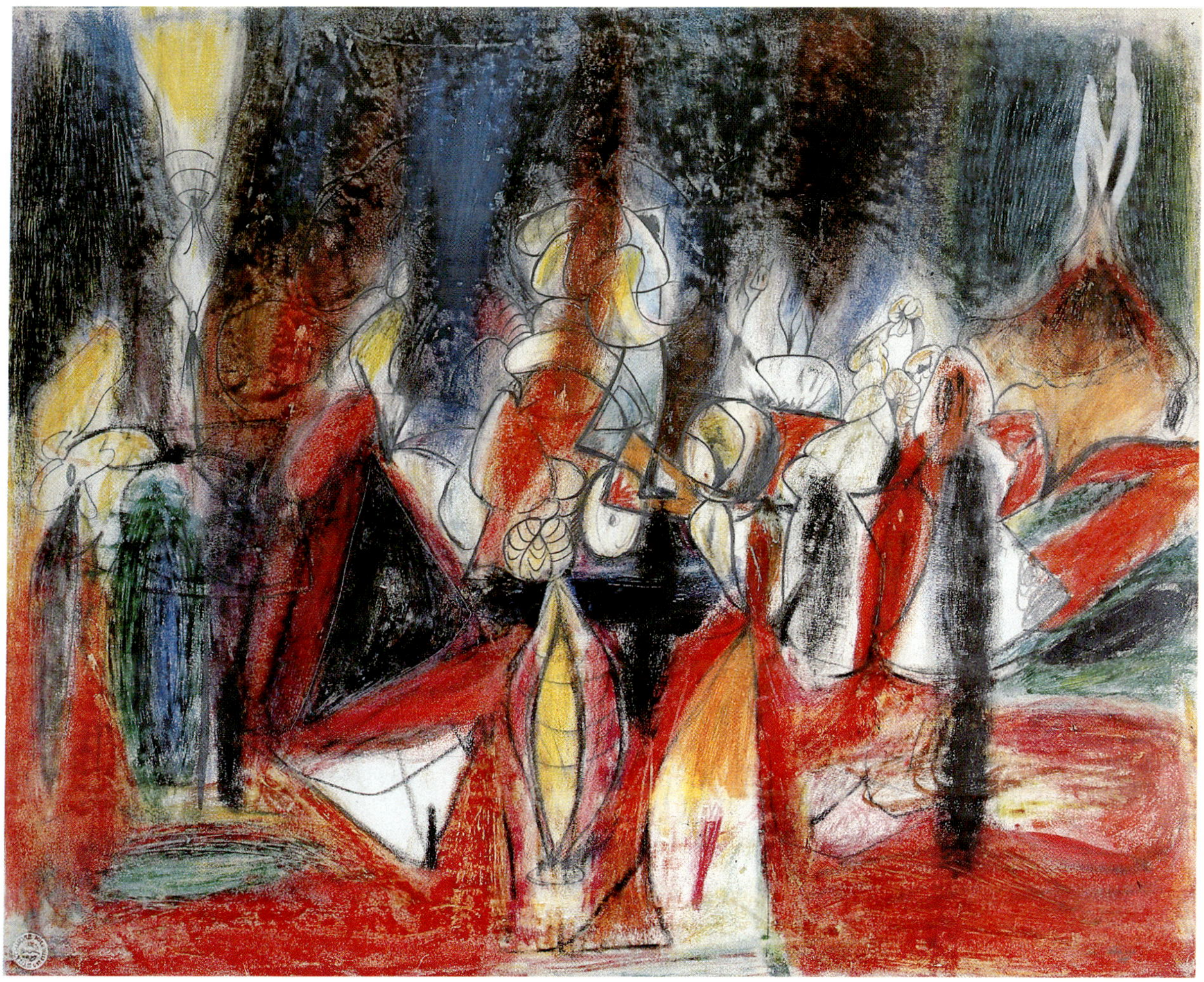

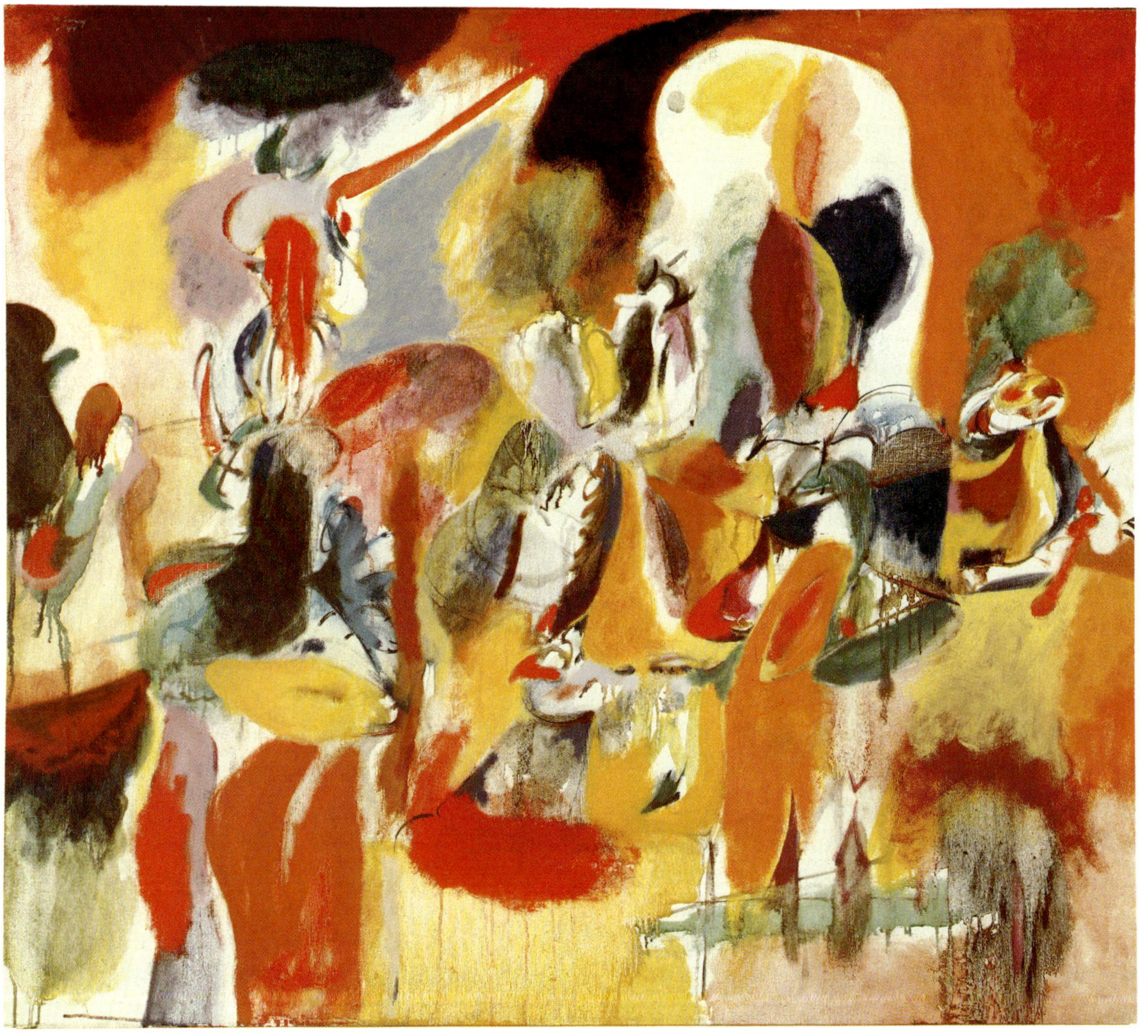

160. *Water of the Flowery Mill.* 1944
Oil on canvas, 42 1/4 × 48 3/4″
Collection The Metropolitan Museum of Art, New York,
George A. Hearn Fund, 1956

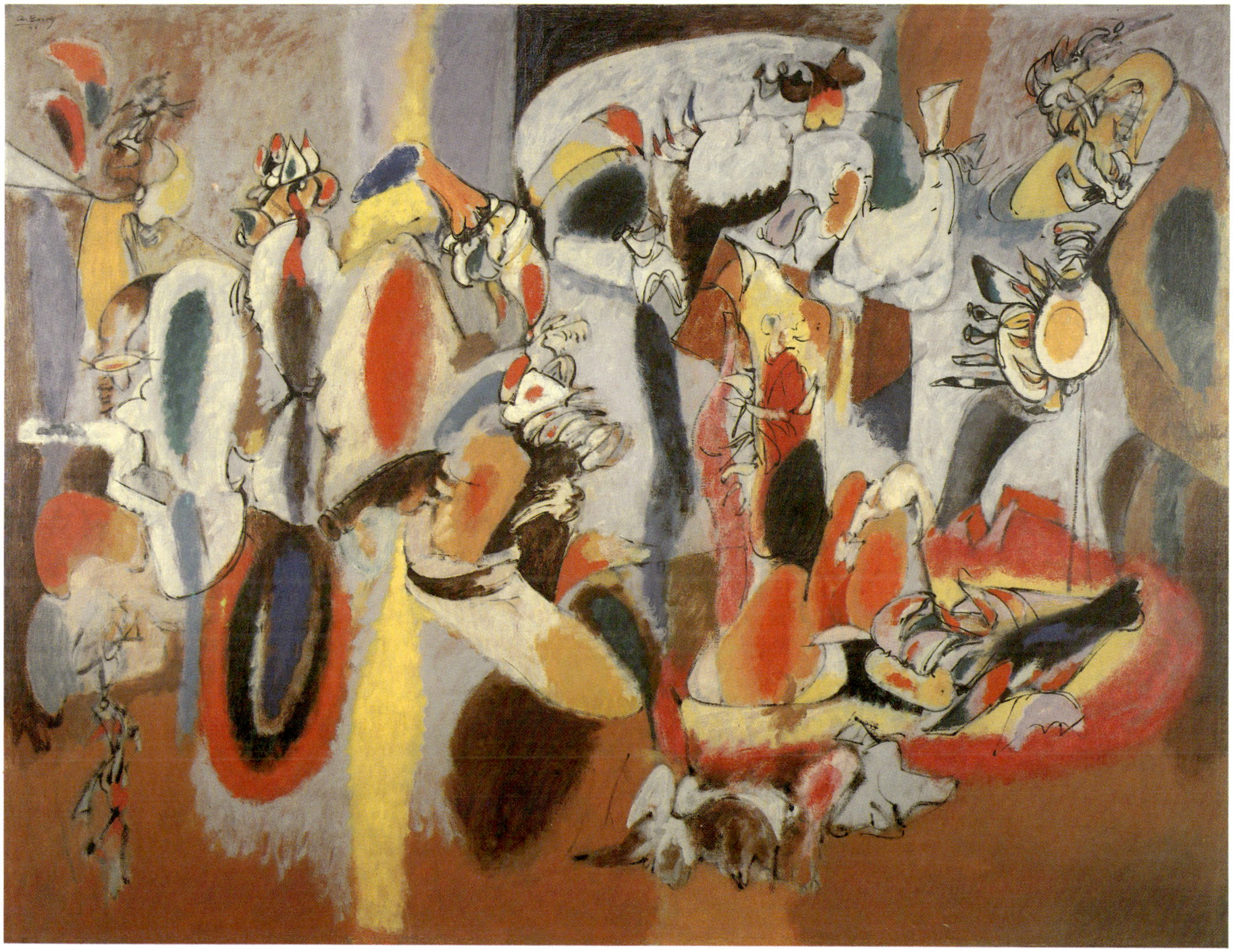

161. *The Liver is the Cock's Comb.* 1944
Oil on canvas, 72 × 98″
Collection Albright-Knox Art Gallery, Buffalo, New York,
Gift of Seymour H. Knox, 1956

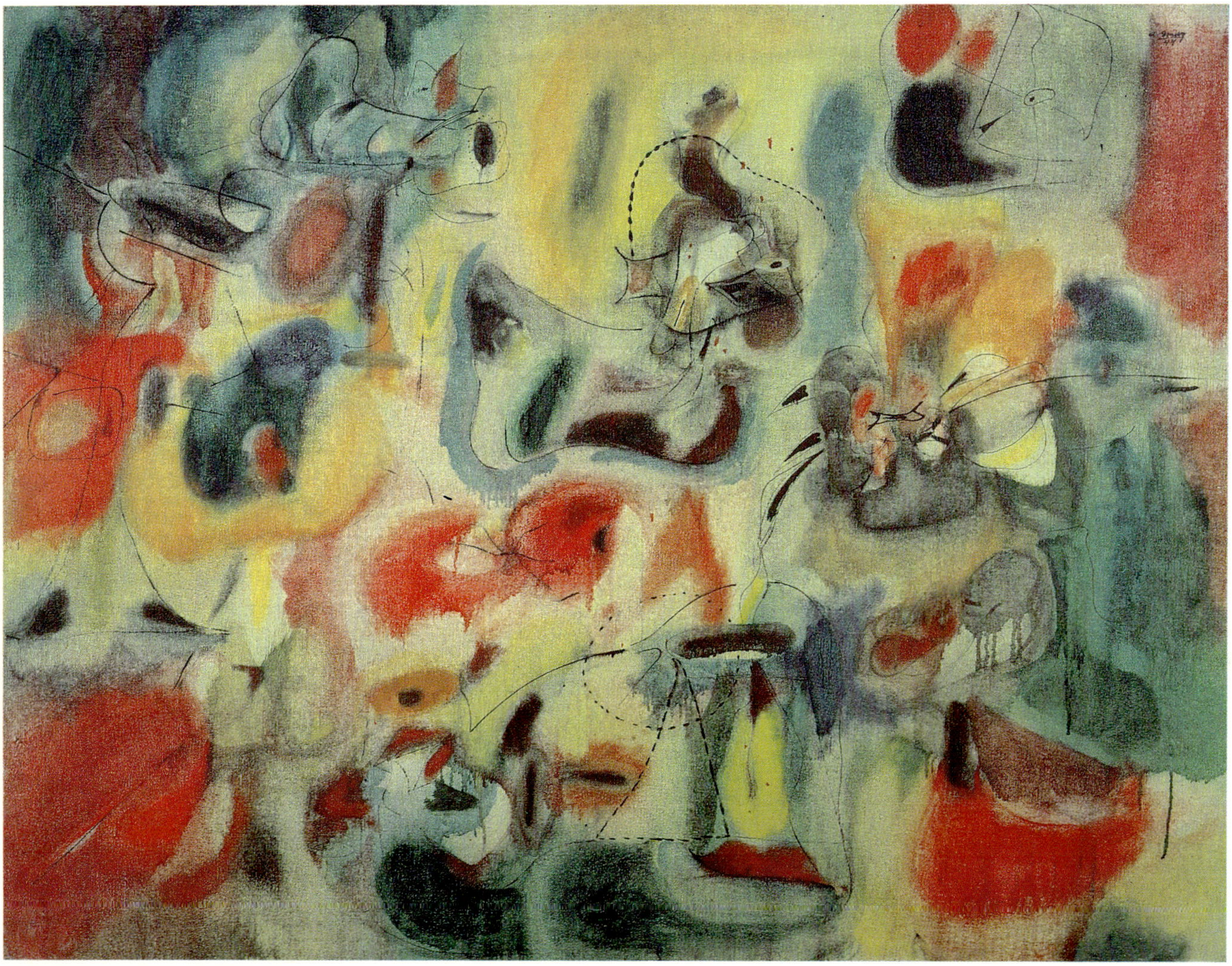

162. *The Sun, The Dervish in the Tree*. 1944
Oil on canvas, 35 3/4 × 47″
Collection Graham Gund

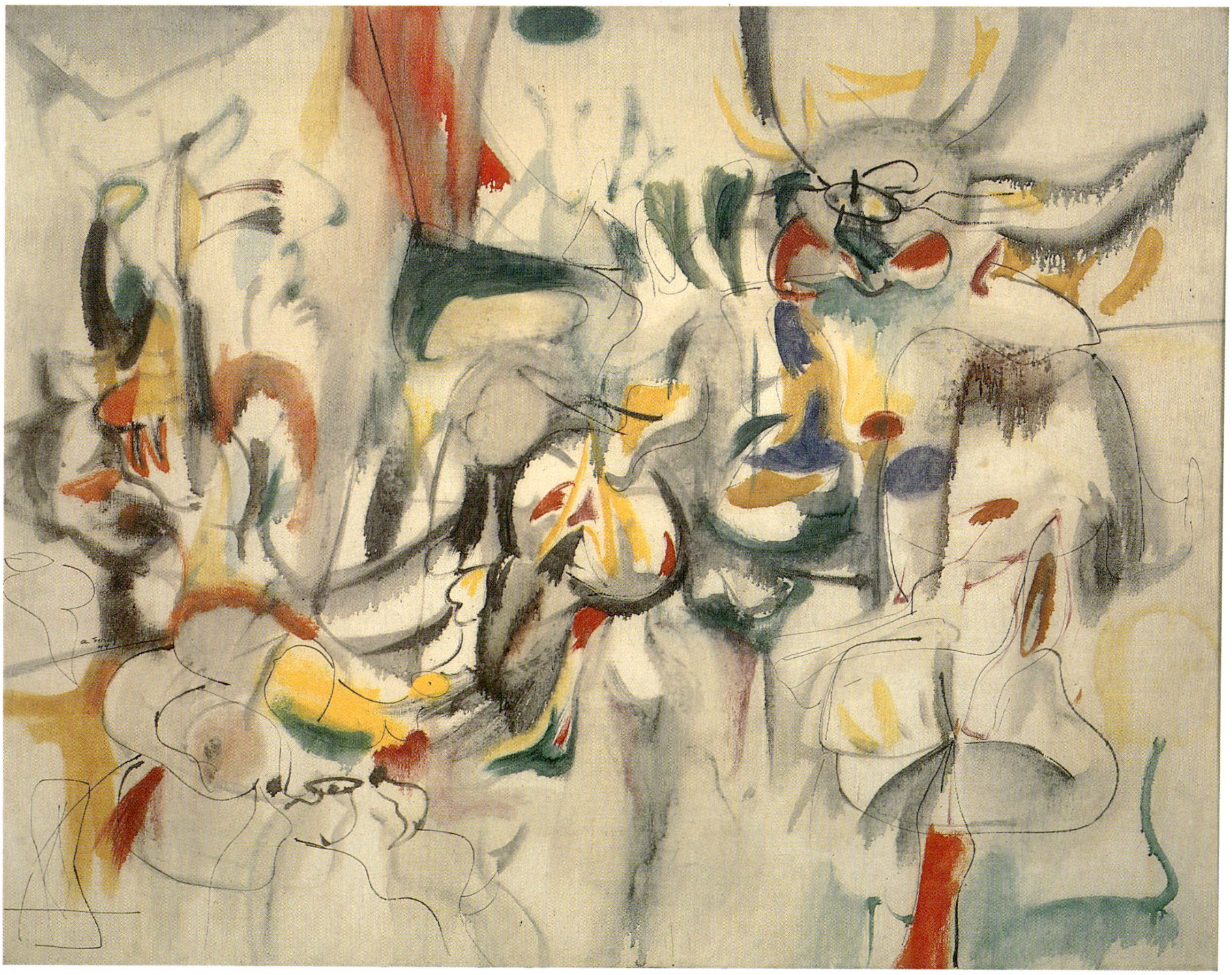

163. *To Project, To Conjure*. 1944
Oil on canvas, 35 3/4 × 46 3/4″
Collection Sue and David Workman

164. *How My Mother's Embroidered Apron Unfolds in My Life*. 1944
Oil on canvas, 40 × 45″
Collection Seattle Art Museum, Gift of Mr. and Mrs. Bagley Wright

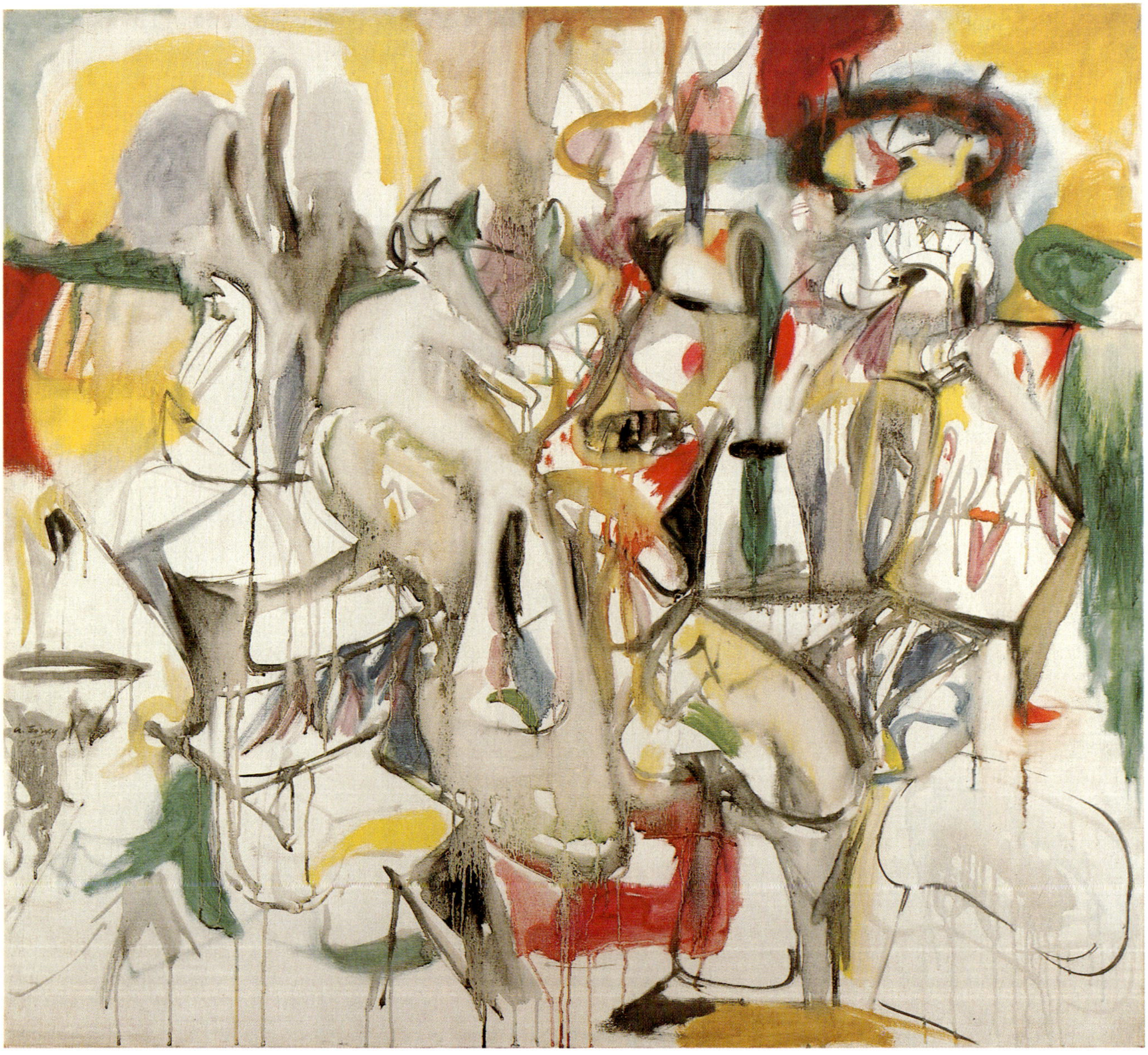

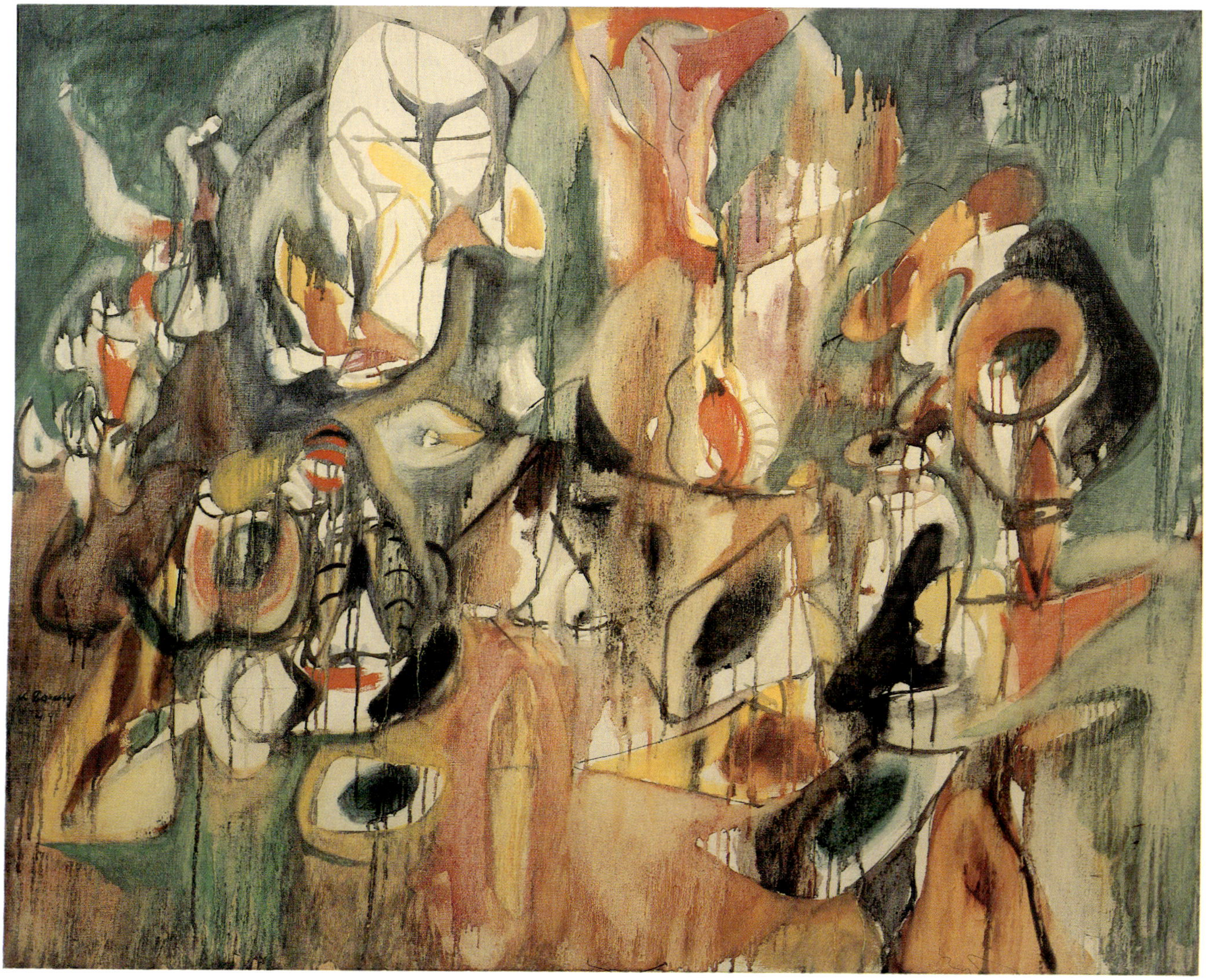

165. *One Year the Milkweed*. 1944
Oil on canvas, 37 × 47″
Collection National Gallery of Art, Washington, D.C.,
Ailsa Mellon Bruce Fund

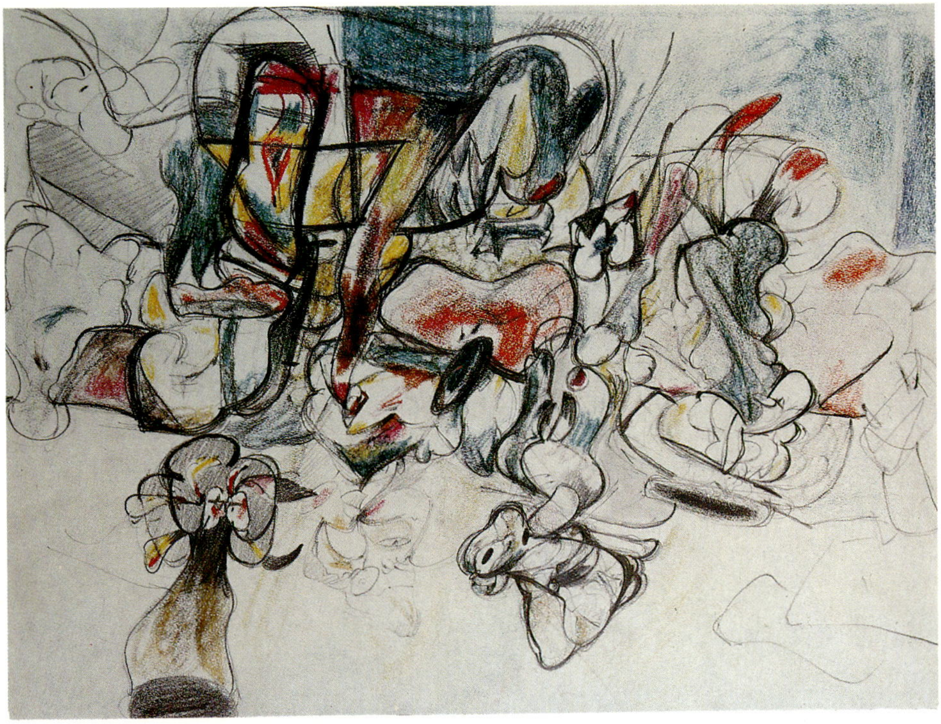

166. *Drawing*. 1943–44
Pencil and crayon on paper, 17 × 23″
Private Collection

167. *The Leaf of the Artichoke Is an Owl*. 1944
Oil on canvas, 28 × 36″
Collection The Museum of Modern Art, New York; Fractional Gift of Sidney Janis

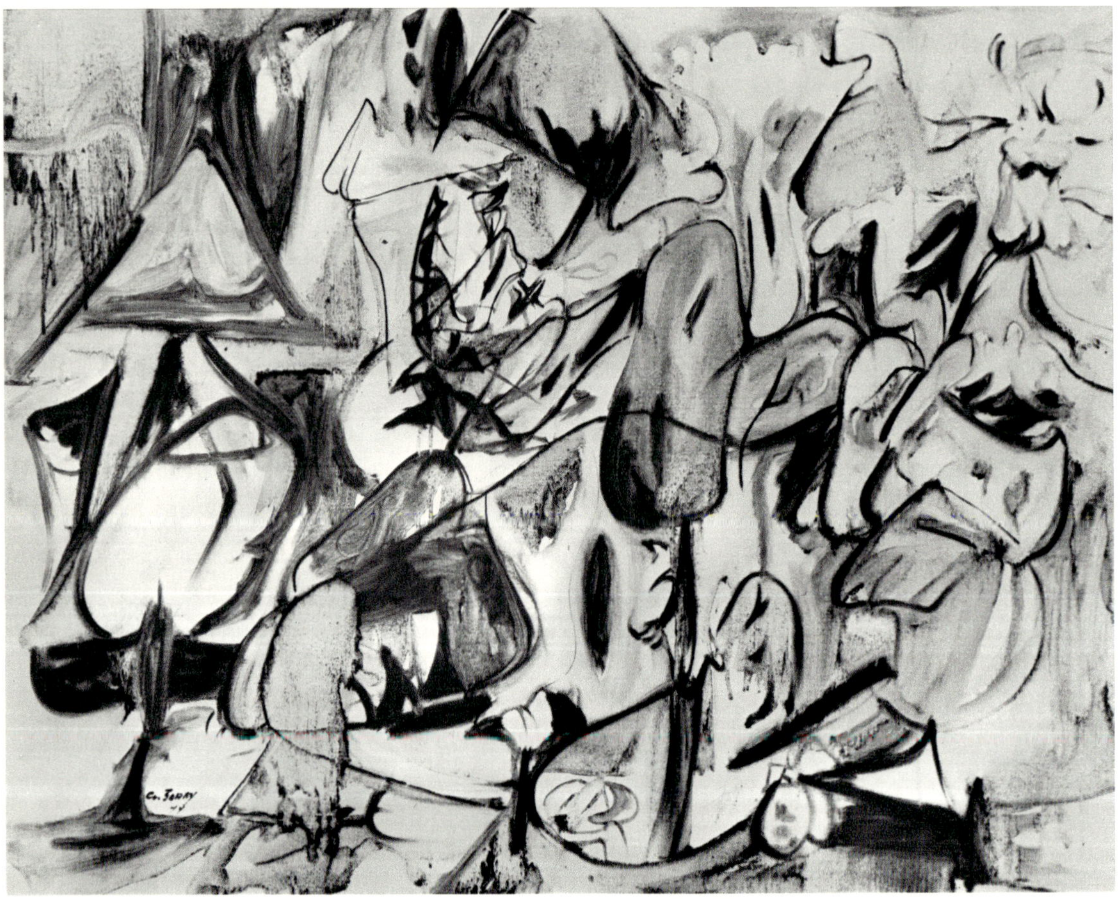

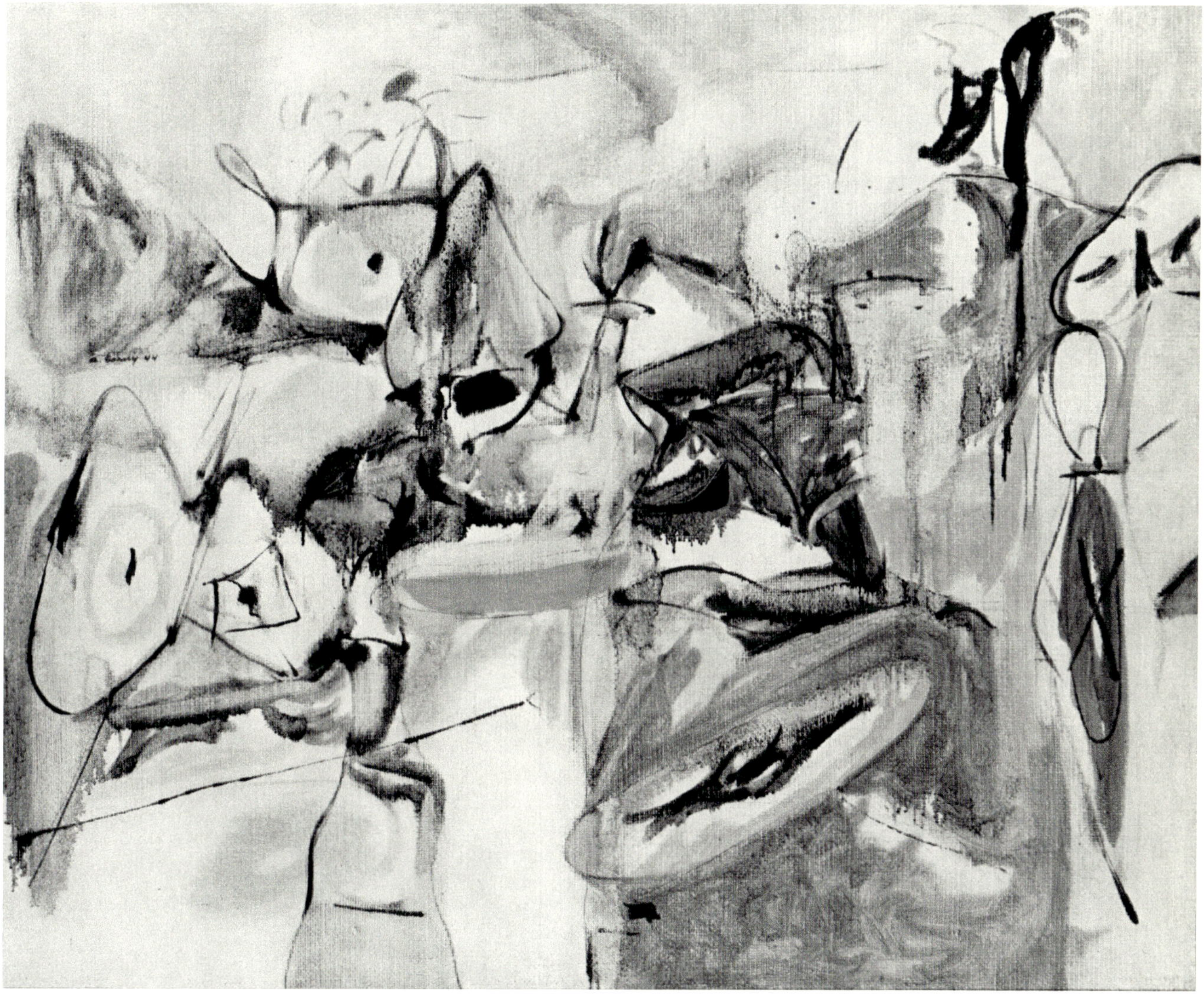

168. *Cornfield of Health II.* 1944
Oil on canvas, 30 1/8 × 37 3/4″
Collection Nelson Gallery-Atkins Museum, Kansas City
(Friends of Art Collection)

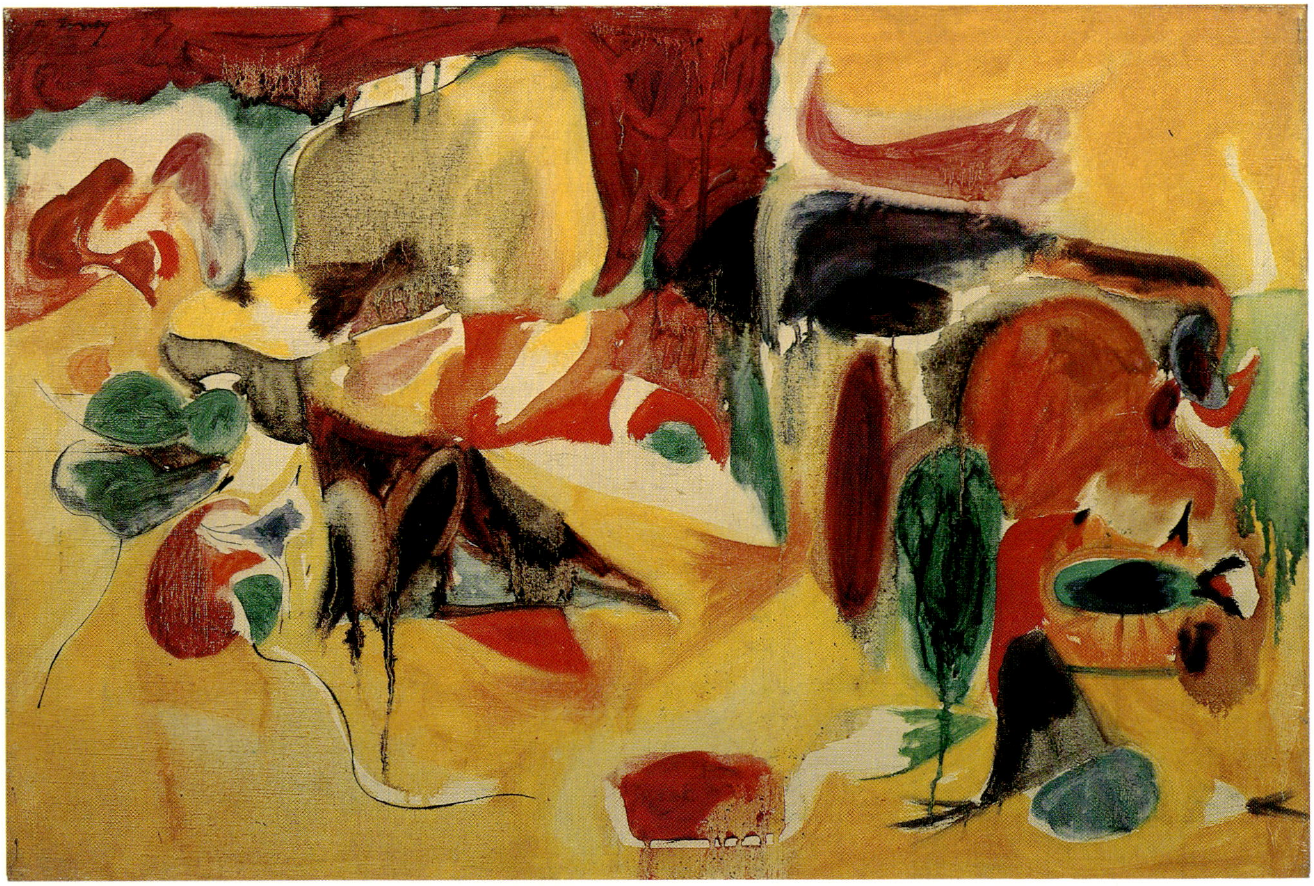

169. *Untitled*. 1944
Oil and pencil on canvas, 19 3/4 × 29 7/8″
Collection Australian National Gallery, Canberra

170. *Apple Orchard*. 1943–46
Pastel on paper, 42 × 52″
Private Collection

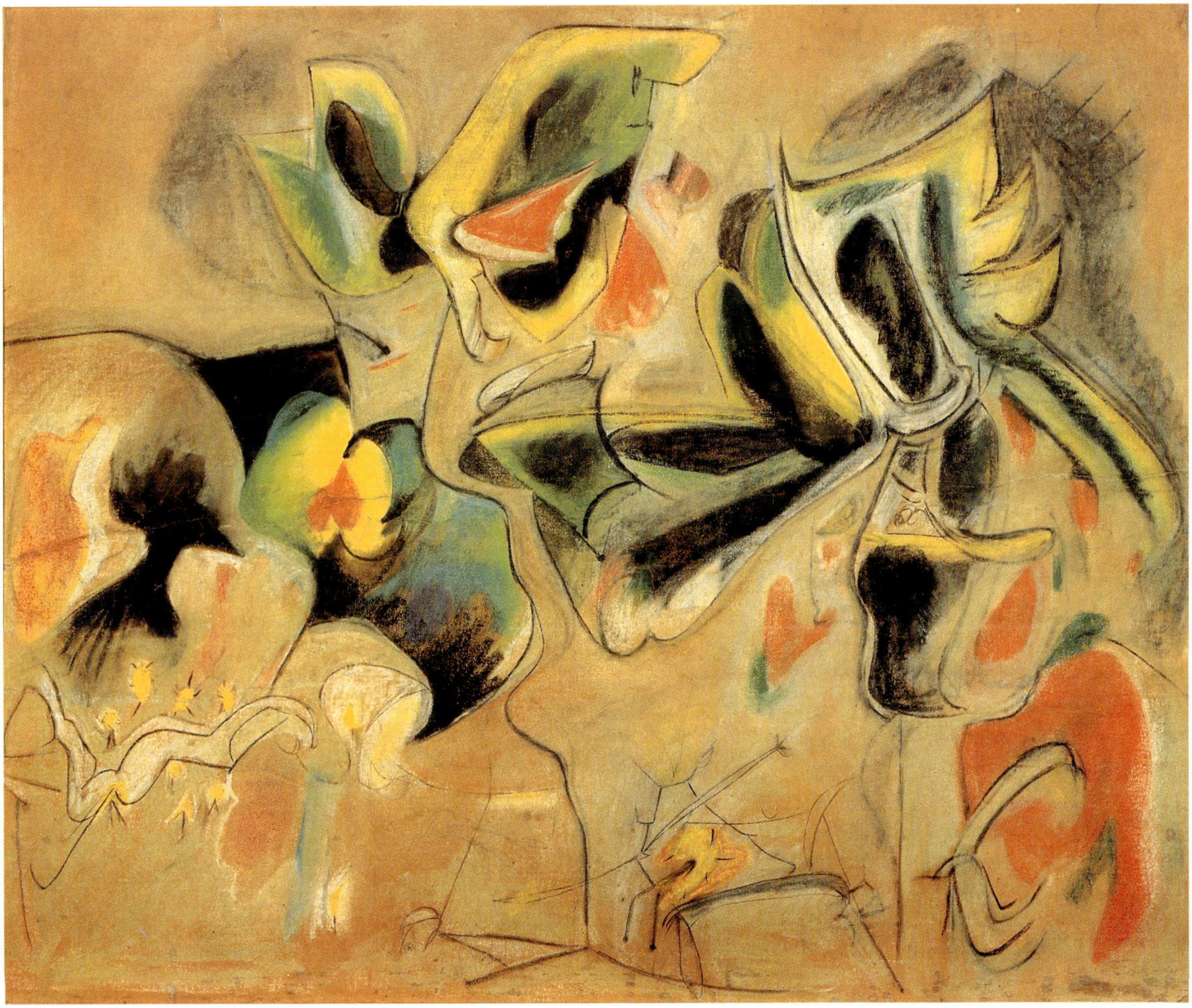

171. *Virginia Landscape.* 1944
Oil on canvas, 36 × 46 1/2″
Collection American Broadcasting Companies, Inc., New York

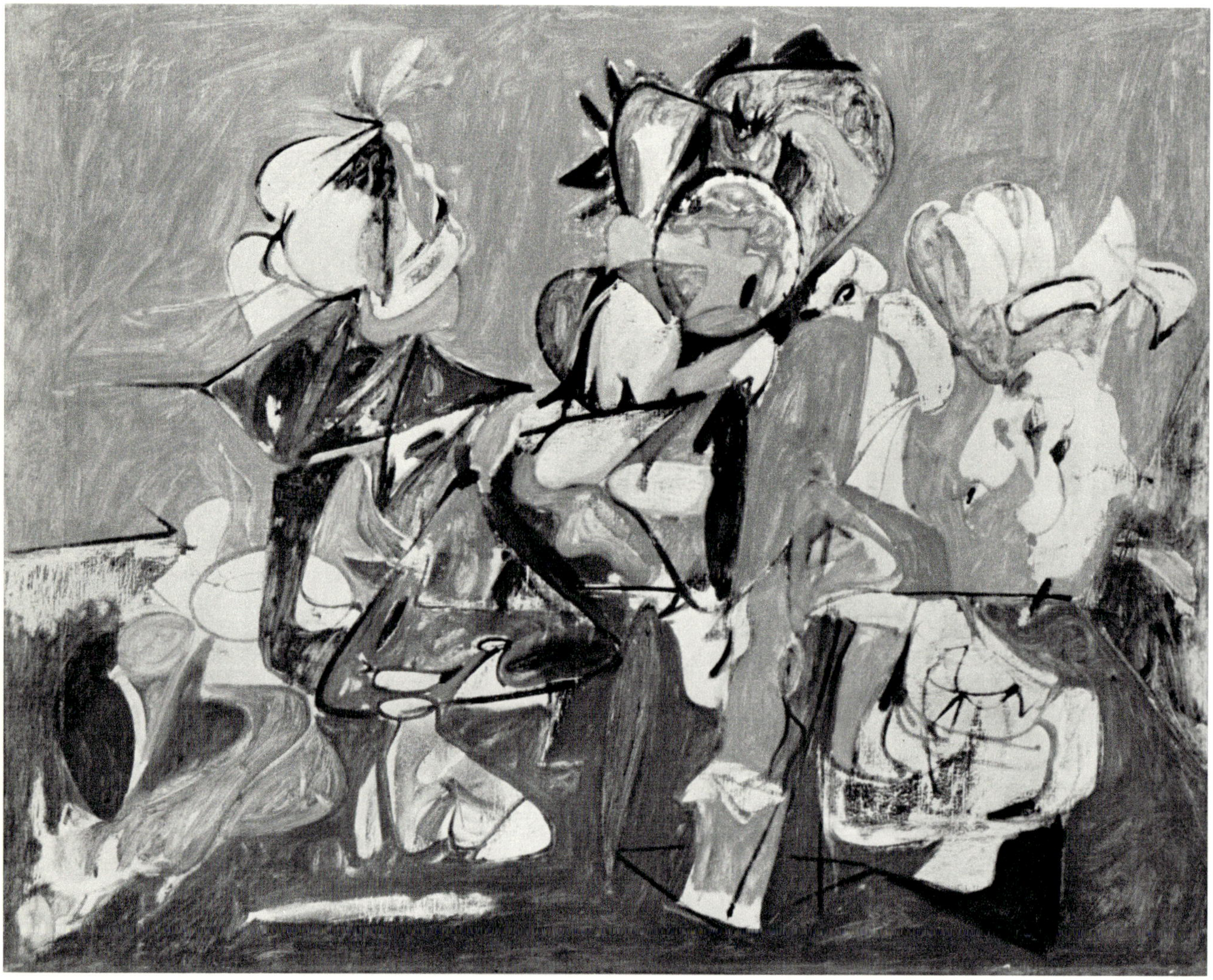

172. *Theme for From a High Place.* 1945
Oil on canvas, 18 × 22″
Collection American Broadcasting Companies, Inc., New York

173. *From a High Place.* 1946
Oil on canvas, 16 7/8 × 24 1/4″
Private Collection

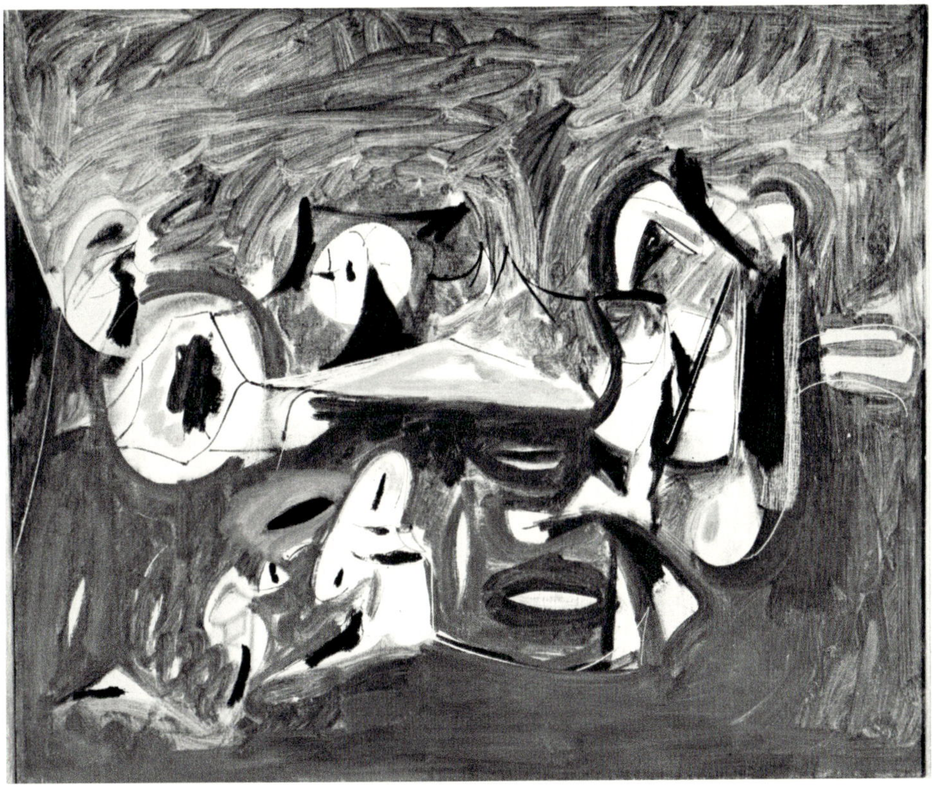

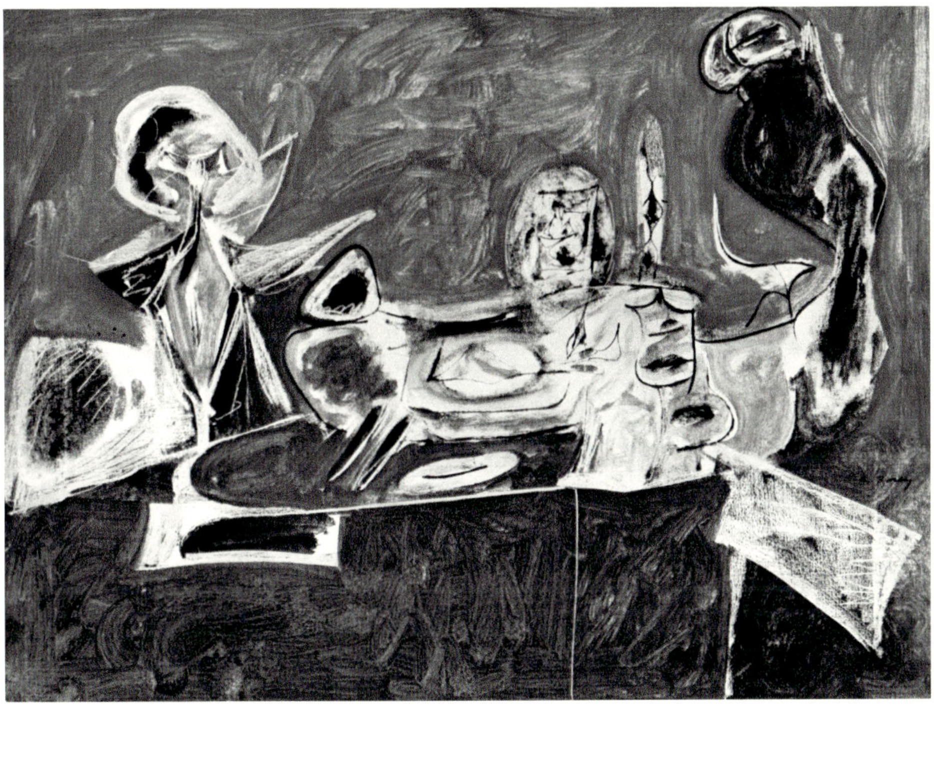

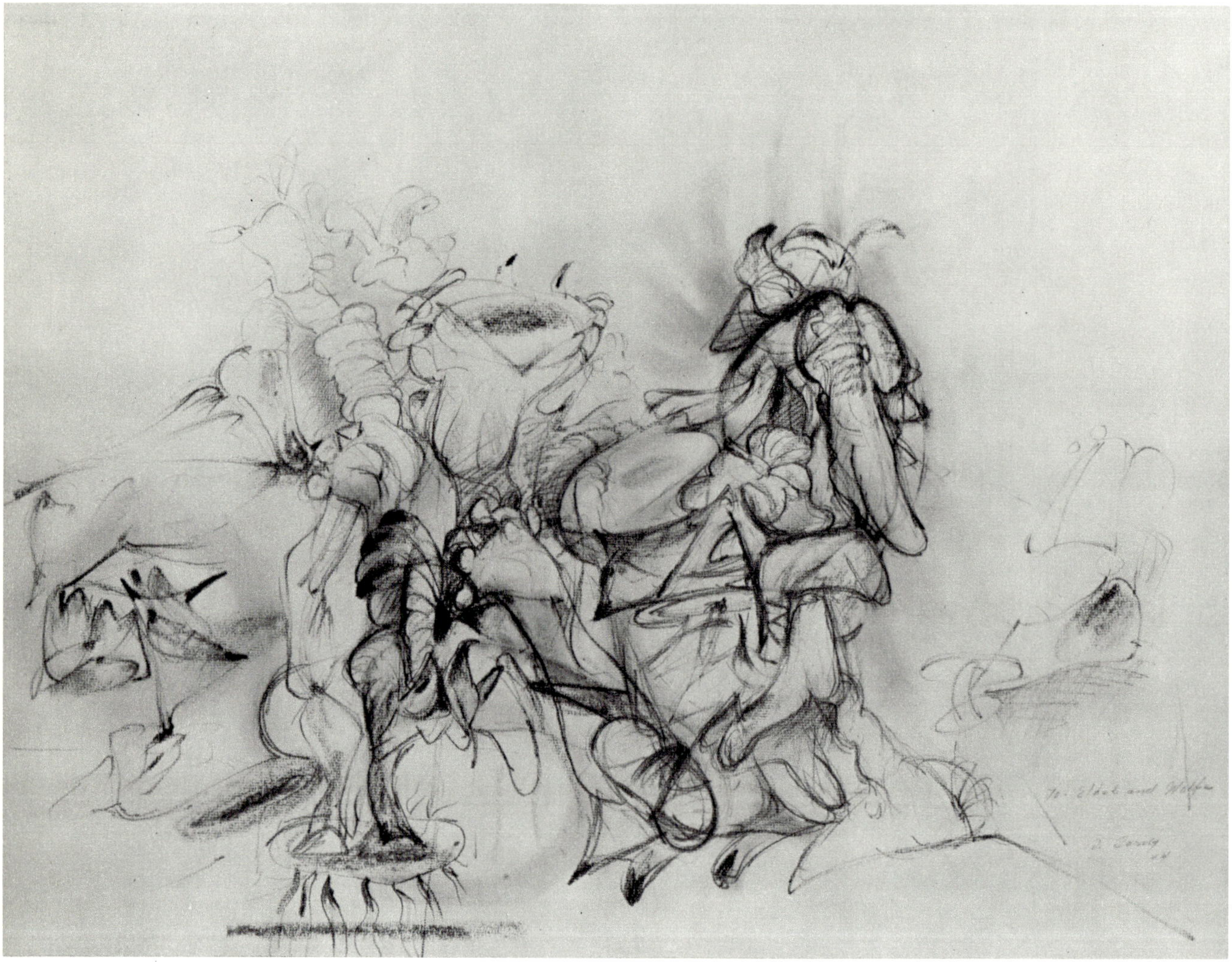

174. *Untitled*. 1944
Pencil and crayon on paper, 19 × 25″
Collection Ethel K. Schwabacher, New York

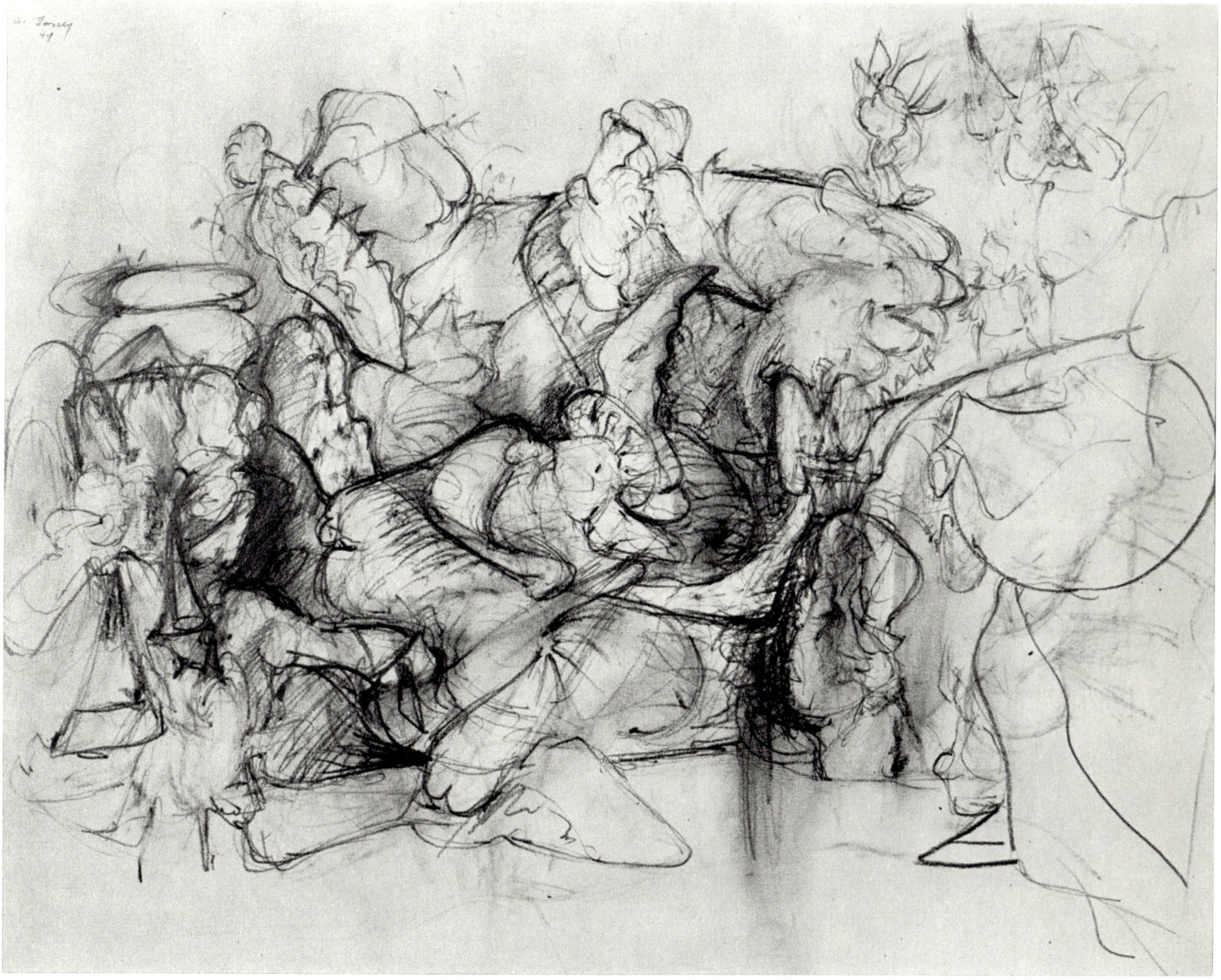

175. *Drawing*. 1944
Pencil and crayon on paper, 18 3/4 × 24 3/4″
Private Collection, Detroit

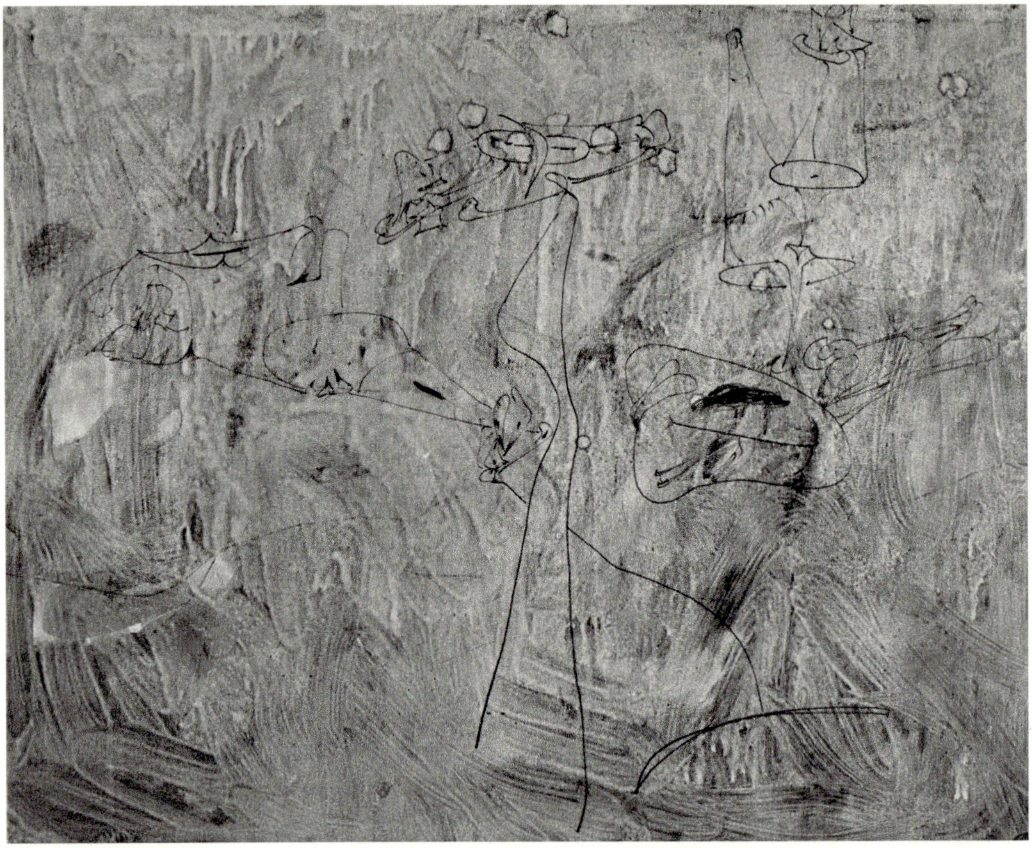

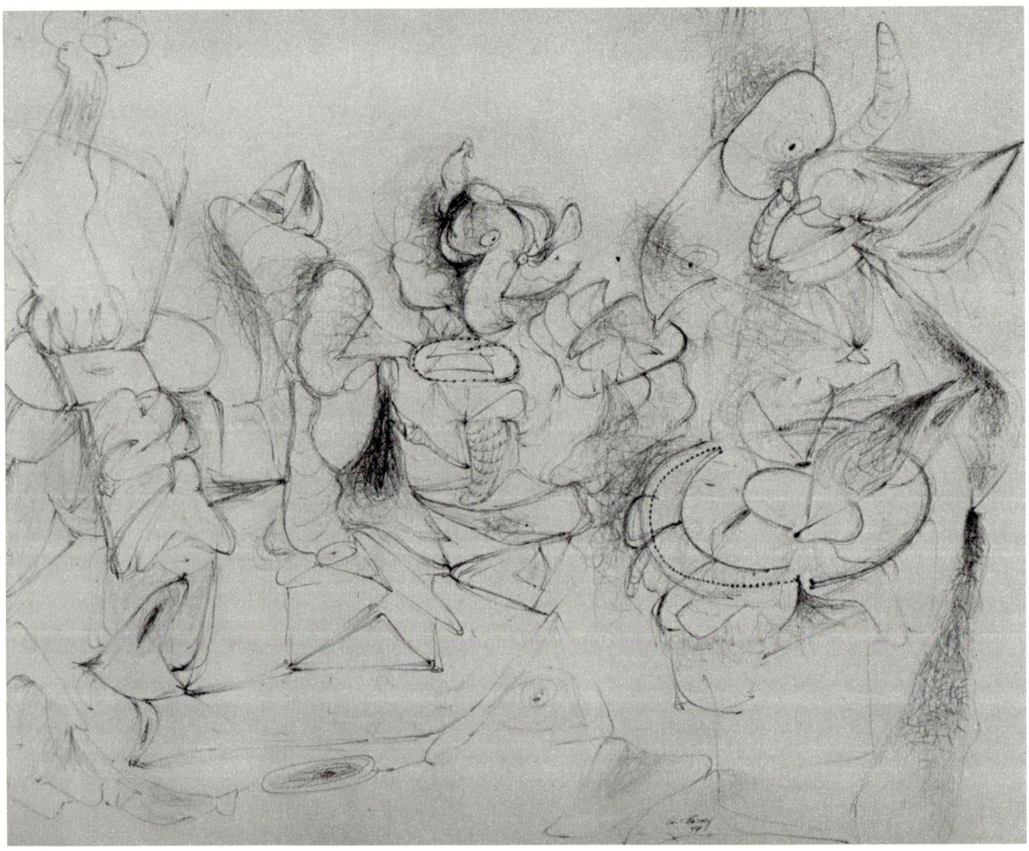

176. *Untitled*. 1945
Wash and pencil on paper, 18 1/2 × 24 1/2″
Collection Washington Arts Consortium,
Eastern Washington State Historical Society

177. *Untitled*. 1944
Pencil and crayon on paper, 19 1/4 × 24 1/4″
Collection Dr. and Mrs. Martin L. Gecht

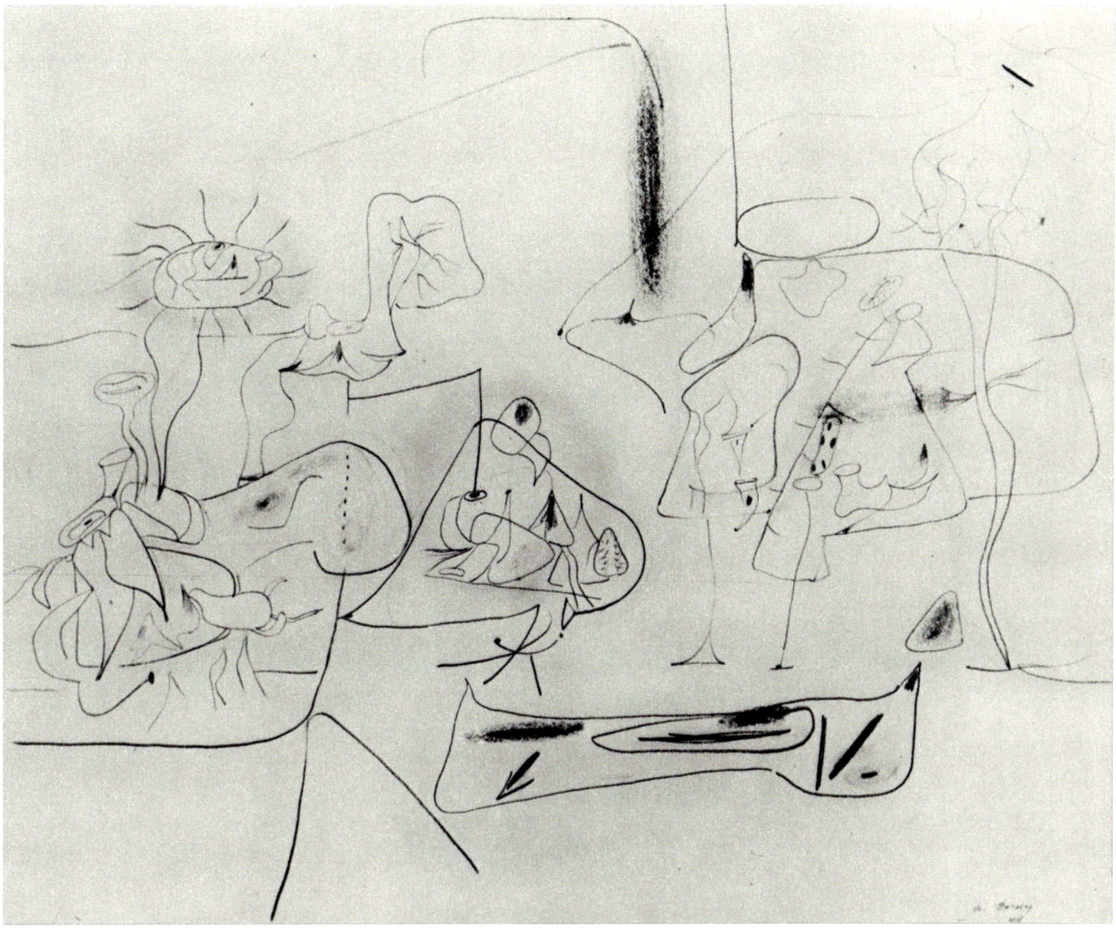

178. *Untitled*. 1944
Pencil and crayon on paper, 19 × 25″
Collection Julien Levy; Courtesy Richard L. Feigen & Co.

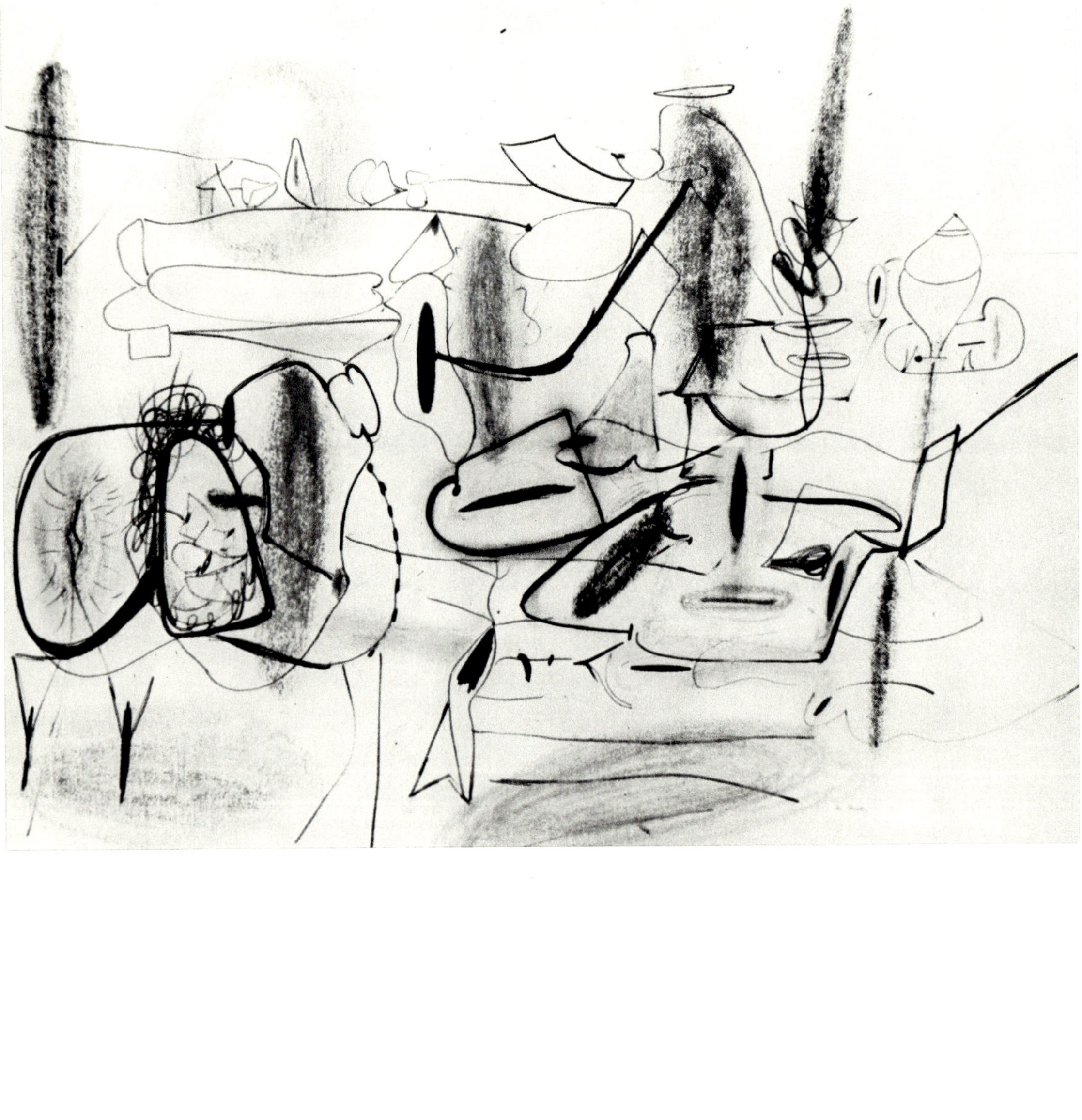

179. *Untitled*. 1944
Pencil and wax crayon on paper, 19 1/4 × 25 3/8″
Private Collection

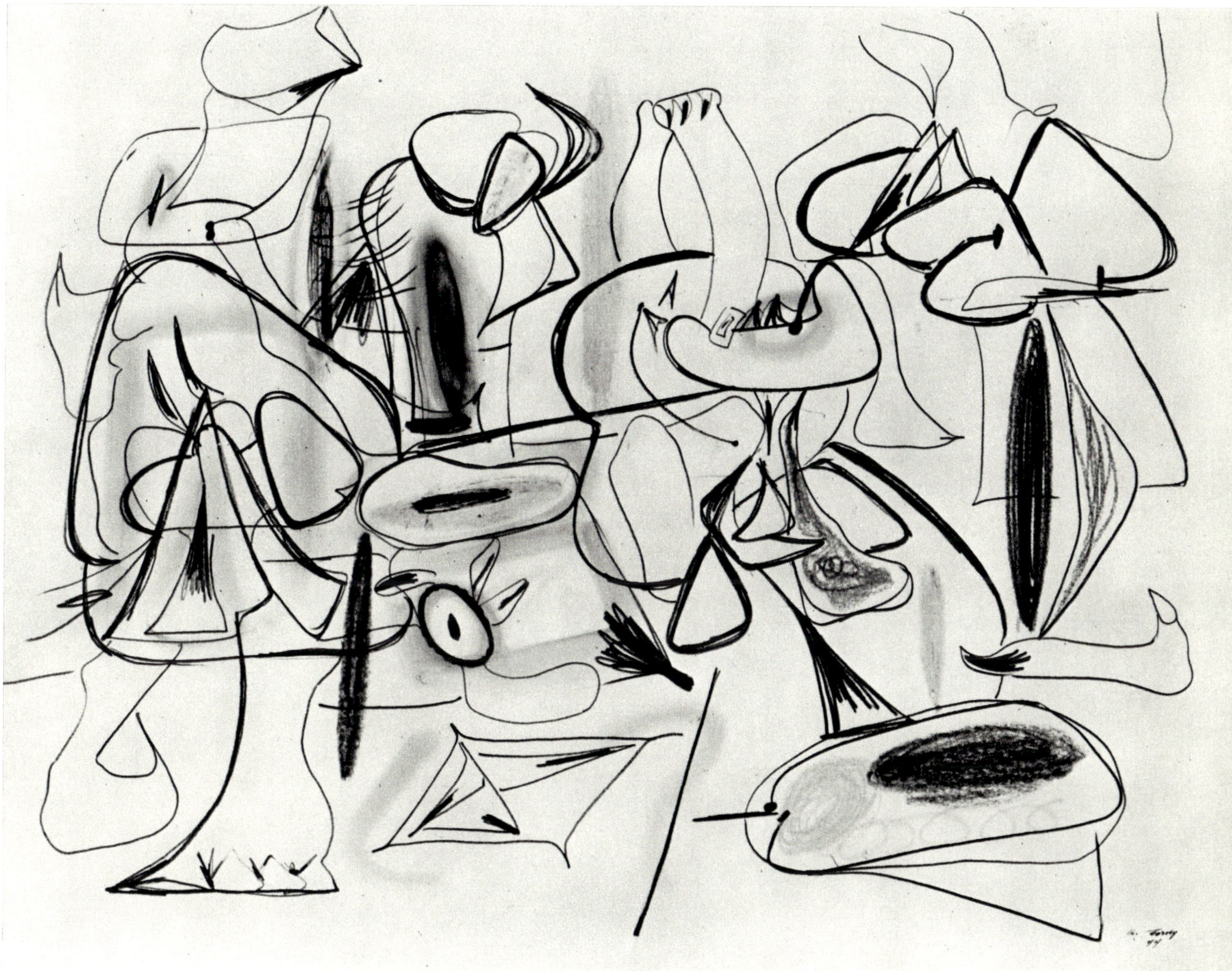

180. Study for *They Will Take My Island*. 1944
Wax crayon and pencil on paper, 22 × 30″
The Brooklyn Museum, Dick S. Ramsay Fund

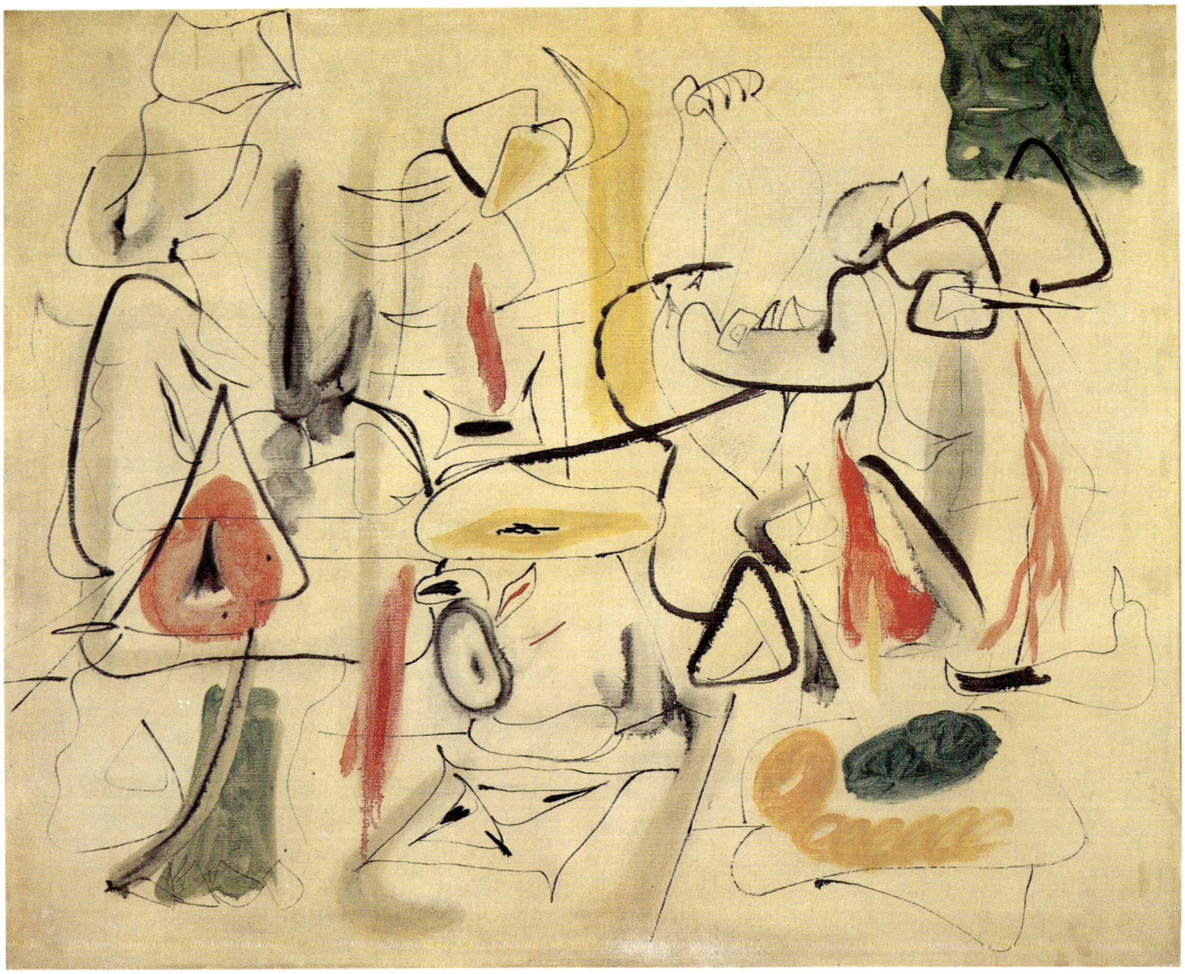

181. *They Will Take My Island*. 1944
Oil on canvas, 38 × 48″
Collection The Art Gallery of Ontario, Toronto; Purchase with Assistance from The Volunteer Committee Fund, 1980

182. *Painting*. 1944
Oil on canvas, 69 3/4 × 65 3/4″
The Peggy Guggenheim Collection, Venice,
The Solomon R. Guggenheim Foundation

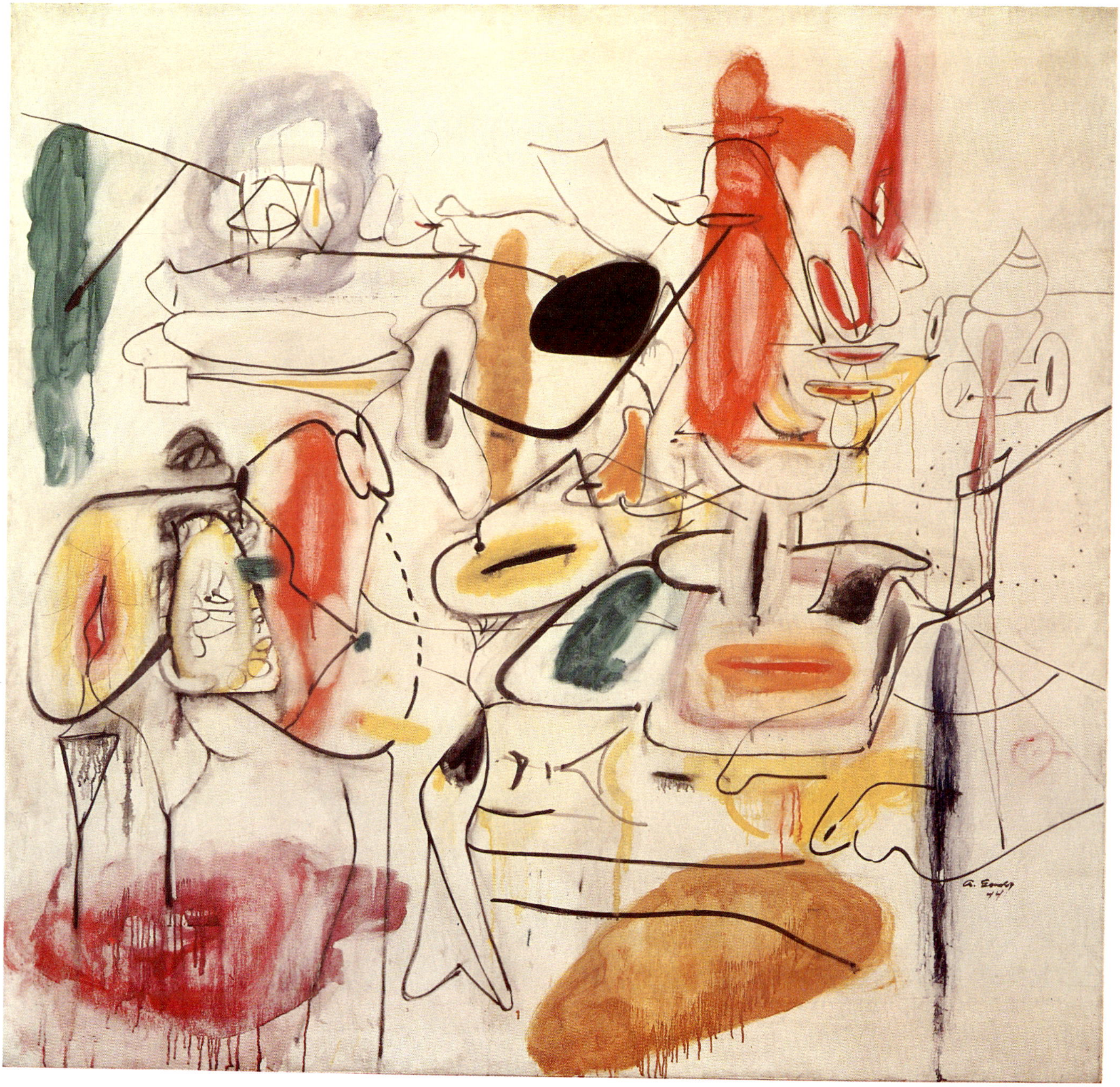

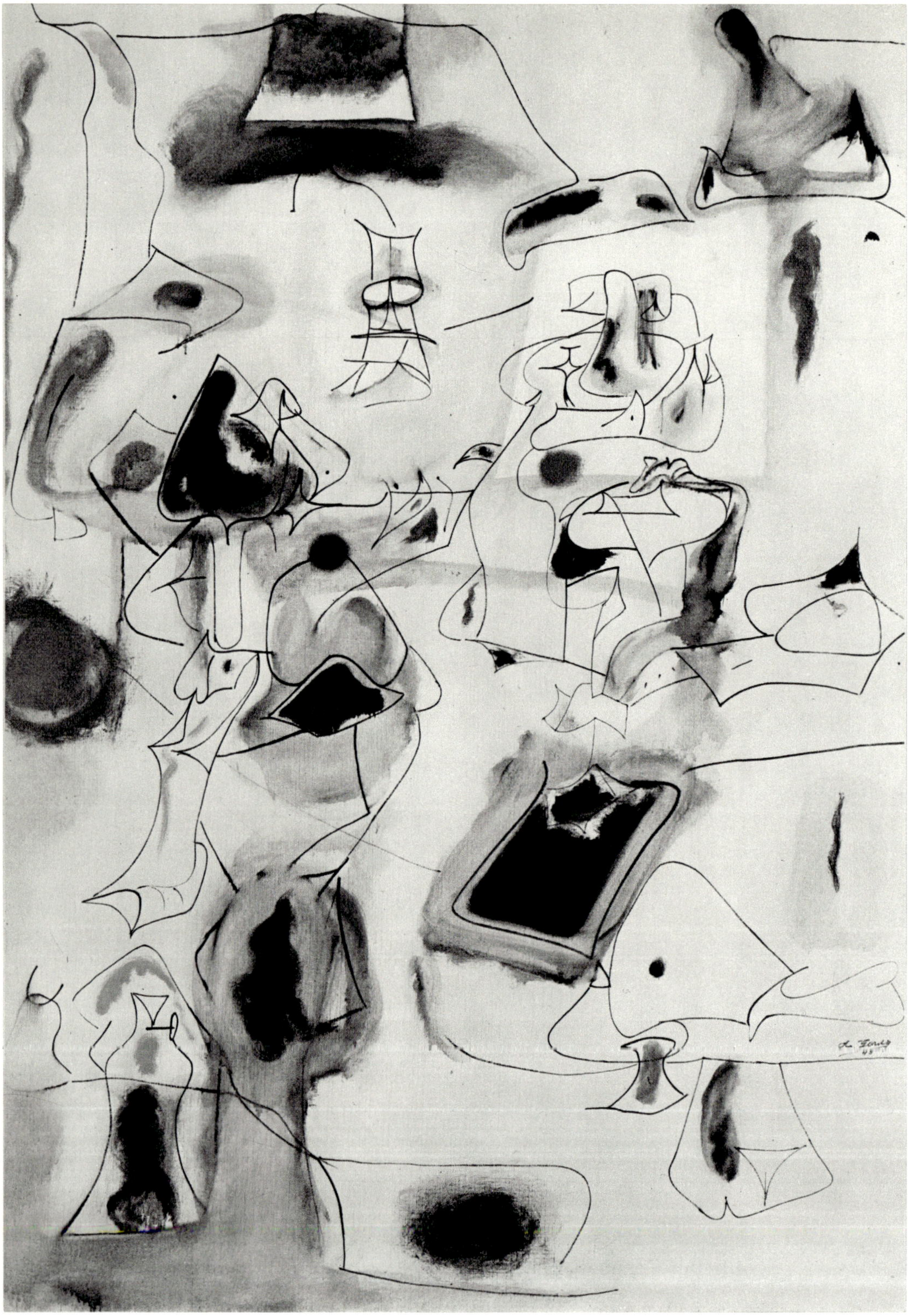

183. *The Unattainable*. 1945
Oil on canvas, 41 5/8 × 29 1/4″
Collection The Baltimore Museum of Art, Museum Purchase

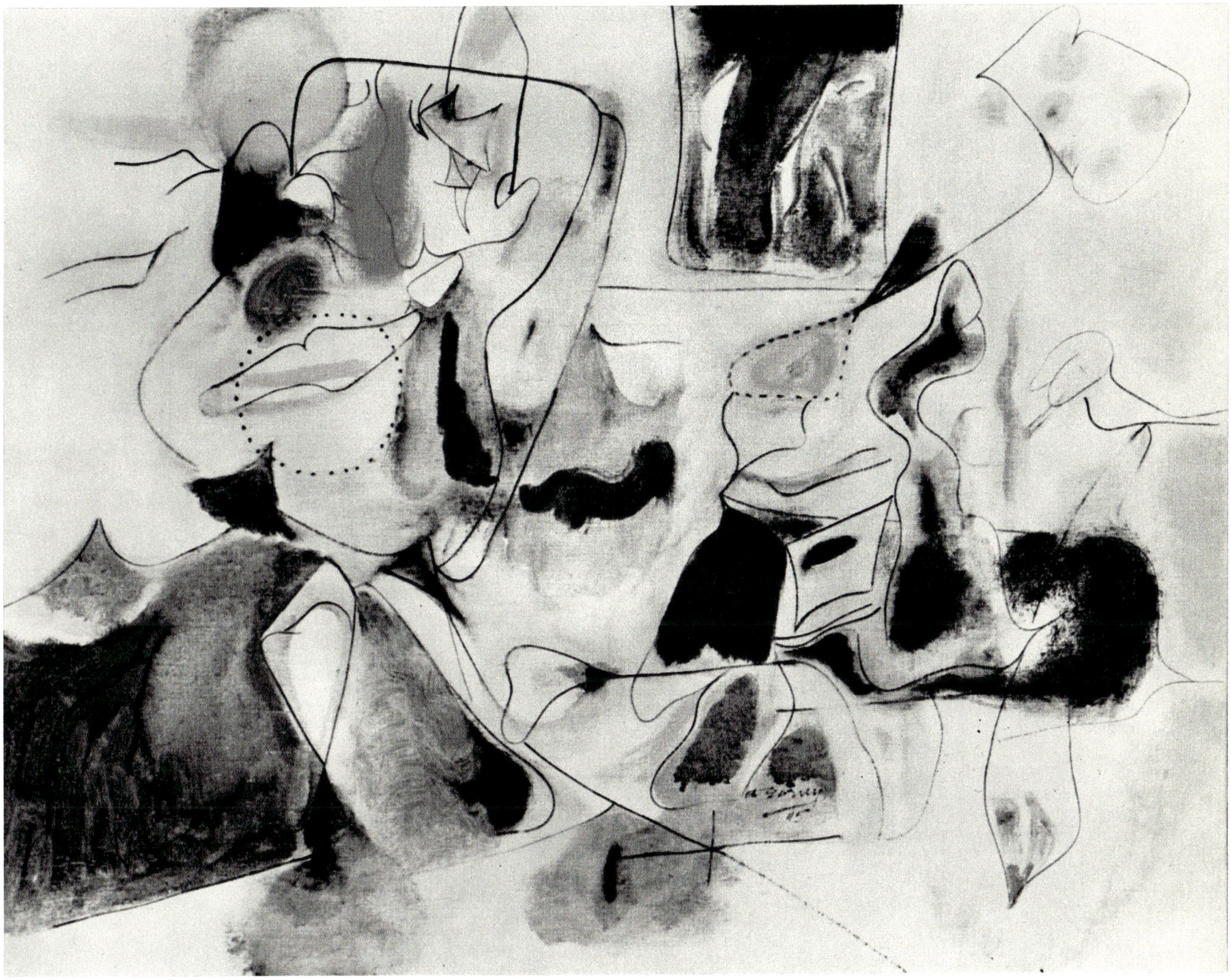

184. *Impatience*. 1945
Oil on canvas, 24 × 36″
Collection Mr. and Mrs. Sidney Kohl, Milwaukee

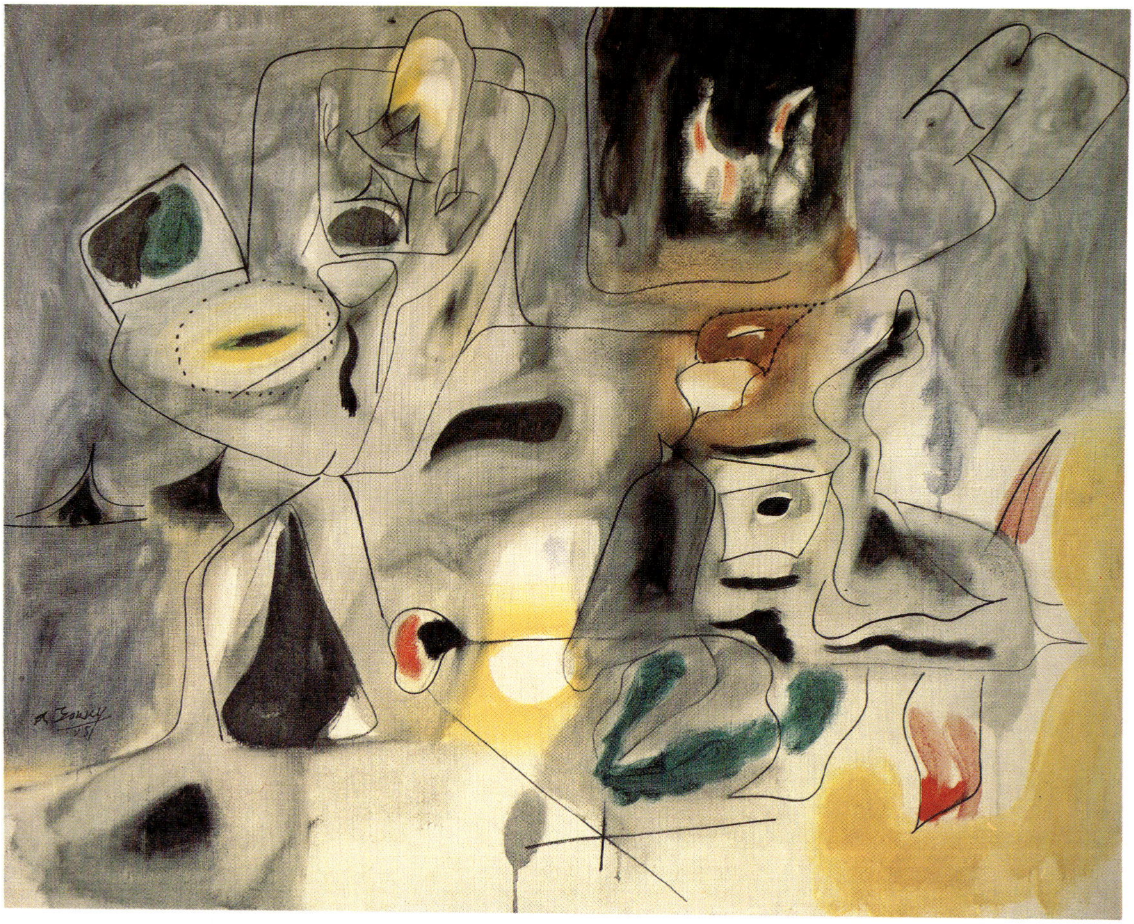

185. *Hugging*. 1945
Oil on canvas, 25 1/2 × 32 5/8″
Thyssen-Bornemisza Collection, Lugano

186. *Diary of a Seducer*. 1945
Oil on canvas, 50 × 62″
Collection Mr. and Mrs. William A.M. Burden

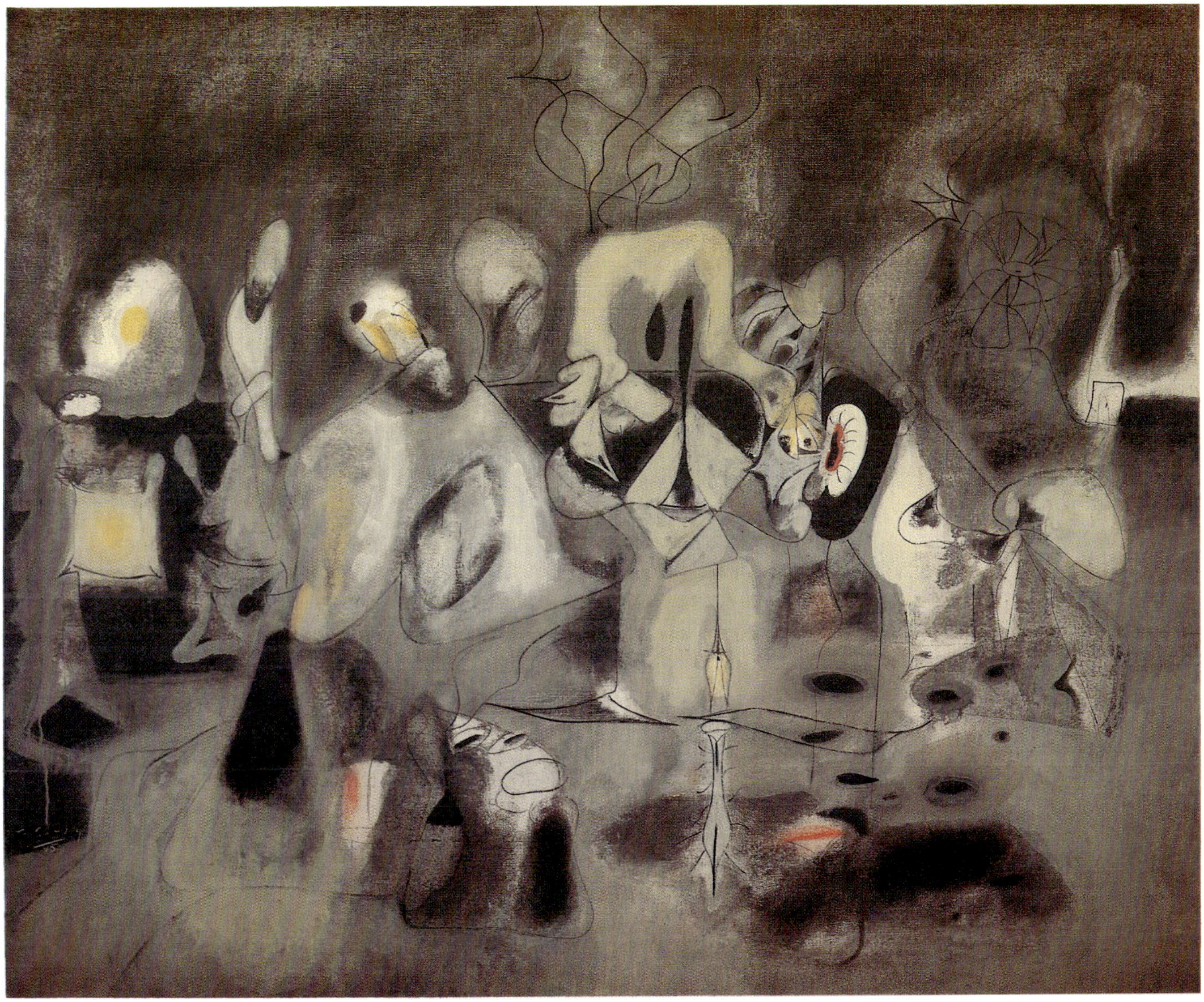

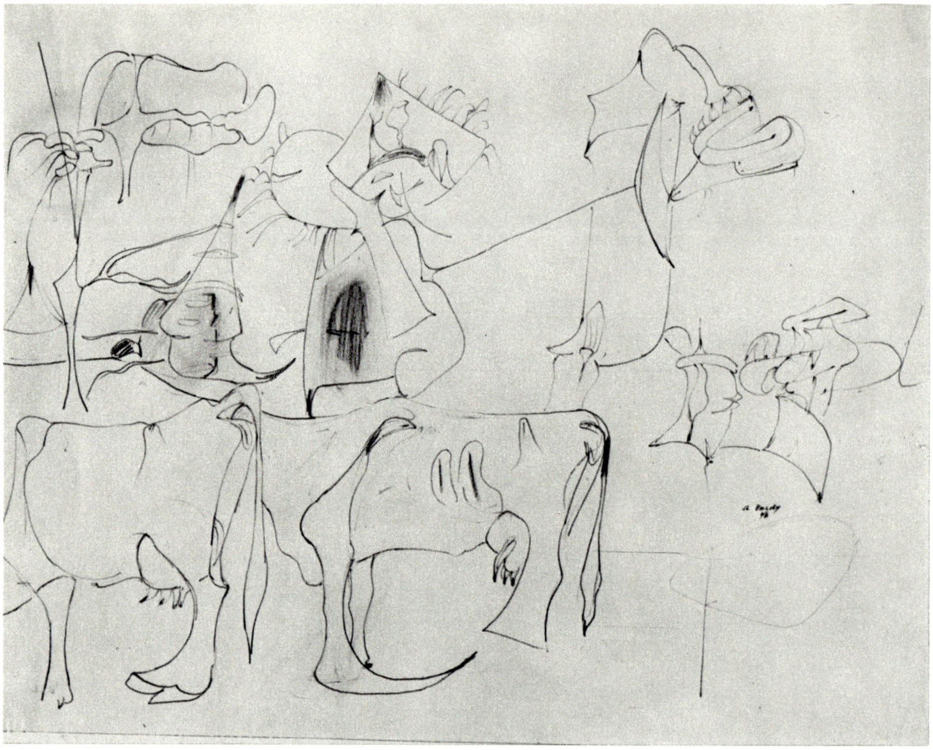

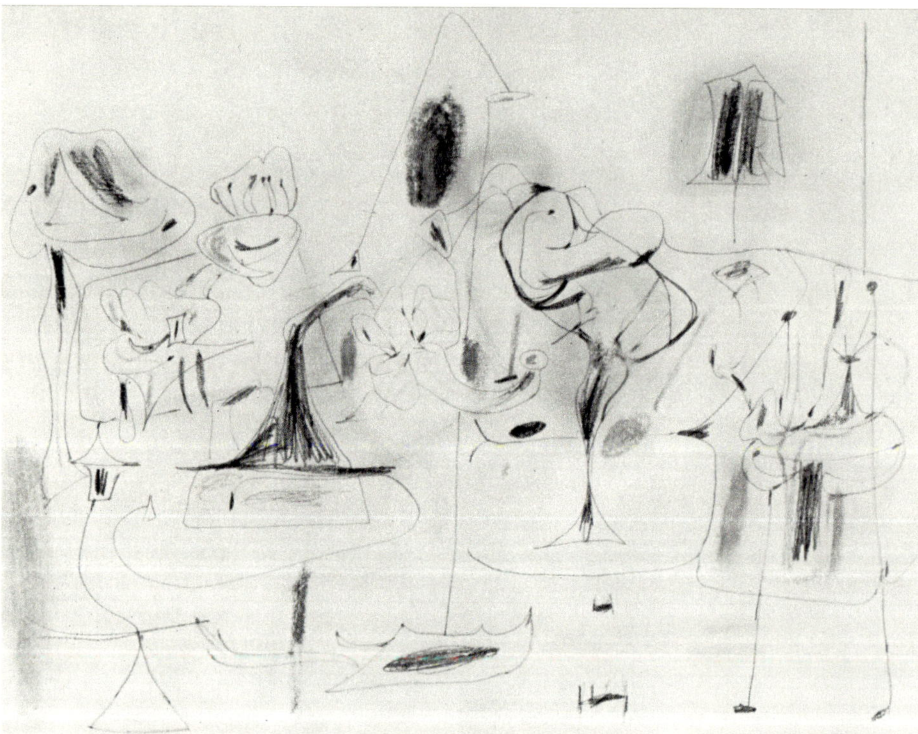

187. *Drawing*. 1946
Pencil on paper, 18 7/8 × 24 7/8″
Collection Yale University Art Gallery, New Haven,
Gift of Julien Levy

188. *Landscape*. 1945
Pencil and crayon on paper, 18 5/8 × 24 3/4″
Private Collection

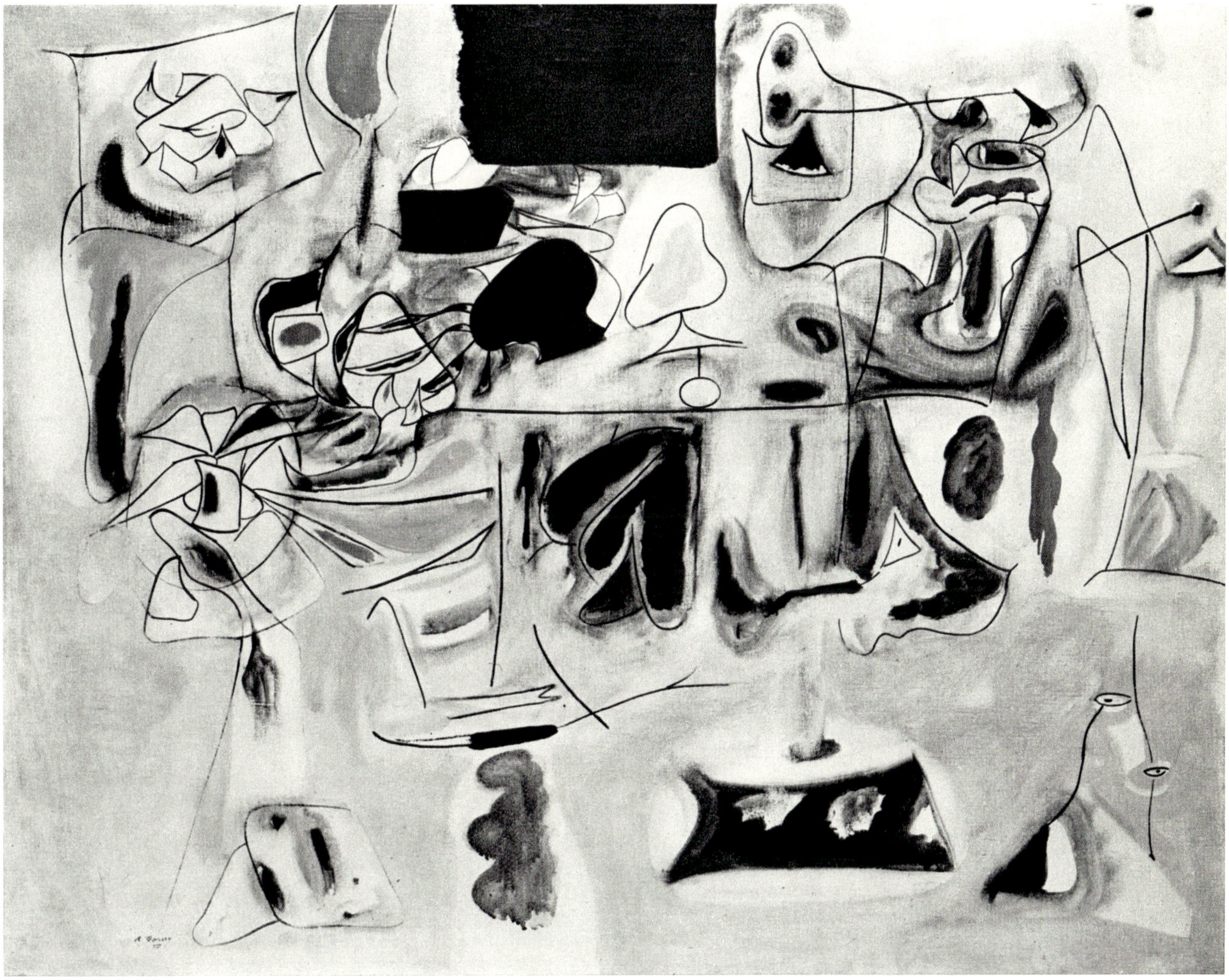

189. *Landscape Table*. 1945
Oil on canvas, 36 × 48″
Collection Musée National d'Art Moderne, Centre National
d'Art et de Culture Georges Pompidou, Paris

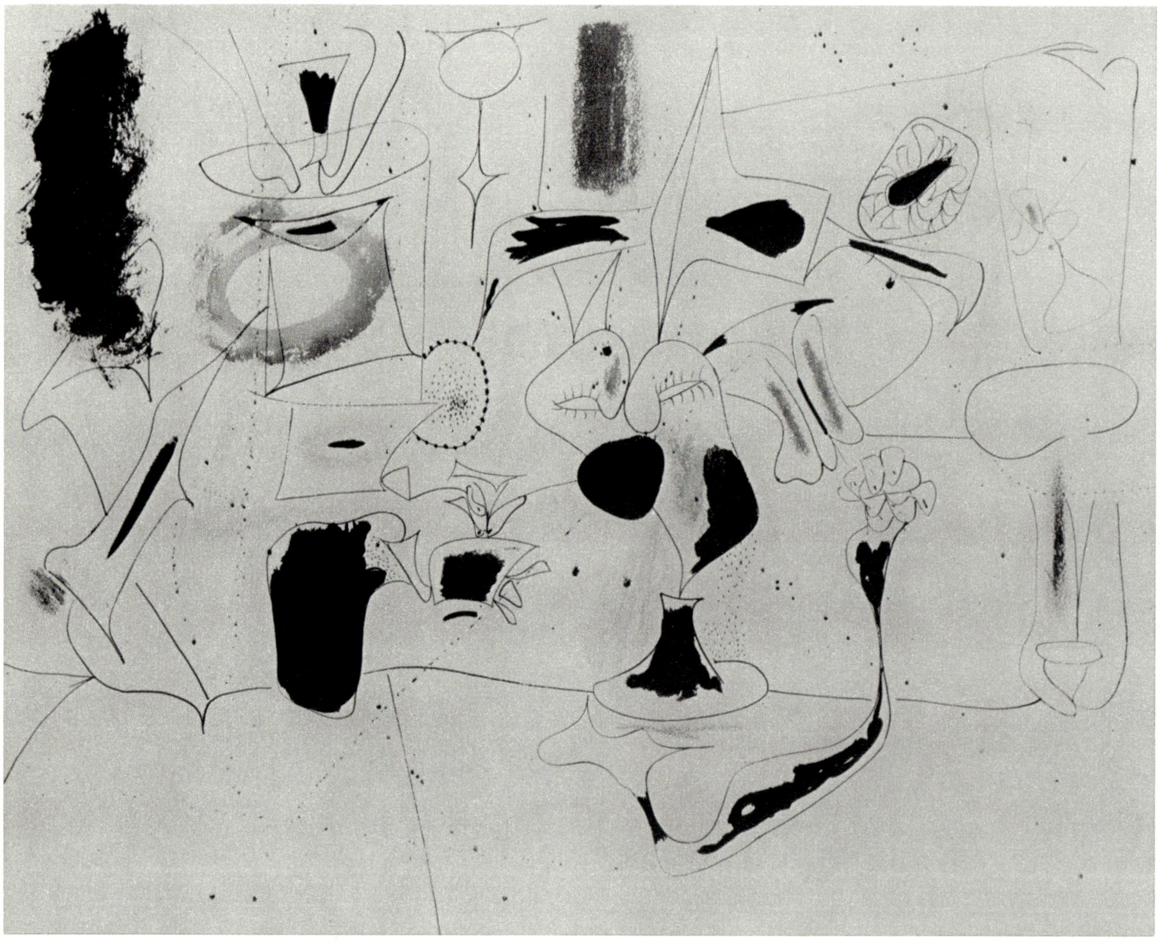

190. *Composition.* ca. 1945–46
Pen and ink on paper, 20 × 26″
Private Collection

191. *Delicate Game*. 1946
Oil on canvas, 34 × 44″
Collection Edwin Janss, Jr.

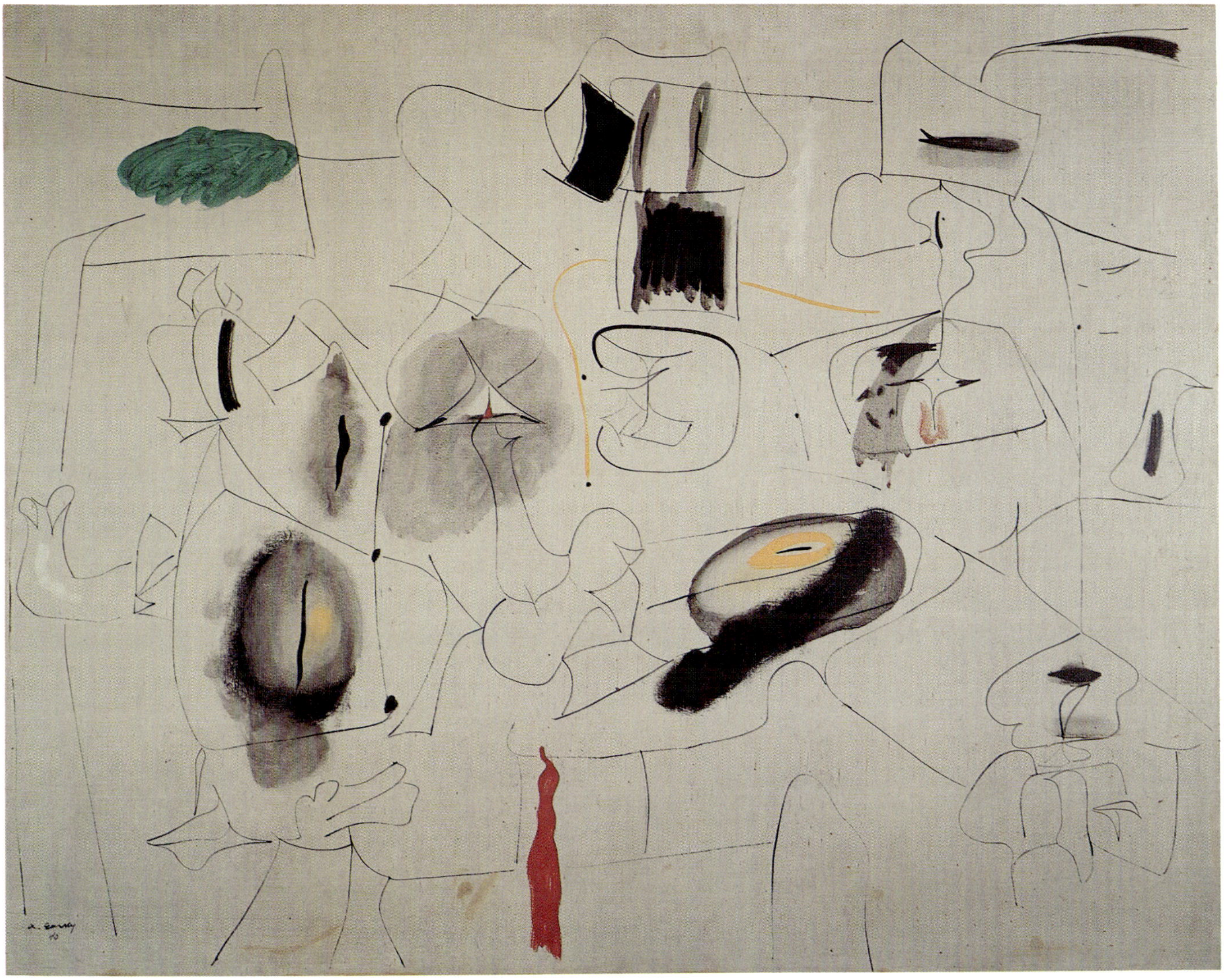

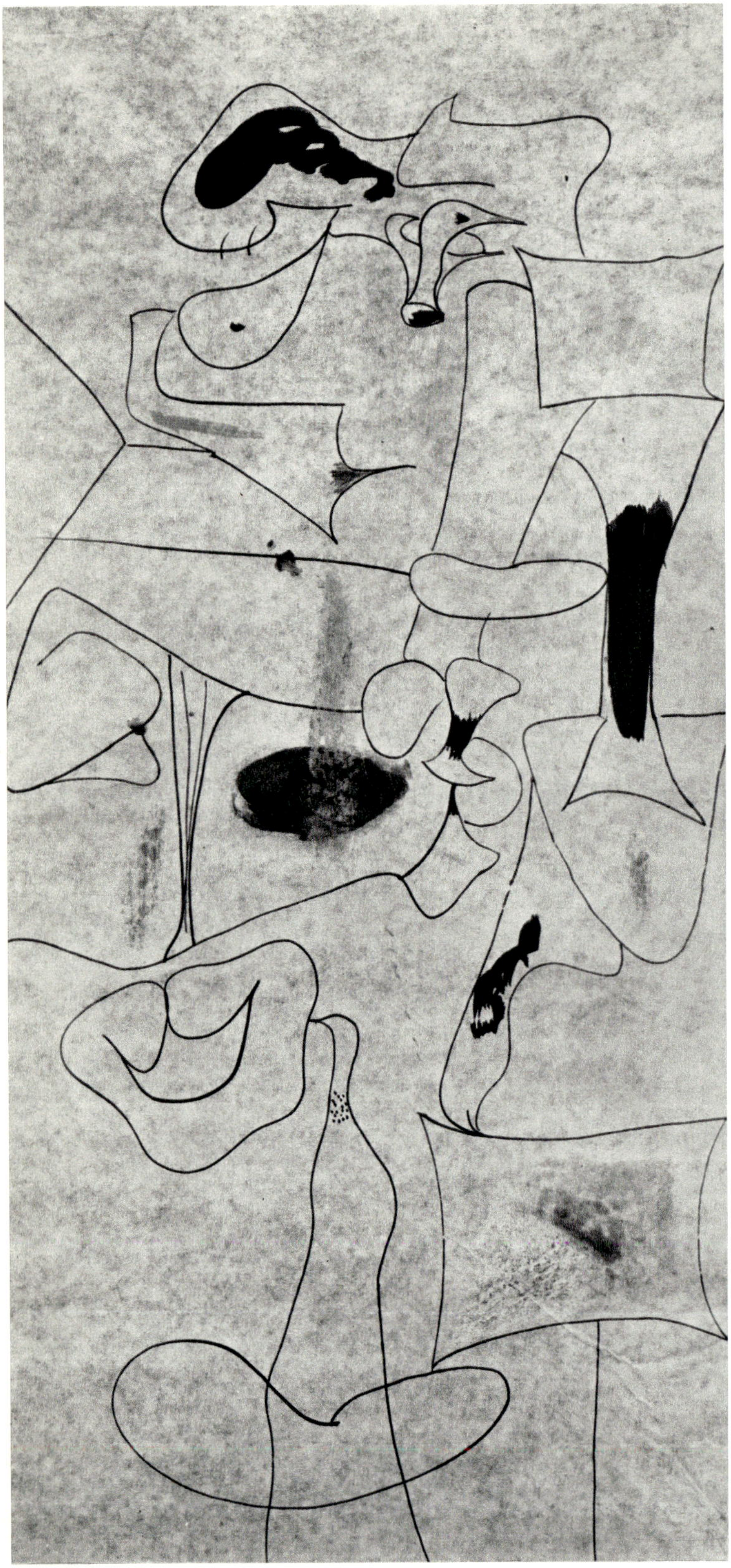

192. *Untitled.* ca. 1945–46
Ink and crayon on brown paper, 27 3/4 × 13″
Collection Mr. and Mrs. E. A. Bergman

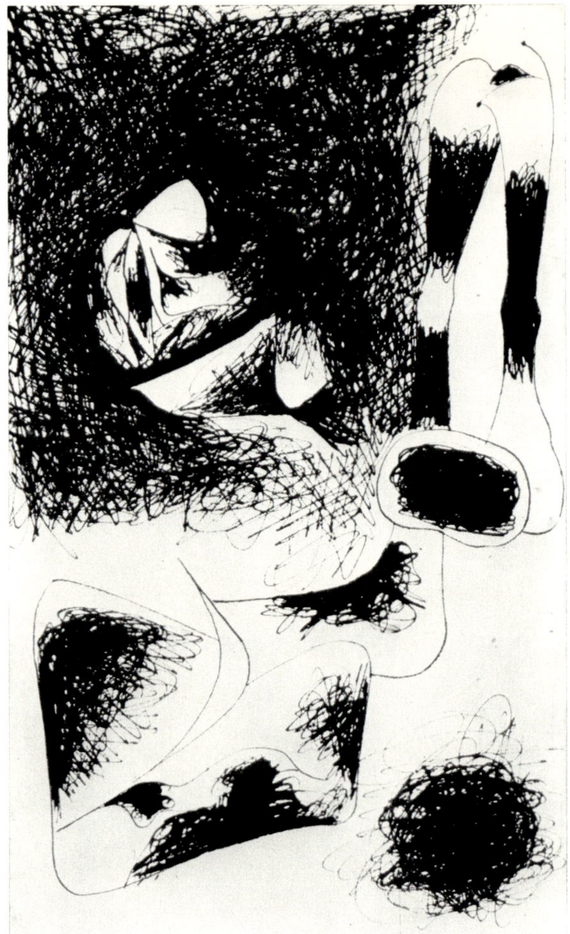

193. *Nude.* 1946
Pen and ink on paper, 9 1/2 × 6 1/4″
Private Collection

194. *Nude.* 1946
Oil on canvas, 50 1/8 × 38 1/8″
Collection Hirshhorn Museum and Sculpture Garden, Smithsonian Institution, Washington, D.C.

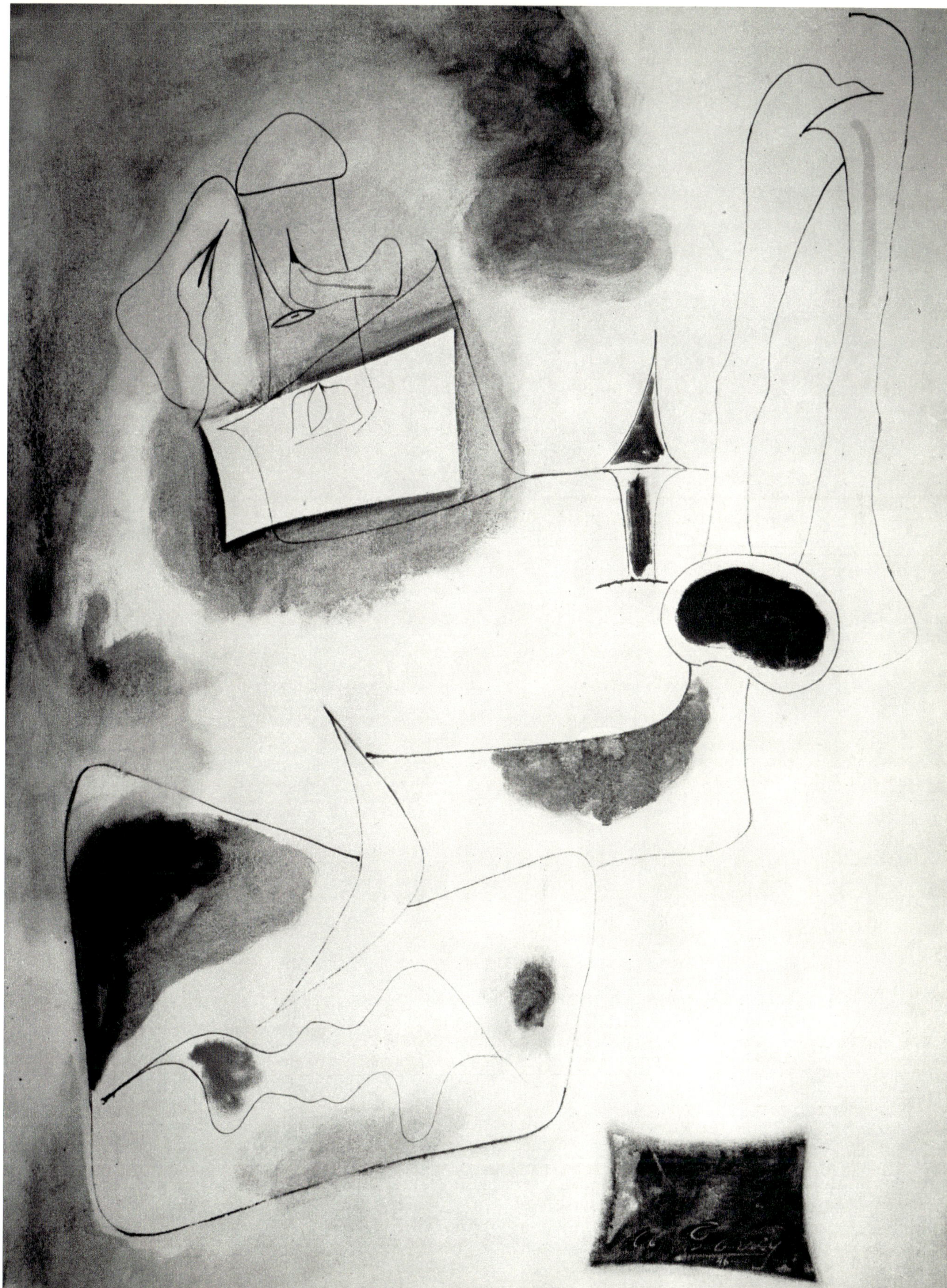

195. *Charred Beloved I.* 1946
Oil on canvas, 58 5/8 × 39 3/4″
Collection Gerald S. Elliott, Chicago

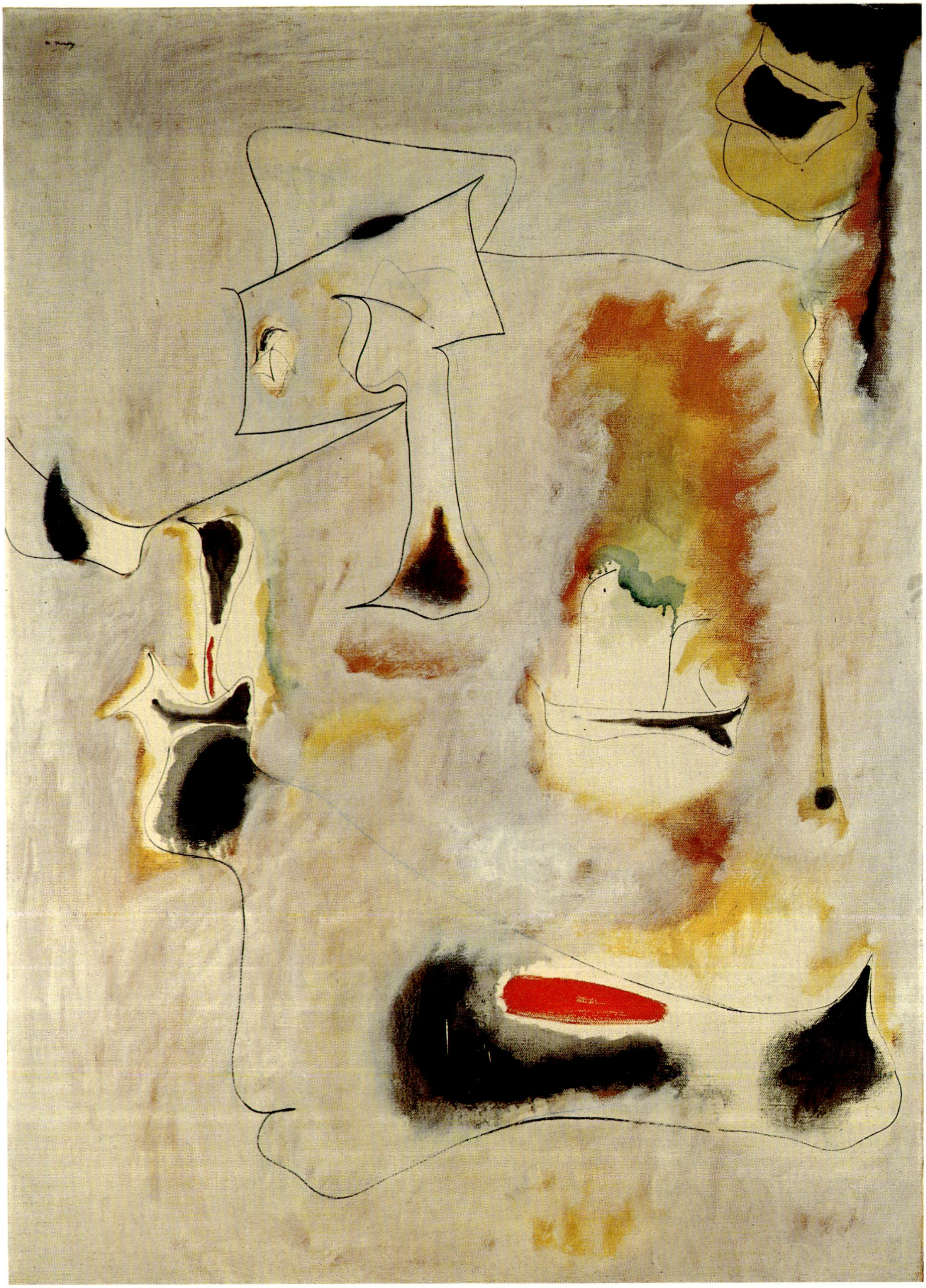

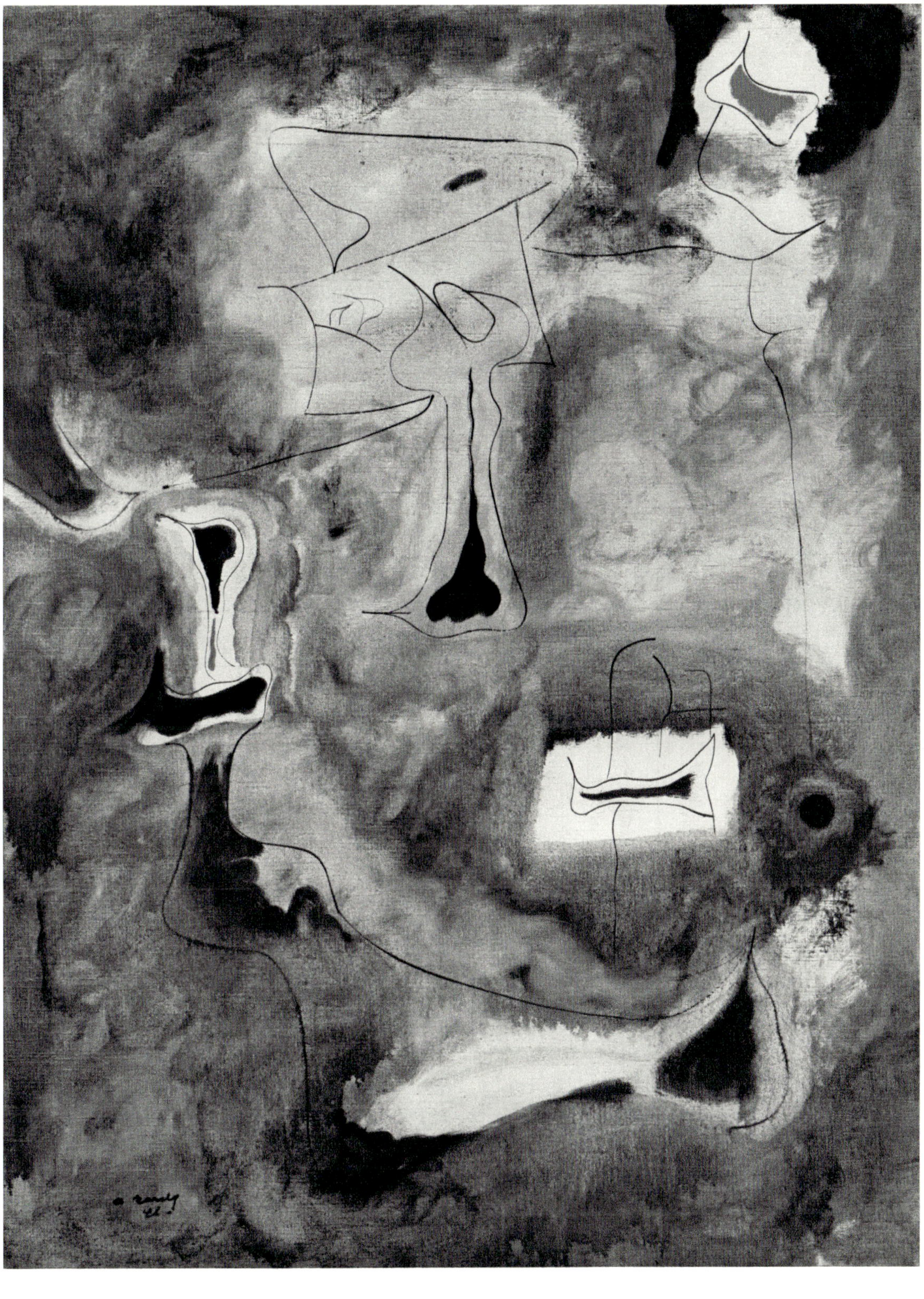

196. *Charred Beloved II*. 1946
Oil on canvas, 53 15/16 × 40″
Collection National Gallery of Canada, Ottawa

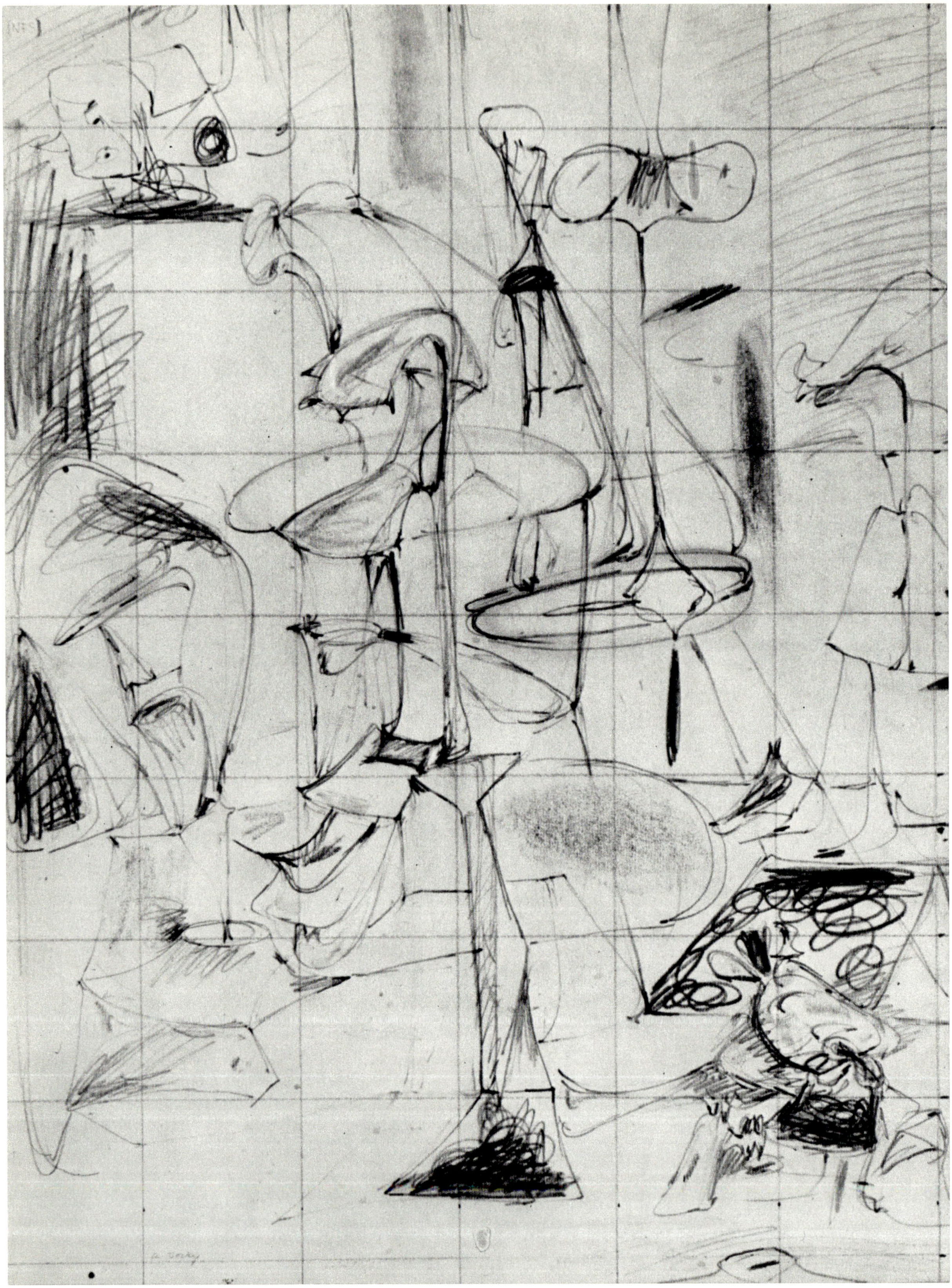

197. Study for *The Betrothal*. ca. 1946–47
Pencil and crayon on paper, 24 × 18 1/2″
Courtesy Xavier Fourcade, Inc., New York

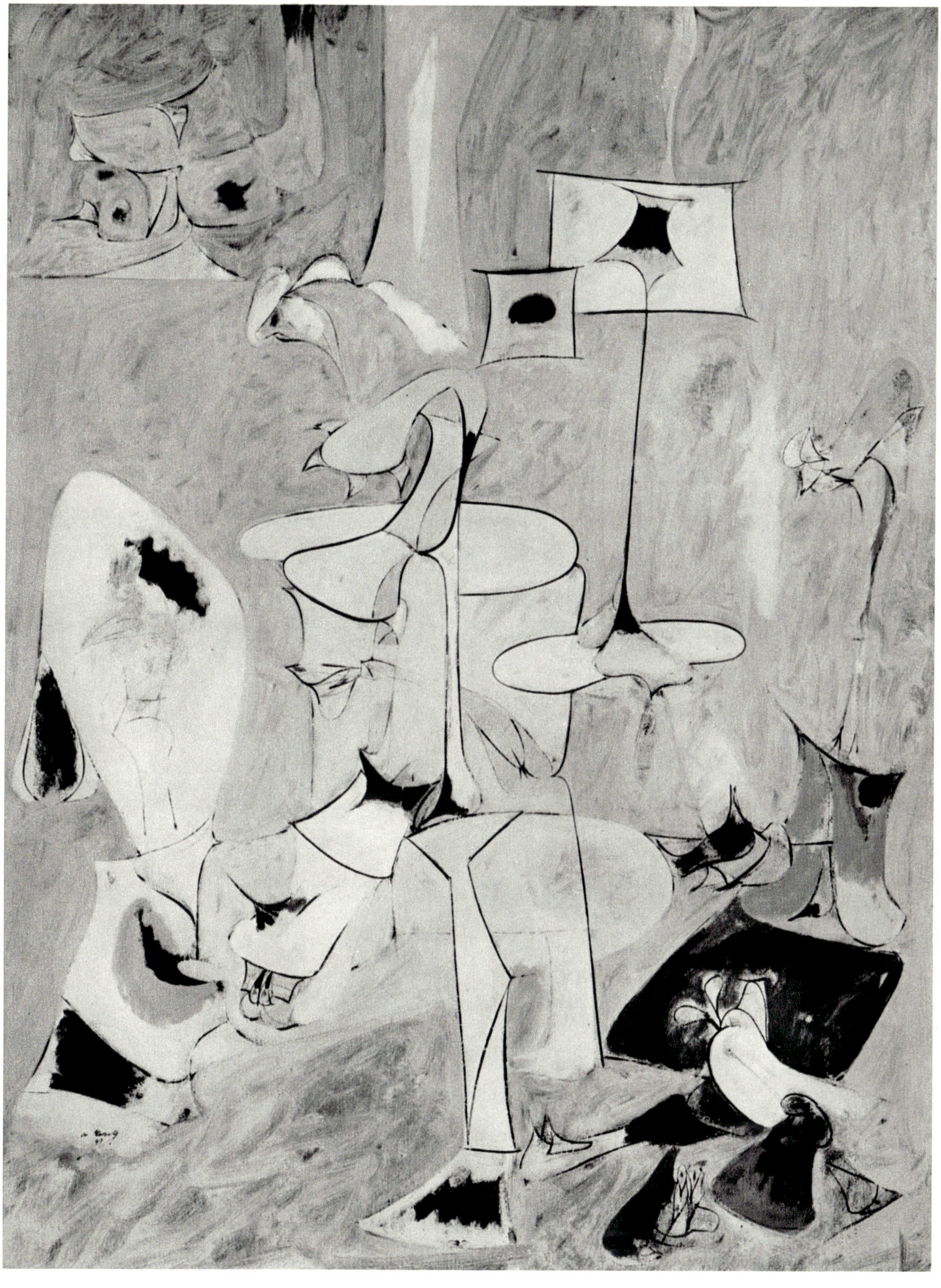

198. *The Betrothal II.* 1947
Oil on canvas, 50 3/4 × 38″
Collection of the Whitney Museum of American Art, New York. Purchase

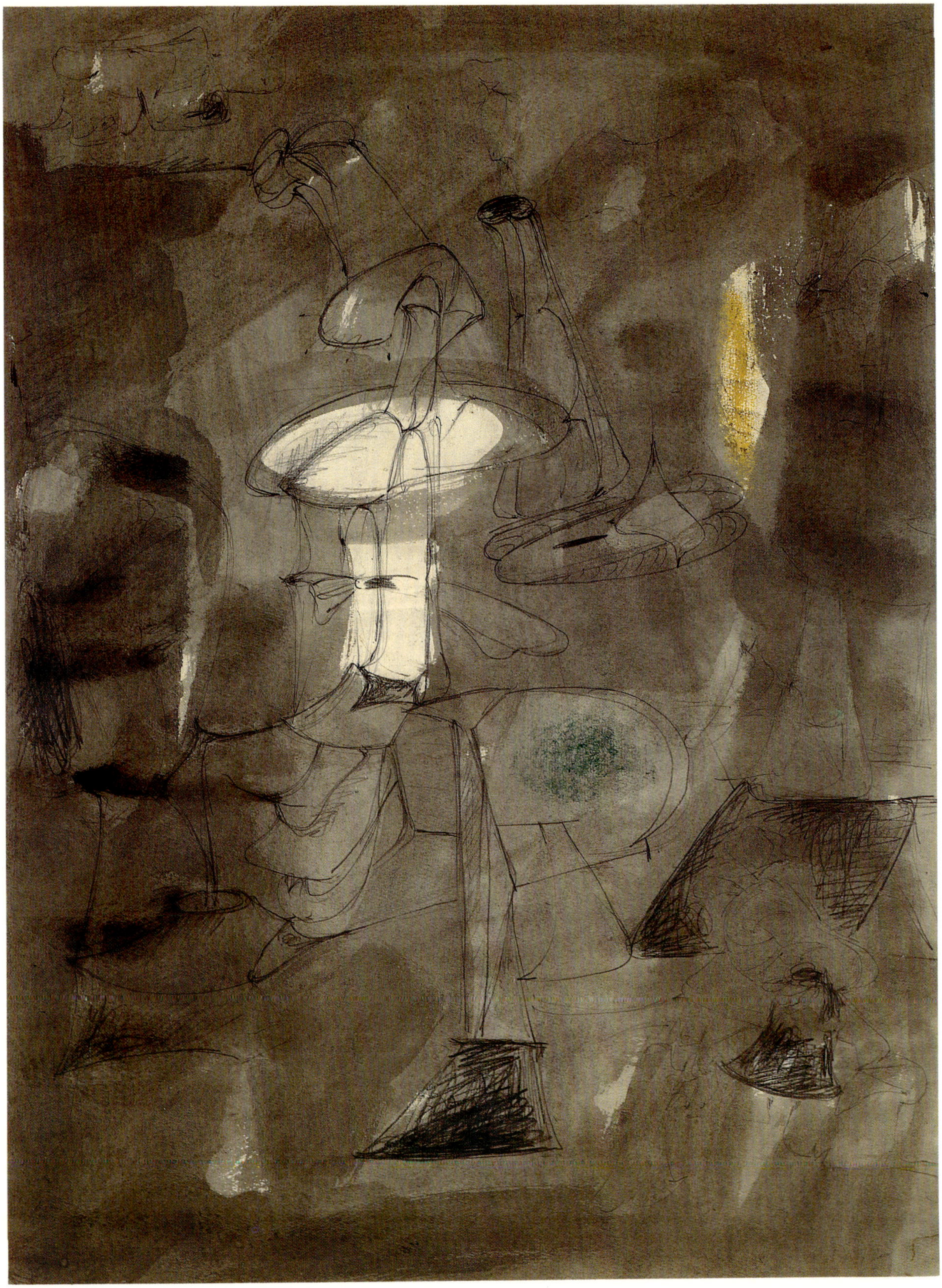

199. Study for *The Betrothal.* ca. 1946–47
Watercolor and pencil on paper, 23 1/2 × 17 1/2″
Collection Dr. and Mrs. L. Keoshian, California

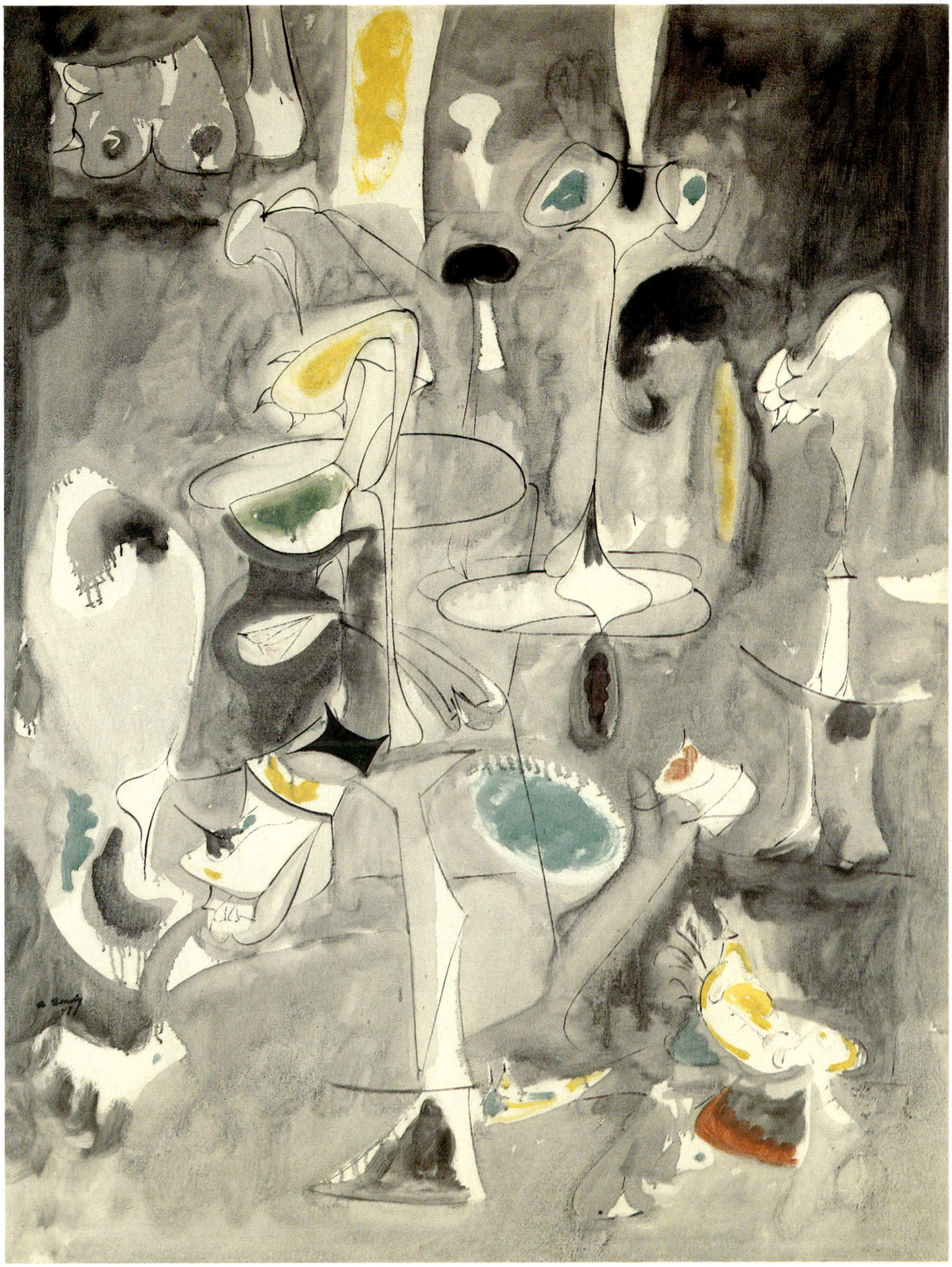

200. *The Betrothal*. 1947
Oil on canvas, 50 5/8 × 39 1/4″
Yale University Art Gallery, New Haven, The Katharine Ordway Collection

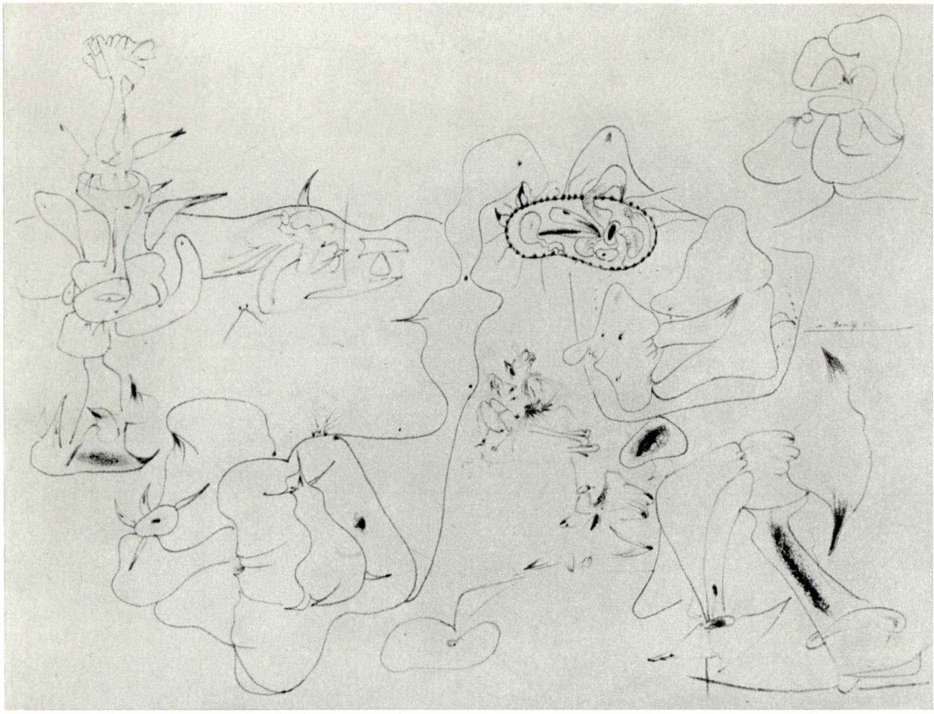

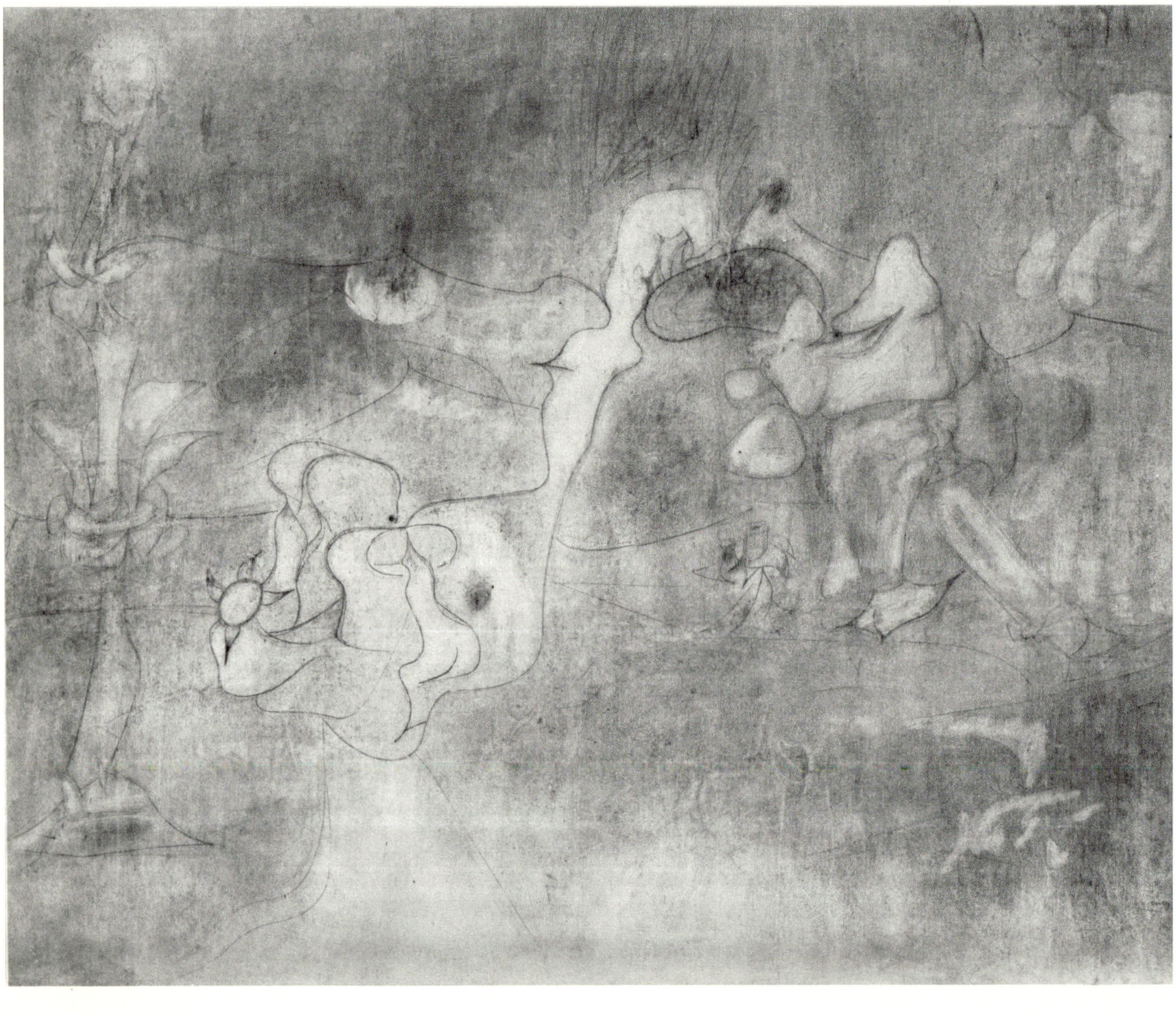

201. Study for *The Plough and the Song*. 1944
Pencil and crayon on paper, 19 × 25 1/2″
Allen Memorial Art Museum, Oberlin College, Oberlin, Ohio,
Friends of Art Fund, 56.1

202. Study for *The Plow and the Song*. 1946
Pencil, charcoal, crayon, pastel and oil on paper, 47 7/8 × 59 3/8″
Collection National Gallery of Art, Washington, D.C., Avalon Fund, 1971

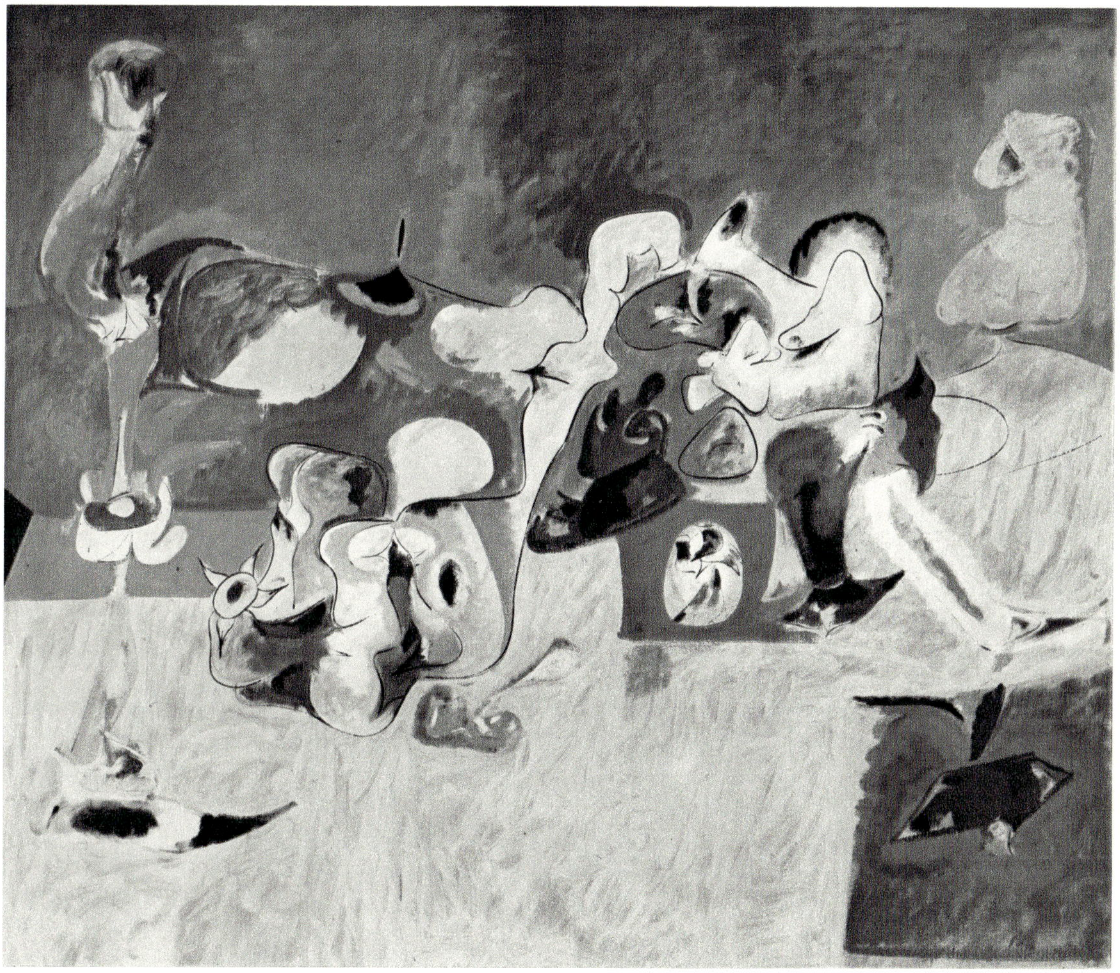

203. *The Plough and the Song No. 2*. 1946
Oil on canvas, 51 7/8 × 61 3/8″
Courtesy of The Art Institute of Chicago,
Mr. and Mrs. Lewis Larned Coburn Fund, 1963

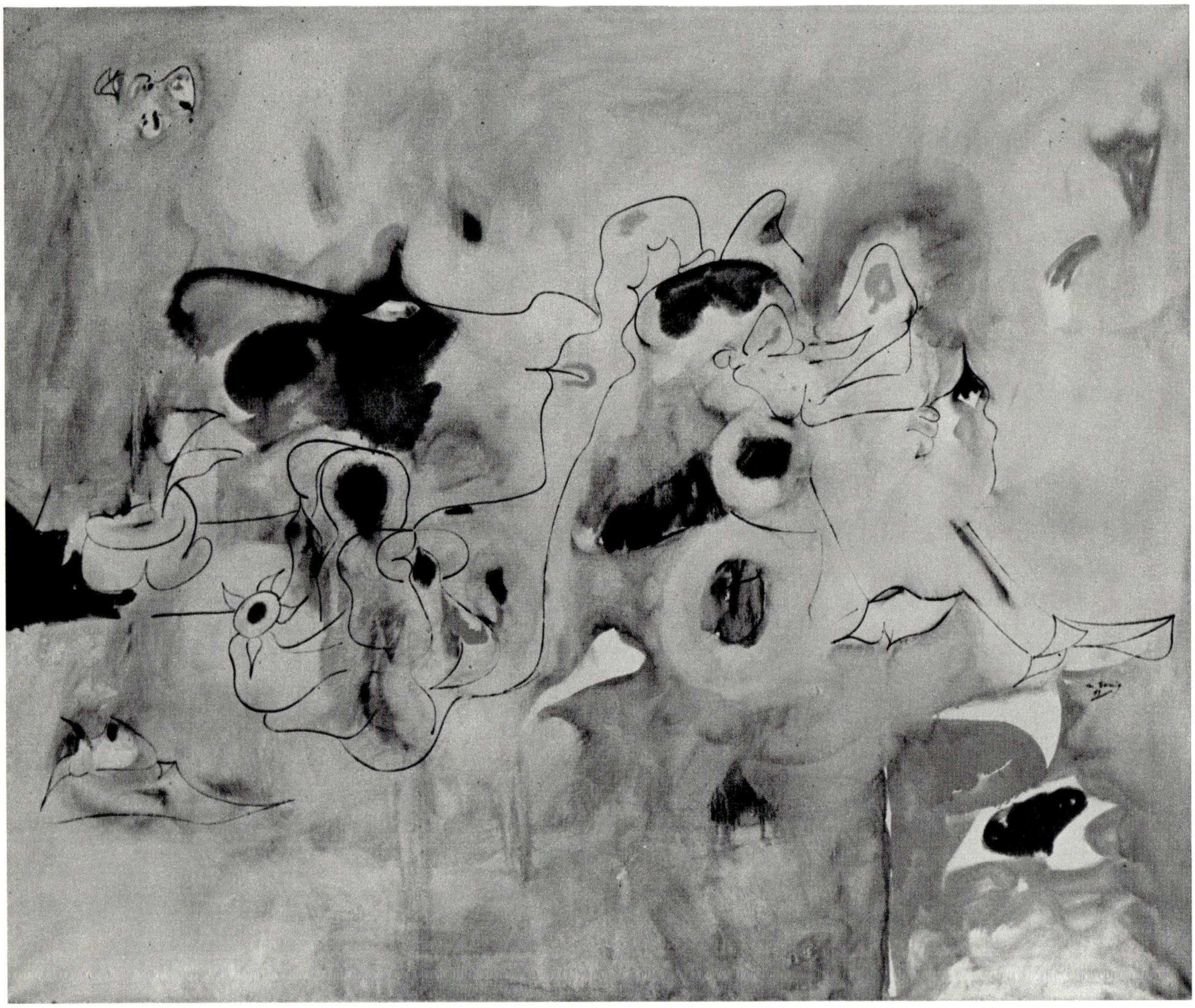

204. *The Plough and the Song*. 1947
Oil on canvas, 50 3/4 × 62 3/4″
Collection Allen Memorial Art Museum,
Oberlin College, Oberlin, Ohio, R. T. Miller, Jr. Fund, 52.16

205. *The Plow and the Song*. 1947
Oil on burlap, 52 1/8 × 64 1/4″
Collection Milton A. Gordon, New York

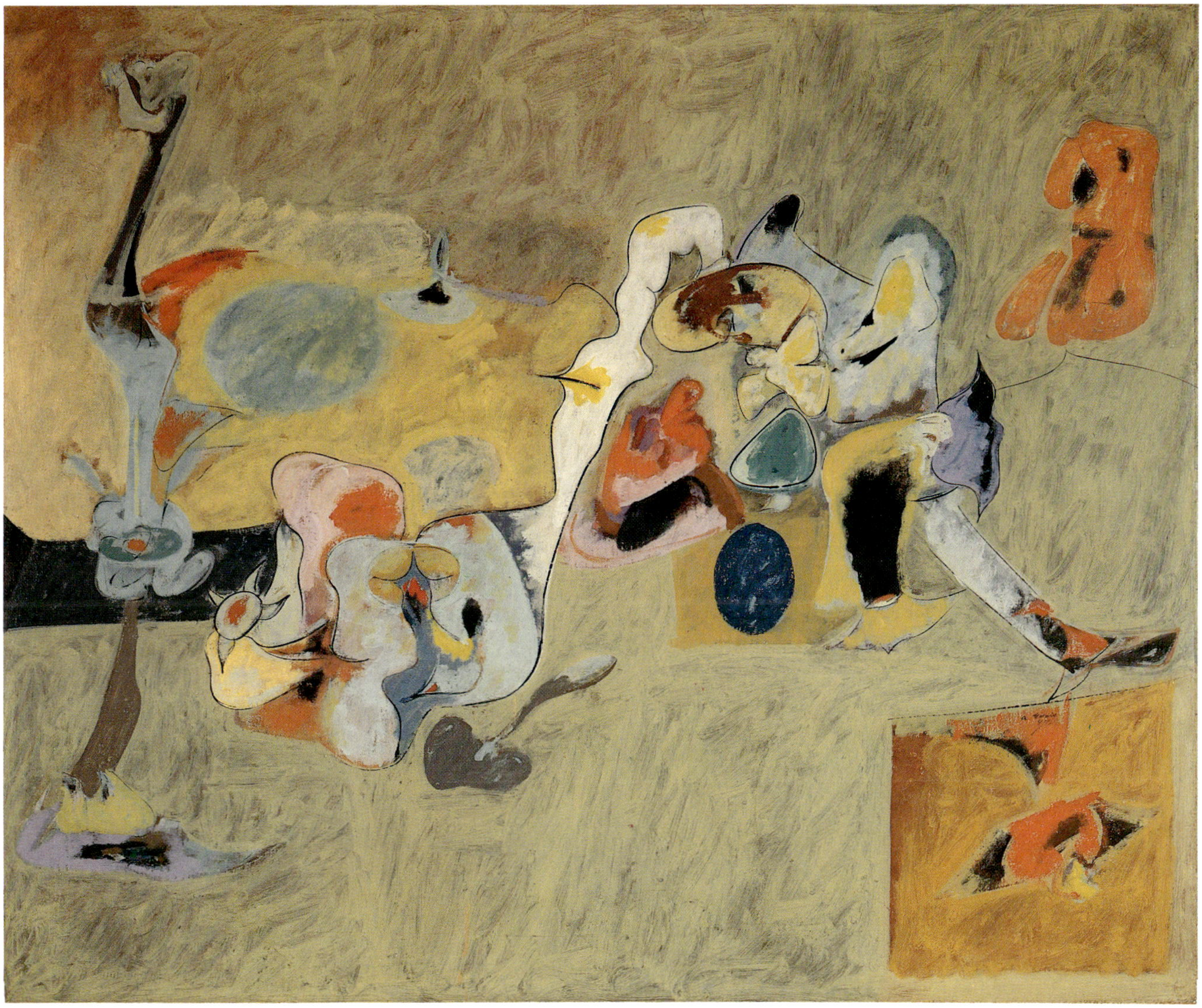

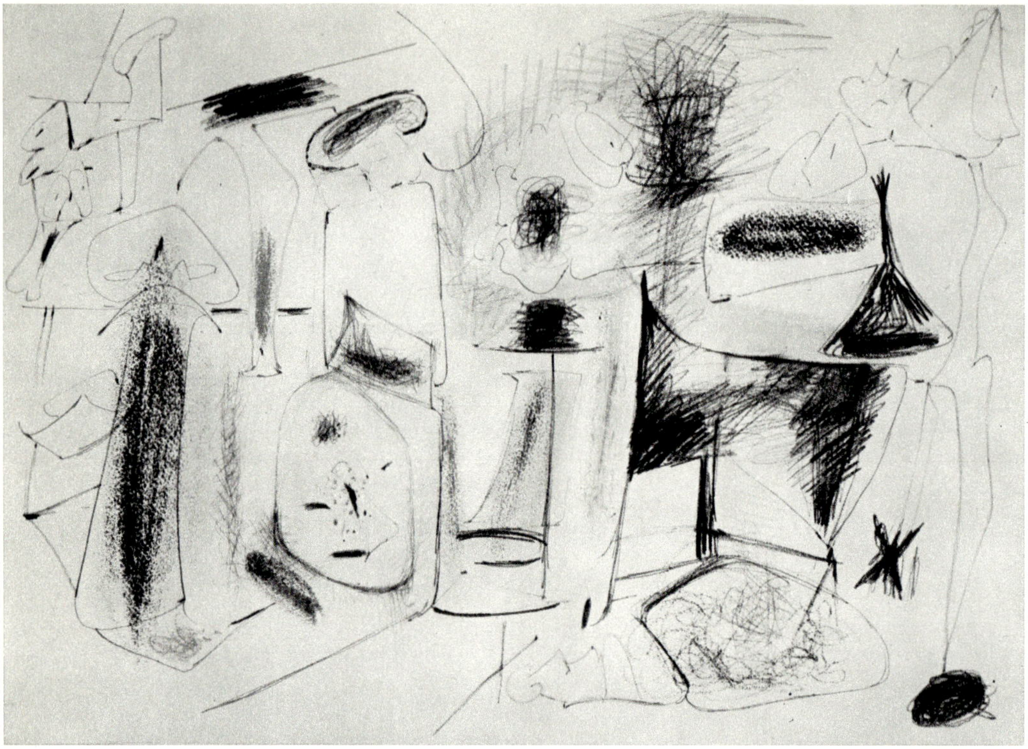

206. *Untitled*. ca. 1946
Pencil and crayon on paper,
15 × 22 1/2″
Collection Ethel K.
Schwabacher, New York

207. *Untitled*. 1946
Pencil and crayon on paper,
21 × 29″
Private Collection

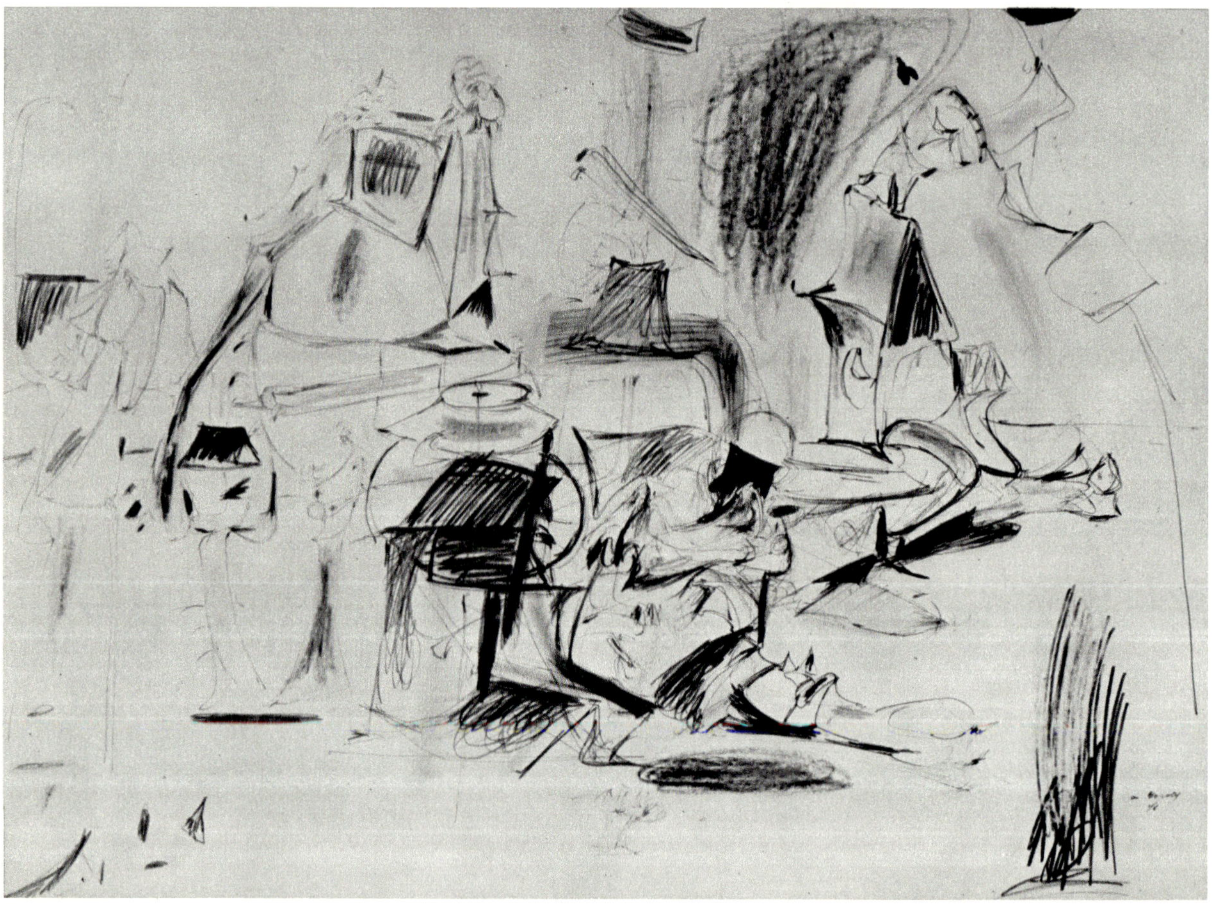

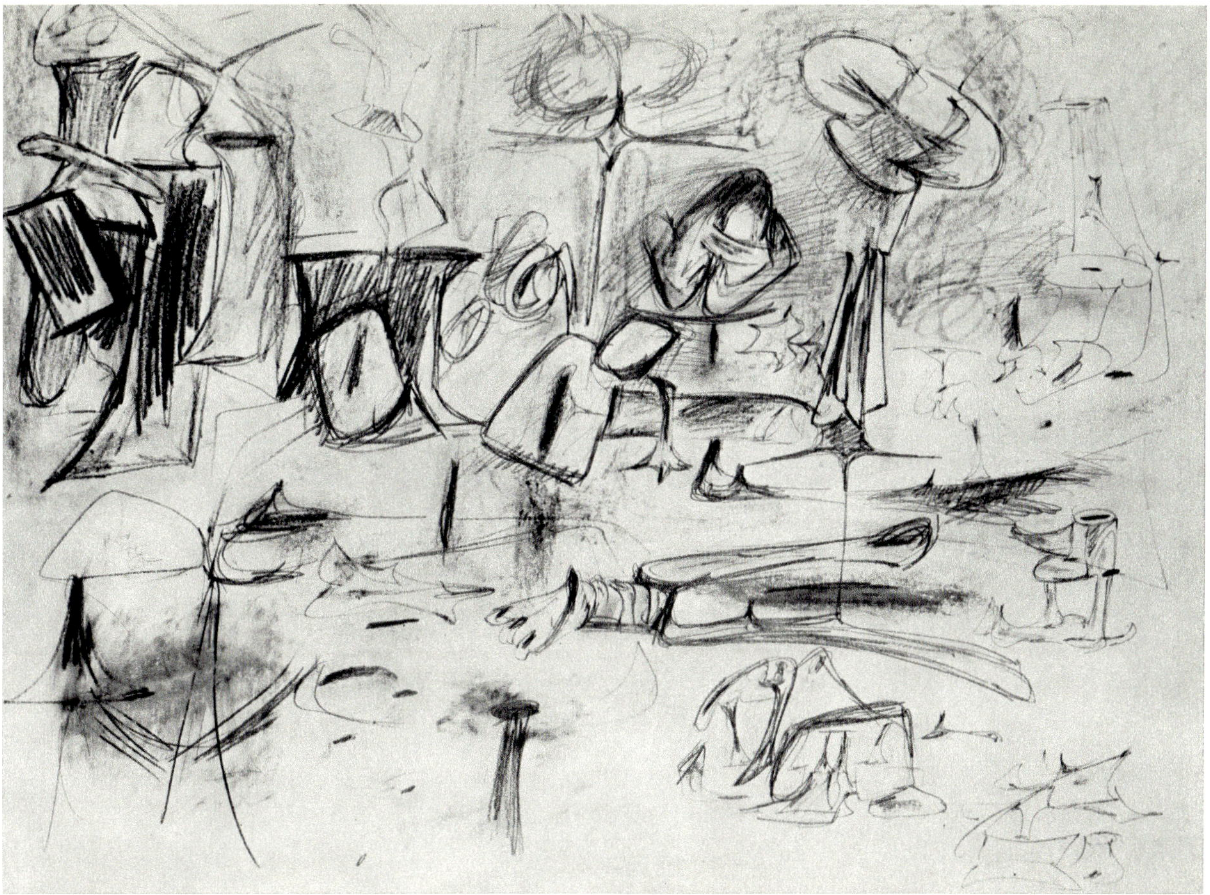

208. *Fireplace in Virginia.* 1946
Pencil and crayon on paper,
21 3/4 × 29 1/2″
Private Collection

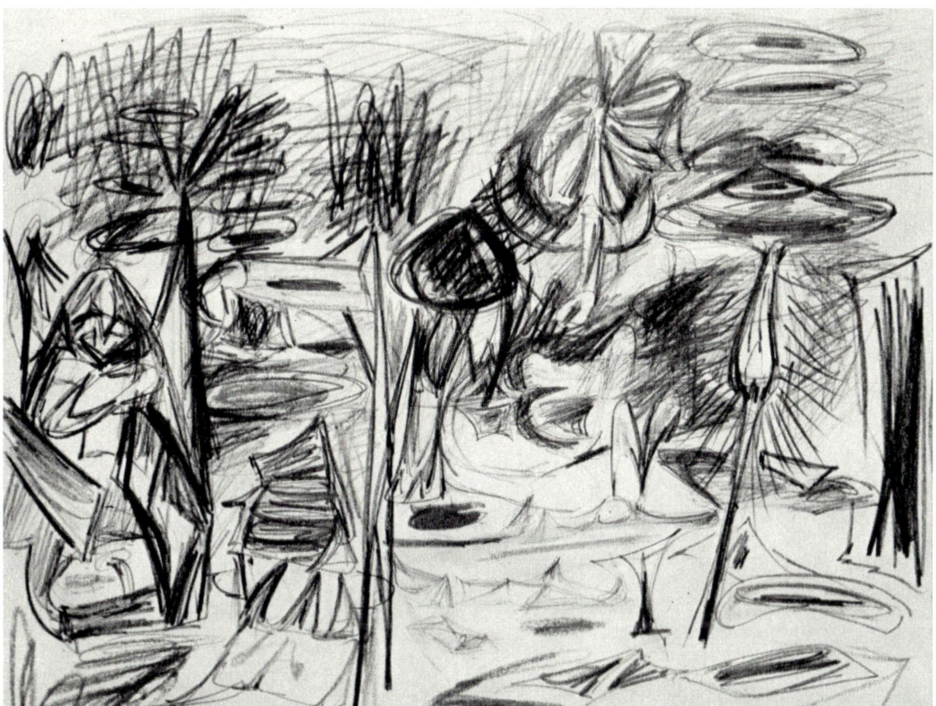

209. *Untitled.* 1945–46
Pencil and crayon on paper,
17 × 21 7/8″
Private Collection

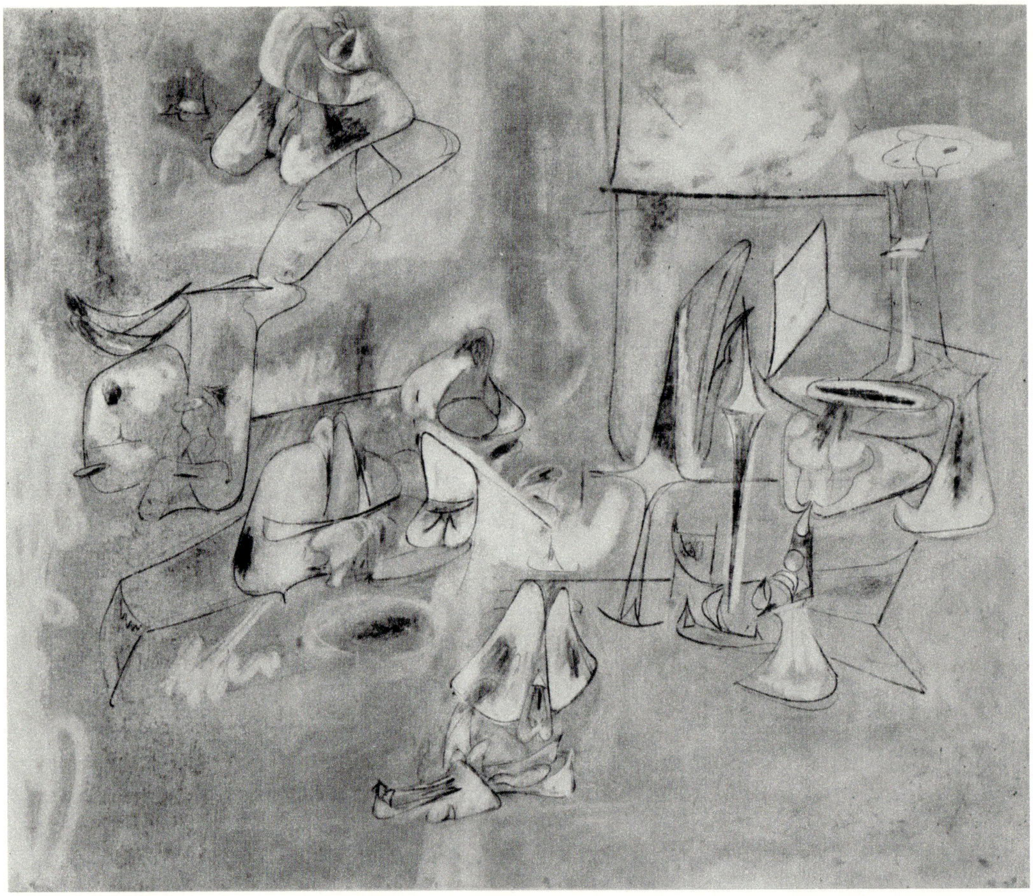

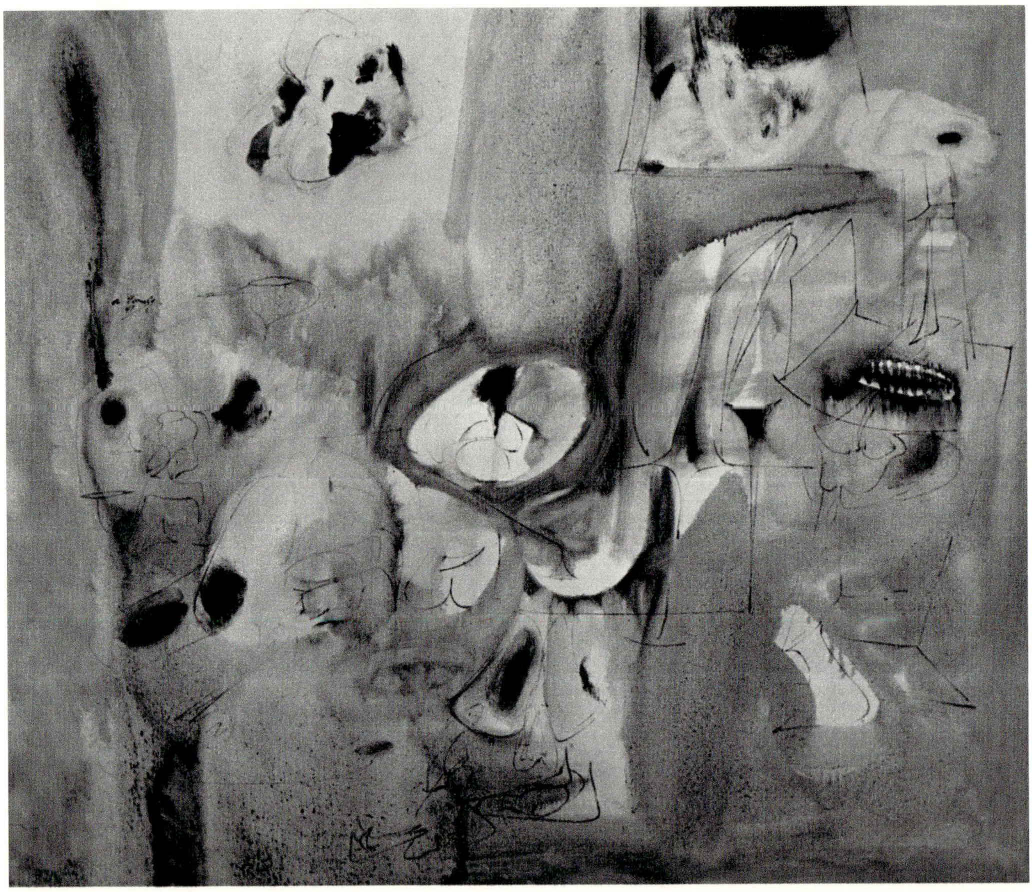

210. Study for *The Calendars*. 1946
Charcoal and chalk on paper mounted on board, 33 × 40 1/2″
Fogg Art Museum, Harvard University,
Cambridge, Massachusetts, Gift—Mrs. Culver Orswell

211. *Making the Calendar*. 1947
Oil on canvas, 34 × 41″
Collection Munson-Williams-Proctor Institute,
Utica, New York, Edward W. Root Bequest

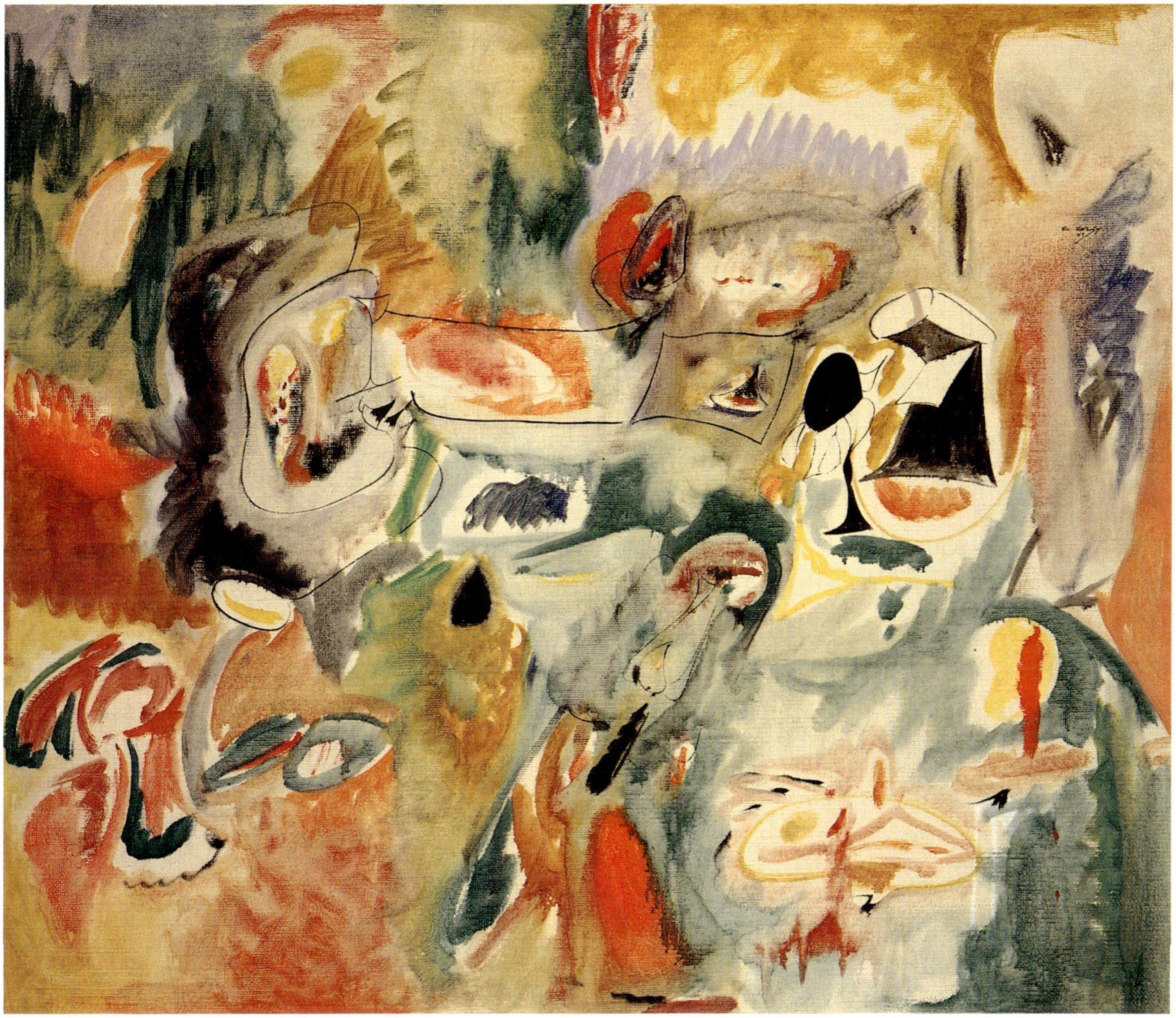

212. *Year After Year*. 1947
Oil on canvas, 34 × 39″
Collection Mr. and Mrs. Gifford Phillips, New York

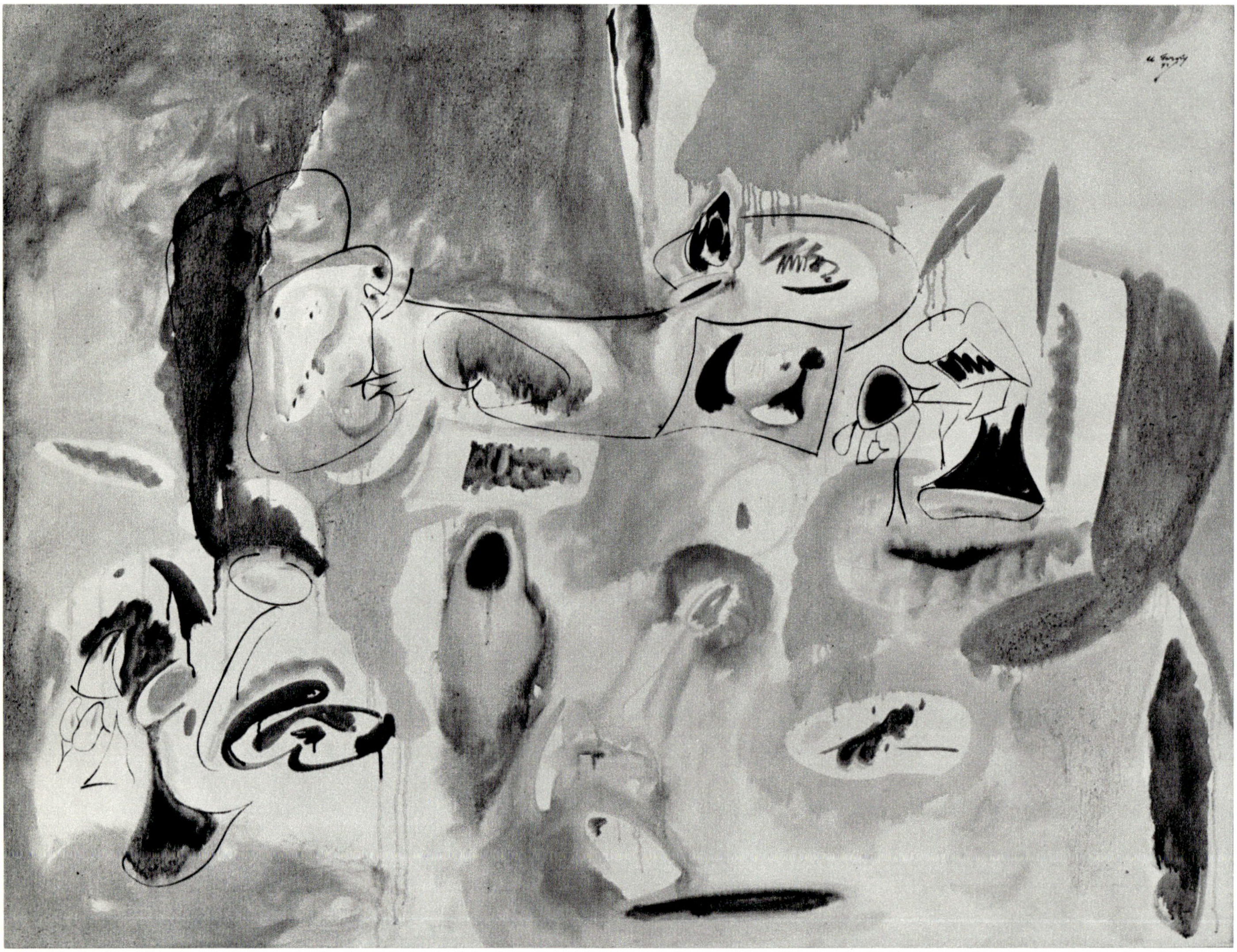

213. *Plumage Landscape*. 1947
Oil on canvas, 38 × 51″
Collection Australian National Gallery, Canberra

214. *Untitled* (*Drawing for Agony*). 1946
Pencil and wax crayon on paper,
18 1/8 × 23 5/8″
Collection The Solomon R. Guggenheim
Museum, New York,
Gift of Rook McCulloch, 1978 78.2516

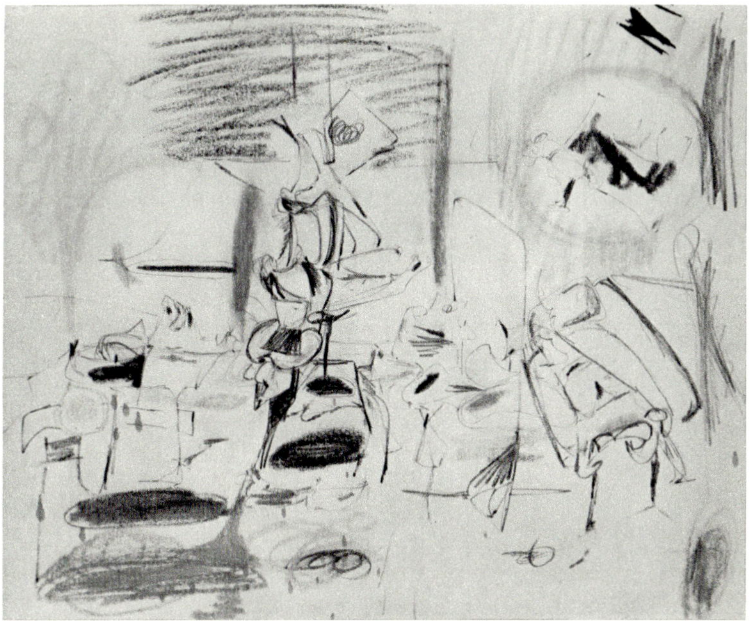

215. *Untitled*. ca. 1946
Pencil and pastel on paper,
24 1/8 × 18 3/4″
Collection Mrs. Satenig Avedisian
on loan to Museum of Fine Arts, Boston

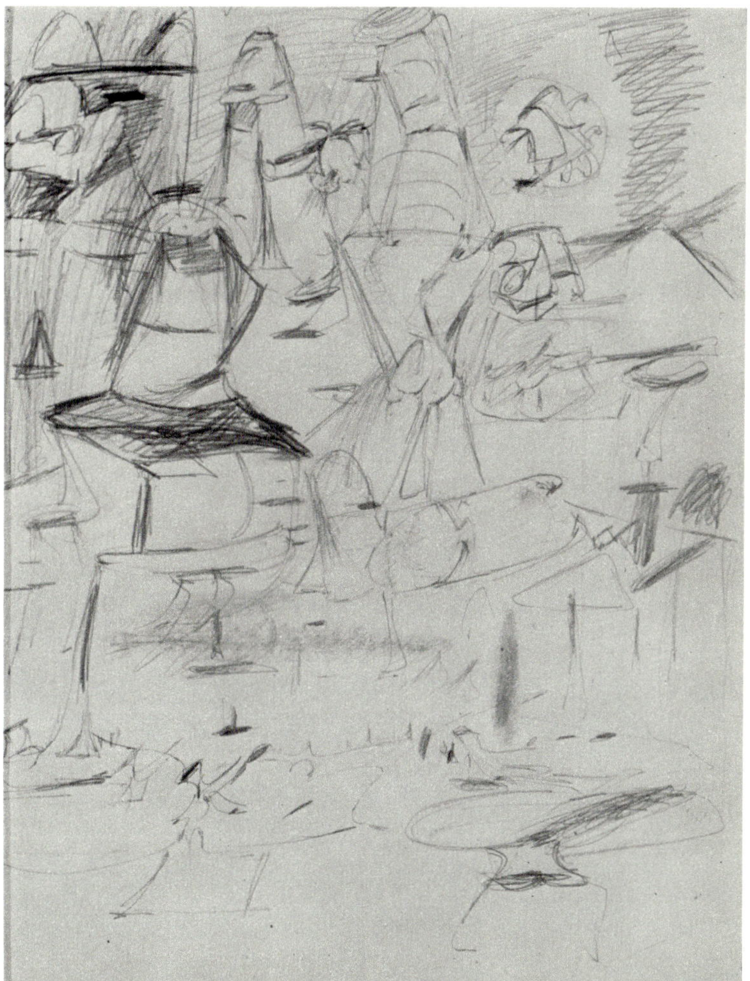

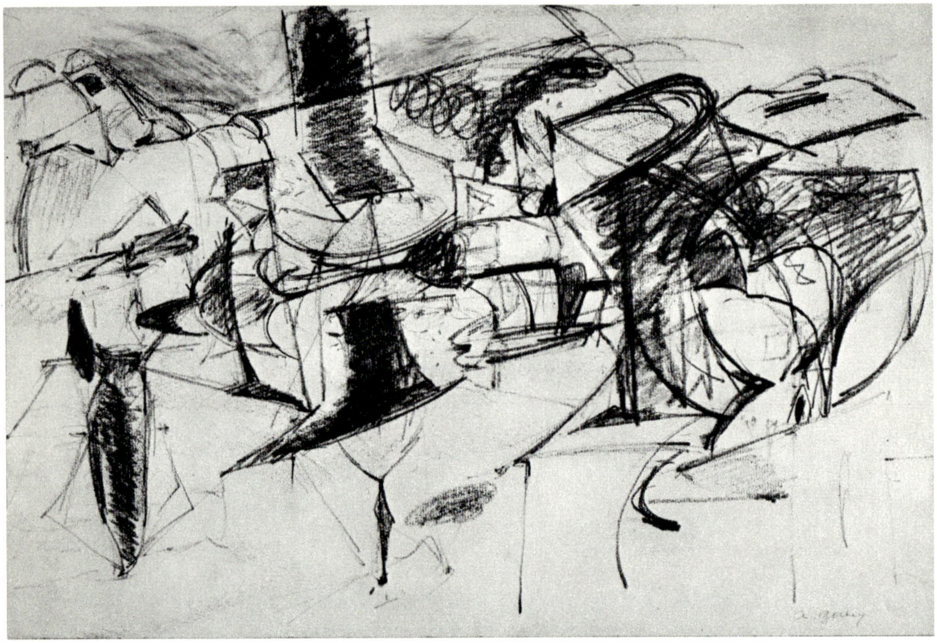

216. Study for *Agony*. ca. 1946
Pencil and crayon on paper, 13 × 19″
Collection Steingrim Laursen, Copenhagen

217. Study for *Agony*. 1947
Crayon and pencil on paper, 19 × 24″
Collection Mr. and Mrs. S.I. Newhouse, Jr.

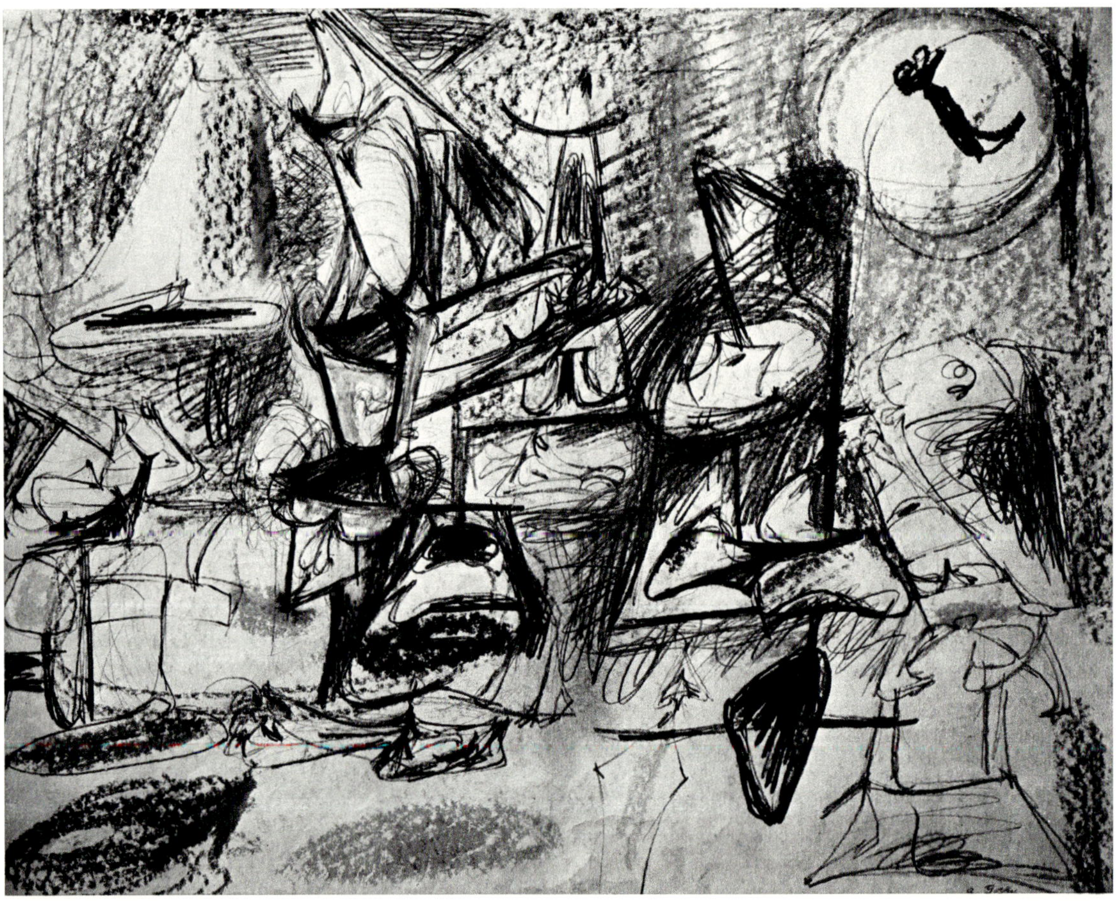

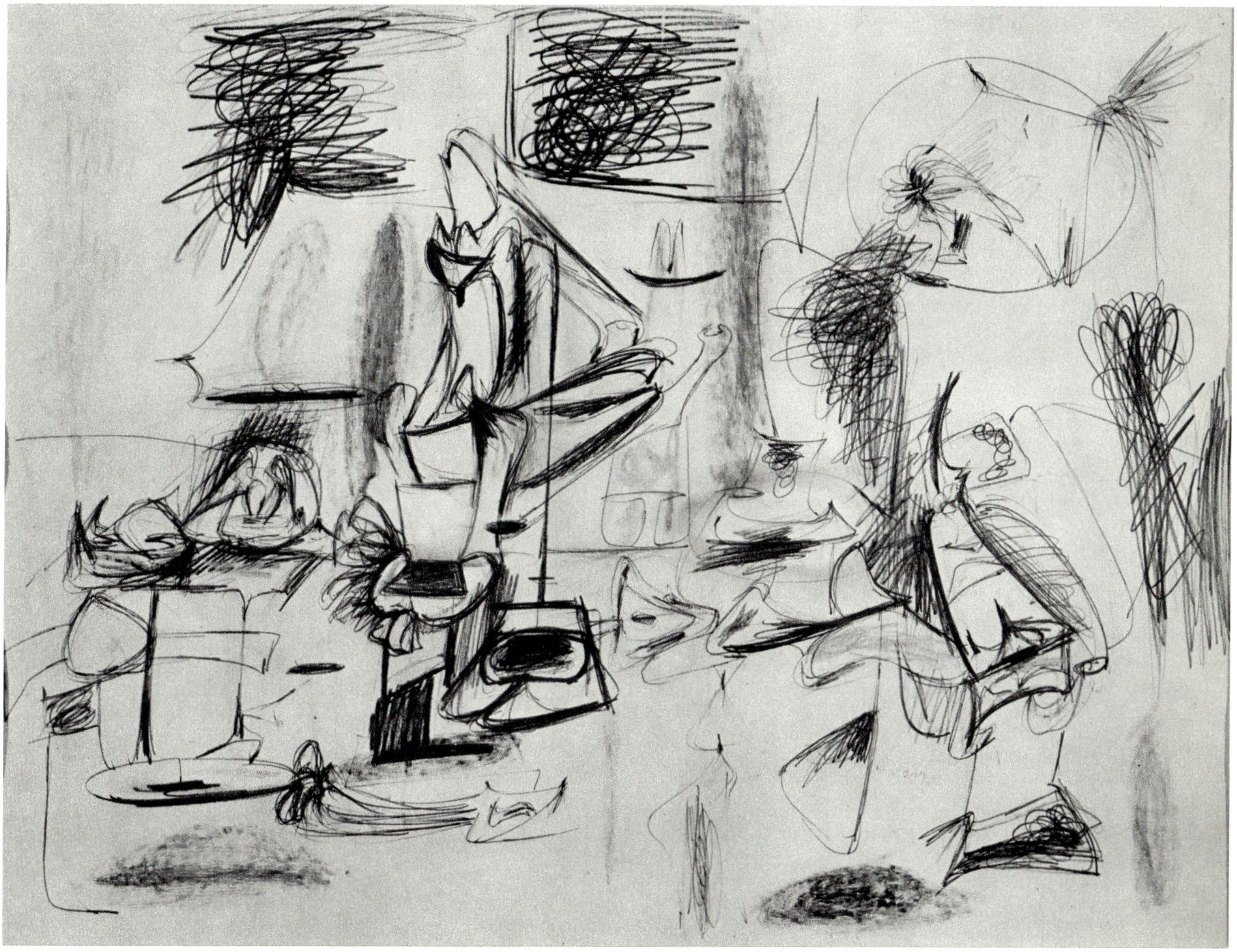

218. Study for *Agony I*. 1946–47
Pencil, crayon and wash on paper, 21 3/4 × 29 1/2″
Collection Sarah Campbell Blaffer Foundation, Houston

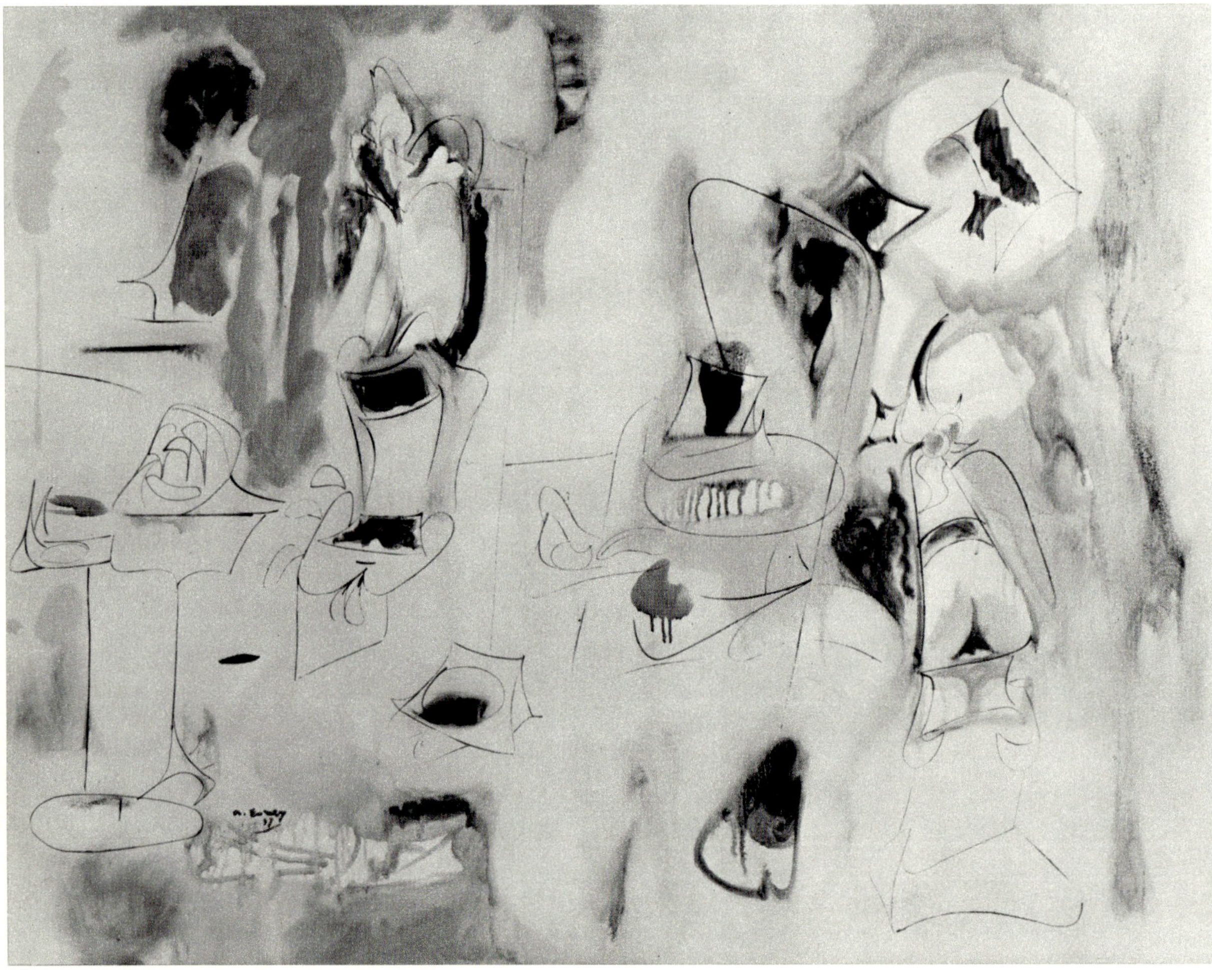

219. Study for *Agony*. 1947
Oil on canvas, 36 × 48″
Private Collection

220. *Agony*. 1947
Oil on canvas, 40 × 50 1/2″
Collection The Museum of Modern Art, New York,
A. Conger Goodyear Fund

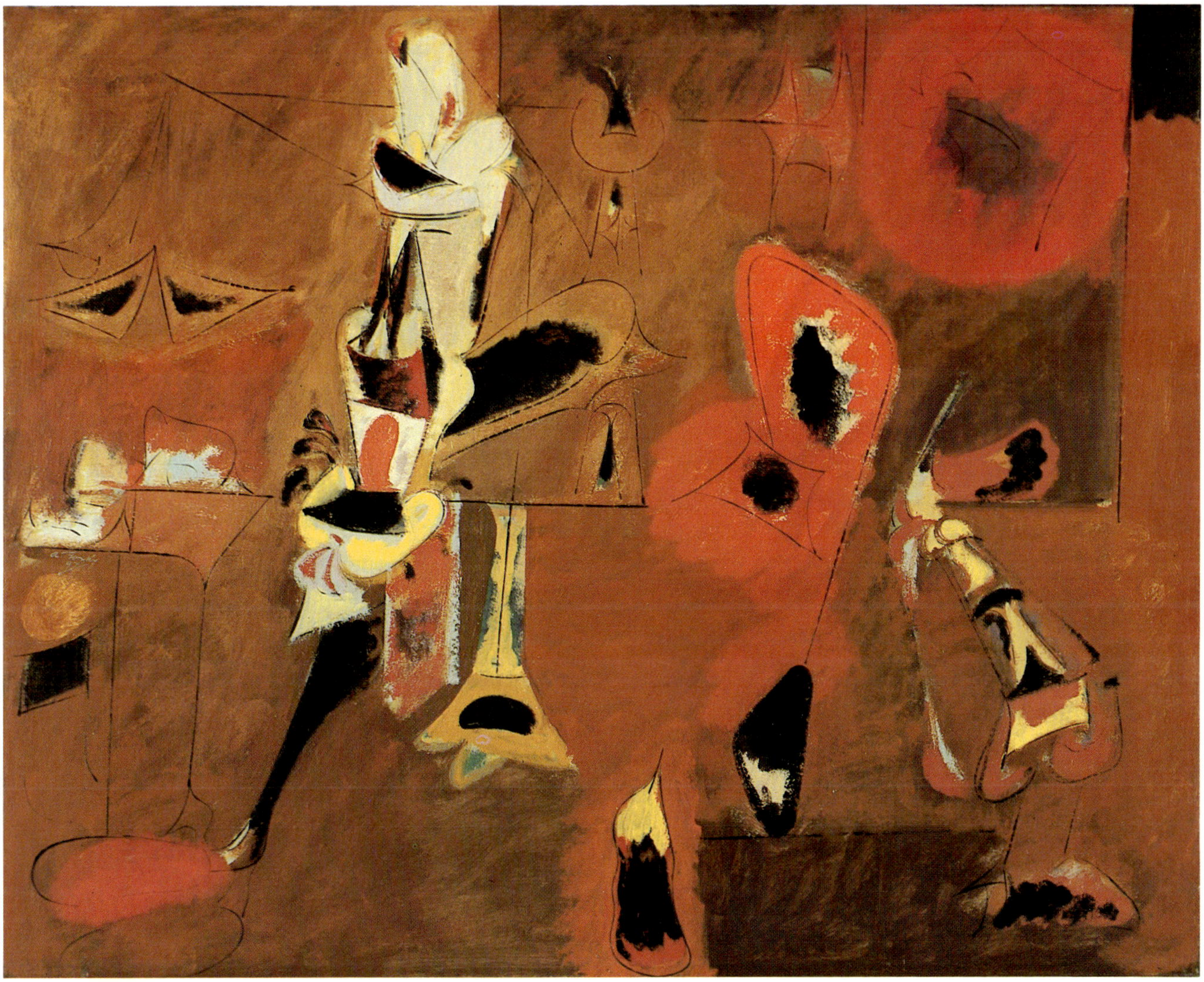

221. *Untitled*. 1946
Pencil and wax crayon on paper, 22 1/2 × 28″
Private Collection

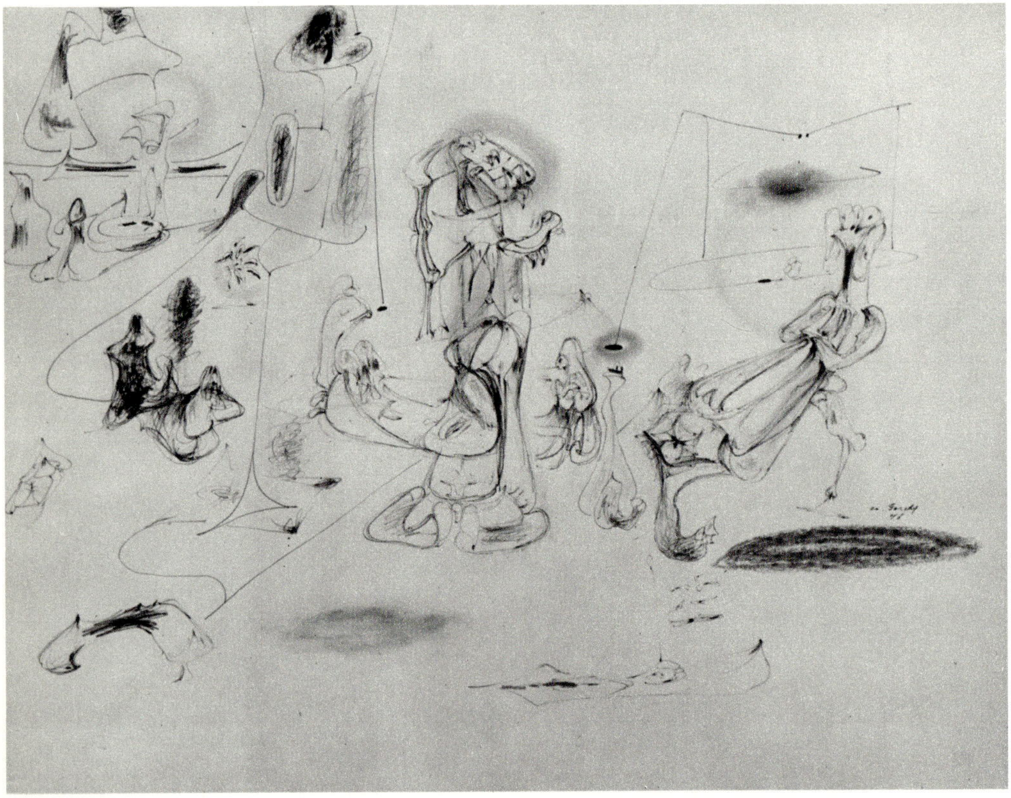

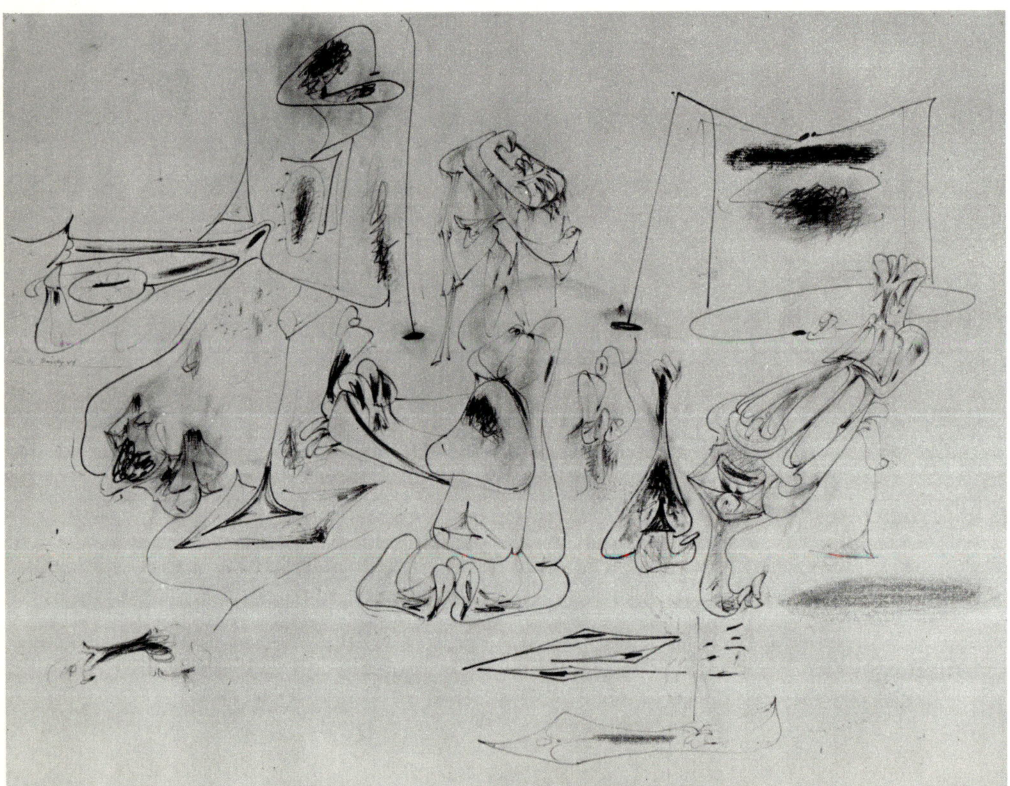

222. *Pastoral*. 1947
Pencil on paper, 19 × 25″
Private Collection

223. *Untitled*. ca. 1946
Wash, ink, watercolor, pencil and wax crayon on paper, 18 1/8 × 23 3/4″
Collection The Solomon R. Guggenheim Museum, New York, Gift of Rook McCulloch 76.2276

224. *Untitled*. 1946
Pen, pencil and wash on paper, 18 1/2 × 24 1/2″
Private Collection

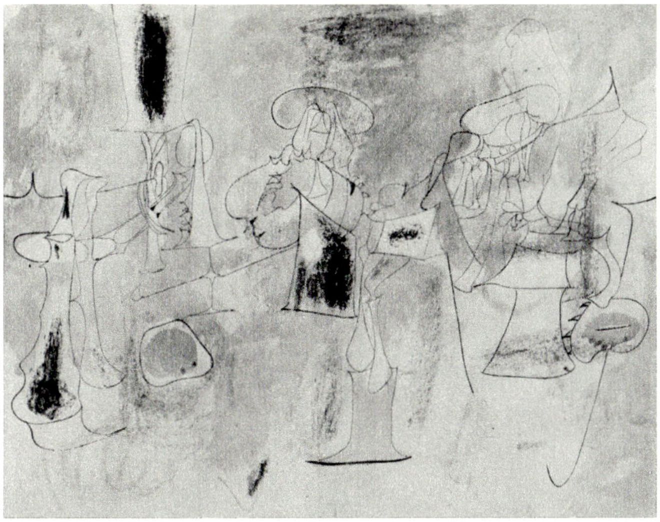

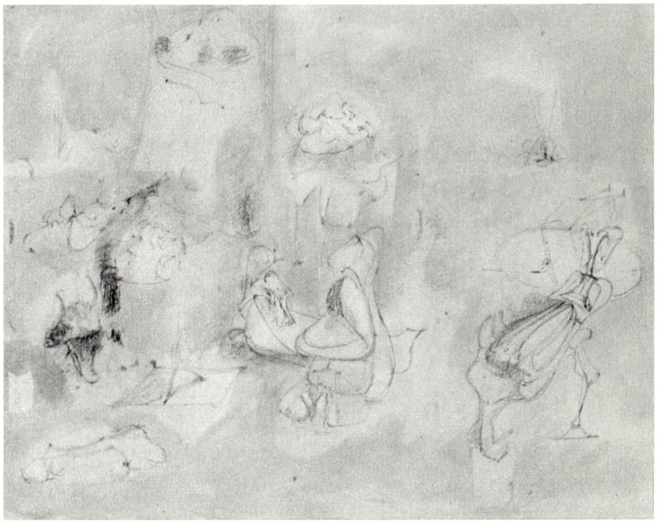

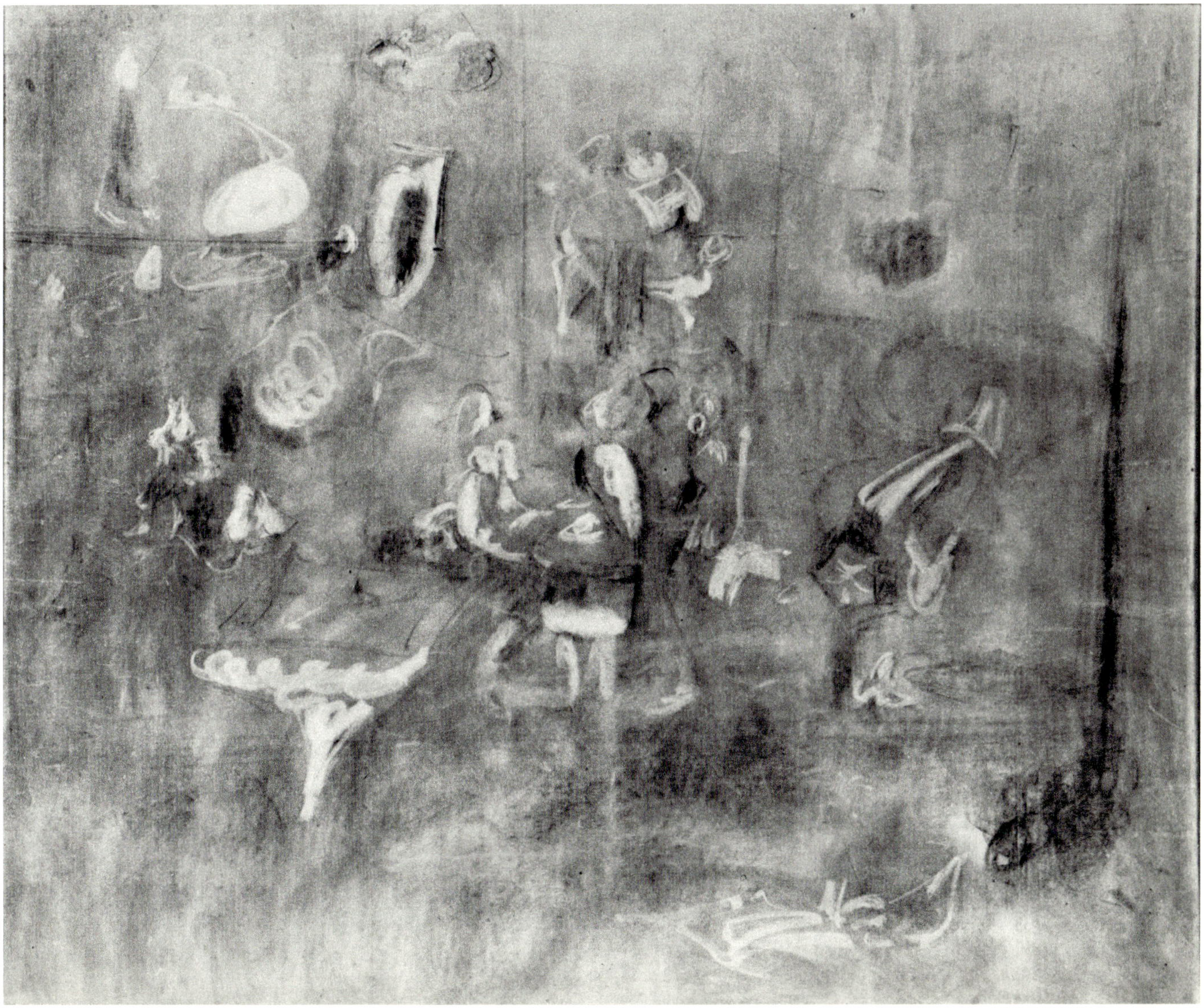

225. *Grey Drawing* (*Pastorale*). 1946–47
Charcoal on paper, 50 1/2 × 62″
Private Collection

226. *A Fireplace in Virginia*. ca. 1946
Pen, pencil and wash on paper, 12 1/2 × 9 1/2″
Collection Duncan MacGuigan, New York

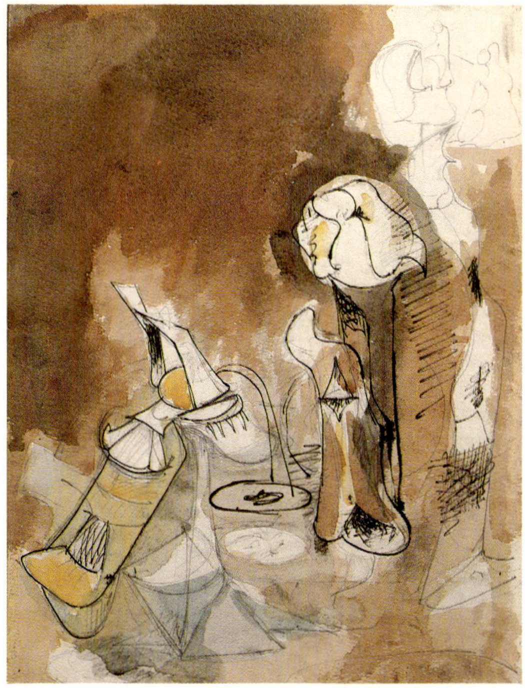

227. *Pastorale*. 1947
Oil on canvas, 44 × 56″
Private Collection

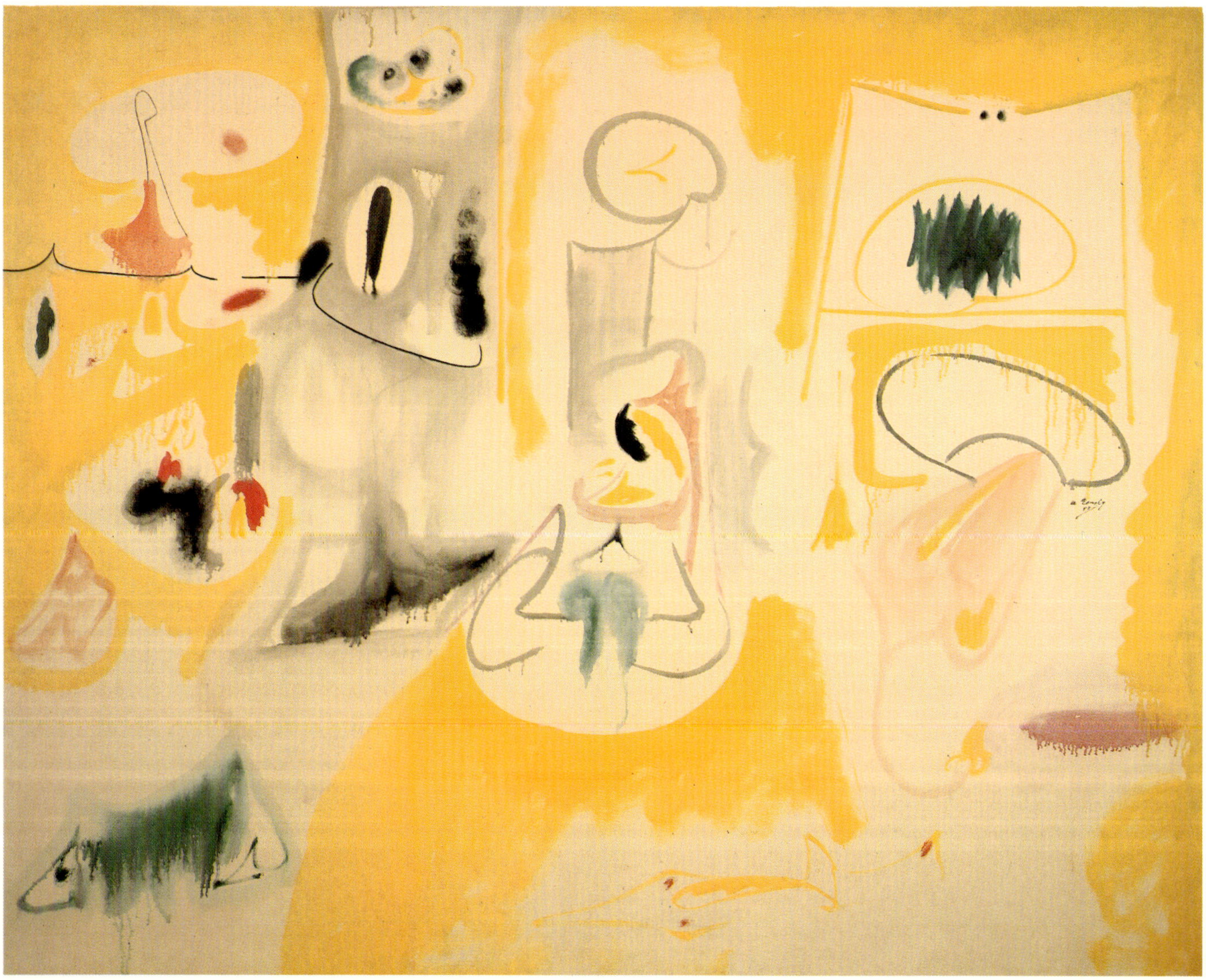

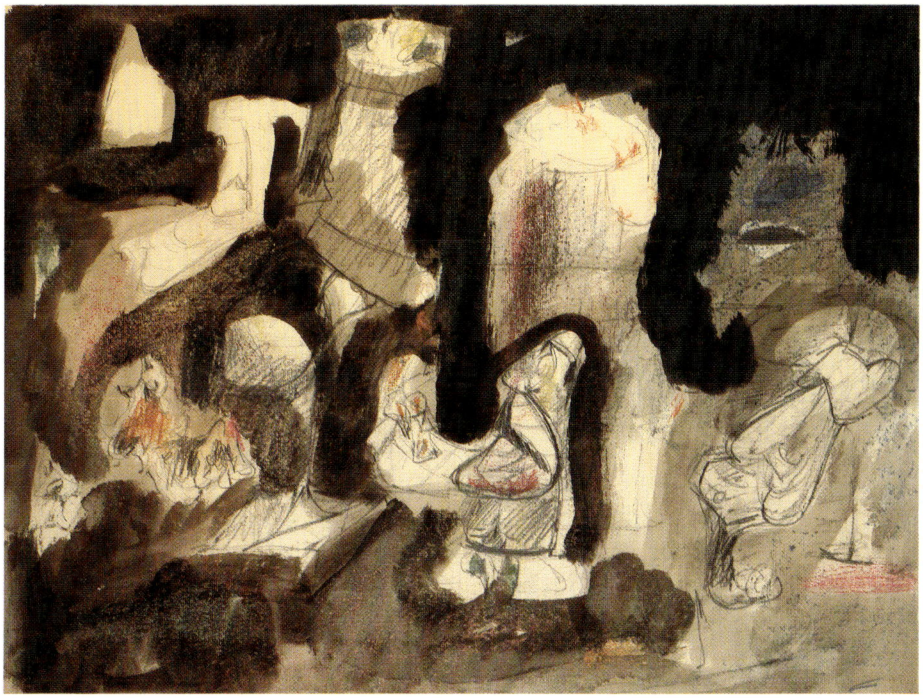

228. *Untitled*. ca. 1946
Pencil, pastel and wash on paper, 18 3/4 × 24 5/16″
Collection Mrs. Satenig Avedisian on loan to Museum of Fine Arts, Boston

229. *Terra Cotta*. 1947
Oil on canvas, 44 1/4 × 56″
Frederick Weisman Family Collection

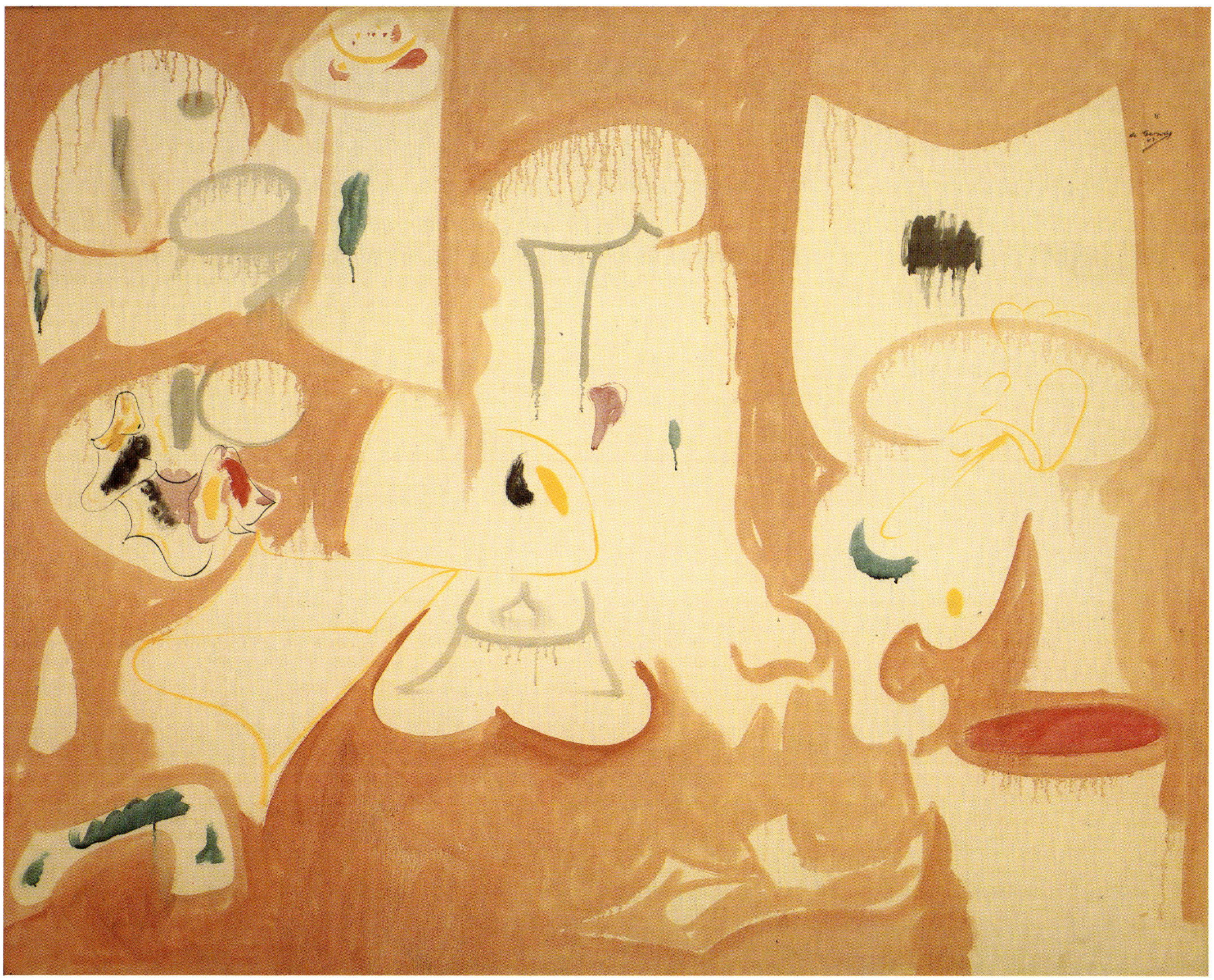

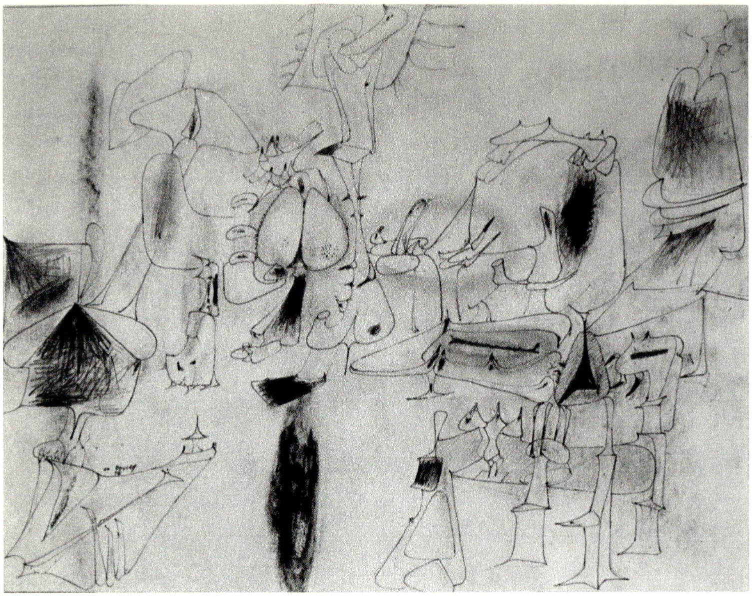

230. *Untitled*. 1946
Pencil, watercolor and crayon on paper, 18 1/2 × 24″
Collection Mr. and Mrs. Harry W. Anderson

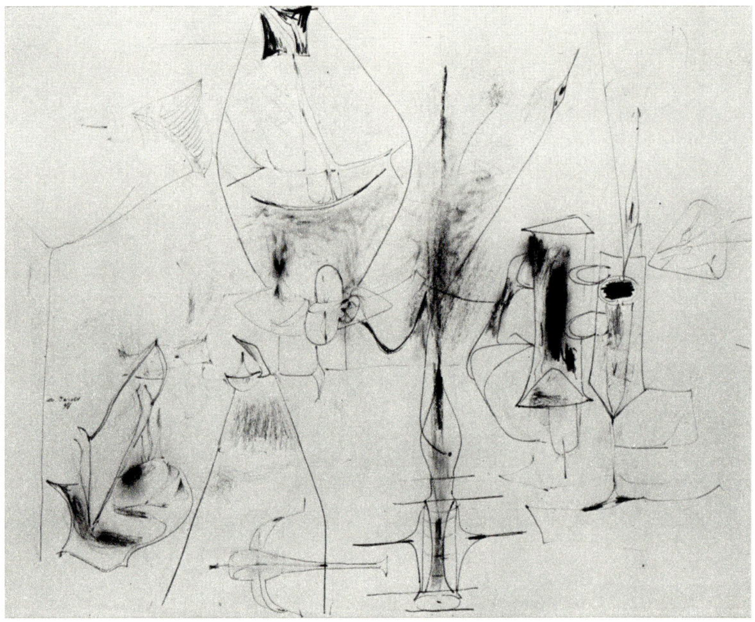

231. *Untitled*. 1946
Pencil and crayon on paper, 19 × 24″
Courtesy Sidney Janis Gallery, New York

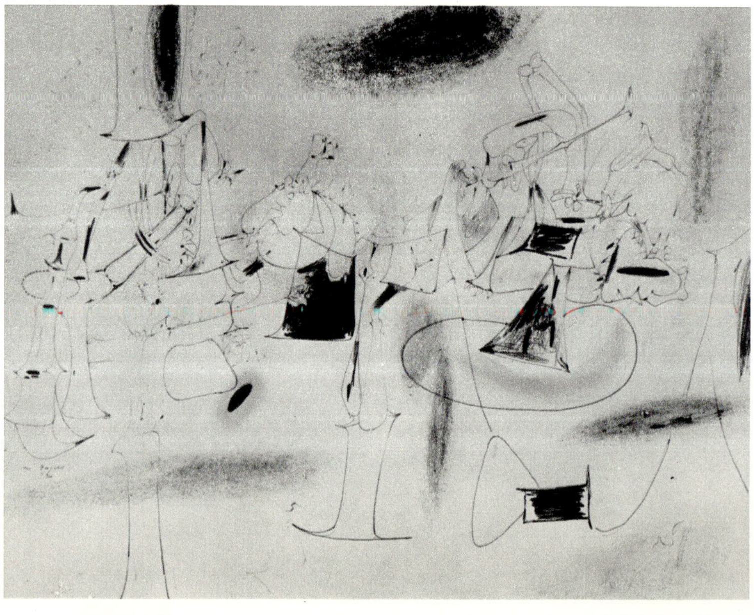

232. *Untitled*. 1946
Pencil and crayon on paper, 18 1/2 × 24 1/2″
Collection Julien Levy; Courtesy Richard L. Feigen & Co.

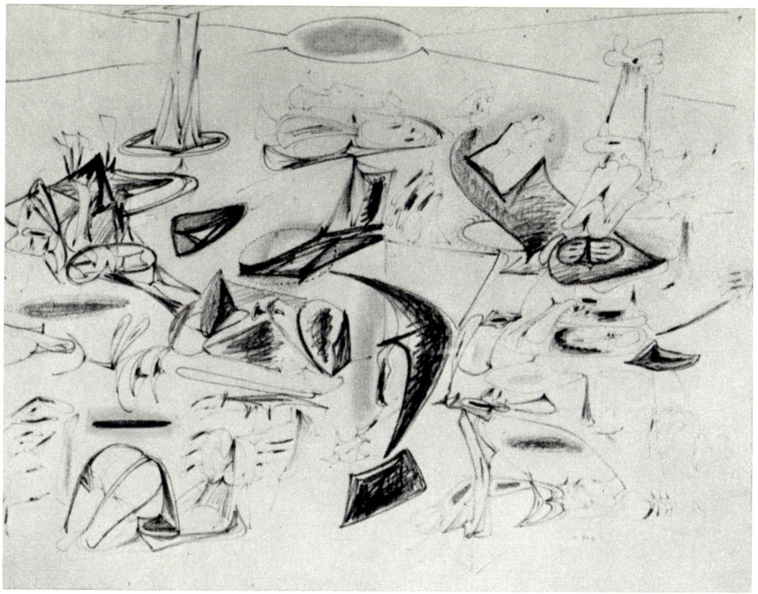

233. *Virginia—Summer*. 1946
Pencil and crayon on paper, 18 × 24″
Private Collection

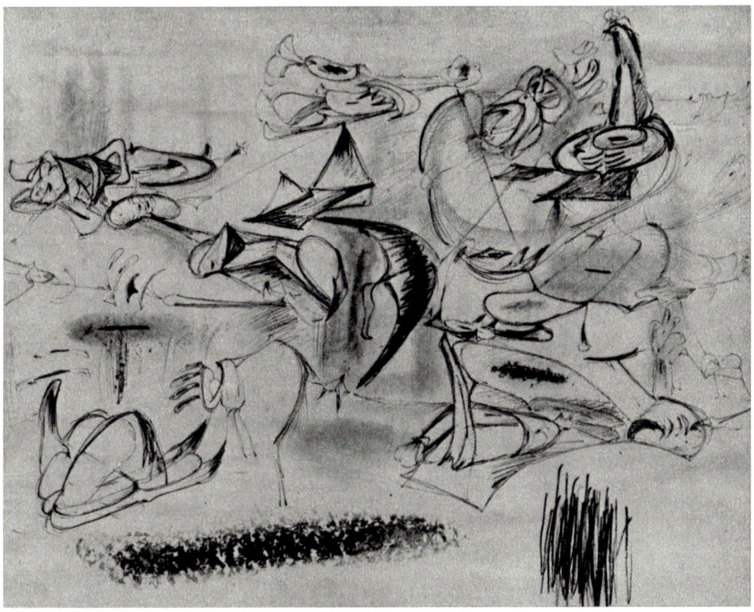

234. *Summer*. 1946
Pencil and crayon on paper, 18 7/8 × 23 5/8″
Private Collection

235. *Untitled*. ca. 1946
Pencil on paper, 18 1/2 × 25 5/8″
Collection The Solomon R. Guggenheim Museum, New York, Gift of Rook McCulloch 79.2575

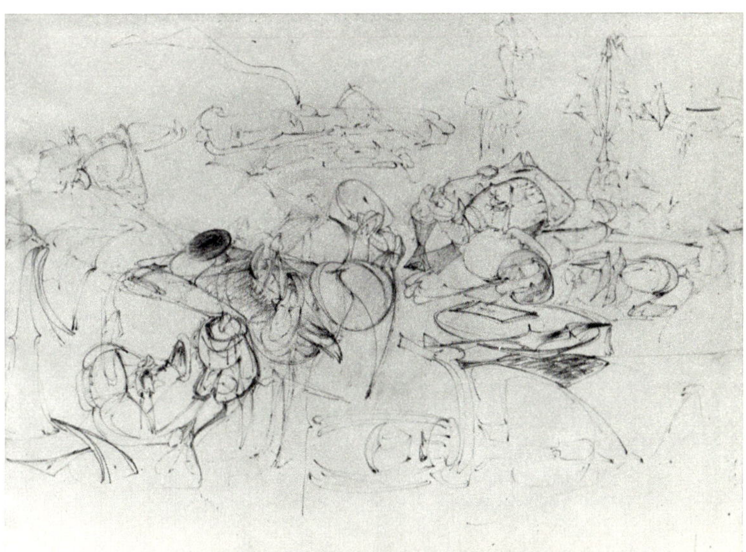

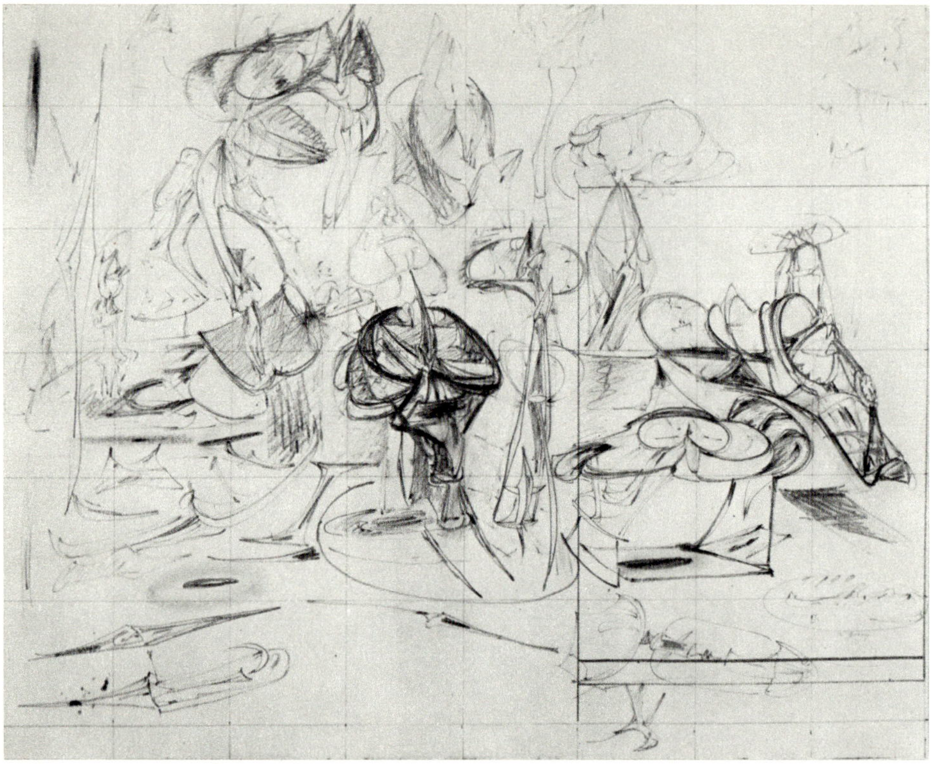

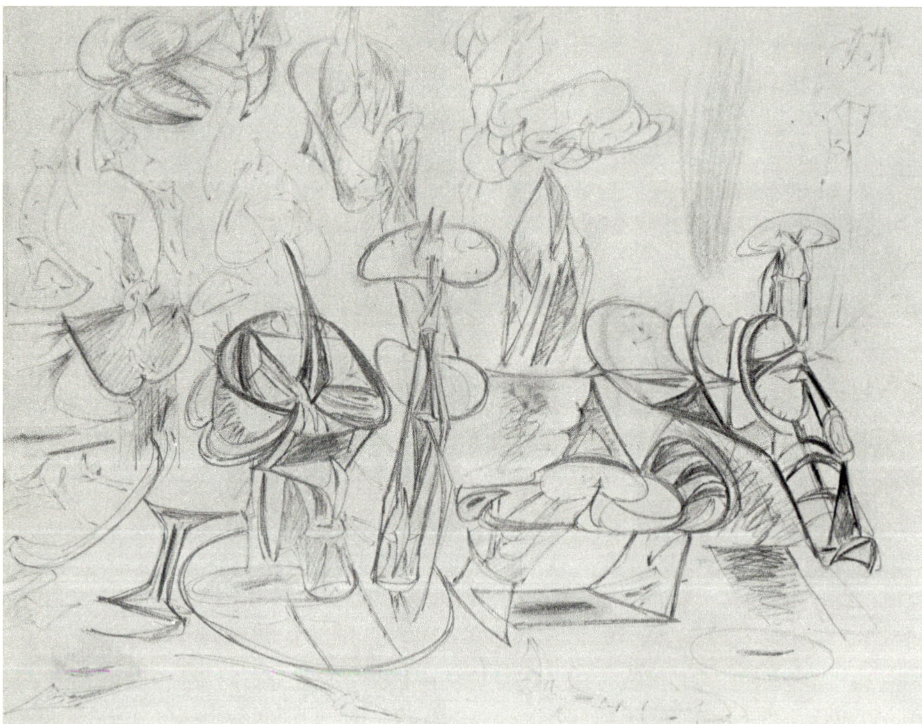

236. Study for *The Orators*. ca. 1947
Pencil and sargent crayon on paper, 19 × 24 1/2″
Private Collection

237. Study for *The Orators*. 1946–47
Pencil on paper, 18 3/4 × 24 1/2″
Private Collection

238. *The Orators*. 1947
Oil on canvas, 60 × 72″
Private Collection, New York

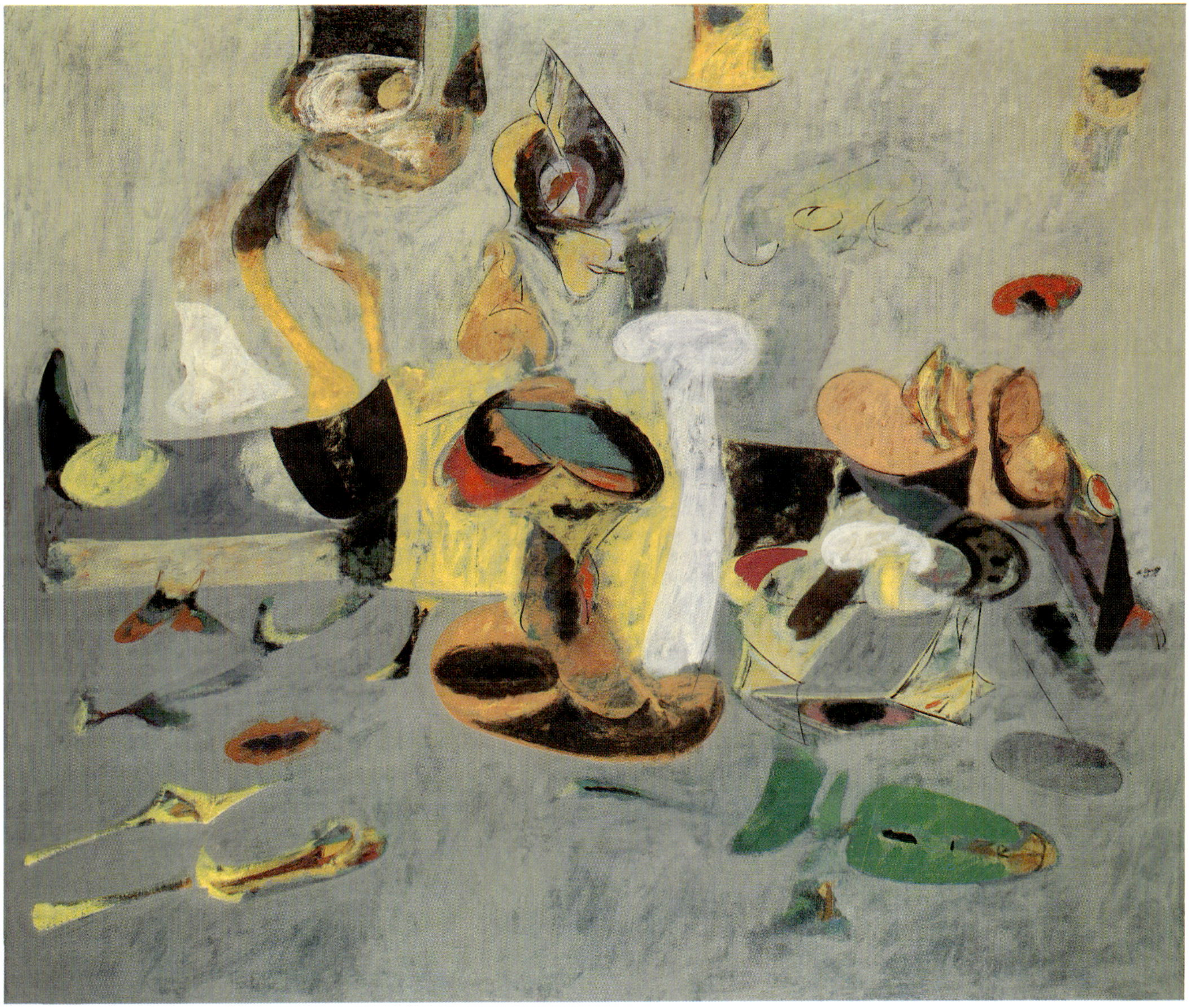

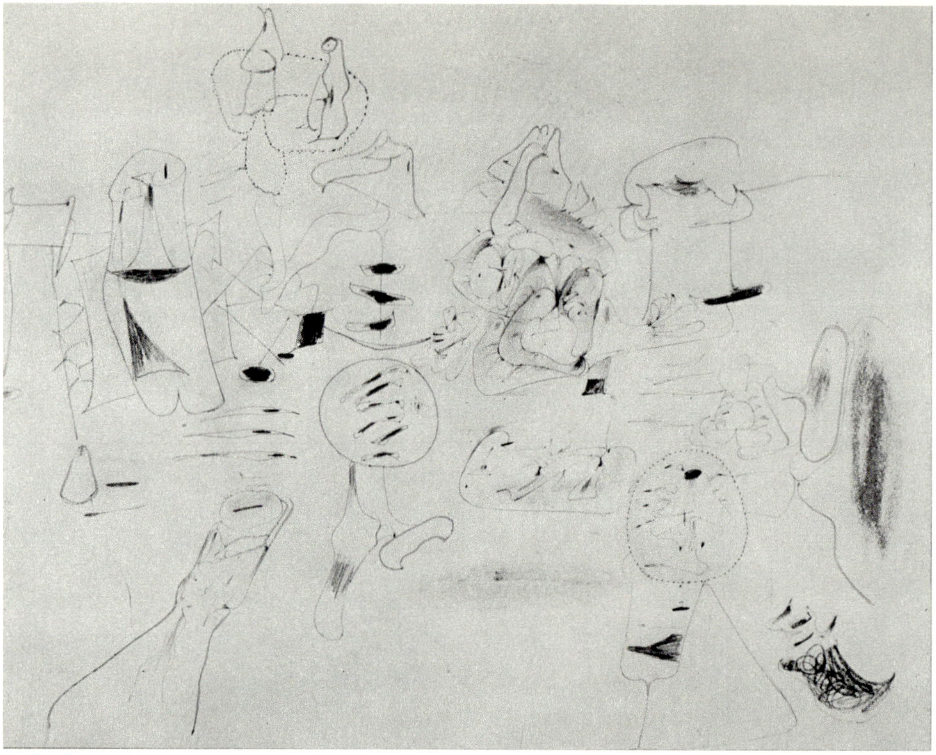

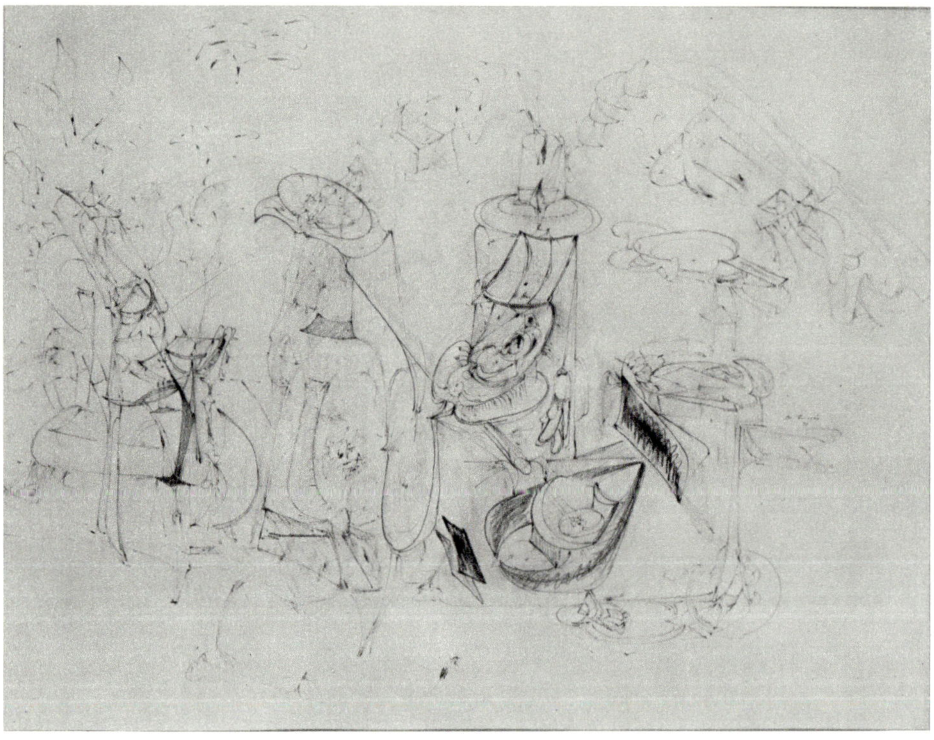

239. *Abstraction.* 1946
Pen and ink and crayon on paper, 18 1/2 × 24 3/8″
Courtesy of Indiana University Art Museum, Bloomington

240. *Composition II.* 1946
Pencil and crayon on paper, 18 7/8 × 25 1/4″
Collection The Baltimore Museum of Art

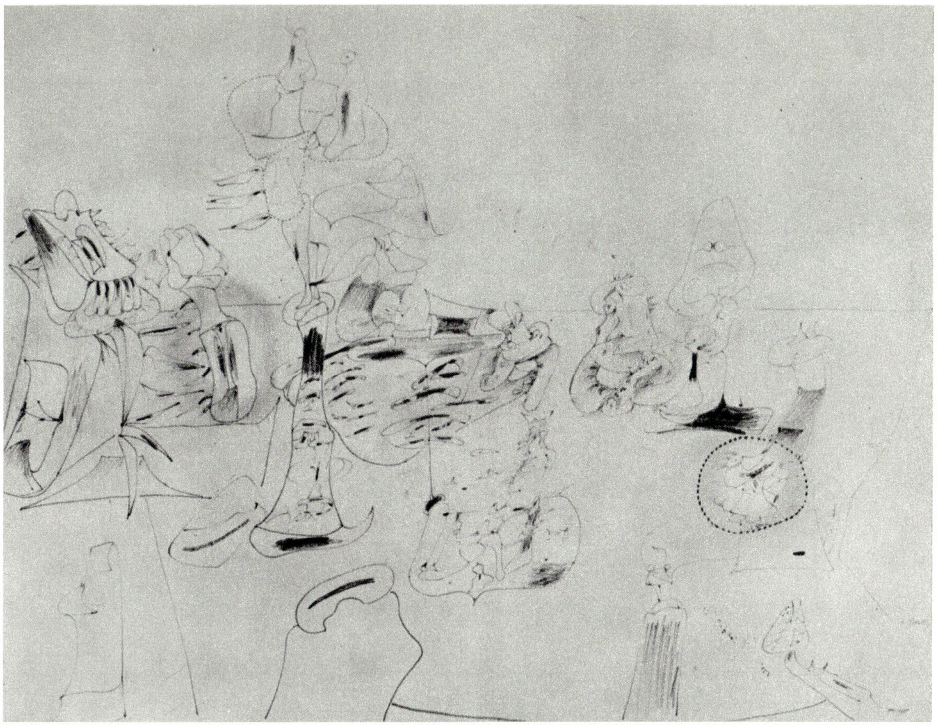

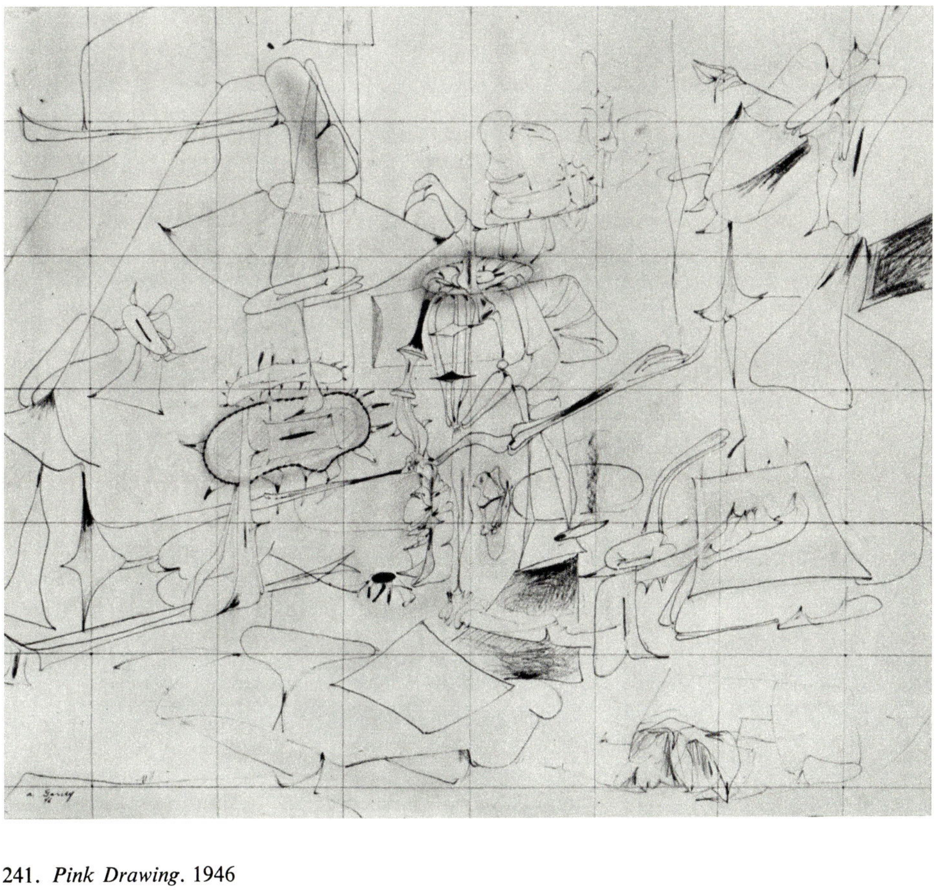

241. *Pink Drawing*. 1946
Pencil and crayon on paper, 19 × 25″
Private Collection

242. Study for *Dark Green Painting*. 1946
Pencil and crayon on paper, 19 × 24″
Private Collection

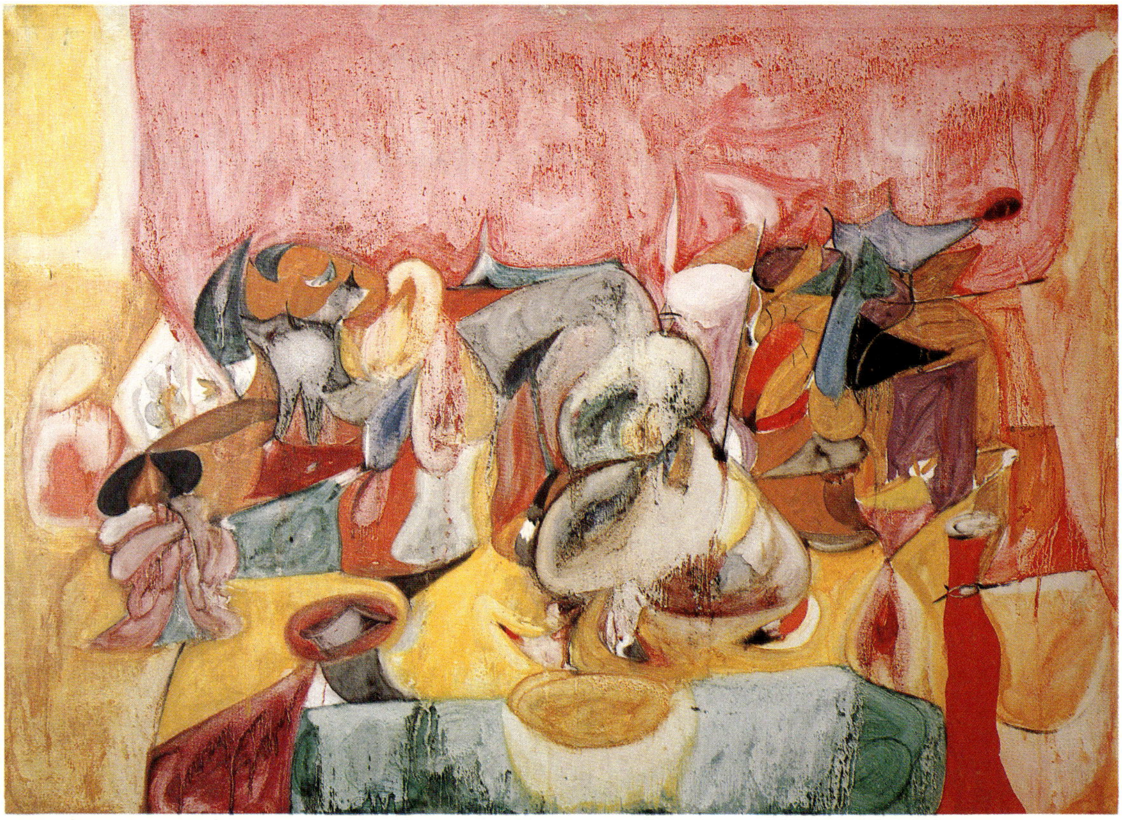

243. *Scent of Apricots.* 1947
Oil on canvas, 31 × 44″
Collection Mr. and Mrs. Joseph Randall Shapiro,
Oak Park, Illinois

244. *Dark Green Painting*. ca. 1948
Oil on canvas, 43 7/8 × 55 7/8″
Philadelphia Museum of Art:
Lent by Mr. and Mrs. H. Gates Lloyd

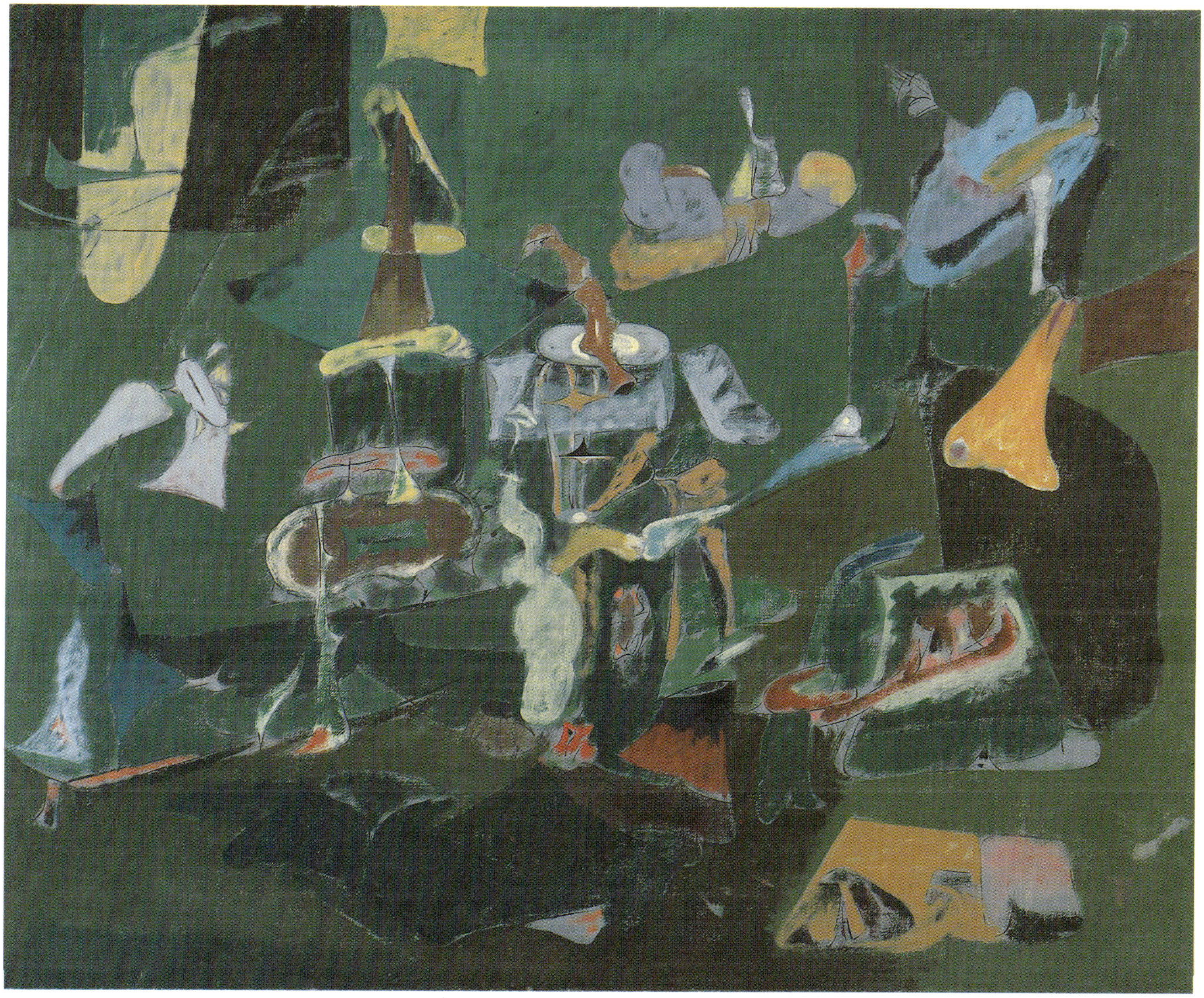

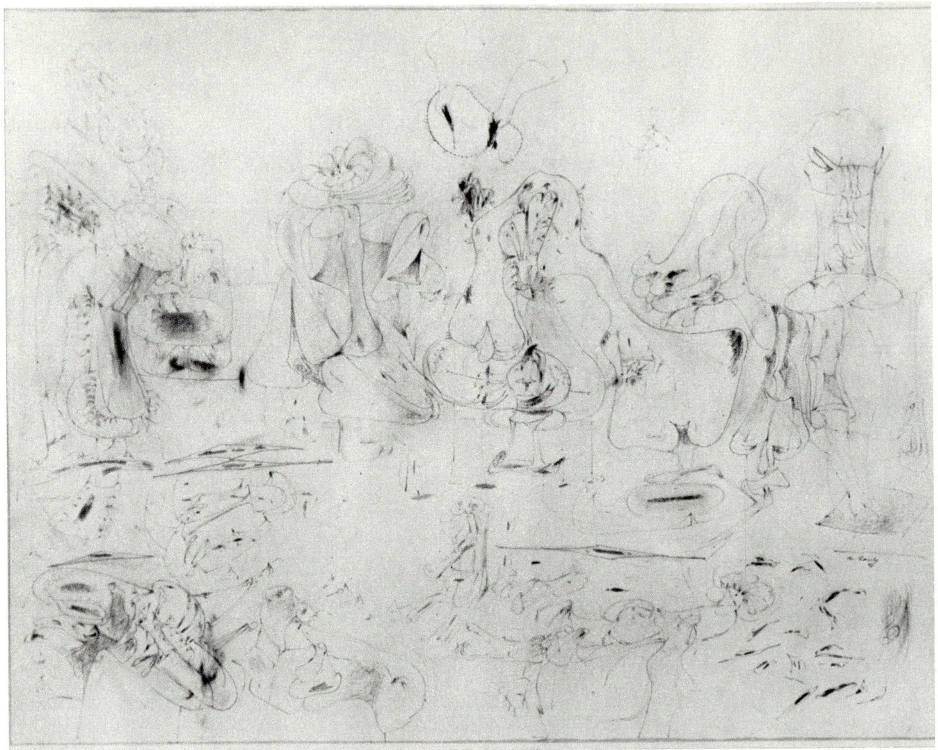

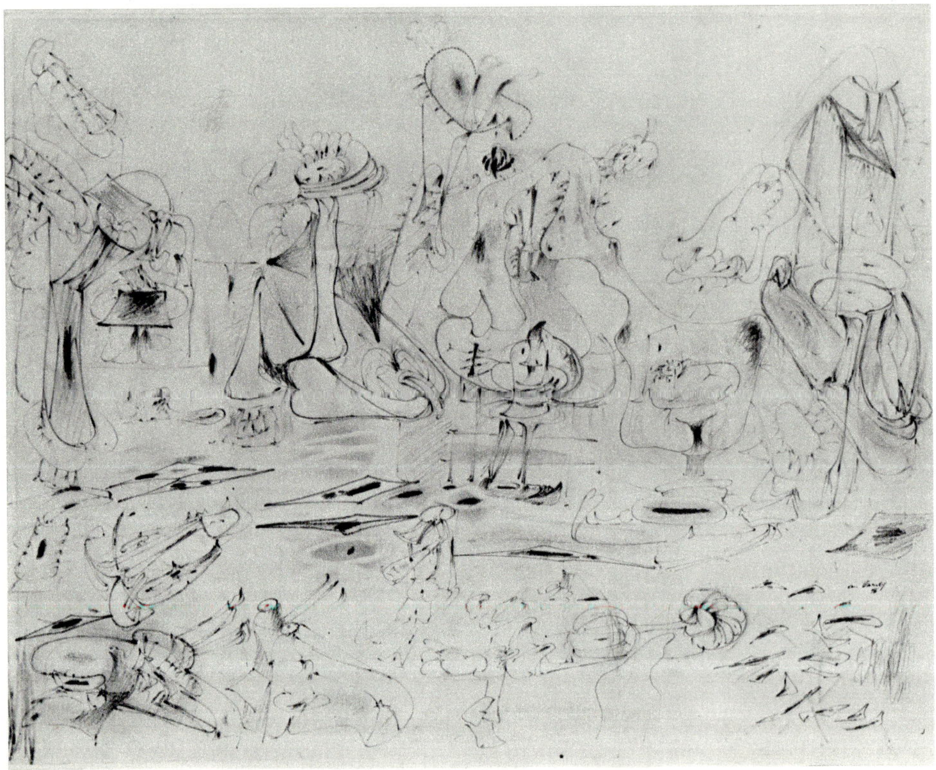

245. Study for *Summation*. 1946
Crayon and pencil on paper, 18 1/2 × 24 1/2″
Collection of the Whitney Museum of American Art, New York,
Gift of Mr. and Mrs. Wolfgang S. Schwabacher

246. Study for *Summation*. 1946
Pencil and colored chalk on paper, 18 1/2 × 24 3/8″
The Museum of Modern Art, New York;
The Sidney and Harriet Janis Collection

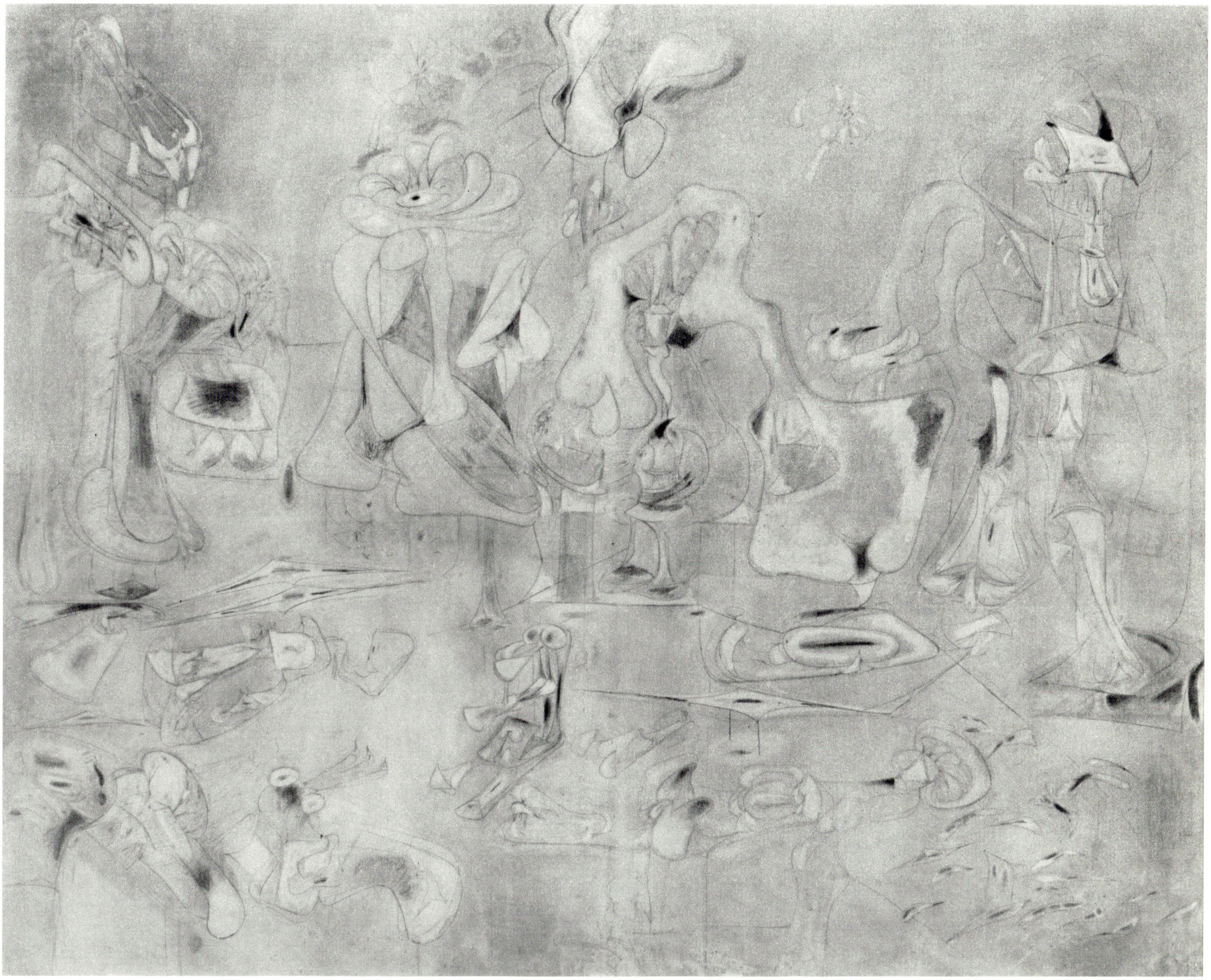

247. *Summation*. 1947
Pencil, pastel and charcoal and paper mounted
on composition board, 79 5/8 × 101 3/4″
Collection The Museum of Modern Art, New York;
Mr. and Mrs. Gordon Bunshaft Fund

248. *The Limit*. 1947
Oil on paper mounted on burlap, 50 3/4 × 62 1/2″
Private Collection

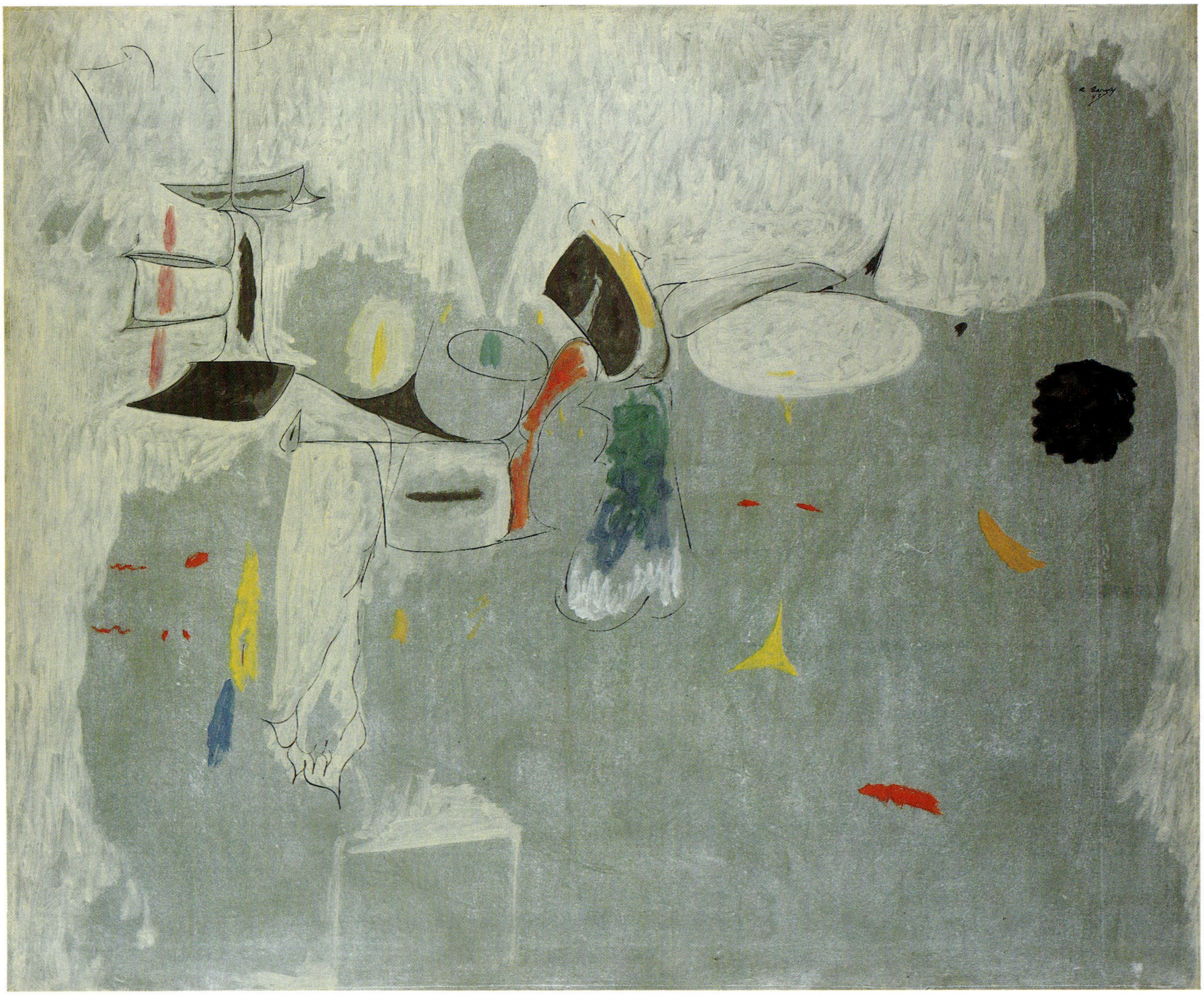

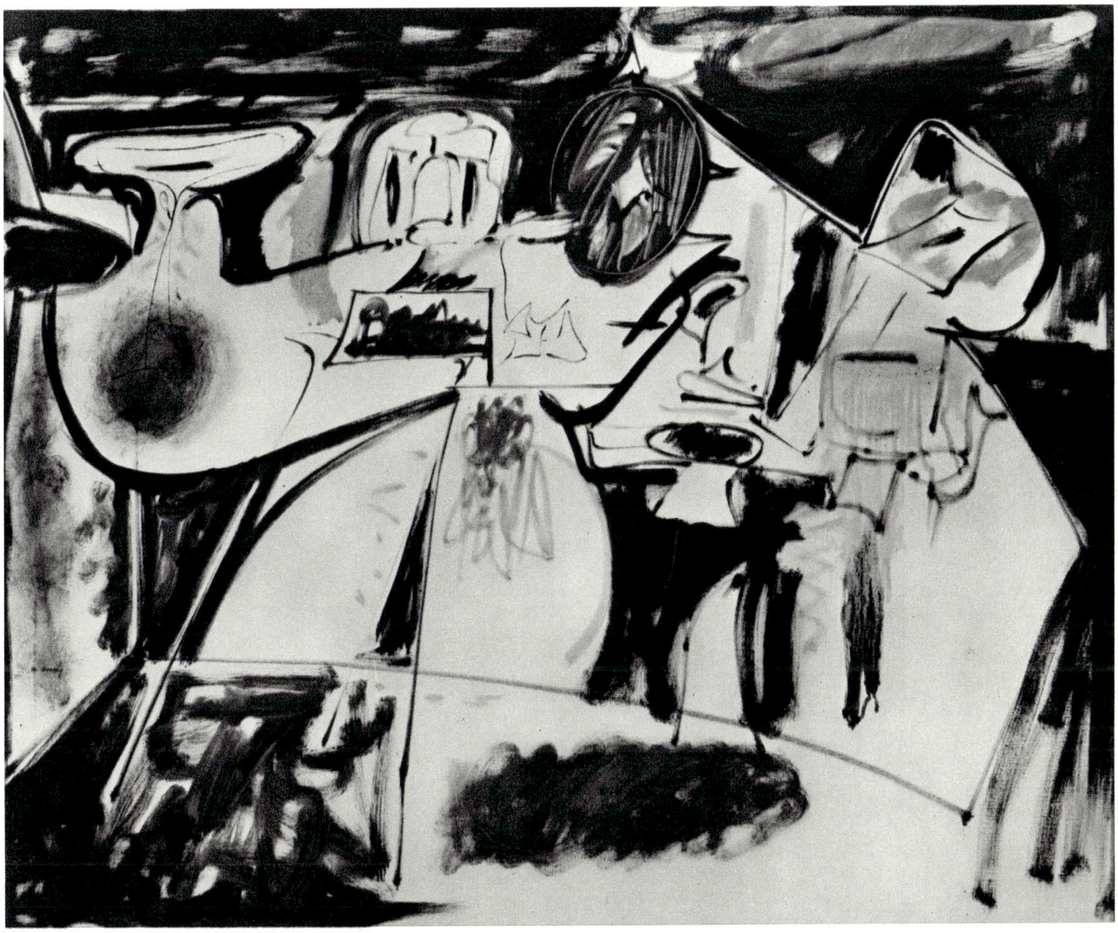

249. *Last Painting*. 1948
Oil on canvas, 30 3/4 × 39 3/4″
Thyssen-Bornemisza Collection, Lugano

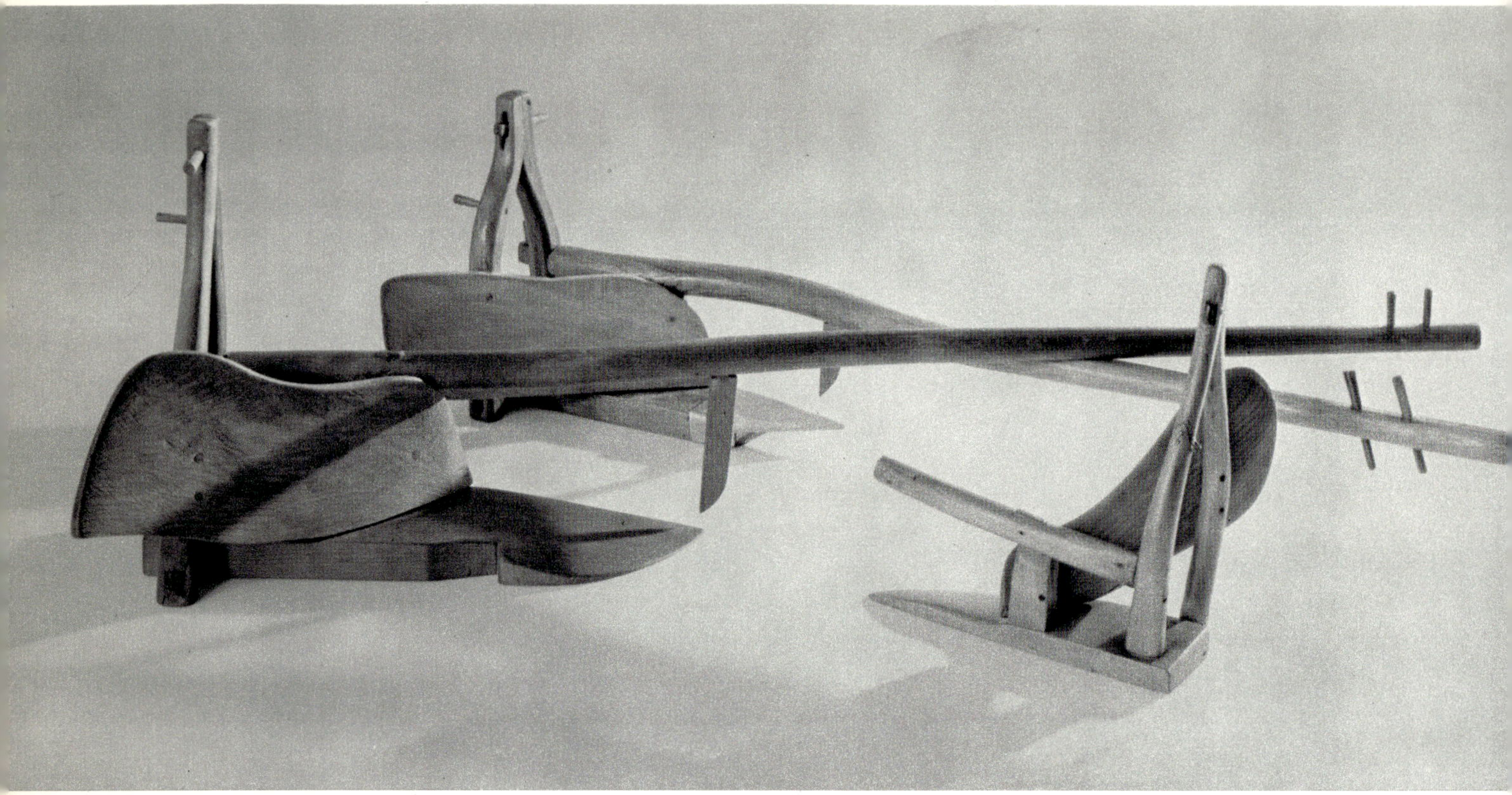

250. *Armenian Plows*. 1944, 1945, 1946
Wood
Mooradian Collection

Chronology

1904

April 15 — Born Vosdanik Adoian in village of Khorkom, Vari Haiyotz Dzor (literally "Lower Vale of the Armenians"), province of Van, east Armenia. Van center of ancient Armenian culture; renowned for its manuscript and wall paintings, architecture and sculpture.

First son of Sedrak Adoian (1863–1947), trader and sometime carpenter, and Shushanik der Marderosian (1880–1919), descended from fifth-century Armenian Apostolic Church priests. Named for mother's ancestral hometown of Vosdan. Later received as middle name Manuk (or Manook) in honor of paternal grandfather, in accordance with Armenian tradition. Older stepsister Akabi (Ahko) (1896–1971) and sister Satenik (born 1901).

1906

September 27 — Sister Vartoosh born. Gorky remains close to her throughout his life.

1908 — Father emigrates to United States, settling in Providence, Rhode Island, to escape draft into Turkish army which forces Armenians to fight fellow countrymen.

Vosdanik reportedly speaks for first time under tutelage of cousin Kevork Kondakian.

1908–1909 — Begins to draw and carve.

1909–1910 — Attends St. Vardan's Armenian Apostolic School in Khorkom; studies drawing, writing and vernacular Armenian. Learns classical Armenian (*Grabar*) from mother.

ca. 1910–1913 — Turkish nationalist ideology emerges; Armenians resist Turkification.

1910

Summer — Vosdanik attends funeral of maternal grandmother Lady Hamaspiur, purportedly source for *The Orators*, 1947 (cat. no. 238).

September — Adoians move to Van city; rent single-room apartment in walled city center. Akabi (now married to Mkrdich Amerian) lives nearby.

Vosdanik and Satenik attend Husisian School, affiliated with Armenian Apostolic Church.

November — Family moves to suburb of Aikesdan. Vosdanik and Vartoosh attend The American Mission School, founded by Congregational Church of America, from now until 1915.

Vosdanik meets Manuk (Moorad) Mooradian, who becomes close friend and later marries Vartoosh.

1912 — In Van city, Vosdanik and mother pose for photograph to send to father in Providence; picture later source for *The Artist and His Mother*, 1926–36, and 1929–42 (cat. nos. 75, 76).

1914

Summer — With advent of World War I, Turkish government intensifies persecution of Armenians and readies genocide campaign.

October 31 — Turks enter war as allies of Germany.

November — Turkish Army begins siege of Van (center of Armenian independence movement); Aikesdan, including Adoian home, shelled. Family takes shelter in east Aikesdan.

1915

April 24 — Official beginning of massacres and mass deportations of Armenians.

June 15 — Adoians evacuate Van with thousands of compatriots on eight-day, 100-mile journey on foot to frontier of Caucasian Armenia. Few survive these death marches.

June 23 — Family reaches Igdir.

June 25 — They arrive in Ejmiadzin; stay three weeks.

July 16	Adoians reach Erevan (now Yerevan) in Caucasian Armenia and establish residence. Vosdanik attends Temagan Boy's School; to help support family, works at carpentry, comb carving and printing.
	By year's end Turks exterminate about 1,500,000 Armenians.
1916	
October 9	Akabi and Satenik emigrate to America.
1918	
May 28	Declaration of independence of short-lived Armenian republic. Economic conditions catastrophic; refugees experience severe famine and deprivation in winter of 1918–19.
August 18	Threat of civil war forces Adoians to leave Yerevan for Tiflis. Lady Shushanik becomes critically ill from malnutrition, and family is forced to suspend journey only eight miles from Yerevan; they stay in Shahab in partially roofless one-room hut.
December 18	Mother's condition worsens; family returns to Yerevan.
1919	
March 20	Lady Shushanik dies at age thirty-nine.
May	Vosdanik and Vartoosh travel with family friend Kertza Dikran to Tiflis.
August	Vosdanik and Vartoosh go to Batum on Black Sea; remain three weeks.
September	Children sail to Constantinople; live in tents provided for Armenian refugees in Haidar Pasha. Befriended by Sedrak and Verghinay Kelekian, who take them in; Kelekians' son buys them tickets to United States.
1920	
January 25	Children leave Constantinople by merchant ship for Athens, remaining fifteen days at port city of Patras.
February 9	Depart Patras for America, via one-day stop in Naples, aboard Italian liner S.S. *Presidente Wilson.* List of Manifest of Alien Passengers for United States Immigration Officer at Port of Arrival includes no. 2 Manouk and no. 3 Vartanouche Adoian, students.
February 26	Arrive Ellis Island, New York; detained for three days.
March 1	Vosdanik and Vartoosh officially admitted to United States; met by Akabi's husband who takes them to Watertown, Massachusetts, to stay at family home on Coolidge Hill Avenue.
April	Vosdanik goes to Providence, Rhode Island, to stay with father, whom he sees for first time in twelve years.
	John Graham, born Ivan Dombrovski, arrives in New York from Russia via Warsaw.
1921	
January-June	According to records of Rhode Island Superintendent of Schools, Manoog Adoian, born March 15, 1903, enrolled in Bridgham Junior High School in Providence, having previously attended Old Beacon Street School. Father listed as Hagop Adoian (possibly Gorky's stepbrother); address listed as 207 Pond Street, later changed to 22 Cranston Street.
Summer	Leaves Providence and returns to Amerian residence in Watertown at 86 Dexter Avenue.
	Vosdanik and Vartoosh employed at Hood Rubber Co., probably through Mkrdich Amerian who works there; Vosdanik fired after two months for drawing on frames in which shoe soles are transported.
Fall	Visits Providence briefly and studies at Technical High School there.
Winter 1922–1924	Attends New School of Design, 248 Boylston Street, Boston, directed by Douglas John Connah, portrait painter and illustrator. Frequents museums; washes dishes in a restaurant for his meals.
1924	
Spring	Earliest known painting, *Park Street Church* (cat. no. 1), executed during recesses at New School of Design, signed "Gorky, Arshele": first appearance of pseudonym. Variant spellings Archele, Archel and Gorki, used prior to ca. 1932 when he begins consistently to employ Arshile Gorky.
	Employed as assistant instructor of life-drawing class at New School of Design, his first teaching experience.
	André Breton's first *Surrealist Manifesto* published in Paris. J.B. Neumann establishes New Art Circle Gallery, New York. Shows Arp, Alexander Calder, Kandinsky, Klee, Max Weber and others.
Late 1924	Moves to New York City.
1925	
January 9	Enrolls at National Academy of Design in New York as day student in life-drawing class with Charles Hawthorne. Address on application is 1680 Broadway; date and place of birth given as

April 1902 in Kazan, Russia. Leaves Academy after one month.

Probably attends New York branch of the New School of Design Inc. at 1680 Broadway, address he had given as his own. School moves to 145 East 57th Street in 1926. Mark Rothko says "Gorky was the monitor of the class in which I was enrolled."

January — Visits Boston briefly.

October — Enters Grand Central School of Art, New York, as student. Shortly thereafter made instructor of sketch class.

The Daniel Gallery, New York, *Blue Four: Feininger, Klee, Kandinsky, Jawlensky.*

1926

January 7–30 — The Art Center, New York, *Memorial Exhibition of Representative Works Selected for the John Quinn Collection.* Includes Braque, Cézanne, Derain, Ingres and Picasso.

January — First issue of *Cahiers d'Art*, founded by Christian Zervos, published in Paris: important link for American artists to European avant-garde. In 1926 articles appear on de Chirico, Léger, Miró, Picasso and others.

August 15 — Willem de Kooning arrives in United States from Rotterdam and settles in Hoboken.

September — Appointed full member of faculty of Grand Central School of Art by Edmund Greacen, Director, to instruct evening Life and Antique classes. Remains on faculty until 1931. As recorded in "Fetish of Antique Stifles Art Here, Says Gorky Kin" in *The New York Evening Post*, September 15, "he is a cousin of the famous writer, Maxim Gorky," his studio is on West 50th Street and he believes "Cézanne is the greatest artist . . . that has lived."

November — Poem "Thirst" published in *Grand Central School of Art Quarterly.*

November 19, 1926–January 1, 1927 — The Brooklyn Museum, *An International Exhibition of Modern Art.* Organized by Société Anonyme. 307 works by artists from twenty-three countries, including Arp, Braque, de Chirico, Kandinsky, Klee, Miró and Picasso. First showing of Duchamp's *Large Glass.* Ninety-one of these paintings shown at Anderson Galleries, New York, *44th Exhibition of the Société Anonyme*, January 25-February 5, 1927.

December 18–31 — Durand-Ruel Gallery, New York, *Exhibition of Paintings by The Impressionists.*

Paints Post-Impressionist and Cézannesque still lifes, landscapes and portraits (see cat. nos. 3–9, 15); works from antique casts, for example *The Antique Cast*, 1926 (cat. no. 2).

Edith Gregory Halpert establishes The Downtown Gallery to promote work of American modernists. Shows Stuart Davis, Reuben Nakian, Max Weber and others.

1926 — Hans Burkhardt enrolls in Gorky's class at Grand Central School of Art; continues to study with him privately until 1937. Nathan Bijur takes instruction from Gorky; studies with him until 1929.

1927

April 23 — Frick Collection buys Ingres' *Mme de Haussonville*, 1845.

April — First issue of *Transition* published in Paris: devoted to contemporary literature, drama, cinema, art; subsequent number includes first English translation of poems by Paul Eluard. Reproductions of de Chirico, Masson, Miró appear in late 1920s, early 1930s.

December 12 — The Gallery of Living Art, New York University, opens at Washington Square. Albert E. Gallatin's collection of works by artists "living or recently deceased," including Braque, de Chirico, Miró and Picasso.

December 27 — Wildenstein & Co., New York, *Drawings by Picasso.*

Begins romance with Armenian model Sirun Mussikian; meets fellow Armenian Raoul Hague through her.

Meets Saul Schary, who becomes lifelong friend.

De Kooning moves to New York; lives in Greenwich Village.

ca. 1927 — Takes studio at 47a Washington Square South, at corner of Sullivan Street.

1928

January 23–February 11 — Valentine Gallery, New York, *De Chirico.* First one-man show in United States.

January 28 — Wildenstein & Co., New York, *Loan Exhibition of Paintings by Paul Cézanne under the auspices of Mrs. Chester Dale.*

February 10–March 3 — Arts Council Gallery, New York, *50th Exhibition of the Société Anonyme.* Includes de Chirico, Stuart Davis, Kandinsky, Klee, Léger.

Walter Murch takes Gorky's life class at Grand Central School of Art; subsequently studies privately with him for two years.

1928–1929 Meets John Graham.

Late 1920s Paints Synthetic Cubist still lifes after Braque and Picasso (see cat. nos. 19, 21, 22).

Meets David Burliuk.

De Kooning meets Graham and, through him, Gorky.

1929

January Gallery of Living Art, New York [Group Exhibition]. Includes Braque, Cézanne, de Chirico, Gris, Klee, Léger Matisse, Miró and Picasso.

November 8 The Museum of Modern Art, New York, opens with *First Loan Exhibition: Cézanne, Gauguin, Seurat, Van Gogh.*

Introduced to Stuart Davis by Graham; the three become close friends. Meets Sidney Janis, introduces him to Davis, Graham and de Kooning.

1930

January 18–March 2 The Museum of Modern Art, New York, *Painting in Paris.* Includes fifteen Picassos, eleven Matisses, several de Chiricos, Légers and Mirós. First showing in United States of Picasso's *Seated Woman*, 1927 (fig. 15).

April 11–26 The Museum of Modern Art, New York, *An Exhibition of Works by 46 Painters and Sculptors Under 35 Years of Age.* Gorky's first group exhibition. Catalogue reads:

> *Archele Gorki*
> *Born 1903, Nizhu-Novgorod*
> *Studied there and in Tiflis and three months under Kandinsky in 1920. To America 1922 . . . .*
> *81.* Still Life
> *82.* Still Life
> *Courtesy the J.B. Neumann Gallery, New York*
> *83.* Still Life [cat. no. 20]
> *Collection Nathan Bijur, New York*

July 1 *Still Life* (cat. no. 81, above) returned to Gorky at 47a Washington Square South.

October 1–November 1 John Becker Gallery, New York [Picasso Drawings and Gouaches].

October 20–November 8 Valentine Gallery, New York, *Joan Miró.* First one-man exhibition in United States.

Meets David Smith through John Graham; meets Chaim Gross.

Picasso's neoclassical *Ovid's Metamorphoses* etchings reproduced in *Cahiers d'Art*, no. 10.

Graham begins yearly trips to Paris, becomes friendly with Picasso, André Breton, Eluard. Keeps friends in New York abreast of artistic developments in Europe.

Early 1930s Moves to new studio at 36 Union Square; he keeps it for remainder of life.

1931

January Valentine Gallery, New York, *Abstractions of Picasso.*

January 1–February 10 Société Anonyme, New York, *Special Exhibition Arranged in Honor of the Opening of the New Building of the New School for Social Research.* Gorky's first exhibition with Société Anonyme; shows *Improvisation.*

February 3–21 Durand-Ruel Galleries, New York, *Fernand Léger.*

February Tristan Tzara's article on Picasso's collages published in *Cahiers d'Art*, vol. 6, no. 2. Gorky begins own collages shortly thereafter.

May 17–September 27 The Museum of Modern Art, New York, *Memorial Exhibition: The Collection of the Late Miss Lillie P. Bliss.* Includes Cézanne, Gauguin, Matisse and Picasso.

June 2–22 The Downtown Gallery, New York, *Paintings, Watercolors, Drawings, Sculptures by Leading Contemporary American Artists.* Gorky shows *Still Life.*

September 3 "Stuart Davis," critical appraisal of this artist's work, written by Gorky at Davis' request, published in *Creative Art*, vol. 9. Here Gorky states: "Has there in six centuries been better art than Cubism? No. Centuries will go past—artists of gigantic stature will draw positive elements from Cubism."

October 5–25 The Downtown Gallery, New York, *Artists' Models: Figure Paintings by Leading Contemporary American Artists.* Gorky shows *Head.*

October John Becker Gallery, New York, *Léger.*

November 18 Whitney Museum of American Art, New York, opens.

November Wadsworth Atheneum, Hartford, *Newer Super-Realism.* First major Surrealist exhibition in United States. Travels to Julien Levy Gallery, New York, as *Surrealist Group Show*, January 9–29, 1932. Includes Joseph Cornell, de Chirico, Dali, Ernst, Masson, Miró and Picasso.

December 7–31 The Downtown Gallery, New York, *American Print Makers: Fifth Annual Exhibition.* Gorky shows three lithographs, priced at twelve dollars each:

Painter and Model (cat. no. 25); *Mannikin; Self Portrait.*

December 28–31 — Valentine Gallery, New York. *Since Cézanne.* Includes Braque, Léger, Miró, Picasso and others.

Starts sketchbook of neoclassical figures similar to those of Picasso of 1920s.

Meets Dorothy Miller and Holger Cahill, who study painting with him briefly; he primarily lectures from books on David, Ingres, Copley.

ca. 1931–1932 — Begins Nighttime, Enigma and Nostalgia drawings, influenced by de Chirico, Picasso and Uccello.

1932

January 17–February 11 — Pierre Matisse Gallery, New York, *André Masson.*

February 1–20 — Valentine Gallery, New York, *Fernand Léger.*

Winter — Urges Julien Levy to see Graham's work; Graham in turn suggests he look at Gorky's drawings. Gorky tells Levy: "I was *with* Cézanne for a long time, and now naturally I am *with* Picasso." Levy replies he will give him an exhibition "someday, when you are *with* Gorky." (Julien Levy, *Memoir of an Art Gallery*, New York, 1977, p. 238)

March 3 — Gorky and Professor Frank Jewett Mather, Jr., of Princeton, deliver lectures, "Two Views on Modern Art," at Wells College, Aurora, New York.

May 10 — Vartoosh and husband Moorad return to Armenia. Gorky, who cannot afford to accompany them, corresponds regularly.

Spring — Special Picasso issue of *Cahiers d'Art*, vol. 7, no. 3–5.

October — Zervos publishes first volume of Picasso catalogue raisonné. Twenty-eight more volumes follow 1932–74.

November 1–25 — Pierre Matisse Gallery, New York, *Miró.*

November 22–December 15 — Pierre Matisse Gallery, New York, *Henri Matisse.* Fifty drawings.

November 26–December 30 — Julien Levy Gallery, New York, *Etchings by Pablo Picasso.* Illustrations for Balzac's *Le Chef-d'Oeuvre Inconnu*, published in 1931.

Gorky's *Objects*, 1932 (cat. no. 39), illustrated in no. 3 of *Abstraction-Création Art Non-Figuratif*, magazine of international artists' association of same name founded in Paris in 1931.

Wilmington Society of Fine Arts, *Exhibition of Russian Painting and Sculpture.* Gorky shows *Composition* and *Portrait.*

1932–1933 — Meets Isamu Noguchi.

1933

March 6–April 1 — Valentine Gallery, New York, *Picasso.*

December 20 — Joins Public Works of Art Project (PWAP), government agency which aids unemployed artists. Paid average of $37.38 per week.

December 20 — Submits written proposal for mural to PWAP: sketch will be pen and ink and measure 30 × 123″

December 29, 1933–January 18, 1934 — Pierre Matisse Gallery, New York, *Joan Miró: Paintings.*

Léger's *The City*, 1919, reproduced in *Cahiers d'Art*, no. 3–4; style and iconography probably influenced Newark Airport murals, specifically panel *Activities on the Field*, 1936.

Begins friendship with Peter Busa; meets Reuben Nakian, who is of Armenian descent.

Late 1933–Early 1934 — Meets fellow artist and neighbor Jacob Kainen, who sits for portrait. Remain friends until Kainen moves to Washington, D.C. in 1942.

1934

January — Ethel Schwabacher and Mina Metzger begin private study with Gorky three hours a day, three days a week; continue through summer 1935. Gorky often takes them to Metropolitan Museum to draw after Old Masters.

January 10–February 9 — Pierre Matisse Gallery, New York, *Joan Miró.*

February 2–15 — Mellon Galleries, Philadelphia, *Arshile Gorky.* First one-man exhibition. Includes thirty-seven numbered, untitled paintings from 1926–30. Checklist with statements by Stuart Davis, Harriet Janowitz, F.J. Kiesler and Holger Cahill, who writes that Gorky has "an extraordinary inventiveness and fertility in creating special arrangements, both precise and harmonious and he contributes to contemporary American expression a note of intellectual fantasy which is very rare in the plastic art of this country."

February 28–March 28 — The Forum, RCA Building, Rockefeller Center, New York, *First Municipal Art Exhibition.* Sponsored by Mayor Fiorello La Guardia. Gorky shows *Organization No. 4* (oil), *Nighttime of Nostalgia* (pen and ink), *Kiss* (lithograph).

March 7 — Submits progress report to PWAP, indicating his mural is to be titled *1934*, and is suitable for installation in uni-

	versities, technical or engineering schools or in the New York Port Authority.
April 29	Dropped from PWAP roster; PWAP dissolves on June 30.
April 29–May 27	Pierre Matisse Gallery, New York, *André Masson.*
	Artists' Union formed in New York, with local chapters elsewhere, "to unite all artists . . . in their struggle for economic security and to encourage a wider distribution and understanding of art." ([Preamble to Artists' Union Constitution], *Art Front*, no. 1, November 1934) Calls for non-discriminatory permanent Federal Art Project to employ needy artists and for establishment of Municipal Art Center in New York.
	Gorky joins Artists' Union but will not participate in political activism. Balcomb Greene recalls: "He attended Union meetings, served on committees, and spoke with much feeling on many issues. He considered it his mission to instill into the rank and file of the organization a respect for art and a suspicion of the political adventurer. He would gain the floor on the most inauspicious occasions and declaim about the contours of Ingres . . . he seemed to give the impression that Ingres might at any moment lend his support to the cause." ("Memories of Arshile Gorky," *Arts Magazine*, vol. 50, March 1976, pp. 109–110)
	Gorky's lack of political commitment causes termination of friendship with Stuart Davis.
November	*Art Front*, official organ of Artists' Union and Artists' Committee for Action, begins publication, continues until December 1937. Contains reproductions of art works, reviews, criticism, reports on Union activities.
November 21–December 10	Julien Levy Gallery, New York, *Paintings by Salvador Dali*.
December 25	Vartoosh and Moorad return from Armenia; stay briefly with Gorky at 36 Union Square.

1935

January 10–February 9	Pierre Matisse Gallery, New York, *Joan Miró 1933–34.*
February 12–March 22	Whitney Museum of American Art, New York, *Abstract Painting in America.* Catalogue by Ethel Schwabacher. Gorky shows *Composition no. 1*; *Composition no. 2*; *Composition no. 3*; *Organization.*
	Gorky, Stuart Davis, Graham, de Kooning, Edgar Levy and Mischa Resnikoff had informed Whitney that they would exhibit only if all were included. However, Davis and Gorky alone were shown; Gorky claims his work was sent without his knowledge.
March 25	Son Karlen born to Vartoosh and Moorad in Boston.
April 5–24	The Arts Club of Chicago, *Sidney Janis Collection of Modern Paintings*. Gorky shows *Composition*, 1932. Also includes Dali, de Chirico, Gris, John Kane, Klee, Léger, Matisse, Mondrian and Rousseau.
July	Applies to Emergency Relief Bureau for home relief; receives $24 per week.
August	Works Progress Administration/Federal Art Project (WPA/FAP) established (Holger Cahill, Director). Consists of Easel, Mural, Graphic, Sculpture Divisions. Most extensive of New Deal art relief programs.
	Gorky assigned to Mural Division (Burgoyne Diller, Director), at $103.40 per month. Begins *Aviation* mural designs for Floyd Bennett Field; these are to incorporate photographs by Wyatt Davis, brother of Stuart.
	Pierre Matisse Gallery, New York [André Masson].
September-October	Boyer Galleries, Philadelphia. One-man exhibition of pen and ink drawings.
	Lectures on abstract painting at Boyer Galleries in conjunction with exhibition.
	Vartoosh, Moorad and Karlen come to live with Gorky; remain until late 1936.
September 30–October 24	The Museum of Modern Art, New York, *Fernand Léger.*
October	Guild Art Gallery, New York [Group Exhibition]. Gallery's inaugural show. "Archile Gorky's handsome abstract decoration . . . may be said to dominate the show." (*The New York Times*, October 13, 1935, p. X 19)
November 24	Delivers lecture "Methods, Purposes and Significance of Abstract Art" at Guild.
November 19–December 21	Pierre Matisse Gallery, New York, *26 Works by Giorgio de Chirico.*
December 16, 1935–January 5, 1936	Guild Art Gallery, New York, *Abstract Drawings by Arshile Gorky*. Includes fourteen untitled works; *Enigmatic Tryptich*; *Night Time Nostalgia*; *Composition*; *Detail for Mural*. "These are not simply studies, but complete large scale compositions in black and white, carefully and skilfully [sic]

elaborated, with a result in the ensemble that is brilliantly effective." (*The New York Post*, December 21, 1935)

December 27 — Federal Art Project Gallery, New York, *Murals for Public Buildings.* Gallery's inaugural show opens. Mayor La Guardia attends opening, says of Gorky's *Aviation*: "I am a conservative in my art, as I am a progressive in my politics. That's why I perhaps cannot understand it." (*New York Herald Tribune*, December 28, 1935)

December — Alfred H. Barr, Jr. chooses Gorky's WPA mural design from two proposals submitted to him. Subsequently, idea of using photographs is dropped, and mural is reassigned to Newark Airport Administration Building.

Between 1935 and 1937 paints ten panels in oil on canvas in seventh-floor workshop of Federal Art Project Building at 6 East 39th Street.

Marries Marny George; they soon divorce.

1935–36 — Works on Khorkom paintings (cat. nos. 99, 100). Corresponds about artistic philosophy with cousin Ado Adoian, member of Armenian Communist Party in Yerevan.

1936

February 1–29 — J.B. Neumann's New Art Circle, New York, *Vasily Kandinsky.*

March 2–April 19 — The Museum of Modern Art, New York, *Cubism and Abstract Art.* Organized by Alfred H. Barr, Jr.

March 16–April 4 — Guild Art Gallery, New York, *Drawings, Small Sculpture, Watercolors.* Includes Gorky, Boris Aronson, Ben-Schmuel, Lloyd Ney, Anna Walinska and others.

Spring — Castigates Social Realists and condemns propagandistic illustrations as "poor art for poor people" in speech at Artists' Union.

June — Boyer Gallery, New York, *Modern American Paintings.* Includes Gorky and others.

September — New York City Art Commission approves Gorky's mural for Newark Airport Administration Building entitled *Aviation*, oil on canvas, 1500 square feet. WPA/FAP Model-Making Division executes maquette showing placement of ten panels.

September 14–October 12 — The Museum of Modern Art, New York, *New Horizons in American Art.* Survey of the first year's work done under WPA/FAP. Catalogue lists:

Arshile Gorky: Aviation: Evolution of Forms Under Aerodynamic Limitation. *Ten Panels in second floor foyer Administration Building, Newark Airport, N.J. Oil on canvas. 1530 Sq. Ft. Catalogue nos. 20. One completed panel, oil on canvas* [Activities on the Field]. *21. Model showing interior with murals. 22. Photograph of largest panels.*

Also includes Byron Browne, Francis Criss, Stuart Davis, Balcomb Greene, de Kooning, Jan Matulka and George McNeil.

Selected works shown at The Newark Museum as *Old and New Paths in American Design 1720–1936*, November 15-December 28.

November — Vartoosh moves to Chicago, resumes lengthy correspondence in Armenian with Gorky.

November 10–December 10 — Whitney Museum of American Art, New York, *Third Biennial Exhibition of Contemporary American Painting.* Gorky shows *Organization.* Also includes Stuart Davis, Graham, Saul Schary, Raphael Soyer.

November 20–December 26 — Pierre Matisse Gallery, New York, *Joan Miró Retrospective.*

Julien Levy publishes *Surrealism.* Gorky immediately reads entire book in back room of Levy's gallery.

December 9, 1936–January 17, 1937 — The Museum of Modern Art, New York, *Fantastic Art, Dada, Surrealism.* Organized by Alfred H. Barr, Jr. Includes Americans Peter Blume, Calder and Cornell; Gorky not shown.

December 18 — Frederick Kiesler, "Murals Without Walls: Relating to Gorky's Newark Project," published in *Art Front*, vol. 2. First magazine article on Gorky; concepts and methods of modern mural painting are discussed.

Romance with painter Corinne Michael West.

1937

February — Photograph of Gorky working on Newark Murals published in Kiesler's "The Architect in Search of . . .," *The Architectural Record*, vol. 81, p. 12.

February 18–March 6 — Syracuse Museum, New York, *Art Here.* Includes Gorky and others.

May — Probably speaks before American Federation of Artists, Washington, D.C.

June 9 — Newark Airport murals unveiled at Administration Building.

June 12–October 31 — Dallas Museum of Fine Arts, *Greater Pan American Exhibition: Art of the*

	Americas, Precolumbian and Contemporary. Gorky shows *Organization no. 2*, lent by Boyer Galleries.
Summer	Is permitted to engage in easel painting in his studio while employed by WPA/FAP Mural Division; continues to do so until summer 1941.
	Around this time begins paintings based on Picasso's studio interiors, for example *Composition with Head*, ca. 1934–36; *Still Life on the Table*, ca. 1935; *Organization*, ca. 1936 (cat. nos. 79, 80, 81).
November 10–December 12	Whitney Museum of American Art, New York, *Annual Exhibition of Contemporary American Painting.* Gorky shows *Painting*, 1936–37 (cat. no. 102): acquired by Whitney, this is his first museum purchase.
	John Graham's *System and Dialectics of Art* published in New York. Gorky, Breton, Eluard, Tzara, Zervos and others included in section entitled "Good Taste."
	Nierendorf Gallery, New York, *Kandinsky: A Retrospective View.* Organized by College Art Association.
	Gorky and de Kooning attend first meeting of American Abstract Artists; neither joins.
1937–38	Works in freer biomorphic style influenced by Miró and Masson, for example *Enigmatic Combat*, 1937; *Argula*, 1938 (cat. nos. 104, 120).

1938

January 1–27	Gallery of the Architecture Building, University of Illinois, Urbana-Champaign, *Exhibition of Contemporary American Painting.* Travels to University Gallery, University of Minnesota, Minneapolis, as *Third Annual Exhibition of Contemporary American Painting at the University of Minnesota*, February 4–23. Gorky shows *Still Life*, lent by Boyer Galleries.
January	Begins studies for murals for 1939–40 New York World's Fair Marine and Aviation Buildings. Sometime this year, study for Marine Building rejected in favor of work by Feininger.
February 23–March 19	Pierre Matisse Gallery, New York, *Fernand Léger.*
April 18–May 7	Pierre Matisse Gallery, New York, *Joan Miró: Recent Works.*
May-July	Musée du Jeu de Paume, Paris, *Trois siècles d'art aux Etats-Unis.* Organized in collaboration with The Museum of Modern Art, New York. Gorky shows *Painting*, 1936–37 (cat. no. 102).
October 24	Nierendorf Gallery, New York, *Paul Klee: A Choice Collection of the Master's Work from 1923–28.*
October 25–November 12	Pierre Matisse Gallery, New York, *Léger.*
November	Receives cut in WPA salary to $91.00 per month.
	Boyer Gallery, New York [One-man Exhibition].
	Nierendorf Gallery, New York, *Three Masters of the Bauhaus: Kandinsky, Klee, Feininger.*
	Included in James Johnson Sweeney, "L'art contemporain aux Etats-Unis," *Cahiers d'Art*, vol. 13, no. 1–2, pp. 45–52. *Painting* (cat. no. 102) reproduced.

1939

January 16	Leaves WPA/FAP to complete murals for World's Fair Aviation Building.
March 21–April 17	Julien Levy Gallery, New York, *Dali.*
Late Spring	New York World's Fair opens in Flushing Meadow, Queens; continues through summer 1940. Gorky's mural *Man's Conquest of the Air* (now destroyed) installed in Aviation Building.
May 5–27	Valentine Gallery, New York. First exhibition of Picasso's *Guernica* in United States. Organized by American Artists' Congress to benefit Spanish Civil War Refugees. Gorky, Leo Katz and Walter Pach hold panel discussion in conjunction with exhibition.
May 20	Naturalized as United States citizen.
June 1	Museum of Non-Objective Painting opens in New York; renamed The Solomon R. Guggenheim Museum in 1952.
June 9	Reinstated on WPA/FAP.
August	Receives second cut in WPA salary, now to $87.60 per month.
September	Outbreak of World War II and subsequent invasion of France causes many European artists, primarily Surrealists, to flee to United States through 1941.
Fall	Applies for John Simon Guggenheim Foundation Fellowship; requests Holger Cahill to write in support of application and writes to Max Weber on October 21, asking to use his name as reference. Fellowship not granted.
November 1	Yves Tanguy arrives in New York.
November 1939–January 1940	The Museum of Modern Art, New York, *Picasso: Forty Years of His Art.*

	Organized by Alfred H. Barr, Jr.
	Matta moves to New York, where he remains until 1948.
	Dali arrives in New York; remains through 1948.
	Nierendorf Gallery, New York, *Kandinsky.*
1940	Begins Garden in Sochi series (cat. nos. 121–125).
January 10–February 18	Whitney Museum of American Art, New York, *Annual Exhibition of Contemporary American Painting.* Gorky shows *Head Composition.*
March	Pierre Matisse Gallery, New York, *Joan Miró: Early Paintings.*
April 16–May 7	Julien Levy Gallery, New York, *Matta.* First exhibition in New York.
September	First issue of *View*, Surrealist magazine founded by Charles Henri Ford, published; continues until 1947.
	Gorky requests use of classroom to teach camouflage course at Grand Central School of Art, but is advised to wait a few months because draft may limit enrollment.
October	Mondrian arrives in New York; remains until his death in 1944.
Fall	Meets Gordon Onslow-Ford, who was lecturing on Surrealism at The New School for Social Research.
November 27, 1940–January 8, 1941	Whitney Museum of American Art, New York, *Annual Exhibition of Contemporary American Painting.* Gorky shows *Oil Painting*, 1938.
December 17	Reinstated on WPA.
Early 1940s	Gorky teaches camouflage course at Grand Central School of Art; course announcement he writes published in school catalogue, 1942. Betty Parsons meets Gorky and takes camouflage and drawing class from him: "He was a marvelous teacher who, as soon as anybody started to get skillful, would go and get a bottle of ink and piece of string, dip the string in the ink and say now draw with it. That taught us alot."
1941	
January 16	The Museum of Modern Art, New York, acquires *Argula*, 1938 (cat. no. 120), gift of Bernard Davis, Gorky's friend and early collector, and *Objects*, 1932 (cat. no. 39), purchased from the artist.
March	Nierendorf Gallery, New York, *Kandinsky.*
April 7–26	Buchholz Gallery, New York [Group Show]. Includes Klee, Léger, Masson and Picasso.
April 19–27	The Metropolitan Museum of Art, New York, *A Special Exhibition of Contemporary Painting in the United States.* Gorky shows *Argoola*, 1938 (cat. no. 120).
June-December	*La Pintura Contemporana Norteamericana.* Organized by The Museum of Modern Art, New York, in collaboration with The Brooklyn Museum, The Metropolitan Museum of Art, New York, Whitney Museum of American Art, New York, and The Coordinator of Commercial and Cultural Relations between American Republics. Traveled throughout South America. Gorky shows *Argula*, 1938 (cat. no. 120).
July 2	Resigns from WPA/FAP.
	Jeanne Reynal, mosaicist, offers to try to arrange exhibition for Gorky in San Francisco. Gorky drives across country with Noguchi, Noguchi's sister, Agnes Magruder and two other friends. Noguchi recalls: "He'd be always seeing some peasant woman up in the sky. And we had terrible arguments about it because I said, 'that's just a cloud.' . . . And then he'd go on about some of his childhood recollections, which seemed to tinge everything he saw." (Karlen Mooradian, "The Philosophy of Arshile Gorky," *Armenian Digest*, vol. 2, September-October 1971, p. 60)
July 17	Arrives in San Francisco.
July	Max Ernst emigrates to United States; marries Peggy Guggenheim in September. After brief stay in New York travels across country. Remains in United States until 1953.
August 9–24	San Francisco Museum of Art, *Arshile Gorky.* Shows ca. twenty paintings, including *Portrait of my mother*, 1921, charcoal drawing (cat. no. 72); *Portrait of my sister*, 1923; *Image in Xhorkom*, 1934; *Xhorkom*, 1934; *Portrait*, 1938; *Enigmatic Combat*, 1937 (cat. no. 104), lent by Miss Jeanne Reynal: she gives painting to Museum this year.
August	Murals (now destroyed) for Ben Marden's Riviera nightclub, Fort Lee, New Jersey, installed. Gorky quoted in Malcolm Johnson's "Café Life in New York," *The New York Sun*, August 22, p. 15: "I call these murals non-objective art . . . but if labels are needed this art may be termed surrealistic. . . ."
September 15	Marries Agnes Magruder in Virginia

	City, Nevada. Calls her "Mougouch," Armenian term of endearment.
September 26–November	Gorky and Agnes visit Mooradians in Chicago on return journey to New York.
November 12–December 30	Whitney Museum of American Art, New York, *Paintings by Artists under Forty*. Gorky shows *Painting*, 1936–37 (cat. no. 102).
November 19, 1941–January 11, 1942	The Museum of Modern Art, New York, *Joan Miró and Salvador Dali*. First Miró retrospective.
	André Masson arrives in New York; remains until 1946.
	André Breton emigrates to United States.
	Gorky meets Matta Echaurren. Levy says Matta urged Gorky to mix turpentine freely in his paints and thus achieve the liberty of fresh, airy improvisation. (Julien Levy, *Arshile Gorky*, New York, 1966, p. 24)
Late 1941	Applies to draft board to serve in camouflage unit; rejected as overage.

1942

January 5–26	R.H. Macy Department Store, New York [Group Exhibition]. Organized by Samuel Kootz. Includes Gorky, Gottlieb, Graham, Carl Holty, Jan Matulka and Rothko.
January 25–February 28	City Art Museum, St. Louis, *American Art*. Gorky shows *Argula*, 1938 (cat. no. 120).
February 28–March 31	The Davison Art Rooms of Olin Library, Wesleyan University, Middletown, Connecticut, *Oil Paintings, Watercolors and Prints lent by the Yale University Art Gallery from the Collection of the Société Anonyme—Museum of Modern Art: 1920*. Gorky shows *Forms*, ca. 1931-32 (cat. no. 40).
March	Pierre Matisse Gallery, New York, *Artists in Exile*. Includes Breton, Chagall, Ernst, Léger, Jacques Lipchitz, Matta, Mondrian, Amédée Ozenfant, Tanguy and others.
April	Special issue of *View* devoted to Ernst.
May	Special issue of *View* devoted to Tanguy.
June	Upon request of Dorothy Miller writes statement on Garden in Sochi series (see essay, p. 46).
	First issue of *VVV*, magazine founded and edited by David Hare with Breton and Ernst as editorial advisors.
June 30–August 9	The Museum of Modern Art, New York, *New Rugs by American Artists*. Gorky shows *Bull in Sun*, 1942, executed by V'Soske, two preliminary studies and design in gouache (cat. no. 118). Writes to Dorothy Miller on June 26: "The design on the rug is the skin of a water buffalo stretched in the sunny wheatfield. If it looks like something else then it is even better!"
Early Summer	Spends three weeks at Saul Schary's farm in New Milford, Connecticut; does studies from nature which initiate major stylistic redirection as reflected in *The Pirate I*, 1942; *The Pirate II*, 1943; *Waterfall*, ca. 1943 (cat. nos. 126, 127, 129).
July 1	The Museum of Modern Art, New York, acquires *Garden in Sochi*, 1941 (cat. no. 124), partial gift of Mr. and Mrs. Wolfgang S. Schwabacher.
October 14–November 7	Whitlaw Reid Mansion, 451 Madison Avenue, New York, *First Papers of Surrealism*. Includes Duchamp, Kiesler, Klee, Masson, Matta, Miró, Picasso, Tanguy and young Americans, among them William Baziotes, Hare and Robert Motherwell.
December 9, 1942–January 24, 1943	The Museum of Modern Art, New York, *Twentieth-Century American Portraits*. Gorky shows *My Sister, Ahko*, 1917 (cat. no. 64).

1943

February	Gorky hosts dinner at his studio in honor of Léger.
February 23–March 20	Buchholz Gallery, New York, *Paul Klee and André Masson*.
April 5	Julien Levy Gallery, New York [Matta Drawings].
April 15	First daughter, Maro, born.
June 17–July 25	The Museum of Modern Art, New York, *Painting and Sculpture by Young Americans*. Gorky shows *Garden in Sochi*, 1941 (cat. no. 124).
July	Gorkys vacation at home of Agnes' parents, Admiral and Mrs. John H. Magruder II, Crooked Run Farm, in Hamilton, Virginia. Gorky makes drawings (see cat. nos. 134–138, 142, 145, 146) out of doors and writes to Vartoosh: "The state of Virginia reminds one of Armenia's lowlands . . . although it is less majestic."
November 23, 1943–January 4, 1944	Whitney Museum of American Art, New York, *Annual Exhibition of Contemporary American Art*. Gorky shows *Shenandoah Landscape*, 1943, pencil and crayon.

1944

February–December	*Abstract and Surrealist Art in the United States*. Organized by Sidney Janis and San Francisco Museum of

Art. Traveled to Cincinnati Art Museum, February 8–March 12; The Denver Art Museum, March 26–April 3; The Santa Barbara Museum of Art, June-July; San Francisco Museum of Art, July; Mortimer Brandt Gallery, New York, November 29–December 30. Gorky shows *The Liver is the Coxcomb.* Also includes de Kooning, Gottlieb, Motherwell, Pollock and Rothko.

April — James Johnson Sweeney, "Five American Painters," *Harper's Bazaar*, vol. 78, pp. 122, 124. Article on Gorky, Milton Avery, Morris Graves, Matta and Pollock. "Arshile Gorky's latest work shows his realization of the value of literally returning to the earth . . . . last summer Gorky decided to 'look into the grass' as he put it. The product was a series of monumentally drawn details of what one might see in the heavy August grass."

Spring — Returns to Crooked Run Farm; spends nine months there.

May 24– October 15 — The Museum of Modern Art, New York, *Art in Progress: XV Anniversary Exhibition for The Museum of Modern Art.* Gorky shows *Garden in Sochi*, 1941.

October 31–November 25 — Buchholz Gallery, New York, *The Blue Four: Feininger, Jawlensky, Kandinsky, Paul Klee.*

Winter — Accompanies Noguchi and Jeanne Reynal to Margaret La Farge Osborn's dinner in honor of Breton, whom he meets for first time.

November–December — Sidney Janis' *Abstract and Surrealist Art* published in conjunction with presentation of traveling show *Abstract and Surrealist Art in the United States* at Mortimer Brandt Gallery, New York.

1945 — Lives for nine months in Roxbury, Connecticut, at home of David Hare. Writes to Vartoosh, July 4: "We were on the farm with Agnes for nine months last year. We returned to New York and two months later came here."

Julien Levy becomes Gorky's dealer; he shows his work annually through 1948.

March 6–31 — Julien Levy Gallery, New York, *Arshile Gorky.* Shows *How My Mother's Embroidered Apron Unfolds in My Life*, 1944 (cat. no. 164); *Horns of the Landscape*; *The Leaf of the Artichoke Is an Owl*, 1944 (cat. no. 167); *Love of a New Gun*, 1944 (cat. no. 144); *Pirate*, 1942; *One Year the Milkweed*, 1944 (cat. no. 165); *The Sun, The Dervish in the Tree*, 1944 (cat. no. 162); *They Will Take My Island*, 1944 (cat. no. 181); *Water of the Flowery Mill*, 1944 (cat. no. 160); drawings.

Checklist with "The Eye Spring: Arshile Gorky" by André Breton: "The eye-spring . . . Arshile Gorky—for me the first painter to whom the secret has been completely revealed! . . . In short, it is my concern to emphasize that Gorky is, of all the surrealist artists, the only one who maintains direct contact with nature—sits down to paint *before* her." Coins term "hybrids" for Gorky's forms, which he describes as "the resultants provoked in an observer contemplating a nature spectacle with extreme concentration, the resultants being a combination of the spectacle and a flux of childhood and other memories. . . ."

New edition of Breton's *Surrealism and Painting*, first published 1928, appears: concluding chapter devoted to Gorky.

May 14–July 7 — 67 Gallery, New York, *A Problem for Critics.* Includes Gorky, Arp, Gottlieb, Lee Krasner, Hans Hofmann, Miró, Picasso, Pollock and Rothko.

May 17–June 17 — California Palace of the Legion of Honor, San Francisco, *Contemporary American Painting.* Gorky shows *Composition*, lent by Jeanne Reynal.

June 14 — Writes to Vartoosh from Roxbury: "[I've] been working vigorously on many works which deal in truth with our Armenian world. Often I elaborate on *The Plow and The Song.*"

July 4 — Writes to Vartoosh: "This is the first year that I am working without any financial worries. . . . Mr. Levy sold seven of my pictures."

August 8 — Daughter Yalda born, name soon changed to Natasha.

September–November — Gorkys move in with friends, architect Henry Hebbeln and wife Jean, in Sherman, Connecticut. They convert barn into studio for Gorky. Friends and neighbors in Connecticut include Peter Blume, Malcolm Cowley, Louisa and Alexander Calder, Muriel and Julien Levy, Hope and Saul Schary, Kay Sage and Yves Tanguy.

November 27, 1945–January 10, 1946 — Whitney Museum of American Art, New York, *Annual Exhibition of Contemporary American Painting.* Gorky shows *Journal d'un Seducteur*, 1945 (cat. no. 186).

1946

January 26 — Fire in Sherman studio destroys about twenty-seven paintings, including two of The Plow and the Song theme, drawings and books.

February — Undergoes colostomy operation for cancer, Mount Sinai Hospital, New York.

February 5–March 13	Whitney Museum of American Art, New York, *Annual Exhibition of Contemporary American Sculptures, Watercolors and Drawings.* Gorky shows *Anatomical Blackboard*, colored pencil and crayon (cat. no. 149).
February 16–March 9	City Art Museum, St. Louis, *39th Annual Exhibition—American Painting.* Gorky shows *Number 242*, lent by Julien Levy Gallery.
Late February	Wolfgang Schwabacher secures grant for Gorky from New Land Foundation for $1500 a year.
April 9–May 4	Julien Levy Gallery, New York, *Paintings by Arshile Gorky.* Greenberg calls the eleven oils exhibited "some of the best modern painting ever turned out by an American." (*The Nation*, vol. 162, May 4, 1946, p. 552)
Summer	Returns to Crooked Run Farm; concentrates on drawing because studio/barn had burned. On November 17 writes to Vartoosh: "This summer I completed many drawings—292 of them. At no other time have I ever been able to draw this much and they are truly excellent."
September 10–December 8	The Museum of Modern Art, New York, *Fourteen Americans.* Gorky shows *The Artist and His Mother*, 1926–29 (cat. no. 75); *Garden in Sochi*, 1941 (cat. no. 124); *The Diary of a Seducer*, 1944 (cat. no. 186); *The Unattainable*, 1945 (cat. no. 183); *Water of the Flowery Mill*, 1944 (cat. no. 160); *Landscape Table*, 1945 (cat. no. 189); *Nude*, 1946 (cat. no. 194); *Childs Companions*, 1945; *Anatomical Blackboard*, 1943 (cat. no. 149); *The Backbone of My Ancestor was Far Away*, 1944; *The Visible Monument-Soft*, 1944. Also includes Hare, Motherwell, Noguchi, Theodore Roszak, Saul Steinberg and Mark Tobey.
Late November	Returns to New York with Agnes and children.
December 10, 1946–January 16, 1947	Whitney Museum of American Art, New York, *Annual Exhibition of Contemporary American Painting.* Gorky shows *Nude*,1946 (cat. no. 194).
	Makes two illustrations for Breton's book of poetry, *Young Cherry Trees Secured Against Hares.*
	Miró arrives in New York on way to work on mural in Ohio; Gorky holds party in his honor at 36 Union Square.
	Moves permanently to Sherman but maintains New York studio. Hebbelns transform farmhouse into modern home with one wall made of glass for Gorkys.
January 17	Gorky expresses objections to lack of seriousness in Surrealist art. Writes to Vartoosh: "Surrealism is academic art under disguise and anti-aesthetic and suspicious of excellence and largely in opposition to modern art."
February 15–28	Hugo Gallery, New York, *Bloodflames.* Catalogue with text on Gorky by Nicolas Calas. Includes Hare, Wifredo Lam, Matta, Noguchi and others.
February 18–March 8	Julien Levy Gallery, New York, *Arshile Gorky: Colored Drawings.*
March 11–April 17	Whitney Museum of American Art, New York, *Annual Exhibition of Contemporary American Sculpture, Watercolors and Drawings.* Gorky shows *Colored Drawing*, 1947, pencil and crayon.
April 15–June 1	The Museum of Modern Art, New York, *Drawings in the Collection of The Museum of Modern Art.* Gorky shows *Objects*, 1932 (cat. no. 39).
July-August	Galerie Maeght, Paris, *Le Surréalisme en 1947: Exposition Internationale du Surréalisme présentée par André Breton et Marcel Duchamp.* Last major Surrealist group exhibition. Gorky shows *How My Mother's Embroidered Apron Unfolds in My Life*, 1944 (cat. no. 164), and others.
November 6, 1947–January 11, 1948	The Art Institute of Chicago, *Abstract and Surrealist American Art.* Gorky shows *The Sun, The Dervish in the Tree*, 1944 (cat. no. 162).
November 19, 1947–January 4, 1948	California Palace of the Legion of Honor, San Francisco, *2nd Annual Exhibition of Paintings.* Gorky shows *Nude*, lent by Julien Levy.
December 6, 1947–January 25, 1948	Whitney Museum of American Art, New York, *Annual Exhibition of American Painting.* Gorky shows *The Calendars.* Greenberg calls it "the best painting in the exhibition and one of the best paintings ever done by an American." (*The Nation*, vol. CLXVI, January 10, 1948, p. 52)

1948

January 27	Gives *The Betrothal* (cat. no. 200) to International Rescue Committee.
January 31–March 21	Whitney Museum of American Art, New York, *Annual Exhibition of Contemporary American Sculptures, Watercolors and Drawings.* Gorky shows *The Betrothal*, crayon.
February 9	Talcott B. Clapp, "A Painter in a Glass House," *Sunday Republican Magazine* (Waterbury, Connecticut), p. 6. Article includes interview with Gorky.
February 16	Photographs of Gorky at home in "the Glass House" published in *Life*, vol. 24, pp. 90–92. Article about remodeled house.

February — Sedrak Adoian. dies in Providence at age eighty-five; Gorky not told.

February 29–March 20 — Julien Levy Gallery, New York, *Arshile Gorky*. Shows *White Abstraction*, 1934; *Garden in Sochi*, 1941; *The Liver is The Coxcomb*, 1944 (cat. no. 161); *The Pirate*, 1945; *Delicate Game*, 1946 (cat. no. 191); *Good Hope Road*, 1946; *Impatience*, 1946 (cat. no. 184); *Soft Night*, 1948; *Sculptured Head*, 1932; drawings.

Greenberg writes: "What is new about these paintings is the unproblematic voluptuousness with which they celebrate and display the process of painting for their own sake. With this sensuous richness . . . Gorky at last takes his place . . . among the very few contemporary American painters whose work is of more than national importance." (*The Nation*, vol. 166, March 20, 1948, p. 331)

June 26 — Neck broken and painting arm immobilized in accident in automobile driven by Julien Levy.

mid-July — Wife leaves with both children.

July 21 — Writes "Goodbye My Loveds" in white chalk on wooden picture crate in Sherman studio and commits suicide by hanging.

Lisa Dennison Tabak

Selected Exhibitions and Reviews

I. Selected Group Exhibitions and Reviews

The Museum of Modern Art, New York, *An Exhibition of Work by 46 Painters and Sculptors Under 35 Years of Age*, April 11–26, 1930. Catalogue

Société Anonyme, New York, *Special Exhibition Arranged in Honor of the Opening of the New Building of the New School for Social Research*, January 1–February 10, 1931

The Downtown Gallery, New York, *Paintings, Watercolors, Drawings, Sculptures by Leading Contemporary American Artists*, June 2–22, 1931. Catalogue

The Downtown Gallery, New York, *Artists Models: Figure Paintings by Leading Contemporary American Artists*, October 5–25,1931. Catalogue

The Downtown Gallery, New York, *American Print Makers: Fifth Annual Exhibition*, December 7–31, 1931

Wilmington Society of Fine Arts, *Exhibition of Russian Painting and Sculpture*, 1932. Catalogue with text by Christian Brinton

The Forum, RCA Building, Rockefeller Center, New York, *First Municipal Art Exhibition*, February 28–March 31, 1934. Catalogue with text by Holger Cahill

Laurie Eglington, "Municipal Show of American Art Opens to Public," *Art News*, vol. 32, March 3, 1934, p. 3

"Ceremonies Mark Official Opening of Municipal Show," *Art News*, vol. 32, March 3, 1934, p. 6

"Hosannas," *Art Digest*, vol. 8, March 5, 1934, p. 12

Boyer Galleries, Philadelphia [Group Exhibition], 1934

Whitney Museum of American Art, New York, *Abstract Painting in America*, February 12–March 22, 1935. Catalogue with text by Ethel Schwabacher

Guild Art Gallery, New York [Group Exhibition], closing October 28, 1935

Edward Alden Jewell, "In the Realm of Art: Campfires on Olympus Slopes," *The New York Times*, October 13, 1935, p. x9

Federal Art Project Gallery, New York, *Murals for Public Buildings*, opening December 27, 1935

"W.P.A. Murals Are Too Much for LaGuardia," *New York Herald Tribune*, December 28, 1935

Guild Art Gallery, New York, *Drawings, Small Sculptures, Watercolors*, March 16–April 4, 1936

Boyer Gallery, New York, *Modern American Paintings*, opening June 15, 1936

The Museum of Modern Art, New York, *New Horizons in American Art*, September 14–October 12, 1936. Catalogue with text by Holger Cahill

The New Yorker, vol. 12, September 26, 1936, p. 30

Whitney Museum of American Art, New York, *Third Biennial Exhibition of Contemporary American Painting*, November 10–December 10, 1936. Catalogue

The Newark Museum, *Old and New Paths in American Design, 1720–1936*, November 15–December 28, 1936. Catalogue with text by Holger Cahill

"Opens Exhibit of Federal Art," *Newark Evening News*, November 7, 1936, p. 24

"W.P.A. Workers Exhibit Art in City Museum," *Newark Star Eagle*, November 7, 1936, p. 3

"Goodness Gracious! Is Aviation Really Coming to This?," *The Newark Ledger*, November 8, 1936

Syracuse Museum, New York, *Art Here*, February 18–March 6, 1937. Catalogue with text by Ruth Lawrence

Dallas Museum of Fine Arts, *Greater Pan American Exhibition: Art of the Americas, Precolumbian and Contemporary*, June 12–October 31, 1937

Whitney Museum of American Art, New York, *Annual Exhibition of Contemporary American Painting*, November 10–December 12, 1937. Catalogue

University Gallery, University of Minnesota, Minneapolis, *Third Annual Exhibition of Contemporary American Painting at the University of Minnesota*, February 4–28, 1938. Catalogue

Musée du Jeu de Paume, Paris, *Trois siècles d'art aux Etats-Unis*, May-July 1938. Organized in collaboration with The Museum of Modern Art, New York. Catalogue

Boyer Galleries, Philadelphia [Group Exhibition], 1938

The George Walter Vincent Smith Art Gallery, Springfield, Massachusetts, *Collection of the Société Anonyme—Museum of Modern Art: 1920*, November 9–December 17, 1939. Catalogue

Whitney Museum of American Art, New York, *Annual Exhibition of Contemporary American Painting*, January 10–February 18, 1940. Catalogue

Whitney Museum of American Art, New York, *Annual Exhibition of Contemporary American Painting*, November 27, 1940–January 8, 1941. Catalogue

The Metropolitan Museum of Art, New York, *A Special Exhibition of Contemporary Painting in the United States*, April 19–27, 1941. Catalogue

La Pintura Contemporana Norteamericana. Organized by The Museum of Modern Art, New York, in collaboration with The Brooklyn Museum, The Metropolitan Museum of Art, New York, Whitney Museum of American Art, New York, and The Coordinator of Commercial and Cultural Relations between American Republics. Catalogue in English and

Spanish with text by Helen Appleton Read. Section I, *Mexico and The West*, traveled to Santiago, Chile; Lima, Peru; Quito, Ecuador, June–December 1941. Section II, *East Coast*, traveled to Buenos Aires; Montevideo, Uruguay; Rio de Janeiro, Brazil, July–December 1941. Section III traveled to Bogotà, Colombia; Caracas; Rio de Janeiro; Havana, July–December 1941. All three sections shown at The Metropolitan Museum of Art, New York, as *A Special/Exhibition/of/Contemporary Painting in the United States*, April 19–27

Whitney Museum of American Art, New York, *Paintings by Artists Under Forty*, November 12–December 30, 1941

R. H. Macy Department Store, New York [Group Exhibition], January 5–26, 1942. Organized by Samuel Kootz

City Art Museum, St. Louis, *American Art*, January 25–February 28, 1942

The Davison Art Rooms of Olin Library, Wesleyan University, Middletown, Connecticut, *Oil Paintings, Watercolors and Prints lent by the Yale University Art Gallery from the Collection of the Société Anonyme—Museum of Modern Art: 1920*, February 28–March 31, 1942

The Museum of Modern Art, New York, *New Rugs by American Artists*, June 30–August 9, 1942. Checklist

The Museum of Modern Art, New York, *Twentieth Century Portraits*, December 9, 1942–January 24, 1943. Catalogue with text by Monroe Wheeler

The Museum of Modern Art, New York, *Recent Acquisitions: The Work of Young Americans*, June 17–July 25, 1943

Whitney Museum of American Art, New York, *Annual Exhibition of Contemporary American Art*, November 23, 1943–January 4, 1944. Catalogue

Abstract and Surrealist Art in the United States. Organized by Sidney Janis and San Francisco Museum of Art. Catalogue with text by Sidney Janis. Traveled to Cincinnati Art Museum, February 8–March 12, 1944; The Denver Art Museum, March 26–April 3; The Santa Barbara Museum of Art, June–July; San Francisco Museum of Art, July. Traveled with separate catalogue published as Sidney Janis, *Abstract and Surrealist Art in America*, New York, 1944, to Mortimer Brandt Gallery, New York, November 29–December 30

M[aude] R[iley], "Whither Goes Abstract and Surrealist Art?" *Art Digest*, vol. 19, December 1, 1944, pp. 8, 31

The Museum of Modern Art, New York, *Art in Progress: XV Anniversary Exhibition for The Museum of Modern Art*, May 24–October 15, 1944. Catalogue with text by James Thrall Soby

The Art Institute of Chicago, *Modern Art in Advertisement*, April 27–June 23, 1945. Catalogue with text by Carl Schniewind

67 Gallery, New York, *A Problem for Critics*, May 14–July 7, 1945

Maude Riley, "Insufficient Evidence," *Art Digest*, vol. 19, June 1, 1945, p. 12

California Palace of the Legion of Honor, San Francisco, *Contemporary American Painting*, May 17–June 17, 1945. Catalogue with text by Jermayne MacAgy

Museum of Art, Carnegie Institute, Pittsburgh, *Painting in the United States*, October 11–December 9, 1945. Catalogue

Whitney Museum of American Art, New York, *Annual Exhibition of Contemporary American Painting*, November 27, 1945–January 10, 1946. Catalogue

Whitney Museum of American Art, New York, *Annual Exhibition of Contemporary American Sculptures, Watercolors and Drawings*, February 5–March 13, 1946. Catalogue

City Art Museum, St. Louis, *39th Annual Exhibition-American Painting*, February 16–March 9, 1946. Catalogue with text by Charles Nagel, Jr. published in *Bulletin of the City Art Museum, St. Louis*, vol. XXXI, no. 1, 1946

Whitney Museum of American Art, New York, *Annual Exhibition of Contemporary American Sculpture, Watercolors and Drawings*, March 11–April 17, 1946. Catalogue

The Museum of Modern Art, New York, *Fourteen Americans*, September 10–December 8, 1946. Catalogue edited by Dorothy C. Miller with statements by the artists

Robert Sunley, "Fourteen American Artists," *Critique*, vol. 1, October 1946, p. 21

Whitney Museum of American Art, New York, *Annual Exhibition of Contemporary American Painting*, December 10, 1946–January 16, 1947. Catalogue

Hugo Gallery, New York, *Bloodflames*, February 15–28, 1947. Catalogue with text on Gorky by Nicolas Calas, p. 8

Whitney Museum of American Art, New York, *Annual Exhibition of Contemporary American Sculpture, Watercolors and Drawings*, March 11–April 17, 1947. Catalogue

The Museum of Modern Art, New York, *Drawings in the Collection of The Museum of Modern Art*, April 15–June 1, 1947

Galerie Maeght, Paris, *Le Surréalisme en 1947: Exposition Internationale du Surréalisme présentée par André Breton et Marcel Duchamp*, July–August 1947

The Art Institute of Chicago, *Abstract and Surrealist American Art*, November 6, 1947–January 11, 1948. Catalogue with texts by Katharine Kuh and Frederick Sweet

California Palace of the Legion of Honor, San Francisco, *2nd Annual Exhibition of Paintings*, November 19, 1947–January 4, 1948. Catalogue

Downtown Community School, New York [Group Exhibition], opening December 6, 1947

Whitney Museum of American Art, New York, *Annual Exhibition of Contemporary American Painting*, December 6, 1947–January 25, 1948. Catalogue

Clement Greenberg, "Art," *The Nation*, vol. CLXVI, January 10, 1948, p. 52

Whitney Museum of American Art, New York, *Annual Exhibition of Contemporary American Sculptures, Watercolors and Drawings*, January 31–March 21, 1948. Catalogue

La XXIV Biennale di Venezia: La Collezione Peggy Guggenheim, Venice, May 29–September 30, 1948. Catalogue with texts by Bruno Alfieri and Peggy Guggenheim

Los Angeles Art Association Gallery, *The Artist as Collector*, April 1949

A.M., "Works Hung by 'Artist as Collector,'" *Los Angeles Times*, April 24, 1949, part IV, p. 3

Samuel M. Kootz Gallery, New York, *The Intrasubjectives*, September 15–October 3, 1949. Catalogue with text by Samuel M. Kootz

Margaret Breuning, "Kootz Reopens," *Art Digest*, vol. 23, September 15, 1949, p. 15

Colorado Springs Fine Arts Center, *New Accessions, U.S.A., from Great Britain, The United States and France, with Sculpture from the United States*, November–December 1949

Virginia Museum of Fine Arts, Richmond, *American Painting 1950*, April 22–June 4, 1950. Catalogue with text by James Johnson Sweeney

Philadelphia Museum of Art, *Masterpieces from Philadelphia Private Collections, Part II*, May 2–September 15,

1950. Catalogue published in *Philadelphia Museum Bulletin*, vol. XLV, Spring 1950

La XXV Biennale di Venezia, Venice, June 3–October 15, 1950. Catalogue with text "Gorky, Pollock, de Kooning" by Alfred H. Barr, Jr.

Stedelijk Museum, Amsterdam, *Surréalisme & Abstraction: Choix de la Collection Peggy Guggenheim/Surrealisme & Abstractie: Keuze uit de Verzameling Peggy Guggenheim*, January 19–February 26, 1951. Catalogue in French and Dutch. Traveled to Palais des Beaux-Arts de Bruxelles, March 3–28, 1951. Traveled with separate catalogue in German with text by Max Bill to Kunsthaus Zürich, as *Moderne Kunst aus der Sammlung Peggy Guggenheim*, April–May 1951

The Museum of Modern Art, New York, *Abstract Painting and Sculpture in America*, January 23–March 25, 1951. Catalogue with text by Andrew Carnduff Ritchie

Delius Gallery, New York, *Still Lifes and Flowers, Old & New*, March 27–April 28, 1951

La Galeria Arquitac, Guadalajara, Mexico, *Arshile Gorky y Arte Contemporaneo Norteamericano*, April 5–21, 1951. Checklist

The Brooklyn Museum, New York, *Revolution and Tradition: An Exhibition of the Chief Movements in American Painting from 1900 to the Present*, November 15, 1951–January 6, 1952. Catalogue with text by John I. H. Baur

D[orothy] S[eckler], "The American Conflict: Rebel and Conformist," *Art News*, vol. 50, December 1951, pp. 21, 58–59

Sidney Janis Gallery, New York, *American Vanguard Art for Paris Exhibition*, December 26, 1951–January 5, 1952. Traveled to Galerie de France, Paris, 1952

Wildenstein & Co., New York, *XXth Century American Paintings*, February 21–March 22, 1952

Sidney Janis Gallery, New York, *Season's Resumé*, April 28–May 31, 1952

State University of Iowa, Iowa City, *Fourteenth Annual Fine Arts Festival: Contemporary Art in Iowa*, June 15–August 1, 1952

Burliuk Gallery, New York, *Exhibition of Works of Art by Noted American Artists from the Collection of Marussia Burliuk*, November 16–29, 1952

Wildenstein & Co., New York, *Landmarks in American Art 1670–1950*, February 26–March 28, 1953. Catalogue with text by John I. H. Baur

All India Fine Arts & Crafts Society, New Delhi, *2nd International Contemporary Art Exhibition*. Traveled to five cities in India, 1953

Eloise Spaeth, "Synthesis of Arts in America: 20 Contemporaries," *The Hindustan Times*, May 6, 1953, art supplement, n.p.

Sidney Janis Gallery, New York, *9 American Painters Today*, January 4–23, 1954

Belle Krasne, "Nine American Painters, Nine American Worlds," *The Art Digest*, vol. 28, January 15, 1954, pp. 10–12

Modern Art in the U.S.A. Organized by The International Council of The Museum of Modern Art, New York. Separate catalogue in language of each country with texts by some or all of following: Holger Cahill, Mildred Constantine, Greta Lieberman, Edward Steichen. Traveled to Musée National d'Art Moderne, Paris, as *Cinquante ans d'art aux Etats-Unis*, March 30–May 15, 1955; Kunsthaus Zürich, as *Moderne Kunst aus U.S.A.*, July 16–August 28; with two catalogues to Museo de Arte Moderno, Barcelona, as *El Arte Moderno en el Estados Unidos* (architecture), and Palacio de la Virveina, Barcelona, as *3 Bienal Hispano-Americano de Arte: El Arte Moderno en el Estados Unidos* (painting, sculpture, prints), September 24–October 24; Haus des Deutschen Kunsthandwerks, Frankfurt, as *Moderne Kunst aus U.S.A.*, November 13–December 11; Tate Gallery, London, as *Modern Art in the United States*, January 5–February 12, 1956; Gemeentemuseum, The Hague, as *50 jaar moderne kunst in de U.S.A.*, March 2–April 15, with one catalogue to Wiener Secession Galerie (painting, sculpture, prints, architecture) and Neue Galerie, Vienna (photography), as *Moderne Kunst aus U.S.A.*, May 5–June 2; with one catalogue to Kalemagdan Pavilion (painting, sculpture), ULUS Gallery (prints, photographs), Fresco Museum (architecture), Belgrade, as *Savremena utmetnost U.S.A.D.*, July 6–August 6

Meyer Schapiro, "The Younger American Painters of Today," *The Listener*, vol. LV, January 26, 1956, pp. 146–147

San Francisco Museum of Art, *Art in the 20th Century*, June 17–July 10, 1955. Catalogue with text by E. Morris Cox and Grace L. McCann Morley

Milwaukee Art Center, *55 Americans*, September 9–October 23, 1955. Checklist

Walker Art Center, Minneapolis, *Expressionism 1900–1955*, January 26–March 11, 1956. Catalogue with texts by H. H. Arnason and Sidney Simon

Museum of Art, University of Michigan, Ann Arbor, *Drawings and Watercolors from the Oberlin Collection*, March 11–April 1, 1956

National Gallery of Canada, Ottawa, *Some American Paintings from the Collection of Joseph H. Hirshhorn*, January 10–31, 1957. Catalogue with text by R. H. Hubbard. Traveled to Montreal Museum of Fine Arts, March 20–31; The Art Gallery of Toronto, April 12–May 26; Stratford Arena, Ontario, July 1–August 31; Winnipeg Art Gallery, Manitoba, October 6–November 3

The Brooklyn Museum, *Golden Years of American Drawings: 1905–1956*, January 22–March 17, 1957. Catalogue with text by U. E. Johnson

William Rockhill Nelson Gallery of Art and Atkins Museum of Fine Arts, Kansas City, Missouri, *Some Points of View in Modern Painting*, February 10–March 10, 1957. Checklist

The Baltimore Museum of Art, *Modern Art for Baltimore*, February 23–March 17, 1957

Sidney Janis Gallery, New York, *8 Americans*, April 1–20, 1957. Catalogue

J[ames] S[chuyler], "Reviews and Previews," *Art News*, vol. 56, April 1957, p. 11

Albright Art Gallery, Buffalo, *Contemporary Art: Acquisitions 1954–1957*, May 15, 1957–February 15, 1958. Catalogue

Poindexter Gallery, New York, *The 30's: Painting in New York*, June 1957. Catalogue edited by Patricia Passloff with texts by Edwin Denby and the artists

Clement Greenberg, "New York painting only yesterday," *Art News*, vol. 56, Summer 1957, pp. 58–59, 84–86

Wadsworth Atheneum, Hartford, *Connecticut Collects: An exhibition of privately owned works of art in Connecticut*, October 4–November 3, 1957. Catalogue with text by Charles C. Cunningham

Dallas Museum of Contemporary Art, *Abstract by Choice*, November 19–December 31, 1957. Catalogue with text by Rual Askew

Whitney Museum of American Art, New York, *Nature in Abstraction*, January 14, 1958–March 16, 1959. Catalogue with text by John I. H. Baur. Traveled to The Phillips Collection, Washington, D.C., April 2–May; Fort Worth Art Center Museum, June 2–29; Los Angeles County Museum of Art, July 16–August 24; San Francisco Museum of Art, September 10–October 12; Walker Art Center, Minneapolis, October 29–December 14; City Art Museum, St. Louis, January 7–February 8, 1959

Avant-Garde Gallery, New York, *Gorky, Lanskoy, GenPaul: Early Paintings*, April 4–May 3, 1958. Catalogue

The New American Painting. Organized by The International Council of The Museum of Modern Art, New York. Separate catalogue in language of each country with texts by Alfred H. Barr, Jr., Porter McCray, reprinted texts by participating artists. Traveled with additional catalogue text by Arnold Rudlinger to Kunsthalle Basel, as *Die neue amerikanische Malerei*, April 19–May 26, 1958; Galleria Civica d'Arte Moderna, Milan, as *La Nuova Pittura Americana*, June 1–29; Museo Nacional de Arte Contemporaneo, Madrid, as *La Nueva Pintura Americana*, July 16–August 11; Hochschule für Bildende Kunste, Berlin, as *Die neue amerikanische Malerei*, September 1–October 1; Stedelijk Museum, Amsterdam, as *Jong Amerika schildert*, October 17–November 24; Palais des Beaux-Arts de Bruxelles, as *La nouvelle peinture américaine*, December 6, 1958–January 4, 1959; with additional exhibition and additional catalogue texts by Sam Hunter and Jean Cassou to Musée National d'Art Moderne, Paris, as *Jackson Pollock et la nouvelle peinture américaine*, January 16–February 15; with additional catalogue text by Gabriel White to Tate Gallery, London, as *The New American Painting*, February 24–March 22; The Museum of Modern Art, New York, as *The New American Painting*, May 28–September 8. Traveled in part to Albany Institute of History and Art, New York, as *The New American Painting*, September 25–October 25

Sidney Janis Gallery, New York, *X Years of Janis: 10th Anniversary Exhibition*, September 29–November 1, 1958. Catalogue

The Cleveland Museum of Art, *Some Contemporary Works of Art*, November 11–December 31, 1958

Sidney Janis Gallery, New York, *8 American Painters*, January 5–31, 1959. Catalogue

Museum Fridericianum, Kassel, Germany, *II. Documenta'59, Kunst nach 1945: Internationale Ausstellung*, July 11–October 11, 1959. Catalogue with text by Werner Haftmann

Klaus Jürgen-Fischer, "Die II. Documenta in Kassel—Fuzit eines Unbehagens," *Das Kunstwerk*, vol. 13, August 1959, p. 41

Sokolniki, Moscow, *American Painting and Sculpture: American National Exhibition in Moscow*, July 25–September 5, 1959. Organized by Archives of American Art, Detroit. Catalogue in English with text by Lloyd Goodrich

University Art Museum, University of California, Berkeley, *Art from Ingres to Pollock*, March 6–April 3, 1960. Catalogue with texts by Herschel B. Chipp and Grace Morley

Walker Art Center, Minneapolis, *60 American Painters 1960: Abstract Expressionist Painting of the '50's*, April 3–May 8, 1960. Catalogue with texts by H. H. Arnason and Herbert Read

Herbert Read and H. Harvard Arnason, "Dialogue on modern U.S. painting," *Art News*, vol. 59, May 1960, pp. 33–36

Otto Gerson Gallery, New York, *11 Modern Works Lent by Distinguished Artists, Writers, Architects*, February 28–March 25, 1961

John and Mable Ringling Museum of Art, Sarasota, *The Sidney Janis Painters*, April 8–May 7, 1961. Catalogue with texts by Dore Ashton and Kenneth Donahue

Williams College Museum of Art, Williamstown, Massachusetts, *An Exhibition of Works of Art Lent by the Alumni of Williams College*, May 5–June 16, 1962

Sidney Janis Gallery, New York, *10 American Painters*, May 8–June 3, 1961. Catalogue

I[rving] H. S[andler], "Reviews and Previews: Ten Americans," *Art News*, vol. 60, Summer 1961, p. 10

Sidney Janis Gallery, New York, *11 Abstract Expressionist Painters*, October 7–November 2, 1963. Catalogue

The Solomon R. Guggenheim Museum, New York, *20th Century Master Drawings*, November 6, 1963–January 5, 1964. Catalogue with texts by Emily Rauh and Sidney Simon. Traveled to University Gallery, University of Minnesota, Minneapolis, February 3–March 15; Fogg Art Museum, Harvard University, Cambridge, Massachusetts, April 6–May 24

Des Moines Art Center, *Art in Iowa from Private Collections*, October 19–November 24, 1963

The Minneapolis Institute of Art, *Four Centuries of American Art*, November 27, 1963–January 19, 1964. Catalogue with text by Marshall B. Davidson

Robert Elkon Gallery, New York, *Selected Paintings and Drawings by 20th Century European and American Artists*, November 1963

National Gallery of Art, Washington, D.C., *Paintings from The Museum of Modern Art, New York*, December 16, 1963–March 22, 1964

Rose Fried Gallery, New York, *Modern Masters*, January 11–February 15, 1964

Yale University Art Gallery, New Haven, *Ernst and Gorky from the Collection of Julien Levy*, March 19–May 3, 1964

City Art Museum, St. Louis, *200 Years of American Painting*, April 1–May 31, 1964. Catalogue with texts by Charles Nagel and Merrill C. Rueppel

Fine Arts Gallery, Indiana University, Bloomington, *American Painting 1910–1960*, April 18–May 10, 1964. Catalogue with text by Henry R. Hope

Fogg Art Museum, Harvard University, Cambridge, Massachusetts, *Within the Easel Convention: Sources of Abstract Expressionism*, May 7–June 7, 1964. Catalogue with text by Rosalind Krauss

The Solomon R. Guggenheim Museum, New York, *American Drawings*, September 17–October 22, 1964. Catalogue with text by Lawrence Alloway. Traveled to Museum of Art, University of Michigan, Ann Arbor, November 11–December 13; Grand Rapids Art Museum, Michigan, January 10–February 7, 1965; University Gallery, University of Minnesota, Minneapolis, February 24–March 21; Seattle Art Museum, April 8–May 2; The Denver Art Museum, June 6–July 4; Dallas Museum of Fine Arts, July 25–August 22; The Columbus Gallery of Fine Arts, Ohio, September12–October10; Krannert Art Museum, University of Illinois, Champaign, November 15–December 5

Rose Art Museum, Brandeis University, Waltham, Massachusetts, *The Painter and the Photograph*, October 5–November 1, 1964. Checklist

Emily Genauer, "Painting What The Camera Saw," *New York Herald Tribune*, October 25, 1964

Tate Gallery, London, *The Peggy Guggenheim Collection*, December 31, 1964–March 7, 1965. Catalogue with texts by Peggy Guggenheim and Herbert Read

M. Knoedler & Co., Inc., New York, *Lawyers Collect*, January 13–30, 1965

The Brooklyn Museum, *Paintings from the Joseph H. Hirshhorn Foundation Collection: A View of the Protean Century*, February 8–April 5, 1965. Catalogue with text by H. H. Arnason

Providence Art Club, Rhode Island, *Critic's Choice: Art Since World War II*, March 31–April 24, 1965. Catalogue with texts by Thomas B. Hess, Hilton Kramer and Harold Rosenberg

Everhart Museum, Scranton, Pennsylvania, *Non-Objective Paintings from the Michener Collection*, May 1–30, 1965

Los Angeles County Museum of Art, *The New York School: The First Generation, Paintings of the 1940's and 1950's*, July 16–August 1, 1965. Catalogue with excerpts from texts by Lawrence Alloway, Robert Goldwater, Clement Greenberg, Harold Rosenberg, William Rubin and Meyer Schapiro and reprinted texts by participating artists

Allan Stone Gallery, New York, *De Kooning, Pollock, Newman, Gorky, Cornell*, October 26–November 13, 1965

National Collection of Fine Arts, Washington, D.C., *Roots of Abstract Art in America, 1910–1930*, December 2, 1965–January 9, 1966. Catalogue with texts by Adelyn Breeskin, Duncan Phillips, John Marin, David Scott and Alfred Stieglitz

Fondation Maeght, St. Paul de Vence, France, *Dix ans d'art vivant: 1945–1955*, April 9–May 31, 1966. Catalogue with text by François Wehrlin

Seven Decades, 1895–1965: Crosscurrents in Modern Art, April 26–May 21, 1966. Organized by Public Education Association, New York. Catalogue with text by Peter Selz. Exhibition divided among New York galleries: Paul Rosenberg and Co., 1895–1904; M. Knoedler & Co., Inc., 1905–1914; Perls Galleries, E. V. Thaw & Co., 1915–1924; Saidenberg Gallery, 1925–1934; Stephen Hahn Gallery, 1925–1934; Pierre Matisse Gallery, 1935–1944; Andre Emmerich Gallery, Galleria Odyssia, 1945–1954; Cordier and Ekstrom, Inc., 1955–1965

Allentown Art Museum, Pennsylvania, *New Acquisitions 1963–1966: The James A. Michener Foundation Collection*, May 13–July 5, 1966

Sidney Janis Gallery, New York, *2 Generations: Picasso to Pollock*, January 3–27, 1967. Catalogue

Marlborough-Gerson Gallery, New York, *The New York Painter, A Century of Teaching: Morse to Hofmann*, September 22–October 14, 1967. Catalogue with texts by Milton W. Brown, Howard Conant, Ruth Gurin and Albert Ten Eyck Gardner

M. Knoedler & Cie, Paris, *Six peintres américains: Gorky, Kline, de Kooning, Newman, Pollock, Rothko*, October 19–November 25, 1967. Catalogue with reprinted texts by participating artists

Stedelijk van Abbemuseum, Eindhoven, The Netherlands, *Kompass III: Schilderkunst na 1945 uit New York: Paintings after 1945 in New York*, November 9–December 17, 1967. Catalogue in Dutch and English with text by Jean Leering. Traveled with separate catalogue in German and English with text by Leering to Frankfurter Kunstverein as *Kompass New York*, December 30, 1967–February 11, 1968

Galleria Civica d'Arte Moderna, Torino, *Le Muse Inquietanti: Maestro del Surrealismo*, November 1967–January 1968. Catalogue

M. Knoedler & Co., Inc., New York, *Space and Dream*, December 5–29, 1967. Catalogue with text by Robert Goldwater

John Ashbery, "They Came from Inner Space," *Art News*, vol. 66, December 1967, pp.48–49, 58

The Museum of Modern Art, New York, *The Sidney and Harriet Janis Collection*, January 17–March 4, 1968. Catalogue with text by Alfred H. Barr, Jr. Traveled to The Minneapolis Institute of Arts, May 15–July 28; Portland Art Museum, Oregon, September 13–October 13; Pasadena Art Museum, November 11–December 15; San Francisco Museum of Art, January 13–February 16, 1969; Seattle Art Museum, March 12–April 13; The Detroit Institute of Arts, July 14–August 17; Albright-Knox Art Gallery, Buffalo, September 15–October 19; The Cleveland Museum of Art, November 1, 1969–January 4, 1970. Traveled under auspices of The International Council of The Museum of Modern Art with separate catalogue in language of each country to Kunsthalle Basel, February 28–March 30; The Institute of Contemporary Arts, London, May 1–31; Akademie der Künste, Berlin, June 12–August; Kunsthalle Nürnberg, September 11–October 25; Württembergischer Kunstverein, Stuttgart, as *Von Surrealismus bis zur Pop Art*, November 12–December 27; with no catalogue to Palais des Beaux-Arts de Bruxelles, January 7–February 11, 1971; with separate catalogue with text by Helmut R. Lepplen to Kunsthalle Köln as *Von Picasso bis Warhol*, March 5–April 18

Art Gallery, University of California, Irvine, *Twentieth-Century Works on Paper*, January 30–February 25, 1968. Catalogue with text by James Monte. Traveled to Memorial Union Art Gallery, University of California, Davis, March 26–April 20

University Art Museum, University of Texas at Austin, *Painting as Painting*, February 18–April 1, 1968. Catalogue with texts by Dore Ashton, Louis Finkelstein and George McNeil

Finch College Museum of Art, New York, *Betty Parson's Private Collection*, March 13–April 24, 1968. Catalogue with text by E. C. Goossen

Rosalind Constable, "The Betty Parsons Collection." *Art News*, vol. 67, March 1968, pp. 48–49, 58–60

The Museum of Modern Art, New York, *Dada, Surrealism and Their Heritage*, March 26–June 9, 1968. Catalogue with text by William S. Rubin. Traveled to Los Angeles County Museum of Art, July 16–September 8; The Art Institute of Chicago, October 19–December 8

National Collection of Fine Arts, Smithsonian Institution, Washington, D.C., *Contemporary American Art*, May 3–June 1, 1968

Honolulu Academy of Arts, *Signals in the Sixties*, October 5–December 10, 1968. Catalogue with text by James Johnson Sweeney

Riverside Art Center and Museum, University of California, Riverside, *Dada, Surrealism and Today*, October 7–28, 1968. Traveled to San Francisco Museum of Art, November 11–December 8; University Art Museum, University of Texas at Austin, January 6–27, 1969; St. Cloud State College, St. Cloud, Minnesota, February 14–March 9; University of Manitoba, Winnipeg, March 24–April 14

Whitney Museum of American Art, New York, *The 1930's: Painting and Sculpture in America*, October 15–December 1, 1968. Catalogue with text by William C. Agee

The Solomon R. Guggenheim Museum, New York, *Works from the Peggy Guggenheim Foundation*, January 16–March 23, 1969. Catalogue with text by Peggy Guggenheim

The Museum of Modern Art, New York, *The New American Painting and Sculpture: The First Generation*, June 18–October 5, 1969. Checklist with anonymous text

Charlotte Lichtblau, "The First Generation," *Arts Magazine*, vol. 43, Summer 1969, pp. 37–39

M. Knoedler & Co., Inc., New York, *Gorky, de Kooning, Newman*, June 26–September 20, 1969

The Metropolitan Museum of Art, New York, *New York Painting and Sculpture: 1940–1970*, October 16, 1969–February 1, 1970. Catalogue with reprinted or revised texts by Michael Fried, Henry Geldzahler, Clement Greenberg, Harold Rosenberg, Robert Rosenblum and William Rubin

Mahonri Sharp Young, "The Metropolitan Museum of Art Centenary Exhibitions—I: The New York School," *Apollo*, vol. 90, November 1969, pp. 426–432

University Art Museum, University of

Texas at Austin, *Selected Paintings from the Michener Collection*, November 2, 1969–January 5, 1970

Pasadena Art Museum, *Painting in New York: 1944 to 1969*, November 24, 1969–January 11, 1970. Catalogue with text by Alan R. Solomon

The Art Galleries, University of California, Santa Barbara, *Trends in Twentieth Century Art: a loan exhibition from the San Francisco Museum of Art*, January 6–February 1, 1970. Catalogue with text by Alan Story

The Wilmington Society of Fine Arts, Delaware Art Center, *Contemporary American Painting and Sculpture from New York Galleries*, April 2–26, 1970

Joslyn Art Museum, Omaha, *The Thirties Decade: American Artists and Their European Contemporaries*, October 10–November 28, 1970

Baukunst, Cologne, *Der Geist der Surrealismus*, October–November 1971

The Minneapolis Institute of Arts, *Drawings and Watercolors from Minnesota's Private Collections*, May 13–June 15, 1971. Catalogue with text by Edward A. Foster

Albright-Knox Art Gallery, Buffalo, *Abstract Expressionism: The First and Second Generations in the Albright-Knox Art Gallery*, January 19–February 20, 1972. Catalogue

The Cleveland Museum of Art, *Cleveland Collects Contemporary Art*, July 11–August 20, 1972. Catalogue with text by Edward B. Henning

University of Maryland Art Gallery, Department of Art, University of Maryland, College Park, *The Private Collection of Martha Jackson*, June 22–September 30, 1973. Catalogue with texts by David Anderson, Adelyn Breeskin and Elayne H. Varian. Traveled to Finch College Museum of Art, New York, October 16–November 25; Albright-Knox Art Gallery, Buffalo, January 8–February 10, 1974

National Gallery of Art, Washington, D.C., *American Art at Mid-Century I*, October 28, 1973–January 6, 1974. Catalogue with texts by William C. Seitz and participating artists

The Hayden Gallery, Massachusetts Institute of Technology, Cambridge, *Drawings by Five Abstract Expressionist Painters: Arshile Gorky, Philip Guston, Franz Kline, Willem de Kooning, Jackson Pollock*, February 21–March 26, 1975. Catalogue with text by Eila Kokkinen. Traveled in part to Museum of Contemporary Art, Chicago, January 10–February 9, 1976

M. Knoedler & Co., Inc., New York, *American Works on Paper 1945–1975*, November–December 1975

The Edmonton Art Gallery, Edmonton, Canada, *The Collective Unconscious: American and Canadian Art: 1940–1950*, December 5, 1975–January 18, 1976. Catalogue with text by Karen Willen

The Solomon R. Guggenheim Museum, New York, *Twentieth Century American Drawing: Three Avant-Garde Generations*, January 23–March 28, 1976. Catalogue with text by Diane Waldman. Traveled with separate catalogue in German with text by Diane Waldman to Staatliche Kunsthalle, Baden-Baden, May 27–July 11; Kunsthalle, Bremen, July 18–August 29

Hirshhorn Museum and Sculpture Garden, Smithsonian Institution, Washington, D.C., *The Golden Door: Artist Immigrants of America 1876–1976*, May 20–October 20, 1976. Catalogue with texts by Daniel J. Boorstin and Cynthia Jaffee McCabe

The Museum of Modern Art, New York, *The Natural Paradise: Painting in America 1800–1950*, October 1–November 30, 1976. Catalogue with texts by Kynaston McShine, Barbara Novak, Robert Rosenblum and John Wilmerding

The Solomon R. Guggenheim Museum, New York, *Acquisition Priorities: Aspects of Postwar Painting in America; Including Arshile Gorky: Works 1944–1948*, October 15, 1976–January 16, 1977. Catalogue

Milwaukee Art Center, *From Foreign Shores: Three Centuries of Art by Foreign Born American Masters*, October 15–November 28, 1976. Catalogue with text by I. Michael Danoff

M. Knoedler & Co., Inc., New York, *Works on Paper/Collages and Drawings by Arshile Gorky, Robert Motherwell and David Smith*, October 19–November 20, 1976

Tyler Art Gallery, State University of New York College of Arts and Sciences, Oswego, *The New Deal for Art*, January 25–February 13, 1977. Organized by the Gallery Association of New York State. Catalogue with texts by Gerald E. Markowitz and Marlene Park. Traveled to The Picker Gallery, Colgate University, Hamilton, New York, February 27–March 20; Albany Institute of History and Art, May 17–June 8; Delaware Art Museum, Wilmington, July 29–August 28; Munson-Williams-Proctor Institute, Utica, September 4–September 25; Fosdick-Nelson Gallery, New York State College of Ceramics at Alfred University, October; Grey Art Gallery and Study Center, New York University, November 17, 1976–January 3, 1977; Huntington Galleries, Huntington, West Virginia; January 10–February 3

Xavier Fourcade, Inc., New York, *Works on Paper, Small Formats, Objects: Duchamp to Heizer*, February 15–March 19, 1977

The Bell Gallery, List Art Building, Brown University, Providence, Rhode Island, *Graham, Gorky, Smith and Davis in the Thirties*, April 30–May 22, 1977. Catalogue

Musée National d'Art Moderne, Centre National d'Art et de Culture Georges Pompidou, Paris, *Paris-New York*, June 1–September 19, 1977. Catalogue

Museum of Fine Arts, Houston, *Modern American Paintings 1910–1940: Toward a New Perspective*, July 1–September 25, 1977. Catalogue with text by William C. Agee

Royal Scottish Academy, Edinburgh Festival, *Modern Spirit: American Painting 1908–1935*, August 20–September 11, 1977. Catalogue with text by Milton W. Brown. Traveled to Hayward Gallery, London, September 28–November 20

San Jose Museum of Art, California, *Post War Modernism*, November 4–December 31, 1977

Herbert F. Johnson Museum of Art, Cornell University, Ithaca, New York, *Abstract Expressionism: The Formative Years*, March 30–May 14, 1978. Organized in collaboration with the Whitney Museum of American Art, New York. Catalogue with texts by Robert Carleton Hobbs and Gail Levin. Traveled to Seibu Department Store, Tokyo, June 17–July 12; Whitney Museum of American Art, New York, October 5–December 3

Wellesley College Museum, Wellesley, Massachusetts, *One Century: Wellesley Families Collect*, April 15–May 30, 1978. Catalogue

Montgomery Museum of Fine Art, Montgomery, Alabama, *American Art 1934–1956: Selections from the Whitney Museum of American Art*, April 26–June 11, 1978. Catalogue with texts by Tom Armstrong and Diane J. Gingold. Traveled to Brookes Memorial Art Gallery, Memphis, June 30–August 6; Mississippi Museum of Art, Jackson, August 21–October 1

National Gallery of Art, Washington, D.C., *American Art at Mid-Century: The Subjects of the Artist*, June 1, 1978–January 14, 1979. Catalogue with texts by E. A. Carmean Jr., Thomas B. Hess and Eliza E. Rathbone

Williams College Museum of Art, Williamstown, Massachusetts, *Documents, Drawings, and Collages: Fifty American Works on Paper from the Collection of Mr. and Mrs. Stephen D. Paine*, June 8–30, 1979. Catalogue

The Cleveland Museum of Art, *The*

Spirit of Surrealism, October 3–November 25, 1979. Catalogue with text by Edward B. Henning

The David and Alfred Smart Gallery, University of Chicago, *Abstract Expressionism: A Tribute to Harold Rosenberg: Paintings and Drawings from Chicago Collectors*, October 11–November 25, 1979. Catalogue

The Contemporary Arts Center, Cincinnati, *The Modern Art Society, The Center's Early Years 1939–1954: An Exhibition in Celebration of the 40th Anniversary of the Contemporary Art Center*, October 12–November 26, 1979. Catalogue with texts by Peggy Frank Crawford, Rita Rentschler Cushman, Edward H. Dwight, Ruth K. Meyer, Betty Pollack Rauti and Robert Stern

Salander-O'Reilly Galleries, Inc., New York, *Works on Paper*, November 7–December 1, 1979

II. One-Man Exhibitions and Selected Reviews

Mellon Galleries, Philadelphia, *Arshile Gorky*, February 2–15, 1934. Checklist with texts by Holger Cahill, Stuart Davis, F.J. Kiesler and Harriet Janowitz

C.H. Bonte, "In Gallery and Studio," *Philadelphia Inquirer*, February 11, 1934

Boyer Galleries, Philadelphia [Arshile Gorky], September 1935

"Exhibition Talks Planned by Boyer," *Philadelphia Record*, October 13, 1935

Guild Art Gallery, New York, *Abstract Drawings by Arshile Gorky*, December 16, 1935–January 5, 1936. Checklist with text by Holger Cahill

Jerome Klein, "Gorky Exhibits Abstract Works," *New York Post*, December 21, 1935

"Arshile Gorky Exhibits," *Art Digest*, vol. 10, January 1, 1936, p. 21

James W. Lane, "Current Exhibitions," *Parnassus*, vol. 8, March 1936, p. 27

Boyer Gallery, New York [Arshile Gorky], 1938

San Francisco Museum of Art, *Arshile Gorky*, August 9–24, 1941

Alfred Frankenstein [Review], *San Francisco Chronicle*, August 17, 1941, p. 11

Alexander Fried, "Gorky Oils of Surrealist School," *San Francisco Examiner*, August 17, 1941

Emilia Hodel, "Léger's [. . .]," *San Francisco News*, August 17, 1941, p. 8

Julien Levy Gallery, New York, *Arshile Gorky*, March 6–31, 1945. Checklist with "The Eye Spring: Arshile Gorky," by André Breton (translated by Julien Levy). Reprinted in: Schwabacher, 1957, see Monographs, p. 280; as "Arshile Gorky: the Eye-Spring," *It Is*, no. 4, Autumn 1959, pp. 56–57; in Washburn Gallery Catalogue, 1978, See One-Man Exhibitions, p. 277

Maude Riley, "The Eye-Spring: Arshile Gorky," *Art Digest*, vol. 19, March 15, 1945, p. 10

"The Passing Shows," *Art News*, vol. 44, March 15, 1945, p. 24

Robert M. Coates, "The Art Galleries," *The New Yorker*, vol. 21, March 17, 1945, p. 77

Clement Greenberg, "Art," *The Nation*, vol. 160, March 24, 1945, pp. 342–343

Julien Levy Gallery, New York, *Paintings by Arshile Gorky*, April 9–May 4, 1946

"Reviews and Previews," *Art News*, vol. 45, April 1946, p. 54

Judith Kaye Reed, "Salvaged from Fire," *Art Digest*, vol. 20, May 1, 1946, p. 13

Clement Greenberg, "Art," *The Nation*, vol. 162, May 4, 1946, p. 13

"New York Exhibits," *MKR'S Art Outlook*, no. 11, June 1946, p. 7

Julien Levy Gallery, New York, *Arshile Gorky, Colored Drawings*, February 18–March 8, 1947

Alonzo Lansford, "Concentrated Doodles," *Art Digest*, vol. 21, March 1, 1947, p. 18

"Reviews and Previews," *Art News*, vol. 46, March 1947, p. 43

Julien Levy Gallery, New York, *Arshile Gorky*, February 29–March 20, 1948

Sam Hunter, "Modernism By Four, Abstraction, Surrealism In Current Shows," *The New York Times*, February 29, 1948, section 2, p.8

Clement Greenberg, "Art," *The Nation*, vol. 166, March 20, 1948, pp. 331–332

Clement Greenberg, "Art Chronicle," *Partisan Review*, vol. 15, March 1948, p. 369

"Reviews and Previews," *Art News*, vol. 47, March 1948, p. 46

Julien Levy Gallery, New York, *Arshile Gorky, 1905–1948*, November 16–December 4, 1948. Checklist

Henry McBride [Review], *The New York Sun*, November 17, 1948

Sam Hunter, "Chiefly Abstract," *The New York Times*, November 21, 1948, section 2, p. 9

Clement Greenberg, "Art," *The Nation*, vol. 167, December 11, 1948, p. 676

"Reviews and Previews," *Art News*, vol. 47, December 1948, pp. 53–54

Kootz Gallery, New York, *Selected Paintings by the Late Arshile Gorky*, March 28–April 24, 1950. Checklist with text by Adolph Gottlieb

Margaret Breuning, "Fifty-Seventh Street in Review: A Memorial for Arshile Gorky," *Art Digest*, vol. 24, April 1, 1950, p. 18

Howard Devree, "By Contemporaries: Museum Shows Its Recent Acquisitions—Gorky, Lebrun, de Martini, Dozier," *The New York Times*, April 2, 1950, p. 8

Weldon Kees, "Art," *The Nation*, vol. 170, April 8, 1950, pp. 333–334

Thomas B. Hess, "Reviews and Previews," *Art News*, vol. 49, April 1950, p. 45

Clement Greenberg, "Art Chronicle," *Partisan Review*, vol. 17, May/June 1950, pp. 512–513

Whitney Museum of American Art, New York, *Arshile Gorky Memorial Exhibition*, January 5–February 18, 1951. Catalogue with text by Ethel Schwabacher and biographical notes by Lloyd Goodrich. Traveled to Walker Art Center, Minneapolis, March 4–April 22; San Francisco Museum of Art, May 9–July 9

Aline Louchheim, "Contemporary Art in New York," *The Atlantic Monthly*, vol. 186, December 1950, pp. 65–66

"Whitney Honors Gorky," *Art Digest*, vol. 25, January 1, 1951, p. 6

Howard Devree, "Whitney to Offer Arshile Gorky Art," *The New York Times*, January 4, 1951, p. 27

Carlyle Burrows, "Memorial Show of Arshile Gorky Art will open at Whitney Museum Today," *The New York Herald Tribune*, January 5, 1951, p. 19

Howard Devree, "A Memorable Year," *The New York Times*, January 7, 1951, section 2, p. 2

Emily Genauer, "Art and Artists: The Whitney's Memorial Exhibition: The Arshile Gorky Tragedy," *The New York Herald Tribune*, January 14, 1951, section 4, p. 6

"Gorky: Was He Tops or Second Rate?," *Art Digest*, vol. 25, January 15, 1951, pp. 9, 30

Robert M. Coates, "The Art Galleries: Moderns—Past and Present," *The New Yorker*, vol. 26, January 20, 1951, pp. 60, 62–63

Manny Farber, "Art," *The Nation*, vol. 172, January 27, 1951, p. 92

The Gotchnag (The Armenian Weekly), vol. LI, January 27, 1951, pp. 82–83

Elaine de Kooning, "Gorky: Painter of His Own Legend," *Art News*, vol. 49, January 1951, pp. 38–41, 63–66

"Fiery River of Images," *Pictures on Exhibit*, vol. 13, January 1951, pp. 4–5

"Modernist at Art Center," *Minneapolis Sunday Tribune*, March 4, 1951, p. F 13

Huldah Curl, "Arshile Gorky Memorial Exhibition," Walker Art Center, Minneapolis, *Notes and Comments*, vol. 5, March 1951, pp. 1–2

Alfred Frankenstein, "Around the Local Art Galleries," *San Francisco Chronicle*, May 13, 1951, p. 28

Louise Ballard, "Art," *Arts & Architecture*, vol. 68, May 1951, pp. 10–11

Kootz Gallery, New York, *Drawings in Color by Arshile Gorky*, January 23–February 10, 1951

J[ames] F[itzsimmons], "Fifty-Seventh Street in Review: Arshile Gorky," *Art Digest*, vol. 25, February 1, 1951, p. 19

R[obert] G[oodnough], "Reviews and Previews," *Art News*, vol. 49, February 1951, p. 46

Paul Kantor Gallery, Los Angeles, *Arshile Gorky: Paintings and Drawings, 1928–1937*, opened June 12, 1952

The Art Museum, Princeton University, Princeton, New Jersey, *Arshile Gorky: A Loan Exhibition of Paintings and Drawings*, October 5–26, 1952. Checklist

William Seitz, "A Gorky Exhibit," *Daily Princetonian*, vol. 76, October 14, 1952, p. 2

Sidney Janis Gallery, New York, *Arshile Gorky in the Final Years*, February 16–March 14, 1953. Poster/Checklist

Stuart Preston, "Tradition To Novelty," *The New York Times*, February 22, 1953, section 2, p. 10

Robert M. Coates, "The Art Galleries: All Moderns," *The New Yorker*, vol. 27, February 28, 1953, pp. 83–84

James Fitzsimmons, "57th Street: The Late Gorky," *Art Digest*, vol. 27, March 1, 1953, p. 16

Henry McBride, "By Henry McBride: Success at Last," *Art News*, vol. 52, April 1953, pp. 66–67

Martha Jackson Gallery, New York, *Gorky, Works of the Middle Period/Trökes, Recent Gouaches and Drawings*, March 27–April 24, 1954

Sam Feinstein, "Fortnight in Review, A Gallery Itinerary," *Art Digest*, vol. 28, April 15, 1954, p. 21

Fairfield Porter, "Reviews and Previews," *Art News*, vol. 53, April 1954, p. 53

Sidney Janis Gallery, New York, *Drawings for Principal Paintings by Gorky*, September 26–October 22, 1955

Emily Genauer, "Gorky, Now Legend, in Week's New Shows," *The Herald Tribune Book Review*, October 2, 1955, p. 10

Stuart Preston, "Modern Work In Diverse Shows," *The New York Times*, October 2, 1955, section 2, p. 15

Hilton Kramer, "Drawings from Gorky's Last Years at the Janis Gallery," *Arts*, vol. 30, October 1955, pp. 48–49

Fairfield Porter, "Reviews and Previews," *Art News*, vol. 54, November 1955, p. 50

Dore Ashton, "Drawings at the Janis Gallery," *Arts & Architecture*, vol. 72, December 1955, p. 34

Galleria dell'Obelisco, Rome, *Arshile Gorky*, opened February 4, 1957. Checklist with text by Afro Basaldella

La Loggia, Bologna, *Disegni di Arshile Gorky*, March 28–April 9, 1957

Sidney Janis Gallery, New York, *Thirty Three Paintings by Arshile Gorky*, December 2–28, 1957. Catalogue

Carlyle Burrows, "Gorky's Art Show Provocative," *The New York Herald Tribune Book Review*, December 8, 1957, p. 14

Howard Devree, "Diverse Moderns—Gorky in Retrospect—Others," *The New York Times*, December 8, 1957, p. 24

Bennett Schiff, "In the Art Galleries," *The New York Post*, December 8, 1957, p. 7

Robert M. Coates, "The Art Galleries," *The New Yorker*, vol. 33, December 14, 1957, pp. 141–142, 145

James Schuyler, "Reviews and Previews," *Art News*, vol. 56, December 1957, p. 10

"Exhibition at Janis Gallery," *Arts*, vol. 32, December 1957, p. 52

Dore Ashton, "Gorky & Contemporary American Painting," *Arts & Architecture*, vol. 75, January 1958, pp. 6, 34

Dore Ashton, "Lettre de New York," *Cimaise*, sér. 5., no. 3, January/February 1958, pp. 36–37

Pasadena Art Museum, *Paintings by Arshile Gorky*, January 3–February 2, 1958

Jules Langsner, "Los Angeles, Gorky: Myth vs. Reality," *Art News*, vol. 56, February 1958, p. 47

Sidney Janis Gallery, New York, *Late Drawings by Arshile Gorky*, September 28–October 24, 1959. Catalogue with anonymous text

Stuart Preston, "Modern Pioneers," *The New York Times*, October 4, 1959, section 2, p. x13

Hubert Crehan, "Gorky," *Art News*, vol. 58, October 1959, p. 12

James R. Mellow, "Late Drawings of Arshile Gorky," *Arts*, vol. 34, October 1959, pp. 55–56

Dore Ashton, "Art," *Arts & Architecture*, vol. 76, December 1959, p. 7

Martica Sawin, "New York Letter," *Art International*, vol. 3, December 1959, p. 10

University Gallery, University of Minnesota, Minneapolis, *Gorky Drawings*, October 27–December 2, 1960

David Anderson Gallery, New York, *Arshile Gorky: Drawings 1929 to 1934*, February 3–March 1, 1962. Catalogue

"The Bitter One," *Time*, vol. 79, February 23, 1962, p. 83

Max Kozloff, "New York Letter," *Art International*, vol. 6, April 1962, p. 42

S[idney] T[illim], "Gorky," *Arts Magazine*, vol. 36, April 1962, pp. 49–50

Sidney Janis Gallery, New York, *Paintings by Arshile Gorky from 1929 to 1948*, February 5–March 3, 1962. Catalogue

Stuart Preston, "An International Gathering," *The New York Times*, February 11, 1962, section 2, p. 15

"The Bitter One," *Time*, vol. 79, February 23, 1962, p. 83

L[awrence] C[ampbell], "Reviews and Previews," *Art News*, vol. 61, March 1962, p. 12

Max Kozloff, "New York Letter," *Art International*, vol. 6, April 1962, p. 42

S[idney] T[illim], "Gorky," *Arts Magazine*, vol. 36, April 1962, pp. 49–50

Everett Ellin Gallery, Los Angeles, *Arshile Gorky: 40 Drawings from the period 1929 through 1947*, April 9–May 5, 1962. Catalogue

XXXI Biennale Internazionale d'Arte: Arshile Gorky, Venice, June 16–October 7, 1962. Catalogue with text by Umbro Apollonio, pp. 113–116

Renato Barilli, "La Pittura di Arshile Gorky," *La Biennale di Venezia*, no. 43, April/June 1962, pp. 11–17

Umbro Apollonio, "Una Retrospettiva alla Biennale: Gorky," *Le Arti*, May 1962, p. 32

Mario Monteverdi, "La Biennale del pressappoco," *Corriere Lombardo—Milan*, June 14, 1962

"Sei rassegne retrospettive sessanta

esposizione italiani," *Il Gazzettino*, Venice, June 15, 1962

Heinz Keller, "Venedig XXXI Biennale," *Werk*, no. 49, sup. 183, August 1962, pp. 183–187

"Visita alla Biennale e prime imagini," *Domus*, no. 393, August 1962, p. 21

Henry Galy-Carles, "La Biennale de Venise: Les Rétrospectives d'Odilon Redon et d'Arshile Gorky," *Aujourd'hui*, vol. 6, September 1962, p. 39

Milton Gendel, "The Venice bazaar, 1962," *Art News*, vol. 61, September 1962, pp. 21–23, 53–54

Guy Habasque, "La XXXIe Biennale de Venise," *L'Oeil*, no. 93, September 1962, pp. 32–41, 72–73

Robert Melville, "Exhibitions: The Venice Biennale," *Architectural Review*, vol. 132, October 1962, p. 285

Klaus Jürgen-Fischer, "XXXI Biennale Venedig," *Das Kunstwerk*, vol. 16, September 1963, p. 3

Arshile Gorky Drawings. Organized by The International Council of The Museum of Modern Art, New York. Catalogue with text by Frank O'Hara. Traveled to Newcomb College, Tulane University, New Orleans, September 23–October 14, 1962; Chatham College, Pittsburgh, October 29–November 19; Watkins Institute, Nashville, Tennessee, January 9–30, 1963; Spiva Art Center, Joplin, Missouri, February 7–28; Smith College Museum of Art, Northampton, Massachusetts, March 15–April 5; Marshall College, Huntington, West Virginia, April 22–May 13; with bilingual catalogue to Seibu Department Store, Tokyo, July 26–August 11; to Westmar College, LeMars, Iowa, September 2–23; Washington University, St. Louis, October 4–25; The Arts Club of Chicago, November 10–December 15; Indiana University, Bloomington, January 2–23, 1964; Wells College, Aurora, New York, February 7–28; Northern Illinois University, DeKalb, March 16–April 6; The Jewish Museum, New York, April 21–June 22; under auspices of United States Information Service with catalogue *Zeichnungen von Arshile Gorky* with text by Frank O'Hara to Badischer Kunstverein, Karlsruhe, July 6–August 5; Hamburger Kunstverein, Hamburg, August 7–September 4; Amerika Haus, Berlin, September 11–October 6; Museum Folkwang, Essen, October 15–November 15; under auspices of Arts Council of Great Britain with catalogue with text by Frank O'Hara to York City Art Gallery, December 5–30; Institute of Contemporary Arts, London, January 6–February 13, 1965; Midland Group Gallery, Nottingham, February 20–March 6; City Gallery of Art, Bristol, March 13–April 3; Scottish National Gallery of Modern Art, Edinburgh, April 10–May 1; with additional exhibition, *Arshile Gorky, Paintings and Drawings*, see Tate Gallery, 1965, p. 277, to Palais des Beaux-Arts, Brussels, May 27–June 27; with catalogue *Arshile Gorky, Schilderijen en Tekeningen* with texts by J.C. Ebbinge Wubben and Robert Melville to Museum Boymans-van Beuningen, Rotterdam, July 24–September 5; with catalogue *Gorky* with text by Frank O'Hara to Museum des 20. Jahrhunderts, Vienna, September 18–October 17; with catalogue *Desenhos de Gorky* with text by Frank O'Hara to Sociedade Nacional de Belas Artes, Lisbon, November 23–December 23; with catalogue *Tegninger av Arshile Gorky* to Kunstnernes Hus, Oslo, January 22–February 13, 1966; with catalogue *Teckningar av Arshile Gorky* to Lunds Konsthall, Lund, Sweden, March 5–April 1; with catalogue *Zeichnungen von Arshile Gorky, 1905–1948* with text by Frank O'Hara to Kunstmuseum Basel, Offentliche Kunstsammlung, April 30–June 5; with catalogue *Arshile Gorky* with text by Frank O'Hara to Galerija Grada Zagreba, Zagreb, Yugoslavia, June-July; Galerija Doma Omladine, Belgrade, October 6–16; Galleria Nazionale d'Arte Moderna, Rome, April 2–May 15, 1967; with additional exhibition from The International Council of The Museum of Modern Art, New York, *Robert Motherwell: Works on Paper* with catalogue *"Sobre papel": Obras de Arshile Gorky* with texts by Jorge Romero Brest, Frank O'Hara and Waldo Rasmussen to Centro de Artes Visuales del Instituto Torcuato Di Tella, Buenos Aires, Argentina, November 29–December 23; with catalogue *"Sobre papel": Obras de Arshile Gorky y Obras de Robert Motherwell* with texts by Frank O'Hara and Waldo Rasmussen to Museo de Bellas Artes, Caracas, January 21–February 14, 1968; with catalogue *Dibiyos de Arshile Gorky y Obras Sobre Papel de Robert Motherwell* with texts by Frank O'Hara and Waldo Rasmussen to Biblioteca Luis Angel Arango, Bogotà, March 21–April 11; Galeria Universitaria Aristos, Mexico City, May 3–June 5

Brian O'Doherty, "Gorky: Private Language, Universal Theme," *The New York Times*, May 10, 1964, section 2, p. 17

Otto Breicha, "Wien: Arshile Gorky, Zeichnungen," *Werk*, vol. 52, November 1965, p. 271

C.H., "Basel: Zeichnungen von Arshile Gorky," *Werk*, vol. 53, June 1966, pp. 133–134

The Museum of Modern Art, New York, *Arshile Gorky, 1904–1948*, December 19, 1962–February 12, 1963. Catalogue published as William C. Seitz, *Arshile Gorky: Paintings, Drawings, Studies*, New York, 1962, foreword by Julien Levy. Traveled to The Washington Gallery of Modern Art, Washington, D.C., March 12–April 14

Jane Debran, "The Genius of Gorky on View," *Brooklyn Eagle*, December 28, 1962

"Tardy Tribute to a Tragic Figure," *Life*, extra New York edition, December 29, 1962, pp. 52–53

"The Bitter One," *Newsweek*, vol. 60, December 31, 1962, p. 39

Suzanne Kiplinger, "Arshile Gorky," *The Village Voice*, January 3, 1963, p. 9

Harold Rosenberg, "The Art Galleries, Art and Identity: The Unfinished Masterpiece," *The New Yorker*, vol. 38, January 5, 1963, pp. 70–77. Slightly revised in Rosenberg, 1964, see General Books, p. 279

Hilton Kramer, "Art," *The Nation*, vol. 196, January 5, 1963, pp. 38–39

Alfred Frankenstein, "Gorky's Stature Keeps Growing," *San Francisco Chronicle*, January 6, 1963

Betty Kaufman, "Arshile Gorky," *Commonweal*, January 25, 1963, pp. 473–475

George Dennison, "The Crisis-Art of Arshile Gorky," *Arts Magazine*, vol. 37, February 1963, pp. 14–18

Stuart Preston, "New York," *Burlington Magazine*, vol. 105, February 1963, p. 84

Jean M. White, "Modern Art Gallery to Open Exhibit," *The Washington Post*, March 8, 1963, p. A7

Leslie Judd Alexander, "Gorky, Greene Are on Exhibit," *The Washington Post*, March 17, 1963, p. G6

Lawrence Alloway, "Gorky," *Artforum*, vol. 1, March 1963, pp. 28–31

Dore Ashton, "New York," *Das Kunstwerk*, vol. 16, April 1963, p. 31

Dore Ashton, "New York Commentary," *Studio*, vol. 163, May 1963, pp. 182–183

Irving Sandler, "New York Letter," *Quadrum*, no. 14, 1963, pp. 115–124

The San Diego Art Institute and La Jolla Art Center, *Arshile Gorky: Paintings and Drawings 1927–1937, from the Collection of Mr. and Mrs. Hans Burkhardt*, February 21–April 7, 1963. Checklist with text by Hans Burkhardt

J[on] R[euschel], "Arshile Gorky," *Artforum*, vol. 1, May 1963, pp. 46–47

G.S.S., "Gorky, when the going was rough," *Art News*, vol. 62, April 1963, pp. 27, 67

Tate Gallery, London, *Arshile Gorky, Paintings and Drawings*, April 2–May 2, 1965. Catalogue with texts by Robert Melville and William C. Seitz

Francis Hoyland, "The Composer," *The Listener*, April 15, 1965, p. 568

H.P., "Exhibition of Gorky Paintings at the Tate," *The Irish Times*, April 28, 1965

James Burr, "Cross-currents in Contemporary Art," *Apollo*, vol. 81, April 1965, p. 330

Alastair Gordon, "Art in the Modern Manner," *Connoisseur*, vol. 158, April 1965, p. 260

Keith Roberts, "London," *Burlington Magazine*, vol. 107, May 1965, pp. 270–271

Joseph Rykwert, "Mostre a Londra," *Domus*, no. 428, July 1965, p. 63

Cyril Barrett, "London Commentary," *Das Kunstwerk*, vol. 19, August 1965, p. 28

University Art Gallery, University of California, Berkeley, *Arshile Gorky, Paintings and Drawings—1927–1937*, May 7–31, 1965

Gallery Lounge, San Francisco State College, *Arshile Gorky, Paintings and Drawings from 1927–1937*, September 14–October 10, 1965

West Gallery, Pennsylvania Academy of Fine Arts, Philadelphia, *Paintings and Drawings by Arshile Gorky*, November 8–December 10, 1967. Checklist

Richard Feigen Gallery, Chicago, *Arshile Gorky: Drawings from the Julien Levy Collection*, March 18–April 26, 1969. Catalogue

J. Millard Tawes Fine Arts Center, University of Maryland Art Department and Art Gallery, University of Maryland, College Park, *The Drawings of Arshile Gorky*, March 20–April 27, 1969. Catalogue by Brooks Joyner with texts by William H. Gerdts and George Levitine

Hathorn Gallery, Skidmore College, Saratoga Springs, New York, *The Drawings of Arshile Gorky*, October 21–November 9, 1969. Catalogue

M. Knoedler & Co., Inc., New York, *Gorky: Drawings*, November 25–December 27, 1969. Catalogue with text by Jim M. Jordan

M[iriam] B[rummer], "Arshile Gorky," *Arts Magazine*, vol. 44, November 1969, p. 62

Hilton Kramer, "Arshile Gorky: Between Two Worlds," *The New York Times*, December 7, 1969, p. 29, section 2. Reprinted in Kramer, 1973, see General Books, p. 279

Louis Finkelstein, "Becoming is Meaning: Gorky as a Draftsman," *Art News*, vol. 68, December 1969, pp. 44–47

Dore Ashton, "New York Commentary," *Studio International*, vol. 179, February 1970, pp. 73–74

Jerrold Lanes, "New York," *Artforum*, vol. 8, February 1970, p. 74

Carter Ratcliff, "New York Letter," *Art International*, vol. 14, February 1970, pp. 77–78

The J.L. Hudson Company Gallery, Detroit, *Arshile Gorky Drawings*, January 7–February 7, 1970

Galerie Dieter Brusberg, Hannover, *Arshile Gorky*, June 8–September 12, 1971

Galleria Galatea, Turin, *Arshile Gorky*, February 29–March 27, 1972. Catalogue with text by Tommaso Chiaretti

Dunkelman [Gallery], Toronto, *Arshile Gorky, 1904–1948*, October 14–28, 1972. Catalogue

Joyce Zemans, "Arshile Gorky, Dunkelman Gallery," *Artscanada*, vol. 29, December 1972/January 1973, pp. 79–80

Allan Stone Gallery, New York, *Arshile Gorky, Paintings and Drawings*, November 14–December 22, 1972

April Kingsley, "Reviews and Previews," *Art News*, vol. 72, January 1973, p. 18

April Kingsley, "New York Letter," *Art International*, vol. 17, February 1973, p. 42

Ellen Lubell, "Reviews," *Arts Magazine*, vol. 47, February 1973, p. 83

Ruth S. Schaffner Gallery, Santa Barbara, *Arshile Gorky, Drawings and Paintings from 1931 to 1940*, March 25–April 29, 1973

William Wilson, "In the Southern California Galleries: from Gorky to Ron Davis," *Art News*, vol. 72, Summer 1973, p. 25

Oklahoma Art Center, Oklahoma City, *An Exhibition of Drawings by Arshile Gorky*, October 28–November 25, 1973. Catalogue with text by Karlen Mooradian. Traveled to Arkansas Art Center, Little Rock, December 18, 1973–January 6, 1974; New Orleans Museum of Art, January 19–February 17; Amarillo Art Center, Texas, March 10–April 7; University Museum, Illinois State University, Normal, April 21–May 19

M. Knoedler & Co., Inc., New York, *Arshile Gorky: Works on Paper*, January 9–February 1, 1975

Hayden Herrera, "Arshile Gorky: Works on Paper," *Art News*, vol. 74, March 1975, pp. 97–105

W. Neil Marshall, "Arshile Gorky," *Arts Magazine*, vol. 49, April 1975, p. 71

Roberta Smith, "Reviews," *Artforum*, vol. 13, April 1975, p. 75

Nina Bremer, "Arshile Gorky: Works on Paper," *Pantheon*, vol. 33, July-August-September 1975, p. 277

University Art Museum, University of Texas at Austin, *Arshile Gorky: Drawings to Paintings*, October 12–November 23, 1975. Catalogue with texts by Alice Baber, Donald B. Goodall, Isobel Grossman, Hayden Herrera, Jim M. Jordan, Karlen Mooradian, Reuben Nakian, Harry Rand, Ethel Schwabacher and the artist. Traveled to San Francisco Museum of Art, December 4, 1975–January 12, 1976; Neuberger Museum, State University of New York, Purchase, New York, February 10–March 14; Munson-Williams-Proctor Institute, Utica, New York, April 4–May 9

David Bourdon, "Gorky Translated Through Tragedy," *The Village Voice*, vol. 21, March 1, 1976, p. 99

Hilton Kramer, "Gorky–Separating the Artist from the Myth," *The New York Times*, February 22, 1976

Arshile Gorky: Paintings & Drawings 1975–76. Organized by The Arts Council of Great Britain. Catalogue with text by John Golding. Traveled to The Museum of Modern Art, Oxford, December 19, 1976–January 16, 1977; Serpentine Gallery, London, March 12–April 11

James Burr, "Round the Galleries: The Last Seven Years," *Apollo*, March 1977, p. 219

Washburn Gallery, New York, *Arshile Gorky—In Memory*, November 2–28, 1978. Catalogue with reprinted texts by André Breton and Willem de Kooning

Susan Grace Galassi, "Arshile Gorky," *Arts Magazine*, vol. 53, February 1979, p. 20

Richard Whelan, "Arshile Gorky," *Art News*, vol. 78, January 1979, pp. 139, 144

The Newark Museum, *Murals Without Walls: Arshile Gorky's Aviation Murals Rediscovered*, November 15, 1978–March 15, 1979. Catalogue with texts by Ruth Bowman, Jim M. Jordan, Samuel C. Miller and Francis V. O'Connor and reprinted texts by Frederick Kiesler and the artist. Traveled to Memorial Art Gallery, University of Rochester, New York,

July 1–August 6; Hirshhorn Museum and Sculpture Garden, Smithsonian Institution, Washington, D.C., October 4–November 25

Sam Hunter, "Mural, Mural, Behind the Wall," *New Jersey Monthly*, vol. 2, October 1978, pp. 44–47

Vivien Raynor, "Art People: Phantom Mural Flys Again," *The New York Times*, November 10, 1978, p. C 21

"Murals without Walls," *The Newark Museum News Notes*, November 1978, pp. 1–2

John Russell, "Art: Lost Murals of Arshile Gorky," *The New York Times*, November 24, 1978

"Airport Archaeology," *Art in America*, vol. 65, January 1979, p. 146

"Gorky's Murals without walls: Newark Museum," *Progressive Architecture*, vol. 60, January 1979, pp. 23–24

John Ashbery, "Sweet Arshile, Bless Your Dear Heart," *New York Magazine*, February 5, 1979, pp. 52–53

E. Schwartz, "Gorky murals: a bit of detective work," *Art News*, vol. 78, February 1979, pp. 136–137

Xavier Fourcade, Inc., New York, *Arshile Gorky, Important Paintings and Drawings*, April 3–28, 1979. Catalogue

Hilton Kramer, "A Rare Gorky and Prints of Prendergast," *The New York Times*, April 13, 1979, pp. C 1, C 24

Hirshhorn Museum and Sculpture Garden, Smithsonian Institution, Washington, D.C., *Arshile Gorky: the Hirshhorn Museum and Sculpture Garden Collection*, October 4–November 25, 1979. Catalogue with text by Phyllis Rosenzweig

Selected Bibliography

I. General

A. BOOKS

John D. Graham, *System and Dialectics of Art,* New York, 1937. Reprinted as *John D. Graham's System and Dialectics of Art,* Marcia Epstein Allentuck, ed., Baltimore, 1971

Jerome Mellquist, *The Emergence of an American Art,* New York, 1942, p. 169

Samuel M. Kootz, *New Frontiers in American Painting,* New York, 1943, p. 49

Sidney Janis, *Abstract and Surrealist Art in America,* New York, 1944, p. 120

André Breton, *Le Surréalisme et la Peinture,* New York, 1945, pp. 196–197

Yale University Art Gallery, New Haven, *Collection of the Société Anonyme,* 1950, pp. 34–35. Text by George Heard Hamilton

John I.H. Baur, *Revolution and Tradition in Modern American Art,* Cambridge, Massachusetts, 1951, pp. 70–71

Thomas B. Hess, *Abstract Painting: Background and American Phase,* New York, 1951, passim

Modern Artists in America, Robert Motherwell, ed., New York, 1951, passim

Selden Rodman, *The Eye of Man,* New York, 1955, pp. 122, 136–137

William C. Seitz, *Abstract-Expressionist Painting in America: An Interpretation Based on the Work and Thought of Six Key Figures,* Ph.D. dissertation, Princeton University, 1955, passim. Publication forthcoming

Rudi Blesh, *Modern Art U.S.A.: Men, Rebellion, Conquest, 1900–1956,* New York, 1956, pp. 132, 244–245, 257–259

Lloyd Goodrich, "Arshile Gorky" in *New Art in America: Fifty Painters of the 20th Century,* John I.H. Baur, ed., Greenwich, Connecticut, 1957, pp. 188–191

Marcel Brion et al., *Art Since 1945,* New York, 1958, pp. 289, 293, 294, 296, 297, 300, 301, 304, 308, 326

Stuart Preston, "Painting in the United States: 1885–1957" in *Modern Art, A Pictorial Anthology,* Charles McCurdy, ed., New York, 1958, pp. 146, 204

Lloyd Goodrich and John I.H. Baur, *American art of our century,* New York, 1961, pp. 114–117

Clement Greenberg, *Art and Culture: Critical Essays,* Boston, 1961, pp. 112, 125, 195, 212, 213, 214, 216, 220, 230, 231, 233, 234, 235

Dore Ashton, *The Unknown Shore: A View of Contemporary Art,* Toronto, 1962, pp. 23, 29, 42, 46, 48–55, 71, 82, 207–208

Thomas M. Messer, "Gorky" in *La Galerie des Hommes Célèbres,* Bernard Dorival, ed., Paris, 1964, pp. 208–211

Harold Rosenberg, *The Anxious Object: Art Today and Its Audience,* New York, 1964, pp. 26, 99–106, 109, 261, 249

Henry Geldzahler, *American Painting in the Twentieth Century,* New York, 1965, pp. 152, 179, 180–182, 183, 188, 191, 197

Edward F. Fry, *Cubism,* New York, 1966, pp. 66–67

Theories of Modern Art: A Source Book by Artists and Critics, Herschel B. Chipp, ed., Berkeley, Los Angeles, 1968, pp. 510, 532–536

Francis V. O'Connor, *Federal Support for the Visual Arts: The New Deal and Now,* Greenwich, Connecticut, 1969, passim

Harold Rosenberg, *Artworks and Packages,* New York, 1969, pp. 68, 136, 191, 202, 212, 216, 222

Irving Sandler, *The Triumph of American Painting: A History of Abstract Expressionism,* New York, Washington, D.C., 1970, passim

Paul Cummings, *Dictionary of Contemporary American Artists,* New York, 1971, p. 143

Stuart Davis, Diane Kelder, ed., New York, 1971, pp. 178–183, 192–194

Dore Ashton, *The New York School: A Cultural Reckoning,* New York, 1972, pp. 1, 2, 3, 16, 20, 22–23, 25, 27, 31, 47, 61, 68, 75, 94, 96, 99, 100, 109, 113, 119, 123, 124, 147–148, 155, 159, 164, 166, 173

Three Generations of Twentieth-Century Art: The Sidney and Harriet Janis Collection of The Museum of Modern Art, New York, 1972, pp. 98, 114, 115, 184. Texts by Alfred H. Barr, Jr. and William Rubin

Sam Hunter, *American Art of the 20th Century,* New York, 1972, pp. 160, 165, 167, 168, 171, 172, 189, 191, 211, 213, 216

The New Deal Art Projects: An Anthology of Memoirs, Francis V. O'Connor, ed., Washington, D.C., 1972, pp. 59, 60, 65, 70, 108, 116, 130, 204, 213, 224, 229, 232, 235, 236, 237, 244, 257, 321, 323

Harold Rosenberg, *The De-Definition of Art,* New York, 1972, pp. 35, 64, 100, 101, 130, 131, 147, 183, 185, 186, 189, 193, 194, 218

Hilton Kramer, *The Age of the Avant-Garde: An Art Chronicle of 1956–1972,* New York, 1973, pp.300, 313–315, 327, 349, 351, 393, 421

Richard D. McKinzie, *The New Deal For Artists,* Princeton, New Jersey, 1973, p. 166

The Genius of American Painting, John Wilmerding, ed., London, 1973, pp. 252, 254, 261–263, 265, 267–268, 270, 271,

272, 281, 284, 288, 289, 290, 332

Art for the Millions: Essays from the 1930's by Artists and Administrators of the Works Progress Administration Federal Art Project, Francis V. O'Connor, ed., Greenwich, Connecticut, 1973, pp. 24, 30, 31, 70–71, 72, 73, 278, 299, 303

Brian O'Doherty, *American Masters: The Voice and the Myth*, New York, ca. 1973, pp. 53, 57, 126, 156, 157

Lawrence Alloway, *Topics in American Art Since 1945*, New York, 1975, pp. 19, 20, 21, 22, 25, 26

Readings in American Art 1900–1975, Barbara Rose, ed., New York, 1975, pp. 98, 107–110, 186

Barbara Rose, *American Art Since 1900*, New York, 1975, pp. 104–105, 106, 120, 123, 125–127, 129, 131, 139, 142–147, 154–156, 159, 162, 179, 263

Julien Levy, *Memoir of an Art Gallery*, New York, 1977, pp. 128, 136, 156, 259, 278, 280–285, 287–294

Milton W. Brown, *American Art: Painting, Sculpture, Architecture, Decorative Arts, Photography*, New York, 1979, pp. 457–458, 477–479

B. ARTICLES

James Johnson Sweeney, "L'art contemporain aux Etats-Unis," *Cahiers d'Art*, Paris, vol. 13, no. 1-2, 1938, pp. 45–52

Clement Greenberg, "Art Chronicle: The Decline of Cubism," *Partisan Review*, vol. 15, March 1948, pp. 366–369

Peter Blanc, "The Artist and the Atom," *Magazine of Art*, vol. 44, April 1951, pp. 145–152

William Seitz, "Spirit, Time and 'Abstract Expressionism,'" *Magazine of Art*, vol. 46, February 1953, pp. 80–87

Clement Greenberg, "'American-Type' Painting," *Partisan Review*, vol. 22, Spring 1955, pp. 179–196. Reprinted in Greenberg, 1961, see General Books, p. 279

Sidney Geist, "Prelude: The 1930's," *Arts*, vol. 30, September 1956, pp. 49–55

William Rubin, "The New York School—Then and Now, Part II," *Art International*, vol. 2, May-June 1958, pp. 19–22

Lawrence Alloway, "The New American Painting," *Art International*, vol. 3, no. 3-4, 1959, pp. 21–29

Robert Goldwater, "Reflections on the New York School," *Quadrum*, no. 8, 1960, pp. 17–36

Dore Ashton, "Seven American Decades," *Studio*, vol. 165, April 1963, pp. 148–153

Edward B. Henning, "In Pursuit of Content," *The Bulletin of the Cleveland Museum of Art*, vol. 50, October 1963, pp. 218–239

Franz Schulze, "On Modern American Painting," *Apollo*, vol. 78, October 1963, pp. 274–280

Dore Ashton, "La voix du tourbillon dans l'Amérique de Kafka," *XXe Siècle*, nouvelle série, XXVIe année, May 1964, pp. 92–96

Richard Armstrong, "Abstract Expressionism Was an American Revolution," *Canadian Art*, vol. 21, September 1964, pp. 263–269

Kenneth B. Sawyer, "The Grossman Collection, U.S. collectors of modern art—2," *Studio International*, vol. 169, February 1965, pp. 82–87

Clement Greenberg, "America Takes the Lead 1945–1965," *Art in America*, vol. 53, August-September 1965, pp. 108–109

Lawrence Alloway, "The Biomorphic Forties," *Artforum*, vol. 4, September 1965, pp. 18–22

Max Kozloff, "The Critical Reception of Abstract-Expressionism," *Arts Magazine*, vol. 40, December 1965, pp. 27–33

Thomas M. Messer, "Kandinsky en Amérique," *XXe Siècle*, no. 28, December 1966, pp. 111–117

Rosalind Constable, "The Betty Parsons Collection," *Art News*, vol. 67, March 1968, pp. 48–49, 58–60

Francis V. O'Connor, "New Deal Murals in New York," *Artforum*, vol. 7, November 1968, pp. 41–49

Dore Ashton, "Response to Crisis in American Art," *Art in America*, vol. 57, January 1969, pp. 24–35

Jacob Kainen, "Prints of the 30's: Reflections on the Federal Art Project," *Artists Proof*, vol. 11, 1971, pp. 34–41

Susan C. Larson, "The American Abstract Artists: A Documentary History," *Archives of American Art Journal*, vol. 14, no. 1, 1974, pp. 2–6

Ellen H. Johnson, "American Art of the Twentieth Century," *Apollo*, vol. 103, February 1976, pp. 128–135

Hayden Herrera, "We Were the Cafeteria People," *Mulch*, vol. 304, Spring-Summer 1976, pp. 41–57

Hayden Herrera, "John Graham: Modernist Turns Magus," *Arts Magazine*, vol. 51, October 1976, pp. 100–105

Stephen C. Foster, "Making a Movement Modern: The Role of the Avant-Garde Critic," *Art International*, vol. 20, October-November 1976, pp. 59–61, 63

Eila Kokkinen, "John Graham During the 1940s," *Arts Magazine*, vol. 51, November 1976, pp. 99–103

"Early Abstract Expressionism: The 1940s," *Flash Art/Heute Kunst*, no. 86–87, January-February 1979, pp. 26–28

II. On the Artist

A. MONOGRAPHS

John Loftus, *Arshile Gorky*, Master's thesis, Columbia University, 1952

Ethel K. Schwabacher, *Arshile Gorky*, New York, 1957. Preface by Lloyd Goodrich, Introduction by Meyer Schapiro, letters and statements by the artist

Alfred Frankenstein, "An American Artist's Tragic Insights," *New York Herald Tribune Book Review*, December 22, 1957, p.6

Stuart Davis, "Handmaiden of Misery," *Saturday Review*, vol. 40, December 28, 1957, pp. 16–17

Robert Rosenblum, "Arshile Gorky," *Arts*, vol. 32, January 1958, pp. 30–33

Mardiros Sarkisian, "Arshile Gorky—A Struggle for Recognition," *Hoosharar*, vol. 45, February 1, 1958, pp. 6–9

Sonya Rudikoff, "Gorky and Tomlin," *Partisan Review*, Winter 1958, pp. 157–160

Fairfield Porter, *Art News*, vol. 62, May 1958, p. 43

Robert F. Reiff, *College Art Journal*, vol. 18, *Winter* 1959, pp. 191–192

Harold Rosenberg, *Arshile Gorky: The Man, the Time, the*

Idea, New York, 1962

Robert Goldwater, "The Genius of the Moujik" *Saturday Review*, vol. 45, May 19, 1962, p. 38

Sidney Geist, "Gorky/Rosenberg: two reviews," *Scrap*, no. 8, June 14, 1962, pp. 1–3

Paul Goodman, "Portrait of the Artist" *Partisan Review*, vol. 29, Summer 1962, pp. 448–450

Harold Rosenberg and Paul Goodman, "Gorky and History: an Exchange," *Partisan Review*, vol. 29, Fall 1962, pp. 587–593

Robert Reiff, "Harold Rosenberg: Arshile Gorky," *Art Journal*, vol. 22, Spring 1963, pp. 148–152

Julien Levy, *Arshile Gorky*, New York, 1966

James R. Mellow, "The Most Elegant Stylist," *The New York Times Book Review*, March 31, 1968, pp. 6–7.

Gorky Drawings, New York, 1970. Facsimile reproductions

Robert F. Reiff, *A Stylistic Analysis of Arshile Gorky's Art from 1943–1948*, New York, 1977 (photo reprint of Ph.D. dissertation, Columbia University, 1961)

Karlen Mooradian, *Arshile Gorky Adoian*, Chicago, 1978

Karlen Mooradian, *The Many Worlds of Arshile Gorky*, Chicago, 1980

Jim M. Jordan and Robert Goldwater, *The Paintings of Arshile Gorky: A Critical Catalogue*, New York, forthcoming

Harry Rand, *Arshile Gorky: The Implications of Symbols*, Montclair, New Jersey, forthcoming

B. ARTICLES

"Newark's Verdict is Awaited on Arshile Gorky's Murals," *Newark Star-Eagle*, November 12, 1936, p. 4

Frederick J. Kiesler, "Murals without Walls: Relating to Gorky's Newark Project," *Art Front*, vol. 2, December 1936, pp. 10–11. Reprinted in The Newark Museum, *Murals Without Walls*, 1978–79, see One-Man Exhibitions, p. 277

Malcolm Johnson, "Café Life in New York," *The New York Sun*, August 22, 1941, p. 15. Includes statement by Gorky

Milton S. Fox, "Camouflage and the Artist," *Magazine of Art*, vol. 35, April 1942, pp. 136–137, 154, 156

James Johnson Sweeney, "Five American Painters," *Harper's Bazaar*, vol. 78, April 1944, pp. 122, 124

Talcott B. Clapp, "A Painter in a Glass House," *Sunday Republican Magazine* (Waterbury, Connecticut), February 9, 1948

"Old House Made New," *Life*, vol. 24, February 16, 1948, pp. 90–92

"Arshile Gorky Dies," *Art Digest*, vol. 22, August 1, 1948, p. 27

Malcolm Cowley, "Arshile Gorky—A Note from a Friend," *New York Herald Tribune*, September 5, 1948, section 6, p. 3

"Arshile Gorky," *Art News*, vol. 47, September 1948, p. 56. Obituary

Willem de Kooning, "Editor's letters," *Art News*, vol. 47, January 1949, p. 6

Lewis Balamuth, "I Met A. Gorky (1938)," *Color and Rhyme*, vol. 19, 1949, pp. 2–3

Mary Burliuk, "Arshile Gorky," *Color and Rhyme*, vol. 19, 1949, pp. 1–2

"Our Editorial," *Color and Rhyme*, vol. 19, 1949, p. 1

Alfred H. Barr, Jr., "Gorky, de Kooning, Pollock," *Art News*, vol. 49, Summer 1950, pp. 22, 60. Reprinted in "Towards a Definition of Abstract Expressionism," in *The Baltimore Museum of Art News*, vol. 22, February 1959

Elaine de Kooning, "Gorky: Painter of His Own Legend," *Art News*, vol. 49, January 1951, pp. 38–41. Occasioned by Whitney Museum of American Art, New York, Gorky exhibition, 1951, see One-Man Exhibitions, p. 274

Stuart Davis, "Arshile Gorky in the 1930's: A Personal Recollection," *Magazine of Art*, vol. 44, February 1951, pp. 56–58. Occasioned by Whitney Museum of American Art, New York, Gorky exhibition, 1951, see One-Man Exhibitions, p. 274

Lloyd Goodrich, "Eight Works by Arshile Gorky With Notes by Lloyd Goodrich," *Magazine of Art*, vol. 44, February 1951, pp. 59–61

Lloyd Goodrich, "Homage to Gorky." Unpublished manuscript dated February 1951, on deposit in Gorky file, Whitney Museum of American Art, New York

Balcomb Greene, "Essay on Gorky." Unpublished manuscript dated February 1951, on deposit in Gorky file, Whitney Museum of American Art, New York

James Thrall Soby, "Arshile Gorky," *Magazine of Art*, vol. 44, February 1951, p. 56

William C. Seitz, "Arshile Gorky's 'The Plow and the Song,'" *Allen Memorial Art Museum Bulletin*, vol. 12, Fall 1954, pp. 4–15

Karlen Mooradian, "Arshile Gorky," *The Armenian Review*, vol. 8, Summer 1955, pp. 49–58

Arti Visive, no. 6–7, Summer 1957. Special Gorky issue in Italian and English with text by Toti Scialoja and excerpts from Schwabacher, 1957, see Monographs, p. 280

Meyer Schapiro, "Gorky: The creative influence," *Art News*, vol. 56, September 1957, pp. 28–31, 52. Reprinted in Schwabacher, 1957, see Monographs, p. 280 and Meyer Schapiro, *Modern Art, 19th and 20th Centuries: Selected Papers*, New York, 1978

Alain Jouffroy, "Arshile Gorky et les secrets de la nuit," *Cahiers du Musée de Poche*, no. 2, June 1959, pp. 75–85

Harold Rosenberg "Arshile Gorky: The Last Move," *The Hudson Review*, vol. 13, Spring 1960, pp. 102–111

Milton Resnick, ". . . A Distant Eye-Time," *Scrap*, no. 8, June 14, 1962, p. 2

Dore Ashton, "Arshile Gorky peintre romantique," *XXe Siècle*, no. 19, June 1962, pp. 76–81, English translation, pp. 127–128, 130, 132, 134, 136. Reprinted in *XXe Siècle*, no. 40, June 1973, pp. 87–91

Mardiros Sarkisian, "Gorky," *Ararat*, vol. 3, Summer 1962

Harold Rosenberg, "Arshile Gorky: his art and influence," *Portfolio & Art News Annual*, no. 5, 1962, pp. 100–114

William S. Rubin, "Arshile Gorky, Surrealism and the New American Painting," *Art International*, vol. 7, February 25, 1963, pp. 27–38. Portions delivered as lecture of same title, The Museum of Modern Art, New York, in conjunction with *Gorky* exhibition, 1962–63, see One-Man Exhibitions, p. 276. Reprinted in The Metropolitan Museum of Art, New York, *New York Painting and Sculpture*, 1969, see Group Exhibitions, p. 272

George Dennison, "The Crisis-Art of Arshile Gorky," *Arts Magazine*, vol. 37, February 1963, pp. 14–18. Occasioned by

The Museum of Modern Art, New York, *Gorky* exhibition, 1962–63, see One-Man Exhibitions, p. 276, and publication of Rosenberg, 1962, see Monographs, p. 280

Margaret Osborn, "The Mystery of Arshile Gorky: A personal account," *Art News*, vol. 62, February 1963, pp. 42–43, 58–61. Occasioned by The Museum of Modern Art, New York, *Gorky* exhibition, 1962–63, see One-Man Exhibitions, p. 276

Donald Malafront, "Mystery of Newark mural revealed in story of Gorky," *Newark Star-Ledger*, March 17, 1963

Robert Reiff, "The Late Works of Arshile Gorky," *Art Journal*, vol. 22, Spring 1963, pp. 148–152. Revised chapter from Reiff, 1977, see Monographs, p. 281

Nick Dante Vaccaro, "Gorky's Debt to Gaudier-Brzeska," *Art Journal*, vol. 23, Fall 1963, pp. 33–34

Jo Miller, "The Prints of Arshile Gorky," *Brooklyn Museum Annual*, vol. 6, 1964–65, pp. 57–61

"Baltimore Museum of Art: Two Works by Arshile Gorky," *The Burlington Magazine*, vol. 107, January 1965, p. 54

Karlen Mooradian, "The Unknown Gorky," *Art News*, vol. 66, September 1967, pp. 52–53, 66–68

Karlen Mooradian, "Arshile Gorky: The Prompter," *Harvard Art Review*, vol. 2, Winter 1967

Karlen Mooradian, "The Gardener from Eden," *Ararat*, vol. 9, Winter 1968, pp. 2–13

Karlen Mooradian, "The Philosophy of Arshile Gorky (Vosdanik Adoian)," *Armenian Digest*, vol. 2, September-October 1971, pp. 52–74

Karlen Mooradian, "The Crisis of Cultural Identity in the Art of Arshile Gorky and Reuben Nakian," *Armenian Digest* (New York), October 1973, pp. 36–40, 61

Ararat, vol. 9, Winter 1973, Special Gorky issue with articles:
"Chronology of Vosdanik Adoian (Arshile Gorky)," pp. 3–5

Karlen Mooradian, "The Man from Van," pp. 6–8

Karlen Mooradian, "A Sister Recalls: An Interview with Vartoosh Mooradian," pp. 9–18

"The Letters of Arshile Gorky to Vartoosh, Moorad and Karlen Mooradian," pp. 19–43

Karlen Mooradian, "Remembrances of Gorky, Conversations with Milton Resnick, Robert Jonas, Willem de Kooning, Reuben Nakian, Max Schnitzler and Yenovk der Hagopian," pp. 44–55

Jean-Luc Bordeaux, "Arshile Gorky: His Formative Period (1925–1937)," *American Art Review*, vol. 1, May-June 1974, pp. 94–102

Nicolas Calas, "A Tough Nut to Crack," *Artforum*, vol. 13, May 1975, pp. 48–49

Hayden Herrera, "Gorky's Self Portraits: The Artist by Himself," *Art in America*, vol. 64, March 1976, pp. 56–64

Arts Magazine, vol. 50, March 1976. Special Gorky issue with articles:

Stewart Buettner, "Arshile Gorky and The Abstract-Surreal," pp. 86–87

Gene Davis, "Gorky Taught Me That: A Remembrance of Arshile Gorky," p. 81

Balcomb Greene, "Memories of Arshile Gorky," pp. 108–110

Hayden Herrera, "The Sculptures of Arshile Gorky," pp. 88–90

Jeffrey Hoffeld, "Arshile Gorky; Collecting and Connoisseurship," pp. 106–107

Jim M. Jordan, "Arshile Gorky at Crooked Run Farm," pp. 99–103

Jacob Kainen, "Memories of Arshile Gorky," pp. 96–98

Diane Karp, "Arshile Gorky's Iconography," pp. 83–85

Francis V. O'Connor, "The Economy of Patronage; Arshile Gorky on the Art Projects," pp. 94–96

Harvey Quaytman, "Arshile Gorky's Early Paintings," pp. 104–105

Harry Rand, "The Calendars of Arshile Gorky," pp. 70–80

Robert Reiff, "Arshile Gorky's Object Matter," pp. 91–93

Barbara Rose, "Arshile Gorky and John Graham: Eastern Exiles in a Western World," pp. 62–69

Nicolas Calas, "Letters to the Editor," *Arts Magazine*, vol. 50 June 1976, p. 110

Grace Glueck, "Art People," *The New York Times*, December 17, 1976, p. C 18

"Cheating the philistines," *Art News*, vol. 76, September 1977, pp. 20–22

M. P. Lader, "Graham, Gorky, de Kooning, and the 'Ingres Revival' in America," *Arts Magazine*, vol. 52, March 1978, pp. 94–99

Duncan MacMillan, "The Outsider: Gorky and America," *Art International*, vol. XXIII, Summer 1979, pp. 104–106

Terukazu Suenaga, "Mirror of Memory: Gorky's Cruel Change," *Mizue*, no. 894, September 9, 1979, pp. 5–45

Barbara Rose, "Gorky, Tragic poet of Abstract Expressionism," *Vogue*, vol. 169, October 1979, pp. 355, 386

Michael FitzGerald, "Arshile Gorky's 'The Limit,'" *Arts Magazine*, vol. 54, March 1980, pp. 110–115

III. By the Artist

[Interview with Gorky] in "Fetish of Antique Stifles Art Here, says Gorky Kin," *New York Evening Post*, September 15, 1926. Reprinted in Rosenberg, 1962, see Monographs, p. 280

"Thirst," *Grand Central School of Art Quarterly*, New York, November 1926. Poem, reprinted in Schwabacher, 1957, see Monographs, p. 280

"Stuart Davis," *Creative Art*, vol. 9, September 1931, pp. 212–217. Reprinted in part in Schwabacher, 1957, see Monographs, p. 280 and Chipp, 1968, see General Books, p. 279

"My Murals for the Newark Airport: An Interpretation," December 1936. Prepared for *Art for the Millions*, Emanuel Benson, ed., never published. Various versions subsequently published in Schwabacher, 1957, Rosenberg, 1962, see Monographs, p. 280; Chipp, 1968, O'Connor, 1973, Rose, 1975, see General Books, pp. 279–280; The Newark Museum, exhibition catalogue, 1978, see One-Man Exhibitions, p. 277; typescript version "General Description of Newark Airport Murals" on deposit in Gorky file, Whitney Museum of American Art, New York

"Garden in Sochi," June 26, 1942. Manuscript on deposit in Collections Archive, The Museum of Modern Art, New York. Reprinted with one line omitted in Schwabacher, 1957, see Monographs, p. 280; in part in Chipp, 1968, see General Books, p. 279; *Arti Visive*, 1957, see Articles, p. 281

"Camouflage," *Grand Central School of Art Catalogue*, New York, 1942. Course announcement, reprinted in Schwabacher,

1957, and Rosenberg, 1962, see Monographs, p. 280

André Breton, *Young Cherry Trees Secured Against Hares*, New York and London, 1946. Drawings by Gorky

Miscellaneous papers on deposit in Gorky file, Whitney Museum of American Art, New York; also Arshile Gorky File, the Whitney Museum Papers, microfilm roll numbers: N659–N662 in The Archives of American Art, Smithsonian Institution

IV. Films

Armenian General Benevolent Union of America, Spotlight on Armenians Series, *Windows to Infinity : The Life and Work of Arshile Gorky,* March 4, 1979. Interviews with Ruth Bowman, Jim Jordan and Karlen Mooradian. Color videotape

WNET Thirteen, Dateline: New Jersey, *Mural Without Walls*, 1979. Produced by Elizabeth Davis. Color videotape

Photographic Credits

Color

Courtesy Albright-Knox Art Gallery, Buffalo: cat. no. 161
Courtesy E. A. Bergman: cat. no. 159
Geoffrey Clements: cat. nos. 75, 125, 198
Courtesy James Corcoran Gallery, Los Angeles: cat. no. 238
Courtesy Andrew Crispo Gallery, New York: cat. no. 185
Mary Donlon: cat. nos. 7, 54
Courtesy Gerald S. Elliott, Chicago: cat. no. 195
Courtesy Richard L. Feigen Gallery: cat. no. 126
Courtesy Xavier Fourcade Inc., New York: cat. nos. 15, 43, 78, 81, 100, 169
Courtesy Graham Gund: cat. no. 161
Greg Heins: cat. no. 170
Scott Hyde: cat. no. 136
Bruce C. Jones: cat. nos. 64, 77, 153, 163, 165, 227, 248
Courtesy Dr. and Mrs. Leo A. Keoshian: cat. no. 199
Paul M. Macapia, Seattle Art Museum: cat. no. 164
Courtesy Duncan MacGuigan: cat. no. 226
Geraldine T. Mancini: cat. no. 200
Robert E. Mates, assisted by Aida Mates: cat. nos. 18, 90, 145, 152, 181, 186, 214
Robert E. Mates and Mary Donlon: cat. nos. 135, 157, 182
Photographic Services, The Metropolitan Museum of Art: cat. no. 160
Courtesy Museum of Fine Arts, Boston: cat. nos. 122, 146, 228
Courtesy The Museum of Modern Art, New York: cat. nos. 120, 220
Courtesy National Gallery of Art, Washington, D.C.: cat. no. 76
Courtesy The Newark Airport Art Collection, The Port Authority of New York and New Jersey: cat. nos. 87, 88
Courtesy David Nisinson: cat. no. 137
Courtesy Philadelphia Museum of Art: cat. no. 244
Courtesy Mr. and Mrs. Gifford Phillips: cat. no. 212
Eric Pollitzer: cat. nos. 22, 149, 229
Courtesy San Francisco Museum of Modern Art: cat. no. 104
Courtesy Mr. and Mrs. Joseph Randall Shapiro: cat. no. 243
Joseph Szaszfai: cat. no. 12
F. J. Thomas Photography: cat. no. 191
Courtesy Frederick Weisman Family Collection: cat. no. 158

Black and White

Courtesy Allen Memorial Art Museum, Oberlin College: cat. nos. 201, 204
Courtesy American Broadcasting Companies: cat. nos. 171, 172
Courtesy Art Gallery of Ontario, Toronto: fig. 14
Courtesy The Art Institute of Chicago: cat. nos. 44, 72, 155, 203
Oliver Baker: cat. no. 3
Courtesy Baltimore Museum of Art: cat. nos. 114, 183, 240
Courtesy Barnes Foundation, Merion, Pa.: fig. 5
Courtesy Mrs. Michael Berberian and Mrs. Satenig Avedisian: fig. 1
Courtesy E.A. Bergman: cat. nos. 9, 45, 133, 192
Courtesy The Brooklyn Museum: cat. no. 180
Geoffrey Clements: p. 15, cat. nos. 102, 245
Courtesy Reynolds Brown: fig. 42
Courtesy Sidney Janis Gallery, New York: fig. 10
Courtesy Cleveland Museum of Art: cat. nos. 138, 143
Courtesy James Corcoran Gallery, Los Angeles: cat. no. 8
Mary Donlon: cat. nos. 19, 57, 96, 98, 116, 147
Jerome Drown: cat. no. 121
eeva-inkeri: cat. no. 106
Philip Evola: cat. no. 85
Courtesy Richard L. Feigen Gallery: cat. no. 178
Courtesy Fogg Art Museum, Harvard University, Cambridge, Mass.: cat. nos. 107, 210
Courtesy Xavier Fourcade Inc., New York: frontispiece; p. 39 top; cat. nos. 10, 16, 23, 26, 35, 37, 79, 80, 89, 92, 101, 103, 115, 193, 207, 213, 241
X. de Gery: cat. nos. 11, 230
Courtesy The Peggy Guggenheim Collection, Venice, The Solomon R. Guggenheim Foundation: fig. 16
Harland's Camera Graphics: cat. no. 131
Greg Heins: cat. no. 222
Hickey-Robertson: cat. no. 218
Courtesy Susanne Hilberry Gallery: cat. nos. 55, 61, 217
Courtesy Hirshhorn Museum and Sculpture Garden, Smithsonian Institution, Washington, D.C.: cat. nos. 62, 63, 65, 66, 91, 93, 95, 99, 100, 128, 156, 194
Courtesy B.C. Holland Gallery, Chicago: cat. no. 177
Bruce C. Jones: cat. nos. 4, 41, 99, 154, 173, 219, 242, 248, 249,
Courtesy Jim Jordan: cat. no. 20
Courtesy Knoedler & Co., New York: cat. nos: 38, 48–50, 52, 56, 70, 73, 82, 83, 105, 108, 110–113, 141, 179, 188, 197, 208, 209, 221, 224, 225, 233, 234, 237
Courtesy Steingrim Laursen: cat. no. 216
Paulus Leeser: cat. no. 11
Courtesy Los Angeles County Museum of Art: cat. no. 13
Andrei Lovinescu: cat. no. 184
Courtesy Lowell Art Association, Massachusetts: cat. no. 1
John Mahtesian: cat. no. 250
Robert E. Mates, assisted by Aida Mates: cat. nos. 34, 47, 67, 69, 94, 109, 117, 130, 174, 205, 206

Robert E. Mates and Mary Donlon: figs. 40, 41; cat. nos. 5, 25, 27, 60, 223, 235
Courtesy Pierre Matisse Gallery, New York: fig. 39
Photographic Services, The Metropolitan Museum of Art: figs. 28, 29; cat. no. 6
Courtesy Dorothy C. Miller: cat. no. 119
Courtesy Donald Morris Gallery, Detroit: cat. nos. 17, 71, 175
Courtesy Munson-Williams-Proctor Institute, Utica, New York: cat. no. 211
Courtesy C. A. Muschenheim: cat. no. 84
Service Photographique du Musée National d'Art Moderne, Centre National d'Art et de Culture Georges Pompidou: cat. no. 189
Courtesy Museum of Fine Arts, Boston: figs. 2, 3; cat. no. 215
Courtesy The Museum of Modern Art, New York: figs. 7, 8, 15, 18, 19, 22, 23, 24, 32, 33, 36, 38, 43; cat. nos. 31–33, 36, 39, 68, 86, 118, 122, 124, 148, 167, 246, 247
Courtesy National Archives and Record Service, Washington, D.C.: p. 40
Courtesy National Collection of Fine Arts, Smithsonian Institution, Washington, D.C.: cat. no. 14
Courtesy National Gallery of Art, Washington, D.C.: figs. 6, 27; cat. nos. 74, 196, 202
Otto E. Nelson: cat. nos. 28, 42, 46, 231
Courtesy William Rockhill Nelson Gallery of Art, Kansas City, Missouri: cat. no. 168
Courtesy Philadelphia Museum of Art: figs. 13, 20, 21, 26, 34, 37
Photography Inc., Toledo: cat. no. 140
Piaget: cat. no. 139
Eric Pollitzer: fig. 35; cat. nos. 29, 30, 51, 53, 97, 132, 144, 232, 236
Courtesy V.V. Rankine: p. 49 bottom
Courtesy Mrs. Alexander Sandow: p. 39 bottom
Ben Schnall, Life Magazine, Courtesy Time Inc.: p.50 bottom
Courtesy Maro Gorky Spender: p. 49 top right
Courtesy Statens Museum fur Kunst, Copenhagen: fig. 4
Ken Strotham: cat. no. 239
Joseph Szaszfai: fig. 12; cat. no. 187
Courtesy The Tate Gallery, London: cat. no. 129
Courtesy University Art Museum, University of Texas at Austin: cat. no. 21
Herbert P. Vose: cat. nos. 151, 190
Courtesy Washington Art Consortium, Washington State University, Pullman: cat. no. 176
Courtesy Whitney Museum of American Art, New York; photos by Geoffrey Clements: p. 49 top left; figs. 8, 11, 31
Courtesy Yale University Art Gallery, New Haven: fig. 44; cat. no. 40
Courtesy Natasha Gorky Young: p. 18

12,000 copies of this catalogue typeset by Samhwa Printing Co., with text set in 10 point Times New Roman 327, English Monotype, headings set from Times New Roman 327 display matrices. Printed by Nissha Printing Co. in four color offset and gravure. Smythe sewn and bound by Taikan-Sha, March 1981, for the Trustees of The Solomon R. Guggenheim Foundation.